Praise for *Reading*

"Elizabeth Pryor's magnificent *Reading the Man* forever buries the tired assumption that the real Robert E. Lee can never be found. Her exhaustive research and beautiful prose recover the many layers of Lee's being. . . . Pryor's intriguing conclusion reveals her brilliance as a biographer. She never loses her empathy or her critical eye for this immensely complicated Virginian."

—Peter Carmichael, *Virginia Magazine of History and Biography*

"Pryor has taken an icon and given us the soul of a complex man and his turbulent age, and has delivered it wrapped in lithe and graceful prose that many novelists might envy. She has, in short, written a masterpiece."

—Fergus Bordewich, author of *Bound for Canaan*

"Pryor . . . may not have intended to create a sensation, but her materials and insights offer a new study of Lee that at once builds on the work of previous biographers, and goes them one better."

—Ruth Ann Coski, *North and South Magazine*

"A humane, judicious and graceful exposition of Robert E. Lee the man. . . . Pryor's copious endnotes show a mastery of the vast body of scholarly and non-scholarly literature on Lee."   —Wayne Wei-siang, *The Weekly Standard*

"Brilliant . . . Ms. Pryor turns out to be a shrewd and astute exegete of this most enigmatic of men. . . . The book becomes a kind of dialogue, not only between the correspondents who are quoted, but between the author and her subjects, between our century and theirs."

—Eric Ormsby, *The New York Sun*

"Admirable . . . Pryor's *Reading the Man* will stand out both for its originality, as well as for the keenness of its perceptions and conclusions. This is truly the first indispensable book on Lee since Douglas Southall Freeman's magisterial biography of the 1930s."

—William C. Davis, author of *Jefferson Davis, the Man and His Hour*

"Pryor writes with a sure hand, informed by strong research. . . . She impressively captures Lee's character and personality and seeks to understand 'what constitutes heroism.'"   —David W. Blight, *The Boston Globe*

"Revolutionary and vital. Absolutely indispensable . . . Elizabeth Brown Pryor and her extraordinary new book . . . have single-handedly revived what was hitherto unrevivable. . . . A masterpiece of biographical examination."
—Matthew Penrod, supervisory park ranger, Arlington House

"Fresh and compelling . . . [Pryor] trains a dispassionate eye on her topic and refrains from both psychoanalysis and moralizing. She also takes pains to contextualize Lee within the norms of his time and place, not ours. . . . Mary Chesnut, writing her now-famous diary during the first summer of the war, doubted if anyone could know Robert E. Lee. Thanks to Pryor's inspired detective work, we can finally edge closer to saying we do."
—Joseph Pierro, *Civil War Times Illustrated*

"Her Lee is an intriguing person. There is a depth of emotion that emerges from Lee's private letters that we don't associate with the Lee of myth. . . . This is probably the first truly objective biography of Lee."
—W. Todd Groce, *Savannah Morning News*

"Pryor is probably the first person to locate and read the vast majority of the surviving Lee family papers. . . . She has produced a monumental work."
—Richard W. Hatcher III, *Post and Courier* (Charleston)

"Excellent . . . [Pryor] reminds us that history is not just a recitation of facts, dates, and events."   —Charles F. Bryan, Jr., *Richmond Times Dispatch*

"If you love Lee or hate him, you've got to read this book. From the old Confederates to the Lee haters, they all got it wrong. This is a book that ought to be read by everybody."   —Kirk Wood, *Montgomery Advertiser* (Alabama)

"The Civil War's 'Marble Man' just got a lot less rigid, and a lot more interesting."   —Clint Schemmer, *The Free Lance-Star* (Fredericksburg)

PENGUIN BOOKS

READING THE MAN

Elizabeth Brown Pryor has combined careers as an award-winning historian and a senior diplomat in the American Foreign Service, most recently as senior adviser to the Commission on Security and Cooperation in Europe of the U.S. Congress. Her biography *Clara Barton, Professional Angel* is considered the authoritative work on the founder of the American Red Cross.

Robert E. Lee, about age thirty-eight, with his son Rooney.

Elizabeth Brown Pryor

Reading the Man

A Portrait of Robert E. Lee
Through His Private Letters

PENGUIN BOOKS

PENGUIN BOOKS

Published by the Penguin Group

Penguin Group (USA) Inc., 375 Hudson Street, New York, New York 10014, U.S.A.
Penguin Group (Canada), 90 Eglinton Avenue East, Suite 700, Toronto, Ontario, Canada M4P 2Y3
(a division of Pearson Penguin Canada Inc.) • Penguin Books Ltd, 80 Strand, London WC2R 0RL,
England • Penguin Ireland, 25 St Stephen's Green, Dublin 2, Ireland (a division of Penguin Books
Ltd) • Penguin Group (Australia), 250 Camberwell Road, Camberwell, Victoria 3124, Australia
(a division of Pearson Australia Group Pty Ltd) • Penguin Books India Pvt Ltd, 11 Community Centre,
Panchsheel Park, New Delhi – 110 017, India • Penguin Group (NZ), 67 Apollo Drive, Rosedale,
North Shore 0632, New Zealand (a division of Pearson New Zealand Ltd) • Penguin Books (South
Africa) (Pty) Ltd, 24 Sturdee Avenue, Rosebank, Johannesburg 2196, South Africa

Penguin Books Ltd, Registered Offices:
80 Strand, London WC2R 0RL, England

First published in the United States of America by Viking Penguin,
a member of Penguin Group (USA) Inc. 2007
Published in Penguin Books 2008

1 3 5 7 9 10 8 6 4 2

Copyright © Elizabeth Brown Pryor, 2007
All rights reserved

Grateful acknowledgment is made for permission to reprint
excerpts from the following copyrighted works:
John Brown's Body, by Stephen Vincent Benét. Copyright © 1927, 1928 by Stephen Vincent Benét. Copyright
© renewed 1955 by Rosemary Carr Benét. Reprinted by permission
of Brandt & Hochman Literary Agents, Inc.
"Burnt Norton" from Four Quartets by T. S. Eliot. Copyright 1936 by Harcourt, Inc. and renewed
1964 by T. S. Eliot. Reprinted by permission of Harcourt, Inc. and Faber and Faber Ltd.

THE LIBRARY OF CONGRESS HAS CATALOGED THE HARDCOVER EDITION AS FOLLOWS:
Pryor, Elizabeth Brown.
Reading the man : a portrait of Robert E. Lee through his private letters / Elizabeth Brown Pryor.
p. cm.
Includes bibliographical references and index.
ISBN 978-0-670-03829-9 (hc.)
ISBN 978-0-14-311390-4 (pbk.)
1. Lee, Robert E. (Robert Edward), 1807–1870. 2. Lee, Robert E. (Robert Edward), 1807–1870—
Correspondence. 3. Generals—United States—Biography. 4. Generals—Confederate States
of America—Biography. 5. United States—History—Civil War, 1861–1865—Personal narratives,
Confederate. 6. Confederate States of America. Army—Biography.
I. Lee, Robert E. (Robert Edward), 1807–1870. II. Title.
E467.1.L4P795 2007
973.7′3092—dc22
[B] 2006047218

Printed in the United States of America • Set in Minion and Minion Expert

To the memory of another great southern gentleman

DONALD WAYNE HOWARD

1953–2004

Worshipped, uncomprehended and aloof,
A figure lost to flesh and blood and bones,
Frozen into a legend out of life,
A blank-verse statue—
                                How to humanize
That solitary gentleness and strength
Hidden behind the deadly oratory
Of twenty thousand Lee Memorial days,
How to show in spite of all the rhetoric,
All the sick honey of the speechifiers,
Proportion, not as something calm congealed
From lack of fire, but ruling such a fire. . . .

A Greek proportion—and a riddle unread.
And everything we have said is true
And nothing helps us yet to read the man. . . .

                    Stephen Vincent Benét, *John Brown's Body*

Contents

Preface

ROBERT E. LEE's personal saga is one of the most riveting stories of American history. It is a family tale; a national epic; a theater piece worthy of Shakespeare. I entered this drama quite literally through the rear stage door. On a summer day many years ago I climbed the back steps to Arlington, and walked into Lee's house and life. I was there for a temporary job with the National Park Service, working on research for the restoration of the property, and was given access to letters and papers that at that time were restricted for general use. To say they were a revelation would be a powerful understatement. Like so many Americans, I knew a little of Lee's story, or at least was familiar with its exoskeleton. I was aware that Lee was a regional icon, and that generations had been taught to revere his ability to inspire devotion and to lose with dignity. I also knew he had grown to be a polarizing figure, a symbol of values both lofty and low. Agnostic myself, I was neither filled with awe for Lee, nor disdainful of his decisions. Like his acquaintance Mary Boykin Chesnut, I thought him too "cold and quiet and grand" to be of much interest.[1] The very name "Robert E. Lee" I knew to be an artifice, for neither he nor his family and friends ever used it—a fitting pseudonym, I thought, for an empty mythological creature. Until I read his letters it could not have occurred to me to describe Lee with the adjectives that now hurry to my mind: witty, bourgeois, self-justifying, scientific, lusty, disappointed.

"Everything we have said is true," sings poet Stephen Vincent Benét in the epigraph to this book. "And nothing helps us yet to read the man." Benét challenged "picklock biographers" to find a more substantial person; to question the stagecraft surrounding Lee; to find the "man enclosed within that image."[2] Inspired by the resonance of Lee's own words, I set out to do just that.

Along the way I discovered a treasure trove of unpublished or unused documents in scores of archives and attics and trunks. I was greatly aided in

this by Lee's descendants, who generously shared many previously unknown documents with me. At the time of this writing I estimate I have read
about 10,000 manuscript pages written by Lee or his close associates. In so
doing, I have been a privileged listener as he reveals himself. His words show
a far more complex and contradictory man than the one who comes most
readily to the imagination.

Lee's papers have never been collected and published, which seems astonishing given his historical prominence. Only casual collections and an imperfect and strongly edited set of his wartime documents are available in
printed form. Nor did he write a memoir, or any other personal account of
his experiences, though he had hoped to do so. As a result, few people are
aware of Lee's talent for writing. Yet its quality, and the story he tells, are so
compelling that even had he not distinguished himself as a general, his family correspondence would still be considered an extraordinary record of the
nation's development.

Many of Lee's personal letters were lost in the upheaval of war. Some
have been recently rediscovered. Others are still missing. The unavailability
of so many documents has created a certain void, which in turn has fostered
Lee's remoteness and the mythology that surrounds him. In the last dozen
years many letters have been quoted, often with great skill. But no matter
how faithful the process, by definition such excisions also cut away context
and meaning. Moreover, hundreds of books have been written about Lee, a
historiographical overload. It seems the more that is written about him, the
more he has become obscured.

So we need a pathfinder through this secondhand wilderness, and what
better guide than Lee himself? For his letters wonderfully illuminate his
personality. Because he had no premonition of fame, never saw himself as a
tragic, heroic figure, they are written unself-consciously. He was more careful during and after the war, of course, but for the most part Lee allows
himself to be remarkably open. He is so candid that at times there is a
voyeuristic sense to reading the letters. They also reveal the pressures on his
character and its development over time. His was not a static personality
that seamlessly flowed from high achievement at West Point to battlefield
brilliance. Irreverent letters from his twenties differ considerably—and sometimes sadly—from the sober, philosophical missives of the wiser, but scarred
and aging man.

With these letters we cannot just admire or reject one aspect of Lee. They
are not a kind of character compass that points forever in one direction. The
letters force us to embrace a multifaceted man. Lee the flirt, the man handi-

capped by passivity and indecision, the racial supremacist, the humorless sermonizer, and the merry companion must be conformed with Lee the natural leader, the sentimental lover of children and animals, the indifferent engineer, the aggressive warrior. His words can distress as much as they charm. We cannot compartmentalize him, and we cannot simply lionize him. His letters show him to be too human for that.

There is a certain responsibility to interpreting precious pieces of our past. Although this book is filled with new material, it is not meant to be a sensationalist biography. Nor is it a cradle-to-grave chronology, a detailed description of military movements, or an exhaustive analysis of the Civil War. Those books have already been written. Debunking the Lee mythology is also not the point of this book. Rather, it is to amplify our understanding of what constitutes heroism, and how as an ordinary person Lee faced the vagaries of the human condition. These letters help us to understand his prominence and to move out of our own moment to connect with a larger collective experience.

In wanting to respect both Lee's fine expressive talent and the larger import of his writing, I decided to publish the entire text of selected letters and use them as departure points for what I call "historical excursions." These essays take us where the letters lead, meandering through family upheavals, societal change, and the development of America's martial institutions. I was inspired in this by the many pleasurable hours I have spent in the company of my sister, Dr. Beverly Louise Brown, who is an art historian. Her ability to illuminate the hidden mysteries of a masterwork made me believe that this could be done with equal effect using manuscripts. An untutored viewer sees a picture, has an emotional and visual first reaction to it, identifies its shapes or images. But when an expert points out the factors that influenced the artist, how he or she mixed the paint and chose the colors, where the subject was found and what is behind the iconography, the painting becomes something more than it was. In the same way, interpreting Lee's letters for the reader lends them context and heightens their value. My hope is that those who read this book will give careful attention to the documents themselves— which are stirring, thought-provoking, and amusing—perhaps rereading them at the conclusion of each "excursion." For in the end it is Lee's writing that will endure and his voice that needs to be heard. Any outside interpreter is but a midwife, delivering his vital words into a different place and time.

It is hard to overstate the importance of letters in an era that had few means of personal communication beyond conversation and handwritten notes. Personal messages still oiled most everyday interactions, from wooing a spouse to pursuing a career. Recognizing this, Lee's mother, Ann Hill Carter Lee, once admonished her second son, Smith, for inattention to his letter-writing responsibilities. With a timeless mother's plea, she writes: "I . . . now have arrived at the disagreeable point in my letter, the obligation I feel to chide you for never writing to your Mother more especially as her health is so impaired." Her wounded feelings aired, Ann Lee then offered a spirited treatise on the importance of skillful composition. "A man that cannot write a good letter on business or on the subject of familiar letters will make an awkward figure in every situation and will find himself greatly at a loss on any occasion," she cautions Smith. "Indeed I cannot imagine how he could pass through life with satisfaction and respectability."[3]

The growth of transportation systems and an increasingly educated population encouraged the habit of letter writing after 1800. By the mid-nineteenth century it is estimated that 95 percent of New Englanders and 80 percent of southern whites were literate. Many were also traveling, exercising their right to explore and settle the vast American continent, and to describe the experience to those left behind. Technological advances revolutionized the production of paper so that it was more available, less expensive, and of better quality than ever before. In a prescient move, the young American nation developed a fledgling postal system, expanding on the pioneering work Benjamin Franklin had done as postmaster in Philadelphia.[4] Prior to this, as a grandfather of Lee's wife grouchily remarked, there had existed only "a damn'd confounded, pretended Post Office here, w[hi]ch keeps Letters as long as they think fitt; it is a generall Grievance to ye country. . . ."[5] This situation began to be redressed in 1778 by a series of sorting techniques and post roads—U.S. Highway 1 is laid out on the original mail link between the Atlantic seaboard colonies—and grew in fits and starts with the addition of riverboat and railway lines, stagecoaches, and contracted carriers. By 1828 Congress had established thousands of new postal routes. Service still remained chaotic, but it gradually became faster and more reliable. Most important, post riders were personally selected for their integrity, and letter writers began to have confidence in the system. For all of its colorful bumblings—and there were many—the new American postal system was a tremendous improvement over the uncoordinated and unreliable delivery methods that had existed previously. Indeed, it was beyond anything the world had ever seen, creating social unity and facilitating commerce in a huge and diverse nation.[6]

Conditions in early-nineteenth-century America meant that letter writing became a commonplace activity, no longer the preserve of the rich, who had the education, leisure, and expensive paper to indulge it. Not only were the time and materials available, it became a fashionable pastime, and the art of expressing emotions and painting descriptions with words was highly prized. Tutors, academies, and writing manuals encouraged both men and women to express themselves vividly and to reveal their innermost sentiments with sincerity and personality.[7] The result is something of a bonanza for the historian of this period. The rise in schooling, with efforts toward the standardization of grammar and penmanship, make the letters more readable than earlier epistles. The charming eccentricities of punctuation and spelling contained in Ann Lee's letters had all but disappeared in the letters her son Robert was writing to his friends. More people also wrote letters, representing a wider spectrum of the population. Personal correspondence had greatly increased by the 1820s, when Mrs. Lee chastised the recalcitrant Smith, and the figure grew exponentially until the popularity of the telephone consigned both everyday chitchat and important business dealings to a recordless void.

This is one of the reasons that the Civil War stands as a great expressive moment in American history. Never before had this country produced such an outpouring from statesmen and common foot soldiers, plantation mistresses and self-styled journalists. All of them had an opinion, and all of them felt impelled to offer it. For the first time, a majority of the population had the ability to write it down. The lingering identification that many Americans still feel for that war comes in large part from the haunting letters that tell us what it was like to be there.

Of the records left to the antiquarian, letters are among the most revealing. They are of the moment and written to specific persons, who can generally be identified. They offer the historian a way to peek into daily lives and see how people interacted—what they talked about to each other and how they expressed it. Memoirs and journals, written with or without ulterior motives, and the more austere accounts in newspapers and public papers, are one-sided, or geared to an impersonal audience. They cannot match the conversational quality of a letter. Compare, for example, George Washington's personal correspondence with his diaries, which contain year after year of minimalist notations. "At home all day. About five o'clock poor Patcy Custis Died Suddenly," was all Washington recorded on June 19, 1773, the day his stepdaughter passed away from epilepsy. It was in a *letter* to his friend Burwell Bassett that he poured out his heart, describing how the family had reached "the lowest ebb of Misery."[8]

Smith Lee never did overcome his disinclination to write letters, but it is clear that brother Robert followed his mother's advice, and, in fact, repeated it to his youngest daughter some thirty years later. "It is said that our letters are good representatives of our minds . . . They certainly present a good criterion for judging of the character of the individual," he told her. "You must be careful that yours make as favorable an impression of you as I hope you will deserve."[9] Lee's letters did make a good impression. Business was conducted promptly and correctly, in a formal style borrowed from the previous century. To these correspondents he "remained y^r most ob^t servant, RE Lee." With his friends and family, however, he developed a more intimate style, sometimes signing himself "thy doughty Bob." Despite his skill, Lee complained about the burden of letter writing. "I *abhor* the sight of pen and paper," he once confided to a West Point friend, "and to put one t'other requires as great a moral effort as for a cat to walk on *live coals.*"[10] Yet, because he spent so much of his time traveling for his profession, correspondence became an important outlet for him. The thousands of letters that survive in libraries and private collections reveal his need to reach out across an emerging nation to his friends and relatives. During the Civil War, when his burden was very great, it must have been a tremendous release, for he writes a note to some member of the family nearly every day. He wrote when he was lonely, and when he was stimulated by new sights and adventures, and he also wrote when he had nothing to say. He could say nothing very well indeed, and some of the most revealing letters are filled more with everyday chatter than historic import. They give us our most tantalizing glimpse of a man who did not open himself easily, but spoke with engaging wit and feeling when he did.

Throughout his life Lee writes as if he were having a conversation, leaping enthusiastically from topic to topic. Think of them as telephone transcripts, as literary snapshots, and the intimacy of the letters will be apparent. Moreover, he had a good observer's eye. "Posterity loves details," the nineteenth-century historian Benson Lossing once told Lee's father-in-law.[11] Lossing would have delighted in Robert Lee's letters. They are filled with punchy conversations and period tidbits that delight the amateur reader as well as the professional historian. In only rare instances are they tedious or boring. Whatever else he was, Lee was immensely likeable. His letters are very good company.

Many of the messages are intensely personal. In fact, one suspects that Lee would have detested the publication of his family correspondence. Always on guard against too much familiarity, he zealously protected the sanctity of private exchanges. Markie Williams, who was a confidante of Lee and a cousin of his wife, Mary, once described a fireside tea at which Mrs. Lee was gleefully reading aloud from the family's extensive collection of old letters. When she read an early-eighteenth-century love note from Colonel

William Byrd to his future wife, and queried whether or not she should publish it, her husband reacted strongly. "Cousin Robert thought it contained too vividly the feelings of a man—did not like to hear it read jestingly, although it was written so many years before," observed Markie.[12] He was even more direct to a comrade who in 1863 wanted to use a sympathy letter to raise funds for the Confederate effort. "It was intended for no eye but [the mother's]," Lee wrote. "If she is willing for its publication & you think it will in any way serve your purpose . . . I shall not object—But I never write but for those whom my letters are addressed."[13]

Lee composed most of his letters unself-consciously, but does that mean that we can accept them as completely straightforward reflections of his thoughts and intentions? Probably not. No human being is completely guileless, even those we most venerate. People write and speak from a variety of motives, sometimes two or three simultaneously. Writing letters gives time for contemplation and, when called for, artifice. Letter writers have the luxury of forethought and, if they are shrewd, also know that written language can last beyond an impulse, and deserves careful crafting. Consider a letter from Clara Barton, who nursed the wounded of both sides during the Civil War. It was composed in the tense hours before the battle of Fredericksburg in December 1862, when she and the soldiers who surrounded her knew that a great contest would take place the next day. Writing to her cousin Elvira, she says:

> Five minutes time with you, and God only knows what that five minutes might be worth to the—may be—doomed thousands sleeping around me. It is the night before a "battle." The enemy, Fredericksburg, and its' mighty entrenchments lie before us—the river between. At to-morrow's dawn our troops will essay to cross and the guns of the enemy will sweep their frail bridges with every breath. The moon is shining through the soft haze with a brightness almost prophetic; for the last half-hour I have stood alone in the awful stillness of its glimmering light gazing upon the strange, sad scene around me striving to say, "Thy will, O God, be done." The camp-fires blaze with unwonted brightness, the sentry's tread is still but quick, the scores of little shelter tents are dark and still as death; no wonder, for, as I gazed sorrowfully upon them, I thought I could almost hear the slow flap of the grim messenger's wings as one by one he sought and selected his victims for the morning's sacrifice.[14]

It is hard to imagine a more sensitive and theatrical description than this. And it is the genuine article: a firsthand account written at the scene of the event. Still, we must question its complete sincerity, since Clara Barton was desperately seeking money and backing in the small towns of Massachusetts for her battlefield succor. She was aware that Elvira was likely to publish such a gripping letter in local newspapers to aid her work. Does this diminish the emotion or the credence? It only puts it into perspective. In like manner we sometimes see Robert Lee posture and dodge in his letters, phrasing them to his advantage, and frequently invoking high motives to cloak self-serving actions. Should this signal the fall of a hero? Of course not. In some cases his wiles simply make us chuckle; at other times, these very human frailties make his truly noble actions all the more impressive.

Sitting at a laptop desk, Lee wrote his letters on ivory or blue paper, often on one big sheet that was doubled to make four pages, then folded again, the address written on the center of the final page, and sealed. Because of the standardized paper size, the length of many of the letters is about the same—rather like using twentieth-century airmail forms.[15] Letter and address made one neat packet until envelopes became more common in the 1840s. Lee used a steel pen and black or blue ink and wrote in an elegant hand, with elongated tails and loops on the letters *b, f, l,* and *p.* He drew exaggeratedly large script for the letters *c* and *s* at the beginning of many words, making it difficult to know whether or not he intended to capitalize them. When he was young he learned to pen the gracious clef-shaped *f* to indicate a double s, as had been the custom in the previous century, and he used this notation throughout his life. He liked & and &c signs, and he always shortened *Christmas* to *Xmas.* Exclamation points are rare. The first pages of Lee's letters are finely drafted, but toward the end, when time and page space put him under pressure, he often began to scrawl a little. Though the letters are still easy to decipher, he once apologized to his mother-in law for what he termed "scraggy chirography," and messages that had the appearance of "ancient epistles."[16]

Part of the appeal of these letters is that they exist at all. This is a marvel on several levels. That they have not disintegrated, but remain legible and intact, is due to the fine quality rag paper on which most were written. This linen-and-cotton-based material began to be replaced by more perishable paper made of wood pulp around 1863. Today's letters would not hold up nearly as well as these.[17] The second wonder is that in the rough-and-ready world of frontier America they were ever received. The U.S. postal system was farsighted in its determination to bind the country together, but the realities of actually delivering the mail were uncertain at best. Ann Lee's letter to Smith was delivered in person, courtesy of a Mr. Delany, and many en-

Savannah 22 Nov 1861

My darling daughters

I have rec'd your joint
letter of the 24th Ot: from Clydale. It was
very cheering to me - the affection & sympathy you
expressed were very grateful to my feelings. I wish
indeed I could see you, be with you & never
again part from you. God only can give me
that happiness. I pray for it night & day. But
my prayers I know are not worthy to be heard.
I rec'd your former letter in western Virginia
but had no opportunity to reply to it. I enjoyed
it nevertheless. I am glad you do not wait to
hear from me, as that would deprive me of the
pleasure of hearing from you often. I am so
pressed with business. I am much pleased at
your description of Stratford & your visit. It is
endeared to me by many recollections & it has
always been a great desire of my life to be able
to purchase it. And that we have no other home,
& the one we so loved has been so fully polluted,
the desire is stronger with me than ever. The
horse chestnut you mention in the garden was
planted by my mother. I am sorry the vault
is so dilapidated. You did not mention the
Spring, one of the objects of my earliest recollection

ABOVE AND FOLLOWING PAGE: *A letter written by Lee on November 22, 1861, to his
daughters Annie and Agnes. The signature "RE Lee" is the one he used all his life.*

I am very glad my precious Agnes that you have become so early a riser. It is a good habit, & in these times for mighty ends advantage should be taken of every hour.

I regretted much at being obliged to come from Richmond without seeing your own mother. I hope she is well & happy with her 9th child. Fitzhugh you may have heard has come in to see his little wife.

This is my second visit to Savannah. I have been down the coast as far as Amelia Isd to examine the defences. They are fine indeed & I have laid off work enough to employ our people a month. I hope our enemy will be polite enough to wait for us. It is difficult to get our people to realize their position.

I have seen good old Mrs. Mackay, now 85, & her daughters Mrs. Joseph Stiles (the mother of your friends) & Mrs. Elliott. Mrs. Wm H Stiles is in Cass with her 9th children. Henry & Holt Stiles are here. You may have heard that Mr. Low has been captured on his way from England & that Mrs. Low is with the Glens in Baltimore. She I presume will soon be here, but he will be detained by our Yankee enemies. Give much love to all with you. Sweet Annie is here. Corresponding I have with sweet Margaret to win a place in Carrie's heart.

Good bye my dear daughters. Your affectionate

R E Lee

Miss Annie & Agnes Lee

velopes in Robert Lee's hand carry words like "Politeness of Mr. Barry" or "Politeness of Major Erving."[18] The invention of stamps was enthusiastically embraced by the Lees, and helped eliminate the need for hand carrying. Not only was it cheaper than the earlier fee—which could be hefty and which the recipient had to pay—but the stamps more reliably stayed on the letter than did the temporary post office labels that preceded them.[19]

The development of stamps did not eliminate all the uncertainty from postal delivery, however. An 1850s letter from Lee, stationed at an army outpost in the Texas wilderness, would have traveled some 1,600 miles through desert, prairie, mountains, and forest. Carried first by mule train, then by riverboat, railroad, and wagon, it would finally be picked up in Alexandria, Virginia, and delivered to the family seat at Arlington in the hands of Perry Parks, a slave.[20] Letters from home were very important to Lee, and his correspondence frequently contains elaborate instructions for directing the missives, including complex arrangements with Mississippi steamboat captains and western cavalry units.[21] "Your kind letter of the 4th Ap[ril] has had a weary journey," Lee told one of his favorite cousins. "It followed me to the Rio Grande, slowly finding its way from point to point, did not reach Fort Brown till after my departure, & has but within a few days got back to its point of starting. But I have enjoyed it, Cousin Anna, just the same as if it were fresh from your presence, and it recalled all that you described vividly before me."[22] Amazingly, letter after letter did reach its intended recipient, and was read and answered with enough immediacy to allow a kind of dialogue. A member of the family noted that the arrival of the mailbag on a winter evening at Arlington was always "a peculiar source of pleasure."[23]

What seems even more remarkable is that the letters managed to survive a time of cataclysmic war. We know that the Lees carefully preserved the family's private papers while they lived at Arlington, as did most of their friends. Americans of all classes valued their precious letters and characteristically saved them for future generations. Ann Lee tells Smith, "Keep my letters that you may read them when I can write no more—They will awaken your Mother's great fondness for you and perhaps prove incentive to the cultivation of these virtues she was most desirous you should possess."[24] Before the days of the photo album, letters were the only way a family had to record its history, glimpse into its past, recall the personalities of departed relatives and friends. "No doubt the literary world will be vastly benefitted by the publication of our correspondence," twenty-four-year-old Robert Lee wrote his fiancée with unwitting prescience. The day of Lee's funeral, his wife reopened that same packet of love letters and sighed over the intervening years and events.[25] Like Mary Lee, those who were feeling low found the faded documents comforting: "Often when I feel lonely and melancholy," wrote a contemporary, "I take [my letters] from my pocketbook and read them as I would converse with a friend and pour over their dear contents, a fount of tears to ease the burden of my lonely heart."[26] No wonder they were carefully laid away in trunks or kept in packets tied with ribbons. This was tangible nostalgia.

The Lees were particularly sensitive to the importance of family papers. Ann Lee's husband, Revolutionary War hero Light-Horse Harry Lee, had been forced by ill health and questionable financial speculation into West Indian exile when Robert was a young child. He died before he could return home, and what exposure Robert had to his father's tastes and philosophy must have come through his letters. In later life he edited some of them, egged on by his older brother Carter, and must have tried to match his scanty memories with the author of the effusive correspondence.[27] The woman Robert married, Mary Anna Randolph Custis, was a granddaughter of Martha Washington, and a virtual guardian of the nation's history. Part of her inheritance was a cache of Washington and Custis family papers that chronicled the early drama of the republic. Cousin Markie Williams found that the documents were often handled casually, many of them lodged in a garret with old deer antlers, molding volumes of the classics, and roosting chickens, which laid eggs among the precious Washington memorabilia. "The Hens have absolutely imbibed a taste for literature & go up to lay on clasic lore," she noted drily.[28] Archival conditions aside, a great deal of verbal reverence was bestowed on the Washington papers, and Mary Custis Lee delighted in bringing them out for guests and bundling them up to take to dinner parties, where everyone was kept laughing over the "idiocincricies of our ancestors." "Reading these old letters, seems to have become quite a mania with dear Cousin M.," noted Markie. "At all hours of the day may she be seen, coming in or sitting down with her arms or lap full of moth eaten letters, some of wh[ich] by date are one hundred & fifty years old." Cousin M. also dispensed autographs as she saw fit. Evidently she was disinclined to give any to Markie—also a Washington granddaughter—despite the young cousin's broad hints and visible disappointment.[29]

Few of the Washington letters survived the Civil War. When Federal troops stormed Arlington in May 1861, Mrs. Lee removed some of the papers to neighboring family plantations for safekeeping. Others remained for a time at the house, guarded by a servant who had stayed on during the Yankee occupation. Soldiers saw them scattered around the attic with other eighteenth-century papers, and picked up a few as souvenirs.[30] The Lees kept some Washington memorabilia with them throughout the war, but most was given to relatives or buried near the Virginia Military Institute in Lexington to secure it from the looting parties of General David Hunter. One collection of irreplaceable relics was stolen during an 1864 raid on a cousin's estate, Kinloch, by Federal cavalry men, who opened every drawer and trunk in the house and poked through haystacks and icehouses, finally making off with a ring containing the first president's hair, as well as mementos of Light-Horse Harry Lee and invaluable family papers.[31] When Mary Lee dug up the buried trunks after the war, she found Washington's letters had rotted, and she wept bitterly as she burned the fragments. The precious few that remained intact were saved for her children.[32]

But Robert E. Lee's letters did survive, or at least a great many of them. Why this is so has remained a puzzle for many years. No doubt before the war they were stashed in the Arlington attics, among the chickens and ancient dust. After 1861 there must have been a hint that they would have a larger importance, but there are few clues to their whereabouts during the war. Cousin Markie tried to rescue some when she visited Arlington a few months after its occupation.[33] A soldier who was stationed in the house in 1862 "rummaged up in the vast garret" and found several trunks full of Lee's letters, dated from "twenty years or more."[34] H. L. Wright, one of many blue-coated soldiers who carried off keepsakes, wrote a somewhat abashed note to Lee's daughter Mary in the 1880s, returning letters from her father and J. E. B. Stuart. Similar notes, postmarked Illinois or Massachusetts, were received from time to time by the Lee descendants.[35] In 2002 an enterprising great-great-grandson, together with the Burke & Herbert Bank & Trust Company, found another cache of papers, kept by the Lees' eldest daughter in the vault, a fabulous treasure which this author was greatly privileged to explore.[36] Lee himself believed all his private letters had been destroyed, and never recovered them during his lifetime.[37]

In fact, more than a thousand letters had survived the sacking of Arlington, the penetration of Union forces into Virginia, the burning of Richmond, and the final flight of Lee's immediate family to lower Virginia. At some point the Lee descendants again came into possession of them, though they are still today not sure how it happened. That the letters were saved may perhaps be due to an extraordinary, ironic circumstance. The man who turned Arlington into a cemetery, ensuring that the Lees could never return, was named Montgomery Meigs. He had been a colleague of Robert Lee when they were young men, but remained with the Union in 1861. Despite Meigs's detestation of all regular army officers who chose to align themselves with the South, his daughter married a cousin of the Lees, Joseph

Hancock Taylor. As the family story goes, one day after the war she and her husband rode on horseback up to the mansion, where Taylor had played as a child. Entering the house, now an army office, he went over to a piece of paneling and pushed a secret spot. The wall opened, and behind it were the Lee letters, which were later returned to the family. And that is all we know, for no records confirm the tale.[38]

However they were saved, Lee's letters offer an extraordinary national and family chronicle and the greatest insights we have into his personal development. Through them a figure trapped in statues and "the sick honey of the speechifiers" is filled with life. Both illuminating and mysterious, these precious scraps of paper give us a glimpse into a guarded soul.[39]

Reading the Man

Chapter One

Torn to Pieces

My dear Sister

I have been delayed writing to you for some days, & a visit from Mrs Lee has been the cause. She is our relation & our mother's earliest friend. It is fitting that I should explain the reason why I do now what I ought to have done a week since, & as the cause is Mrs Lee I cannot do better than explain Mrs Lee. In fact I am glad of the chance—I have an overflowing of the heart whenever I think of her & an outpouring of the spirit is the only relief

Very fine women (you may doubt me) are rather rare here. Female talent has generally received a wrong direction. I have seen many a worn out Coquette, many a heartless Belle that wanted but the first impulse to have been made useful & happy. I have heard of many instances of rare capacities—but waste followed possession as tho' it were irresistible—In fact it may have been so—Society (that of Virginia I mean) was full of splendid meteors: if a woman had been inclined to pursue a right path there was no steady light whereby she could discern it. But Mrs Lee need not have been in Virginia to have been pronounced excellent—There is no circle—none on earth—of which she would not be an ornament. She commenced life a spoiled child—a beauty & fortune—but Heaven has used her as its purest gold & all that died under the torture were her imperfections.

My Mammy you know was a beauty & fortune too in her day—Nancy Lee & herself were pretty much brought up together—Mrs L the eldest by a year. General Lee, at that time at the head of everything in Virginia, was in love (honestly they say) with Mrs Carter. He was handsome, of splendid talents, & Governor of the State. Mrs Carter (then Miss Farley) & Mrs Lee (then Miss Carter) were living together during the General's suit to Miss F—As desperately as was General Lee in love with Miss Farley was Miss Carter with General

Lee, & at the same time compelled to witness his devotion to another object. His repeated visits to Miss Farley & utter neglect of her preyed upon her health, but drew nothing from her of unkindness to her fortunate cousin, & her only interference, & that against herself, was when General Lee had made his offer & Miss Farley avowed that she should reject it—She then said—"O stop, stop Maria—You do not know what you are throwing away." Maria however, persisted in throwing it away, & then in the face of decency & delicacy he made an offer to her, which she <u>could</u> <u>not</u> resist, & became his delighted Wife, but to find in the short space of an fortnight that her affections were trampled on by a heartless & depraved profligate. I am right as to time. One fortnight was her dream of happiness from which she awoke to a life of misery. Her fortune was soon thrown away upon his debts contracted previous to marriage; she was despised & neglected, & he, who in his outset of life bid fairer for a glorious termination of it than perhaps any man in America, died a Vagrant & Beggar.

General Lee at the time of his marriage with her was a widower. By his first marriage he had two children—one—a daughter,—married & proved to be everything that was abominable—the other, a son—was the kindest & to his new mother & her children the most affectionate relation on earth. Mrs L. herself had five children. Just as Carter Lee (whom you recollect in college) had proved himself a fine fellow, her eldest daughter Ann was attacked with a dreadful complaint in the hand &, after a year's residence in Philadelphia for the sake of medical assistance & after sufferings of a most horrible sort, was informed that her life was to be saved only by the amputation of her arm. The mother had infused a portion of her own heroism into her daughter & about six months since, after eighteen months exercise of it, the sweet little creature was pronounced convalescent—one misery ceased but to prepare the way for a greater—Henry Lee—her Husband's Son—a gentleman of great fortune & talents—more distinguished perhaps than any young man in Virginia for excellence of various sorts—His genius, liberality, his devotion to his mother's family & promise of eminence being the theme of every one—was convicted of crimes of the blackest dye. He married a Lady of fortune & her sister lived with them. He was her guardian. He seduced her under circumstances too—too—horrible to mention & blackened with his disgrace everyone that bore his name. This—the last fatal—fatal—stroke seems to have left no phial unemptied. And yet when you see her you do not require the consideration of her suffering to give interest to her. Her simple dignity, her most admirable understanding & manners—excite enough of admiration without any appeal to sympathy.

This is the history of the Lady who had kept my letter back & it is a most edifying one—Misery & temptation have beset her from the outset & their only

*effects have been to raise her nearer to Heaven. Carter and her youngest
Daughter Mildred were with her—They left us this morning*

*10th Sep: After writing the foregoing I stopt for breath as well I might—You see
that the panting continued for four days—Finding myself better in wind than
I was, I go at it again*[1]

>—⊹—○—⊹—<

THE STORY of each man's life begins before his birth. Some say that
Robert Edward Lee's personal history commenced with Richard the
Lionheart, others have maintained that it could be traced to the Holy Scrip-
tures. For practical purposes it starts here, as a family tale, handed down in a
letter written by Samuel Storrow, the cousin of Lee's mother. The writing is
clearly cathartic, and Storrow says he "stopt for breath" as he finished the sorrowful saga of Ann and Henry Lee. A reader two centuries later feels much
the same way. Accusation and intrigue are packed into nearly every sentence,
and at the end of the page it appears that the author might not have finished
yet, for he states: "Finding myself in better wind than I was, I go at it again."
We do not know whether he continued to write or if he ever sent the letter.
Someone had second thoughts about the wisdom of preserving such an indictment, however, for it was found ripped into small pieces, evidently destined for the dustbin. What is even more fascinating is that someone else
reconsidered that decision, and saved every tiny piece; indeed, hid them for
generations, until latter-day historians reassembled the mosaic.

What then are we to make of this exposé, penned three years after the
death of Henry Lee and thirty years after the events it describes? We know
the author had credibility, for he was the son of Maria Farley, the beauty
who rejected Henry Lee's proposal. But why would Storrow hold on to his
bitterness for such a long time? What was his motive in resurrecting family
gossip that might best be forgotten? How should we interpret the ambivalent action of shredding and then safeguarding this fragile piece of history?
Most important, how much of this scandalous tale about Robert E. Lee's
parents is true?

Henry Lee III lived his life in high relief. Born in 1756, the eldest son of Henry
Lee of Leesylvania, he grew up with all the advantages of one of Virginia's
premier families. His mother, Lucy Grymes, had been courted by George
Washington, and his father was a respected local figure whose chief interest

was breeding horses. At the age of fourteen, "Harry" was sent to Princeton, where he studied the classics and jurisprudence, his "fine genius" standing out among such classmates as Aaron Burr, James Madison, and the poet Philip Freneau.[2] It was at Princeton that Harry Lee was exposed for the first time to revolutionary sentiment. The students hung Tories in effigy and used their commencement address in 1773 to warn that "angry tumults" would not subside "Till foreign crowns have vanished from our view."[3] Harry returned to Virginia's Northern Neck to find that his father was also speaking out in favor of "preserving our libertys if necessary at the Expense of our Blood."[4] He was seen to be a promising, if somewhat arrogant young man. (Contrasting his own brilliance with his parents' mediocre intellect, he quipped: "Two negatives make a positive.") Plans were made for him to study law in London, but as tensions with England mounted, it became increasingly apparent that Harry Lee would not be pursuing a British legal career.[5]

In 1776, on the nomination of Patrick Henry, Lee was appointed captain of cavalry in his cousin Theodorick Bland's Virginia regiment. The following year that regiment joined the Continental Army. From the start Lee drew attention for his coolness and for a certain dash that set him apart as an officer. He took noticeable trouble to care for his men and horses, spending a good deal of his personal wealth outfitting his troops.[6] Lee used his men as special forces, scouting, harassing the enemy, and conducting some critical foraging for the bleak winter encampments at Morristown and Valley Forge. The small horse corps was so agile that Lee gained the nickname "Light-Horse Harry." Washington, commending Lee's "exemplary zeal, prudence and bravery," convinced the Congress to promote him to major, and to create a special "partisan" (or quasi-guerrilla) unit under his command. Called Lee's Legion, the 300 troops were equipped with green jackets, bearskin helmets, and long-bore pistols. They were granted an extraordinary amount of independence, essentially reporting only to the commander in chief.[7]

Light-Horse Harry had an instinctive understanding of the strategy Washington needed to follow if he were to outmaneuver the British imperial force. He knew his commanding general—a former surveyor—valued intelligence about terrain and enemy concentrations, and that surprise was an important weapon for the patriots. He perfected a style that might be called "calculated daring," a willingness to take risks and to challenge superior forces, but only under conditions that he had assessed personally and with tactics that were of his own design. At the same time he showed a genius for leadership. Though short and weak—"not qualified, in personal strength to make a heavy charge in battle"—Lee was a fine horseman and looked splendid in his tall leather hat, topped by a white horsehair plume.

He forged such a bond with his men that they followed the boldest orders, certain they would be led to triumph and safety.[8] Henry Banks, who knew the legion, later wrote, "Both cavalry and infantry were like a band of brothers, having entire confidence in each other, and all having equal confidence in, and personal esteem for, their commander, Lee."[9]

Intellect, illusiveness, and speed were Harry Lee's tools. His legion became known for actions that distracted and hampered the enemy, buying time for the Continental Army. In 1779 at Paulus Hook, New Jersey, the legion gave major service by capturing a British garrison that commanded the New York harbor. Lee, who had designed the operation with Washington's blessing, relied on stealth and audacity to overtake the greater force, with scarcely any loss of American life. For this, arguably his most splendid achievement of the war, he was awarded an official citation and a gold medal from Congress.[10] Finding that Lee preferred staying with his own troops to a prestigious staff position, Washington sent him with his ablest general, Nathanael Greene, to take on

Henry Lee, painted by Charles Willson Peale around 1782.

INDEPENDENCE NATIONAL HISTORIC PARK, NATIONAL PARK SERVICE

the defense of the South. Greene arrived in North Carolina to find the army ("if it deserved the name of one") greatly lacking, and he augmented his inadequate troops with auxiliary actions by Lee's Legion. He used them to harass the British supply lines and cut off their communications, and partnered Light-Horse Harry and Francis Marion—the "Swamp Fox"—to create an unpredictable and mobile guerrilla band in the Carolinas. Often fighting boot-to-boot, Lee's men "performed wonders" for Greene's forces at the battle of Guilford Courthouse in 1781. The engagement essentially crippled Cornwallis's army, though it was technically a win for the British. Lee later gave himself credit for conceptualizing a follow-up campaign that capitalized on the British weakness, forcing their retreat to Virginia, where they entered the trap that led to their surrender.[11]

"For rapid marches," Greene wrote him, "you exceed Cornwallis and everybody else."[12] Lafayette also took the trouble to express his "high opinion"

of the legion and to offer them some embellishments for their uniforms—
"lace, swords and feathers"—lately brought from France.[13] Light-Horse Harry
stood with Lafayette when Cornwallis surrendered, and another admiring
general, the unrelated but equally colorful Charles Lee, summed it all up:
"Major Lee . . . seems to have come out of his mother's womb a soldier."[14]

But he was as young and brash as the revolutionary politics he was defending, and his passion sometimes outstripped his prudence. Jealous fellow officers started to question whether there was not more bravado than
valor in Lee, and if his enthusiasm was but a ploy to gain attention from the
high command. He was court-martialed for unorthodox actions taken at
Paulus Hook, and though he was acquitted, the event left him resentful and
disillusioned.[15] Washington remained his loyal champion and gently tried to
curb Lee's sometimes overzealous instincts. "The measure you propose of
putting deserters from our Army to immediate death would probably tend
to discourage the practice . . . ," the general told him in 1779. "I think that
the part of your proposal which respects cutting off their heads and sending
them to the Light Troops had better be omitted."[16] Ugly accusations continued during the Carolina campaign, especially after an episode known as
"Pyle's Hacking Match," at which the legion surprised John Pyle's three
hundred loyalist militia men, slashed or shot to death ninety of them, and
wounded most of the rest. The incident had been started by the British, and
Lee called the whole encounter "unintentional," but it left a set of questions
that were difficult to answer.[17] Exhausted emotionally and physically after
nearly seven years of war, and believing he had been slighted in the official
approbations of General Greene, Lee announced he would leave the army. It
was a painful decision for a man who had loved the stimulation and camaraderie of field life. Those who wished him ill said his patriotism was evoked
only in the intensity of battle, and that after the surrender he lost interest in
the patient work needed to finish the war. Greene, however, retained his admiration, and chose to consider Lee's departure a furlough. Light-Horse
Harry was in such a pitch of despair that he left his beloved legion without
an official farewell. "The ceremony of parting from you & my friends is so
affecting, that I wish to decline it personally," he told Greene.[18]

Windburned and weary, Henry Lee returned in the spring of 1782 to the
Northern Neck of Virginia. He was twenty-six years old, a genuine war hero,
now with the rank of lieutenant colonel. During the Yorktown campaign he
had been posted in the neighborhood, and he seems to have reached an understanding with his cousin Matilda Lee, for he married her a few weeks
later.[19] The "divine Matilda" was evidently everything her name implied:

adroit at repartee, fond of playing Scarlatti on the harpsichord, and blessed with a "heavenly mildness" of character. At the death of her brother, she had come into possession of "Stratford" and an impressive fortune. The bridegroom was genuinely in love, and it appeared the couple would settle into the life of the privileged gentry. They made elegant improvements to staid, boxy Stratford, and with charm and lavish hospitality gave it a coveted reputation. To all appearances Henry had attained everything promised by the fight for independence: tranquillity, opportunity, and domestic happiness. Yet he was inexperienced and impatient with plantation management, and as his boredom grew, so did his dabbling in land ventures and local politics. The picture left of him at this time is of a man in nervous motion: a figure streaking across the countryside, a pack of dogs trailing after his horse.[20]

Henry Lee was not alone in his restlessness. Few revolutionary leaders retired easily into the peace they had battled so hard to win. Those who had articulated the principles of independence and successfully fought the British were now asked to design an unprecedented framework for governing. In the years following the war, when national structures were barely formed and not fully accepted, they were, in essence, inventing a nation. This was delicate work, and the revolutionary generation found that they were not of one mind about how it should be done. There was spirited discussion about whether the federal or state governments would hold the most power, about national finance, voting rights, military needs, and the character of the premier governmental offices. Debate over these issues did not end with the framing of the Constitution, but turned to prolonged partisan rivalry, with an animosity scarcely equaled since in American politics. The decade of the 1790s was noisy, passionate, and dangerous. Thomas Jefferson wrote that men who had been intimate all their lives now crossed the street to avoid each other, "lest they be obliged to touch hats." It was small comfort that the intensity of debate reflected the importance of the issues.[21]

With his election to the Continental Congress in 1785 Henry Lee entered this high-stakes game. He continued to play a part in politics for fifteen years, as partisan, congressman, and governor of Virginia. Generally following the Federalist principles of his idol Washington, Lee believed that narrow interests should be subordinated to overarching national concerns. He fought for Virginia's ratification of the Constitution, championing the opening "We the People" against "We the States" and defending the need for a robust central system and a professional army. With wit and eloquence he won the day against opposing orators Patrick Henry and his cousin Richard Henry Lee.[22] Lee again took action on behalf of a strong national system in 1794, when President Washington called on him to lead 13,000 militiamen against the Whiskey Rebellion, a small popular protest over an excise tax on spirits. Washington thought the movement was a challenge to the young federal government and gave Lee the title of major general and the authority to prove that the new system could defend its decisions. Though Lee and his men acted admirably—essentially quelling the "rebellion" by their mere presence—it was an unpopular move, for which even the untouchable Washington was vilified. Henry Lee, at that time governor of Virginia, returned to Richmond to find that he had the reputation of an "exterminator" and that he had been removed from office. Feeling betrayed, Lee became enmeshed in the ugly backbiting of the day. He quarreled with Patrick Henry over trade and western expansion, and began a lifelong feud with Jefferson after he allegedly slighted Lee in front of Washington. A republican who tried to engage Harry in friendly debate at dinner the following year found him "hurt beyond description from the late political occurrences in the country" and noted that in their discussion "political hostility immediately ensued."[23]

Lee's personal life during these years was as unstable as the political scene. His was a volatile nature, one that perhaps served him better in war than in peace. A cousin had once worried about a certain "wild and savage humor" that threatened to undermine Henry's fine intellectual skills. Another relative, visiting with the Lees, left a picture of home life that was far from serene: "vexation—torment—torture . . . Matilda crying, Nancy pouting— Harry Lee ranting—delightful group for a social party. . . ."[24] Matilda's health was precarious and finally gave way during childbirth in 1790. The loss of his beloved wife and infant child, followed two years later by the unexpected death of his eldest and dearest son, devastated Henry Lee. He poured out his anguish to sympathetic James Madison, sorrowing that the "domestic calamity which stirs me to the quick . . . has removed me far from the happy enjoyment of life."[25] He sought solace first in politics—he was elected governor at this time—but later considered distracting himself by a return to arms, "the best resort for my mind in its affliction." His thought, he told Washington, was to fight with the revolutionaries in France, much as Lafayette had joined forces with the colonists. Washington quietly steered him away from the plan, advising that as he was governor "of a respectable State, much speculation would be excited by such a measure." Seeing the wisdom of Washington's advice, and resigned to his life in civil society, Lee turned to another diversion: the pursuit of pretty women.[26]

"I am in love with every sweet nymph," Henry Lee wrote to Alexander Hamilton from the shabby governor's mansion in Richmond, "but am not so far gone with anyone yet as to think of matrimony."[27] He indulged in flirtations and began traveling to nearby plantations to meet the daughters of leading families. He used all of his charms—which were considerable—to woo several young women. Lee was a handsome man of thirty-seven, a fascinating talker who loved to quote the classics, and a romantically grieving widower. He drove a shiny "chariot" harnessed to six sleek horses, and as Samuel Storrow tells us, was "at the head of everything in Virginia." No wonder a young lady such as Ann Hill Carter would become smitten, and exclaim at the prospect of such a catch. Yet something underlying Henry Lee's notes to Hamilton and Washington smacks of desperation, or at best a lack of discrimination in his courting. If Storrow is right, he turned from one girl to another, pursuing "Nancy" Carter "in the face of decency & delicacy" when rebuffed by Maria Farley, whom he had noticed only after telling Hamilton of his infatuation with a Miss Allen in Philadelphia. Nor does the sequence of Lee's letters point to a passionate love match with Miss Carter. On April 29, 1793, he wrote to Washington of his strong interest in going to France, never mentioning an imminent wedding—if anything, Lee was seeking solace in the excitement of warfare. On May 6, only a week after this correspondence, and just two days after Maria Farley's wedding to William Champe Carter, Lee impatiently confided to Hamilton: "I mean now to become a farmer & get a wife as soon as possible."[28] Evidently the most available option was nineteen-year-old Miss Carter. Perhaps sensing ambivalence, Ann's generous and kind father, Charles Carter, wrote to Henry on May 20 that since he had given up the prospect of fighting with the French, there was no real objection to Lee's marriage with his daughter, but found it prudent to note that he expected him to be "a most affectionate and tender Husband." Given Lee's inclinations and Ann's feelings, Carter drily remarked, the sooner the wedding "takes place, the better—"[29]

A month later, on a sticky June evening, Ann Hill Carter and Governor Henry Lee were married in the mahogany and sterling splendor of Shirley, the Carters' hospitable home. Newspapers paid tribute to the nuptials of "Virginia's favorite young soldier," and George and Martha Washington congratulated Light-Horse Harry on having exchanged the "rugged and dangerous field of Mars for the soft and pleasurable bed of Venus." Washington was said to have given Ann his portrait miniature as a wedding gift, and she wore it as a pendant when her own likeness was painted. Aligned to the wealth and power of the Carter family, with gallantry in his past and the promise of a great future, at least one biographer believes that this wedding marked the apogee of Henry Lee's life.[30]

Decades later the groom would say that the day was "marked only by the union of two humble lovers," and there is every reason to believe that Henry Lee should have cherished Nancy Carter.[31] She had been the favorite in her large family of twenty-two siblings, a lovely olive-skinned, black-eyed young woman, with a serene manner and grave humor. She was unusually well educated, loved to ride horseback, sang sweetly, took pleasure in the beauty of nature, and had an innate dignity that impressed nearly everyone who met her.[32] Samuel Storrow thought she was a bit spoiled, and some of her letters do show a tendency toward selfishness—she rather condescendingly wrote her Virginia cousins from Philadelphia, for example, that it "was unreasonable to imagine I could find leasure to remember country friends while immersed in the pleasures of a city life."[33] But overall, Ann Hill Carter Lee left an impression of intellect and elegance. Four days after the wedding at Shirley, a guest wrote this description:

> Sent for to dine at Shirley in a private way with Governor Lee, who was married on Tuesday evening last to Miss Nancy, a young lady of whom ever since my acquaintance in the family, I had formed a very high opinion. She appears to me to possess in a very peculiar manner, all those virtues & qualifications so desirable in a wife—and which are calculated to insure happiness in an affluent state of Matrimony.[34]

Had Nancy Lee's "virtues and qualifications" been enough to "insure happiness," her story might have ended very differently.

Though controversy over the Whiskey Rebellion removed him from the governorship the year following his marriage, Henry Lee continued to be an active political commentator, and was elected to Congress in 1799. This was a happy time for the Lees. They enjoyed a sophisticated life in the temporary capital at Philadelphia, and reveled in the antics of their eldest son, Charles Carter Lee. Carter, as he was called, would later remember his parents playing chess together, the light of the fire glowing on their faces, and how he had ridden on the shoulders of his father to attend the theater, which Henry Lee adored.[35] Perhaps it was the theater that inspired Lee's finest contribution during these years. He had a great gift for spontaneous and expressive oratory, a talent that stood out even in an era of pleasing rhetoric. When Washington returned to his hometown, Alexandria, Virginia, just before becoming the first president, Lee was asked to write a tribute from his neighbors. Leaning against the mantel at his cousin Philip Fendall's house, he impulsively dashed off a perfect salutation to this "best of men . . . and most beloved fellow-citizen."[36] He found the same easy eloquence at the death of his one-time nemesis, Patrick Henry. Hearing the news at dinner, Lee called for paper and pen and wrote a striking and beautiful elegy. "Mourn, Virginia, mourn," it began, "say to rising generations—Imitate my Henry."[37] His most enduring fame also sprang from this ability to express the nation's unfolding drama. While in Philadelphia, word came of George Washington's death, and Lee was asked to give a funeral oration before the Congress. In stirring fashion he articulated both his own love and the lasting reverence the nation would feel for its founder: "First in war—first in peace—and first in the hearts of his countrymen." Half a century later, Henry's son Robert would proudly carry a little clipping of this speech in his pocket diary, written by the father he had barely known.[38]

From the time he was a young man, Henry Lee had seen grandeur in America's future, had hailed her noble political experiment and embraced the prospect of developing the country's resources. One of the goals of the Revolution had been to halt the British exploitation of valuable American property, unleashing its vast potential for national prosperity. During the years the republic was forming, there was an exhilarating rush to anticipate patterns of settlement, trade, and technology; to clear forests, build roads, and establish canal routes. Many men saw this in terms of personal advantage; it was not unusual, therefore, that Lee would feel keenly the possibility of the moment, and join the sport with unbridled optimism. He began to buy large tracts of land, often unseen and always on credit, and entered into some highly speculative commercial schemes. All of his contemporaries were doing the same, and his partners were the most illustrious names in the nation—Lee's mentor Washington among them.[39]

Unfortunately, the risks Lee had taken in the fury of battle and in the cacophonous world of politics were modest compared to his financial dealings. In just a few years he was caught in an astonishing maze of promissory notes, nerve-jarring payment schedules, and "a combination of bargains which could hardly benefit one party without injury to the other."[40] Lee engaged in speculation with the financier Robert Morris, loaning him $40,000 under circumstances that Morris later denied. He then unwisely bought some shares Washington was trying to unload in the ill-fated Great Dismal Swamp Company and tried to develop a settlement at the falls of the Potomac, which he tactlessly named "Matildaville" after his first wife.[41] He borrowed tens of thousands of dollars from his brothers, so much that Richard Bland Lee ultimately forfeited his plantation and would write to President Madison for help against the "Heavy misfortunes" imposed on him by the "indiscretions of a beloved Brother."[42] Lee sacrificed huge acreage from his estates and erratically bought and sold slaves. He then embroiled both Washington and Jefferson in deals that involved selling the same tract of land to two buyers.[43] Washington took the high road, calling the transaction a mistake and stating that he could "hardly think it possible that Genl Lee could so far forget what was due to his own character as to sell the land I had purchased of him to Genl Spottswood." Jefferson, however, chose to make the matter public.[44] By 1787 Lee was already so mistrusted that he was insulted in his father's will, which left him only minor property and assigned the family stewardship to his four younger brothers. On her deathbed Matilda Lee put Stratford and the rest of her estate in trust for her children. Charles Carter had done the same, protecting his daughter's inheritance "from the claim, demand, let, hindrance or molestation of her husband, General Henry Lee or his creditors."[45]

Although an intelligent man, Lee was by no means clever at investments. Not only did his enthusiasms outpace his common sense, he did not really understand the complex system of financing that supported his speculation. Business transactions had traditionally been a matter of friendship and trust, nowhere more so than among the intertwined families of Virginia's Northern Neck. In the formative years of the republic these methods were in a transitional stage, moving from the eighteenth-century informality of gentlemen's agreements to more impersonal, rigid, and self-interested structures. The old system by which credit ran on yearly accounts—and debts often went unpaid until death—could not suffice for the burgeoning commercial world of the early national period.[46] Henry Lee never really grasped this change. Moreover, he unwisely mixed politics and business in transactions that would be considered unethical today. Though he deplored Hamilton's plan to underwrite the national and state debts, for example, he tried to get advance information about the arrangement, so that he could profit by it. People came to suspect that Lee had little talent for business, but quite an eye for the shady deal.[47]

Creditors appeared at Stratford, demanding payment in slaves, livestock, and furnishings. Some personally seized the possessions while Lee was away making more deals.[48] In one remarkable performance, Light-Horse Harry revived his foraging skills by charging across the property of a man who had confiscated goods at Stratford, trampling the grass, killing an ox, and taking away furniture, liquor, even "knives Forks Spoons Dishes sheets Blankets. . . ."[49] Friends began to talk. Elizabeth Collins Lee, who had shared the joys and sorrows of young motherhood with her sister-in-law Ann, wrote that she and her husband were concerned "on account of Genl. Lee . . . business with him for the last five years has produced to us anxiety and unhappiness."[50] Court cases were now so plentiful—"I would give $250 to have Genl Lee arrested in Fairfax," began one suit—that Lee had to physically dodge the law. He hooked a huge chain across the doorway at Stratford to bar entry, and peered out apprehensively at the slightest sound.[51]

Samuel Storrow accuses Harry Lee—a "heartless & depraved profligate"—of destroying his bride's happiness in just two weeks. "I am right as to time," he states emphatically. Despite some pleasant days in Philadelphia, it is clear that anxiety soon displaced harmony, though just how quickly this began we cannot say with certainty. Scarcely two years into the marriage, Henry was selling lands belonging to his wife, and the sheriff was at the door questioning whether she had agreed to the transactions.[52] Increasingly Ann would have to constrict her needs and her pride. She suffered from what she termed "dropsy," possibly a disease of the heart or kidneys, and pronounced herself "much afflicted."[53] Henry was gone a good deal of the time, slaves and furnishings were confiscated, and Stratford's imposing rooms were uncomfortably cold, lonely, and bare.[54] "I have long since, ceased to regret such privations," she staunchly told a friend who tried to lend her some servants. What she most keenly felt was the loss of her carriage and the isolation it brought her. In February 1799 she confided to her sister-in-law that she had not left the house since the previous August, and that she could "with much truth be said to live 'the World forgetting by the World forgot.'"[55] As her husband's misfortunes brought down others, the once laughing Nancy Lee mourned the loss of her affectionate companions. She wrote to one family who had been ruined by Henry, that "my mind often recurs to you with mingled sensations of pleasure and regret. . . . I consider you among the number of those dear friends whom fate has probably forever severed me from—" To a woman who held that the society of dear friends was "one of the greatest gratifications allowed us in this life," the undeserved ostracism cut her heart with an "affliction, which death only can obliterate."[56]

She was left to raise the family largely on her own as well. Henry and Matilda's two surviving children, Lucy Grymes and Henry IV, were unhappy and resentful.[57] There was also a trio of her own children: charming Carter had been joined by a frail sister, Anne, and a lusty brother, Smith. In the spring of 1806 Ann Lee realized she was pregnant again. She traveled to Shirley in July to seek comfort in her family, only to find that her father had died shortly before her arrival: "the eyes that used to beam with so much affection on me, were veiled for ever!" Distraught, she begged her husband to come with a carriage to bring her home and to take responsibility for her

Stratford, birthplace of Robert E. Lee.

JESSIE BALL DUPONT MEMORIAL LIBRARY, STRATFORD

and the children. "Oh! My dearest Mr. Lee," she implored him, "remember, that your poor afflicted *Fatherless* wife, can now, only look to you, to smooth her rugged path through life, and soften her bed of death!"[58] The carriage did not arrive until November or December, and then its drafty condition left Mrs. Lee shivering in sickness when her third son was born at Stratford on January 19, 1807. She named him Robert Edward, after two favorite brothers. Her sister-in-law, Elizabeth Lee, had written to her in jubilation about the prospect of her own new son, but Ann did not share their joy. Nor was Henry Lee home for the birth. By the time he arrived a few weeks later, he was completely distracted—enmeshed in a dispute with Thomas Jefferson over whether or not he had ever supported the renegade Aaron Burr.[59]

Lee's political squabble with Jefferson was the least of his troubles, for by now his creditors were taking serious legal actions against him. He tried to evade them, moving from place to place and hiding behind his barricaded door. Fifteen months after Robert's birth, however, he was forced to surrender to the sheriff of Westmoreland County. Kept in a twelve-by-fifteen-foot cell, in the same courthouse where George Washington had once cast a ballot electing him to Congress, Lee was sunk into a slough of despair. Once he had written of a friend who was confined for debt that it "would have been comparative humanity to have put him to death rather than thus detained." Another warrant was served against him on April 24, 1809, and Lee was moved to the Spotsylvania County jail—"this depot of misery," as he called it. He had been arrested against a small writ for $425, plus damages, but the collective embarrassment of his affairs was large and complex, and even Lee admitted "the thing is so obscured & so mixed . . . that I cannot speak with any precision thereon."[60] He was in debt to twenty creditors, his brothers, and both of his fathers-in-law, as well as the estates of Patrick Henry and George Washington. He had even borrowed money for the two quires of paper he purchased to write a diatribe against Jefferson. Lee had thought all might be righted if only he could collect from Robert Morris, but it appears that Morris had at least partially compensated him already, through the transfer of some 90,000 acres of land in the Allegheny mountains.[61] To obtain release from prison, Lee paid most of his debts in land. A sampling of these conveyances suggests the extravagance of his speculation: 40,000 acres in Hampshire and Hardy counties to erase one debt; 28,300 acres in Westmoreland to secure another; 50,000 acres in Bath County to one creditor; and the deeds to two coffee estates in Santo Domingo to offset other liabilities. In 1810 he surrendered his life interest in Stratford to his eldest son Henry, and wrote up a final "schedule" of his necessary payments. On March 20, he was finally "discharged from the custody of the Sheriff . . . having complied with the act . . . for relief of Insolvent Debtors."[62]

To overcome his terror and humiliation in prison, Lee embarked on a writing project that fixed his mind on the glorious days of the Continental Army. Initially he hoped to write a biography of his esteemed commander, Nathanael Greene, who had died in 1786. After Lee appealed to his old comrades for their recollections, however, the project broadened into a history of the war in the southern colonies, with Lee's Legion playing a starring role. During those dismal days, Light-Horse Harry sat writing on the courthouse lawn, where he had been allowed to venture, his big bold script slashing across the pages, much as he had once dashed across the countryside. He wrote an astonishing 600 pages in that year, frankly personal, and all in heroic style. In 1810 it was the best account to date of the actions in the South, and it remains today a standard reference work for that theater of the Revolution. Though some later criticized Lee's book as self-serving, it was in fact a wonderful achievement for a man in distress, without access to official papers or even proper writing conditions. One admirer praised his "surprising quickness and talent" with words: "a genius sudden, dazzling, and always at command." Lee hoped for a "big run" and as partial fulfillment of his debt signed over the rights to his brother Richard Bland Lee.[63]

Even Henry's release from prison and hopes for the new book, however, could not halt the family's downward spiral. Ann Lee had been so ill after the birth of Robert that a friend believed she would "not long be a traveller in the rugged paths of this world." Her "heavy calamities" continued when her favorite sister died a few weeks later, and reached new depths with the loss of Stratford. Mrs. Lee staunchly put off those who offered her sanctuary from her husband, but did insist on the right to determine her own home.[64] She chose to move to Alexandria, but was forced onto the charity of her Fitzhugh cousins, whose own fortunes had suffered from Henry Lee's imprudence. Some scholars have maintained that debt was so common in southern society as to be a unifying link between gentlemen, with little dishonor attached. Perhaps so, but Harry Lee had worn out the unspoken statute of limitations.[65] A few of his compatriots from the war maintained that his "talents must again be brought into action," and he was allowed to rejoin the bench of the local magistrates, but the revolutionary generation considered honor and integrity necessary for the development of the republic, and Lee was never again considered for national office. In the leading families it was said that sons and cousins were warned against dealings with him, and at least one newspaper referred to him as "that Swindling Henry Lee." His old friend James Madison, now president, was busy bailing out Lee's relatives and did not answer his letters, though when war scares arose with Britain Madison considered calling up the old soldier. By then, however, Lee's final calamity had commenced.[66]

He had persisted in his staunchly Federalist views, escalating his partisan disputes by hinting at Jefferson's incompetence as governor of Virginia during the Revolution and acting as advocate for a mutual friend who accused the third president of attempting to seduce his wife. For his part, Jefferson spoke openly of the Lee family as "those insects."[67] In 1812, with republican sentiment prevalent and war looming, Henry Lee sided with Baltimore printer Alexander Hanson, whose newspaper, the *Federal Republican*, had been highly critical of the Madison administration, and whose printing press had been destroyed in retaliation. When the printer returned to Baltimore to reestablish his paper and his right to freedom of speech, Lee was there. According to his account, this was mere chance, though Lee would later be charged with having been instrumental in arranging a face-off with Hanson's detractors. On the night of July 26, 1812, a barrage of insults hurled by street ruffians deteriorated into a full-scale riot. When Lee and a dozen other supporters tried to defend Hanson's property, they were threatened by a mob that began to grow in size and inebriation. Baltimore's mayor had Hanson's men removed to the jailhouse, ostensibly to protect them, but the mob broke down the door, viciously attacking them with swords and clubs. The rabble tried to cut off Lee's nose, sliced through his cheekbone instead, brutally beat him, and, when they believed he was dead, poured hot candle wax into his eyes to verify the fact. Lee barely survived, and was so injured that he was taken to Pennsylvania for safety. When he returned to his family weeks later, they wrote that his "wounded spirit & debilitated body" had "received such a shock—that he cannot hope for vigorous health again."[68]

General Henry Lee was fifty-six years when he rejoined Ann and his children in Alexandria. John Jay and a few others tried to encourage him, but he was desperately maimed and demoralized, and tottered around the town, a notorious and frightening figure. He seems to have become something of an old crank, expounding on the foolishness of war with Britain and hurling epithets at those who would not join him in a game of chess.[69] Creditors again began to hound him, and though under a court injunction to remain in the area, in early 1813 he took passage on a ship bound for the West Indies, abandoning his family to the pity of their kin. It was one of his old schemes, meant to elude responsibilities he could not meet and salve his lacerated body and spirit. His brother Edmund wrote that he intended to return in a few months, and prayed he would do so, for he was liable for the bail. As he told Sheriff Luther Martin, "If I should be obliged to pay this money, it will be almost my ruin. . . ."[70] But Henry Lee would not return, and his outsized, contradictory life continued to embitter those he left behind.

That Samuel Storrow's accusatory letter would end in shreds was emblematic of Henry Lee's career. It is hard to come to easy conclusions about Light-Horse Harry, and perhaps that is why Storrow's letter was both destroyed and preserved, an outward expression of the ambivalence Lee has inspired. For every stirring word of praise there is an equally strong piece of damnation; for every noble action, a seemingly despicable deed. He was never boring, always quick to charm, but hard to admire unconditionally. Yet many of Lee's most controversial acts resulted from true conviction. He had fervently believed in American independence, and for the rest of his life staunchly defended the patriot foot soldiers who had borne the burden of its defense. No voice rang louder or more eloquently for a central government that could protect individual liberties while unifying the disparate interests of the states. He understood, too, that such a government might sometimes have to be defended by force, and lived out his principles, whether advocating the creation of a national army, leading troops in the Whiskey Rebellion, or defending freedom of the press in Baltimore. And he passionately believed in the promise of America, in the possibilities for national expansion, the opportunities for wealth, and the historic destiny that this implied.

Patriot, profligate, American Cicero: since his own day, Light-Horse Harry Lee has defied anyone's ability to make a seamless whole of his difficult life. Still, after his death in 1818, one could have expected the controversy to quiet down. The puzzle is why Samuel Storrow wrote such a passionate letter three years later. Storrow says that his interest in the whole business had been rekindled by his encounter with Ann Lee at Farley. But there is another clue, and it lies in the date of the letter: "Sep 6 21"—September 6, 1821. Only a few months earlier a new scandal had arisen at Stratford, this one involving Henry's eldest son, and it had riveted the neighborhood. Just as Storrow recounts, Henry Lee IV had seduced his young ward, the sister of his wife. An infant child was discovered dead. There was talk of murder and embezzlement, and Henry IV began to be called "Black-Horse Harry." Among those present at Stratford when the terrible discoveries were made was Henry's fourteen-year-old half brother Robert.

Chapter Two

Perplexity

Ever since I left you my dear Smith, which has been long too long, you have been almost always present to my mind

I long to get a thorough knowledge of you, which I am deprived of & the most proper period of y^r life will pass before I can execute my wish unless I soon see you.

But my dear son we can interpose a little remedy at once by writing to each other—I set now the example, you will surely follow it, & let me read you as soon as I land in America—y^r dear mother will forward it to me.

Never mind what you tell me, so that [it] is about yrself & Robert

The good old greys are gone I hear—where is my little grey & how is the dog

Do you market as well as Carter did & are you as kind dutiful & affection-ate to y^r dear mother as he was—which do you most love Anne or Mildred

write & tell me everything which concerns you as fast as you can

    ever my dear son

    your loving father HL

Master Sydney S. Lee[1]

. . .

Alexandria July 17th 1816

My dear Carter,

I received your letter acknowledging mine enclosing money—I shall not be at home when your bills will next become due. . . . You will do well to write for no more, than is absolutely necessary, and to demand as little as possible for what is called pocket money—It is now ascertained beyond a doubt, that all of my expenses must be diminished. . . . Have sent off two of the servants. . . . I fear the next sacrifice must be the horses—We have very seldom more than one dish on the table of meat, to the great discomfort of my young Ladies & Gentle-

men. . . . *Ann prefers fowls, but they are so high, that they are sparingly delt in;
and if brought to table, scarcely a <u>back</u>, falls to Smith & Robert's share. . . .*
     Farewell my dear Child
          Ann H. Lee[2]

. . .

Nassau 4th 16

My dear Fish
     *I am still struggling with the effects of the outrage I suffered soon after I
dined with you in Washington & I confide with [a] celebrated Spanish Physician who cures every body not actually in the arms of death. But my debility &
the daily medicine has put me in disgust of every thing eatable in my command.*
     *I therefore avail myself of Captain Ross Brig James, who sails tomorrow for
N York & will return here—He is so civil as to say he will bring the few articles
you will be so kind as to procure for me. He takes with him an Turtle which I
hope may get safe to you.*
     *It is 22 wt & said to be very fat—the only article here which you can
desire—I have not seen it, as I scarcely ever leave my room*
     *I think I could occasionally eat some of y[r] beef—send me three <u>flanks</u> well
cured & three ribs fresh. Let them be of the smallest size you can get as they better will suit me—3 or 4 venison hams as many gallons pickled oysters done up
of the largest & fattest oysters in the old manner when more pains were taken
with all our works than latterly—the common way of pickling them now spoils
them 12 lb best potted back country butter of the best quality 25 wt buck wheat
meal & as many lbs pilot bread with one barrel pippins. 12 small sprouts of the
Court [apple] tied up in a small bundle, incased with dirt at their roots—this
for a gentleman wishing them here to try if they will grow here. Now my dear
Fish excuse the trouble I impose by asking these triffles.*
     *Naught but my situation could induce me so to trouble you, & the impossi-
bility of communicating with my own home from hence, no vessel every having
gone since I have been here to the Chesapeake.*
     *If you ever see John Jay the man of my heart after Washington died, present
me to him & to Harrison Bayard. Col Smith & Jon Lexington remember me
with real esteem. In y[r] self & Lady & children I wish every good advance.   H Lee*

     *Please to notice Captain Ross for his kindness to me & put my let[r] to the post
office.*[3]

. . .

Sudley March 4th 1821

My dear Mary

When I parted with you I expected to see you again in a few days, but Aunt Calverts health has improved so much it is not necessary I should be there, and although It would give me much pleasure to spend some time with her, it would be exceedingly inconvenient for me to leave home at this time. I intended writing to you by the last post but my mind has been in such confusion for a week past I could not do anything. A day or two before my Husband left me he received a Letter from Uncle R.S. requesting his immediate attendance in Westmoreland, and giving the dreadful information of Betsy McCarty having been seduced by H Lee, he says every vile art was used to accomplish this deed of darkness; and H Lee left home the day after the discovery was made to him and he did not suppose would ever return. My Uncle said, she had had a child, but leaves us all in the dark about particulars; poor wretched Ann was quite ignorant of the whole transaction at the time he wrote and also the poor Old Grandmother. William wrote me a few lines from Alexandria saying there were a number of Horrible tales in Town; one of which was that HL had killed the child by laying it as soon as born in an out House during the severe weather where it was found frozen. I do not think this can be true; or my Uncle would have said something about it, and it is improbable, as there is a vault in the garden; and an unoccupied wine vault under the cellar besides many other places about the House, more convenient and likely to be chozen. Yet it often has happened that an overruling providence deprives a guilty wretch of his accustomed craftiness; and leads him to do the very thing; most likely to bring him to justice. If this story is true it is certain the degraded man can never return, for he would have to stand a trial for his Life. What will be done with the deluded Girl I know not; my Uncle says she is more to be pitied than condemned; but I shall not think so, unless I see her spend the balance of her Life in penitence and prayer.

Dear miserable Ann I should think would be more likely to recover her composure if removed out of the neighborhood; and I intend to solicit her coming to Live with us. Oh Mary! How great is the debt we owe to restraining grace; but for that, might we not have been as vile in the eyes our fellow creatures, as we have often been in the eyes of him who see'th the secret chambers of the Heart?

Nancy Rose and myself were lamenting the ungodly Lives of our relations when I was last in Westmoreland concluded by joining to express our apprehension that some great affliction would attend those who had received so many favours; without acknowledging the hand from whence they came: my Uncle now reaps the fruits of his pride and indulgence, he brought those girls up to

think they were too grand to be advised by two poor old women—consequently
Ann engaged herself without asking any advice and poor Soul was married to
disgrace and misery. The other was always self willed, and unruly, and when I
was in Westmoreland, I saw improprieties, which caused a suspicion to cross
my mind; which I banished immediately, as an uncharitable suggestion of the
evil one. These reactions are made in confidence to you. When my Husband re-
turns you will see him before I shall and hear all the particulars for he will
know it is useless for him to attempt to conceal anything.

We seem to lead a very fashionable life, for he has been more from Home in
the last 12 months, than for many preceeding years taken together. But I trust
the same will never happen again; we must now be prudent and saving that we
may have something to lend into the Lord who has thus far upheld us, and Oh
Mary he never leave[s] us to ourselves. The girls send much Love to you and
Sally wishes you to take the missionary Herald for her and have it sent to Chan-
tilly. May there be some word in it directed by the blessed spirit to cause light
to shine on the darkness which surrounds her is the fervent prayer of your
AC R[obertson][4]

⊳⋅◇⋅⊲

T HESE LETTERS are among the most revealing sources we have about
Robert E. Lee's troubling childhood. We have no firsthand account of
Lee's boyhood days, and he is infrequently mentioned in the correspondence
of his parents, so each scrap is as precious as it is rare. These emotive letters
introduce us to Robert's intimate family: notorious half brother Henry;
scholarly bon vivant Carter and ebullient Smith; sister Anne who was a nervous invalid, known for her "wild childish manners"; and Mildred, considered "the flower of the Lees, by a long way."[5] The juxtaposition of Ann Lee's
growing financial anxiety and the continued self-indulgence of her profligate
husband and stepson could not be clearer. Desperation and despair seep
through the pages, as her loving concern turns to gritty determination. By
the end of this tense family correspondence we are left unsure about what is
sincere and what may smack of guilt or opportunistic manipulation. If in
reading these missives it seems that historical import lies buried beneath domestic detail, read again. For in the trivial lies the potent; and our own discomfort mirrors the perplexing atmosphere of Lee's formative years.

"Had I not escaped from my country, the climate must have finished me ere
now," Light-Horse Harry Lee told President James Madison, soon after he
sailed away in 1813. It was true that he had been badly weakened by his en-

counter with the Baltimore mob, and the family clung to this explanation for his disappearance.[6] It is also clear that his creditors were on the offensive again and that to avoid another turn in debtor's prison he had to elude them.[7] For close to five years he remained on the move in the West Indies, seeking in Nassau what he could not find in Port-au-Prince, restless for something—serenity, or vigor, or release. During this time he was genuinely ill, racked with bodily torments that affected his digestion and bladder. The descriptions left of him depict a man without an anchor, sometimes fascinating his acquaintances, sometimes shouting obscenely with pain.[8]

To the end he was Harry Lee, who liked his Madeira, indulged his powerful will, and could never resist the siren call of a wager. During the early years of his exile Lee speculated on shipping ventures that might breach the wartime blockade of the Chesapeake Bay. When they did not pay, he racked up debts and "lived on his Wits and the donations of credulous persons," giving worthless notes against a fictitious account with a Savannah banking house.[9] Intermittently he wrote lengthy epistles to his family, extolling the virtues of truth, early rising, and the study of Cicero.[10] He was particularly fond of clever, amiable Carter, whom he expected to restore the family's greatness.[11] The letters, full of advice that he himself had not heeded, seem to have been more a catharsis than a genuine influence on the Lee sons. Most of them were addressed to Carter, then studying at Harvard, and it is unclear if Robert ever saw them. Apparently many of them were not sent at all, and to Carter's bewilderment were delivered nearly two decades later.[12]

It is hard to say how the letters that did arrive were received. Henry, Lucy Grymes, and Carter, the three eldest children, had known their father and tasted his charm, and they would defend him for the remainder of their lives.[13] Carter recalled that "my rambles with him were my chief delight" and remembered the excitement of lavish feasts, famous guests, and foxhunting with Stratford's pampered hounds, Hotspur and Stormer. He recorded the way Harry liked to teach the children little classical mottoes or read beautiful passages from the *Iliad,* his fine voice like "a trumpet with a silver sound."[14] Carter consecrated the days in sentimental poetic sketches, recalling Stratford's "flower enameled lands" where "We boys without our hats would run/All careless of the burning sun."[15] Ann Lee's younger children knew this world only fleetingly, visited more in their imaginations than in reality. Henry treated them like a footnote in his life; we have only those few fond lines to Smith—and none at all to Robert. Harry's neglect was joined with sickness and war to make the family's existence increasingly precarious. By the time of her death, Lee's mother could no longer pay a ten-dollar debt.[16] "God of heaven, how cutting to my heart the knowledge of y^r situation," Harry would wail when he heard of his family's increasing poverty, but it did not keep him from surreptitiously ordering sides of beef and gallons of oysters for himself.[17] Once the fulcrum of their pride, he was now the agent of their despair.

When Henry was forced to relinquish his life interest in Stratford, Ann Lee insisted on settling in Alexandria, where congenial friends and the protective shield of numerous relations would ease her life. The official family story was that the move was made for the purpose of educating the children, and there may have been some truth in that assertion.[18] Soon after Henry's release from jail, Ann Lee began to cajole family members into helping locate a house. There was no money for rent, so her relatives' largess became a critical element of the search.[19] In late 1810 the family packed a few possessions— the tradition is that they took only a clock and Robert's cradle—and moved first to a small house on Cameron Street, and later to a larger building on Oronoco Street. This was Alexandria's heyday as a commercial port, and the town was attractive and intriguing, laid out in wide streets lined with handsome brick buildings. It was Federalist almost to a man, having nurtured some of the most distinguished founders of the country, many of whom were still alive, and others, such as Washington, who were so immediate to memory that "they were constantly obtruding on the conversations of . . . remaining friends."[20] Carter Lee thought that Alexandria abounded in delights for a boy, with its ever-changing river, tall-masted ships along the wharves, and a market piled high with local delicacies.[21]

Ann Lee and her brood would change residences several times during their years in Alexandria, but it was 607 Oronoco Street that provided the backdrop for most of Robert's childhood memories. The red brick house was a gracious late Georgian structure, with elegant proportions and some lovely details, including plaster moldings and ornate Prussian gray marble mantelpieces. In back were slave quarters and a large garden where Robert recalled playing among the snowball bushes. He probably slept in a finished garret room, above his mother's chamber, on the east side of the house. Though it was seemingly luxurious, architectural analyses of the house hint at the difficult state of Ann Lee's finances. William Henry Fitzhugh, the kinsman who generously lent it to the Lees, did not paint the interior during their occupancy, and the wood fires and smoky lamps left the walls sooty and peeling. Half of the house was listed on fire insurance policies as a separate dwelling, apparently rented out to gentlemen boarders, who shared a kitchen and other amenities with the Lees. Neighbors recalled that it was located at the edge of town, in an area known to be swampy, mosquito-infested, and unhealthy.[22]

Looking at Robert Lee's childhood is something like peering through a half closed door. We catch tantalizing glimpses, but much is obscured in the hazy light of memory or lost in hushed tones. There are only a few small things that we really know. He was bashful; to tease him, his sisters and brothers liked to "scream with glee and laughter" when he lost a front tooth. He was

The Lee family home at 607 Oronoco Street, Alexandria.
LIBRARY OF CONGRESS

often sickly, worrying his mother to the point that she took him to the New Jersey seashore for his health. There he had a pet lobster and a pet hummingbird, early signs of his lifelong love of animals. Both of these creatures died on the same day, and Robert sadly buried them in the sand with an epitaph written by the renowned jurist Horace Binney: "Here lies a lobster mourned by friends & foes / Tread lightly on him, or he'll bite your toes."[23] Later in life he fondly remembered swimming in the Potomac, playing by the spring at Stratford, and seeing his mother plant a horse chestnut tree on the estate.[24]

Each day the Lee household was buttressed by morning and evening prayers, and Robert once told a clergyman that his mother taught him the church catechism before he was able to read.[25] All of the children received a good education. Robert seems to have gone first to family plantation schools in Fauquier County, then began attending the Alexandria Academy when he was about fourteen. This was a first-class school with a distinguished pedigree, where he learned classical languages and literature—Caesar, Virgil and

Tacitus, Homer and Xenophon—as well as algebra, the first six books of Euclid, and some "inferior branches" such as English grammar. He enjoyed the company of his cousin Cassius Lee during his three years there, distinguished himself for "gentlemanly deportment," and would later acknowledge the "affectionate fidelity" of his teacher William Leary.[26] When he was seventeen, Ann Lee scraped up the ten-dollar tuition Robert needed to enter a school that had been opened by Benjamin Hallowell, a gifted Quaker educator. Hallowell's school was unusually advanced for a southern educational institution, with a shelf full of sophisticated calculus books, a chemistry lab, and a "magic lantern" that illuminated astronomical slides. All of this suited Robert's goal of improving his technical skills before he departed for West Point, where he had been accepted as a cadet. Hallowell noticed the studious young man, particularly the polish with which he completed each project.[27] Ann Lee rounded out the education by sending her children to their cousins' dancing lessons, defending the art for its cultivation of grace, even when it was questioned in some religious circles. Two decades later Robert would also insist that his children learn to dance, claiming he would rather have them "pierced by a hundred Mexican balls" than see them become as lifeless as "Hallowells boys."[28]

Carter Lee would leave vivid recollections of a boyhood spent trapping squirrels and rabbits, stealing the neighbors' apples, playing "marbles, hopscot, bat, bandy-prisoners-base" and sneaking into the Methodist church to gawk at their emotive services.[29] One can imagine that Robert's boyhood was similar. Certainly somewhere along the line he learned to shoot, skate, ride, and hunt on foot, activities he continued to enjoy as an adult and passed along to his own boys. It was an era without many rule-laden games—companionship was largely spontaneous and unstructured—but the boys seem to have had their own code of conduct that later formed the core of their manly values. A young girl whose brothers played with the Lees remembered hearing them talk "about self defense, righting the wronged, protecting the persecuted, never provoking a fight; but if once engaged in it, it was the duty of a boy to fight like fury, and never give up until he had punished the boy who struck first."[30] Role-playing aside, probably what the boys prized most about hunting in the forest and the adventure of mock battles was the way these pursuits released them from the constraints of home.[31]

It is not clear how often Robert escaped the domestic scene on Oronoco Street. In the years following Harry Lee's departure, his mother became increasingly ill and depressed. In her younger days Nancy Lee had been known for her grace and her subtle humor, but as an older woman she is generally described in terms of stoic fortitude. It is clear that she did a remarkable job of raising her "young Ladies & Gentlemen." She read them the Bible, forbade them to wager on their chess competitions, worried constantly that they would fall into "idleness and dissipation."[32] She told her sons that one or two glasses of wine with dinner were convivial and healthful, "but for the third—look for my ghost in it warning you against it."[33] Despite her thin purse, Ann Lee's children were educated, accomplished, and kind. What she could not supply in material possessions or paternal pride she gave them in breeding, an elusive but instantly recognizable quality of affability and manners that was noticed by virtually all who met her quintet of sons and daughters.[34] But hardship also seems to have given Ann Lee a dogged, humorless approach to life and a large share of self-pity, apparent in her letters to Smith and Carter, and vividly recalled by her closest friends.[35] Sadly, we have little direct evidence of tenderness on her part. Our best clues are found in the high regard all of Ann Lee's children retained for her, or in descriptions of the family, which invariably portray them as close and loving.[36]

She had much to lament and much to worry her, and doubtless she genuinely needed assistance. She also required considerable cheering. With his older brothers away, and his sisters too young or too delicate to care for their mother, Robert took on the responsibility. Alexandrians remembered him engrossed in housekeeping, racing home at school recess to assist his mother with chores or take her for a pleasure ride in the carriage. Evidently he mixed his mother's medicines, was her "outdoor agent and confidential messenger," and played the clown to make her laugh, all of which increased her reliance on him.[37] He was by all accounts devoted to her, and perhaps also unusually anxious for her approval. He certainly won her esteem and enlarged his influence at home, and it may be here that we see the first signs of a lifelong use of irreproachable conduct as an agent of power. One cousin who was in the room when Robert departed for West Point remembered how his mother wailed, "Sally, you know what I have lost. He is son, daughter and everything to me."[38] No doubt Robert's service was an excellent lesson in self-denial, and it seems to have brought out a genuinely nurturing side that he would later exhibit with his own family. Yet it placed him in a kind of inverted relationship in which the child becomes the caretaker and the responsible adult the dependent. An early biographer, who knew the family, postulated that it "must have cut him off somewhat from the natural overflow, the fresh spontaneousness of boyish spirits. I think he showed the effect all his life."[39]

One day in early April 1818, Ann Lee received a hurried message from her brother-in-law Richard Bland Lee. "My dear Madam," it began: "It is my painful duty to announce to you the death of your husband—He died at a friends house in Cumberland Island Georgia on the 25th March." No further particulars were given, and the short note ended with the hope that she might find "abundant consolation in the virtues of your excellent & promising children."[40] Word must have reached Henry Lee's eldest son the same day, for he also wrote to Ann, but in more emotional tones. "To the grief of a wife and of a son—no human power can afford consolation," he commiserated. "Together we have felt the bounty of his heart—together we have experienced the hardness of his fortune—together let us mourn the affliction of his parting."[41]

Dramatic to the last, Light-Horse Harry Lee died as he had lived, caught between degradation and honor. Sensing the life ebbing from his feeble form, he persuaded a ship captain to give him passage to the southern United States, where he hoped to rejoin his family. When he could not raise the money required to pay his debts before leaving Nassau, he swindled an elderly lady into paying them, giving her worthless scrip in return. By now a shabby old man, with no fortune but his war stories, he embarked with one tattered bag and a cask of Madeira. Often in tremendous pain, he passed the voyage alternately shouting curses and entertaining those on board "with the most agreeable and interesting conversation spiced with numerous anecdotes of the revolution."[42] As the vessel neared the Georgia coast it became clear that he could go no farther, and he asked to be put off at Dungeness, the citrus-and-magnolia-scented estate owned by the daughter of his old commander Nathanael Greene. Amazed at the specter that had appeared on their wharf, the family took Harry Lee in, just as he had hoped. "I am come purposely to die in the house and in the arms of the daughter of my old friend and compatriot," he announced, and that is exactly what he did. His feisty spirit did not succumb easily, and he lingered for fifteen days, often screaming or throwing boots at the servants in his agony. When the end came, he was treated with the greatest respect, not only by General Greene's relatives but by a naval group anchored close to Dungeness. Officers from the U.S. *John Adams* laid their swords across his breast and carried the coffin to the family cemetery; an army band played the dead march; the ships' minute guns fired their loftiest salute. The years of deception and defeat were left unmentioned. As a volley of musketry sounded over the grave, a witness noted only that "one of the patriots that the country . . . so frequently speak of" had been lost.[43]

There are conflicting reports about how the family in Alexandria reacted. Letters exist that suggest there had been a continued affection between Henry and Ann, as well as some collaboration on domestic matters, and a family story states that every day she wore a black-and-gold brooch containing a lock of her husband's hair.[44] However, more than a year before her husband's death Ann Lee was already referring to herself as a widow, and it may be that by April 1818 she had long accepted his loss. After she received the news, she evidently went into tight-lipped isolation, lying in her darkened room for weeks. When the man who had accompanied Lee from Nassau called to offer condolences—and collect a debt—she reportedly refused to meet with him.[45] Carter Lee probably expressed the family's official line when he said that "a disposition to aim too high, or at too much" was what had ruined his "great father, in dispite of his mighty prowess."[46] The details of General Lee's tortured end may have been kept from the younger children. A few weeks before his own death, Robert was troubled when an account of his father's final misery, including the temper tantrums, was published by a man who had been present. Mary Lee, writing for her husband, asked Carter to confirm it, saying that the story had distressed him and was "not at all consistent with what he has always heard."[47]

For nearly a century it has been believed that the atmosphere and events of early childhood have significant emotional and behavioral consequences. For a child the departure or death of a parent is a seminal experience. Robert Lee's youth was not easy, and it was punctuated with some melodramatic episodes that must have been perplexing to a developing boy.[48] He was six years old when his father sailed for the West Indies. He had seen little of him in those few years, what with debtor's prison, the endless search for land deals, and the long recuperation from the wounds sustained in Baltimore. Those injuries had made him a frightening figure, with a swollen black face and desperate look. One little girl who saw Harry Lee at church with his family recalled how he was whispered about in the town and how his penetrating look terrified her: "the bright black eyes were shining under white bandages that bound his brow and others passing over his head and under his chin . . . his fiery eye alarmed me whenever it fell on me."[49] It must have been a powerful image to a small boy: a man—a great man—*his* father—crippled and humbled, the object of horror and gossip. Over the years many writers have tried to evaluate Lee's attitude toward his father, and some have laid him on the psychobiographical couch, extrapolating from slim evidence a series of intense and sometimes destructive feelings. Armchair analysts have blamed his father's disgrace and abandonment for Robert Lee's adult depression, his "failure" as a father, a powerful rage on the battlefield, his desire to please his mother, and a hypothetical case of foot fetishism.[50] To step into the psychohistorical world of inference and conjecture is a dangerous business, however. We have no clinical evidence, and each of the Lee

brothers developed a distinctive personality, which ranged from highly conscientious to profligate, so that no simple model of response to Henry Lee's
tragedy can be drawn. Indeed it may be that the difficulties of Robert's
childhood galvanized his will to succeed rather than led him to despair. Andrew Jackson, who suffered similar boyhood losses, thought the experiences
had strengthened him. "It was this that gave me knowledge of human nature," Jackson told a young contemporary, "it was this that forced into action all energies of my mind, and ultimately caused me to progress through
life as I have done."[51]

What then can be said with certainty of Lee's reaction to his famous, and
infamous, father? To start with, Robert barely knew Light-Horse Harry Lee.
Piecing together dated letters and court records, it seems that altogether he
spent only about thirty-four months in the company of his father. The most
extended periods took place when he was under two and a half, and after
Harry was maimed and badly wounded in spirit. In his voluminous correspondence Robert refers to his father only a few times, and some analysts
have made much of this. However, he mentions his mother no more, and
she was said to be the object of his great affection. It is also true that Robert
never named a child after his father—something that has also been raised as
an indication of filial ambivalence. Nonetheless, he did not balk at "Henry"
as an auxiliary name for his second son, William Henry Fitzhugh Lee. He
also urged his brothers to carry on the name (which Smith and Carter did),
lightheartedly begging them to do so quickly because he could not "defer
my claims to it much longer." In fact, when Carter finally heeded his suggestion, Robert pronounced it a clear indication that the boy would "be good
as well as great."[52]

Whether his heart held Henry Lee in admiration or at a cautious distance
we also do not know, for his renown may have been as intimidating to a
small lad as his deformities. Henry Adams, who came from a similarly illustrious family, felt "branded" by his ancestors' achievements, and though he
acknowledged that it could be an entry ticket to certain circles, he felt the
expectations were also a handicap. "One had to pay for Revolutionary patriots. . . . Such things warp young life," Adams wrote, and proceeded to spend
a lifetime searching for a separate identity.[53] Robert did record seeing his father's swords, and two legionnaire pistols, and perhaps these military trappings inspired his choice of profession.[54] Then again, he may have been
captivated by Alexandria's militia ground, where the boys liked to hang
about on muster day, or by his cousin Hill Carter's much-heralded performance during the War of 1812. What we know for certain is that he claimed
that a taste for military trappings had "clung to me from boyhood."[55] Some

have postulated that Ann Lee took care to praise Henry to his children, reminding them of his heroics even under the duress of his desertion; others
believe that she did everything possible to convince Robert that he should
not emulate his father.[56] Whatever the case, it is clear that in later life Robert
felt some pride in his father. When a stranger told him of his relatives' role
in the American Revolution, Lee wrote fulsomely of "the pleasure I feel in
learning that your ancestors were fellow-soldiers with mine," saying they
had a "hereditary bond of amity."[57] When he was about thirty, he had his father's portrait by Gilbert Stuart copied for his parlor wall.[58] At least twice he
went out of his way to visit his father's grave on Cumberland Island, and he
did so in dignity and peace, calling it "the last tribute of respect that I shall
ever be able to pay. . . ."[59] As a West Point cadet he would choose friends
whose fathers had fought alongside Light-Horse Harry. Joseph E. Johnston
noted that in fact this was the first foundation of their lifelong friendship.[60]
Perhaps the most tantalizing tidbit is that Lee appropriated his father's birthday, giving it as his own, in the first letter we have in his hand.[61] General
James Longstreet recalled that Lee only rarely spoke of his father, "but when
he did, he was far more charming than he thought."[62]

There are also indications that Robert knew the family situation was insecure. He once noted that he ate very little as a child, shunning most food.[63]
He told his fiancée that family troubles had led him to believe he would lead
a life of isolation and probably never be able to marry.[64] He was well aware
that his father was in exile and generally out of communication. Whether
related to this or not, as an adult he was quite anxious that his own children
might not know him. "Do not let them forget me," he begged his wife during the Mexican War. "Talk to the children of me. Teach them to love
me. . . ."[65] Lee became obsessive about paying debts and was repulsed by the
thought he might ever be considered a swindler, though his wife linked this
to his "admirable mother" rather than his father's lesser reputation.[66] The
next generation was also aware of their grandfather's excesses. Hearing that
Light-Horse Harry may have acquired some Revolutionary War relics illegally, Fitz Lee wrote to one of Robert's daughters, "Oh! Suppose our Grandfather did not pay Capt Massie . . . Oh Mildred I fear he did wrong."[67]
Robert Lee read all of his eldest brother's ill-conceived diatribes, which in
defending Light-Horse Harry also resurrected the malicious talk about him,
and he once spoke of the need to "resuscitate" the family name.[68] Even if the
kinfolk were discreet about Harry's history, everyone else in the small
Alexandria community knew all the excruciating details. Since he had not
developed a clearly formed personal image, Robert was subject to the con-
fusing impressions others had about his father.

Among the most revealing documents about Lee's relationship to his father is the introduction he wrote for a new edition of Light-Horse Harry's *Memoirs of the War in the Southern Department of the United States*, published in 1869. Carter, ever on the alert for an opportunity to revive the Lee reputation, harnessed his now-celebrated brother to finally lay to rest any doubts about his family's greatness.[69] Robert was reluctant, and only accepted the project after Carter had assembled letters, obituaries, and other materials.[70] The "biographical sketch" is actually a scrapbook of articles and descriptions written years earlier by other authors, all laudatory, and all reminiscent of Light-Horse Harry's elaborate self-justifications. Robert Lee's role as biographer seems to have been minimal—he dutifully pasted the pieces together, but never adds personal anecdote or interpretation. He was openly anxious that nothing be included that could cause any but kindly feelings, and the result is an anodyne narrative. At Carter's insistence he did add a number of spirited epistles from Light-Horse Harry, but many of these had arrived decades after they were written, too late to guide the formation of young minds or soothe the wounds left by desertion. These letters are particularly fascinating for what Lee edits out of them. The compulsive, rambling quality is gone, the erratic phrases and repetitions eliminated, and tidy paragraphs replace the large scrawling pages of the originals. Where Harry's advice seems embarrassingly at odds with his own character, it too is modified. A letter Carter thought particularly significant—in which Harry consigns Smith and Robert to Carter's care, professes pacifism, and expresses doubt about the divinity of Christ—has been entirely omitted, and with it some of the more intriguing aspects of Harry's persona. This pastiche feels more like a detached paper cutout than the work of an affectionate heir who recalled the advice and whimsicalities of a glorious, if eccentric, father. Perhaps Lee was in denial about the painful realities of his father's life and needed to create through other people's impressions an image that would finally feel unified and comfortable. Perhaps he simply did not know the man and had nothing more to say.[71]

He was "a boy without a childhood," some of his analysts would say, but the evidence is not that bleak. Lee himself referred more than once to the "happy days of my boyhood."[72] One of the reasons for this was the network of kin that Ann Lee and her children enjoyed. She had chosen wisely in moving to Alexandria, where community and family were quite literally synonymous. Three uncles and a dozen cousins lived within five blocks of them. William Meade, another cousin, was the rector of Christ Church, and it was with him that Robert studied his catechism. Charles Lee, one of Light-Horse Harry's brothers, who had been attorney general of the United States, welcomed Ann Lee into his well-appointed home on North Washington Street. Uncle Edmund was mayor of the town. From the time Robert was a tiny boy, Henry Lee thought him "a copy of my brother Edmund," and the comparison is interesting, for Edmund Lee was an austere, pious man, who kept the town and the vestry of Christ Church in strict order. William Meade, who was trained to be charitable, found him a "man of great decision and perseverance in what he deemed right," but obstinate, unpopular, and committed to doing his duty "regardless of all others." However, Edmund Lee also shepherded the town through its golden age, as well as the War of 1812.[73] After the death of Henry he was given particular responsibilities for the guardianship of Robert. A half dozen other men also watched out for the boy—William Henry Fitzhugh, George Washington Parke Custis, Thomas Turner, Philip Fendall, and Hill and Bernard Carter. Robert remembered these men and their kindness to him all his life,

Ann Hill Carter Lee.
WASHINGTON AND LEE UNIVERSITY

and in the absence of his own father they must have provided some reassurance and masculine companionship.

The intertwined families were also extremely social, hosting soirees in town and passing long weeks together in the country. Alexandrians of that period recalled that young and old attended the same parties, the children sometimes sitting at side tables but fully participating in the merriment.[74] Robert was open in his fondness for Kinloch, Shirley, Eastern View, and Arlington, where he was caught up in the beauty of wooded hills, wide rivers, and the joyous melee of multiple cousins.[75] These comfortable periods with his kin had a larger social context, for strong, interconnected families were vital to the preservation of a traditional, hierarchical social order. Within an extended family the lengthy periods of intimate living, reinforced by copious correspondence, offered emotional well-being and an irreplaceable web of important connections. Family groups sometimes acted as a business enterprise or loan institution, increasing their capital through collaborative ventures or pooled land holdings. Ann Lee had found her relatives to be an informal insurance policy, and for the elderly they often provided similar emergency assets. Such clan networks fostered biological and political structures that were nearly tribal, making it unlikely that the outside world could either fully enter them or work their demise.[76]

The connections of the Lee family were of tensile strength. For decades Lee ancestors had extolled the virtues of intermarriage and blood-related business arrangements. One of the earliest Lee settlers remarked that "the first fall and ruin of families and estates was mostly occasioned by imprudent matches."[77] Succeeding generations took heed, until the family was as intertwined as a "tangle of fishhooks."[78] Philip Fendall, one of Ann Lee's most generous supporters, offers a good example. His first wife was a cousin, Sarah Lettice Lee. After her death, he married Elizabeth Lee, the widow of Philip Ludwell Lee, the heir of Stratford, whose daughter Matilda had been Light-Horse Harry's "divine" first spouse. Fendall's third wife was Mary Lee, Harry's sister. Robert Lee's immediate family had similarly complex connections. His half sister Lucy married his mother's brother Bernard Carter, making Bernard simultaneously his uncle and his stepbrother. Bernard and Lucy's son Charles Carter was both Robert's first cousin and his nephew.[79] The large family could confuse even the hardiest genealogist and sometimes caused Lee amused frustration. Speaking of a family reunion before his marriage, he told his brother, "There was Miss Ladonia too, Cousin Anne Butler Berkeley, with all her Brothers & Sisters. 25 Misses Nelson & as many Misters &c. &c. &c. &c. I returned to Norfolk with them at night. Saw there Uncle Edmund, Cousins R^{cd} B. Lee, John Lee U.S.N., Sally, Nancy, Randolph, Tom Turner, & in fact if I was to mention them all you would cut your throat in despair."[80]

Despite his light tone, the close extended family had a deep impact on Lee's life. He would name his children after them, seek their advice on private legal matters, lend them money when he had little to spare, and arrange his social life around their joys and sorrows. He counted on them to be compatible boarding-school roommates for his sons and daughters, to sell him sound horses, deliver notes, hire his slaves, and advance his professional interests. Not surprisingly, the wife he chose was a member of this clan. Lee's children would also marry cousins, deepening the nearly unfathomable ties.[81] Despite some strong connections in the army, Lee always felt most comfortable within this closed society. Carter Lee reflected his brother Robert's thoughts when he wrote: "I am happy every where, & under almost any circumstances, but . . . I find from reiterated experience that I prefer the country to the town, & my own kith & kin to any one elses."[82]

Among the family members who were given special responsibility for Robert was his half brother Henry. Henry Lee IV was twenty years older than Robert, and was widely thought to be among the most promising young men in America. He had a fleshy face, with a nose that was "rather meaty," but he was witty and erudite, much sought after as a companion.[83] Around 1810 Henry entered local politics, representing Westmoreland County in the Virginia House of Delegates, and during the War of 1812 he was appointed a major in the infantry, where he evidently acquitted himself well. On his return he made a bid for his father's old congressional seat, but lost. His closest associates praised his "brilliant conversational powers" and encouraged Henry to use "the wandering enthusiasm of your genius" fully. His friends also needled him about a darker side, an arrogance laced with sarcasm, which stood in the way of success. Henry chose not to listen, refusing "to steal one moment from lavacious mirth, or the pleasures of the table."[84]

On his return from the army, Henry reopened Stratford and began to reverse its sad state of disrepair. Like the other Lees, he loved the estate, romantically describing it as a "place of solitude, of nooks & of shade . . . & the music of the wild winds."[85] In 1817 his ability to re-create the lavish hospitality of "divine Matilda's" day was enhanced by his marriage to Anne McCarty, a seventeen-year-old heiress from the Westmoreland neighborhood, whose regal carriage, blue-black hair, and thoroughbred family impressed all who met her. Stratford was generously opened to the Lee brothers and sisters, and Henry's "genius, liberality, his devotion to his mother's family & promise of eminence" became "the theme of every one."[86] It appears from family papers that Robert and his siblings spent a good deal of time there, particularly after William Henry Fitzhugh sold the Oronoco Street house in 1818. "Be pleased to assist Smith & Robert in their preparations & departure for this place," Henry wrote to Philip Fendall a few months after Light-Horse Harry's death. "I should & we should all be glad if you w^d accompany them."[87] The census records for 1820 also suggest that they were living at Stratford, for although only Henry Lee was listed by name, the other members of the household correlate by age and gender to Ann Lee and her offspring.[88] Thus it was that Robert, then a young adolescent, was present at the estate when two tragedies struck.

In the fall of 1818 Anne McCarty Lee gave birth to a daughter, named Margaret. Evidently she was a charming little girl, adored by both parents. Barely two years later the child reenacted a shocking scene from Stratford's past. One of the notable features of the house was a long flight of exterior stairs that swept up from the driveway to a grand ceremonial entrance hall on the second floor. Sometime around 1780, the heir to Stratford, four-year-old Philip Ludwell Lee, had fallen down those stairs to his death. Now, two generations later, Margaret stumbled in the same way, leaving her mother in despair.[89] Inconsolable, she turned to laudanum, with its soothing opiates, and to the comfort of her sister. Elizabeth McCarty, then sixteen, was as striking as Anne, with a glorious mane of mahogany curls. On her arrival at Stratford, Henry Lee was made her guardian, the protector of her welfare and her considerable property. As Anne became more and more indisposed, Henry and Elizabeth were thrown together "in a state of unguarded intimacy." Lee had long been known as a ladies' man who seduced his friends' sisters and laughed at their lovelorn notes. One abandoned lover remembered her "feelings were *exquisite*" on the night Henry "partook" and that the arrival of a message from him "arous'd yes arous'd all my former feelings . . . but no Henry Lee yet appear'd." Now Lee took similar advantage of his vulnerable ward. As Ann Robertson's shocked letter at the opening of this chapter attests, the discovery of a dead child in an outbuilding, stillborn or murdered, created a public scandal.[90]

"Poor Mrs. Lee and the innocent sweet Ann," Nelly Custis Lewis wrote of Robert's mother and sister during this trauma.

> Major H Lee . . . has seduced his sister in law, Miss McCarty, defrauded her of her great part of her property, & they would have gone to South America together after deserting his wife had not Miss McC's unexpected confinement disclosed the nefarious business. He is justly detested, & she is miserable—has returned to her poor Grandmother who must think that she has lived too long.[91]

Elizabeth McCarty was indeed miserable. She wrote tearfully that she was almost "overpowered by a sense of desolation & desertion . . . left friendless & alone . . . ," and asked that others not forsake her "for my mother's sake, who tho' she (as an angel) must blame, still loves & pitys her unhappy child."[92] In contrition she cut off the beautiful auburn ringlets, which she said were the cause of the attraction, and kept her head close-cropped for the rest of her life. Her sister Anne languished for years in complete despair and became addicted to opium.[93]

The extended Lee kin were concerned about the effect this would have on the more innocent members of the family. "You have no doubt heard of H. Lee's adventure & Miss McC—s disgrace, therefore I can *will not* sully this paper with the relation of such black deeds . . . ," wrote one of Robert's aunts. "I have been wretched about my poor Sister L[ee]'s boys, being confined to such a malignant spot of vice . . . it is a most improper place for them."[94] Carter, who took Henry's part, did not improve the situation. "I am sorry to hear that Carter is travelling about with his vile Brother," wrote one relative in irritation, adding darkly: "They are both *Deists*."[95] The Carter family arranged to have Smith and Robert removed, but the effect of the incident must still have been stunning. Not only was the family again plunged into disgrace, but the boys were of an impressionable age, their sexuality just forming and their future security not well assured. Normal desire must have now been confused with lust and degradation, and with consequences of outsize proportions. Moreover, the rumor that Henry had embezzled Elizabeth McCarty's fortune was true. The financial ruin of the Lees was sealed.[96]

Some of Henry Lee's friends stood by him, questioning whether he was "never to be forgiven for one sin?" Most people shunned him.[97] Henry tried to appear contrite, but could not refrain from loudly disputing those who doubted his morality or from starting a legal battle over the exact definition of incest. Finally, in a particularly contemptible document, he wrote a justification of his adventure, comparing it to Thomas Jefferson's pursuit of a friend's wife and ending with the braggadocio that he had succeeded in his seduction "in less than three years and [Jefferson] failed confessedly after a perseverance of more than twelve."[98] His unwise pronouncements tainted the whole family, and like a bad penny they kept turning up, haunting his brother Robert for years. Unwelcome in polite American society, Henry exiled himself to Paris, where he continued to misspend what was left of the family funds and began to pen long, rambling defenses of his father, full of poisonous words against not only Jefferson but James Madison and others who had long befriended the Lees. Each one of Henry Lee's works simply resurrected the talk of intemperance and profligacy among the Lees. "If I can believe the papers your situation has had no mollifying influence upon your pen," Carter told his brother, telling him that words such as "malignant" were being linked to his name.[99] Finally, when Henry's extravagance and dishonor forced the family to break up their last home, even loyal Carter lost heart. "I have never felt so sensibly the utter demolition of the fortune of the whole race of Lees," Carter wrote pointedly to his unrepentant brother.[100]

In many ways the crisis provoked by "Black-Horse Harry" was more damaging than his father's mistakes. The elder Lee had been a genuine hero, and the disgrace of debt was a comparatively acceptable one. Henry IV had overstepped the bounds of decency, however, taking crude advantage on all sides and coupling it with self-righteous harangues that would have been repellent under the best of circumstances. The combination of these catastrophes was devastating and had real consequences for Robert Lee as he entered young manhood. Leading families questioned the Lees' desirability as suitors, and Robert came to believe that he would have to remain single. There are also indications that it depressed his spirit, for he once said he had been for "years in the habit of repressing my feelings." He told intimate acquaintances that he had no idea how to remedy the family calamities other than to try "to escape the sins into which they have fallen. . . ."[101] Whether conscious or not, what can be said with certainty is that Robert E. Lee chose a path quite different from that of the senior Lees. As a concerned father; as a careful investor; as an ambitious careerist; in the abnegation of his strong sexuality; as a man nearly fanatically obsessed with duty and correct behavior, he sidestepped the foibles he had been exposed to in his youth. Only in the exigency of war would he finally honor his father with emulation.

Chapter Three

The Torchbearers

Office of the Col Soc. Washington
Sept 7 1825

My Dearest Sister & Friend

The military bands and the patriotic citizens are assembling to pay their last honours to the venerable Lafayette. A large company of gentlemen (Mr. Custis of the number) yesterday dined at the Presidents, and Arlington house in the evening was brilliantly illuminated. As the night was dark, and as Philip and myself managed the lights with some ability, the effect was fine, & seemed I doubt not, to the good general like the affectionate smile of our country's Genius, upon the melancholy of his regretted departure. In one or two hours, he will be on board the boat, which is to convey him to the Brandywine. Perhaps the Christian could offer up no prayer at a moment like this, more consonant to his feelings, than that this venerable man may after the few years of this life, find the repose and rewards of a Christian warriour in the Kingdom of Jesus Christ!

It gives me extreme pain my excellent sister to hear that you are unwell. Let it be, I pray you; your first object to preserve the health which all, except perhaps yourself, consider invaluable. If any shadows darken your mind, the sunlight of the best and most affectionate Society will I trust dispel them, and especially do I hope & pray that He who never forgets us in affliction will be present to cheer & to bless.

Mr. Custis accompanied the General to the Brandywine, to return on friday. Washington Peter has recovered. I have the life of Lafayette by R Waln of Philadelphia which I wish to send you but fear I may have no opportunity.

We are waiting with anxiety to [torn] that our agent in Norfolk [torn] chartered a vessel for Liberi[a]. I fear delay in this expedition will be considerable. We are without a sufficient number of Emigrants. I shall come to Frederick if possible. You will see a very warm, _perhaps imprudent_ article, on slavery in *the Last Christian Observer. Assure Mrs Page of my deep and sincere regard. To Miss Mary let her, as at all times, [be] affectionately remembered & my best respects for Miss Stuart. In the purest & warmest friendship, yours RR Gurley*

Mrs Custis

P.S. I should have told Miss Mary that her beautiful print of Gen Lafayette is now hanging in the parlour.[1]

>‑‑◆‑‑○‑‑◆‑‑<

R OBERT E. LEE ENTERED young manhood in an era that expressed strong reverence to revolutionary leaders and the ideals they served. No one embodied this heroic period more dramatically than the Marquis de Lafayette. On September 7, 1825, the day this letter was written, Lafayette was departing on the U.S. ship *Brandywine,* after a nostalgic thirteen-month sojourn in the United States. On his last night in the national capital, the aging general dined with the president, as clergyman Ralph Randolph Gurley tells us, and then crossed the Potomac River to Arlington, where he was given a splendid send-off. There was an emotional round of toasts, the passionate words set against the brilliant illumination of bonfires and glowing torches.[2] One guest wrote of the throngs straining to touch Lafayette's hand and of the magical procession as he returned to Washington. Lafayette's entourage created a "fairy-like" scene as it slowly crossed the bridge, the lights from the torchbearers "doubly reflected in the water on either side . . . thus magnifying & multiplying both the object & the light, placing as it were, our nations benefactor in a resplendent *halo* of glory—"[3]

The description leads us to the doorstep of George Washington Parke Custis, whose home was the backdrop for this occasion. It is to his wife, Mary Lee Fitzhugh Custis, and her daughter that Ralph Gurley wrote his evocative letter. Although no one in 1825 could have predicted that one day the estate would serve as an emerald pall for America's war dead, Arlington was already becoming a hallowed place. Custis—"the heir of Washington"— had been raised at Mount Vernon. He dedicated his life to promoting the principles of the American Revolution, and his home was a virtual shrine to the memory of the nation's first president. The mansion's fine edifice mirrored the aspirations of the new federal city across the river, and its heritage and beautiful acreage caused it to linger in the hearts of the families who called it home. Robert E. Lee, who knew it from boyhood, felt so strongly about Arlington that he would declare it the place in the world where his affections were most firmly rooted. That attachment in turn influenced one of the most momentous decisions in U.S. history.

It was shrewd old James Monroe who orchestrated Lafayette's trip as a grand finale to the era of good feeling he had ushered in. The nation had developed greatly during his presidency, witnessing unprecedented technological advances, westward expansion, and a population boom that had added six stars to the flag. Unfortunately, much of the idealism and accord of the revolutionary period had eroded in the bitter political atmosphere of the early republic, or was squandered amid the increasingly materialistic culture that accompanied this time of extraordinary opportunity. Monroe thought the country would benefit from a reinvigoration of the old principles, particularly as the revolutionary generation passed away. In addition, the previous year the president had issued his Monroe Doctrine, an unequivocal statement of American resistance to foreign ambitions, and he wanted to underscore that point to several European leaders. What better way to tie the country together and rekindle the spirit that had stirred patriots nearly half a century before than to reclaim its near-legendary champion, whose acts had known no partisanship, and whose name was revered in every section of the land? In 1824 Monroe wrote to Lafayette, inviting him to return to the United States as the "Nation's Guest." Eager to escape proroyalist factions in the French government, and anxious "to see for himself the fruit borne on the tree of liberty," the sixty-six-year-old marquis accepted.[4]

Lafayette had expected to spend four months in the United States, but the acclaim he received was so immediate and so overwhelming that he extended the visit to more than a year. During this time he visited every state, traveling by boat, carriage, railroad, and horseback; an exhausting journey, but fabulous in the patriotic love he inspired. Everyone knew his story: how he had left for America in 1777, a member of the French nobility, with everything to lose, but inspired by a love of liberty that would infuse his whole life; how he had used his influence with the French monarchy to gain material and political support for the patriots; how he had won the confidence of George Washington with his dazzling performance at battles such as Monmouth and the lead-up to Yorktown—a major general at age twenty-four. Alongside his American brethren Lafayette had pledged his life, his fortune, and his sacred honor to the cause of independence, and no one had lived up to that pledge more truly. Now, nearly fifty years later, he was greeted by scores of veterans, by bands and parades, bonfires and bouquets, in every town he visited, many of them changing their name in his honor. Thirty thousand people came to the wharf on his arrival in New York, a record in its day. In New England old soldiers donned their ragged uniforms; a "Lafayette March" was premiered; and the rush of emotion nearly overwhelmed their visitor. Dolley Madison wrote from her Virginia estate, where Lafayette stayed several days, that she had "never witnessed so much enthusiasm as his appearance occasioned here and at our court house, where hundreds of both sexes collected together to hail & welcome him."[5] A souvenir industry sprang up, perhaps the first of its kind in America, with Lafayette whiskey bottles and Lafayette snare drums sold alongside the marquis's memoirs. Young Robert Lee's math tutor, Benjamin Hallowell, brought his bride out to see the great man and wrote an amusing parody of the popular enthusiasm.

> Each lover of Liberty surely must get
> Something in honor of La Fayette
> There's a La Fayette watch-chain, a La Fayette hat,
> A La Fayette *this,* and a La Fayette *that.*
> But I wanted something as lasting as life
> As I took to myself a La Fayette wife.[6]

Public tributes matched the splendid trappings. The phrases were florid, but their grandiosity could not mask the sincere feelings of America's citizenry. As Lafayette prepared to depart, on the day after Arlington's splendid illumination, the newly elected president, John Quincy Adams, spoke for the nation in a faltering voice. "We shall look upon you always as belonging to us, during the whole of our life, as belonging to our children after us," he said. "You are ours by . . . [the] patriotic self-devotion with which you flew to the aid of our fathers at the crisis of our fate; ours by that unshaken gratitude for your services which is a precious portion of our inheritance."[7]

Lafayette's extraordinary reception was also a manifestation of the near cult worship for George Washington that was growing during this time. Washington's pivotal role in designing the new nation had started to take on mythical proportions—though the deeds themselves were not always above criticism. What was collecting in the public consciousness, however, was an admiration based less on specific military or political accomplishments than on inner qualities that were thought to represent the "republican" virtues of obligation and disinterestedness. This definition of leadership differed considerably from the European concept, which held that intellect, talent, or physical appearance virtually compelled the public to follow a specific person. In America the idea was growing that it was civic service and self-sacrifice that commanded respect, and that those qualities were essential for maintaining the purity of the democratic experience. Washington, who had regularly subordinated his own interests to those of the nation, came to personify this ideal. His earliest publicist, Parson Weems, went to some trouble to stress this side of his character, and when the facts did not suffice, supplanted any doubt by inserting some instructional tales, such as the cherry tree and hatchet incident. What resulted was an almost mystical veneration of the first president—indeed, near canonization by the centennial of his birth in 1832. Twenty years earlier John Adams had already complained of the "idolatrous worship paid to the name of George Washington," and a Russian visitor remarked that every American home seemed to contain his picture.[8] A few years later, while traveling on the frontier, Robert E. Lee found much the same thing. Jared Sparks's biography of Washington had recently been published, and to Lee's surprise even the humblest cabin boasted an edition, often in calfskin binding—"ranged along side of the Bible."[9] Lafayette, who was closely associated with Washington's gallant actions, was also seen as an exemplary self-sacrificial soldier and statesman, who had acted without financial or political motives, and sometimes to his personal detriment. It was this example of "disinterested" involvement that did much to reanimate a country which, in its futuristic pursuit of happiness, sometimes took a nobler past for granted.

Although Alexandria was a small place, it would not be outdone in its welcome for the Nation's Guest, for this was considered George Washington's hometown. Lafayette made several visits there, but his official entry was on October 16, 1824. The procession included 2,000 militiamen, artillery salutes, bands, and a carriage holding George Washington's war tents. Lafayette entered the town "amid the wildest popular demonstration of joy and affection," making his way to the center, where a magnificent arch had been built over King Street. At the top of the arch sat a live eagle, and as the hero passed under it, the bird obligingly spread wide its wings and gave a mighty screech—encouraged, said some, by a small boy with a pin placed nearby. Alexandria's streets were lined with young girls in white dresses, throwing nosegays, and the windows were filled with ladies waving their handkerchiefs, among them Mary Anna Custis and her mother. Years later Mary told a friend that her attention had been drawn that day by her seventeen-year-old cousin Robert Lee, who as junior marshal was taking his first steps in the military pageant that was to define his life.[10]

Lafayette was en route to Mount Vernon and a commemoration at York-town, but a neighbor reported that he took the time to call on the widow of his friend Light-Horse Harry Lee. The local newspaper reported that he again paid his respects on a "flying visit" on December 14, when he dined with Mrs. Lee.[11] We have no account of these conversations, but one hopes that Robert Lee was present and that he had an opportunity to hear of the great adventure General Lafayette and his father had shared. They had been young men together in the Revolution, both favorites of Washington, both fighting under the banners Lafayette had brought from France, which brazenly proclaimed "Ultimo Ratio" ("Final Reckoning") to their enemies. Harry Lee had loved to tell a story about the Yorktown surrender, when the American and French troops presented themselves in parallel lines and the conquered British had to march between them. Hoping to snub the Ameri-cans, who they considered rabble, the British looked toward the French. Lafayette glanced over to Lee's Legion and mischievously ordered his band to play "Yankee Doodle"—so loudly that it forced those surrendering to turn away, their faces now directed to the Americans.[12]

With all the celebrity and tradition he represented, Lafayette's visits to the Lee family must have been as awe-inspiring as his call at Arlington, if more modest in scale. Robert had just been accepted to West Point, and he was poised in impatient anticipation of his future. There is something pleas-ing in the idea of the old warrior meeting a young man just on the thresh-old of his own patriotic career; an encounter between the generation that had given so much for pure principle and the new Americans who would profit by it, embellish it, and squander it too, and in the end test with their own lives the vitality of those ideals. It is not hard to imagine that the mus-ketry and music of Lafayette's reception in Alexandria made an impression on Robert Lee. But perhaps he also sensed the larger message of this na-tional celebration: that at the heart of glory was sacrifice.

Thus Marie-Joseph-Paul-Yves-Roche-Gilbert du Motier, Marquis de Lafay-ette, paraded his way through twenty-four states. George Washington Parke Custis accompanied him on many of his official activities, and it was entirely appropriate that he do so. Custis had been raised at Mount Vernon, knew Washington intimately, and was a veritable memory bank of facts about him. His grandmother, Martha Dandridge Custis Washington, had been a widow with two children when she married Washington. The couple remained childless, and Washington treated his stepchildren, and later his two youngest stepgrandchildren, as his own. Lafayette remembered little "Tubs" as an inte-gral part of Mount Vernon, "holding fast to one finger of the good general's remarkable hand" as he waved farewell in 1784.[13] He and his sister Nelly were somewhat intimidated by the formidable Washington—"Altho' he was kind . . . we felt [we] were in the presence of someone who was not to be trifled with"—but they cherished every recollection. After Washington died in 1799, the grandchildren inherited many of the possessions that were closely associated with this greatest of heroes.[14] For the rest of his life Custis would be the self-appointed curator of Washington's memory, becoming, in the words of one of his contemporaries, "the living link between the patriots of the old war and the present custodians of the prize which they won."[15]

At Martha Washington's death, Custis tried to buy Mount Vernon, but Bushrod Washington, who had inherited the property, chose not to sell.[16] Custis moved instead to a tract of land left to him by his father, 1,100 acres located just across the Potomac River from the fledgling national capital. Originally he meant to call the property Mount Washington, but in the end settled on Arlington, after the original family estate on the Eastern Shore of Virginia. For a time the young man lived in a small cottage near the river, but when rats and humidity destroyed some of his irreplaceable artifacts, he determined to build a house on higher ground. The structure he envisioned was ambitious in size and design and carefully situated so that its classical facade would be visible from some distance.[17] The prevailing style of the early 1800s was still Georgian, but Custis engaged an architect—probably George Hadfield, one of the early designers of the Capitol building—who used the Grecian elements just coming into vogue to plan a mansion that mirrored the imposing public buildings being constructed across the river. The classical features—the fine prospect and white columns—all bespoke hospitality and grandeur. These are now almost stereotypically associated with a genial southern way of life, but in 1803 Custis was ahead of his time by nearly two decades in incorporating the style into domestic architecture. Inside, the design was as striking as the exterior, with eighteen-foot ceilings, lovely large arches separating the rooms, and shimmering fanlights. Custis did not have the funds to complete the entire house at once, so it would be a progressive work—two smaller wings built first and the center section constructed around 1818. Twenty years later the process continued—in 1839 Custis wrote his wife that he was painting the woodwork for the first time.[18] Arlington would not be truly completed until the 1850s, when Robert E. Lee oversaw the finishing of a large parlor. Yet from the start it was a dominant feature of the local landscape, drawing the capital city's monumental promise out across the river to the Virginia farmlands George Washington had loved. Robert E. Lee would one day describe it as "a House any one might see with half an eye."[19]

Arlington House around the time of Lafayette's visit.
VIRGINIA HISTORICAL SOCIETY

With the completion of the north wing, Custis crowded the Mount Vernon memorabilia into the small space and then moved in another precious occupant: his new wife. Custis had known Mary Lee Fitzhugh from childhood, and when they married in July 1804, they were already linked through numberless family and social associations. Mary—or Molly, as she was called—was the daughter of William Fitzhugh of Chatham, one of Washington's greatest friends, and sister of the William Henry Fitzhugh who had befriended Ann Carter Lee on her move to Alexandria; indeed the Custis-Fitzhugh wedding is thought to have taken place at 607 Oronoco Street, the home Fitzhugh later lent to the Lees.[20] Custis's choice of Molly Fitzhugh as a partner was as sagacious as his design of Arlington House. A portrait of her painted around the time of the marriage shows a demure woman with curly, light brown hair, a long oval face, and a sweetly calm expression, dressed in the appealing style of Jane Austen's heroines.[21] She loved reading, and spent fifty years developing the estate's grounds, to rapturous praise.[22] An early opponent of slavery, she personally oversaw its comparatively benign direction at Arlington. Every description throughout her long life reflected the image of a superior person: pious and industrious, but affectionate, welcoming, and above all sympathetic.[23] Molly Custis, wrote one admirer, lived with a "charming simplicity and sincerity," performing "innumerable acts of courtesy, kindness and benevolence."[24]

Aware of her strong sympathetic powers, Molly nurtured acquaintances and kin, but she especially doted on her daughter Mary, the only one of her four children to survive infancy. The child was vivacious and bright, a favorite because of her unaffected nature and her efforts to please friends.[25] Given her antecedents, it was expected that she would play a dazzling role in the social life of the new nation. One gentleman who noticed mother and daughter at a public event around the time of Lafayette's call remarked that the younger Mary was the "observed of all observers," her personal attractions much admired and her attire and deportment bespeaking "her rank and bringing up."[26] The welcoming embrace and memorable character of Molly Custis, and her daughter's wit and broad interests, would give an engaging warmth to Arlington that made it stand out among other congenial homes.

The contrast between Mary Fitzhugh Custis's quiet grace and the untamed exuberance of her husband added to Arlington's unique personality. From childhood, G. W. P. Custis had been gregarious and charming, but undisciplined in his pursuits, more given to enthusiasm than diligence. George Washington worried about this, complaining that the boy ignored "every thing that did not tend to his amusements." The older man sought to animate Custis with his wisdom and strength, but was disappointed. His ward continued to be more concerned with "chariots" and monogrammed livery than with public service, was expelled from the College of New Jersey (Princeton), and was hauled before a local magistrate for stealing two silver spoons from Gadsby's Tavern.[27] Though he would forever identify with his adopted parents, the young man was indeed a Custis, taking after his equally self-indulgent father, Jacky, and an eccentric line of ancestors, who lived in colorful local lore long after they left this world.[28] Of medium height, with a florid face and prominent nose, he was an unforgettable character, exuding, as his daughter rather wryly noted, a "vivacity of temperament."[29] A friend who visited Washington Custis around the time of Lafayette's tour portrayed him as "rather awkward in his movements, blunt in the expression of his opinions, and rough, though genial, in his manners." Careless of his appearance, Custis wore knee breeches years after they had gone out of fashion and wandered around the Arlington grounds wearing an old straw hat. He adored cats, fiddle music, and hunting and was an avid dancer, considering himself an expert in "cutting the pigeon wing" during a lively Virginia reel.[30] Custis indulged these tastes at Arlington Spring, where he built a dancing pavilion and picnic ground for use by the whole neighborhood. He could often be found there, swapping "anecdote for anecdote and joke for joke" with the picnickers. He sometimes brought out his violin to entertain the crowds with marches and dancing tunes, and frequently treated the folks to a rousing impromptu speech.[31] An acquaintance looked back with pleasure on Custis's affability, recalling "the blending of good humor, cordiality, interest in those whom he addressed,

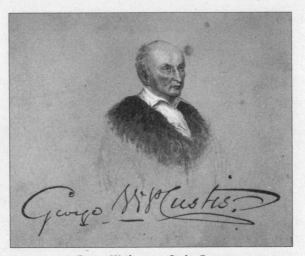

George Washington Parke Custis,
proprietor of Arlington and Lee's father-in-law.
ARLINGTON HOUSE, THE ROBERT E. LEE MEMORIAL, NATIONAL PARK SERVICE

with the richness of poetic imagination, throwing light and joy upon all around."[32]

Especially welcome were relatives associated with Mount Vernon, such as the Peters, Fitzhughs, and "Stewarts" who were present at Lafayette's torchlit evening. All of these families were closely linked by bonds of business, kinship, and hallowed memory.[33] Many of them were also related to the Lees—Molly Fitzhugh Custis herself being a Lee. She befriended her young cousins, Robert, Smith, and Carter, and made sure they were also regular visitors to Arlington. Carter was especially close to the kindly woman, confiding his disappointments in love and his loneliness and sending her poetry and rosebushes in appreciation of her sympathetic ear.[34] On one of Lafayette's visits to Arlington, the Lee brothers were invited to share the special occasion and enjoyed a long chat with the general and his son.[35] Smith Lee made Arlington his "headquarters" when on shore leave from the navy, and Mary Custis Lee liked to remember how as children she and Robert had planted a long line of trees together near the house, which grew into a magnificent alleé.[36] Robert developed "the tenderest affection" for Mrs. Custis, regarding her as a surrogate mother, and at her death would be so overcome that he went through a period of serious depression and spiritual questing.[37] He held the same esteem for the colorful master of the house, who like his wife showed a sympathetic interest in Ann Lee and her children and liked having them at Arlington. Robert would gratefully acknowledge the debt that he owed Custis, "whose affection I experienced in boyhood," writing that he had "been to me all a father could."[38] For the rest of his life Arlington would be as close to a real home as Robert Lee was to experience.

By the time of Lafayette's visit, Custis's chief passion was the protection of George Washington's name, fame, and personal possessions. He was so well established as the guardian of the Washington legacy that many assumed he, not Dolley Madison, saved Gilbert Stuart's portrait when the British burned the White House in 1814.[39] Arlington's walls were covered with family pictures, and some of them, such as Charles Willson Peale's 1772 painting of Washington, were already well known. Revolutionary War tents and regimental flags captured from British and Hessian troops were sometimes set up on the lawn, and despite having "suffered from the tooth of Time," they never failed to evoke national pride. Washington's deathbed was in the house, as were trunks full of his papers, and even the coverlet under which he had expired. Visitors could see Martha Washington's tea table, the heavy Mount Vernon silver service, and a huge porcelain punch bowl with a ship painted on its interior, the veteran of many a Mount Vernon fête.[40]

Yet Arlington was far from a drear reliquary. The Washington artifacts were not merely for show; the items were lovingly used by the family, who relished their historic associations.[41] There were no public museums in America at that time, only a few private "cabinets" of rare and curious objects. By amassing this rich collection and willingly making it available to the public, Arlington's master presaged a national preservation movement that would not begin for a half century. He was not a perfect curator in the contemporary sense of the word—in his enthusiasm to give away mementoes, he broke up irreplaceable sets of china, cut up battlefield memorabilia, and excised signatures from the bottom of priceless letters. What distinguished Custis was that he understood the importance of tangible signs and symbols, and how every little story was a hinge that connected generations. In his hands these objects linked people to their heritage. It was not only by conserving the frayed canvas of Washington's tents that Custis fostered the nation's pride—but by cherishing the very fabric of the man.

The respect Lafayette showed Washington Custis proved to be more than a passing honor: it inspired him to strengthen his dedication to the principles of his adopted father. During the year Lafayette spent in the United States, Custis had an opportunity for many conversations with the old gentleman, and he drew him out, recording his memories of the Revolution's glory days and of his hope that its ideals would spread across the world. On one visit Washington Custis conversed about a plan for gradual emancipation of the family's slaves, for Lafayette believed it a barbarous institution, in decline everywhere except the United States, and had gone so far as to request that those slaveholders lining his travel routes not be accompanied by their human property.[42] Custis published a series of fascinating articles based on these conversations, which were well received by the public. Their success encouraged him to begin compiling a similar set of "recollections" about Washington, which were also published serially, and which won the praise of noted historians. Custis had never missed an inauguration, a Washington's Birthday celebration, or the festivities on the Fourth of July, but now he more regularly addressed the public, standing not so much for specific political interests—though he was an ardent Federalist—but for the broader platform of democracy. Believing, as did Lafayette, that the principles of liberty must be promoted in the Old World as well as the New, he spoke out for the oppressed Poles, Greeks, and Irish, and sponsored rallies on Saint Patrick's Day to underscore his point.[43]

Custis also began to look for opportunities to celebrate America's unparalleled potential.[44] He adopted Washington's interest in agriculture, experimenting with horticultural methods and sheep husbandry that might be particularly appropriate for Virginia's terrain. He excited interest in these activities by sponsoring an annual "sheep shearing" at Arlington that encouraged the development of strains truly adapted to native conditions. Some saw these as thinly veiled political rallies, held on the anniversary of Washington's first inauguration, and with a strong push for the national self-sufficiency that had been preferred by the Federalists. But Custis viewed them in the larger context of scientific husbandry and the need for America to wean itself from practices that encouraged imitation or dependence on European nations.[45]

At the same time, Custis fostered American originality in the arts. He had imbibed a love of the theater from Washington, and now he began to write plays—with the pen of an amateur to be sure, but good enough to be professionally produced. Custis chose to explore native topics, such as the story of Pocahontas or the effect of burgeoning technology on the pristine wilderness. These formed a part of the era's self-conscious effort to define a distinctively American culture, and he took as his friends others who were working to the same end, including the writer Washington Irving and painters Charles Willson Peale and his talented sons.[46] Perhaps inspired by the Peales, Custis also began to paint battlefield scenes, with Washington in martial glory. These were large canvases, depicting multiple figures, rearing horses, and all the chaos of combat—quite a bold project for an untutored artist. The drawing and perspective were primitive, but as Custis's daughter would remark, they were "spirited and original," falling somewhere between tableaux and folk art. Nonetheless, their conception and historical accuracy were notable. At least one, a monumental rendition of the battle of Princeton, was exhibited in the Capitol until some senators asked that it be removed.[47]

In life as in art, Custis was unpretentious; still, not everyone admired Arlington's proprietor. One critic, complaining about his enthusiasm for the erection of a Washington Monument, played off his interest in sheep breeding by referring to him as "the little Arlington Ram" who was "butting at the *whole nation* for delaying the monument."[48] Another, having heard the "little son of a step-son" speak at one too many ceremonial events, referred to him as "the inevitable Custis."[49] Many of the complaints were politically motivated, often appearing in the anti-Federalist newspaper *The Spirit of Seventy-Six*.[50] Custis's zeal was bound to elicit comment, and even son-in-law Robert and his brother Carter lightheartedly joined in the mockery. "Montgomerie has *failed*," Robert Lee mischievously remarked, referring to one of Custis's historical plays. "The 'big Picture' has been exhibited in the Capitol, and attracted some severe animadversions from the Critics which he says were levelled at his *Politics*!!" It would seem, Carter rejoined, "that the man of many muses is in many troubles."[51]

Such irreverent remarks about Custis's earnest efforts fill pages of the Lee brothers' correspondence, and they are interesting for more than their youthful chortles.[52] The boys had grown up in a time when popular fancy was hooked fast to the heroic Washington, and of course their own father had hugely respected his Revolutionary mentor. Connections among the families associated with Mount Vernon were multifaceted and close. These were potent influences, as were the trappings of Washington's life which filled the homes of those related to the original "first family." Washington

memories and Washington memorabilia were a part of Robert Lee's everyday experience. This, and the fact that Lee resembled Washington in certain
ways—powerful physical presence, personal reserve, and a near fanatical
adherence to self-defined "duty"—have led generations of popular writers
and even top-flight historians to envision a mystical bond between the two
men. In some cases this has gone so far as to be characterized as "idolization" by Lee—a willful modeling of his character around the first president.
Pronounced differences of style and temperament between the two men
would be disregarded in the desire to forge this link. The legend was extended in the late nineteenth century as Confederate nationalists increasingly used Robert E. Lee to justify their "second American Revolution." Lee's
moral fiber was perceived as a symbol of southern virtue, and it was augmented by connecting it to Washington's untarnished greatness. As with
many myths, the story has been repeated so many times, each generation of
historians citing and reiterating the inaccuracies of the last, that the false assumptions have come to have a life of their own.[53]

In ten thousand letter pages Robert Lee mentions Washington fewer than
two dozen times. He remarks on the public's interest in its leader; mentions
that he looked over a popular biography sent to him by a friend; notes the
celebration of his birthday. Most of these comments are quite casual. In his
most enthusiastic writing on the subject, Lee, like others of his day, points to
Washington's wisdom and integrity, and particularly praises his valedictory
address to the American people, which, ironically, cautioned against growing sectionalism.[54] But even in his most fulsome expression, the remarks are
general, steeped in the national pride of the day, rather than personal feelings. Never does Lee say he idolizes Washington, or that he hopes to emulate
him.[55] The closest Lee came to a conscious association was after the war,
when he struggled to come to terms with his decision to join the Confederate cause, and cites Washington's change from British to American allegiance
as an example of an earlier crisis of loyalty.[56] But this was after the fact. During those terrible days of 1861 he used Washington's name quite differently—
as justification for maintaining the Union.[57]

Yet the false fittings have continued to be jammed together. One writer
states forthrightly that Lee's mother selected and promoted Washington as
a role model, citing no source save a series of fanciful biographers.[58] The fact
that Lee was born in the same county as the nation's founder, on the banks
of the same river, is invoked as proof of a spiritual tie—yet brother Black-
Horse Harry was also born there, with no discernible traces of Washington's
lofty character.[59] Lee's father is said to have instilled a love of Washington in

his sons, something that might be well conjectured, but is not stated in any of Light-Horse Harry's admonitory letters to his boys.[60] It is true that Lee was surrounded by sacred paraphernalia from this national hero, and that he sometimes enjoyed handling it, but this in itself is no grounds for the assumption that he felt anything beyond a normal curiosity about historic relics. Henry Adams, for example, was similarly steeped in Revolutionary artifacts and lore, and his response was to feel burdened by it.[61] Incredibly, for there is not one shred of proof, Lee's most quoted biographer asserts that he was taught to revere Washington "above his father and every other man."[62] The evidence is to the contrary, for his brother Carter makes clear that as much as he admired the nation's father, no one displaced Light-Horse Harry in the Lee household. None of the associations Lee had with the Washington legend indicates that he held the great man in anything more than the general high regard that permeated early-nineteenth-century society. Those who would wishfully make Lee a disciple of George Washington—whether explicitly or "almost without being conscious of it"—have taken some leaps of imagination to bridge the factual void. When Lee does meet a man he admires extravagantly and wants to emulate, he is not shy about expressing it, or declaring his fealty. But that would be a different general in a different war.[63]

Lee never hinted that his father-in-law's home inspired a reverence for Washington, but he was open in his love for the place. He was not alone in this, for Arlington seems to have been held in a special affection by all those who knew it well. The splendid view; the impressive facade of the house; the tangled gardens where jasmine, roses, lilies of the valley, and tall lilies bloomed "in unconstrained delight"; the ancient trees; and of course the glowing friendship of Molly and Washington Custis made it an unforgettable spot.[64] People spoke warmly of the other estates in the family's circle—Ravensworth, Tudor Place, Woodlawn, Riversdale, and Goodwood—each had its own cachet. But nearly every mention of Arlington carries with it an exclamation point, or superlative adjective. "Lovely Arlington! Scene of brightest pleasures!" wrote a friend of Mrs. Custis.[65] "Beautiful Old Arlington!" Robert Lee's nephew would exclaim, recalling his boyhood days there. "Its broad portico and widespread wings, held out open arms as it were, to welcome the coming guest. . . . Its halls and chambers were adorned with patriots and heroes . . . and without and within, history and tradition seemed to breathe their legends upon a canvas as soft as a dream of peace."[66] This highly personal estate, and the spirit that had created it, enveloped them all in tenderness. "I will only add . . . that my heart leaps within me at the thought of soon revisiting Dear A—& all its inmates scenes & associations—," Robert E. Lee once declared. A few days later, musing again about Arlington, with its warmth, animation, and quirky splendor, he would conclude that it was here that his "affection & attachments are more strongly placed than at any other place in the World."[67]

Chapter Four

The Long Gray Line

Sir

Having just heard that it was always agreable to you to receive from every applicant for a Cadets Warrant, a statement of his age, studies, &c., made by himself, I take the earliest opportunity of sending you the following.

I completed my eighteenth year on the 29th of last January, I have read, besides the small authors which are generally begun with, Caesar, Sallust, Virgil, Cicero, Horace, and Tacitus of the Latin Authors, and the Graeca Minora, the Graeca Majora, Xenophon, Homer, Longinus of the Greek, and have studied Arithmetic, Algebra, and the first six books of Euclid.

In confirmation of my statement I enclose you the certificate of Mr Leary which though less flattering and rhetorical than that which Mr Garnett was so kind as to send you is more precise and satisfactory.

*I remain Sir your most
Obedient servant R.E. Lee*

Alex^a, Febr^y 28th 1824.[1]

A T WEST POINT they talk of the "Long Gray Line"—a timeless procession of cadets in smoke-colored uniform; an inspiring continuum of pride and service. Robert E. Lee was part of that line, and the U.S. Military Academy was a potent influence in his life. This unprepossessing note launched him on two careers: his military profession and a lifelong commitment to letter writing. It is the earliest document we have in his hand, and it has been lost for nearly a century and a quarter. Evidently taken from government files after the Civil War and given to a private collector, the letter was rediscovered through a facsimile printed in a San Francisco newspaper in 1886. Because it is our first glimpse of Lee from his own description, it has intrinsic importance but it also gives us a few insights into his young character. The statement Lee gives of his age, for example, raises some intriguing questions. Traditionally Robert's birthday was January 19, not January 29, which is in fact the birth date of his father. The accepted year for his birth is also 1807, which would have made him seventeen rather than eighteen in February 1824. Despite these lapses in exactitude, the application is tinged with a little moral superiority, lauding one sponsor's precision over another's flattering words—the same fussy trait that would cause his mother-in-law, his children, and his wartime staff to despair.[2] Lee was finally accepted at the academy and excelled there, and its tradition and training became touchstones in his life. The only strong friendships Lee would form outside his kinfolk were established at West Point, and his eldest son, Custis Lee, his nephew Fitz Lee, and assorted young cousins would follow him in the long line of cadets. By the time he became superintendent of the institution in the 1850s, West Point's customs and idealism had folded over him like the leaves of a bud, forming complex overlapping layers around the core of his personality.

Government records tell us that Robert Lee of Virginia attended West Point from July 1825 to July 1829; that he graduated second in a class of forty-six, with no demerits for misconduct; that from his second year he was a staff sergeant and in his final year Adjutant of the Corps of Cadets, the highest honor at the academy. He was also tapped in 1826 to be an assistant professor of mathematics, an indication of his superior abilities in that field.[3] Lee had wanted badly to enter the academy, but to do so he had to curry the kind of political favor he would later come to hate. Nelly Custis Lewis, half brother Henry, and cousin William Henry Fitzhugh used their influence to help him gain access to senators and Cabinet members whose recommendation was key to securing a place.[4] When Robert received the appointment from Secretary of War John C. Calhoun, it was tinged with a bit of disappointment, for in his eagerness to please everyone Calhoun had appointed too many Virginians. Lee was told—as was his classmate Joseph E. Johnston—that he would have to wait a year before entering.[5] Some biographers have proposed that he went to the academy in order to spare his family the cost of a college education. Actually Lee himself stated that his mother tried to talk him out of going to West Point, but he believed the notorious actions of his father and brother had precluded any chance of a normal life—and he might as well embrace the romantic world of a soldier. In addition, he recalled, a fascination with the military life had "clung to me from boyhood."[6]

We know that Lee wrote letters home from West Point, but none of these have surfaced.[7] Fortunately the skeletal official records can be fleshed out by the evocative letters and diaries of his fellow cadets. From these we learn that Lee's generation arrived at West Point by boat, thrilled by the splendid Hudson River scenery but almost entirely ignorant of what awaited them. Lee's insistence on accompanying his son to the Point a quarter century later may have stemmed from his recollection of that perilous moment when, jumping off the boat, he was greeted by an old one-armed academy retainer who proffered a hook instead of a hand. Entering boys were asked to write their names on a slate, then escorted directly to the unknown terrors of the superintendent's office and the entrance exam. The exam was not really hard, only some simple exercises in reading, writing, and arithmetic. It was the subsequent daily testing of the academy that ultimately would prove the mettle of the men. Nonetheless, it was a tense moment when the results were announced. One of Lee's classmates recalled that the selection took place on the evening of June 27, 1825, and that the names of those who had passed were read in alphabetical order. The new cadets were ordered to step forward four paces, with two dozen luckless young men left in their rear. The next morning they were marched to summer encampment, divided into two companies and issued tents. The first assignment for the "newies"—as plebes were then called—was to dig the "sink," or outdoor latrine.[8]

Sketch of a "newie" arriving at West Point, drawn by James McNeill Whistler when he was a cadet. Published 1906 in The Golden Age.

The "newies" embarked on a regimen that challenged both physical and mental endurance. They learned to adapt to days that began with reveille and morning drill, followed by classes until late afternoon. The evening parade signaled supper, study, and lights out at nine. They were measured for their dress uniforms, cut so tightly through the chest that they virtually trussed the cadets into a ramrod stance.[9] That summer the task before them was to learn how to drill. To teach precision marching, shallow trenches were dug twenty-eight inches apart, over which the squads were marched until they were able to step that distance uniformly.[10] Abner R. Hetzel, a cadet who arrived two years before Lee, wrote to his father that the first day after selection "I was taken out to drill & sure you never saw a more awkward creature in your life than I was or appeared to be. . . . To display the chest, draw in the Corporation, draw the chin in perpendicular to the Chest, hold the hands down so as to touch the seam of the Pantaloons, & take care don't bend the elbows, keep the Shoulders drawn back & always be sure to keep the feet in an angle of 45° etc., etc."[11] The older classmen thought the new men looked ridiculous, and they stood around the edges of the drill, joking and wondering if they had ever been so clumsy. But hazing of "newies" was strictly forbidden by Superintendent Sylvanus Thayer. Alfred Church, a year senior to Lee, recalled with gratitude that upperclassmen "instead of making me stand on tip-toe on one foot, tossing me in a blanket, or smoking me out, treated me with kindly interest, gave me correct information on what I was to do, and how to do it, in other words treated me as a true gentleman ever treats his fellows. . . ."[12]

On September 3, 1825, having survived summer camp, the class of 1829 signed articles binding them to serve five years. The oath taken by Robert E. Lee and his classmates would challenge many in the decades to come:

> I do solemnly swear that I will bear true allegiance to the United States of America, and that I will serve them honestly and faithfully against all their enemies or opposers whatsoever; and observe and obey the orders of the President of the United States. . . .[13]

When Robert Lee donned the cadet's form-fitting gray jacket in 1825, he was entering an institution still evolving alongside the young United States. Since the country's birth there had been a national debate about the place of a professional military in a democracy. George Washington, whose experience with militia units had not always been felicitous, originally favored the creation of a trained officer corps, as did Alexander Hamilton and Lee's father. There were equally strong voices on the other side—those who, like Jefferson, thought defense a prerogative of the states, or disliked any group that even vaguely resembled a powerful national army, so reminiscent of the oppressive military units kept by European monarchs. The compromise they reached was to create a very small regular army for peacetime that could be expanded by adding militiamen in times of crisis. In 1802 West Point was made the seat of regular army training, with defensive fortification its essential mission. Confidence in the militia was not increased during the War of 1812, when many citizen soldiers fled or refused to fight, and this reinvigorated the call for a professional military program. When John C. Calhoun was appointed secretary of war in 1817 he saw quickly that the institution needed to be buttressed against foes who thought it a superfluous luxury, or a dangerous training ground for political operatives. He took a personal interest in the academy, appointing Thayer, a West Point graduate who had distinguished himself in the recent war with Britain, as superintendent. Together the two revolutionized not only military training but scientific education in the United States.[14]

The course they put together was one of the most ambitious in the world and ultimately produced the first corps of professional engineers in the United States. It was based on the curriculum of the French École Polytechnique, the leading institution of its kind in that era, and was designed to cultivate a habit "of investigation and reasoning that excludes, absolutely, all specious and sophistical conclusions."[15] Cadets were on probation the first six months, their studies limited to mathematics and French, the military lingua franca of the era. After probation they began a rigorous program of mathematics, practical sciences, and engineering, embellished with a few courses in philosophy and history. The cadets studied advanced calculus, trigonometry, and descriptive geometry to aid them in planning fortifications, and natural sciences such as biology and astronomy to help them assess terrain and master positioning. They also learned surveying and spent long hours perfecting the draftsmanship needed to plot maps and draw intricate structural diagrams. Always there were the endless drills, riding practice, and instruction in tactics and artillery. Lee added to his load by paying for extra tutorials in fencing and geology.[16] The lessons were densely packed with material; moreover, the classes were oral and every cadet was ranked on a daily basis.

The course was still experimental in the late 1820s, and far too difficult for many who attempted it. Nearly half of Lee's entering group left before graduation, but he excelled in the demanding atmosphere. He got perfect scores in the military classes and near perfect in moral philosophy, chemistry, and French, placing him third in his class the first year and second thereafter.[17] Jefferson Davis, who was in the class of 1828, later noted that he thought the emphasis on science played to Lee's strengths. Others would write that it was nearly impossible to get scores such as his without rare mathematical ability.[18]

In spare moments the cadets were responsible for polishing guns and barracks furniture and acting as the "orderlies" who enforced discipline.[19] The daunting winter terms were relieved by summer encampments, pleasant in their change of rhythm. Here too, however, the cadets were tested, drilling ten hours a day, or arduously dragging cannons into place, all the while enduring primitive outdoor conditions. "We were huddled into cramped and miserable tents exposed to the broiling sun and the pelting storm," groused one of Lee's classmates. "The solace of an Indian fire was even denied to our drenched and benumbed limbs."[20] During the summer they also learned to dance, hilariously swaying to the music, without benefit of female partners.[21] That Lee found it all quite challenging is evident from the emphatic advice he gave his son when he entered West Point: "I pray you may have *strength fortitude* & *capacity* to accomplish the course before you. . . . It will require a *firm resolve* on your part; *persevering industry* & a *courageous heart*."[22]

The competition was keen. Leonidas Polk, class of 1827, told his father that the pressure to excel gave him no possibility of escaping grueling hours of study.[23] Lee was crowded at all times from below and was never able to best his nemesis, Charles Mason—a taciturn but prodigiously talented New Yorker, who won perfect scores in every math, chemistry, philosophy, and engineering course he took, as well as flawlessly performing at artillery and tactics. In multiple courses Lee received 299½ out of a possible 300. Mason consistently achieved 300. Like Lee, he departed West Point without a single demerit. After graduating first in the class, Mason left the army and had a distinguished career as a federal judge and the commissioner of patents. Years later he would have reason to look wistfully at the comparative success of his rival. "General Lee is winning great renown as a great captain," Mason confided to his diary in 1864. "Some of the English writers place him next to Napoleon and Wellington. I once excelled him and might have been his equal yet perhaps if I had remained in the army as he did. I sometimes regard his fame as a reproach to myself. . . ."[24]

In 1825 Superintendent Thayer had been in charge of the academy for eight years and was just hitting his stride. A quiet and dignified man, he interested himself in every detail of the West Point operations, from the need for running water in the barracks to relations with the skeptical Congress. He sat at a desk that had a pigeonhole for every cadet, and at a glance he could assess the academic, financial, and moral standing of each one—something that profoundly unsettled some boys. Along with his rigorous curriculum, Thayer had designed an elaborate social structure that instilled discipline and rewarded diligence. The year Lee arrived at the Point, Thayer inaugurated a unique demerit system, which is still one of the defining features of the academy. Passionately committed to the idea of equality, Thayer envisioned a ranking system that undercut any idea of favoritism. Finances were also controlled so that no single cadet was more privileged than the others. Under Thayer's direction cadets were denied any support from home and made to live on the $28 a month they received for food and rations, out of which they were obliged to pay for uniforms, books, blankets, and other necessities of daily living. Most were in perpetual debt to the tailor, barber, and bookseller, and Thayer liked it that way, for he saw pocket money as a temptation to either vice or elitism.[25] Understanding the need to win influential friends for the academy, Thayer also instituted a system of public examinations. These not only ensured that the assessments were scrupulously fair but brought accomplished men such as Sam Houston and Washington Irving to participate in the process. The exams, held each January and June, were conducted orally, so that the "Board of Visitors" and instructors could openly quiz the cadets,

Sylvanus Thayer, superintendent of West Point, 1817–1833, painted by Robert W. Weir.
WEST POINT ART COLLECTION, UNITED STATES MILITARY ACADEMY

with no possibility of cheating or obfuscation. A question posed to Lee's Descriptive Geometry class in June 1827 was as follows:

> To pass a plane to the surface of the helicoide, the point of control being on a given helix, and a plane to be parallel to a given right line. To determine the intersection of a Cylinder whose case and direction of its right lined elements are known with a given plane. To pass a Plane through any Element of the helicoide, and find the points in which it cuts the outward helix of the Screw. To find the intersection of a plane passing through a given line, with the surface of the Screw.[26]

The polished performance of the cadets greatly impressed the Boards. "Thirteen young men were under the screw four hours . . . ," wrote the Harvard educator George Ticknor, who examined Lee in 1826. "It was as nearly

perfect as anything of the kind ever was." That each board published a report to Congress, and returned home extolling the virtues of Thayer and his
academy, did a great deal to foster its reputation for excellence.[27]

Thayer was bound to a system that accorded class rank, privileges, and
punishments on the basis of conformance with his strict standards. This,
however, did not mean that he lacked partiality toward certain members
of the corps. He did not, for example, care for Jefferson Davis, who was an
indifferent student and came within eleven demerits of being dismissed.
Thayer called him "a recreant & unnatural son," and harbored his mistrust
over thirty years.[28] On the other hand, he liked Cadet Robert Lee. He recognized his academic excellence by making him an assistant professor, chose
him to be a cadet officer at the first opportunity, then vaulted him over the
unstoppable Mason to be Adjutant of the Corps. The increased duties taxed
both time and patience—another cadet would complain that appointment
as an officer caused him to lead a "thankless dogish life"—but Lee would
later appreciate the importance of this appointment. It taught him how to
lead, he claimed, and gave him an appreciation for the difficulties of his
superiors, making him "more liberal, more just."[29] Superintendent Thayer
must have seen in Lee the reflection of his own traits: the punctuality, precision, and reserve that characterized his style; the self-discipline and follow-
through he esteemed; the unmistakable air of command. In outlook, carriage,
and commitment to excellence the two men were unmistakably similar. Lee
so clearly mirrored Thayer's manner and principles that it is hard not to
conclude the superintendent was an important professional and personal
model. If Thayer did not instill these values in Lee, his example must have
strongly reinforced them.[30]

Certainly Cadet Lee never resisted his superintendent's exacting regulations, as did so many members of the corps. Thayer had established an elaborate labyrinth of requirements, which embraced stance, attire, attitude,
academic preparation, and the larger transgressions of insubordination or
absence without permission. It was all part of his vision of creating a class of
professional military men whose service was predicated not on loyalty to
a ruler, as in Europe, but on dedication to a set of values that would honor
the nation. To do so, he believed that officers must be molded—essentially
stripped of their individuality and inculcated with rigorous habits of discipline and duty. Thus formed, they would not only make reliable warriors
but overturn the popular fear of a military rabble terrorizing the populace.
In daily practice this program was almost impossible to uphold without error. The meals at the academy were stunningly bad, for example, and some

errant cadets were given demerits simply for bringing extra food into their rooms. Demerits were given for slouching, for folding clothes without precise corners, for accidentally stepping out of line.[31] Constrained by the bleakness of the barracks, many found ways of sneaking out at night. "Benny Haven's" was the destination of choice, and demerits skyrocketed alongside its popularity. An off-limits temple of food, drink, and sympathy, it catered to the extracurricular needs of the cadets. Generations of the Long Gray Line added verses to the rousing song "Benny Havens O!" which included the memorable lyrics:

> Come seize your glasses fellows and stand up in a row. . . .
> In the army there's sobriety, promotions very slow
> And we'll sigh our reminiscences of Benny Havens O:
> O Benny Havens O! O Benny Havens O!
> We'll sigh our reminiscences of Benny Havens O![32]

The biannual Board of Visitors might note that "the moral discipline of the Institution is perfect," but the cadets knew otherwise.[33] Samuel P. Heintzelman, who entered West Point the year before Lee, kept careful note in his diary of drinking in the guardhouse, of bringing nitrous oxide—laughing gas—to the barracks, of New Year's grog, and of cadets being fired at by a local man because they were chasing his daughters.[34] Even Lee and Mason, who graduated without a demerit, may actually have received them. Jefferson Davis thought so: "It is stated that [Lee] had not then a 'demerit' mark standing against him, which is quite credible if all 'reports' against him had been cancelled, because they were not for wanton or intentional delinquency."[35] During the writing of Douglas Southall Freeman's *R. E. Lee*, historians at West Point told the author that they doubted anyone could pass through the institution without actually receiving a demerit, pointing to a long-established system of having them erased for good behavior or working them off. "It seems impossible that not only a cadet, but several, could have been here for four years and never had any record against them," they concluded.[36] Nonetheless, Lee's page on the official Record of Delinquencies shows that he received no negative reports. Indeed, it is filled with the overflow sins of a classmate with the memorable name Pleiades Orion Lumpkin.[37]

In one notable instance during Lee's cadet years, the delinquent actions of the corps nearly jeopardized the academy's political standing. Lee's class had entered as a rowdy group. One week after their selection they celebrated the Fourth of July by excessive drinking, forming a provocative snake dance, then arriving at guard post so tipsy they could not stand.[38] Incensed, Thayer announced a moratorium on possession of alcohol, even for the traditional celebrations at Christmas and Washington's Birthday. As the winter holidays drew near, Jefferson Davis and some of the other Southerners nonetheless determined to host a festive eggnog party. They acquired the necessary ingredients—probably from Benny Haven's—and timed the toast for 1:30 a.m. on Christmas morning. The party took place in the North Barracks, where Lee roomed, and many of his friends were there, but Lee and buddy Joe Johnston declined their invitations. When the event got out of hand, several officers looked in to see what was happening. "A large number of cadets got on a spree, and became excessively riotous," recalled an eyewitness, "setting all officers at defiance and even, with a drawn sword, chasing one to his room—throwing missiles through the halls, breaking windows and the railings of the stairs, &c."[39] Drunken cadets reeled from room to room. Mathematics professor Ethan Allen Hitchcock was hit by a small log. Finally the cadets began firing loaded guns. After several hours, the "Eggnog Riot," as it became known in West Point lore, was halted, with 70 of the Academy's 250 cadets implicated. Thayer was as aghast at the threat to West Point's reputation as he was at the evidence of massive defiance. He knew that any report stating that nearly a third of the cadets had been accused of drunken revelry would give his opponents a pretext for closing the academy. With great dexterity he sorted the more serious offenders from standers-by and, using his detailed knowledge of the character and record of each cadet, finally identified and charged the nineteen guiltiest cadets. Of these, twelve were ultimately dismissed. Seven were pardoned or had their sentences commuted by President John Quincy Adams, at Thayer's recommendation. The others received lighter punishments, including Jefferson Davis, who had slipped into his room to vomit at a fortuitous moment. Lee and Johnston, of course, were exonerated. But doubtless they listened soberly when President Adams came to West Point to admonish the "Young Men from whom their Country had a right to expect better things." While those who had committed the offenses were responsible, Adams noted, the shame of the affair "of necessity is shared with them by the dearest of their friends."[40]

Some of Robert Lee's associates had been involved in the Eggnog Riot, but for the most part he steered away from Jefferson Davis and his crowd. The Southerners did band together, however. Lee's friendships show a predilection for comrades who came from the slave states, and especially those whose fathers had fought in the Revolutionary War. Joe Johnston was among them, his father Peter having served with Light-Horse Harry in Lee's Legion. Hugh Mercer, though a year older, was another kindred spirit with

Virginia antecedents, and another son of the Revolution: his grandfather was the great General Hugh Mercer, whose life was lost at the battle of Princeton. Dick Tilghman of Maryland, a descendant of Washington's aide-de-camp Tench Tilghman, was also a favorite compatriot. Lee's best friend—and the one with whom he maintained close relations after West Point—was "Jack" Mackay of Savannah, who also claimed a heritage of patriot action. Lee was friendly with others whose names would be linked to his—P. G. T. Beauregard, Leonidas Polk, Albert Sidney Johnston—but his mainstays were Mackay, Mercer, Tilghman, and Joe Johnston, all top scholars who generally avoided trouble and saved their "raisins" (as money was popularly called). "We had the same intimate associates," Joe Johnston recalled of Lee,

> who thought as I did, that no other youth or man so united the qualities that win warm friendship and command high respect. For he was full of sympathy and kindness, genial and fond of gay conversation, and even of fun that made him the most agreeable of companions, while his correctness of demeanor and language and attention to all duties, personal and official, and a dignity as much a part of himself as the elegance of his person, gave him a superiority that every one acknowledged in his heart.[41]

One of the hallmarks of Lee's leadership was this physical presence, which was evidently apparent from his teenage years. Mercer and Jefferson Davis remembered him as strikingly handsome, with a natural charisma that lent force to every undertaking. As adjutant Lee had a frustratingly managerial job, without the glory of leading the cadets in parade. (That job went to the Corps captains, of which Charles Mason was one.) However, Benjamin Ewell, who was a cadet from 1828 to 1831, remembered that Lee would pass down the lines of inspection giving a little nod or smile to those whose bearing was particularly fine. Once Ewell was so acknowledged, and he recalled, "I felt as if I had received a nod from Olympian Jove."[42] A cousin who saw Robert when he was home on furlough was also struck by his presence. "He was dressed in his cadet uniform of West Point, gray with white bullet buttons, and every one was filled with admiration of his fine appearance and lovely manners."[43] Years later Johnston would muse, "In youth and early manhood I loved and admired him more than any man in the world."[44]

"I am this moment from the examination hall," Jack Mackay wrote excitedly to his mother on June 15, 1829. "I have passed satisfactorily to myself on every subject, and the game is now over. . . . Our class will be relieved from

duty at the Military Academy this evening, or tomorrow at the farthest."[45]
Mackay would graduate eighth in the class, and Lee, never able to overcome
Charles Mason, would graduate in second place. For this honor he was entitled to choose his branch of service, and he selected the prestigious Corps
of Engineers. Like classes before them, the new graduates ceremoniously
smashed their slates on the boulders dotting the parade ground. Then they
fired off mortars and howitzers in celebration, and, if they followed the pattern, set the woods on fire with their homemade imitations of "Greek fire."[46]
Mackay and friends were taking a restful trip to Niagara Falls, but Lee, now
brevetted second lieutenant, made a sober journey home to his mother's
sickbed.[47] Before he left, he sat with the others to hear Mason's valedictory
address. "I have said to myself," Mason told his colleagues, "that . . . when I
am listening as the whispers of Fame float by and when I view the catalogue
of her favorites I shall behold some name that brings up the recollections of
the exercises here undertaken."[48]

Friendship, respect, and achievement. All of this should have combined
to inspire pride and loyalty for West Point. Not everyone expressed nostalgia for the academy, however, and Lee departed with a lasting ambivalence.
It was—and remains—one of the most formidable educational experiences
in America. "There is no child's play there," was Lee's sober comment.[49] He
and his colleagues arrived at West Point from highly personal worlds, which,
no matter how troubled or untidy, were far removed from the austerity and
drudgery of the cadets' regimen. Many felt keenly the subordination of their
personality to the military ideal. The prowess and individuality that had
gained them the opportunity at West Point was systematically broken down
in the attempt to cast a new character, and many boys felt a near loss of self
in the process. Thayer thought the young men would need to know how to
survive under any conditions, and however right this was in theory, the reality
caused actual deprivation. Cadets were allowed just one candle to study by,
and the rooms were so cold that they huddled with blankets around their
shoulders. The work calendar was 363 days long, with only Christmas and the
Fourth of July as respites. Charles Mason called the life of a cadet "wretched"
and another West Point graduate would later remember his resentment at
the "continued hardship of unremitting study; the freedom of action fet-
tered; the orders and requirements which could never be evaded. . . ."[50] Jack
Mackay told his mother that he left West Point "with very little regret and
very few thanks for the expensive complement paid me."[51] Others felt they
were living a life devoid of adult dignity. On reaching his majority, a cadet
under Lee's superintendence in the 1850s wrote bitterly to his sister that he
"used to think it would be *very high* to be 21, and my own master, and so per-

haps it would be if I was a Cit[n] but to be in the army, it makes no difference how old a fellow is; he is never his own master."[52] Even the cadet officers felt pinched and stressed. They might be allowed to keep their lights on after hours, but they were pressed from all sides, unable to please either their superiors or the corps.[53] Indeed Lee draws the uncomfortable conclusion for us: "The great mistake of my life was taking a military education."[54]

Just how West Point influenced Lee's military outlook and his political or strategic thinking is a vexing question. Perhaps the school's most important effect on its cadets was to instill patriotic values and a commitment to public service. Those founding the academy were determined to create a corps of dedicated professionals who identified as much with national unity as they did with military principles. Thayer relentlessly reinforced these ideas until he had transformed a socially and regionally diverse group of young men into the most nationally focused professional cadre in the country.[55] In addition, West Point taught the craft of the soldier—the discipline, drill, technical language, and use of armaments that gave men occupational competence. Many resented the academy's austerity and rigor, but in Lee's case it played to his natural asceticism. As cadet adjutant, he gained important experience in management and the ability to lead younger men. He also became a competent engineer who could design and build bridges, forts, roads, and boats.

Outside these technical skills it is dangerous to draw simple conclusions about West Point's military influence. The curriculum stressed the construction of fortifications and operational expertise; it did not teach battlefield maneuvers to any great degree, and little time was spent on war games or other theoretical pursuits. Military analysis, to the extent that it existed, focused on informal discussions of the American Revolution and the Napoleonic Wars, including the War of 1812. These conflicts had been pathbreaking in military terms, and offered some indicators of the future nature of combat. Both had departed, for example, from traditional battle tactics, in which lines of troops met in rigid formation and fired at each other with unreliable short-range weapons. Moreover, Napoleon had overturned the idea that siege was the pinnacle of warfare; he avoided defensive positions, preferred to destroy an army than a fort, and to do it he relied on mobility, subterfuge, or wars of attrition. His innovations included the use of field engineering and feeding his troops on the move, either off the land or through well-conserved supplies. In addition, his talent as a statesman showed how civil development and skillful diplomacy must accompany field activities if military success was to be lasting.[56] Antoine-Henri Jomini's earliest catalog of tactics, also based on experience with Napoleon's armies, was available to Lee in French and was also excerpted in a standard text on military science used at West Point. Some have pointed to Jomini as a major influence on Lee, particularly his discussion of combined defensive and offensive maneuvers to "stupefy the moral powers of his enemies." Perhaps all of this historical philosophy did affect Lee's command in the fields of Virginia. If so, Lee himself never overtly drew the comparison.[57]

The West Point library also held a poor translation of Simon François Gay de Vernon's book on field fortifications, which extolled the virtues of earthworks, but for the most part cadets were taught tactics with General Winfield Scott's all-American *General Regulations for the Army,* which was largely bureaucratic in nature. Carl von Clausewitz's meditations on the political and strategic consequences of military action, which again drew on Napoleonic principles, were also available in French, though it is not known whether Lee ever read his work. Clausewitz underscored the relation of military science to the larger concerns of the society and the need for soldiers to subordinate themselves to statesmen. War could not, in his view, exist for its own purpose, but must always carry out a political design. Lee also read—or reread—Machiavelli during his cadet years.[58] Something of each of these works can be found in Lee's generalship, but there is no perfect correlation. One of Lee's contemporaries remarked that the texts available to the cadets of their generation were so poor, and the translations so riddled with mistakes, that textbooks really did not influence the students; it was the personal experience of the teachers that carried the most weight. If this is so, it would have been the philosophic Ethan Allen Hitchcock and haughty Cadet Commandant William Jenkins Worth who molded his thought.[59] Worth had distinguished himself as aide-de-camp to Scott in the War of 1812 and was an acolyte of his teachings. Lee would work closely with Scott, Hitchcock, and Worth during the Mexican War, reinforcing the theory in Scott's manuals with impressive firsthand knowledge.[60]

At the turn of the twentieth century a debate rose about whether cadets of the 1820s had been taught constitutional law from textbooks that promoted the right to secession. For the first two years of Lee's cadetship, William Rawle's *A View of the Constitution of the United States* was the required reading. Rawle, a Pennsylvanian and staunch supporter of the Union, pointed out that tragic results would arise if the federal compact were to be broken. But he was firm about the *right* of a state to secede and of its people to select a preferred form of government. Apparently in 1828 this work was replaced by James Kent's *Commentaries on American Law,* which was far more Federalist in nature. Lee also reread the "Federalist Papers" during his time as a cadet. Whatever the classroom or barracks discussions may have been, Lee developed views on secession that were not precisely in keeping with Rawle. Though he would have agreed that governments should reflect the will of the people, he also branded secession itself as "revolution." The right he defended was to maintain the Constitution as it stood, not the right to abandon it.[61]

In the end it was probably West Point's system of thinking that had the most lasting effect on Lee. Part of this was the dedication and uncompromising attention to duty that was the backbone of a trained professional army. It was the mastery of rigorous assessment, however, that set Thayer's soldiers apart. Cadets at the blackboard were taught to solve problems, not just in mathematical terms but with an eye to anticipating difficulties and formulating creative responses. Those responses began with a set of theorems and structures, but they did not end with them; the most successful learned to adapt scientific principles to new conditions and unknown situations, and reckon with the intellect as well as the eye. The Civil War was a tour de force of military art, in part because the leadership on both sides had learned so well the lessons of multiple variables, intrepid calculation, and implacable assurance. Coupled with a powerful dose of national identity, it was an impressive style of leadership training. This was the enduring tradition of West Point. It is the most tragic of ironies that the nation turned these innovative techniques against itself. Thayer could not have imagined in the heady days of West Point's development that his brilliant plan of officer formation would have consequences as terrible as they were unforeseen.

Chapter Five

Long to Be Remembered

Ravensworth
13ᵗʰ July 1831

So, Captain, you would not come up to Arlington on that memorable Thursday. But I gave you the severest scolding you have had this many a day, from which I hope you will derive great benefit. However you would have seen nothing strange, for there was neither fainting nor fighting, nor anything uncommon which could be twisted into an adventure. The Parson had few words to say, though he dwelt upon them as if he had been reading my Death warrant, and there was a tremulousness in the hand I held, that made me anxious for him to end. I am told I looked "pale and interesting" which might have been the fact. But I felt as "bold as a sheep" & was surprised at my want of Romance in so great a degree as not to feel more excitement than at the black Board at West Point.

The Party all kept together till the following Tuesday, when most of them departed, particularly the Gentlemen. Some of the Ladies remained the rest of the week, and we were then left alone. I would tell you how the time passed, but fear I am too much prejudiced to say anything more, but that it went <u>very</u> rapidly & still continues to do so. We are this far on our way to the upper country, where we shall spend the remainder of my leave of absence, and I there hope the Mother & Daughter will recover from the effects of an attack of the Fever & Ague they have lately undergone. Their health has been reestablished though not their looks. We shall return to the District about the first of August & you may expect me down in the <u>first</u> Boat in that Month. I purchased in Alexandria some few Articles which I directed to be sent by the Potomac to your care, & are to go down next Friday. May I trouble you to have the Bedstead placed in the larger room, (of the two in the Wing) since the <u>Madam</u> prefers that, and such other articles as you may think fit, the rest can be placed in the small room. All Feather beds have been forbid the apartment under pain &c and as I could not *procure a Palliasse, the Mattress must answer for the present. The Box of articles I will not trouble you to open or arrange, as I can do that in five minutes after my arrival, and this closes the list of commissions. There is nothing now here except a second edition of the Ingham affair which has been put to press since the arrival of the President & all of which you will get by the Papers. I was over in Washington last Monday, saw the Genl & Mrs. G[ratiot] the first of [whom] was not very well. They talk of going N before going to Old Point. Col. Thayer had arrived that day & was with the Genl. Poor Mansfield had been ordered on to consult Genl Bernard & arrived the very day he resigned, so that he has to go back to N. Port. I was very anxious to see M. but could not find him. Remember me kindly to Mrs. Hale & tell her I am constantly reminded of her by the Good People I am with & that the Madam looks forward with great pleasure to forming her acquaintance. I long to hear little Miss Rebecca's "Lee", "Lee" & to see whether Miss Kate is still as "Bwack as Wee". I write in great haste, with the servant waiting to take this to the Office which will give him a long ride because I <u>actually</u> could not find <u>time</u> before I left the District for anything but——— Remember me to every one & Excuse Dear Capt. all the trouble I have given you & Believe me*

Yours truly & sincerely

RE Lee

P.S. They are all talking around me at such a rate that I hardly know what I have written & despair of <u>reading</u> it. But please send the boat out for me that first trip the P. makes in August

> *To*
> > *Capt. A. Talcott*
> > > *Corps of Engrs.*
> > > > *Fortress Monroe*
> > > > > *Virginia*[1]

>⊷·0·⊶<

A WEDDING. A time of intensity. The merriment, the feasting, the gathering of friends and relatives—all mark the fusion of families and the private merger of two dreams. The outward show of gaiety can also mask uncertainty, however, and this marriage, which took place between Mary Anna Randolph Custis and Robert Edward Lee on June 30, 1831, had its share of anxiety. Robert is the one who has left us the most vivid descriptions of the event, and also a sense of the strong sentiment that evolved from this bonding. Together the Lees would face challenges they could not possibly have imagined on that happy summer evening. And together they would forge a marriage as original as the two individuals who entered into it.

In June 1829 Robert Lee graduated from West Point and was commissioned a second lieutenant in the Army Corps of Engineers. His achievement was tinged with sorrow, however, for while his classmates went on a celebratory trip to Niagara Falls, Lee took a somber journey home to the deathbed of his mother.[2] At fifty-six, Ann Lee's delicate constitution was finally exhausted, and she died on July 10. According to those present, Robert was nearly beside himself, taking on his old role as nurse, mixing medicines and doing what he could for her comfort. Ann Lee evidently was content only when he was in the room. When the end came, one cousin recalled, Robert's distress was "excessive." Too overcome to attend the funeral, "he paced to and fro, the floor of the bedroom in inconsolable grief."[3] His brother Carter spoke for all of Ann's children, now scattered about the eastern seaboard, when he bewailed the loss of a family home. "I am left by myself to reflect on how melancholy it is that there will soon be no longer a roof under which we can be gathered as our home," he wrote to Robert. "This happening at the very time of your departure seems to complete the overthrow of that domestic happiness, which after all the heart appears most to rely on."[4]

As if to magnify their grief, Black-Horse Harry's awful business again surfaced. Andrew Jackson had chosen to befriend Henry Lee IV, going so far as to invite him to stay at "The Hermitage." In return Henry was supposed to write campaign literature, including a biography of the general. When Jackson was elected president, Lee had hopes of receiving a lucrative office, a necessity now that his public disgrace and financial irresponsibility had lost him Stratford.[5] Though the biography seems never to have been finished, Jackson did appoint Henry Lee to be U.S. consul to Algiers. In a move reminiscent of his father, Lee sailed away quickly, before he had to face further court proceedings on the still-unpaid settlement of Elizabeth McCarty's estate. But the Senate, on a unanimous vote, chose not to confirm Lee's appointment. The proceedings were loud, public, and piercing. Henry was forced to leave his post and live in exile in Paris, and the rest of the Lee clan had to relive the humiliation of their family indiscretions.[6]

It was in this disturbed mood that Robert Lee settled into his first army post. He had been sent to Cockspur Island, Georgia, where a fort guarding the approach to Savannah was to be built. The one consolation in the hot, poorly supervised, and mosquito-infested assignment was the proximity of Jack Mackay's family. Jack had five sisters, all attractive and merry, and they embraced the young Virginian in their Broughton Street home as if he had been a lifelong friend. Lee seems to have had a particular affection for Eliza Mackay; they struck up an intense flirtation, complete with mischievous letters and vows of eternal fidelity. But Eliza and her sisters had other suitors, and Lee was left depressed and terribly lonely. Having heard nothing from his family, he composed a sad letter to Carter, saying that he could "no longer refrain from begging you to write & that quickly"—for, as he noted, "I feel, and doubly feel, a hundred times more wretched than the day we parted."[7] His misery must have increased when he received news a few weeks later that his family's generous protector, William Henry Fitzhugh, had unexpectedly died at the age of thirty-two.

William Henry Fitzhugh's death was a sorrowful blow to the Lees, but it was a major calamity for the Arlington household. Fitzhugh was the only brother of Molly Custis, and a most beloved uncle of her daughter Mary. He had been an exceptional young man: wonderfully handsome, known for his liberality and charity, an early opponent of slavery, and a benefactor to many of his relatives, the Lees notably among them. His death was mysterious, which increased the family's gloom. He had been slightly indisposed while on a visit to his wife's girlhood home, took some medicine, became violently ill, and within a few minutes threw himself back on his pillow and expired.[8] As his niece would lament, he had been "torn from us all by a lightening flash," leaving them in "utter wretchedness." At first Mary Custis felt only a small sadness at her uncle's passing, confiding to her diary her "feeling of regret that my mourning dress would prevent my entering gay society the winter succeeding."[9] Then, on a visit to her devastated aunt, she was suddenly struck by the transience of these temporal conceits, and the experience provoked an intense spiritual catharsis. Mary described it as the defining moment of her life, a revelation so swift and penetrating that it interrupted all conscious thought and superseded every other concern. The experience also initiated a significant change in her character. Where she had once enjoyed self-indulgence, she was now determined to shape a more mature and selfless nature.[10]

As the only surviving child of the Custises, Mary probably had been a bit spoiled. Arlington, with its scores of servants, lush surroundings, and near-royal Washington associations, was the kingdom of her childhood. She grew up with an uninhibited personality, a quick temper, a clever intellect, and a mind of her own. She was more skilled in the arts of painting and prose than her amateur father, and as one of her daughters later noted, she possessed "the real artist temperament," revering nature and caring little for outward structures—such as time—or for societal pretensions—such as dress. Her "artist temperament" fostered some irascibility as well, which manifested it-self in acerbic comments. "She spoke whatever came in her mind—but it was over in a moment," observed one family member.[11] Mary had been ed-ucated well for a girl of her day, studying history, Greek, and rhetoric in ad-dition to embroidery. A surviving copybook shows some excellent attempts at essay writing and philosophical thought—and also a lack of sustained ap-plication. At the same time she was brave and morally strong, and had in-herited her mother's sympathetic nature—a girl more challenging and more interesting than the predictable local belles.[12]

Historians have had a field day with Mary Custis's sharp features and sometimes equally sharp personality. "By her late teens she was a spoiled, unpleasant woman accustomed to lavish parties and the incessant atten-tions of her father," one Lee biographer has written. Another was harsher still: "Expressed bluntly . . . Mary was careless, self-centered, dependent, undisciplined, and dull."[13] Somehow, however, the more one reads about Mary Custis, the more appealing she becomes. A brunette with cinnamon-brown eyes, she attracted many admirers, who praised her "placid and win-ning face" and laughing expression.[14] In 1830 her portrait was painted by Auguste Hervieu, and the picture shows a thoughtful girl with a rich pile of curled hair.[15] When she was about fifteen, her aunt, Nelly Custis Lewis, found her wonderfully appealing and told a close friend that she "would love this sweet modest girl, so humble & gentle with all her classical attainments. She has wit & satire too, when they are required."[16] Robert Lee's sister Mildred, who was a confidante in the years of their girlhood, begged for letters from her, praising "the talent which you possess in such an imminent degree to entertain and amuse one."[17] Yet another cousin, describing Mary and her mother, remarked: "I wish you knew them. They are my favorite Aunt and Cousin, so good and so very intelligent."[18]

And to top it all, Mary was evidently an accomplished flirt. One of her chums teased her in 1825 about the "*mischief* you are making upon the un-fortunate youths *around you*," exclaiming, "pray what have you done with poor Mr Carter—Mr Lloyd—*Mr Lee* & . . . a dozen or more swains who seem to be dying with the prevailing Love fever of the day."[19] "Mr. Lee" could have been Robert—for he teasingly referred to a flirtation with Miss Custis the previous Christmas—or it could have been either Smith or Carter, both of whom notoriously haunted Arlington "to kneel at [her] shrine." There were rumors of other distinguished suitors, including dashing Sam Hous-ton, then a congressman in his early thirties.[20] Though she enjoyed the at-tentions of the young men who came to call, Mary pronounced herself an "*impregnable fortress*" and also earned a reputation for a quick, barbed

Mary Anna Randolph Custis, by Auguste Hervieu, 1830.

repartee, which, a confidante noted, proved "so fatal to the beaux."[21] Such a woman, with her imposing background, her watchful parents, her distinctive personality and self-absorption, was not easy to court. In 1827 Aunt Lewis commented that Mary Custis was "still unattached. There are few worthy of her I think."[22] In 1829 Mildred Lee advised her to carry out resolutions she had "so long formed of repressing and softening" her disposition, and under her tutelage, and the influence of religious awakening, something did come about—a kind of epiphany, which led the girl to shed her self-gratifying amusements.[23] Mary once had told a friend that she would not stand godmother to her daughter because she could not promise "for another what I have never performed myself—to make a solemn vow to renounce for the child those pomps and vanities of the world in which I so much delight." Now she agonized over her willful nature and asked God to lead her away "from pride, selfishness, indolence."[24]

So it was that two spirits came together in the summer of 1830, both buffeted by loss and uncertainty, one homeless and unsettled, the other committed to pursuing a new and demanding path. When weather and water halted the operations at Cockspur Island, Lieutenant Lee was granted a furlough, and he chose to spend it in the company of his kin in northern Virginia. Those who encountered him around this time, at Kinloch, Eastern View, Ravensworth, and Arlington, remembered Robert Lee as "bright, animated and charming." Lee had inherited his mother's dark curls and rich coloring—he always referred to his complexion as "black" and laughed at his perpetually red nose. It is to this he is referring when he asked Captain Talcott if his little friend was still "as Bwack as Wee." The eyes that would one day smolder on the battlefield were hazel brown in the parlor, framed by elegantly curving eyebrows. Everyone commented on his fine appearance in uniform and his lovely manners, but mostly they remembered his enjoyment of flirtation and repartee—"as full of life, fun, and particularly of teasing, as any of us."[25]

Just what led the two childhood friends to move from cousinly friendship to lovers' intimacy, we do not know. In 1824 Robert was apparently courting all the neighborhood belles; his brother Carter laughed at "the old fellow Bob" trying to choose between several Washington beauties and two Miss Campbells: "I left him there a fortnight since in the picturesque situation of the ass starving between two bundles of hay."[26] There is some indication that Robert, for all his flirtation, was hesitant when it came to serious courtship. He enlisted his sister to transmit his admiring thoughts to Mary, and shows uncertainty in his earliest letters to her. Among Carter Lee's papers was a two-part poem, entitled "Robert to Miss Polly"—Polly being a nickname for Mary. In it Robert laments that Miss Polly has so many beaux "That I alas! must be of those / Who dare not meet such charms as hers." In the answering couplet Miss Polly remonstrates: "Tell him that faint-heart never won Fair Lady . . . / None but the brave deserve the fair."[27] Perhaps it was this encouragement that bolstered his spirit; in any case, around the spring of 1830 Lee's letters begin to show a marked interest in Mary Custis. "Tell [her]," he wrote to his brother Carter, who was staying at Arlington, "that if she thinks I am going to stay here after you go away, without hearing any thing of her . . . she is very much mistaken. So . . . she must write to me & if she does not I'll tell her mother. Or if she will say that I may write to her, she will have to answer me through common politeness."[28]

That summer the romance grew more serious, leading to their engagement by September. The glimpses we have of their courtship are endearing: Mary resisting the advances of "worldly young gentlemen who flattered my vanity & pleased me in spite of myself"; Robert buying flowers that he could not afford for Mary and all of her visiting friends; the two reading Sir Walter Scott together in the wide breezy hall parlor at Arlington; a laughing pair as they walked or rode together in the estate's luxuriant park.[29] According to one family tradition it was while Mary was cutting Robert a piece of fruit-cake in the Arlington dining room that he leaned toward her and asked her to share his life.[30] By the time Robert had to return to Savannah, Miss Custis could write the delicious news to her friends. "Never was I surrounded with more of the joys of life than at this time," she confided to one of her girlhood companions. "I am engaged to one to whom I have been long attached— Robert Lee."[31] The prospective groom also announced the betrothal. "Strange things have happened here this Summer," he wrote to Carter from Arlington on September 22. "Charles Henry is engaged. Marietta T. is engaged & last though not least I am engaged to Miss Mary C. . . . That is, she & her mother have given their consent. But the Father has not yet made up his mind, though it is supposed will not object."[32]

They would see nothing of each other in the coming months, but they commenced an exchange of letters that hint at both their closeness and the individuality of each partner. When Robert left Arlington, he took with him a present from Mary: a book of her favorite sermons. He expressed appreciation, but longed so much to see her that the verses swam before his eyes, and while she was contemplating the love of God, he was overtaken by more worldly desires.[33] She encouraged him to write as much as he could, and allowed that her mother no longer thought it necessary to read his missives— "So you are perfectly at liberty to say what you please"—adding demurely that she trusted his "discretion to say only what is right."[34] And he did say just what he pleased. He spoke of his delight in her person, of his longing, and of his desperate loneliness. The stack of love letters he left are among his most agreeable, crackling with sexual tension, filled with irreverent pokes at the military, and always seasoned with his disarming humor. "Do you ever think of me my own sweet Mary?" he taunted her, expressing his frustration at the army that kept him so far away. "I will ask the General for a Furlough & if he will not grant it I will take it. For I declare I cannot wait *any longer*. And He & his Uncle Sam may go to—France—For what I care."[35] "I wish you were here today to amuse me," Mary rejoined. "I wish for you very often, though I am still *content*."[36] Then they waited: for George Washington Parke Custis to give his consent; for Mary to stop hesitating about the date; and for Robert Lee to get a furlough long enough to celebrate the marriage.

Evidently Custis did have reservations—Mary admitted that her father had "not given a decided consent," and her fiancé continued for some time to speak of the upcoming wedding in conjectural terms.[37] Robert allowed that he was "the worst coward" when it came to speaking to her father and cringed at the thought that the decision "should be the wrong one."[38] It may have been reluctance to give up his only daughter that caused Custis to hesitate, but it seems to have been a cautionary feeling about the prospects of Lieutenant Lee. Courtship and matchmaking were a serious business in the early nineteenth century, when not just happiness, but progeny and prosperity were at stake. As an only child, Mary was an important heiress. Her expectations included thousands of acres of prime Virginia land, nearly 200 slaves, and the beautiful seat at Arlington. In addition, William Fitzhugh had sired no children, and his vast property was left to his widow Anna Maria during her lifetime and then to his niece, Mary Custis. She was also Martha Washington's granddaughter, and the Mount Vernon tradition was her birthright. Quite simply, there were few in the United States that could claim a place in society of equal rank. Robert Lee, for all his personal qualities and historic family ties, could not hope to match this. He had a share in some land in the Blue Ridge Mountains—the remnants of Light-Horse Harry's folly—and a few slaves, but nothing that would compare to the Custis patrimony.

Then there was the question of his career. Americans liked war heroes, but they were skeptical about the attributes of regular army officers, whose reputation had been sullied by the frequently disreputable performance of their brethren in the militia. Custis, who had served for a short time as a staff officer during the War of 1812, knew exactly what army life entailed, with its rough men, rough posts, and rough pay, not to mention constant absences from family and friends. Army officers expected their wives to follow them loyally, despite deprivation, and Lee believed in this credo, once telling a military bride that she should never "desert her post, which is by your husband's side."[39] Mary's father had watched his sister Nelly sink into constant worry when her daughter married a soldier, and he may have been unwilling to accept the same kind of anxiety.[40] The Custis family was hardly unique in these attitudes. General Winfield Scott had also struggled with a prospective father-in-law who insisted he must make a choice between the army and his bride. The father of Jefferson Davis's first wife refused his consent on the same grounds, though he was himself an army officer. When Davis and the young woman married without the father's blessing, it led to a lifelong estrangement.[41] Whatever pressure was put on Lee, we know that he resisted. "But what are you talking of Weddings, & my resigning?" he challenged his brother. "The Wedding, if there is one, will not be till next Spring (so she says). And I am not going to resign till God knows when, for I don't."[42]

The real sticking point, however, was the doubt Light-Horse Harry and his eldest son had created about the desirability of the Lee men. The Custises had remained loyal to their Lee cousinry through debt, villainy, scandal, and flight, but the marriage of their only daughter with one of that clan was a different matter. The recent resurrection of Henry Lee's troubles was not a ringing endorsement for a young man intent on proving his worth to one of the great heiresses of the land.[43] His brothers might insist that he was "good enough for any woman," with accomplishments that were "already considerable," but six months after the betrothal Custis had still not given his blessing. Lee considered writing to him again, terrified at what the outcome might be.[44] It was Mary who finally screwed up the courage to speak to her father on the matter, and persuade him that Robert was his own man. Hugely relieved, Robert wrote in appreciation to his bride: "If *you* 'felt so grateful' to your Father for his kindness, what must I feel. . . . I only wish that his 'approbation' in the one case was as well founded as his 'objections' in the other. Of these no one can be more sensible than myself, or less able to devise a remedy. But should I be able to escape the sins into which they have fallen, I hope the blame which is justly their due, will not be laid to me."[45]

The Lees also had questions about the alliance. Mary's spontaneous conversion was well known among the family members, and they were worried that it might prove oppressive for the disinclined Robert. Revivalism was popular in the early nineteenth century, and the Lee brothers whispered that it had "afflicted the sweet girl with a little of that over-righteousness which the blue-lights brought into Virginia." Carter, for one, hoped the impending marriage would "cure her mind of this disorder."[46] Henry was also surprised by the match, for he was certain "that Robert cannot be older than Miss Custis."[47] He appears to have been nearly correct about this, for the family Bible shows clear tampering with her birth date, changing it from October 1807 to 1808. The earlier date is validated by a letter written in December 1807, praising Mrs. Custis's new daughter, unequivocally identified as "Mary Anna Randolph." Another note, also penned months before the date in the Bible entry, was addressed to "my dear little cherub Mary Anna."[48]

Most important, Mary had her own qualms about the match. It was she who insisted on waiting nearly a year to be wed, opting for postponement even as the day grew close. Women of this time were far from giddy about the prospect of marriage, and more likely than men to view the transition with foreboding. Concerned about separation from their families and the gamble they were making on their future, many young women were inclined to prolong the engagement period. Betrothal initiated a time of withdrawal from the support and laughter of a girlhood circle and a wary entry into the responsibilities of adulthood. An engagement also signaled the end of the heady period of courtship, the one time in her life a belle could count on the deference of men, which was apt to disappear as soon as the flirtation stopped. Nothing illustrates this so starkly as the remarks made by MEA Lewis, a few years after her cousin Mary Custis was married. "The gentlemen in this District seldom find a Lady interesting enough after she is engaged to ride to see her. . . . My Cousin Mrs Lee and Mrs Powell . . . spent the winter after they were engaged here; and not one of their numerous acquaintances called once to see them. Sad! Sad! is it not."[49] For women, marriage could also mean the loss of personal liberty and the beginning of an existence in which a man's wishes shaped her fate. Alexis de Tocqueville, who arrived in America the year the Lees were wed, observed that unmarried girls in America were relatively free in comparison to their European sisters, but that "the independence of women is irrecoverably lost in the bonds of matrimony."[50] Added to this was the loss of virginity, a pivotal event for most young women, and the very real fear of mortality during childbirth. In light of these factors, marriage for many girls denoted separation and death as much as it did union and fresh life.[51]

Mary Custis had all of these issues to consider as she contemplated what she called her "new situation." She was far from single-minded in her desire to wed. She discussed the advantages of spinsterhood with Robert's sister, frustrated her fiancé by repeatedly delaying the wedding, and would one day caution her daughters and others of marriageable age to appreciate their "blessed" single state and not be in a hurry to leave it.[52] She was additionally concerned with the way her forthcoming responsibilities might impact her religious contemplation. Her search for faith was entirely genuine, and indeed dominated the year prior to her wedding. Though the rounds of visiting relatives continued, and Mary would express pleasure at being immersed in the "joys of life," the diary she kept in 1830–31 is filled only with her desire to find peace in biblical principles, overcome worldly aspirations, and serve her God. She believed her fiancé did not exhibit enough spirituality, and once remarked that he lacked "the one thing needful without which all the rest may prove valueless."[53] She spent much of their engagement year proselytizing to a good-humored, but unrepentant, Robert.[54] Lee is never mentioned directly in her writings, and only indirectly in terms of apprehension about the distraction he might cause to her spiritual quest. "O Lord suffer me not to be drawn aside from Thee in the new situation I am about to enter on," she prayed two weeks before the nuptials, "but with a single eye may therein live to thy service & by a blameless life & conservation endeavor to shew forth thy praise."[55]

Mary was conflicted enough that, after postponing the wedding several times, she would have begged a few months more, but the impatient Robert plunged ahead and officially requested a furlough for late June 1831. When Mary tried to put the day off just two weeks before the wedding, Robert teasingly pointed at the courage "oozing out at your finger ends," but firmly added: "No Miss Molly it is too late to change your mind now. . . ."[56] Then it was Robert's turn to feel nervous. "The day has been fixed and it is the 30th of June," he informed Carter. "I can tell you I begin to feel right *funny* when I count my days."[57] With only a few weeks to plan for the event, both bride and groom began to make hurried preparations. Robert had originally wanted the simplest sort of ceremony: he romantically imagined arriving at Arlington in the dewy dawn with a minister in tow and intercepting Mary on her morning walk. But the Custises had other ideas, and finally Robert acquiesced with a perceptible groan.[58] Anticipating a house full of guests, Mary and her mother beseeched relatives and friends to loan cake baskets, mattresses, candlesticks, and servants. Robert was concerned by his attire, and anxiously sent Smith on a chase for epaulettes and implored Carter to deal with the tailor. "I believe I will wear my uniform coat on the important night," he told his brother, "& therefore the *white* pantaloons must be in character. . . . Let the material of all be the best & *don't* let him charge too much."[59] Mary chose a half dozen bridesmaids, and Robert struggled to find an equal number of available groomsmen. Standing with the bride were

Robert Lee in the dress uniform of a lieutenant of engineers, by William E. West, 1838.

cousins and childhood friends. Smith Lee was best man, and Robert's West Point and army colleagues filled out the male side. Lee tried to entice both Andrew Talcott and Carter to come. "Can you come on to see it well done?" he asked anxiously, then held out an enticement: "I am told there are to be *Six* pretty bridesmaids, Misses Mason, Mary G., Martha, Angela, Julia & Brittania & you could have some fine kissing. For you know what a fellow you are at these weddings."[60] In the end neither Carter nor Talcott could attend, and Lee left Old Point alone on June 29, stopping one final time at the flower shop, where so much of his precious lieutenant's pay had been spent. He rode up "pale and breathless," the florist recalled, "and cried out as he approached, 'Pierce, old boy, make me six bouquets, and don't spare pains or expense. It's the last you will get out of me, for I am going to be married on Thursday night, and then the girls may gather wild flowers.' "[61]

The night of the wedding was one of steady rain, but guests remembered that the bride's "beautiful home was most happy and bright."[62] The minister, the Reverend Reuel Keith, was caught in a shower while riding to Arlington, arrived drenched to the skin, and was obliged to dress in the clothes of Mr. Custis, who was several inches shorter and wider than he. The situation caused much glee among the wedding party, but dignity was restored when the parson covered his ill-fitting garments with clerical robes. Tradition says that Nelly Custis Lewis was there to play the piano as Mary came down the stairs with her father, and that a bell of flowers hung from the graceful arches of the parlor where the couple stood. Bridesmaid Marietta Turner would write that her cousin, "always a modest and affectionate girl, was never lovelier and Robert Lee with his bright eyes and high color was the picture of a cavalier."[63] The service was conducted "in a quiet way" and, as Robert tells us, was solemn enough to remind him of a death warrant. Mary was nervous—her hand shook as Robert held it—and the groom seems to have been a bit intimidated as well, self-deprecatingly describing his feelings as "bold as a sheep."

After the ceremony there was a supper and dancing, and the celebration carried over to the servants' quarters, where it was said that unlimited food and drink were provided.[64] The party kept going for several days in an atmosphere that Dolley Madison liked to term "Virginia hilarity."[65] Washington's punch bowl was filled to the brim each night, and Mr. Custis would allow the company to drink until the hull of the frigate painted in the bottom came into view—then everyone was sent to bed. Flirtation and jesting were the chief occupations of the wedding guests. Bridesmaid Angela Lewis reported that some of the gentlemen were more enticing than others, one of the groomsmen nearly spoiling the merriment by being unable to converse on anything "other than *sensible* subjects."[66] The whole party then traveled on to neighboring estates for a continuation of the festivities. Evidently such extended wedding parties were a purely Virginia custom, for when Lee tried to explain the whole business to Georgian Jack Mackay, he had to give up. "It is useless for me to tell you of the doings on such occasions. Come to Virginia, get married, and then you will know it."[67]

Some of the friends brought gifts: a pair of delicate etched-glass decanters that were given to the Lees can still be seen at Arlington. More enduring still were the sentimental memories of the event. "The evening was one long to be remembered," concluded bridesmaid Marietta Turner many years later. "The elegance and simplicity of the bride's parents, presiding over the feast, and the happiness of the grinning servants . . . remain in my memory as a piece of Virginia life pleasant to recall."[68]

"I take this occasion to congratulate you on the *happy* Union of Robert & Miss Custis they are worthy of each other," wrote Lee's first cousin, Zaccheus Collins Lee, a few days after their wedding.[69] Cousin Zaccheus's comments proved insightful. The marriage of Robert and Mary Lee would become a partnership of unusual equality, the strength of each spouse reinforcing the relationship—but not without some sparks in the burnishing.

It is tempting to view the Custis-Lee wedding as the merger of two old and distinguished Virginia houses. Some have gone so far as to hint that Mary had few available options, and that Lee's motive for the marriage was to revive his family's reputation and fortune. Robert Lee's status and financial security were undoubtedly enhanced by the union, but his courtship letters show him to be passionately smitten. Moreover, the old assumption of matrimony-as-business was radically changing by the 1830s. The popular eighteenth-century view had been that marriage was either an unapologetic economic alliance or a coupling fitted for low, snickering humor. In the early years of the nineteenth century, however, attitudes were shifting in favor of relationships grounded in friendship and mutual support. Marriage with a true companion, which eased the burdens of life and inspired introspection and self-sacrifice, was seen to be part of the happiness that Americans were entitled to pursue. In a culture that still legally and socially curbed the freedom of women, a "companionate" marriage—one in which the partners showed care and understanding—could help bridge the gender difference and overcome social restrictions. Some scholars have proposed a pattern for southern marriages that was based on starkly separate worlds for husband and wife, in which male patriarchs consciously isolated women by expecting them to live up to unrealistic ideals, or established nonnegotiable boundaries that often resulted in hostility and bitterness. Such a model has no resonance for the Lees' marriage, which embraced the individuality of both partners, and even on bad days was predicated on communication and mutual commitment.[70]

During their engagement Robert Lee had been the more ardent of the two, and it appears that from the outset he also liked the reality of the connubial state more than did his wife. Early on he told Jack Mackay that he "would not be unmarried for all you could offer me. Hope never again to interfere in the remotest way with the prerogatives of you Bachelors. A Bad life (for me) to lead, Flat, stale & unprofitable."[71] In this he seems to have been typical of men of his age, who saw marriage as a refuge from the strains of career competition and enjoyed not only the regular sexual contact, but the domestic comfort and community they received in it. In general during the antebellum period men were also in control of their homes, and the pursuits of the family were frequently ordered around their pleasure.[72] Women were more skeptical of the arrangement, which often resulted in a jolting drop from the status of beloved daughter to that of subservient wife, or put high-reaching individuals in conflict with personal goals. They could also find themselves subordinated to the unreasonable whims of their husbands— or to household drudgery, the rigors of childbearing, societal constraints, and inequitable laws.[73]

Mary Lee seems also to have been typical here. Her earliest comment on her "new situation," penned four days after the nuptials, showed concern that "in the circumstances with which I am surrounded my poor vain foolish heart has been too much drawn aside from Thee, Oh my Father. . . ." Throughout her life she continued to feel anxiety about the way marriage distracted her from her devotions.[74] Clearly claustrophobic, she went a step further and defined a distinctive role for herself, which was independent of either the expectations of society or those of her husband. From her perspective, this was totally appropriate. Mary was certainly Robert's intellectual and cultural equal, and his superior in social rank. She read four newspapers a day and was used to conversing with the leading figures of the nation, who had shared the family table since she was a child. She had grown confident in this environment, where her opinions were respected. She also came from a long line of spirited Custis women who had been tough and durable enough to challenge male authority. Her mother had lobbied effectively for both religious and social reform, and she counted some incipient feminists among her acquaintances, including Robert's younger sister.[75] She saw few reasons to follow unquestioningly her husband's lead in matters where she trusted her own judgment. "Altho' my accounts may not seem to you very clear according to your nice mode of keeping yours," Mary shot back when Robert appeared to question her handling of the family finances, "there is no one more particular to pay all I owe to the uttermost farthing. Do not be uneasy about me—"[76] Moreover, she expected him to project the same independence. "Mr. Lee desires me to say something handsome for him," she announced when he tried to get her to tend to his social obligations, "but I think he is well able to deliver his own messages—"[77]

Mary Lee also knew her mind in daily living and showed no inclination to conform to Robert's style. He was patient, painstaking, and often passive; she was quick, creative, and volatile. He delighted in the children and was intensely engaged in their development—she called them "my brats," suffered neuralgia from the noise and confusion, and easily passed them off to the servants.[78] Like her father, Mary cared little for fashion, preferring to dress informally and comfortably, if not eccentrically, and throughout the nearly forty years of their marriage she exasperated Lee by appearing in clothes he felt were unsuitable. The stories about her wardrobe are wonderful. She once was seen at a fashionable resort in a calico dress and blue cotton stockings she had knit herself. She made a frantic search for gloves before an important address by her father, and when they could not be found donned a tatty old pair that were entirely "unharmonious with the rest of her dress." During a party before the war Lee surreptitiously approached a female acquaintance and said, "Will you please tell Mrs. Lee that her [under]skirt is longer than her dress? If I tell her she will pay no attention to it."[79] Once when Mary had been ill, her hair became so snarled in bed that "on her first sitting up took the scissors & cut it all off." When it started growing out, she again became annoyed, and, Lee told a friend, "when I left today she talked of having it shaved off and I expect on my return to find her *bald*."[80] Mary Lee similarly dismissed her husband's obsession with household order and punctuality, which she saw as the unpleasant harping of a martinet. "Tell the Ladies that they are aware that Mrs. L. is somewhat addicted to *laziness & forgetfulness* in her Housekeeping," Lee only half jokingly told the Talcotts, and to Mary he implied that the slave Cassy, whom he had previously disdained, was the superior housekeeper. Mary's response was to tell her mother, who scolded Robert for his nagging.[81]

The dissimilar personalities caused real frictions in the early years of their marriage, and voices were often raised. Robert "does scold me early & late," Mary complained. Lee groused in his turn, describing how he had "so many accounts to settle" with his wife and announcing publicly that her "*forte* is to give *advice*."[82] When Robert failed to provide enough information on the doings of some favorite cousins, a shouting match ensued. "My dame made many an exclamation at these omissions which I echoed back in the profoundest manner," Lee admitted, "notwithstanding which the Sin was visited upon poor innocent me, because 'that was just my way,' & 'so unsatisfactory.' "[83] As the years went on, however, they learned to accept their differences and, where compromise could not be found, to narrow the gap between them. Mary became a tolerable housekeeper, and Robert tried to stop bullying. "I don't know that I shall ever overcome my propensity for order & methodology," he admitted to his wife. "But I will try. And as I have lately learned such good reasons against it I hope they will weaken my idea of their necessity, which will tend much to diminish my predilection."[84] One of the Lee children recalled how their contradictory perceptions of timeliness came to be accommodated. "My father was the most punctual man I ever knew. . . . He used to appear some minutes before the rest of us, in uniform, jokingly rallying my mother for being late, and for forgetting something at the last moment. When he could wait no longer for her, he would say he was off and would march along to church by himself. . . ."[85]

Robert and Mary Lee had grown up together, were distantly related, and had a commonality of background that should have made for a smooth entry into married life. Unfortunately, in addition to their strong and distinct personalities, they had a third party to contend with: the U.S. Army. The requirements of the military and Mary's intense love for Arlington were at odds with each other, causing the most serious disagreement of their marriage. Shortly before their marriage, Robert Lee predicted that Mary, sheltered for so long, might have trouble adjusting. He was soon proven right. She began to be homesick almost immediately after her wedding, describing herself forlornly to a friend as "a wanderer on the face of the earth and know not where we are going next."[86] Her husband, still in honeymoon spirits, was stunned when she returned to her mother just months into the marriage. It was the beginning of a lifelong pattern, whereby both partners felt drawn to the Custis estate, but diverged on whether it should become their permanent home. At the beginning Lee addressed the situation with humor: "Just as I have despaired of ever hearing from you again, my dear Mary, & was consulting with Dick how he & I could cut our throats in the *easiest* manner, one of the Boatman stepped up & said there were two letters on my table . . . [this] makes *two long* weeks since I last heard from you. This will never do Molly. . . ."[87] Soon, however, he grew more serious, questioning whether they should be apart and whether dependence on her family was a wise choice, even in the short term.[88] He was up against some formidable opponents. His mother-in-law, as well as a host of allied relatives, encouraged

Mary to remain at her parents' home. Believing that her mother was ill, she lingered at Arlington, and when she returned to Old Point she brought Molly Custis with her.[89]

Society expected a wife to cleave to her husband's bosom—the popular image of the time was of a vine clinging to a sturdy oak. However, as a friend would proudly observe, Mary Lee "never did come to heel."[90] In the 1790s her grandmother, Ann Randolph Fitzhugh, had written a finely crafted booklet for her daughters, which counseled finding a man of understanding and then "falling in with his inclinations as much as possible." If Mary ever saw this well-intentioned advice, she ignored it.[91] Her strongest allegiance was already fixed to her parents, and her religiosity had also given her something that consoled, guided, and fulfilled her that was outside of her husband. She was never disloyal or unsupportive, but she had an identity beyond matrimony and chose to honor it. Robert teased her about her independent ways, calling her the "vixen in the family, whose husband tried in vain to conquer her."[92] He was clearly unhappy with her hesitation to fully embrace the army life he had chosen. "This is a terrible life we lead Molly, unsatisfactory, profitless & irksome," he wrote once when she had left him to return to Arlington.[93] One again feels his discomfort in the counsel he gave a new army bride in the 1850s. Cautioning her not to desert her husband, he advised, "I consider it fatal to the future happiness of young married people, upon small provocation, to live apart. . . . The result is invariably that they cease to be essential to each other."[94] Of course Mary Lee did take on the burdens of army life to a considerable degree. In the years before the Civil War she traveled to every one of Robert's posts, save the Mexican War and the wilderness of Texas, spending more than half of her life at military outposts. But she felt lonely and awkward in new places, and thus the tension continued until the day the war forced them to flee Arlington.[95] Mary saw their destiny as an extension of her childhood, with its loving care and family associations. Robert wanted a more autonomous profile, a life that included his kin, but also moved beyond their boundaries. In the end both got their way: Arlington remained home, and Lee held on to the army, which gave him the freedom and adventure he needed.[96]

It is fascinating to read about this marriage, which appears so familiar to modern sensibilities. Neither partner chose to relinquish personal desires completely, yet both contrived to maintain the viability of the relationship. Robert realized he should stop moralizing and bring joy into the household, and Mary grew to understand her role in enhancing their life together rather than indulging her own amusement. They fought it out or toughed it out, and in the end they were able to look beyond their differences to build a hard-wearing bond, characterized by affection, humor, and cooperation. Contrast the tone of this circa 1852 letter from Mary to her mother with the couple's arguments twenty years earlier. "Robert proposed to me last week to go on & stay with you 'till the first of August but . . . he really leads such a *fatiguing* life I thought he' ought to have some comfort at home. . . ."[97] They endured years of separation, but it gave them a chance to appreciate each other and to savor some little prerogatives that were not available within a confined relationship. For her part, Mary came to revere her husband's "excellent judgment" and to be as proud of him as she was of her illustrious ancestry.[98] The marriage was perhaps more essential to Robert than to Mary Lee—he writes as if adrift whenever apart from her—but it provided important emotional substance to them both. Perhaps more than anything they were friends, and their love shines through in hundreds of letters we were never meant to read. "I am always longing for the hour that will again unite us & more & more wish for its arrival," Robert wrote tenderly in 1835; and then a few years later: "I am anxious, my dear Mary, to get back to see you all. . . . I dream of you and the dear little children nearly every night." As the army ordered him to Texas in 1860, he lamented, "It was very sad to leave you and my departure grows harder to bear with years." And, most poignantly, on June 30, 1864, from the trenches of besieged Petersburg: "Do you remember what a happy day thirty-three years ago this was. How many hopes and pleasures it gave birth to!"[99] Mary, less demonstrative in her letters, revealed her deep attachment in prayer, calling on God to "take that loved one of my soul under thy fatherly care."[100] When death finally parted them, she deeply missed his "strong arm and loving heart" and admitted she knew not how to "continue my weary pilgrimage alone."[101]

Chapter Six

Seven Arias

I was delighted my dear Mother by the reception of your letter & the news it contained. How is that dear Mama? Tell her I deeply sympathize with her in her suffering & hope that the pleasure she experiences in her little boy amply compensates her for all she has gone through. It is strange how my heart yearned towards him as soon as I heard of his existence. In anticipating that event I felt no other interest in him, than was connected with the safety & well-being of his Mother, but no sooner was I conscious of his birth, than all my affections were awakened. Perhaps it was from your telling me he resembled Rooney. Poor little red thing, how strange he must feel. Can't Mama find him a better name. Tell her I am much flattered by the selection but think if he is to walk in the footsteps of his illustrious brother, as well as into his pants, he deserves a better. What would she think of <u>John</u> <u>Tyler</u>? I am truly grateful my dear Mother at the happy issue of this event. I have prayed daily & fervently that it might be safe & propicious for our dear Mary & that she may now be preserved in health & comfort. I know you will do every thing that the kindest & most affectionate Mother can do to affect that object, but I am very uneasy lest trusting in her strength, she may commit some imprudence that may prove injurious. What nurse has she with her? Do charge her from me to do or <u>suffer</u> nothing but what she <u>knows</u> to be proper & beg that poor Mama to be patient & not to <u>experiment</u> where the risk is so great & the result may be so ruinous. Tell her I long to see her & be with her & nothing but the impracticality of my doing so prevents me.

Tell the Major I am much obliged to him for his letter & thank him for his hearty congratulations. I will make every exertion to get on as soon as my business will allow & I can get permission, & that it will give me pleasure to do all in my power to render him a straight & circumstantial account of the affairs at his estates on the Pamunkey. It will not be possible for me to leave here (I think) before the 15 or 20 of December, in which case, should he not have found a suitable manager, It might then be difficult to do so, in as much as those following that business, may have made their engagements for the year. If he approves of it, I will write to Hill Carter, & ask him to recommend some suitable person & get his <u>present</u> opinion (his <u>former</u> one I know) of Mr. Frank Nelson, the rate of wages &c & any thing else he may have to suggest. Please let me know his views on the matter when you next write.

I am glad to hear of the well doing of those dear children. Nobody can know how I want to see them. Tell Wiggy I will give her that little baby, but she must not take all the clothes off of it as she does off of her Julia. I am sure Mother you will be pleased with the proficiency of that Rooney. He is a smart fellow but does not confine his search after knowledge to <u>books</u>. He puts in requisition all objects that come within his reach & finds much to improve him in the savoury compositions of cakes, pies & such things, as well as in the productions of nature such as apples & peaches. He is charmed with the study of natural history, particularly with that of the horse & all belonging to him, & will spend days in riding & driving that noble animal, without giving the least signs of weariness. I am sure he will profit by your instructions Mother, but pray don't let him infect you with his <u>zeal</u> & lay yourself up. Tell those little daughters to get their sweet mouths ready for I shall kiss them off when I get there. I brought Smith down with me Saturday ev^g & he spent Sunday with me. He is very well & hearty & sighing after Nannie & his boys, to whom he hopes to be able to pay a visit as soon as he can learn what are to be his future movements. I went up yesterday to Govrs Is^d to witness the reception of Genl Bertrand & to gratify my desire to see him. He is a fine looking old man very plain & gentlemanly in his appearance, with a great deal of composure in his look & manner & is hale, hearty & active. He visited the Independence, North Carolina & the Navy Yard & was suitably recd at all. He was accompanied by the Govr of the State, Mayor, City Authorities , & a long cortege of militia officers in full feather. I am very sorry to hear of Mr. Marshall's ill health, & have been anxious about him for some time. He has a fancy to doctor himself & I think is too fond of calomel. Poor Uncle Wms how distressed he must be. How does he bear Charlottes death. It will make his own easier & I hope happier. To lose two such daughters as Bella & Charlotte I should think would destroy his happiness in this world. I have written you a hurried letter Mother. The night is the only time I can devote [to] it, & I was prevented from commencing till late by a visit from some of the young gentlemen of the Garrison. I will attend to your commission about the cambric. The Stantons & our neighbors are all well. I went up to inform the former of the good news & was invited up to se Mrs. S. & her scion. She looks very well & sent *her love to you all & her sympathies & congratulations to Mary. Her little boy was making so many faces that I could not see his right one. They had just weighed him & I think he weighed 5½ lbs! Misses M & S are still in the city. Do write soon Mother & tell me how Mary is & how she deports herself now that she is the Mother of <u>six</u> children. Best love to all. Very truly & aff^y your son RE Lee*[1]

. . .

Wm H Fitzhugh Lee
Cambridge Mass:

Ringgold Bks: Texas
1 Nov 1856

Your letter of the 22nd Sept my dear Son has just been handed to me by a courier from San Antonio. It was as unexpected as welcome, for I had not looked for so much pleasure until my return to San Antonio. I am very glad to find that you are again at your college, well & happy, & delighted to learn that you have determined to complete your course, & are earnestly, faithfully & regularly studying. I think if you will persevere you will not only find your studies easy & agreeable, but also that it is entirely within your power, to take a respectable if not a high standing in your class. You must not think me so unreasonable as to expect you "to be proficient in <u>every</u> branch of literature", but I do expect you in graduating to have, what you say you will have, "a good foundation for pursuing the studies of any profession", & of being also <u>above</u> "the general run of educated men" as regards scholarship, gentlemanly deportment & virtue. Is that asking too much? I cannot believe you <u>inferior</u>, & I am sure you do not wish to prove yourself so. You are right to defer making your final decision of a profession until you graduate, & I would not recommend you to do otherwise, for in the next two years, your tastes & feelings, may undergo a great change. My only object has been to bring the subject to your consideration, to let you feel its necessity & to prepare you for it, that you might shape your course & studies accordingly.

I regret as much as you can your disappointment in not getting to West Point. But it is solely because you wished it. I think you can be as useful, & consequently, as happy in other walks of life. You may have liked the life of a soldier, or as hundreds of others whom I know, had you been able to pursue it, become heartily tired of it. My experience has taught me to recommend no young man to enter the service. Those who prefer it, I am happy to see in it, but in the 5th Regt of Infr, now encamped near me, it is common even among the young officers who graduated under my superintendency, as well as among captains who were cadets with me to hear the wish constantly reiterated, that they could earn their bread in some other way. You see therefore all do not love *it who are in it, & it must be acknowledged: it is a hard & thankless life. But should the life be so agreeable to you, it may not be impossible for you still to enjoy it. There are every year a number of young men from civil life appointed in the Army. There have been several this past June, & must be so as long as the yearly numbers of resignations continue as great. I see no reason why you should not get one of these appointments, if you desire & deserve it. None could present a higher recommendation than a distinguished graduate of Harvard University, with a fair name, fair fame, health & strength. With the knowledge you may acquire there, & with the devotion which you say you feel to the Service & an earnest application to your duties, I will guarantee in a year or two, you will be as well qualified as the graduates of W.P. generally are. I think therefore you are wrong "to curse the day you went to college", & trust it is in words, thoughtless words, & not in reality, you do so. What could you have done more proper? Do not regret the past therefore, but look to the future. The coward looks back, the brave ahead.*

It is true as you say, that your sojourn at Cambridge has separated us "by distance", but I feel no separation on my part "in <u>heart</u>". If it has made you "cold & uncommunicative", it has but animated me with a more intense anxiety & yearning for your welfare & happiness. If by endeavoring to direct you to virtue & deter you from vice, to shew you the beauty of wisdom & the evil of folly; to inspire you with a love of the noble characteristics of man, & a detestation for the passions of a brute; is deserving of having my "opinions & love less valued["], then I am rightly served. If you could hear the beating of my heart for you, in the long wakeful hours of night; & feel the anxious throbbing of my brain for your future, during the busy hours of day, you would find little cause to say that you had lost a "devoted father", whatever truth there may be in your assertion, that I had lost "an affectionate son". An "undutiful" one I cannot say you have been; nor have I seen a lack of affection. I pray God I may never see it, never think it, never believe it. But that in his mercy, I may first be cold in my grave, & feel the green grass growing over my heart.

I too enjoy the retrospect of our former life. I still feel the glow of your infant cheek as I carried you in my arms. I yet feel your arms clasping my neck as I swam with you on my back & love to think of the many, many times I have hugged you to my heart. Those days as you say, have passed, but as happy ones may be before us. They may bring everything for our "approval" & produce nothing for our "disapproval". I trust they are not distant. I long for their arrival. I long to have you near me, with me, to see you, hold you, talk to you. But that cannot be now, for the duty of each keeps us apart. I cannot leave mine & you must perform yours. Let it then be done, so as to give us mutual pleasure. I can see no reason why your being at <u>college</u> should interrupt it. There can be

but one right & wrong, there as here. I think I know the first, however prone I
may be to follow the last. If you will pursue the first, you may feel as well as-
sured of my approbations there, as if with me here. I fear this is not the letter
you desired. But when I think of the momentous question before you, & that
your present as well as future weal, may depend upon its determination, I can-
not treat it as if writing to a boy of __nine__, but must speak as if dealing with a
man of __nineteen__. I can neither divest myself of my responsibility or exonerate
you of yours. But I am done. Very truly &c.
     RE Lee[2]

>─◄◆►─○─◄◆►─<

CHILDREN WERE THE OPERA in Robert E. Lee's life. It was through them that his spirits soared or plunged into deep notes of dejection. As one reads these letters, the intense emotion he felt for the seven "little Lees" is so clear and so touching that it is in a sense superfluous to try to embellish his words in any way. Every powerful chord is here: the precariousness of pregnancy and birth, and fear of a child's loss; the fatherly admonitions on education and courage; the strong affection and gentle whimsy. Humor and warmth are combined with anxiety and guilt, for Lee's army responsibilities created a serious conflict with his desire to be an effective parent. Because he cared so deeply for his offspring, and wanted so much for their future, his voice could also at times become shrill, striking a stern, inflexible tone that few other subjects would bring forth. Thrown into the role of absentee father, he found his ability to impart discipline, wisdom, or love was limited, and often linked to the uncertain arrival of the mailbag.

Lee's instinctive bond with children was clear to everyone who met him. Nieces and little cousins recalled how he would habitually swing them up from the ground to share a seat on his horse. In St. Louis he encountered a party of young girls in white frocks and pantalets and called it the "prettiest sight I have seen in the West, and perhaps in my life." During the Civil War a reporter remarked on the fact that a child "thrown among a knot of strangers would be inevitably drawn to General Lee first in the company, and would run to claim his protection." One story was told about a small girl who asked the great general for a lock of hair. "You shall have it," he replied, and he put his head in her lap while she clipped off a little piece above his neck.[3] Such ease was in sharp contrast to the more reticent impression that Lee gave to adults. He was naturally paternal, liked the role, and developed it throughout his life. A good part of his reputation for leadership would one day stem from adopting a fatherly style that gave his troops confidence and inspired them to uncommon gallantry.

Lee's attachment to children blossomed with the birth of his own sons and daughters. In the first fourteen years of their marriage Robert and Mary Lee produced seven children, four girls and three boys, and with each addition Pa'a, as they called him, would nearly shout with exaltation. "I have got me an heir to my Estates!" proclaimed the nearly penniless second lieutenant after the birth of his first son. "Aye a Boy! To cherish the memory of his *Father* & walk in the light of his renown!"[4] The arrival of girls elicited equal jubilation. "How is the little darling with the bright eyes?" he asked anxiously after his eldest daughter, and he pronounced Agnes, a later addition to the family, "the finest child that was ever seen."[5] All of the children were given affectionate nicknames. The impressive name of the eldest—George Washington Custis Lee—was shortened to "Boo" and later to "Custis"; little Mary Custis was "Daughter"; William Henry Fitzhugh won the name "Rooney" until his father thought it undignified and began calling him Fitzhugh. Anne Carter became "Annie" and her sister, Agnes, near in age, was the "Wiggy" who was promised a baby doll in the 1843 letter that opens this chapter. Robert E. Lee Jr. was called "Rob" and his younger sister Mildred became "Precious Life," which her papa thought particularly appropriate to her. In an era of high infant mortality, the Lees were able, with luck and care, to raise them all to adulthood. "We have a nice little panel of them now Mother," wrote Lee after the arrival of his fourth child. "God grant that they may all be preserved to us and grow to be our joy and comfort."[6]

Both Mary Lee and her husband were fond of small children and their correspondence resounds with the discovery of these newly minted people.[7] "Mr. Boo" was "as beautiful as love himself . . . ," Lee wrote with evident pleasure when the boy was nine months old. "He is dabbling in sounds, dipping in locomotion, has two teeth . . . & is biting very hard to get out their fellows."[8] From the start Lee was actively engaged with the children, and with the smaller ones he was quite physically affectionate. One of the most pleasing pictures left to us is a description of family life written by his youngest son. "The two younger children he petted a good deal," Rob reminisced, "and our greatest treat was to get into his bed in the morning and lie close to him, listening while he talked to us in his bright, entertaining way."[9] Lee also treasured these intimate moments, sometimes dreaming that his children were lying beside him when he was away at war, and yearning for the little ones with a direct physicality. "When I call to mind his sure soft person," he sighed when Rob was a baby, "I am almost crazy to press it."[10] With the young children he was a gentle guardian. "It was a raw cold evg," he wrote, creating yet another lovely image. "The stage was crammed with passengers. . . . I had Wiggy in my lap fast asleep whom I was sheltering from the cold wind with my cloak as well as I could. . . ."[11]

As the children grew older, Lee continued to be companionable. "He was always bright and gay with us little folk," Rob attested, and remembered being taught by him to ride, skate, and swim, and how his father built a high

Mildred Childe Lee, called "Precious Life"
by her father.
VIRGINIA HISTORICAL SOCIETY

jump in the back garden to try his skill against the bigger boys. The girls also learned to ride and skate, and he encouraged all of the children to spend as much time as possible getting exercise in the fresh air.[12] Lee loved to laugh and joke with them, calling Annie and Agnes "Dem Hussies" and mercilessly ribbing "Precious Life" about her pet chickens: "I see for them no prospect of peace but the frying pan," he teased.[13] He liked the children's company, and when the family was together he took the boys with him to see the engineering works he was overseeing or on trips into town to do his business.[14] Pa'a was also a great storyteller, and Rob evocatively described the evenings filled with his "bright talk, his stories, his maxims and teachings." Curiously, he liked to have the children tickle his hands and feet while he told his tales, stirring them up with his foot a little when they slacked, and declaring, "No tickling, no story!"—a habit he continued with Agnes until his death. He could recount Sir Walter Scott and had his own anecdotes of the Mexican War or the Indians and rattlesnakes he encountered in Texas.[15] One of Lee's favorite yarns was about a perilous voyage his brother Smith, a U.S. Navy officer, experienced in the Straits of Magellan. For three days, in blinding wind and rain, the ship had been guided by just one man, with a chart and a compass and a bell that faintly sounded instructions to those on deck. He used the thrilling uncertainty of rocks and waves to give his children a memorable notion of steadfastness and courage.[16]

At Arlington there was room enough in the wooded acreage for the children to build tree houses, tend their little gardens, and ride their ponies.[17] Even in this vast play yard, however, the troop of young ones—often augmented by their numberless cousins—made for a chaotic atmosphere. They disliked being in the house, the boys refused to wear their shoes, and the girls threw off their sunbonnets. Mary Lee called them "a most noisy set" and complained that all together they kept up "such a clamour that I can scarcely get a moment to think or read." Her husband suffered their boisterousness as well, once ending a letter with the words "I have been made a horse, dog, ladder, & target for cannon by the little Lees since I have been writing, so I wish you well over it."[18] He cautioned Mary not to be too quick to go visiting with such a mob, fearing the children's discipline had been so lax they would be an imposition. The family does seem to have been something of a road show when they went traveling. Even devoted cousin Edward Turner at Kinloch could not refrain from noting the scene in his otherwise weather-and-crop-filled farm book: "At night Mrs. Custis and Mrs. Lee (her daughter) with a squad of children, negroes, horses, and dogs arrived."[19]

Despite the cacophony, it is clear that the Lees greatly enjoyed the antics of their offspring and that the children were the center of the family. In this they were reflecting a trend in American culture that had been growing since the mid-eighteenth century. In earlier times children had been seen as miniature adults, who arrived on earth with their traits fully formed and their peccadilloes predetermined. Many were considered mere extensions of mature family members, or a prospective workforce for farm or shop. The reasons are not fully clear, but prior to the American Revolution attitudes about children began to change. Perhaps it was the new emphasis on individualism, which encouraged the potential in every person, or transformations in religion and education that saw the formation of character—rather than the repression of sin—as the chief goal of child-rearing. Family affection and family bonds came to be prized as an antidote to a tumultuous world, and the creation of a large and loving clan was portrayed as the ultimate objective of the companionable marriage. Whatever the cause, families began to value the uniqueness of each girl or boy and to enjoy, rather than suppress, their childishness. Playful activities were now seen as a natural part of the growing process. When Rooney ran around the house with his hoop and stick, or "the Hussies" threw their "paper babies" all over the parlor, the Lees' response was to indulge them.[20]

Just as attitudes about childish fun were altering, so were parental roles changing. In the days when both parents were employed close to home, the expectation had been that mother and father would exert equal influence on their offspring, though the father retained the titular position of family head. As industrial and professional careers beckoned in the early 1800s, long-standing patterns of home and work were interrupted, with a greater separation between fathers, who pursued business on the outside, and the women and children who remained at home. Manliness came to be defined less by patriarchal authority than by ambition and achievement. Parenthood from a distance, or on a part-time basis, became the norm, and men's aspirations for their profession and for their offspring were frequently in competition.

Lee was one who tried to fight the trend toward paternal disengagement. He wanted badly to guide his children, and during his absences he read the popular advice books of the day, frustrated at the difficulty of applying their suggestions "to the thousand variations of temper, situation, occasion and opportunity."[21] He tried to remain engaged through not-always-welcome advice to his wife and a constant stream of hortatory epistles to the children.[22] A number of the books he read, including some by authors who were visitors to Arlington, extolled the virtues of increased female interaction with small children. Whether as a result of counsel, conviction, or circumstance, the Lees' child-rearing came to follow a pattern that left the main burdens to Mary Lee and her mother.[23] Lee wanted to be a strong parental presence, but the fact of the matter was that he was absent much of the time. Later generations believed that it was Mary, not Robert, who was the nucleus of the family. "I couldn't tell you his exact words," said one of Rob's daughters, "but Father gave the impression that she was the one who kept the family together. He was doing other things."[24]

So it was to Mary Lee that the day-to-day child-rearing chiefly fell. She suckled them and clothed them, and personally taught them all to read and write. On one day in 1839, when she as yet had only four children, she speaks of nursing little Annie, teaching Boo and Daughter to read two different lessons, caring for her sick mother, and doing all the housework.[25] She was less patient than her husband with the noise and confusion of such a household, often irritated at her inability to pursue the intellectual and artistic pastimes that gave her pleasure. "You know what a monotonous life I lead," she confided to a friend, "and how very stupid the fitting up of 7 children with winter clothes must make one."[26] Once in her frustration she cut off all of Daughter's hair because it would not curl to her satisfaction, then sat down to vent her aggravation at Rooney in a letter that began, "Mr. Rooney is growing up very tall & very bad & his feet grow so fast. . . ."[27] Her chief concern was the state of the children's souls, and her best efforts went to instilling habits of prayer and trust that provided an unshakable base for their own spiritual development. For evangelicals like Mary Custis Lee the goal was to impart the fear of God and a consciousness of right and wrong. Soon after the birth of her eldest child, she wrote in her diary: "O Lord bestow on me a double portion of thy grace that I may train up this young spirit to glory & immortality. . . . This is all I desire for myself & all with whom I have concern."[28] In this she seems to have had some success. Rob recalled how she taught him to study and revere the Bible, precepts that proved a comforting guide in the uncertainties he came to face. One of the most joyous letters Mary Lee ever penned was written the day Annie and Agnes announced their desire to surrender their wills to God. Glowing with enthusiasm, she told her absent husband: "This is a compensation for all of my pains. I must not now complain of anything but pray more earnestly that the rest of my children may be brought easily into the fold of God."[29]

At the age of thirty-eight, Mary Custis Lee ceased bearing children. We do not know exactly why or how this happened, but there is some evidence that it was a conscious decision. The Virginia gentry were becoming aware of the advantages of family limitation by the 1830s. A major treatise on birth control was published the same year the Lees were married, which stressed economic considerations, the health of the mother, the value of each individual child, and the virtues of a manageable family size. Statistics from the time show a sharp drop in marital fertility rates in Virginia for women who had reached age thirty-five, which suggests that they tried to stop producing children when they had delivered what they considered a respectable number.[30] After the birth of Mildred, Lee had written a rather gloating letter to his mother-in-law, in which he attempted to blame the continuous childbearing on Mary's desire to rival fertile King Priam, who had twenty-odd children: "I do hope . . . that Mama will be satisfied for from present appearances she will stop at nothing less."[31] The assertion hardly rings true, for in antebellum southern society it was rarely the wife who desired a large family.[32] Mary, who dreaded pregnancy and suffered greatly during most of the births, must have been alarmed when she looked around at her fecund relatives: a grandmother who bore twenty children: a mother-in-law who was one of twenty-three brothers and sisters; Cousin Mary Carter, who had seventeen confinements during twenty-six long years of childbearing; her cousin Rosalie Calvert, the mother of nine children in twelve years, whose family finally insisted that for the sake of her health she do something to limit her pregnancies.[33] Nonjudgmental Anna Maria Fitzhugh was one of several who had begun to worry about Mary. "She has so many children poor thing that she scarcely knows what to do with them or herself."[34] It is doubtful that she would have resisted any plan to curtail the family's growth, and even Lee, upon hearing of her final difficult labor, acquiesced to the need "that some limit be found which shall in no event be exceeded."[35]

Knowledge of women's fertility cycles was imperfect, and artificial means of contraception were just in their formative stages, but the Lees would have had several options available to them. They unintentionally employed one—later marriage—which helped to delay reproduction. By waiting until she was nearly twenty-four to wed, Mary had eight more years of respite from childbearing than did her mother, who had married at the age of sixteen. It seems clear that she also utilized breast-feeding, which was understood to hinder conception and which could be controlled by the woman. Infant Lees arrived regularly each twenty-one to twenty-four months, with a bit longer interval between the oldest and youngest two. The pattern indicates that they were nursed for a year to eighteen months, when the Lees again quickly conceived another child.[36] The most common and reliable method of birth control was abstinence, but though marriage manuals proclaimed the virtues of self-control, this was very hard for loving couples to accept. Part of the intimacy of the close, compatible marriages then being extolled was the joy of expressing sexuality. Far from being prudishly denied, this was well understood in the early nineteenth century.[37] In addition, the evidence indicates that in Virginia few men were willing to forgo sexual pleasure to spare their wives. Their attitude toward pregnancy reflected pride in the prospect of a child, not fear about the process. In his younger days, at least, Robert Lee seems to have fallen into this category. In 1836, after the birth of little Mary, he wrote that his wife was suffering from a "brain fever" that left her "much shattered," full of anxiety and depression, and that he feared for her recovery. A fortnight later the Lees conceived their third child.[38]

Separation was the surest way of avoiding pregnancy. It was probably

Lee's two-year absence during the Mexican War that most effectively controlled family growth until Mary was closer to menopause.

It must have been a welcome change, for it was clear that the birthing process was not becoming easier for Mary Lee. She seems to have had a natural and trouble-free first confinement. As Robert described it, their son arrived without warning, and Mary was nearly pain-free for much of the birth.[39] The following six were difficult, however, and in at least one case she was in real danger. The perils of childbirth were not a myth in her world. Women endured not only terrible pain but aftereffects, such as infections and seizures, which were potentially fatal. They feared for the life of the child as well. Virginia statistics were among the worst in the nation: the 1850 census shows that mortality from childbirth was nearly double that of New England or most mid-Atlantic states.[40] There is plaintiveness in Mary's response to a friend who had just experienced a difficult delivery: "Poor thing, my 4 weeks confinement & helplessness tho' so far less than hers has made me *truly* sympathetic with her—"[41] To lessen the ordeal, she tried to be near her mother for the births, and the six younger children were born at Arlington, in a small room off the Lees' bedchamber. The Custises were also relieved that they could help her at these times. "I suppose Mary feels a *growing* necessity for being at home early," Molly Custis demurely wrote before Agnes was born, "and I am glad she takes the precaution to get here earlier than she at first did." We know that Mary Lee was attended by a doctor at one birth—this was an emergent trend in the 1830s and '40s—but like most women of her era, Mary was most comforted by the assistance of her mother and other women who may have been in the birthing chamber.[42] Lee was present for the arrival of his first child, but thereafter, whether from distaste, fears for Mary's safety, or distress at his own helplessness, he was pointedly absent, even when it would have been possible for him to accompany her, and even when Mary was clearly anxious for his support.[43]

Many illnesses resulted from multiple childbirths, the legacy of scars and tearing, or chronic fatigue. One suspects that the repeated mention of Mary's ill health in her young womanhood may be an unwitting reference to difficult pregnancies and slow recoveries.[44] She was sick for several months after the births of Mary, Annie, Rob, and Mildred, and finally Lee himself had to acknowledge "all she has gone through."[45] After Mary gave birth to Daughter in 1835, she was dangerously ill from a groin infection. After four months she was still unable to stand and feared she would not walk again. "I get very melancholy accounts of Robert's wife's health—indeed the last I received were very alarming, so much so that I dread the arrival of the next mail," Carter Lee nervously wrote to their brother Henry.[46] To her diary

Photograph of Mary Custis Lee with one of her children,
probably Rob, taken around 1845.
VIRGINIA HISTORICAL SOCIETY

Mary confided the full depth of her despair, writing of her "anguish" over
this "alarming visitation of Providence." She never completely regained her
strength after this time.[47]

The incident changed the Lees' marriage as well. Robert was off on a topographical expedition near the Great Lakes at the time, and when Mary
wrote to him in distress to come home, he replied with a high-handed letter
that advised her that he did not intend to come, that she should stop her

"aggravation" and that he "should rather require to be strengthened & encouraged to the *full* performance of what I am called on to execute, rather than excited to dereliction."[48] Mary said no more, and when her husband finally reappeared at Arlington several months later, he was stunned at her precarious condition. "I never saw a man so changed and saddened," was the impression he left on one cousin. "It has always been painful to me to think of him as he was then."[49] After this a truce seems to have grown up between the two. Mary never again complained to him of her health, though at times it was fully warranted, and Robert made a visible effort to understand her condition, and in time would become a tender nurse.

Although Robert Lee did fairly crow with masculine pride at the birth of each child, his approach to child-rearing was unlike the traditional patriarchal attitude sometimes associated with men of his class and region. Democratizing influences after the American Revolution had brought fathers closer to their youngsters, stressing companionship as well as obedience. At the same time relations between husband and wife were becoming more equal. Far from overemphasizing the male side of the house, for example, all of the Lees' children were evidently named by Mary, and the three eldest, plus "Eleanor" Agnes, were called after venerated members of her family.[50] When he was at home Lee shunned the remote and authoritarian role of paterfamilias and involved himself in a variety of mundane chores having to do with the children's well-being. In addition to sitting up with sick and injured tots, he was concerned about the state of the girls' teeth, the purchase of summer clothes, and the youngsters' eating habits.[51] Though he left the early teaching of the children to his wife, he cared deeply about their education and put quite a bit of effort into finding the best schools, teachers, and curriculum for the older boys and girls. Lee's interest in education again reflected the trends of his time, for parents of the antebellum period had begun to see their largest aspirations in terms of the success of their offspring.[52] Having no patrimony to "settle" on the children, Lee thought the most important legacy he could leave them was a foundation that would allow them to prosper from their own exertions. Lee had a broad vision of education, which embraced dancing and art alongside calculus, and he encouraged his daughters as well as his sons to challenge themselves. Annie and Agnes, for example, were sent in 1856 to an academy to study chemistry, rhetoric, political economy, botany, Latin, French, logic, and geometry.[53] As he tells Rooney in his letter of November 1, 1856, the ideal was not only to acquire a good foundation for pursing a profession, but to be "*above* the

general run of educated men as regards scholarship, gentlemanly deportment & virtues."[54] One of the reasons Lee remained in the army was to pay
for this private schooling, for which he felt particularly responsible.[55]

Lee's close involvement with his children is where we see his deep affection for them turned to action. He was often passive in other areas of his
life, refusing to take major decisions, resigning himself to a religion that required submission to the will of an outside entity, surrendering to the tide
of events rather than attempting to shape them. With his children he was
quite the opposite, constantly delineating specific goals and defining the
path to achievement. He wrote elaborate treatises about the necessity of instilling obedience and self-denial in the children, traits that he considered to
be the foundation of all happiness. For the parents he had even more stringent requirements. They must couple the "mildness and forbearance of the
mother with the sternness and perhaps unreasonableness of the Father" and
never indulge in displays of temper, angry looks, or hasty words. "Before he
can expect to govern a child, a parent must first learn to govern himself," Lee
wrote in an essay entitled "On Education."[56] These ideas were not original
to him: the obsession with industry and self-discipline, belief in steadfast
example, even his moralizing tales—all strongly reflected the wisdom of
the time. Indeed it was an old dilemma in American culture, this desire to
reach for a higher set of ideals while fostering ambition and still retaining a
soft spot for indulgence—and Lee's struggle with it was not always comfortable.[57] What strikes one about Lee's interest in the philosophy of child-
rearing is less the innovation of it than the fervor. He left no such treatises
on military strategy, engineering technique, or the management of men. His
anxiety for raising his children was arguably the central concern of much of
his life.

As a result, Lee's letters on the subject of children are among the most
complex documents we have, showing his gentle wit and painterly ability
with words, but also a side that could be uncomfortably strict and authoritarian. Rob remembered that even though he was "joyous and familiar" with
the children, "exact obedience to every mandate of my father was a part of
my life and being. . . ."[58] He badgered his eldest son nearly to distraction to
distinguish himself at West Point, stating, "You must be No. 1. It is a fine
number. Easily found & remembered. Simple & unique. Jump to it fellow."
He had a long list of prescriptions for the girls, which included being "*regular, orderly & energetic* in the performance of all their duties." He also
wanted them to learn to sing and refused to listen when they protested that
they had no talent. "I cannot admit their assertion that 'they can't,'" Lee
fairly bellows through the paper. "They *can* if they *try* & I say in addition

they *must.*"[59] As the children grew older and Lee grew a little more fanatical in his belief that duty was the cornerstone of character, the admonitions can seem very stern indeed. "The most important things for him to learn at [t]his period of life," he wrote of eleven-year-old Rob, "is obedience, regularity & precision in the discharge of his duties, the necessity of labour, & how to apply his faculties to the best advantage. . . . If he is *made* to know them now, *habit* will make them easy."[60] Lee appears rarely to have punished his children, using instead the specter of disappointing or embarrassing the parents as the worst consequence of misconduct. When eight-year-old Rooney cut off the tips of two fingers with a hay cutter after disobeying his parents, his father pulled out every shame-inducing phrase he could muster: "If children could know the misery, the devastating sorrow with which their acts sometimes overwhelm their parents they could not have the heart thus cruelly to afflict them. May you never know the misery I now suffer . . . !"[61] The girls got similar lessons in culpability. "I am told that you are growing very tall & I hope very straight," Lee wrote to Annie as he became superintendent of West Point in the 1850s. "I do not know what the Cadets will say if the Supt's children do not practice what he demands of them. . . ."[62] Despite the sometimes unforgiving words, in this, as in so many other ways, he was well within the standards of his time. Habits of industry and application were considered essential to the ultimate success and well-being of an individual, and if they could not be instilled by appealing to the child's logic, humiliation would do as a tool.[63] Fortunately, the Lee children had a host of jolly relatives who provided a bit more perspective on life. "That's right my boy work hard and be gay and brave and nothing can hurt you," Uncle William Marshall philosophized to teenage Rooney. "Work hard, don't eat too profusely of the Parisian luxuries . . . be careful to cultivate a power to sleep . . . and you will be a great and good man."[64]

Lee could not take it all so lightly. He was extremely susceptible to his progeny, sometimes maudlinly so, as he was the first to admit. "It is there I am most vulnerable, most sensitive," he told Molly Custis, claiming that God was punishing him through the worry he felt about the children's development.[65] And again to his mother-in-law: "My earnest prayer is that they may continue through life to grow in wisdom & goodness & my greatest wish is that I might be able by example & precept to aid them in that course. When however I look back to my own life I can find nothing to point to in way of the first. . . ."[66] We can only speculate about the cause of his obsession with the children's upbringing or his self-flagellation over parental inadequacy. He may have been expressing guilt about his inability to reconcile professional ambitions and his fatherly role, or perhaps his concern for the children's future simply reflected the love he felt. Some have postulated that this angst was caused by his own near-fatherless state, the lack of a strong paternal example to follow, or the suffering he had consciously or unconsciously undergone when Light-Horse Harry abandoned the family. But we actually do not know—Lee never made any direct references to it, and his strongly conflicted, philoprogenitive nature could also be explained by more positive family traditions or the era's powerful societal transitions.[67]

Perhaps it is true that Lee's apprehension stemmed from a dread of repeating his father's dismal performance: he once fiercely exclaimed that his children "shall not suffer if I have to sell the shirt from my back."[68] Yet in reading this and hundreds of other letters, what is striking is not so much a fear of failure as a tremendous desire to succeed. When Lee became overzealous, it seems more that he was frustrated in having to relinquish the day-to-day guidance he badly wanted to give, and deeply sad at the physical distance between him and his offspring. "Oh what pleasure I lose in being separated from them," he would cry. "Nothing can compensate me for that."[69] The letters were a way to continue his emotional commitment to the little Lees. If at times they seem harsh, the earnest love behind them was never in question. And for all his lecturing, Lee sometimes deftly hit the right note. He is wonderfully wise in the 1856 letter to Rooney, adroitly navigating the shoals and eddies of a rebellious adolescent's emotions. A warning on the indulgence of vice was also endearingly expressed. "I was sorry to see, from your letter to your mother, that you smoke occasionally," he told Rooney. "It is dangerous to meddle with. You have in store so much better enjoyment for your mouth. Reserve it, Roon, for its legitimate pleasure." Or take the witty guidance he gave Precious Life about her spelling. "I notice that you spelt Saturday with two *ts* (Satturday)," he chided her. "One is considered enough in the Army, but perhaps the fashion is to have two."[70]

Some of Robert Lee's actions may seem off-putting in retrospect, but they do not appear to have alienated his children. When Agnes received a letter containing some little rebukes about the need to study, she recorded in her diary only that she had had "such a precious letter from Papa. It was full of strong affection." Annie also longed for her absent father, thought he gave them "such good advice," and admitted to him that she read his letters over and over, "& then could not resist the longing to talk with you even on poor paper."[71] Mildred recalled the dear, amusing notes he penned her when even a little child. "You must be a very great personage now," he playfully wrote from Texas. "Sixty pounds! Enormous. I wish I had you here in all your ponderosity."[72] For the rest of her life she cherished the sentimental man who wrote those words.[73] Lee's sons strove to emulate him well before the war, following him into military careers, despite his recommendation against it. This in itself is interesting, for it shows that the boys were confident enough to challenge their father on a subject about which he felt strongly—as was adventurous daughter Mary, who never did acquiesce to the stay-at-home life Lee would have preferred. The sometimes haranguing letters seem to have been tempered by vivid memories of swimming on their father's back and skating at his side, or of his charming, familiar banter.[74] Only Lee's eldest son appears to have been left with a flavor of dejection and unhappiness, once saying that he had "never had any fun" in his life. Numerous documents suggest that he suffered from depression from the time he was a small boy, however, and it is hard to know what was due to parental treatment and what to temperament.[75]

Much has been made of the fact that none of Lee's daughters ever married. Though he freely admitted how much he needed their presence and that it would "require a *tussle*" to get them away from him, personality and circumstance seem to be as responsible for their maidenhood as any overbearing actions of their papa.[76] Similarly, those who feel that Lee may have overshadowed his offspring neglect to acknowledge the way the Civil War eclipsed everything, far more than could any one person. The Lee children— ages fifteen to twenty-eight at the outbreak of war—were just on the threshold of realizing their identities and launching their dreams. The war came to define them rather than allowing them to find themselves—but that would likely have been the case even without the major part their father played in the conflict.

"What a name and inheritance he has left his children," Mary Lee would write of her husband.[77] She was referring, of course, to his military reputation and the near adulation with which he was held in the postwar South, not to a financial future or aristocratic legacy. Lee himself envisioned a different parental epitaph. Wrestling with the correct course to take, in one of his many agonized letters, he gives the reason for his relentless, emphatic, affectionate guidance. "If they can carry in their memories our unceasing love & anxious efforts for their welfare & happiness," he explained to his wife, "it may, when no other monitor is near, point them in the course they ought to pursue."[78]

Chapter Seven

Pioneers

St. Louis 27th June 1838

Will you tell me my dear Jack, where the "Cherokee Agency near Calhoun Tenn." is? Is it in these United States, or to what country does it belong? Are all avenues of information closed, shut up and cut off; and is there no method of learning what is doing in the world? I tremble my friend least you have been smuggled off the continent, buried alive, and your days lost to you, yea and your nights too. Why you do not know that I am a sojourner in the "Western Metropolis"! Well! the whereabouts of the <u>great</u> can be but little noted in the "Agency", and a man can be better reconciled not to be famous. It is as true Jack as that I am living, that I am <u>here</u>: And what is more my <u>dame</u> and the little Lees are with me. It is a rough country to bring them to I acknowledge, but they smooth it to me most marvelously. You will now know why your letters have been so long reaching me. The first, March 11th must have nearly died of fatigue; as that of May 18th was treading closely on its heels. This last reached me just as I was on the eve of setting off to the Rapids, about a fortnight since; and I sat down and penned a note instantu to the Genl. to know what was the State of the App^r for the imp^t of the Savannah river; the intention of the Dept in regard to it; the prospect of the work going on &c and whether they wanted a good man & true like yourself to take charge of the business. This of course was done in [an] <u>un</u>official way, and I know the Genl will give me all the information in his power, which when rec^d I shall lose no time in handing over to you. But it will take time, Mackay, it will take time.

Why do you allow the "Sovereigns" to bother you? Don't spare them a thought. Do you recollect the Don's injunctions to Sancho, after he had slid from his mule through fright, upon his being questioned as to the cause of certain odours that reached his Highness' nose? "Let it alone Sancho I tell you, the more that you stir it, the more it will stink." I believe though I can appreciate the feelings which have led you to think this seriously of the step you have in view. The manner in which the Army is considered and treated by the Country and those whose business it is to nourish and take care of it, is enough to disgust every one with the Service, and has the effect of driving every good soldier from it, and rendering those who remain, discontented, careless and negligent. The instance that you mention in your own person of the Authorities at W. listening to the miserable slanders of dirty tergivsators and then acting upon such filthy ex-parti evidence is an insult to the Army, and shews in what light its feelings are estimated—and its _rights_ sacrificed at the shrine of popularity. But I am getting angry Mackay and will stop, else I shall be no better than those who have excited my bile. If you could have converted the Mississippi into the Savannah and you had been willing to lend a hand in the manner you speak of, I think together we should have been able to put the rivers in such a state, that Boats would navigate of themselves, if they could only induce the Captain & Eng^r not to blow them up.

I found Bliss, you know _Horace_, in Baltimore this spring laying on his oars and looking out for Rail Roads; and proposed to him to come out with me and take charge of the immediate sup^r of the operations at the Rapids, whereupon he packed up his trunk and came. He is now there getting all things in readiness by the time the river falls. The object is to endeavor to get a channel through the Rapids for S[team] Boats during the stages of low water and will consist in blasting the rock under water and rem[oving] it from the channel. The Lower Rapids are 11 miles long and 250 miles above this. The upper are 14 miles Long and 150 above the Lower. Besides this they have set me to work to do something for this Harbor. There is a large _bar_ as they call it, or rather Island upwards of 200 acres in extent, covered with a growth of cotton wood, which has been growing from year to year, situated at the lower part of the city, and threatens to shut up their Harbor; and Cong. has made an app^r of 50,000 to remedy the evil, and which is about enough to commence it. One half is already spent in S. Boats, Store Boats, Pile drivers &c and we are now at work in building a pier to give direction to the current. I have been also directed to do something to the Missouri, but they have given as yet no money and of course nothing has been done. I wish _all_ were done and I was back again in Virginia. I volunteered my services last year to get rid of the office in W. and the Genl at last agreed to my going—I was cognizant of so much iniquity in more ways than one, that I feared for my morality, at no time _strong_, and had been trying for two years to quit—

I spent last winter in W[ashington] partly on duty and partly not. Had a pleasant time with my friends in Virginia, and am now here working for my country—I have got through with my paper and have hardly <u>commenced</u> talking to you—We really must have a meeting Mackay, for this letter business is all a <u>humbug.</u> Your acct of the Cherokees &c., was very interesting to me. I hope you will be able to arrange matters <u>peacebly</u>. I see the Sav[annah] Papers are throwing out some commendations upon Genl Scott so I suppose his course is satisfactory to them—The Rumours of the disturbances on the N. Frontier you get from the papers. The boys in Wash. hold out hopes of the passage of the Army Bill and think it will go—I hope so but am <u>dubious</u>—I was glad to hear of all in Broughton Street. I think of them every day. The increase of the <u>Gr^d children</u> is delightful but <u>who</u> is doing it Mackay—Mrs. L. joins me in much love to all of them. Your true friend RE Lee.[1]

›·◆›·•·◌·‹•·◆·‹

L IEUTENANT ROBERT E. LEE loved to banter with his West Point friend Jack Mackay, and the jocular tone of this message is so pleasing that it nearly overshadows some revealing remarks about the emerging U.S. Army. The scope of the army's work expanded in the Jacksonian period, yet mistrust of a strong professional military force also grew during these years. The army bill that Lee casually mentions at the end of his letter did go through, enlarging the army for the first time in two decades, but it was hotly debated and highly politicized. The increased bureaucratization and partisan infighting alienated the young soldier until, "fearing for his morality," as he lightheartedly told Mackay, he begged Charles Gratiot, the chief engineer, to let him escape Washington and aid in the improvement of western navigation systems.[2]

For all Lee's facetiousness, it was an important period of maturation for the army. Lee would also personally develop during this time, for he had been sent to the "great Western metropolis" to redirect the channel of the Mississippi River, one of the most demanding engineering projects of the day. Lee's struggle with the stubborn current offers a fascinating snapshot of him as a young scientist. Though later generations have seldom associated him with experimental ecological engineering, Lee was in the very vanguard of American attempts to redesign nature. Reverence for innovation and action, and the desire to exploit the continent's huge potential, was taking hold in the national psyche. Lee and his colleagues in the army may have dreamt of military pageantry and the valor of war, but they were destined to play an equally critical role on a different stage. With their technical education, their discipline and tenacity, the Corps of Engineers would become a driving force in the development of technology and the westward expansion of the nation.

Thirty-year-old Lieutenant Lee arrived in St. Louis at the worst time of year. It was late summer, oppressive with heat, mosquitoes, and the stench of garbage. Cholera and bilious fever were common, and shopkeepers shuttered their windows against choking clouds of dust. "It is *astonishingly* hot here," he told his wife, calculating that it was 97 degrees in the shade and that the powdery dirt was ankle deep in the streets.[3] By 1837 the invention of the steamboat had made the Mississippi River one of the most profitable transportation routes in the country, and St. Louis was a boomtown. The population had more than quadrupled in two decades, and included a colorful array of French trappers, Spanish treasure hunters, and German peasants. Indians also strolled through the streets, demonstrating their skill with the bow and arrow by shooting at the passing crowd. Lee was unimpressed, finding the city dirty, expensive, and chaotic, with inhabitants who were "powerful at a promise, but don't mention the fulfillment."[4] Depressed, he remarked that it was a good thing he had "seen several pretty girls," otherwise he would pronounce St. Louis's prospects "a *'bloody humbug.'*"[5]

Still, as he acknowledged, it was a self-imposed exile, for Lee had jumped at the opportunity to go west. In the chief engineer's office he had heard rumors that the prosperity of St. Louis was about to be undercut by the capriciousness of the river. The Mississippi's current made it a powerfully evolving force, which severed its own branches and carved new bends—in human, not geological, time. At St. Louis deposits had begun to collect as early as 1815, silting up the deep channel and creating obstacles that blocked the port. By the mid-1830s one sandbar, Duncan's Island, had grown into a 200-acre prominence covered with cottonwood trees; another, named Bloody Island, after the hotheads who rowed there to fight duels, had become a notable feature of local lore. The Illinois shore of the river was caving in, and the channel was widening and deepening on that side, raising the possibility of competition from new wharves. Well aware that the course of the river would dictate the course of investments and immigration, city leaders tried to stop the progress of the bars. They dropped tons of sand in wooden boxes at the head of Bloody Island to throw the current toward St. Louis, but the river smashed the boxes and the sand increased the bar. There were primitive attempts at dredging with ox teams, but more silt was deposited and more steamboats grounded. Then, in 1831, St. Louis was made a port of entry for the United States, and the federal government began to have a stake in the efforts. Chief Engineer Gratiot, who came from an old St. Louis family, went out to assess the situation and personally examined the various proposals to halt the damage. After a long lobbying effort by Missouri's powerful senator, Thomas Hart Benton, Congress made the first of several appropriations to redirect the river's current, improve navigation, and save the port.[6]

General Gratiot had a personal interest in rescuing St. Louis, but that was not the reason the army engineers were given the task. By the time Congress approved the Mississippi River project, the army had spent more than a decade working on the internal improvement of the nation. The Corps of Engineers had originally been established in 1802 to construct defensive fortifications. However, as the United States acquired territory, Secretary of War John C. Calhoun realized that the country could never hold the land unless it was surveyed and made accessible to settlement. Calhoun increasingly came to see military needs as indistinguishable from public works. In 1824 he pressured Congress to place the construction of canals and improvement of rivers and harbors under the direction of the army. During the next twenty years the Corps of Engineers became an irreplaceable source of expertise on the waterways, as it would be for exploration, management of territorial lands and native peoples, accurate mapping, and internal communications.[7]

At the time Robert Lee entered West Point, army engineers were charting the Great Lakes, surveying canal routes, and contributing innovative technical and managerial skills to the earliest American railways. Before 1830 the Corps of Engineers could take credit for fourteen roads totaling some 1,900 miles, including the National Road. In 1831 the War Department was given primary authority for topographical work. This came to include the establishment of boundaries and observation of weather conditions and natural resources, as well as recommendations for likely military sites. It was under this aegis that Lee was assigned for several months in 1835 to survey the frontier between Michigan and Ohio, an excursion he enjoyed. In 1838 a distinct Topographical Corps was created. Lee thought this branch of the service appealing and seems to have hoped that he, like his friends Jack Mackay and Joe Johnston, might be tapped for it. "Give me your hand My friend . . . ," Lee exclaimed to Mackay when he heard of his appointment, "you are in the Topogs, which perhaps offers the most pleasant duty of any corps in the Service. It will introduce you to the community at large, give you an opportunity of visiting all parts of the Country, enable you to practice what you have learned, stimulate your farther efforts in science &c. . . ."[8]

The military contribution to developing the vast, uncharted American territory was so extensive that warrior Zachary Taylor would drily note: "The ax, pick, saw and trowel, has become more the implement of the American soldier, than the cannon, musket or sword." At least one historian believes that the western expansion of the country would have been delayed by a decade without the work of the U.S. Army.[9]

Lee, Johnston, Mackay, and their fellow officers were uniquely fitted for this work. West Point was for many years the only academic institution in the United States that stressed mathematical and scientific training. Higher education in the early nineteenth century was still thought to be a process of memorizing classic literature, or studying ancient languages and history, with only the slightest nod to practical application. Harvard did not require students to have even a passing knowledge of arithmetic before 1802, and until 1835 West Point was the only school in America that offered a degree in engineering. West Point also pioneered the American teaching of such subjects as architecture, geology, astronomy, and mineralogy, and Thayer weighted examination points to favor the more exacting technical subjects. It was a measure of Robert Lee's ability that he was chosen in his second year at the academy to be an assistant professor of mathematics, for his fellow professors were in the forefront of the nation's nascent scientific endeavors. If important books were unavailable in English, West Point faculty translated them or wrote their own, and these works became the basis for the study of engineering in many other academic institutions. As colleges slowly adopted similar courses, they hired graduates of the military academy to teach and direct them. Both Harvard and Yale, for example, selected West Pointers to head their first schools of engineering, founded nearly four decades after the academy opened its doors.[10] When Robert E. Lee was commissioned in the Corps of Engineers in 1829, he was as prepared as anyone in the country to embrace the new field of "technology"—a word just introduced into the common vocabulary that same year.[11]

It was with this background that the young engineer began his struggle to constrain the Mississippi's currents. He had only a vague idea how to accomplish it. Navigational engineering was still at a tentative stage. All previous attempts to curb the river's natural inclinations had failed. Army engineers who had begun a similar venture to deepen channels in the Hudson River reported to Congress that the experiment "was a bold one and its success doubtful."[12] Lee learned some lessons from the Hudson project, however, including the need to construct barriers that could channel a current without creating such resistance that the dykes were eventually destroyed. He called on his former boss, Captain Andrew Talcott, who had worked on the Hudson River improvements, for advice, admitting that he was "in despair," he had "so many things to ask."[13] Ultimately, a combination of fragile precedent and trial and error would guide Lee's work.

As Lee told Mackay, he had, in fact, been handed several assignments at once. In addition to the crisis at St. Louis, commercial lobbyists were hoping to clear obstructions that were impeding navigation along the upper reaches of the river. The chief obstacle was a series of rapids 200 miles north of St. Louis, with a high velocity and hidden rock formations that made that section impassable in times of low water.[14] In August 1837 Lee set out to survey the area, map it, and write a preliminary report on both projects. He was accompanied by another army engineer, Montgomery Meigs, whose booming confidence led Lee to declare him "a host in himself."[15] Together they conducted operations from a dugout canoe, Meigs consulting the compass and level lines, making watercolor sketches of the topography, and producing the final maps. Lee recorded the depths and currents of the river and designed a comprehensive plan. Their base camps were "the worst kind of small log cabin," or a filthy room in St. Louis that caused Lee to break out a bottle of cologne and Meigs to declare: "The atmosphere is phaugh!" Together they caught yard-long catfish, hunted wild turkeys from horseback, and encountered a group of Indian chiefs "in full costume . . . with scarlet blankets & Buffalo robes and painted faces—not caricatures." Given the sorrowful part Meigs would play in Lee's later life, one reads of their exuberant adventures with some wistfulness.[16]

But that was a quarter century hence. In late 1837, the work season closed, Lee and Meigs drew their precise and beautiful maps, elaborated their plans, turned east, and made their case to a tightfisted Congress. To overcome the rapids, Lee advocated following the natural channel of the river and blasting out as much rock as necessary to allow steamboats to pass at low water. This was a deviation from earlier plans that had suggested skirting the rapids by building a parallel canal. To salvage the port of St. Louis, he recommended building dikes at either end of Bloody Island, which would prevent the river from cutting a larger channel on the Illinois side and force the water to flow along a prescribed path. Lee also suggested the construction of a wing dam, some 1,300 feet long, that would project diagonally toward the city, pushing away the accumulated sand from Duncan's Island and creating a deep new shipping lane. The dikes were to be built of pilings, surrounded by stones, and filled with brush that would allow for filtration to dissipate the river's force, but also catch its notorious silt and floating branches to stabilize the structures. There was little original in this proposal. The use of dikes, wing dams, and blasting were the standard processes for water management, and many of the techniques had been known in Europe since the eighteenth century. Lee's plan drew heavily on a French textbook on hydrodynamics that had been used at West Point for twenty years, and on recommendations made by Henry Shreve, a celebrated inventor and river man, who had earlier assessed the situation near St. Louis. Only the little inno-

vation of using brush to catch debris that would reinforce the dikes lent a ring of originality to the proposal. Still, it was persuasive enough that the Congress agreed (though ambivalently) to fund the endeavor for two years.[17]

Lee returned to St. Louis in the spring of 1838, having persuaded seasoned army engineer Horace Bliss—the "Bliss, you know *Horace*" of his letter to Mackay—to replace Meigs. He was also confident in the expertise of Henry Kayser, a surveyor born and trained in Germany, who had worked for him the previous year. He hired eighty men to labor on the river, engaged a steamboat, two skiffs, and some large transportation boats, acquired a machine to drive pilings, and found lodging and provisions for the workers. It was a

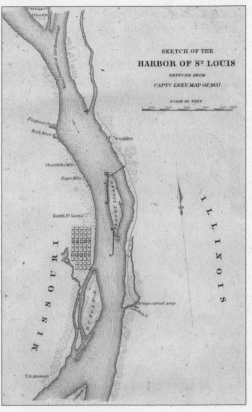

"Sketch of the Harbor of St. Louis," drawn by Lee in 1837.
NATIONAL ARCHIVES

frustrating project, plagued by blistering heat, balky mules, and equally balky workmen, and water levels that seemed always to be either too high or too low to allow any progress. The editors of the *Missouri Republican* cheered them on, noting that since "the commencement of the work it has been prosecuted with great activity, and with unexpected dispatch, when the character of the locality, the scarcity of laborers and other difficulties are considered."[18] Another champion of the endeavor, St. Louis mayor John Darby, recalled many years later how "indefatigably" Lee had toiled. "He went in person with the hands every morning about sunrise, and worked day by day in the hot, broiling sun . . . [and] with his assistant, Henry Kayser, Esq., worked at his drawing, plans and estimates every night till eleven o'clock."[19] The punishing work seemed initially to be paying off: by late 1838 the channel near the wharves had gained both depth and breadth, and Duncan's Island was moving downstream. At the Des Moines rapids Lee and his men had been able to blast and remove thousands of tons of stone, resulting in a passage as wide as eighty feet in some places. After three work seasons there was reason to be optimistic. But Lee was thwarted by the fickle Congress, which failed to appropriate sufficient funds after the panic of 1837, and the interference of irate citizens from Illinois, who had hopes of moving the lucrative channel to their shore. When cannons were fired deliberately at the crew, and an Illinois state court filed an injunction, the project was brought to a temporary halt. Frustrated, Lee told Mayor Darby of his "chagrin and mortification at being compelled to discontinue the work," but, under orders, he returned to Washington in January 1839. When he visited St. Louis again the next year, it was only to see about the dispersal of government property and to tie up some dangling bureaucratic threads. His plans, he confided to Mackay, were "for the present *dished*."[20]

Much of Lee's writing during this period consists of painstaking accounts of monies expended, the condition of equipment, the desire to hire "waders" who would be able to stand in the river all day, or the need for pressed spikes, tar, rice, and "manilla rope."[21] At first glance the letters seem to be little more than a tedious testament to Lee's orderly nature. However, taken as a whole—and there are scores of such records—they reveal a fascinating side of the Mississippi River assignment. This undertaking was the first venture for which Lee had primary responsibility. Far from being the detached, cerebral designer, he was forced to wear many practical hats. In addition to being the chief procurement officer, he was quartermaster ("I shall . . . procure some Keel Boats to quarter the men in &c, have them fitted up for the purpose and bring along such utensils and implements as may be required"); comptroller ("I did not make the alteration as the vouchers were all numbered &c, but we must . . . return the amount this qtr."); and technical expert ("The Pile Engine will have to be 30 to 35 ft. high, worked with a horse. Ram 1600 to 2000 lbs.")[22] For the audience in Washington he had also to act as lobbyist for the continuation of funding, reminding Congress and the War Department that the benefits of the river improvement "would more than authorize ten times the sum, and that the community at large will be repaid an hundred fold."[23] In short, he was the executive director of the project. As such, Lee typified one more contribution the army engineers made to civil society: the introduction of meticulous new methods of administration, groundbreaking for their day.

One of the many visionary reforms Calhoun brought to the army was the creation of an efficient management system that allowed the government to control the largest and most diverse set of enterprises of its day. The military's interests were vast in their scope and ambition, encompassing field armies, Indian agencies (such as the one at which Jack Mackay was serving), coastal fortifications, the development of new munitions, and the bureaucracy of men and matériel—all over a huge, wild, and unknown geographical area. Calhoun, who had witnessed the disastrous inefficiencies of the Corps of Engineers during the War of 1812, was determined to devise a progressive administrative system that would forgo the old "craft" ethos that had relied on instinct and experience rather than clearly defined methods. Calhoun was joined in his task by Sylvanus Thayer, who saw the administrative reforms as a natural outgrowth of the precision he taught at West Point. General Winfield Scott, who would become one of Lee's mentors, was another ally in the plan. In the early 1820s Scott had written the *General Regulations for the Army* (or "Institutes" as he preferred to call them), the first modern management manual published in the United States. It inaugurated a military culture that stressed responsibility, established a chain of command, and delineated a series of authorized procedures for reporting. Calhoun and Scott also devised standardized forms and regulations, so there was uniform accountability, whether at Washington headquarters or fighting the Seminole Indians in Florida. When a young officer such as Lee struggled at an outpost to complete forms in duplicate, to pay accounts to the half penny, or to maintain a daunting schedule of monthly, quarterly, and congressional reports, he was responding to structured management principles that would transform the way that business was conducted in America.[24]

Army modernization spilled over into civilian life through the engineers' participation in public projects. Corps members like Lee who were loaned to build canals, lighthouses, and railroads brought with them the methods being promoted in the military. Instead of relying on intuition or personal whim, army engineers calculated with an eye to efficiency and cost savings and used standardized measures and precise rules when planning their constructions. These concepts were not completely alien to American entrepreneurs, but virtually no business organization of the time could claim

such a detailed corporate structure. The influence was particularly pronounced on the railroads, where military engineers inserted their own hierarchical arrangement into the corporations and infused them with the army's
ethos, procedures, and even its forms. Just as they lent their mechanical expertise to large public projects, the engineers ushered in a new way of thinking about professionalism and the running of diversified corporations.[25]

While Lee was mastering these administrative procedures, he was also
experiencing the new challenge of supervising large groups of men. He was
still growing into his leadership. The workers were impressed, as was nearly
everyone, with his fine physical presence and courtly ways, but he remained
aloof, "never on any occasion becoming too familiar with the men."[26] Despite his own conscientiousness and attempts to compensate for the rough
conditions with double pay, he had trouble inspiring the workers and was
plagued with absenteeism.[27] Once in frustration Lee asked Talcott, who was
working on the lower river, to come and help him, plaintively asking him to
leave his work "at the mouth of the Miss—you had better take hold in the
middle."[28] He essentially deferred to the ideas of Shreve and Chief Engineer
Gratiot, rather than fighting for control of the operation.[29] The low-key style
of management he later used so effectively was also still under development.
Lee's instructions to Henry Kayser, a respected professional peer who handled his boss's personal finances in his absence, were often impatient, and
though never insulting, were far from motivating.[30] This was the harsh note
of inexperience. As he gained confidence and practice, Lee's approach to
command would grow gentler.

Robert E. Lee's immersion into practical science was encouraged by the professional relationships he enjoyed in St. Louis. During his first visit to the
city he met Dr. William Beaumont, a military surgeon who, as Lee wryly
noted, was "at the head of the Profession here so that he can administer food
and Physic in just proportions."[31] On his second sojourn in the city, when he
had brought along his wife and sons Custis and Rooney, they shared quarters with the doctor's family.[32] A fly on the wall of their large parlor would
have had a satisfying earful. In addition to Beaumont and his hospitable
wife Debbie, they were often joined by Ethan Allen Hitchcock, a brilliant
army officer who had taught Cadet Lee mathematics at West Point. Hitchcock was a fine conversationalist, famous for his disdain of "dullards,"
whom he drove away by reading aloud from Spinoza and classical literature.
Lee was also known as a good storyteller, and Dr. Beaumont, who was interested in Shakespeare and self-improvement as well as the makeup of gastric
juices, was not only clever but wickedly outspoken.[33] Hitchcock and Lee vied

in flirtation with Sarah "Tasy" Beaumont, the doctor's lovely and amusing sixteen-year-old daughter. The group spent merry evenings with Tasy at the piano and Hitchcock joining in on the flute, while Lee turned the pages of the music book. The little Lee boys roared around the room pretending to be riverboats, until their father feared they would "keep on so heavy a pressure of steam . . . that they will burst their boilers."[34]

There was serious talk, too, sometimes of army affairs, sometimes of religion or local issues. After a dinner with Senator Benton they compared shocked notes about the untamed Missouri political scene, but they were also well aware of the country's potential and quickly joined the excited speculation on real estate. Beaumont's home had been part of a museum housing the Indian and natural artifacts collected on the Lewis and Clark expedition, and this association heightened their inquisitiveness about the region.[35] It was an age in which scientific method revolved around observation, cataloging natural objects and meticulously recording facts. The exploration and description of North America was a landmark event in scientific circles, and Lee and his fellow officers were contributors to the westward advance of rigorous investigation. Though one Lee biographer has proclaimed him "an engineer, not a naturalist," in fact he was a keen observer, and painstakingly noted the features for which the prairies would become celebrated.[36] Not only did he provide some of the earliest accurate soundings of the Mississippi, he carefully examined nature in all its forms. To Jack Mackay he enthused over land teeming with game: "Why man, in a half an hour you can put up 200 prairie hens, and have a prairie 60 miles in extent to shoot them in. As to partridges you can hardly keep from stumbling over them, and hares and squirrels are out of number."[37] He dug three and a half feet into the soil, found it still rich and black—utterly unlike the familiar Virginia clay—and reported that it was so friable "you could cultivate it with your feet." He wondered at the size and beauty of the black walnut and sugar maple trees, and precisely noted their measurements. Lee was also curious about human life, and along with his catalog of the region's physical features, he remarked on the dangers of vigilante law and appreciated the qualities of the brave pioneer "wimming." "The people are rough, but they will polish," he remarked, and pronounced Missouri "a great country, which will one day be a grand one."[38]

Lee's appreciation for critical observation was reinforced by his relationship with William Beaumont, for the doctor had conducted landmark experiments in physiology that had given him an international reputation. In the early 1820s, while stationed on Mackinac Island, Beaumont treated a wounded French-Canadian fur trader named Alexis St. Martin, who had been shot in the upper abdomen. The damage was extensive, leaving a hole the size of a man's hand, and St. Martin had not been expected to live. Beaumont's skill saved him, but the doctor was not able to completely close the wound, and it healed with an opening between the surface of the body and the stomach. A few years later, Beaumont began to take advantage of the unusual "window" to do experiments on human digestion. He attached pieces of salt pork, stale bread, and cabbage to silk threads, then dangled them in and out of the hole, chronicling the rate of digestion, the temperature of the organ, and the effects of alcohol and exercise on the stomach's action. He established for the first time that the stomach worked alone to digest food; that it was an acidic chemical process; and that the contents of the stomach were digested together, rather than one item at a time. His observations that meat and starchy foods were more easily digested than vegetables, that digestion was aided by mild exercise, and that most people consumed far more than their bodies needed provided a basis for prudent dietary health that is still prevalent today.[39] Beaumont also extracted gastric juice to perform some early "test tube" experiments, and attempted to analyze its composition.[40] For nearly seven years he persuaded the reluctant St. Martin to continue the research. In 1833 Beaumont published a book entitled *Experiments and Observations on the Gastric Juice and the Physiology of Digestion*. The findings were immediately embraced by European and American scientists, with even the popular press acknowledging their value.[41]

Beaumont's revelations were extremely important at a time when virtually nothing was known about bodily processes or the causation of disease. Once more it had been the foresight of the military that had given a push to scientific advance. Notable here was Army Surgeon General Joseph Lowell, who had encouraged his doctors to conduct such experiments.[42] There were few things doctors of this day could be counted on to facilitate competently—they could give smallpox vaccinations, for example, and knew how to set bones, and they had drugs at their disposal that would alleviate pain or relieve constipation. But medical schools were few and driven by commercial interests, and no research hospitals existed at the time.[43] Dissension and competition among practitioners was high, and chicanery was common. Beaumont himself once characterized his contemporaries as buffoons, quacks, or eccentrics.[44] The prevailing remedies for everything that ailed a person—from cholera to arthritis—were those that provoked a visible reaction, positive or not. Hence the bloodletting that might temporarily induce an artificial calm or lower the body temperature; purgatives that showed the quick effect of vomiting or diarrhea; or the "blistering" that was thought to release noxious elements from a raised pustule. Many of these methods were dangerous or even lethal. All were ineffective, pointing up the helplessness of doctors in the face of infection and disease.[45] The Lee family suffered under this ignorance along with everyone else in their society. For years Robert Lee's wallet held a "Prescription for Yellow Fever" that proposed curing the mosquito-borne virus with a purgative to clear the bowels, water and vinegar-soaked cloths to the fevered brow, and, when all else failed, mustard plasters on the soles of the feet. His cousin Hill Carter had a similarly elaborate recipe for reversing the onset of a miscarriage: "copious" bleeding, a grain of opium, and the elevation of the patient's hips above her head. If things turned worse, she was to be "plugged up" and given a mixture of sugar and lead every two hours. Hill Carter's wife lost seven babes in her first dozen pregnancies.[46]

The result was a reliance on home nursing and a general disdain of doctors, which Robert Lee shared. "I have lost a good deal of confidence in Drs & medicine for any protracted sickness," he wrote when in his thirties; and later, when suffering from a bad case of the flu: "I am now under the operation of the mustard plasters & blisters. Tomorrow I am to have 20 leeches & the next day God knows what." Though he would affectionately remember Beaumont, "in his shirt sleeves, with a dose of rhubarb in one hand & a glass of toddy in the other," Lee remained a skeptic and generally advised suffering friends to avoid doctors and embrace exercise and a healthy diet.[47]

Lee enjoyed a promotion to captain while working in St. Louis, and honed skills that would be important for him in the future, notably the ability to cope with changing circumstances and disparate variables, and to synthesize them as he directed an ambitious project. Still, the uncertainty of funding and the endless delays frustrated him, and he grew weary of the project. In addition, despite his curiosity, at heart he was no frontiersman. On his first journey toward St. Louis he had already expressed a nostalgia for Virginia that never really left him.[48] He was alarmed when Indians stopped being picturesque and tried to snatch away two-year-old Rooney—he sent the children home with his wife a few months later.[49] Finally, in 1840, he savored the announcement of his "escape from the West." "I felt so elated when I again found myself within the confines of the Ancient Dominion," he told Cousin Hill Carter, "that I nodded to all the old trees as I passed, chatted with the drivers and stable boys, shook hands with the land lords, and in the fullness of my heart—don't tell Cousin Mary—wanted to kiss all the pretty girls I met."[50]

The river work was left unfinished. Lee recognized and lamented this, but the whims of the waterway, the inadequacy of congressional appropriations, and the experimental nature of the effort dictated that it would be so. Already in 1840 Lee acknowledged that he was "much concerned to find that the river was making an effort to resume its former channel & would probably succeed." The Mississippi had begun to tear breaches in the dikes and to fill up sections of the channel, and he suggested strengthening the pier in front of the town.[51] By 1844 the harbor was again seriously threatened, and the river had apparently worn another channel, again sending water to the Illinois side. Even though he had cleared an impressive pathway through the rapids north of the city, it was still far from navigable. Mark Twain, who knew the Mississippi River with a famous intimacy, could have predicted that Lee's improvements in St. Louis would be temporary. It was near to impossible, Twain averred, to "tame that lawless stream . . . curb it or confine it . . . the West Point Engineers have not their superiors anywhere . . . they conceive that they can fetter and handcuff that river and boss him . . . [they] might as well bully the comets in their courses and undertake to make them behave. . . ."[52] At a distance Lee could do little, and essentially retired from the project, leaving it to the city to find a way to stabilize the reinforcements.[53] Kayser and Mayor Darby devised temporary strategies to keep ahead of the river until 1853, when a new city engineer, Samuel R. Curtis, made essential modifications to Lee's plan and finally secured the port.[54]

Nonetheless, by drawing on previous advances on the Hudson River, refining the work of Henry Shreve, and building up a body of data, Robert Lee had contributed to the future of St. Louis. What he accomplished was to buy time and provide a foundation for those who would find the permanent solution—the time-honored cumulative approach for success in engineering.[55] For this he was remembered with respect, and after the Civil War with proud affection. In his memoirs Mayor Darby thought of Lee as he described the final stretch of a 1,200-mile Mississippi steamboat race that ended at St. Louis on July 4, 1870. Telegraph operators reported the thrilling progress of the great vessels as they roared up the river, faster than the speed of the railroad. The contest could not have taken place, Darby maintained, but for the deep water channeled by a sunburned army lieutenant, attempting to redirect nature against many odds. Newspapers depicted the climactic scene of the race so evocatively that it became firmly fixed in American consciousness and even in popular song. With an enthusiasm that challenged police control, more than a million people crowded onto the levee: all waiting for the boat that bore the young engineer's name—waiting for the boat that would smash every record to win the day—waiting for the *Robert E. Lee*.[56]

Chapter Eight

The Family Circle

From the diary of Martha Custis Williams, Arlington, February 27, 1854:

Uncle said "Well Markie, dear, have you been reading the Bible to poor old mammy?" No I said, not mammy because she was not well enough to come out in the rain, but to the other servants. "Do you know, he said in a half serious half playful manner, that it is my duty [to] confine you a month in jail, in accordance with the laws of the state?—but surely he continued, it can never be wrong to teach them that Holy Book. No Markie, I wont put you in jail I want you here with me too much."

From the diary of Martha Custis Williams, Arlington, March 28, 1859:

. . . I went to dear old Georgetown, to see poor Stasia, to whom I had long promised a visit. The getting to her abode was quite a pilgramage, but I was fully repaid by her hospitable greeting—over & over again, did she assure me, that she was "<u>so</u> glad to see me." How strong the tie that binds one to an old family servant—one who has known you from babyhood & witnessed for all the years of your life, the numerous vicicitudes of the family-circle. It seemed to me a sacred duty to go see Stasia and therefore I selected my birth-day for its fulfillment.[1]

. . .

Arlington, near Alex^a Va.
24 April 1858

Mr. A. E. L. Keese—
    There are two women belonging to the Estate of G. W. P. Custis, now in Washington, where they have been since 1 Jany last. One, black, about 35 years

old, named Caroline Bingham with a child about 6 mos: old, has been seen frequently in the centre market, going & returning by N. 7ᵗʰ st. The other, mulatto, about 23 years old, named Catharine Burke, with a nearly white child about 2½ years old, has also been seen in the centre market. Last Saturday evening she was seen in Mr. Bryans Grocers store near 7ᵗʰ St. with Austin Syphax, a freedman from this place. They report themselves at service with my consent—I have offered $10 for the apprehension of each of these women, upon their delivery in the Jail at Alexᵃ & the expenses of transporting them there.

A robbery of some articles of jewelry has recently been discovered in this house, in which it is believed that one or both of these women are concerned either as principals or accorsorys. You will find an account of it in the Baltimore Sun for the week ending this day—I have offered a reward of $50 for the recovery of the articles & apprehension of the thief.

A mulatto girl of about 14 years old, named Agnes Burke sister to the above Catharine Burke, who was hired in Janʸ last to Mr. I.W. Atkinson, Blksmith in Alexᵃ has recently left her place & is believed to be in Washington, where she has an Aunt Louisa Burke, & Cousin Hilliard Burke Carpenter in the 1ˢᵗ Ward, with other relatives. I will give $10.00 for her apprehension & delivery to Mr. Atkinson in Alexᵃ.

Austin Bingham, brother to the foregoing named Caroline Bingham, a black boy about 19 years old, hired to Mr. Edwᵃ B. Powell in Janʸ last, & who resides on Four Mile Run, just above the old Factory, between this Place & Alexᵃ—left his place yesterday. I will give $10.00 for his apprehension & delivery to Mr. Powell—

All these people are well known in Washington by any of the negroes residing there. I am told a Mrs Fleming Huckster in Centre Market, knows the two women first named & has seen them there. The people from this place, who frequent that market, meet them there.

> *Very respʸ*
> *RE Lee Exʳ of G.W. P.C.*²

>─┼─◄►─○─◄►┼─◄

T HE SOUTH CALLED IT the "peculiar institution." Abolitionists called it the "monster of darkness." Slavery was the consuming political question during Robert E. Lee's lifetime, the crucible over which the nation strained and finally divided. It is also one of the issues around which admirers and detractors have wanted to mold Lee, fitting him to their own predilections. These three documents offer remarkable insights into the reality of life in the black, white, and mulatto Arlington household, where Lee had his most immediate experience of slavery. At first reading the passages seem to be at odds with each other. Two are from a diary kept by Markie Williams during the time she cared for the aging George Washington Parke Custis and acted as mistress of Arlington. Her observations express the bonds of common experience and ties of place she shared with the servants, and a desire that some human warmth might mitigate the severity of the slave system. The exacting hand of the law, dictatorial even on reading the Bible, is expressed here as well—as is the family's willingness to circumvent it. That the relationships in the household were highly conflicted, however, is evident in the third manuscript, written when Robert Lee was executor of his father-in-law's estate. This is a business letter. The business was hunting and catching slaves who had tried to escape from his control.

The Custis family had one of the largest holdings of human property in Virginia. In a day when only 10 percent of slave owners possessed more than 20 slaves, G. W. P. Custis held 196 people in bondage.[3] Some sixty lived at Arlington; the rest populated his Romancoke and White House estates, or were hired out to other masters.[4] Most of the blacks had been inherited from his father or his grandmother, Martha Custis Washington. Those from the Washington household, such as Lawrence Parks and "Old Nurse," were notable personalities, much respected as living links to the first president. When "dear old Mammy" died in 1856, Agnes Lee recalled what "tales she could tell of 'those good old times' of Mrs. Washington's beauty & good management. How 'she was one of the out-door gals & would run to open the gate for the Gen.'" These personal associations contributed to the special prestige of the estate, and historians such as Jared Sparks, who visited Arlington to research Washington's life, sought out the servants and recorded their anecdotes.[5]

G. W. P. Custis's attitude toward his servants differed little from the common views of his contemporaries. He bemoaned the inefficiency of what he termed "the Vulture of Slavery" and in frustration blamed it for all of Virginia's economic ills, concluding that the "foot of the Proprietor is the best manure for the soil, so is the sweat of a *Freeman's* brow. . . ."[6] He was strongly against the slave trade and once offered his James River property as a refuge for some Africans who had been seized from an illegal slaving vessel.[7] He found slave auctions distasteful and refused to speculate in human beings, saying that though "Negro property is of great and increasing value . . . I have no desire to add one more."[8] Yet, like his famous step-grandfather, he liberated neither his slaves nor himself from the system during his lifetime.

It was his wife who finally persuaded him to leave a will ending nearly two centuries of slaveholding by the Custis family.[9]

In his treatment of blacks Custis followed the customs and prerogatives of others of his social class. In the 1820s he declared that he wanted his property "well fed, well clothed, treated fairly & kept in proper subjugation to those who are placed over them."[10] Unfortunately he disliked direct supervision of the workforces and left this to an uneven series of overseers, ignoring day-to-day operations even when it became clear that his estates were gaining a reputation for being out of control. One year the situation became so bad that the estate manager had to defend himself against charges that he starved the slaves, had whipped one to death and drowned others, and that his lax oversight had resulted in a slave stabbing one of the overseers.[11] Arlington's proprietor sold black people when he thought it necessary and gave away human beings as gifts.[12] As justice of the peace, Custis was well aware of the fine points of the slave codes, differentiating between gray areas where he could allow some leniency and situations where he must hew to the law. He might wink at educating the servants after it became unlawful in 1849, and permit a few freed slaves to live illegally under his protection, but in cases with larger social consequences he was firm. Markie Williams witnessed a wrenching scene at Arlington in 1853, when two free blacks, caught without their papers, were brought before Custis. The ultimate punishment for this offense was a return to slavery. Despite the presence of a shocked foreign woman, and the freedmen's plea that they could not understand the law because they were illiterate, they were consigned to jail, their fate to be determined by a white court.[13]

Custis could be generous to Arlington's black people, however, particularly on some large issues of identity and self-respect. Slaves at Arlington lived in family groups, with acknowledged lineages and recorded surnames, apparently of their own choosing. As Robert Lee's letter to A. E. L. Keese shows, whites at Arlington clearly saw the slaves as individuals and were well aware of their relationships and habits. This seemingly commonplace recognition of a family's name or kinship ties was not something that people in bondage could take for granted. Perceiving how names highlighted the distinction between the ruling caste and those it subjugated, many owners called their slaves only by first names, or imposed identities on them, rather than accept those preferred by the servants. Masters frequently took a casual attitude toward familial relations, guarding the flexibility to relocate or dispose of slaves at will. Marriage between slaves had no legal basis in any southern state, and family unity generally lost out to economic considerations, even when a master was placed under intense emotional pressure. Simply put, if one did not recognize the legitimacy of a family, one need feel no remorse at breaking it apart.[14]

At Arlington the situation was better than the norm. Slaves were sold to pay for the construction of the mansion, and into the 1850s Mary Custis Lee saw the auction block as a way to rid the family of recalcitrant blacks. "I wish indeed I could find a purchaser for her for I think she would be much better with an owner who could keep her in order & she deserves no favors," she wrote of one erring servant.[15] On the whole, however, slave sales were a rare occurrence, and there is evidence that the Custises took some pains to hold families together and even to foster "marriage" among their slaves. In the 1840s Mary Custis and her daughter went to elaborate lengths to arrange the wedding of their servant Rose, buying her a bonnet and dress and making it an occasion for the entire estate. They also allowed those "married" outside the property to visit regularly with their partners.[16] The exception to this generally sympathetic approach came during the hiring process, when slave families were often broken up for years at a time. The Custises and Lees, as well as their overseers, appear to have been oblivious of the trauma this caused. Toward the end of the antebellum period, such insensitivity would have dramatic consequences.[17]

Slavery was at heart a system of coerced labor, and it was for this that the black people had been brought to Arlington. Work defined much of the slave's life, yet the slave had but small power to define his work. The blacks had little say in the amount or pace of their labor, or what form it took. Though sometimes performance was rewarded by a better situation, for the most part a slave's fate was determined less by his ability or inclination than by the master's whim. Some of the slaves at Arlington, such as gardener Ephraim Derricks or cook George Clark, were specialists, but most servants lived their lives in the drudgery of hand labor. At best they provided personal services for the family, at the pleasure of the master or mistress.[18]

The slaves carried out an impressive variety of tasks at Arlington. Custis had developed the estate as a gentleman's country retreat, and black people there were never engaged in the kind of single-crop gang labor that was found in the Tidewater tobacco country or the legendary cotton fields of the lower South. Instead they contributed to the mixed farming that reflected Custis's ideal of self-sufficiency, or aided in the development of the property. Mount Vernon servant George Clark worked with his master to build Arlington House, and slaves also erected stables, sheds, and their own dwellings.[19] Some performed a variety of farm chores, from milking cows and harvesting wheat to making cider, with work cycles dictated by the seasons.[20] Perry Parks lit candles, closed the house for the night, and announced every arrival, from casual visitors to the president of the United States.[21] Slaves also watched over the Lee children and nursed them at their breast in their infancy.[22] One servant accompanied hunting parties; another was sent out in front of the carriage on a dangerous icy morning to light the path and cut notches in the wheels should the road prove too slippery.[23] Once, while visiting cousins at Cedar Grove, Annie Lee was startled to find slaves acting as human vehicles. As their boat landed, the African-Americans waded into the river to carry the passengers to shore—including their host, a tall and stout man, who rode in "on the back of a rather small negro."[24] Nor were the slave children exempt from labor. Mrs. Lee admonished Annie to "keep the children at work"; a little black boy made shade for Markie by holding an umbrella over her head in the garden; others amused the Lee babies, gathered black walnuts, or brought dishes into the house.[25]

The servants at Arlington did not gain a reputation for carrying out these responsibilities with a will. Robert Lee was openly disdainful of the slaves' competence, and others affirmed his criticism. Annie Lee regaled a schoolmate with stories of the "laziness of Arlington," and Lee counseled his wife not to expect much of the servants, since it was "almost useless to attempt improvement, or to resist the current that has been so long setting against industry & advancement."[26] Even sympathetic Molly Custis remarked on the insubordination of the servants. When slave Perry Parks explained to her that he was beating a dog because it was necessary to make him mind, she drily supposed that "the absence of that salutary Discipline is what prevents *his* minding."[27] Whether the lax performance was due to incompetence or artfulness is an interesting question. It undoubtedly stemmed partially from the attitude of Custis, who was himself negligent of his duties as master, and came to require little from his servants. But the inefficiency also hints at passive resistance, one of the few ways that slaves could manage to control, however marginally, a system in which the power was so asymmetrical.

Slaves took pride in outwitting their masters, in developing elaborate ways of communicating, and in opposing any kind of work that would turn them into beasts of burden. Left without a say about how they lived and toiled, slaves fought the system as best they could. They delayed and dissembled, broke equipment, and embarrassed the master.[28] Arlington's records are filled with actions that fit this pattern. Once when the woods caught on fire, Perry Parks slowly entered the house, apparently unconcerned, to advise Mr. Custis of the crisis, then waited until his orders were repeated twice before rallying the servants to action.[29] Visitors found their rooms stifled with roaring fires in eighty-degree weather or missed their trains through the dawdling of the Negro driver.[30] One young woman who had been invited to tea had to wait until eight in the evening to be served. When Mary Lee, "fairly provoked," asked why the tea had been delayed, the servants' reply was that they needed milk to serve it properly and that "they *couldn't find anything to milk the cow in.*"[31] Items great and small had a habit of disappearing. Letters were lost en route to the post office, and Mrs. Lee cautioned her daughter to lock up the cellar in her absence "as the wine there is a tempting article."[32] In 1860 Robert Lee complained that after his clothes were packed by house servants Selina and Marcelina, a shaving brush and "my pants, my *new pants* I cannot account for." Finally, resigned to their loss, he sputtered: "They are only one more item to the number that have disappeared. Perhaps taken off by Spirits, I know not where."[33] More serious was a robbery of enough note to be mentioned in the *Baltimore Sun*, as Lee attests in his letter to Keese. Nor were the slaves averse to openly ridiculing their masters. A little black boy mocked one of Mr. Custis's monumental artistic efforts by putting a clownlike dollop of red paint on the nose of a dying warrior.[34] Agnes Lee recalled the disapproval of the slave children when she greedily took some peaches from an orchard, and Annie described the shocked expression of the servants as she tried to single-handedly manure her garden.[35] Ridicule, inefficiency, and irritation were the tools slaves used to prove that the system did not work and that there was a limit to their acceptance of it.

In return for raw labor, it was the master's legal responsibility to provide for the slaves' daily needs in at least a minimum fashion.[36] At Arlington this seems to have been adequate. The servants were decently clothed, their wardrobes augmented by occasional cast-offs from the white family.[37] A clue to the way the masters cut financial corners, while maintaining their benevolent self-image, is found in a letter directing that the Custis slaves should have "wooden soaled shoes. . . . They save two-thirds expense of soal leather, & are far better for the health of the Negroes." Nothing could have been farther from the truth, of course: wooden soles were rough on the feet and detrimental to foot, leg, and back.[38] Slave housing, largely in "mud-chinked, and mud-floored, mud-and-stick huts" near the river, was shabby and cramped, but probably typical of its time.[39] The health of the slaves commanded a good deal of concern. A doctor visited Arlington for slave ailments sixty-two times in the first seven months of 1807, and similarly high rates of medical attention are recorded in the following decades. When "Old Nurse" suffered a severe eye problem, the best surgeon in Baltimore was called in to perform the operation.[40] Even Robert Lee, who was generally unsympathetic to the slaves, often commiserated with them about their health. During his first army assignment he brought one of the old Stratford servants with him to Savannah in hopes of curing what appears to have been consumption. The experiment was doomed, but the story of Lee's considerate treatment of the old man has lived on to this day.[41] To be sure, compassion was coupled with pragmatism in all of this care. The nurturing of life was essential to protect a valuable labor force; in addition, disease could easily become uncontrollable in this small community. In 1836, for example, Lee became concerned when his little boy "Boo" spread the whooping cough to his other children, then to the houseguests, and finally to "all the little Ebony bipeds on the hill."[42] In the tangled web of denial about the humanity of the slaves, the communicability of disease was one human link the whites at Arlington could not afford to ignore.

The modest amount expended for the servants' food at Arlington stands in contrast to the sums spent for clothing and medical care.[43] Bacon and corn were bought to feed the slaves, and fish were salted for their use during the shad and herring runs in the Potomac.[44] Increasingly, however, the blacks fed themselves. G. W. P. Custis had never been a shrewd agriculturalist like his step-grandfather Washington, and over the years he became ever more wrapped up in his artistic and literary pursuits. This, coupled with a long period of agricultural depression in northern Virginia, diminished his ambitions for Arlington.[45] The estate's slaves were allowed to tend their own gardens, to keep chickens, even to sell produce in the markets at Washington and Alexandria.[46] They eagerly sought this privilege, since it generally meant provisions that were substantially better than the standard ration of a peck of corn and pound of fat bacon per week. Slaveholders also amplified their self-image in this way, masking the more brutal aspects of slavery through such seemingly generous policies. Nonetheless, like so many other aspects of slavery, the "privilege" carried a paradoxical twist. Slaves cultivated the coveted gardens on their own time, robbing them of leisure and adding to their labor. The only benefit they theoretically derived from slavery—the assurance of sustenance—was now casually removed from the master's responsibility and put into their own hands.

To further the irony, the favor seemed to make the slaves dissatisfied and demanding. Part of the reason blacks hoped to grow their own food was that it connected them to the product of their labor and increased their ability to maneuver in the world outside the estate. Far from inspiring gratitude, it served ultimately to whet the bondsmen's appetite for freedom and increase the self-sufficiency needed to obtain it. Jim Parks caught the incongruity of the Arlington slaves' quasi-freedom when he recalled: "We used to go to Washington 'cross de long bridge, or we'd dress up and row across. People ud look at us an' say: 'Who's dem fine folks?' Den some'd say: 'Dey's de free Custis niggers.' Dey had dey own horses an' cows, an' raised dey own stuff."[47] This kind of respect lifted the slaves' confidence, so much so that it sometimes caused public protests or encouraged the servants to run away.[48] As Lee's letter to Keese attests, the Custis slaves were granted a good deal of leeway in their movements, only to disappear in distressing numbers. A taste of liberty, a worldview that encompassed life outside the plantation, and an appreciation of what they could achieve on their own became powerful forces in shaping the slaves' aspirations.

The lenience at Arlington reflected the hope that the slaves could be trained into a kind of "gradual emancipation," one that would keep them temporarily in subservience but develop skills needed for eventual freedom. Mary Fitzhugh Custis, who was raised in a home that had great ambivalence toward slavery, was particularly wedded to this philosophy. Both she and her daughter relinquished their rights to slaves they were to inherit from the Fitzhugh estate, in exchange for a legal commitment that would release all of the black children from servitude.[49] For fifty years Molly Custis dedicated herself to the creation of a community at Arlington that would conform to the law but prepare the black people for an independent life. She began educational and religious programs, instructed the Lee children to treat the servants with consideration, and compassionately cared for the sick. Over time, practices such as selling slaves and harsh child labor were discontinued.[50] Her husband admitted that all this was "not according to my notions . . . I have my own notions on those subjects."[51] Indeed, one of the family servants remembered that Custis was "'clined to be rude to 'em in his

A watercolor sketch of a slave leaving for the market, by Mary Custis Lee.

COURTESY OF THE LEE FAMILY AND ARLINGTON
HOUSE, THE ROBERT E. LEE MEMORIAL,
NATIONAL PARK SERVICE

young days," but that under his wife's influence he mellowed.[52] The slave families were well aware of the way that "Mistress" tried to smooth their path. At her death slave William Burke remarked that "her kindness & Instruction to me is what I never can forget."[53] Crusty "Old Nurse," who prided herself on speaking just as she pleased, left this eulogy: "Now, when you consider all things up & down this side & tother, from the beginning to the endeing Mistress was the greatest Lady and the best in the whole land."[54] When Mary Fitzhugh Custis was laid to rest behind her cherished gardens, the pallbearers were family slaves.[55]

Three generations of Arlington women taught the slaves rudimentary reading and writing, laced with scriptural wisdom. Former slaves remembered gathering in a little back room to learn their ABCs, along with such childhood hymns as "Little Drops of Water."[56] Results seem to have been mixed. Robert Lee did not think black people were "as capable of acquiring knowledge as the white man is," but noted that some of the servants "learned to read and write very well." Some extant letters from former Arlington slaves bear out the latter assessment, showing a high degree of literacy.[57] Nonetheless, the teachers sometimes railed against the poor motivation or disappointing progress of their students. Annie Lee ruefully noted that her pupils did not "do us, their masters teachers I mean, much credit."[58] That little slip may have been one explanation for the uneven learning, since the presence of the master, even in the benevolent guise of teacher, could be intimidating. Then there was the fact that the "teachers" were untrained girls. Markie Williams's recollection of these days indicates that her own grasp of spelling and grammar was none too sure: "I went up stairs to hear the children their lessons. They said a spelling lesson, read a Chapter in the Bible & wrote a coppy on their slates." Another complicating factor was that one classroom contained pupils of all ages and abilities. "We have a considerable number of 'ebony mites' as Papa calls them & as no one knows as much as another it makes their instruction very tedious," grumbled Agnes.[59]

The slaves, moreover, may not have valued such book knowledge in the way that the Custis and Lee families did. Extensive networks of practical learning existed among African-American populations. Wisdom about job skills, recipes and remedies, religious and cultural heritage, and endurance under a cruel system were conscientiously passed along among generations. Asked how she knew her catechism so well, Mammy replied that she and others at Mount Vernon had learned from "two old black men, that used to know something and they used to teach the rest of us."[60] Lessons given by white owners were hardly an exercise in filling empty brains, for the slaves had a vast store of knowledge and a realistic understanding of what was relevant to their survival and what was not.[61] In addition, the school was held just once a week, on Sunday, interrupting the only day that the servants were allowed any leisure. As one of Arlington's elite house slaves told Markie, the classes were "just too much *trouble.*"[62]

The main objective of teaching the slaves was to give them religious instruction. Christian teaching was thought to elevate morale, improve the work ethic, and offer eternal salvation in return for obedience, patience, and fealty. As an evangelical Episcopalian, influenced by the religious revivals of the early national period, Mary Fitzhugh Custis was convinced that she was responsible not only for the slaves' physical health but their fitness for eternal life.[63] To promote the spiritual atmosphere at Arlington she included the servants in daily family prayers and had a small log schoolhouse outfitted to hold services every Sunday evening. Blacks and whites worshipped there together, sometimes walking through the woods, conversing pleasantly as they made their way to the church. Biblical texts were carefully chosen, inclining toward the optimistic, and avoiding such difficult passages as the Exodus or those extolling the brotherhood of man. One sermon preserved by Markie Williams stresses the notion of gratitude to the master and acceptance of one's lot in life.[64] Students from the nearby Episcopal Theological Seminary led the congregation, providing an outreach service and honing their preaching skills. The inexperience of the young theologians sometimes resulted in a certain hilarity. "When they get up to discourse, they make all sorts of rare gesticulations & say the most extraordinary things," Cousin Markie confided to her diary, "then partially discovering what they have said, they try to unsay & this always makes things worse. Then they look as if they should expire."[65]

G. W. P. Custis enjoyed these evenings, finding an inner peace that eluded him in formal churchgoing, and a tranquillity that sometimes set him to dozing. He once mentioned that he liked this humble manner of worship, and "that although he paid pew rent in the church at Alexandria, he should never go anywhere but here." Markie Williams agreed. She went to the "little tabernacle in the woods" every week during her residence at Arlington and wrote that "I felt my soul might be more benefited there, than in the gorgeous edifices of Paris." Robert Lee also occasionally attended the church, and was observed to be "singularly alert and reverent in his bearing."[66] The reaction of the servants was more nuanced. One Sunday evening Markie was surprised to hear from a black companion that, although they faithfully appeared at the Episcopal services, one and all considered themselves Baptists, and many of them were members of that church. Markie also learned that the slaves held their own religious services, "preaching and exhortation among themselves at home in the morning," and that many disliked the family's custom of hymn singing, and soberly refrained from the activity.[67] She had an even more intense cultural encounter with slave religion on a visit to Cedar Grove in 1855. Her cousin Ada convinced her to attend a charismatic worship service among the plantation slaves, at which she was pressed into reading and interpreting Scripture. The slaves sang "with the most unearthly voices," flashed whips, writhed, and moaned. As soon as Markie began to read from the Bible, she said, "they began to groan & repeat my words and assent to all I said with earnest gesticulations, in a manner I had never seen them act before. By god's grace, however, I was enabled to restore the solemnity of my feelings. . . ."[68] Doubtless some of the slaves appreciated those Sunday services in the chapel at Arlington. But the Baptist leanings and morning "exhortations" again pointed up the dual culture that existed on the estate: one to which the slaves outwardly conformed, another that expressed their true sentiments and life ways.[69]

Robert Lee and his in-laws were convinced that bondage was a way station for blacks on what they considered to be a necessary journey toward "civilization" and "salvation" and that as slaveholders they were fulfilling God's design. They took some risks in achieving this vision. Antebellum social custom did not approve of instilling notions that would set slaves above their station. Moreover, they were on shaky legal ground. Arlington was located in the District of Columbia until 1847, the year in which Virginia reclaimed its section of the federal city. The laws of Washington, D.C., did not preclude educating slaves or holding religious meetings, as long as they took place before ten o'clock at night.[70] Once the estate came under Virginia jurisdiction, however, the Custises were subject to a more rigid slave code. After Nat Turner's 1831 rebellion, which had been plotted in late-night "religious meetings," whites were highly suspicious of any black gathering or of skills that might allow slaves to forge passes or formulate subversive opinions. In response, the Virginia House of Delegates had passed legislation forbidding the hiring of teachers for black instruction and any nighttime African-American religious assemblages. Technically those at Arlington still could have remained within the law under these conditions, for their teachers and ministers were not paid, and the meetings took place in the daytime. But in 1849 Virginia closed the legal loopholes by making "every assemblage of Negroes for the purpose of instruction in *reading* or *writing* . . . an *unlawful assembly.*" Whites who taught either slaves or free blacks were to be confined to jail for up to six months. G. W. P. Custis, as justice of the peace, was only half joking when he told Markie that he should throw her in jail for teach-

ing the servants. After 1849 the little church in the woods may have remained just within the law, since the new code did not prohibit services led
by white preachers, as long as they were not paid. The slaves' own religious
celebrations, however, were clearly illegal, for the new code prohibited any
meeting at all that was led by a Negro.[71]

The Arlington philosophy, which embraced eventual emancipation but
shunned the notion of an interracial society based on equality, led its owners to participate actively in the American Colonization Society. The society
was founded in 1816 by prominent national leaders—including President
James Madison, John Marshall, Henry Clay, and Daniel Webster—who proposed settling freed slaves in Liberia, a West African state created especially
for this purpose. It was presented as an enlightened response to the potential dangers of a mass of uneducated and underemployed freed blacks, who
were seen as having no realistic chance of succeeding in America, and who
increasingly threatened the guardians of the stratified southern class system. In its early years the society enjoyed a reputation as a practical alternative to perpetual slavery, giving planters the possibility of emancipation
without any lingering responsibility, and offering blacks a kind of pioneer
experience in Africa, which was perceived to be their natural home. The
prestige of the charter members and their well-known religiosity initially
gave the society credibility. William Henry Fitzhugh, brother of Arlington's
mistress, and her cousin William Meade, were charter members of the organization. Meade's opinions illustrated the confusion and sometimes the
duality of purpose that lay behind the society. On the one hand he was candid about his aspirations for the program—the demise of a system he
thought was a burden for whites, and the attractive prospect of promoting
evangelical Christianity in Africa—but on the other he believed that the
slave system was truly wicked and needed to be purged. "We make the sins
of our Fathers our own . . . ," he wrote prophetically to Molly, stating that
slavery was "an evil which grows with our growth & strengthens with our
strength, and will soon outgrow us & beat us to the ground." He, like his
cousin at Arlington, found slavery incompatible with his personal religiosity and promoted colonization in an idealistic spirit.[72] Mrs. Custis also became convinced that Arlington's blacks would profit from emigration, both
materially and morally. "For years this has been the subject of her hopes &
prayers not only for their own benefit but that they . . . might aid in the
mighty work of carrying light & Christianity to the dark heathen countries,"
wrote her daughter.[73] Like her mother, Mary Custis Lee strongly encouraged
the movement, both spiritually and financially, and even the little Lee girls

collected flowers to sell for the cause.[74] George Washington Parke Custis was a more reluctant convert, though he was a member of the organization and spoke at its rallies. Robert Lee never officially joined the society, but he often acted as scribe for his mother-in-law or wife in their business with it.[75] The families' robust words seem to have been somewhat more decisive than their deeds, however. The Lees donated funds to the society well into the 1850s, but the evidence indicates that only a handful of slaves were actually sent to Liberia.[76]

Many who embraced the effort did so believing that it was, in Lee's words, a "noble & Christian enterprize."[77] Its reputation began to suffer, however, when it became clear that some of its followers actually hoped to reinforce the system of slavery by ridding the nation of "the great public evil" of blacks not under direct white control, and removing the disturbing influence of freedmen from the vicinity of their slaves. Abolitionists took issue with the theory that the deportation of freedmen would hasten the demise of slavery and pointed out that there was strong opposition to the idea from the slaves. Many black families had been in America for a century or more and no longer considered themselves Africans. They also heard with alarm the tales of real hardship that was endured by those settling in Liberia.[78] Both Mary Fitzhugh Custis and William Meade were frustrated by the lack of interest the slaves showed in the prospect of deportation. At the death of Mrs. Custis's brother, nearly 250 slaves had been freed with the intention of sending them to Liberia, but to their dismay the family found that "not a single one of them will go to Africa." Duped and swindled when they tried to hire out their labor, and disheartened by the intelligence that "amalgamation [was] out of the question" in the North, the newly liberated people determined not to work at all. "I think freedom is a curse to them in this country," Mary Lee wrote in despair.[79] Controversy about the intent and feasibility of the society's proposals, coupled with the failure of Congress to provide sufficient funding to sustain it, weakened the organization. At the same time those in favor of unambiguous emancipation were gaining vocal authority in the North. Mary Fitzhugh Custis lamented with uncharacteristic bitterness that "the whole New England states are arrayed against us," and her friend Ralph Gurley, head of the Colonization Society, looked with troubled presentment on the situation. "There is a deep, strong & increasing dissatisfaction with slavery, & with the South for doing nothing to ameliorate its condition & ultimately remove it," he wrote in 1842, while on a fund-raising tour of the northern states. "The mind of the North, & especially of the Christian community, is I aprehend becoming more & more alienated from the South."[80] As the abolitionists gained momentum, the

American Colonization Society withered and died. Its legacy was the provocation of an open debate about race relations in the United States and the emigration of some 19,000 blacks to Liberia.[81]

When Markie Williams wrote of the bonds within "the family-circle," she was probably referring to the communal household at Arlington, which formed a distinct economic and social unit. Among the tragedies of slavery, however, was the fact that many who lived in these close plantation environments were family in more than shared experience. Sexual relations between blacks and whites had begun as soon as the first slaves arrived in the New World. By the 1850s, the practice had, in the words of one historian, "reached a crescendo."[82] Virginia and the District of Columbia had tried to restrain such relations, sometimes from moral fastidiousness, more often because of the confusion it caused in the class structure. Despite these efforts, racial intermingling, usually by white males and female slaves, often under conditions of brutality, was a well-understood part of the system.[83] One Lee cousin deplored the fact that a "double standard of living in a spectacular chivalry walked hand in hand with intemperance and moral laxity, open and unabashed. . . . I venture to say that every family has its more or less open secrets . . . but because of the very prudery of the times, buried in the darkest closets of the memory."[84] A former Virginia slave gave horrifying reality to the coercion involved in most of these situations when he wrote: "Did de dirty suckers associate wid slave wimen? . . . Lord chile, dat wuz common. What we saw, couldn't do nothing 'bout it. My blood is bilin' now [at the] thoughts of dem times."[85] Some slave owners who fathered children by their slave women, such as Custis's cousin George Calvert, acknowledged their offspring and took pains to care for them. Others simply ignored what they did not want to acknowledge. A cousin of Molly Custis, reeling from the pain of living alongside a slave who had given birth to the daughter of one of her menfolk, admitted that "in similar cases among us, nothing is ever done, & this makes it difficult for me to act—"[86] Slave codes stipulated harsh sentences against miscegenation for whites as well as blacks, but they were rarely enforced.[87] Moreover, mulatto children inherited the status of the mother, and these children were then forced to live in bondage. Of slavery's many horrors, perhaps none is so shocking as the abuse of black women, and the chilling fact that as the mulatto population grew, increasingly the whites were enslaving themselves.[88]

It appears that Arlington did not escape this sad manifestation of human frailty and unequal power. The Custis family had a reputation for interracial dalliance, and many of the mulatto servants had clearly descended from il-

licit ties. John Custis IV, the great-great-grandfather of G. W. P. Custis, endowed his slave Jack with freedom and grants of land that would have made
him a substantial property holder. John Custis grew so fond of Jack that he
feared the boy's death and wrote, "I am sure I should soon follow him, it
would break my heart, and bring my grey hairs with sorrow to the grave my
lif[e] being wrapt up in his." Evidence points to the fact that Jack was his
son. Later Custis wrote a will that instructed his legitimate son Daniel, in
quite an insulting manner, to provide handsomely for Jack. G. W. P. Custis
told the story differently, concluding that Jack was but an amusement to his
ancestor and that the will had been written to taunt his white son. However,
the legal record shows a consistent pattern of concern that seems to override
assertions that Jack had merely "turned somersets" to secure the affection of
his master.[89] The Custis rumors continued in the next generation. Martha
Dandridge Custis Washington was said to have had a mulatto half sister,
Ann Dandridge, who was kept as a slave at Mount Vernon, and that this sister in turn produced a child by Martha's problematic son Jacky Custis. The
truth of these histories, preserved in family lore but rarely in official record,
is often difficult to verify. What is well established is that the son of Ann
Dandridge, named William Custis Costin, was freed, was well known to
G. W. P. Custis, and was sometimes financially supported by him. Costin became a respected figure in the free black community and a trusted employee
of the Bank of Washington.[90]

George Washington Parke Custis may also have fathered mulatto children. As a young man, both before and after his marriage, Custis began to
free a few of his female slaves and their mulatto offspring, in at least one
case bestowing land along with liberty, and causing even the *Congressional
Record* to note that he showed "something perhaps akin to a *paternal* instinct" in so doing. These were the only slaves he freed before his death. One
of the families, named Syphax, who allegedly stemmed from a relationship
between Custis and Mount Vernon slave Airrianna Carter, stayed on the Arlington property, despite a Virginia law requiring freedmen to move out of
the state. The family produced a number of distinguished civic leaders,
among them William Syphax, whose photographs show a marked resemblance to G. W. P. Custis.[91] Another slave, Lucy Harrison, and her mulatto
offspring were "sold" to distant relatives in Alexandria on the condition that
they be freed. The new owners believed that Lucy Harrison was the daughter of G. W. P. Custis and Mount Vernon servant Caroline Branham. "She
bore a very strong remembrance to his daughter Mary Custis . . . ," confided
one of the Custis cousins. "The children might easily have passed for
white . . . an uncle Uncle William Parke became a wealthy man in Washing-

ton, educated his daughters & sent them west & south where they married white men & occupied excellent positions."[92]

Demographics uphold the evidence of miscegenation at Arlington. It is thought that 9 to 11 percent of the South's population was mulatto between 1850 and 1860, and some scholars put the figure as low as 7.7 percent. The inventory taken at G. W. P. Custis's death, and the 1860 census for Arlington, show that more than 50 percent of the slaves, and all of the free people living on the property, were of mixed race.[93] Acquaintances spoke openly to G. W. P. Custis of "your yellow coloured Servants," using the nineteenth-century term *yellow* for mulatto. Even Cousin Markie remarked on the "little safron colored pupils" she taught.[94] Three of the seven runaways Robert Lee was trying to apprehend were described as mulatto, including a "nearly white" child. A picture of an Arlington slave and his grandson, taken before the war, shows a startling contrast in color.[95] There is no evidence that Lee himself indulged in sexual activity with the slaves, but certainly he was aware of it. "Everyone was so mixed, half-colored and half-white," concluded a daughter of Arlington slaves. "Those were terrible times. Nothing pleasant to think about."[96]

Arlington slave Charles Syphax with his grandchild.

ARLINGTON HOUSE, THE ROBERT E. LEE MEMORIAL, NATIONAL PARK SERVICE

This was the experience of human bondage that most immediately influenced Robert E. Lee. It was, as he would write, a system characterized by "a union of wealth, poverty, want elegance, sloveness."[97] Like all studies of slavery, it is painful to read, invoking private guilt and the anguish of a legacy that cannot be easily overcome. It is particularly distressing because its familiarity and its oppression existed simultaneously. It is clear that the Lee and Custis families genuinely cared for "their people." They took pains to treat them with courtesy, watched after their legal affairs, and enjoyed their company. Treats such as sledding and gifts of dolls or candy for the children coexisted with deprivation.[98] Harsh rebukes there were, but it is also difficult to doubt the genuine emotion in Agnes Lee's tearful farewell to the black people: "each servant, with the parting gift have been told good-by with the wish 'I hope I'll see you *next* summer, well & happy' how truly those words came from my heart. . . ."[99] Mrs. Lee's letters show as solicitous a concern for the servants as for her own relatives. Without question the white families flouted the law to give the slaves some education, and with it, a little chance to dream. When the Lees fled Arlington in 1861, it was to the black housekeeper that Mrs. Lee entrusted the keys, and this servant carried out the responsibility with loyalty and spirit, challenging Union generals to stop their troops from looting.[100]

In 1862 young Robert E. Lee Jr. described the family's still-unfreed slaves at the White House plantation, telling his sister that the "most delightful thing about the place is the set of negroes. They are the real old Virginny kind, as polite as possible devoted to their master & mistress, who are devoted to them & who do everything for them."[101] This was the pleasant, paternalistic world that slave owners liked to portray. The slaves also had their idealized tales of warm bonds and powerful connections. The Syphax family passed down a story that G. W. P. Custis's illegitimate daughter Maria Carter was "raised in the Custis Mansion and educated by the same Tuitor as her half sister Maryanna Custis."[102] Another slave family cherished the tradition that housekeeper Selina Gray had been married in the same room as Robert and Mary Lee, by the same Episcopal minister.[103] In all three of these accounts truth melds into the wistful desire to believe in a harmonious connection between master and slave. They point to the fond fantasy that this household, so interdependent economically, might constitute a true family circle, with shared traditions, genuine respect, and mutual support. The reality of course was far harsher, even at Arlington. That some of these ties existed is indisputable; that blood relations gave the experience a haunting intimacy is strongly implied. Yet the slaves were denied any ability to determine their simplest actions or to define their lives and the fate of their children. Slave women came in for special abuse, but the whipping post in the Arlington slave quarter was a silent testament to the ever-present threat of humiliation for all black people.[104] No matter how close the human bonds, they were always overshadowed by the specter of perpetual servitude and the rigidity of a stratified class system, as Robert Lee's chronic problem with runaways affirms. Ultimately, under the strains of that system the Arlington slaves would begin to openly rebel.[105]

Chapter Nine

Humanity and the Law

18 April 1841
Fort Hamilton

I returned here last night my dearest Mary & found your letter of the 14th written after you had rec^d mine. You will see by mine of yesterdays date that I have given my opinion upon the matter referred to. If the object is to raise the funds desired by Mrs Lewis, you had better make a <u>loan</u> to the Major. Your plan of the purchase I think will bring you nothing but trouble & vexation & it is very problematical whether the condition of Robert will not be injured rather than bettered. In judging of results you must endeavor to lay aside your feelings & prejudices & examine the question as thus esposed. In this matter is everything to be yielded to the servant & nothing allowed to the master? What will be the effect of the precedent upon the rest & the instruction of the example intended to be set as well as the comparisons likely to be made to the prejudice of your father & his authority. Others ought to be considered as well as Robert. If you determine to apply your money in this way I am ready to pay it. So consider well upon the matter & act for yourself.

I rec^d a letter from Hill saying that he had enclosed me a draft for $60 & directed his letter to Arlington. Has it arrived? If it has & is not payable to my <u>order</u> you can retain it for the present. But if it is made payable to my order you will have to send it on for my signature. Ask Smith if he has been able to cash the note I left with him.

As to matters here they are like what they are every where else. All situations have their advantages & disadvantages. Evy one says it is healthy & I should think it was. It is open to the sea, but is more retired, that is farther removed from it than I had supposed. I am told however that the sea breezes are very cool & refreshing. The scene is very animating & interesting. Vessels of all kinds are constantly passing & the view is extensive. The country in the neighborhood is fertile & well cultivated & there are quantities of handsome country seats in all directions. The Q^rs in the Forts are all casemates though & plenty of them. At Fort Lafayette you would be entirely surrounded by water & inconvenienced by few visitors. The Q^rs outside the Fort is an old building with a great many <u>cuddies</u> & small rooms, out of repair, & has not been inhabitable for some years. A nice Yankee wife would soon have it in fine order. I shall consider to whitewash & clean it up, but am afraid can do but little with it before your arrival, as <u>Boss Cropsy</u>, to whom I was shewing it, says all it wants is a woman [in] it. I have got myself a Bedstead, mattress &c a dozen chairs, Pitcher & Basin. You can get anything you desire in N. York but they shew you so many handsome things that it is dangerous to go in the stores. I take my meals in the family of a very good man Mr Church, who is Postmaster, Stage Agent, Coroner, Militia Col Skipper, Builder etc. and seems to embrace in his own person every office & agency—I receive poor encouragement about servants & every one seems to attend to their own matters. They seem to be surprised at my enquiry for <u>help</u> & have a <u>wife</u> too & seem to have some misgivings as to whether you possess all your faculties. You had better arrange all your matters & send off the boxes to ensure there being here when you arrive. The floors are so bad they will have to be covered. What shall it be with carpets or mats? I told you about the Boarding houses. I think they would be very disagreeable & then too we should lose the pleasure which would more than compensate for all the trouble of housekeeping, of having Mother & the Major with us.

I envy you your visits to Colross. I have seen no one here yet that I desire even to behold again. Tell Rose he is a happy fellow. I long very much to see the dear children, & <u>especially</u> Miss Agnes. I told you that she was the finest child that was ever seen but you would not believe me. Are you going to have her christened before you come on? I am very sorry to hear that Mother is so poorly. Tell her if she could only see the <u>lilacs</u> around our Qrs. I think it would revive her. Mr. Church says there are upwards of <u>1000</u> plants. Shall I send her any, for as soon as I get a little time I shall make a dash at them. A lookout has been kept all day for the British steamer but she has not made her appearance yet. The two Spanish frigates have been playing before us all day. They are fine looking vessels & work beautifully. I have been told that no pains or expense have been spared in their build & equipment. They have been built at N.Y. for the Spanish Govt. I rec^d a letter from Uncle Bernard saying he would sail for Europe tomorrow (the 20th). Also one from Capt. Talcott telling me that he had left Mrs T. in N.Y. until his return from Glastonbury which would be in a few days. I have been so much engaged that I have not been able to get up. I shall endeavor to go tomorrow. Remember me to every one very truly & Aff^y RE Lee[1]

THIRTY-FOUR-YEAR-OLD Robert E. Lee penned this message to his wife just after his arrival at a new assignment. He had gone to New York to oversee the construction of four forts that were to guard the harbor—nothing too exhilarating, but the best of the possibilities he had been offered. The letter helps us humanize a hero, setting him amid everyday scenes and everyday problems, worried about housing, anxious over New York store prices. Nonetheless, it would be just a quick glimpse into the domestic life of the 1840s, and of only passing interest, but for the opening paragraph. In this passage a family crisis is addressed, one that points to a central conundrum of slavery, and one on which Robert Lee and his Custis in-laws were at odds.

Mary Lee, wrestling as her mother did to find a way of inserting humanity into an unkind system, seems determined to change the situation of a slave named Robert. It appears this man was on a Lewis family estate, perhaps related to Aunt Nelly Custis Lewis. A plan was afoot to rescue him, either by purchasing and liberating him or bringing him to Arlington's more benign atmosphere. Robert Lee was skeptical about the idea. If the strategy was to help the Lewis family out of debt, he recommended floating them a loan. Any effort to buy the slave he thought ill-advised, however, since it interfered with the prerogatives of the owner. Mary's attitude was not only sympathetic to the slave's situation; it showed a willingness to believe that he had a right to be removed from his domineering master. Lee thought otherwise. He worried that it would set a bad precedent "for the rest" if this slave was treated leniently, undercutting the "instruction" the slave's punishment was supposed to impart. It was the master's privilege to manage his property and to exercise control over his labor force, and he was protected for the most part from questions about his judgment on these matters. This view was reflected in Lee's query—"is everything to be yielded to the servant and nothing to the master?" But it was Mary's money, after all, despite the nineteenth-century reality that if she determined to apply her funds in this way, he "was willing" to pay it. The point of Robert and Mary Lee's disagreement was not just whether to interfere in the unpleasantness of their friends' domestic disputes. It pointed to something more fundamental: a difference of philosophy between those who chose to define their relationship to slavery through the law, and those who hoped to shape it through human interaction.[2]

The opinion Robert Lee voiced from Fort Hamilton reflected views he held, not just in 1841, but throughout his life. Some historians have proposed that he was silent on the subject of slavery, at times boiling down his entire thinking to one long political paragraph he penned in 1856. Actually Lee's letters are peppered with comments about race, servitude, and abolition. Some make statements that by today's standards would be branded elitist, if not straightforwardly racist. Others discuss the day-to-day arrangements of slavery, which Lee never failed to find irritating. There are numerous letters that give clues to his moral and political thinking on the subject. Taken together, they provide abundant detail about Lee's thirty-five-year involvement with the peculiar institution.[3]

The tradition that Robert E. Lee was opposed to slavery has become part of the mythology that surrounds him. Words as strong as "condemnation" and "abhorrence" have crept into the idealistic literature concerning his views on slavery, and some apologists have him "rejoicing" at the thought of its abolition.[4] It is true that Lee seems to have detested the institution, but it was not the depravity of slavery that colored his disdain. There is no evidence that Lee went through the kind of intellectual questioning that permeates the writings of Jefferson, or the philosophical flip-flops that characterized his ancestor Richard Henry Lee's grandstanding on the issue. Nor did he attempt to elaborate a complex alternative morality within the justification of slavery, as did some of his fellow slave owners.[5]

In fact, Lee's political views on the subject are remarkably consistent. He thought slavery was an unfortunate historical legacy, an inherited problem for which he was not responsible, and one that could only be resolved over time and probably only by God. As for any injustice to the slaves, he defended a "Christian" logic of at least temporary black bondage. "The blacks are immeasurably better off here than in Africa, morally, socially & physically," Lee told his wife in the famous 1856 letter. "The painful discipline they are undergoing, is necessary for their instruction as a race, & I hope will prepare & lead them to better things. How long their subjugation may be necessary is known & ordered by a wise and Merciful Providence." He went so far as to believe that the slaves should be appreciative of the situation and showed displeasure at any sign of their "ingratitude." When his father-in-law decided to open the grounds of Arlington to picnic parties in 1839, Lee feared this would dangerously distract the workforce. Not only would it provide an opportunity for "gossip and idleness," it would prove a temptation for Custis's "own people . . . to appropriate the small powers of their labor to themselves. Nothing can add to their little consideration for himself, his kindness and indulgence." Lee might characterize slavery as "an evil in any country" and state that his feelings were "strongly enlisted" for the slaves, but he ultimately concluded that it was a "greater evil to the white than to the black race" and admitted that his own sympathies lay with the whites.[6]

Perhaps more telling than words were Lee's actions in support of slavery. He continued to participate in the system and distance himself from anti-slavery arguments up to and during the Civil War. Neither Nat Turner's rebellion in 1831 nor John Brown's raid at Harper's Ferry in 1859 impressed on him the desperation caused by the bondsmen's situation, though he was in the neighborhood when the first uprising occurred and played a principal role in the Harper's Ferry drama.[7] In 1856, and as late as July 1860, he expressed a willingness to buy slaves. Those blacks who were in his possession were frequently traded away for his own convenience, regardless of the destruction it caused to the bondsman's family. He ignores injustice to the slaves and defends the rights of the slaveholder in both his 1841 and 1856 letters to his wife, and he continued to uphold laws that constrained blacks well after the war. During the brief time that Lee had authority over the Arlington slaves, he proved to be an unsympathetic and demanding master. When disagreements over slavery brought about the dissolution of the Union and he was forced to take sides, he chose not just to withdraw from the U.S. Army and quietly retire, as did some of his fellow officers, but to lead an opposing army that without question intended to defend the right to hold human property. Even taking into account the notions of his time and place, it is exceedingly hard to square these actions with any rejection of the institution.[8]

Lee may have hated slavery, but it was not because of any ethical dilemma. What Lee disliked about slavery was its inefficiency, the messiness of its relationships, the responsibility it entailed, and the taint of it. He resented the fact that slavery had been visited on the South by unwise forefathers, whose decisions, born of expediency and greed, had saddled their progeny with an intractable problem. He did not like politics, and he hated the politicization of his familiar way of life. Lee's childhood exposure to some of the worst elements of the system, the domestic scene at Arlington, where slaves mingled freely in a tense extended family, his stressful responsibilities as a slave owner, and his difficulties as a master during two painful years in the late 1850s, caused him to see the whole system as personally distasteful and endlessly taxing. The experiences also hardened him into acceptance of slavery's worst realities, forming scales that never really fell from his eyes. If Lee believed slavery was an evil, he thought it was a necessary one. The best guardian against any excess of the system was the law. His upbringing, founded on the class and racial prejudices of the day, paralyzed any larger vision.

For contemporary readers, a particularly jarring note in Lee's writings on slavery is his belief that the institution was a greater evil for whites than for blacks. Today, the seeming insensitivity of this remark leaves one questioning Lee's moral perspective. But of course Lee was hardly an isolated purveyor of these views. Leonidas Polk, a fellow West Pointer who left the army to enter the ministry and later became a Confederate general, for example, would join Lee in this chorus. "Talk of slavery! Those madcaps at the North don't understand the thing at all," he exclaimed in 1856. "We hold negroes and they hold us! . . . They furnish the yoke and we the neck! My own is getting sore. . . ."[9] To contemporary ears, such statements smack not only of self-justification, but of a crude indifference to the realities of a brutal system. How could those who had the authority to eradicate the "evil" of the institution be the ones most burdened by it? How in a cruelly one-sided power structure could a man of integrity ask if everything was to "be yielded to the servant & nothing to the master?"

Exposed from an early age to the dilemma of slavery, Lee would have seen the situation differently. To him these statements expressed the irresolvable position of the "responsible" slave owner, who desired both to make a functional, profitable enterprise of plantation farming and to accept limitations that allowed him to live with his conscience. Slaves were difficult property to hold. They required continuous decisions that pitted efficiency against kindness and property rights against humanity. Faced with near bankruptcy, for example, liberty-espousing Thomas Jefferson sold his slaves, but only on his distant plantations so that he would not have to face the reality of what he had done. From childhood Robert Lee had been surrounded by the moral irrationality of such a society. Though his father had sometimes used his artful rhetoric to denounce slavery as an evil, he gained a reputation for cruelty as governor of Virginia when he chose to uphold a law that allowed a heavily pregnant slave woman to be hung for knocking down an overseer who was trying to brutally beat her. His brother Carter described Stratford as a paternalistic haven of solicitous masters and smiling servants, but by the time of Robert's boyhood, financial problems had led to complete chaos in the handling of the family's human chattel. Some slaves were summarily sold alongside land, horses, and furniture. Others were transferred to distant owners or seized for debts, and in one startling instance Henry Lee took an armed band into the house of a creditor and enticed his repossessed servants to escape. The fear and instability caused to black people by such procedures was a sorrowful part of the institution. At a very young age Robert Lee witnessed the confusion and pain it caused for both whites, whose assets and prestige were devastated, and blacks, who suffered personal humiliation, broken families, and the trauma of an uncertain future.[10] The discomfort of the Lee family's participation in the worst aspects of slavery must have been heightened by their move to Alexandria, the very center of the border state slave trade, where coffles of blacks were a daily sight, and some of the largest auction houses in the country were but a few blocks from the Lee residence. "Scarcely a week passes without some of these wretched creatures being driven through our streets . . . ," lamented the *Alexandria Gazette*. "The children and some of the women are generally crowded into a cart or wagon, while others follow on foot, frequently handcuffed and chained together."[11]

The reality was that those who were not scandalized by exposure to such sights became inured to them. George Mason, a liberal founder of the republic, and connected to the Lees by marriage, is unequaled in his description of the moral erosion this caused. His powerful words are all the more unsettling since he was the owner of a large body of slaves, whom he never freed. Nor, for all his political genius, did he ever propose a remedy for the "slow Poison"

> which is daily contaminating the Minds & Morals of our People. Every Gentlemen is born a petty Tyrant. Practiced in Acts of Degradation & Cruelty, we become callous to the Dictates of Humanity, & all the fond feelings of the Soul. Taught to regard a part of our own Species in that most abject & Contemptible Degree below us, we lose that Idea of the Dignity of Man, which the Hand of Nature has implanted on us, for great & useful purposes. Habituated from our Infancy to trample upon the Rights of Human Nature, every generous, every liberal Sentiment, if not extinguished, is enfeebled in our Minds. And in such an infernal School are to be educated our future Legislators & Rulers.[12]

Here, then, was the dilemma of slavery: if one did not openly reject the system, by definition one had to accommodate to it. Accommodation meant accepting the discomfort of moral compromise and exercising power based on oppression. It was this that constituted the insidious "evil" for white Southerners.

Robert E. Lee accommodated. His mother still owned some thirty-five blacks, and his social world was defined by relatives who retained significant slave holdings. His first personal experience as a master came with his mother's death in 1829. Ann Lee left thirty slaves to Robert and his brothers. Since he had just graduated from West Point, in theory his inheritance could have been seen as a basis for launching a new life. However, it is clear that from the outset Lee saw his servants as an uncomfortable stewardship. He declined to attend the meeting called to allocate his mother's servants, sending Smith as proxy. Once given his share, he did not know how to employ this new property. Social pressure and family ties did not allow him to sell them, and Lee resented the care and "useless trouble" that the blacks required. "I do not know what to do with our Georgetonians," he wrote to Mary in 1831, referring to the servants that had been living with his mother when she moved to Georgetown. He did not want Nancy to come and cook for him and could not recommend her to anyone else. He had no idea what to do with Cassy or Jane; he supposed Letitia could be his wife's *femme de chambre*. "In the meantime you may do with them as you please if opportunity offers. But do not trouble yourself about them, as they are not worth it."[13]

His need to supervise the slaves was a perpetual frustration. Despite his wife's assertions that Nancy was "quick & obliging," Lee did not like her and did not want her around. He tried to keep the number of servants with them to a minimum and chose to hire out most of them.[14] When his wife asked his opinion about the comparative merits of two of his slaves, he gave an offhand reply and begged, "But Molly, there is your Mother, my love, consult her about these things, for I know nothing of the matter."[15] He often complained of the poor quality of the slaves' work. Nancy was "a bad cook & washer"; Meriday he thought was "destined to give you trouble . . . if you can only get him to *work*"; the plowmen at Arlington were in the habit of making only superficial efforts, and it "was very hard to get them out of it." In sum, "it would be accidental to fall in with a good one."[16] In 1862, four days before the battle of Fredericksburg, he was still complaining about the family servants: "Perry is very willing & I believe does as well as he can. You know he is slow & inefficient & moves very much like his father Lawrence, whom he resembles very much. He is also very fond of his blankets in the morn. The time I most require him out. He is not very strong either."[17]

For Lee, African-Americans were poor workers and a time-consuming emotional handicap, more trouble than they were worth. His approach, therefore, was to keep himself aloof from the responsibilities of slave management as much as possible. Just how long he owned human property is unclear. As he departed for the Mexican War, Lee wrote a will in which he freed the much maligned Nancy and her children, though what he intended for the others he owned is not stated, nor is it clear whether or not we should assume that a special relationship had inspired Nancy's preferential treatment. Douglas Southall Freeman thought that he liberated all of his slaves after 1847, since he found no tax listing for them after that date. According to a Dr. John Leyburn, who claimed to have interviewed the general before his death, Lee "had freed most of his Negroes before the war," sending some to Liberia. Another account, written by Robert E. Lee Jr., stated that "General Robert E. Lee inherited three or four families of slaves and 'let them go . . . a long time before the war.'" The account states that the reason no formal paper was executed at that time was that he did not want them to have to leave Virginia, which state law required. Hiring records, however, show that Lee himself still owned slaves at least until 1852, and that he used enslaved blacks as personal servants until the end of the Civil War.[18]

It is not clear that Lee "let go" all of his slaves before the war, and indeed he considered buying more. But he did hire them out with great regularity. This gave him the double advantage of getting some return—"rent"—for his property and lightening the duties of oversight. This was a common practice in northern Virginia and the flexibility it gave to the system probably helped slavery to remain viable in some areas of marginal profitability.[19] He seems also to have had hopes that different masters might correct some of the slaves' perceived shortcomings. He was still harping about the unfortunate Philip Meriday when he hired him out in 1852, saying he would lower the price, if only the new master would "make him regular & punctual." Sometimes Lee hired slaves to his brothers or cousins—others he gave to slave dealers to be auctioned off. He particularly chose the latter course after he took over the management of his father-in-law's estate in 1857, finding the hiring system a good source of revenue, but also a way of getting troublemakers out of the way. This was the fate of Ruben—"a great rogue and rascal"—who along with several others had had the temerity to rebel against the system. Three women were also rented away from the area: "I could not recommend them for honesty," Lee noted sourly. Sending the men away from Arlington served as a cautionary lesson for the other slaves, who considered it a fairly severe punishment. It also helped Lee maintain a distance from the unsavory duties of being master.[20]

Lee's need to remove himself as much as possible from the day-to-day oversight of the slaves reflected an elitism that inclined him to react according to preconceived notions about those who were not of his class or race. Both plantation life and the army were hierarchical worlds. Status, class prerogatives, command and obedience, as well as the concept of noblesse oblige were part of the accepted habits of human relations. Lee felt no discomfort in describing "the lower classes" of St. Louis as a "swaggering noisy set, careless of getting work except occasionally" whose children were "dawdling and dirty and uninteresting." "Those of the higher order" he found "very kind

and friendly," if engrossed in business.[21] When he encountered Mexicans
during the 1846–48 war, and in his scouting expeditions in Texas, he found
little to admire in their distinctive way of life, instead finding them "weak"
and "primitive in their habits and tastes."[22] Native Americans also held little
fascination for him. Aside from a few romantic descriptions of their birch-
bark canoes, written to his little children, he found them "hideous" and "uninteresting" and concluded "they give a world of trouble to man and horse
& poor creatures they are not worth it."[23] His letters show personal involvement in the decimation of native peoples during casual encounters on the
prairie, with his accompanying comment that he was "glad of it."[24] As he
prepared for the possibility of fighting on the Seminole frontier, he told
Eliza Mackay Stiles that he was content with a job that was "to keep in subjugation the Indians and the negroes in that quarter."[25] Indeed, much of his
military career was spent in subduing anyone who came into conflict with
white aspirations, be they Mexicans, John Brown's dangerous band, or native tribes.[26] Lee was no Meriwether Lewis or George Catlin—men who had
felt an urgency to record something of the rich cultures they encountered.
His disdain for peoples unlike himself certainly reflected the society he lived
in, but does not rise above it. Whereas some of his fellow officers found the
Indians to be fascinating and honorable, Lee simply dismissed them.[27]
"They are not worth it" was Lee's disdainful phrase for interacting with anyone who was not white.

To manage such a complex world of peoples and cultures, Lee professed
a simple and inflexible social order, as tidy as the mathematical laws that
governed his engineering. "Though climate, government and circumstance
have produced changes in the character of the people," he once wrote, "yet
in all essential qualities they resemble the races from which they are sprung;
and to no race are we indebted for the virtues and qualifications which constitute a great people than the Anglo-Saxon."[28] Blacks were clearly at the bottom of this racial scale. Lee believed that they were innately inferior to
whites and that destiny favored the ascendancy of the Anglo-Saxons.[29] He
would have agreed with his father-in-law, who told his cousin Markie
Williams how he scorned an Irish overseer who "looked upon & associated
with the Negroes as if they were quite on a par with himself. Yes, said he, he
was really as ignorant as *that*."[30] Mrs. Lee, who spoke with sympathy of the
servants, was nevertheless so aware of the social order that she fretted over
whether or not to seat a hired white "mantua maker" at the family dinner
table. The Arlington slaves, either from submission or calculation, parroted
the white notion of an ordered society, which only confirmed the opinions
of patricians like Lee. Markie Williams also recorded a telling conversation

with one servant who allowed that "servants ought to know their places and not be always aiming to be something they cant attain to! For my part, I don't think tis any use for colored people to be spriring to be like white ones—if they were to use soap by the dozens cakes, t'would'nt make no impression on their color, no more can all the airs they put on, make um like the quality." The slave was told that he was right, that everyone in life traveled in a certain sphere, which was theirs to adorn. "Who is more respected than a good servant?" Markie proposed. "Let us then, servants & masters, Children & parents . . . keep within our spheres."³¹ Lee also found comfort in an ordered world designed along lines of class and racial hierarchies. Even in 1865, his world nearly shattered and slavery abolished, he would write that he considered "the relation of master and slave, controlled by human laws, and influenced by Christianity and enlightened public sentiment, as the best that can exist between the white & black races." Concluded Lee: "I would deprecate any sudden disturbance of that relation unless it be necessary to avert a greater calamity to both."³²

These words, which today seem startling, were entirely unremarkable in Lee's world. No visionary, Lee nearly always tried to conform to accepted opinions. His assessment of black inferiority, of the necessity of racial stratification, the primacy of slave law, and even a divine sanction for it all, was in keeping with the prevailing views of other moderate slaveholders and a good many prominent Northerners. They had many justifications for it. Jefferson thought abolition would be like "abandoning children"; Lee thought slavery a kind of "painful discipline" that was part of God's grand design. Defenders sought rational and religious arguments for the perpetuation of slavery, professing to see God's hand in servitude and a divine mission in its conduct. Although they accepted that there were faults in the system, like Mason they neither saw nor created an alternative to it. James Henry Hammond, a leading proslavery writer, espoused the theory of a fundamental incompatibility of the races, which Lee later echoed. "They differ essentially, in all the leading traits which characterize the varieties of the human species, and color draws an indelible and insuperable line of separation between them," Hammond wrote in 1845.³³ Even Abraham Lincoln believed this to be true. He, like others of his time, had to work through the problem of slavery intellectually and emotionally. Yet he never revised his theory of an insurmountable distinction between the races: "there is a physical difference between the white and black races which I believe will forever forbid the two races living together on terms of social and political equality."³⁴

For Southerners of Lee's social strata, this philosophy absolutely precluded freeing the slaves. The chief justification for this was the example of free blacks in the South. Life was difficult for the freedmen, who had trouble finding work, maintaining their legal status, and overcoming the dislike of virtually everyone in their communities. Lee's contemporaries used the widespread contempt for free blacks to raise the specter of a lawless colony of such people, "the most worthless and indolent of the citizens . . . the very *drones* and *pests* of society."[35] The series of debates that took place in the Virginia legislature in 1831–32, following the shock of Nat Turner's rebellion, was the last serious effort in the South to consider general emancipation. At the time these discussions were widely complimented for their eloquent analysis. They broke down from fear and a failure to imagine a different reality. Instead of resulting in a new, humanely based social order, the legislature passed laws that institutionalized a more rigid form of bondage. Thomas Roderick Dew, who wrote a brilliant commentary on the debates called "Abolition of Negro Slavery," inspired a generation of proslavery thought when he concluded that the slaves were not only economically but morally unfit for freedom. Although Lee, Hammond, and others claimed that they accepted the concept of gradual liberation, or maybe manumission followed by deportation, they clung to the notion that any immediate, universal emancipation would lead to an insupportable class of beggars and ruffians, and possibly to anarchy. They were certainly not going to do anything to hasten that day. So unwilling was Lee to take any action that would change the condition of the bondsmen that he deferred the resolution of slavery's injustice to the leveling hand of death. "The poor blacks have a multitude of miseries," he told his wife in 1849. "I hope death that must come sooner or later will end them all."[36]

In his philosophy of slavery, Lee declined either to defend the institution completely or to work to destroy it. Instead he chose to distance himself and to accept an elaborate middle ground that acknowledged its faults, but justified its existence. Lee seems to have thought that laws and social customs might protect both the slave and the master from any excesses. As an alternative to freedom, Lee proposed a kind of vague evolution of the institution, which "a wise and merciful Providence" would direct. It had no precise time frame and no real perimeters, but assumed that "the course of the final abolition of slavery is onward." Here again, Lee's views were in keeping with the political philosophy of his contemporaries. The debates of 1831–32 had also purposefully blurred a clear picture of the peculiar institution's fate. While the delegates had rejected immediate emancipation, they also shunned the idea of perpetual slavery. Instead they approved a statement of future abolition at an undetermined date, dependent on the public will.

Even Thomas Roderick Dew assumed that slavery in Virginia would disappear over time.[37] Failing to develop a policy that could give moral and political direction to the greatest problem of their age, the pro-slavery activists, like Lee, could only describe the future with evasion, denial, and grand illusions.

Apologists for slavery resolved the conflict between their ethical beliefs and their daily practices by defending the master's role as a kind of enlightened despotism. Slaveholders had been wrestling with accusations of "immorality" for many decades. Those who felt they could not create a more equitable social order came to define justice not by the destruction of the institution, but by the way that slaves were treated *within* the system. Patrick Henry had proclaimed this—"let us treat the unhappy Victims with lenity, it is the furtherest advance we can make toward Justice." This was precisely the philosophy that Mary Fitzhugh Custis adopted at Arlington.[38] In their day-to-day existence, tolerant masters would somehow prepare their slaves for freedom and guarantee kind treatment. Elijah Fletcher, an acquaintance of the Lees, may have articulated it best: "Slavery is rather a misfortune than a crime. The present holders of slaves are not censurable for their fathers crimes of introducing them. They are only censurable for not treating those they possess well. We have some free negroes here, and it is a general remark that the slaves who have good masters are in a better situation. To emancipate them at once would be the height of folly and danger." It was a tactical rather than strategic philosophy. At its center was a reliance on the law to justify and control the system. The owners would be both restricted and empowered by law, and would rule with inspired wisdom and compassion for the daily good of the bondsman. Ultimately, however, by this doctrine the slaveholder rejected any personal responsibility for the existence of the institution or for its victims. The fate of those he left to God and the lawyers.[39]

For "progressive" slaveholders, then, here was the way out of the moral straitjacket. Slavery was regrettable, but it was not their fault. To emancipate the slaves immediately would be the "height of folly and danger"; in any case, with good treatment by enlightened owners, the slaves enjoyed a "better situation" than they would in Africa. The law would protect both slave and master. At some imprecise time the institution would fade away.

What this convoluted scheme failed to address was the humanity of the slaves and their innate right to freedom. By Lee's lifetime slavery had become a philosophical morass of property rights, human "inalienable" rights, and political "states'" rights. It became even more complex if you added "humanity" into the mix. "Human rights" is an abstract concept, one that easily slips into definitions that are highly subjective. But individuality and human connections are not abstract, and the most painful contradictions in slavery rose out of its personal relationships. How could one enslave these people with whom one had grown up; and indeed, how could anyone determine who had taken care of whom? How, in the complex interrelated plantation families, could a clear distinction be made between white and black, let alone slave and free? When one had personally witnessed the terrible injustices of the system, how could one continue to uphold it? Lee tried to sidestep it by making the burden greater for the oppressor than for the oppressed and by defining his responsibility strictly by law. The tragedy for Lee is that he never made the transformational leap that would recognize the fundamental human nature of the slaves. George Washington wrestled with it; Abraham Lincoln did as well. Neither of these men ever considered African-Americans their equal. Ultimately, however, they both grasped the fact that what was wrong with slavery was not an absence of sufficient laws, or a need for more humane treatment within an exploitative system. What was wrong with slavery was that it failed to recognize the brotherhood of the human condition. The entangled lives of the slaves and their masters, the emotional, historical, sexual, and communal connections, could mean only one thing: that these beings were equal as part of mankind; equal in their human instincts, passions, desires, and inclinations, including the desire for self-determination. Equal, as Lincoln said, in the "right to eat the bread without the leave of anybody else, which his own hand earns. . . ." Capable, as George Washington finally realized, "of a destiny different from that in which they were born."[40] This was the pivotal insight of *Uncle Tom's Cabin*, which riveted popular attention in 1852; it was the great truth of *Huckleberry Finn,* articulated by Mark Twain, a southern white, born to a slaveholding family. Robert E. Lee would never cross this threshold. He could embrace the need for justice, but it was a justice defined by unjust principles. His racism and his limited imagination meant that he never admitted the humanity of the slaves with whom he lived. In avoiding that truth, he bound himself to slavery's inhumanity.

Chapter Ten

Adrenaline

Hacienda [El Len]cero
18 April 1847

My dearest Mary,

    I am at this magnificent Hacienda of Santa Anna, 8 miles in advance of the main Army, & write a few lines by the courier, who is about starting. My reason for writing is that I presume Genl Scott, who is behind the main Army, will send dispatches to the U.S. that will convey the intelligence of a great victory, & I wish to assure you of my safety, about wh[ich] you might be doubtful if no letter arrived. The battle [took place] this mor^g shortly after Sunrise. The Enemy was strongly [page torn] in the mountain Pass of Serro Gordo. In which there was [page torn] six Forts along a distance of some 2 or 3 miles commanding the whole Pass. The advance under Gen^ls Patter[son & Twi]ggs had been stopped 2 or 3 days before the arrival of Genl Scott & after 2 more days of reconnaissance & preparation their whole line was turned by the left. It was a beautiful operation & came in well after our turning San Juan de Ulua by first taking Vera Cruz. Yesterday by taking [page torn] positions by the extremity of the road that we had made, we were [ob]served by the Enemy who opened a strong fire upon us from a hill under which we [were] advancing on his position, but we [dro]ve him back to his fortified line, & then waited quietly till this [morning] the attack was ordered. By 11 their left was completely turned [and] the Fort crowning the Serro Gorda & the last in the series taken. Their Field batteries [page torn] its foot that were guarding the plain below were also in full retreat. The other Forts finding we were in their rear & all opposition useless sent in a white flag & by 12 the Garrisons of all had surrendered themselves prisoners of War. 5 Gen^ls, 4500 [so]ldiers & I do not know the number of Arms, Guns, Ammunition &c [page torn] about $20,000 & Santa Anna's <u>carriage & leg</u>, with wagons, pack mules &c fell into our possession. I came on with the advance in [pursu]it of the fugitives from the plain, but after reaching this

*place, [finding] men & horses exhausted & that we had not been able to [keep]
up with them, it was considered most prudent to halt. [Unreadable] comfortable quarters, beautifully furnished, & delightfully [situ]ated. What is of more
consequence, we are nearly all safe. Many have been killed & wounded in the
two days fight. Genl Shields is reported badly wounded. Genl Pills slightly, Capt
Mason badly in the leg & several others. My poor Joe Johnston on the second
day after Genl Twigs arrival & before Genl Scott came up was severely but not
seriously wounded. He was fired on by a Picket & was struck by 2 balls one on
the Arm & [the] other above the hip. He is doing very well. Both balls are out.
He is comfortable & the D^{rs.} say it will only confine him a few [page torn]
brother Mr Lane of the Navy, has come up from Vera Cruz but will [page torn]
soon as arrangements can be made will take h[im] aboard ship. His other
brother Mr Lane who is in the rifles w[as] wounded to day. Mr Rhett has escaped & I hope always will. All of our Eng^{rs} are also safe & have done good
work. I am but thankful for my preservation amidst the show[er] of balls that
fell around me & hope I shall be sufficiently gra[teful] to that merciful God,
that extended his powerful hand to me. Give oceans of love to my dear children
& Parents & remember me to all friends. For yourself I am always y^{rs} RE Lee[1]*

⊱──◦──⊰

HANDLING THE SCRAPS of this Mexican War letter is something like
touching a tattered old battle flag. The edges are ragged, the ink so
faint you must arm yourself with a strong magnifying glass and even
stronger patience to decipher it. The delicate condition of the document,
however, cannot mask the elation that flows from every hastily scribbled
line. It was written from the home of the Mexican general Santa Anna, just
hours after the battle of Cerro Gordo, and the faded letterhead on the
stationery—"Secretaria Paticuliar del Presidente de la Republica"—proclaims
the U.S. army's occupation of sensitive territory. This is a victory dispatch:
the proud announcement of a daringly won contest in which Captain Robert Lee of the Engineers had taken a leading part.

The Mexican War was a seminal event in Lee's life. During this conflict
he felt the first seduction of warfare, tasted the sweet satisfaction of outma-
neuvering an opponent, thrilled with the excitement of uncertainty and
danger. In Mexico he also experienced another side of war—the daily discomfort, bickering, and bravado that tarnished the luster of martial glory.
He suffered personal loss there, and knew the hideous sight of a battlefield
littered with the mangled bodies of his compatriots. Most important, the

Mexican War offered an opportunity for Lee to prove himself, both to the army and to his own satisfaction. This was where Robert E. Lee became something more than a fine parade ground soldier or a diligent engineer. This was where he became a warrior.

In the late 1840s Americans were stretching themselves in every direction. It was a period of immense social and economic change; a time of energetic debate about how the legacy of liberty should be developed, and to whom its benefits should apply. Workingmen—slaves—even women began to demand that the promise of America be extended to them. In the arts a national personality was being formed. Stephen Foster was writing "Oh! Susanna" and other popular songs that captured the essence of the age. In their parlors Americans read Edgar Allan Poe's "The Raven" and *Typee*, which brought Herman Melville to fame. P. T. Barnum tested the boundaries of entrepreneurship—and credulity—with a fabulous show displaying "all that is monstrous, scaly, strange and queer." The Smithsonian Institution opened its doors to curious minds in 1846. That same year women stood in line to wonder at the first patented sewing machine—a harbinger of their liberation from the needle. In that time of sentimentality and optimism, Americans believed the potential of their country knew no limits.[2]

The great expanse of North America was one of the elements that captured the national imagination. In 1846 the United States held only half of its present continental territory, and land-hungry citizens were looking for ways to fulfill their dreams of richer pastures. Andrew Jackson's protégé, James K. Polk, had stirred the expansionist spirit during the election of 1844, winning on a platform that proclaimed it was America's "manifest destiny" to reach from sea to sea. Polk gambled that he could achieve his goals bloodlessly, and he was able to bully the British into a favorable settlement on the Oregon Territory. He hoped that an internal revolution in Mexico might result in the peaceful annexation of southwestern lands, but the Mexicans proved to be feistier than the British. The fight for independence in Texas and its "reannexation" to the United States in 1845 were considered acts of war in Mexico, and they felt honor bound to protect their property. Using the disputed boundary of Texas as a pretext, Polk claimed the Mexicans had fired at U.S. citizens on "American" soil. Intending to conduct a limited campaign— just large enough to require a peace treaty that would cede ground—the president convinced Congress to declare war on April 25, 1846.[3]

Polk's ambitious platform was infectious; nonetheless he had his detractors. John Quincy Adams, still in Congress at age eighty-two, thought it little more than a shameless land grab that would extend the reach of slavery. Henry David Thoreau would write his famous essay "On Civil Disobedience" after refusing to pay a poll tax that supported the war.[4] But most of America's 20 million people had expansion on their minds, and despite the cries of opportunism, they embraced the conflict with romantic patriotism. " 'The Mexican War' is the engrossing subject just now with everyone hereabouts—" Anna Maria Fitzhugh told Carter Lee, a few weeks into the fray. "Crowds assemble on the wharves every ev^g to meet the Southern Mail boat . . . decorated with flags, to give notice in advance of our triumphs."[5] Cousin Anna was one who did not approve of the war; Robert also wished he was "better satisfied as to the justice of our cause," but told himself that the duty of a soldier was to follow policy, not make it.[6] His greater concern was that he might miss the fight. He watched in some agony as most of his garrison planned their departure for Texas. "There is nothing but preparation for battle," he told Markie Williams. "The Sharpening of Swords, the grinding of bayonets & equipping for the field, occupy all thoughts & hands."[7] Throughout the spring and summer of 1846, while American forces were beginning their campaigns in northern Mexico and California, Lee was diligently filing reports on the waterproofing of Fort Hamilton's endless masonry ramparts. Finally, on August 19, he received orders to report to General John E. Wool for service in Mexico.[8]

"I believe I am the last man ordered, every one is ahead of me & I am hurrying to endeavor to reach San Antonio de Bexar before the Army moves," Robert told Carter Lee. He learned quickly of war's exhilaration—and its price. On the day he arrived in Texas, Markie's father, Captain William G. Williams, was killed during the American triumph under Zachary Taylor at Monterey.[9] Lee was roused by the sentimental glory of Williams's death "on the field of battle, with the cry of victory in his ear," just as he was by a visit to the Alamo a few days later.[10] In 1836 Antonio López de Santa Anna, Mexico's wily, one-legged general-cum-dictator, had ruthlessly annihilated the little band who held out there for nearly three weeks in the name of Texas independence. Memories of this act, and other unsavory deeds, had been partially responsible for America's enthusiasm for a fight with its southern neighbor. And Santa Anna was a formidable opponent, resilient and difficult to contain. Unbowed by the U.S. Army's early successes, the "Napoleon of the West" redoubled his commitment to "have war not only to the *knife* but to the handle also," raising an army of 18,000 despite an exhausted treasury. A few months later he came within a whisker of defeating Zachary Taylor at Buena Vista. Lee did not know it yet, but one of his chief jobs would be to outwit Santa Anna on questions of terrain and maneuver—matters on which the Mexican general prided himself.[11]

Inspired by the room where Davy Crockett had been killed, Lee, like his fellow countrymen, remembered the Alamo and chafed to get to the action. What he encountered instead in these first months were cumbersome logistics. The army was badly supplied, the quartermaster's office was woefully conducted, and officers had to procure their own uniforms, equipment, and horses. Lee bought a sure-footed, cream-colored mare, "Creole," which he came to love, and struggled to catch up with Wool's forces.[12] He and his servant Jim Connolly had to move cross-country in pitiful conditions. Food was hard cracker and warm water. He made the acquaintance of "prairie flies," and found them so bad that he traveled by night to avoid their eternal biting. When he did find rest, it was "in an ox cart to keep out of the way of the goats & hogs that assembled around me to welcome my arrival." It was only the first of many difficult marches he would endure, some so onerous that men and mules expired along the road.[13] Once he caught up with Wool, he found the regiment a hodgepodge of volunteers and regular troops, with little love lost between them. The volunteers were spirited and tough—it was largely due to their energy that Monterey had been taken—but they lacked the training of the "old army," frequently deserting their posts, and presenting a pathetic spectacle at drill. Lieutenant George B. McClellan, who arrived about the same time as Lee, wrote contemptuously in his diary that "Falstaff's company were regulars in comparison with these fellows. . . . they were dirt and filth from top to toe. Such marching! . . . all hollowing, cursing, yelling like so may incarnate fiends. . . ."[14]

Unfortunately, the work was similarly uninspiring. Lee's early tasks included sounding fords, cutting down banks, and making roads for the passing army, then preparing the lines to cross the Rio Grande. Even this pedestrian activity came to a halt when General Taylor agreed to an armistice that suspended all operations.[15] Annoyed by the lull, and fearful that his ambition for battle would be permanently thwarted, Lee groused: "I only regret that we should be kept here doing nothing. . . . We ought now to be on the march & might have been in position to do signal service." He was further irritated when General Wool employed him to cut roads for a series of excruciating forced marches, called to avoid an enemy advance that proved to be nonexistent.[16]

But the routine logistical role of the engineers was about to be transformed. Lee got a taste of this around Christmas 1846, when yet another rumor about Mexican movements threatened yet another useless tramp across the countryside. Volunteering to scout out the position of the opposing troops,

Lee set off virtually alone on a reconnaissance so daring it nearly frightened away his local guide. Creeping close to the supposed location of the Mexican camps, Lee found them abandoned, discovered that a flock of white sheep had been mistaken for tents, and learned from local drovers that the enemy was a mountain away from their presumed position. With this vital news Lee made a forty-mile night ride alone to Wool's headquarters, interrupted the plans for a pointless maneuver, and then set off again with a cavalry escort to get more precise information.[17] The expertise he used that night—geographical knowledge, the verification of facts, and logical deduction—were all scientific tools, though they were of a different genre than banking streams or constructing batteries. No one understood the utility of these skills better than General Winfield Scott, who was about to arrive in Mexico and swiftly turn the West Point engineers into a potent weapon for the army.

In this highly partisan war, rivalries were intense between political personalities and among generals. Polk purposefully kept Scott, who he detested, out of the conflict until Zachary Taylor's battlefield successes made him such a hero that the president feared—rightly, as it turned out—that "Old Rough 'n Ready" would overshadow his own popularity. Thinking that the elevation of Scott to commander in Mexico might counter Taylor's prominence, Polk dispatched him to the front. He also reluctantly agreed to a plan Scott devised to march overland from the port of Vera Cruz to Mexico City, where he hoped to destroy the Mexicans at their political center.[18] It was not lost on anyone that this was the very route Cortez had followed to conquer the Aztec capital. The challenging terrain, as well as the superior numbers and home advantage of the Mexicans, made it an audacious strategy.

Winfield Scott arrived in Mexico in early 1847. He was a big man, a booming man, a man so imperious that he was called "Old Fuss and Feathers." He wore "all the uniform . . . allowed by law," liked parades, and liked to be at the head of them. Scott had fought heroically during the War of 1812, winning a reputation for originality and courage—as well as for irascibility. His great life work, however, had been the establishment of a professional army, and now he fulfilled his vision by employing the regular officers with real effectiveness. Almost immediately he used his prerogative as commanding general to requisition the best junior men for his own staff. Lee, whom he had met in Washington, was among them, the second of two captains of engineers. Staunchly ethical Ethan Allen Hitchcock was inspector general on the team; other junior officers included P. G. T. Beauregard and George B. McClellan, with cameo appearances by Joseph Johnston and George Gordon Meade—a haunting convergence of historic names. Scott quickly showed his genius at using what he termed his "little cabinet." The engineers knew topography, and they knew how to alter it to facilitate surprise movements. Scott used them for intelligence work as well as fortifications, trusted them, and listened to them. Ulysses S. Grant, who for a time was also a member of his team, noted that he "saw more through the eyes of his staff officers than through his own."[19] Scott believed that battles were won not by throwing quantities of men onto a battlefield, but by what he called "head-work."[20] Captain Robert Lee and the other members of the cabinet were encouraged to innovate and even to dissent.[21] Scott could certainly bellow and bluster, abruptly cutting off the younger aides, particularly when things were going awry, but the staff adored him for the respect and confidence he gave them.[22] "Our Gen¹ is our great reliance . . . ," a somewhat gushing Lee would write. "Confident in his powers & resources, his judgment is as sound as his heart is bold & daring."[23]

The general returned the compliment. From the start Lee would be a star on his staff. Though Lee was not the senior man, Hitchcock referred to him as "*the* engineer," and Scott came to rely on him not only for "head-work" but as a fine operations manager and his chief scout.[24] One of Scott's junior team members left a vivid description of the "little cabinet" at work and the intensity with which Scott listened to Lee's counsel. "I will never forget that evening," wrote Lieutenant Isaac Ingalls Stevens to his wife, "Captain Lee in calm even, well-weighed words, giving a full view of the state of our force, suggesting the various methods of reëstablishing affairs, and proffering his own services and exertions to carry out the views of the general; Scott, composed, complacent, weighing every word he said, . . . and exhibiting entire confidence in the ultimate event."[25] It was Captain Lee's versatility that impressed Scott most, and he found himself writing commendations that praised him for everything from battlefield bravery to the cunning location of a road. The collaboration left Scott with an unshakable belief in Lee's abilities. "The very best soldier I ever saw in the field," the general would write.[26]

Lee got an early opportunity to exhibit his talents. The first objective of the campaign was to take the port of Vera Cruz, which would allow men and supplies to land, and serve as a logistical base. Packed onto boats, the troops hovered offshore for several miserable weeks, Lee in the *Massachusetts* with Scott and seasick bunkmate Joe Johnston. In March 1847 they finally went ashore—in boats designed by Scott expressly for the precedent-breaking amphibious landing—and Lee was put in charge of locating the position of the gun battery and supervising its construction. McClellan, who helped him, wrote at the time that it was a terrible labor, done during the dark hours of the morning, under the dual complications of a chilling storm and sporadic enemy fire. Lee added his own complaints about wet clothes, scanty provisions, and reluctant naval units.[27] Scott had hit upon the idea of using several huge cannons from the ships to pound the castle at San Juan d'Ulloa and the city's other considerable defenses. Lee later relished telling stories about that night, when, using nautical directions "and not a few ex-

Currier and Ives's image of American forces landing at Vera Cruz, 1847.

pletives," the sailors dragged the guns and magazines across torturous sand dunes and into position.[28] Navy men also manned them, including Lee's brother Smith, who had entered the theater a few weeks before. A "perfect storm of iron" began just as the guns were placed.[29] It was a starlit night, with no moon, and one of the naval officers recalled how the procession of burning fuses could be seen tracing the sky in "those beautiful parabolas, peculiar to this kind of projectile" just before exploding with deadly precision. Shells bursting around them, the engineers worked through the night to keep the battery repaired, sometimes firing the cannons themselves, with Lee taking turns at a thirty-two-pounder.[30] He was all the time keeping an eye on his dear Smith, picking him out by his "usual cheerfulness and white teeth," as he later told his wife. "No matter where I turned, my eyes reverted to him," Lee wrote, "and I stood by his gun whenever I was not wanted elsewhere. Oh! I felt awfully, and am at a loss what I should have done had he been cut down before me."[31] The siege was kept up for three days, progressively shattering the enemy fortifications, but Lee's batteries had been so well placed that the Mexican guns did little damage. With the Mexican surrender on March 29, 1847, the Americans had secured their toehold.[32]

This was Lee's first experience under fire. Many of his comrades had fought in the Indian wars of the 1830s, but Lee had never before seen live action. He had not flinched, as had some of the "blue in the gills" recruits at the battery. On the contrary, he and his subordinates had distinguished themselves. At the end of the siege General Scott showed McClellan a victory dispatch he was sending to Washington, which ended with the words "the indefatigable Engineers."[33] It was the beginning of a grand vindication for the professional army Scott and Sylvanus Thayer had so arduously toiled to establish. From then on the proficiency of the corps' trained scientist-soldiers would become "as necessary to [the] army, as sails are to a ship."[34]

For the next six months Lee followed Scott across harsh deserts and mountains, infested with noxious plants, dangerous fevers, and "guerilleros." Mexico City lay seventy-five miles away, and Santa Anna, persuading his government that he could destroy the "Yanqui" army by taking advantage of the rugged natural barriers along the road, gained his government's support to build a defending army three times the size of the American forces. Scott decided to press forward despite this, even when it appeared he would ultimately have to cut his supply lines. In light of the terrain, the unequal numbers and Mexican home advantage, the Duke of Wellington, who was following the army's progress from England, predicted disaster: "Scott is lost—he cannot capture the city and he cannot fall back upon his base."[35]

But Scott, realizing that traditional frontal assault would be useless under these conditions, began to develop a method of warfare that relied on first-rate reconnaissance, unpredictability, bravado, and attacks from the rear and side—his signature "turning" movements that forced opponents to fight at their most vulnerable point. Lee's prowess was critical to the success of this strategy. When Lee wrote his wife that excited letter from Hacienda El Lencero, he had just returned from a battle whose victory had been in large part due to his creative "head-work" and unstoppable resolve. Cerro Gordo, where the engagement took place, was an extraordinarily difficult piece of Mexican property, with the 700-foot "Fat Mountain" at its center, a string of well-placed fortifications, and cliffs, impenetrable chaparral, and a turbulent river protecting its sides. Acting on some excellent preliminary explorations by Lieutenant Beauregard, Lee found a path through the scrubby wasteland on the Mexican left that he thought might be extended to accommodate the army. He had one of his most unnerving experiences of the war during these reconnoiters, for when he and his guide John Fitzwater came upon a spring, they were surprised by the arrival of some Mexicans. Quickly diving under a barely concealed log, Lee and Fitzwater spent the rest of the day in tense misery. A parade of Mexicans visited the waterhole, chatting and sitting on the log, and an equally unremitting swarm of insects devoured the two agonized Americans. Finally under cover of darkness they crept back to the camp. Over the next few days they refined their plan and laid out what Lee called "The Trail." With unimaginable difficulty they enlarged the road at night and hauled dismantled artillery by rope down the ravines in preparation for battle. Grant was one of those who admired the tenacity of Lee and his fellow engineers as they made these preparations, over ground thought to be impassable and without Santa Anna's awareness.[36]

Finally, on April 17 Winfield Scott issued a detailed general order for a multipronged attack. General David Twiggs's forces stormed the heights to carry the fortress, while men under General James J. Shields and Colonel Bennett Riley followed Lee's "Trail" to surprise the Mexicans on the left and rear. Lee personally directed Shields and Riley along the torturous route; that he came under heavy pressure is clear from his own description of the "show[er] of balls that fell around me" and the fact that Shields nearly died of the wounds he suffered in the attack. It had been a tremendously daring gamble, but the conception and execution were exemplary, and it was all over in a morning. Santa Anna was taken unawares while eating a roast chicken, and fled so quickly that he left behind his carriage, a well-stocked money chest, and his wooden leg, just as Lee told his wife. He also left behind a thousand dead and several thousand prisoners, as well as precious materiel and an open road. Scott's casualties totaled 33 officers and 398 men, of whom only 63 were killed.[37]

Once again Robert Lee was singled out for commendation. Riley made special note of the "intrepid coolness and gallantry exhibited by Captain Lee of the Engineers when conducting the advance of my brigade under the heavy flank fire of the enemy." Naval officer Raphael Semmes, who worked with Lee, noted his powerful way of assessing a situation and presenting his observations, as well as a particular knack for topography: "he seemed to receive impressions intuitively, which it cost other men much labor to acquire."[38] About this time one of the lieutenants on Scott's staff also observed that Lee's "power of enduring fatigue is extraordinary, and his strength of judgment and perfect balance are conspicuous."[39] Artillery captain Robert Anderson noted in his journal that Captain Lee should write a military memoir of the battle, his contribution to military science was so great.[40] Neither did Scott, a stickler for unadorned reports, hold back. "I am impelled to make special mention of the services of Captain R. E. Lee, Engineers," he wrote.

> This officer, greatly distinguished at the siege of Vera Cruz, was again indefatigable during these operations, in reconnaissance as daring as laborious, and of the utmost value. Nor was he less conspicuous in planting batteries, and in conducting columns to their stations under the heavy fire of the enemy.[41]

Lee had spent two decades in the Corps of Engineers establishing a reputation for courtesy and competence. In three short weeks during the spring of 1847 he changed his profile to one associated with bold maneuver, steely nerves, and gallantry.

As Scott's forces approached the Mexican capital in late summer, Lee was again called on for surveillance, and for brain work that would overcome seemingly insurmountable obstacles. The army had been kept inactive for much of the summer, partially because of Polk's looming jealousy of Scott, and partially because of the need to await the arrival of volunteer troops. The lull allowed Santa Anna to reconstruct his army and concentrate its power in defense of the capital, but it also proved advantageous to the Americans, who had the benefit of fresh men for their onward push. Scott was again anxious to find a route that would support a stealthy approach by the American forces. The geography was not conducive to this strategy. Mexico City lay in a quagmire of reed beds, lakes, and volcanic waste that required single-file movement along causeways, impeding either quick advance or surprise movements. Lee was once more sent on reconnaissance, this time to see if a path could be found across an old lava bed called the "Pedregal"—whose jagged outcrops blocked clear passage, cutting hooves and flesh like a razor. During several days of adrenaline-pumping adventure, Lee led an advance party, pushing himself "far beyond the bounds of prudence," as one general officer would comment, to discover a trace that he thought could be cleared to support the troops' march and allow for a surprise attack.[42] Lee also discovered that the Mexicans were close enough to open fire on his men as they improved the trace and laid batteries. He had already been working several days without rest, but when scouts rode in to say that Santa Anna had dispatched forces that would block a proposed flanking movement, Lee volunteered to take word to General Scott. It meant that he must recross the treacherous Pedregal, alone—at night—and in a torrential storm. When he miraculously arrived at headquarters hours later with the critical message, he was sent out again into the dark and rain to take a message back to General Twiggs, ordering an assault. Scott later pronounced this foray "the greatest feat of physical and moral courage performed by any individual" during the campaign.[43]

Lee went on to distinguish himself at the field of Contreras. Here he again spied out the terrain, found a narrow ravine that could be exploited to circle

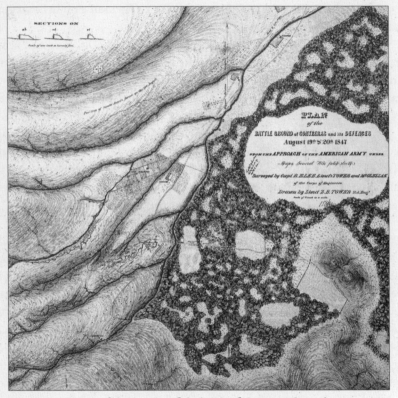

A map of the vicinity of the battle of Contreras drawn by Captain R. E. Lee, showing the formidable Pedregal.

NATIONAL ARCHIVES

behind the enemy, and while General Franklin Pierce feinted a frontal assault, led Twiggs's and Pillow's forces along a route that enabled their attack from the rear. The battle lasted seventeen minutes. The Mexicans lost seven hundred men and precious cannonry; the Americans counted a total of sixty dead and wounded.[44] At the assault on Chapultepec, a few weeks later, which opened the way for defeat of the capital, he worked for sixty hours straight to advance the battle movements. Among his comrades during these tense days were James Longstreet and his protégé George Pickett, and a young artillery officer, Thomas J. Jackson—not yet likened to a stone wall. In the last critical hours of the campaign Lee played a vital role in gathering intelligence, positioning guns and troops, and acting as Scott's trusted messenger, all amid serious fighting and on roads "so beset . . . by robbers & Guerilleros, that it is difficult for even a courier to steal through." Finally, suffering from a minor wound and "pretty well worn out from excessive work night and day," Lee passed out in the saddle, toppling from his horse. That same night Santa Anna evacuated the capital.[45]

The next morning, September 14, 1847, Lee joined "Old Fuss and Feathers" in the full dress parade into Mexico City. Colors were lowered and drums rolled as a victory proclamation was read from the balcony of the Palacio Nacional. It was a splendid vindication for Scott's meticulously designed offensive strategy. He had captured an extensively fortified city with a greatly outnumbered army, which was cut off from its own line of supply and communications. Moreover, using "head-work," he had done it with a minimum of casualties. In England the Duke of Wellington changed the tone of his commentary. "His campaign is unsurpassed in military annals," he wrote of Scott. "He is the greatest living soldier."[46]

All through the dreary, dusty trekking; the apprehension of battle; the solitude and the glory, Lee found his outlet in writing letters. He wrote home regularly once a week, and he wrote when he learned that special dispatches were being sent. In the first three months of his sojourn in Mexico, no mail at all arrived for him, but still he wrote, and the letters he sent into the void tell of his longing and his vulnerability. When, in early December 1846, he was finally handed several envelopes from Mary, he openly expressed his delight—and his frustration that in the midst of a march he had no time to read the messages: "I could do nothing more than recognize the handwriting & put them in my pocket. . . . It was very tantalizing after so long an expectation to carry unopened in my pocket what I so much desired. . . . I could occasionally read a few lines . . . I had not finished it when I arrived at my journeys end. . . . I then had the pleasure of a quiet perusal. . . ."[47] As always, Lee was conscientious about keeping in touch, but the letter writing seems to have meant far more to him than the fulfillment of an obligation. It is a measure of the family's warm relations that this reticent man, so cautious about revealing himself, could be so openly expressive.

Lee's letters from Mexico are a wonderful blend of travelogue, military observation, sweet sentiment, and complaints about fleas, food, and politicians. To his children he wrote about the game little Mexican ponies and described bright local flowers and the hummingbirds he had named for those "saucy little hussies" Agnes and Annie.[48] He compared notes with brother Smith about the best way to procure wine and new shirts—and they both grumbled about the ingratitude of Congress.[49] Lee liked to replay battles with his male correspondents, and he sometimes speculated to Mary about military operations, previewing, for example, Scott's risky cross-country advance. This was a dangerous business, however, since word of this plan had gotten to Santa Anna through the interception of a similar private missive.[50]

Lee was delighted by Mexican chocolate and the way the señoritas discarded their stockings and wore "their polished ankles" instead. "I admire the change most amazingly," he told Jack Mackay.[51] He did not, however, too much admire the Mexicans or their way of life. Lee was not alone in his disdain for the people he termed "cowardly" as well as "idle worthless & vicious." Behind the American excursion into Mexico lay an almost missionary zeal to extend Anglo-Saxon culture southward. Many of his colleagues thought, as did Lee, that they would be doing a noble service by bringing their version of civilization to what they considered a backward and idolatrous region. "I believe it would be our best plan to commence at once," Lee declared, succinctly stating his recipe for progress. "Open the ports to European immigration. Introduce free opinions of government & religion. Break down the power & iniquity of the church. It is a beautiful country & in the hands of proper people would be a magnificent one."[52]

Lee was uncertain whether his letters were received at Arlington, and in fact many seem never to have arrived. He continued to mail them faithfully, and to send his powerful emotions into the uncertainty. "I cannot describe all the love I feel for you & the children, mother & all with you & how often I think of you & how anxious I am for your welfare," he admitted while on a long march. At Christmas he was especially lonely. He amused himself by writing a richly detailed and hilarious description of the officers' Christmas dinner—how it had been interrupted by a false alarm from Santa Anna—and embellished by a centerpiece of oranges and "three bottles of the genuine anchor brand."[53] An "ample supply of the Parras wine" could not soothe his homesickness, however. "I hope good Santa Claus will fill my Robs stockings tonight & that Mildreds Agnes & Annas may break down with the good things," Lee wistfully told his little boys on Christmas Eve. "I do not know what he will have for you & Mary, but if he . . . leaves for you only half of what I wish you, you will want for nothing."[54] With seven children to raise alone, the youngest of whom was only a few months old, Mary Lee also suffered from the separation. She had not heard from her husband in some time, she confided to their old friend Sarah Beaumont; still she could not help but "dread the arrival of each mail & even to contemplate what may be in store for me." After the battlefield deaths of her cousin Captain Williams and Sarah's own young husband, her fears grew. "I cannot see why I should be spared more than others," she wrote. "My only hope is in the forbearing mercy of my God. . . ."[55] She and her Whiggish relatives did not support the war cause and desired that the army would "be withdrawn on any terms." As the conflict continued, Mary despaired of ever seeing her husband again and was filled with "the pains of protracted absence." She and her parents hoped that the Mexican adventure would put an end to Robert Lee's desire to remain in the army.[56]

Lee was given two brevet promotions for valor during the Mexican War. The recognition was not unusual—in an army that had so few ways of rewarding its men, and an age when medals were not yet awarded, brevets became standard issue. Lee outwardly scorned his own, telling Jack Mackay that everyone in the army was his "own trumpeter," and observing that "it is so much more easy to make heroes on paper than in the field."[57] He took the same tone with his father-in-law, peevishly listing a series of officers who had received more brevets than he, and showing resentment that his own laurels had been awarded only for Cerro Gordo, so "that if I performed any services at Vera Cruz, or at the battles around this capital they will go for naught."[58] If he was disappointed in this official recognition, however, he must have been aware of the sincere respect he had earned from his colleagues. When his brother Carter met some officers returning from the front, they assured him "that Robert's is the most enviable reputation in the army."[59] Mary Lee was told much the same thing by General Scott personally, who revered Lee as much for "felicitous execution as for science and daring."[60] A dozen years later, when war clouds again gathered and men's military ability became an urgent issue, one veteran assessed Lee's prospects by saying that if "those who were with him in Mexico should answer, they would immediately declare him to be in all military qualifications without a rival in the Service."[61]

It is hard to know whether Lee was satisfied with his outstanding performance, for he reacted to all praise with calculated modesty. He told his father-in-law that he knew his services "to be small," and his brother that he "did nothing more than what others in my place could have done much better."[62] The gauze of humility thrown round these responses does not quite seem believable. To begin with, it is too much at odds with Lee's genuine achievements. It also seems to mask some anger that he had not been appropriately recognized. Like many of his comrades, he had entered the war with large aspirations. On his arrival in Mexico Lieutenant George B. McClellan forthrightly stated: "I came down here with high hopes, with pleasing anticipations of distinction . . . and acquiring a name and reputation as a stepping stone to a still greater eminence in some future and greater war."[63] Lee echoed these sentiments, saying that although he did not believe in the cause of the war, it was an opportunity in which he "might gain distinction & honour & therefore not to be regretted."[64] His ambition also showed in the way he volunteered for the most difficult duty and sometimes drove himself to the point of collapse. Lee initially *offered* to cross the Pedregal during that dark night—he was not ordered to do so—and he pushed himself, as General Persifer Smith had written, "far beyond the bounds of prudence." The generals above Lee were measuring him, but he was also measuring himself and, as he recognized his strengths, was not averse to promoting them. He wrote, for example, that there were "few men more . . . able to bear exposure & fatigue, nor do I know any of my present associates that have undergone as much of either in this campaign."[65] Whether he was attempting to test himself or to gain respect is not clear—perhaps some of each. Both were understandable impulses for someone who had spent his whole life "preparing & waiting for the events that have occurred."[66] Healthy self-interest was not only normal in these circumstances; it is hard to imagine that one could perfom as Lee did without a strong sense of his own capabilities. What is more intriguing is the resentment he held against those who had received similar recognition for what he considered lesser feats, and the way that he simultaneously felt he had to cloak in exaggerated modesty any pride in his accomplishments.

Some of Lee's irritation may have been rooted in the way the army was treated during the last months of the war. He was immensely proud of the "Long Gray Line," and believed their victory validated the whole principle of West Point training. "You say truly this Mexican affair is a glorious thing for West Point . . . ," he told Mackay, comparing it to the quite inglorious beginning of the War of 1812. "Everyone must see the difference between the commencement of the present war & the last, & everyone must acknowledge that this difference is caused by the difference in the officers."[67] Lee's belief that the professional military had been vindicated would ultimately be borne out, but in the last months of the war the army took some final insults. Most of these stemmed from President Polk's continued jealousy of the heroes who had been made in the war. When quarrels broke out among the strong personalities of Generals Pillow, Worth, and Scott, Polk was quick to take the part of his former law partner, Gideon Pillow. He used Pillow's accusations as a pretext to call a court of inquiry and to relieve Scott of command in Mexico City.[68] Lee and his comrades were aghast. Notwithstanding some colorful peccadilloes and unfortunate rash personal actions, they revered Scott's military assiduity and the aplomb with which he had conducted the occupation of Mexico City. To see him not only underappreciated but vilified was shocking. "The treatment which Gen[l] Scott has rec[d] satisfies me what those may expect who have done their duty," Lee snidely remarked to his father-in-law. "It will be better for me to be classed with those who have failed."[69] As the court of inquiry dragged on in humiliating view of the troops, Lee would publicly stand up for Scott, proving to the old general that he was a man of loyalty as well as bravery, and probably sealing the "almost idolatrous fancy" Scott reportedly had for him.[70] The charges would eventually be dropped, as Lee had predicted, but Scott left Mexico with his victorious army demoralized and his commander's flag furled. At his departure officers stood in the street all night with caps over their hearts in a final tribute to the commander Lee had called "head & shoulders above every man" in the army.[71] "As he drove by it was done in silence, neither party being able to speak," Lee told Carter, "& the murmur of prayers for his safety & happiness was all that could be heard."[72]

To make matters worse, the army had been more or less marooned in the Mexican capital while diplomats and politicians fought over a peace treaty. The negotiations dragged on for months, with the Mexicans showing reluctance to accept anything that legitimized the American aggression, and the army in contemptuous disbelief that Washington would not press its advantage. Lee was among those who continued to be ashamed that the United States had "bullied" Mexico, but he was exultant in the "drubbing" her fighting forces had given their neighbors, and was convinced that the Americans were "the conquerors in a regular war & by the laws of nations are entitled to dictate the terms of Peace."[73] The stalemate continued for five tedious months, the soldiers growing cynical as they passed the time. Lee spent his days drawing meticulous maps of the interior fortifications and roads in Mexico, learning a bit of Spanish, and courting some little Mexican girls with wildflowers.[74] Sometimes the officers made excursions into the countryside, and once they were invited to an elegant picnic, cooked by a French caterer, by the side of a ruined monastery.[75] They formed a drinking and dining society called the Aztec Club, and there Lee mingled with Lieutenants Beauregard, McClellan, and Grant and Captains Joseph Hooker, Phil Kearny, and J. B. Magruder. But as the days wore on, he became increasingly despondent. Captain Magruder remembered that he declined to attend a dinner even when his health was being proposed, preferring to remain in drudgery at his desktop.[76] Homesick, disillusioned, and bored, Lee's thinking about the value of his service began to alter. "I confess there is a change in my feelings now & I should be very happy if I could leave the country tomorrow without dishonour. Judging from the feelings of my acquaintances, there would be a slim army left, if they could get away."[77]

The Mexican War has sometimes been portrayed as a rehearsal for the greater conflict that would commence a dozen years later. This it was not, for in scale and emotion, divisiveness, armaments, mobilization, duration, and consequence it did not begin to compare. In 1847 casualties were counted in hundreds and the enemy was a remote, foreign population; no one could have imagined the slaughter and the sorrow of a true civil war. Nonetheless it was a pivotal experience for many who would participate in both wars, including Robert E. Lee, and it marked the beginning of a kind of combat that would be repeated by many generations of Americans.

We can only speculate on all that Lee may have internalized during his time in Mexico. In basic terms he had a true experience of war. This was no West Point blackboard exercise but warfare in all its tumultuousness—its smoke and noise and fear, and its exhilaration. He was a definitive player in the drama, providing strategies, picking tactical positions, close to the most powerful voices, indeed a voice in his own right.[78] This must have been a heady experience for a genteel thirty-nine-year-old engineer, and it is clear that Lee excelled at this game of wits and the interplay of personalities. If this was war, he liked it. The outfoxing and derring-do seemed to fit some need to surpass others that was part of his character.

He also learned that war is not really glamorous, but tedious and uncomfortable and tragic. The fundamental duality of combat—the intermingling of glory and gore—can never truly be separated, yet often it is, in the strange compartmentalization of memory. The Mexican War was among the most gruesome on record. Eighteen-pound shot tore soldiers to pieces, almost no medical services were available, and, as an officer on Scott's staff recorded, the fields were "scenes of terror." E. Kirby Smith and other of Lee's colleagues described piles of partially decomposed bodies thrown in a pit, "the vultures were already at their widespread feast, the wolves howling and fighting over their dreadful meal."[79] Lee's own blood was spilled in this conflict: he was wounded in the campaign before Mexico City, and had a near escape when an American soldier fired on him and the bullet singed his shirt.[80] Grace Darling, his favorite horse, was said to have been hit seven or eight times, and her rider cannot have been far away from that target. On her back Lee picked his way through a battlefield littered with bodies, mourning the many who were friends.[81] He came also to know two other tragic realities of war: that a single personal experience of death is far more poignant than the gross impersonality of even the most shocking statistics; and that the mind can become inured to unimaginable suffering and inhumanity when served it in daily doses. The large and small experiences do not always mesh in war, and while Lee could express touching concern about the plight of a single soldier—"I doubt whether all Mexico is worth to us the life of that man"—and would weep with Joe Johnston over the killing of Joe's young nephew, he could still gleefully toast the annihilation of thousands of Santa Anna's men.[82]

Lee also had the important experience of working with General Winfield Scott, whom he held in the highest regard. Through him he experienced the power of effective leadership, the way that a commanding officer not only draws the battle plan but compels it to be realized. Scott had a knack for using staff effectively, something Lee would later try to emulate. His very presence had a calming effect on the troops, yet he was bold and implacable, "a great man on great occasions," keeping to his resolve in the face of doubt; always looking for the way to surmount obstacles, a veritable forerunner of the American "can-do" spirit.[83] *Spirit* was in fact a word he liked, and Lee would learn a great deal about its power in his service. Scott may have loved the adornment of finery and feathers, but it was his presence, his confidence in the troops, and the pride he stimulated that gave them their invincibility. Lee would one day rely on the same ingredients to build an army that sometimes had little to fuel it save esprit.

Scott also gave Lee a chance to learn the art of military maneuver from a master. Scott won with smaller forces on unfamiliar territory by overturning the old belief that the key to victory was to throw massed forces into the enemy, with little but raw courage as a tactic. The tricks he used—superior intelligence based on reconnaissance; striking at the political heart of the enemy; imaginative use of the terrain; surprise; flexibility and agility— would become hallmarks of a new kind of warfare. Scott saw frontal assault as a wasteful use of troops—he thought uncertainty, strong artillery support, and attacking the enemy's most vulnerable spots to be more conducive to triumph, and he preferred the offensive to the defensive. His turning movements were so effective against the naive Mexican army that they became the model for many officers, North and South. He kept the larger picture in mind at all times. As he termed it, "I steadily held to the policy not to wear out patience and sole leather by running to the right or left in pursuit of small game. I played for big stakes."[84] Scott was also wedded to the idea of pursuing the enemy after a victory, and he encouraged his officers to take chances in order to do it. To his mind risk-taking was synonymous with maximizing his advantage. Surely this was reinforced to Lee as he contemplated the daring bombardment at Vera Cruz, the odds-off victory at Cerro Gordo, the seventeen-minute rout at Contreras, and the advantage gained by his own two treacherous trips across the Pedregal. That being said, Scott had a strong understanding of the importance of fortification during an advance, and knew that unnecessary exposure should be avoided.[85]

Scott also invented the idea of the generous victor, a principle that still makes Americans proud. There was no international law on occupation— not even a viable model for such—at the time that Scott conquered Vera Cruz, Puebla, and Mexico City. He maintained that he was there not to triumph over a people but to win an enduring peace, and seemed instinctively to understand the importance of keeping the population on his side. He went out of his way to ensure goodwill, paroling prisoners, paying for supplies and property, establishing order, and reining in his troops. He even attended Catholic mass, something that many Americans found anathema in those nonecumenical days, and once was unwittingly caught up, along with Captain Lee, in a large religious procession. "No officer and no man, under my orders, shall be allowed to dishonor me, the army & the U. States," Scott insisted. From Appomattox to World War II, his legatees remembered the principle, overturning the tradition of brutality by victorious armies.[86]

Unfortunately, Winfield Scott did not have the same enlightened instinct about his relationship to the Washington power structure, which, in a democracy, controlled the activities of the army. He had not believed in the righteousness of the war and disliked putting his troops into battle for crass political ends. In the process of forming his novel strategy he created head-on collisions with the president, the Congress, and the press, all of whom were only too willing to sacrifice him when he threatened their authority. As a result he was "fired upon from his rear," which hindered him and temporarily spoiled the great military achievements of the campaign.[87] Captain Lee and his other subordinates were disgusted by the treatment of Scott, but could not have failed to take away some salient lessons about the wisdom of confrontation with a strong commander in chief. Joe Johnston did not take the point as well as he might have, and fifteen years later would find himself similarly thwarted by a headstrong Jefferson Davis, who himself watched Scott's little dramas from the staff of Zachary Taylor. Lee took it in and reinforced his nonconfrontational inclinations.[88]

The Mexican campaign also solidified Lee's relationships within the regular army. It was the first time that officers from all of the branches of the service—engineers and infantry, cavalry and artillery—pulled together on one grand mission. This had been their great moment, indeed Lee's great moment, and in later years, when war came to mean something less triumphal, Lee and the other veterans still took pleasure in recalling the exploits of this first conflict. The army's achievement not only stimulated pride—it gave Lee important insights into the interplay of the various units, as well as the personalities of individual colleagues, and how they reacted to privation and stress. It also brought Lee into contact for the first time with volunteer foot soldiers, so many of whom were to fight under him in the Civil War. Officers like McClellan might scorn the "mustang" soldiers, but the Mexican War actually proved that Calhoun's theory of an "expandable" army—one that coupled trained professionals with enthusiastic citizen soldiers—could be highly effective.[89] Lee probably knew well only a handful of men whom he would later meet on the battlefield—Johnston, Gustavus Smith, McClellan, and Beauregard—but he had the opportunity to observe many more and to understand the kind of men who excelled under pressure. Grant was among those who appreciated the knowledge of character he had picked up during the Mexican War. He used Lee as an example of someone who had lost his mystique through shared experience on the ground. By the time of the Civil War, Grant drily observed, many people had clothed Lee with superhuman qualities: "but I had known him personally, and knew that he was mortal; and it was just as well that I felt this."[90]

There were also things that Lee did not learn in Mexico. Armaments had begun to change at this time, though it was a transitional period. Smoothbore muskets had not yet given way to the more precise and longer-range rifles that would alter the battlefield landscape from 1861 to 1865. From his engineering vantage point Lee did not have close exposure to the developments in ordnance that would make it such a critical factor over the next few years. Nor did Lee truly lead men in the Mexican War. He was adept at guiding forces over roads he had constructed, but the command of large-scale movements was not part of his job in this conflict. In fact, he never had full responsibility for any field force, and supervised only a handful of junior men. Neither did he learn what it was to lose a battle or order a retreat. Scott's string of successes was so bright that the only dim moment—at Molino del Rey near Mexico City—came when faulty intelligence made the cost of that victory questionable.

On May 25, 1848, the Mexican Senate finally ratified the Treaty of Guadalupe Hidalgo, and after twenty eventful months, Lee began his plans to return home. By the terms of the treaty the United States was given clear title to Texas, California, and most of what is today Arizona, New Mexico, Nevada, and Utah, as well as portions of Colorado and Wyoming.[91] With this, and his settlement on the Oregon Territory, Polk had kept his promise of nearly doubling the size of the United States. Mexico was paid $15 million, plus $5 million to settle war claims. Lee thought the terms just, but, like others, noted that many lives might have been saved had the purchase simply been made from the outset.[92] In early June he boarded a steamer with Grace Darling, a dog, and his Irish servant, impatient to get up the long Mississippi. He reached Arlington a few weeks later. Able at last to tell his brother of his safe return, he penned a sentimental note.

Here I am once again, my dear Smith, perfectly surrounded by Mary and her precious children, who seem to devote themselves to staring at the furrows in my face and the white hairs in my head. It is not surprising that I am hardly recognisable to some of the young eyes around me and perfectly unknown to the youngest. . . . I find them, too, much grown and all well, and I have much cause for thankfulness, and gratitude to the good God who has once more united us.[93]

Chapter Eleven

Crenellations

Old Point, Nov. 3, 1831

Give me a post-master for a correspondent, I say. J. Mackay, P.M. That takes my eye. 2 pleasures at once. A letter from the friend, which I love above all things, and if there is another, a perfect martyr to this system of exercise, and it has eaten more of the linings of my waist-coat pocket than "moth and rust." My child, look a little to that lung of yours, and put hay in your boots. It is a kind of provender that suits well any clime that I have been in, and your Southern Market is I believe peculiarly adapted to it. There is an air about a well-feathered nest that nothing can attain to. For it may be said to pull the very stroke-oar of pleasure, or draw the near-wheel of contentment. Oh, by the Gods! Whiskers and moustaches!! . . . It is the essence of strange and unexpected things. I should as soon expect my nose to be white, as you to present so hirsute an appearance. What a producing country that must be on the Mississippi! The atmosphere is certainly saturated with Macassar oil, and combs and brushes the growth of the land.

But, stop, I have something that will strike your ear sweeter than the notes of a flute, or have you heard that your company is to be ordered back to Savannah? God grant that it may be true, for sweet Miss Mary Anderson, who is now in New York, wrote me word that Col. Mercer told her so himself. This is my only authority, nor can I obtain corroboration of the intelligence (which is, I fear, almost too good to be true) though I have been on the qui vive to reduce it to a certainty every since. However we are now in such a military community that a man would not be able to learn whether his throat was to be cut or not. I will explain to you my friend, for I see that thou hast already drawn thyself up in an attitude of curiosity. Hast thou yet to be told that the Artillery School of Practice has been reviewed at this same post, Col. Eustis commanding? And that there are ten comp^{ys} stationed here. Five of the 1st, three of the 3rd, and two of the 4th Artillery? It is even so, Jack Mackay, and Mackays and Frasiers from

Boston, Lyons from New London and Munroes and Gatts from Governor's island are the very ones. So that I have my Joe, even Jos. Johnston with me again,
and Bradford, and Bob Temple, and Gustave Brown (who was the sergeant of
the guard that night in camp) and others, not to mention the old set.

Will you believe me? Tom has been here. I espied his long frame, marching
by the side of a Company across the plains early one morning. The poor devils
of Sub[altern]s are drilled off their feet. They commence at sunrise and drill till
half past eight. When the guard beats for guard mounting, the ones detailed for
guard of course needs be in readiness breakfast and all on time. At nine if the
guard is turned off, the officers must be at their companies and wait—mark me
child—wait Col. Worth's arrival. At ten the drill commences and lasts until
twelve, and at half past three it again commences, and continues till Parade.
And at Tattoo an officer must be present at Roll Call. This is what Dick calls a
short synopsis of the day. The Officer of the Guard is not allowed to leave the
Guard House, his meals are sent to him.

Hugh Mercer came down to see us but was alarmed at proceedings, and
only stayed two days. He left here about ten days ago, was going to New York,
West Point &c, to knock about until the expiration of his furlough, 1st of December. He looks remarkably well, and rails at fortune. I hope he will meet with
the Misses A. at the North. Joe saw Jim Z. at New York. He had been quite sick
and obtained a furlough. He looked badly but was in good spirits. His constant
companion was that phial of Texas whiskey, hermetically sealed to celebrate his
meeting with Dick T. whenever that should take place. Dick left yesterday cursing the whole command for not letting him go a week ago, when he might have
been present at the races on the Central Course. You will see by the papers what
a grand affair they have had this season.—Eclipse took the money.

To John Mackay
     U.S. Artillery
          Fort Jackson
               Louisiana[1]

· · ·

Fort Hamilton
17 June 1845

Col Jos G. Totten
Chief Enginner

Sir

I have rec^d your Circular of the 28th ulto: inquiring whether in case of an increase of the mil establishment at the next Sess. of Cong. I would desire a transfer to the new forces with promotion.

In the event of war with any foreign government I should desire to be brought into active service in the field with as high a rank in the regular army as I could obtain, & if that could not be accomplished without leaving the corps of Engineers, I should then desire a transfer to some other branch of the Service, & would prefer the Artillery. I would however accept no situation under the rank of field officer.

Very resp^y &c^2

. . .

Fort Carroll
20 Augt 1852

Genl: Jos. G. Totten
Chief Engineer
Washington City U.S.

Sir

I have transferred to Lt. W. H. C. Whiting in obedience to your orders, till the arrival of Capt. H. Brewerton, the charge of operations at this place; & have turned over to him all the funds in my hands, together with all the public property of every description belonging to the same.

I shall in further, complying with your orders, present on Monday next the 23d visit to West Point & be prepared to relieve Capt. Brewerton of the Sup^r of the Mil. Academy on the 1st Sept.

It may be satisfactory to you to know that the sea wall on Front 1 has been brought up to low water level, 14 feet high. That not more than one & a half courses of Stones are required on Front 2, to prepare it for the leveling course, which will bring it to the same height. The three bottom courses of stone are laid on Front 3, about one fourth the length of that face.

The foundation piles on the remainder of that Face, are driven, punched down, & sawed off, & the machinery placed on Front 4, ready to commence driving on that Front. About 40 feet of the sea wall on Front 6, adjoining Front 1 has also been brought up to low water level. The filling of the coffer work on Front 1 with concrete has been successfully commenced & sixty feet in length completed.

A tremie of boiler iron has been constructed for the purpose, which operates perfectly satisfactorily, economically & conveniently. There is nothing required for the rapid progress of the work in all its parts, but a sufficient app^r by Congress.

I am very resp^y. Your obd^t Ser
RE Lee B^t Col
Capt Eng^rs.^3

⊱⊶⊙⊷⊰

CRENELLATION was a common word in Robert E. Lee's vocabulary. It refers to a defensive wall with intermittent spaces for lookouts or guns, and is most familiar as the toothed upper level of a castle. Lee would have seen the image of just such a fortress every day, for it was—and still is—the symbol of the Army Corps of Engineers. He would have drawn them by the

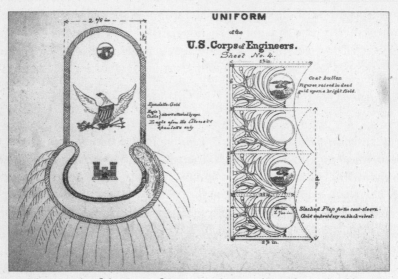

The insignia of the Corps of Engineers, showing the castle as its emblem.
NATIONAL ARCHIVES

dozens in the years when he designed and built defensive fortifications, and worn the insignia on shoulder straps and belt buckles and epaulettes. He also knew the uneven life that came with this association. As these letters indicate, for thirty-four years his world was made up of congressional frustrations and unattainable promotions; bantering camaraderie; boredom and drinking in the garrison; pile drivers, stone foundations, insufficient pay, and the misery of undesirable orders. In many ways the army was his home, the place he grew intellectually and experienced the pleasures of professional collegiality. The scientific training and rigorous military discipline he absorbed there became a fundamental part of his character. But the army was also a burdensome commitment that competed with his strong parental love and his longing for permanent roots in Virginia. Lee never resolved the conflict presented by these opposing loyalties, and he spent years trying to find a solution that would accommodate both. In the end it would take a national calamity to force the choice.

The army Robert Lee entered as a second lieutenant was small and controversial. Except for the brief period of the Mexican War, Congress kept it fluctuating between six and ten thousand men until the late 1850s, despite the fact that the nation's population tripled each decade. The form and nature of the military also continued to generate sharp debate, despite its acknowledged contributions to internal transportation and the protection of white settlers. Some thought any national institution threatened a dangerous centralization of power. Militiamen saw it as an unwelcome challenge to their right to self-protection.[4] Ambitious entrepreneurs loudly objected to the expenditure of citizens' money on a skilled cadre that might supplant local businesses. A populist newspaper, the *Missouri Daily Argus,* had taken just this stand against Lee's navigational improvements on the Mississippi in 1839.[5] General Winfield Scott remarked in exasperation that any lobbying the army did seemed to backfire, giving military leaders the image of "mendicants at the Treasury . . . odious in the eyes of their fellow citizens."[6] Others felt that West Point graduates constituted an intolerable elite, a throwback to the armed feudal classes. The wife of Jefferson Davis recalled how demagogues railed against the officers, calling them "military dandies," "toy soldiers," and "other choice epithets such critics have always in store."[7]

The regular officers did sometimes seem out of place in the wilderness garrisons that made up most of the early postings. Groomed and educated to an exacting standard, they found themselves among rough frontiersmen— thrown out, as one put it, "as a barrier against barbarism."[8] The officers also contrasted sharply with the rank and file, who were recruited from newly arrived immigrants and the itinerant orders of American society. The years of solving elegant mathematical problems and stepping in precision drill at West Point had little application in these environs; nor did many taste the excitement of war until the conflict with Mexico began in 1846.[9] Isolation and deprivation were often their lot, and for much of the early nineteenth century the army was little more than a well-armed constabulary. Some West Pointers felt that exercises such as maintaining peace between natives and settlers or patrolling the borders were futile, and boring to boot. "I am suffocating physically, morally and intellectually," wrote an officer who served with Lee in Texas, "in every way I am fairly gasping for fresh outside air and feel . . . like begging to be taken out and hung for the sake of variety."[10] The monotony of garrison life was broken in some colorful ways— chasing wolves as if at a foxhunt, shooting buffalo and roasting their tongues, or training horses to fight each other in specially constructed barns.[11] However, most of the officers escaped through the gaming and drinking that were a part of every fort. Lee was no teetotaler, and he rarely exhibited a judgmental manner when teasing compatriots about their excessive mint juleps, but privately he regretted the dissipating effects garrison life had on his fellow officers. "It is *impossible* for me to comprehend," he wrote sadly of one fellow officer, who though intelligent and good-looking was intent upon appearing drunk at parade. And a few years later: "I have seen minds, formed for use & ornament, degenerate into sluggishness & inactivity, requiring the stimulus of Brandy or cards to rouse them to action."[12]

One of the compensations for this life of sacrifice was the high degree of comradeship among the officers. Powerful ties were formed during the challenging years at West Point, but some thought that it was in the harshness of active duty that the real attachments developed.[13] The military was a distinct all-male world of strong physicality, where the measure of a man was calculated by deeds and accomplishments, and where there was opportunity for the masculine bonding that Lee clearly valued.[14] His friends were chosen from the same crowd he had enjoyed at West Point—largely Southerners whose academic achievement mirrored his own, and who reciprocated his high regard. Jack Mackay, who loved Shakespeare and fishing and had a dog named Fang, remained Lee's closest friend.[15] As a young man Lee also spent a great deal of time with Joe Johnston, whose career path paralleled his own, and with whom he liked to "prowl around" the garrison, looking for late-night chatter. Except for the prized relationships with his cousins, army connections were the strongest of his life, and Lee never underestimated their importance. "You have often heard me say the cordiality and friendship in the army was the great attraction of the service," he told his wife during one of many ruminations about whether or not to retain his commission. "It is that, I believe that has kept me in it so long, and that which now makes me fear to leave it. I do not know where I should meet with so much friendship out of it."[16]

Robert Lee was a fine colleague throughout his career and was remembered with affection at every rank, even by those who would become his bitterest enemies. Erasmus Keyes, who knew him before the Mexican War, wrote that "although I subsequently met General Lee on several fields of battle, and did my best to kill him . . . yet every palpitation of my heart has been of kindness for him and his, and will be till the end of his life."[17] He was responsible, dedicated, and loyal, but Lee's secret asset seems to have been his lack of pretension. For all his achievement and natural dignity, he was unassuming, given to irreverent joking and harmless high jinks. His nephew Fitzhugh Lee left a delightful image of him riding his horse home one evening in Washington. A fellow officer jumped on behind him, and "the two gaily rode along the great public avenue . . . passing by the President's house, bowing to Cabinet officers, and behaving in a rather hilarious way generally."[18] He wrote wonderful letters to his companions, full of amusing asides and saucy remarks about their flirtations. "Here is our J E Johnston, who has been lately accused of *Blushing*," he wickedly reported to "Delectable Jack," then taunted him as well: "Miss Teaco . . . inquired after *you* Mackay & said a great many pretty things about you, that my modesty forbids me to retell."[19] Lee curbed his irreverence in later years, but never lost his touch for professional companionship.

Lee's letters to army colleagues are as sympathetic and quick to applaud hard-earned success as they are full of witty banter. Rarely does he show any overt competition or indulge in malicious gossip. Interestingly, neither does he often extend himself professionally for his friends. Keyes was one of the few who recalled that Lee had spoken to General Scott on his behalf about a coveted position, and occasionally there are allusions to Lee's intervention for Mackay on some army matter.[20] In general, however, Lee avoided involvement in the affairs of his colleagues. When Dr. William Beaumont ran afoul of the new policies of Surgeon General Thomas Lawson, which interfered with his research and private practice, Lee declined to take up Beaumont's case in Washington. Hiding his reluctance behind some noble-sounding words about the injury his "obtrusive interference" might cause, Lee left it to Ethan Allen Hitchcock to protect the celebrated physician. Despite Hitchcock's spirited defense, Beaumont was ultimately forced out of the army.[21] Lee declined to recommend an officer whose conduct in the Mexican War he had praised because it might be considered "obsessive or out of place," and he refused another because his support would be "of no assistance."[22] In the late 1850s Albert Sidney Johnston's wife recorded in her diary that Lee would not testify on behalf of a close colleague during a court-martial called to defend his character. "He humed and ha'd and at last said . . . he had not observed him particularly and finally left for Clear Fork, a mean act in my opinion when he knows the mans reputation as well as he does."[23] He was more active on behalf of family members, gaining West Point appointments for son Custis and a Lee cousin, and trying to persuade Jefferson Davis, a senator at the time, to get his brother-in-law appointed U.S. district attorney.[24] Even among his relatives, however, he often balked at actively advancing their interests. He repeatedly avoided doing favors for his brother Carter, finally having to admit to him his "entire failure in executing your commissions."[25] Lee also failed—this time disastrously—to follow through on a commitment he had made to be executor for his uncle Bernard Carter, who had not only done that duty for his mother, but had befriended him in his youth. Lee told his ailing uncle that he would undertake the service, but when death arrived he spent considerable effort wriggling out of the obligation, again trying to justify his actions in terms of highest integrity, stating that he did so from the belief that he should be doing his cousins "an injury by accepting." After Lee stepped aside, the will was tied up in acrimonious legal battles for years.[26] It may be that Lee was a better companion than he was a friend.

Robert Lee's army correspondence not only shows his light hand at conversation, it reveals his cynicism about politicians and their role in military affairs. In addition to dispensing gossip among his colleagues, he liked to disparage the political scene in mock confidentiality. During the 1834 congressional session, which debated whether the Bank of the United States ought to transfer its funds to the states, he told Mackay that nothing was discussed in Washington except "Bank, Bank, Deposites, Deposites, speeches, Memorials, wrangling & quarelling & *doubling of fists*—very gay."[27] He referred to politicians as "the Turks & *Haethens*" and decried anyone's ability to "tell what Cong. will do for the plain reason that they do not know themselves."[28] As he scoffed at the legislature, however, Lee also seriously followed the progress of each session's army appropriations and regulation changes. He knew where every bill stood, assessed his chances for promotion if the legislation went through, and encouraged his fellow officers to pay attention to the fine points.[29] In 1844, when Eliza Mackay Stiles's husband was elected to Congress, Lee became an unofficial adviser on the current army bill. He was unsuccessful in his lobbying effort, but retained his interest in political machinations.[30] When isolated on the Texas prairies just before the Civil War, he persuaded his children to run a veritable clipping service for him. "If you see any items in the papers, about the Army, war, troops or matters of interest, clip them out & enclose them in your letters," he suggested.[31]

We have few clues to Lee's political leanings before the war. We do not know how he voted, or even whether he ever spoke his choice, as was the Virginia viva voce custom. The only property he owned—a prerequisite for voting in Virginia, where polls were conducted locally—was in the western reaches of the Old Dominion. There is no record of his participation in party politics, and when Lee wrote assessments of frontier rallies in St. Louis, or key cabinet appointments, he styled them as an observer, disdaining any

partisan fervor. "I forget I never mention Politics," he once wrote to Mackay
after giving a long litany of complaints, "thinking that you see all the *Slang-
whang* in the papers, & care & believe as much as I do." Nor were regular officers encouraged to participate politically—their job was to carry out the
will of the government, not to design the policies. It has been assumed from
the activism of his father and father-in-law, and the long veneration his
family held for Federalist views, that Lee was a Whig until around 1850,
when he clearly began to sympathize with the Democratic Party, which reflected southern priorities on slavery and states' rights.[32] But if all politics is
local, Lee's foremost concern was for the parochial interests of the army, its
troop movements, transfers, and personalities, and how Congress and the
popular will would influence its evolution. These issues affected him personally; they had curtailed the work he began near St. Louis, and he would
be similarly handicapped by insufficient funding in later postings. Even
generous-spirited Lee could not always rise above jealousy and gossip on
these subjects. When one set of officers received news that their temporary
"brevet" ranks had been formalized, Lee cattily remarked that he had gone
along to express his congratulations and that the whole ceremony was "a
complete Farce . . . by far better than *Othello*. . . . Because the *acting* was
real."[33] Therein is contained the secret of Lee's interest in those army bills.
They held the key to promotion—and promotion was a sensitive subject.

Part of the debate about the way a professional military should be constituted was the nature of its officers' rights—how they were to be paid, and
whether promotions should be political or generated from within. The
American public's skepticism about the value of the army meant that for
most of its first half century compensation and promotion were completely
unpredictable. The number of positions at each rank was regulated by law,
and the only way to move up was to fill a slot that had been vacated. Since
there were no annuities, no one left the service. "Few retire and none die,"
was a common lament, and with each congressional session army regulars
hoped the number of positions would be increased, or ways would be found
to muster out the old warriors, some of whom were in their eighties.[34] Rarely
did this happen, and year after year the disappointment resounded. "Oh we
have been horribly shamefully treated . . . ," Lee wrote in 1836, when it
looked as though no promotions were going to be coming through. "In fact
I am in *dis-g-u-s-t*."[35] When openings did occur, they were filled by seniority,
something generally accepted in the corps, but unlikely to inspire the pursuit of excellence among younger officers.[36] The result was a system of
painfully slow promotions with no expectation of advancement based on
merit. Roger Jones, who was adjutant general to Secretary of War Lewis

Cass, made a "conjectural calculation" that it would probably take a newly minted second lieutenant fifty-eight years to attain the rank of colonel.[37] This was an exaggeration, but it felt accurate to those waiting to move up. The situation was relieved somewhat by the lobbying of General Scott, who well realized he could never command the loyalty of career officers if they felt underappreciated, and by the brevet system, whereby honorary promotions were given for unusual valor. The latter carried with it some perquisites in the form of larger rations and the use of a title, and was widely employed during the Mexican War. Though brevets took the place of medals, which were nonexistent at the time, they were never more than a species of quasi-rank, and a quasi-solution to the problem of career advancement.[38]

It took Robert E. Lee close to thirty-two years to rise from West Point graduate to full colonel. From Roger Jones's point of view this may have been a near meteoric rise, yet much has been written about the slow pace of Lee's career. Comparing his record with others who graduated around this time shows him to be just a little ahead of the average. Exact correlations are not easy, because Lee was the only man in his class to pursue a lifetime career in the Corps of Engineers, where promotions were governed by different legislation and were often slower than those in the artillery or infantry. He was behind several of his classmates in promotion to first lieutenant, waiting, for example, seven years to Mackay's four and a half, then got a nice push forward when, two years later, Congress voted to enlarge the army and he was made captain on the same day as the "Delectable Jack." Then for eight long years he languished. During the Mexican War Lee was awarded two brevet promotions for gallantry, but he was given no formal increase in rank until 1855, when Secretary of War Jefferson Davis offered him the lieutenant colonelcy of the 2nd Cavalry, vaulting him over the rank of major and several senior officers in the process. That promotion, his big break, came only with the creation of two new cavalry regiments, and the price was leaving the Engineers and virtual exile from his family. In March 1861 Abraham Lincoln made him a full colonel, in hopes that he would remain with the Federal forces. Lee resigned three weeks later.[39]

Lee cared about promotion, cared a good deal about it in fact, both because he thought the whole system unfair and because the only way to increase his salary was to elevate his rank. As a young officer he frequently had money worries. When contemplating marriage in 1830, he told his brother that his pay was "barely sufficient for one, much less for two," and a few years later he was still complaining that "money is a scarce article with your 2nd

Lt."[40] A decade later, when Congress cut salaries, the situation had grown acute. "I was never poorer in my life," he lamented, "& for the first time I have not been able to pay my debts."[41] Even with his financial woes, he did not like to court political favor to gain promotion, as did many young officers. Joe Johnston was one of these; Lee good-humoredly tolerated his self-promotional activities, but could not bring himself to emulate them, even when he saw how Johnston succeeded.[42] Lee's ambition may have also been undermined by the actions of his superiors, which were often unfortunate. His first boss was the unspeakable Major Samuel Babcock, who augmented his shaky engineering skills by arriving at his post "stupefied with drink," abused his wife, and undervalued his bright lieutenant.[43] His first mentor, Captain Andrew Talcott, left the army to work as a corporate engineer before he could do much to advance Lee's interests. Chief Engineer Charles Gratiot, whom Lee had called "so able a friend and one to whom I was so much attached," ran afoul of the government in 1839 when he unofficially "repaid" himself some money he believed he was owed. Winfield Scott, a roaring lion of a general, had grudges, intrigues, or outright battles with everyone from his courier to the president of the United States. Lee was extremely loyal to these men, and these associations may have caused him collateral damage.[44]

The most Lee could do was to insert himself forthrightly whenever he saw a possible opening. His 1845 letter to the new chief engineer, Joseph Totten, is quite straightforward: if a field corps was to be created, he would leave the Engineers if it would mean a promotion. A few years later he tried to get a friend in the Washington Bureau to recommend him for anything above his official rank of captain.[45] Though for decades he impatiently dismissed his wife's ambitions for him, and avoided interference by his other relatives, finally in 1856, depressed by the realities of his cavalry post, he told Mary that if "anything should turn up in the way of promotion, ask your father if suitable & proper to apply in my behalf."[46] He had his eye on the quartermaster or inspector general's offices, both of which carried the rank of brigadier general, and went so far as to let some concerned citizens, including Governor Henry Wise of Virginia, send a petition in his favor. Again it was not to be. Joe Johnston, who had lobbied aggressively for his brevet ranks to be regularized, and who had curried favor with John Floyd, the current secretary of war, leapfrogged over him for the quartermaster general post. It was one time that Lee had to swallow hard to accept a comrade's good fortune. He had told his wife "not to worry about the Brigadier," but to his son he confided that Johnston had "been advanced beyond any one in the Army & has thrown more discredit than ever on the system of favoritism and making brevets."[47]

Uncertain advancement, interrupted projects, scheming colleagues, financial disadvantage, and what Robert Lee called "the everchanging & tempestuous life" of the regular army all created a painful ambivalence about his career choice.[48] He was not alone in this; in some years army desertions ran as high as one-third of the regular ranks, and the service bled officers as well, particularly in the 1830s, when there were abundant opportunities in the private sector. In 1837, the peak year of this exodus, 117 officers—99 of them West Pointers—resigned, and in Lee's class of 46, only 14 officers stayed in the service more than twenty years.[49] As early as 1834 Lee began feeling that his situation was "worse than being sold to the Dutch for I belong to *Uncle Sam*," and for the next twenty-five years the agonized soul-searching continued.[50] He contemplated following the example of Talcott and Johnston, who had entered civil sector engineering, but failed to take any concrete steps to achieve it: "I am waiting, looking and hoping, for some good opportunity to bid an affectionate farewell to my dear Uncle Sam. And I seem to think that said opportunity is to drop in my lap like a ripe pear, for d—d a stir have I made in the matter."[51] The ripe pear did not drop, and he ruefully admitted that one of the reasons he had remained in the army was that no other opportunity ever presented itself. His family, always hopeful that he would give up the military for country life, increased his doubts. Less than four months after his wedding, his bride, her mother, and the Arlington overseer were already plotting for him to leave the army and take care of the estate. Two years later the family was pushing him to manage their White House plantation on the Pamunkey River.[52] The badgering continued over the years, feeding his defensiveness and his growing guilt about absenting himself from his children. After the anxious years of the Mexican War, everyone joined the chorus. "I wish & pray that he may soon be restored to you . . . & *follow the trade of war no more*," exclaimed Aunt Nelly Custis Lewis.[53] One of the few existing letters from Robert's ebullient brother Smith is also on this theme: "Today's mail brought me a letter from my darling Bob. . . . He seems to grieve over the long separation from his wife & children. . . . I have been think & hoping that he would come in the summer and when we got hold of the old fellow might 'Keep him fast for a time at least—' "[54]

And so the years passed, and Lee's uncertainty increasingly rankled. 1845: "The army in our country is certainly not a desirable profession for any young man who has ability and perseverance to succeed in any other."[55]

1848: "I shall make a strong effort to leave it. My children require more attention than I have ever yet been able to devote to them."[56] 1856: "Unless they give me some position which will enable me to bestow some care upon my family, I feel I shall be obliged to resign."[57] Yet for every resolute assertion there is a corresponding salute to "the kind consideration of my brother officers," to duty, and to the need to support his family and the comfort of a steady income.[58] The Mexican War was a tonic as well, with its excitement, the recognition of his courage, and his pride in the accomplishment of the West Point graduates. The unspoken messages were also there: Lee's intense interest in things military; the romantic ideal of the dashing gentleman soldier, resplendent in gold-laced uniform; his taste for the active life; the change of scenery—and even the escape from family pressures—that the service offered. And so what Lee termed his "halting, vacillating course" continued. "A divided heart I have too long had," he wrote as late as June 1860, "& a divided life too long led. That may be one cause of the small progress I have made on either hand."[59]

Lee's ambivalence toward the army carried over to the engineering work that was his specialty. His first assignment after West Point was to Cockspur Island, off the coast of Savannah, where the task was to locate the site for a fort and construct it on the island's none-too-secure sandy soil. One of the designs that he drew there is considered the original blueprint for what would become Fort Pulaski, but he saw the job as just a series of "little troublesome plans & worse calculations about weight, cost, &c, of Masonry, Lime, sand & such stuff."[60] The following two years he worked on the completion of Fortress Monroe, another coastal defense meant to forestall the kind of destruction the British had inflicted on the country in the War of 1812. Here Lieutenant Lee agonized over the construction of arches, piers, and floor joists that had a way of being carried away by storms.[61] His work on the Mississippi River was the first full-scale operation under his charge, and after this posting he was given responsibility for several other projects. One of these was the upgrade of Fort Hamilton, which protected the harbor and city of New York. During Lee's presence there from 1841 to 1845, he oversaw efforts to waterproof the fort and reinforce its batteries. His letterbooks from this time illustrate the versatility required to manage these early construction sites. From May to November 1842 Lee recorded ordering stone, accounting for funds spent, improving the ventilation of the battery, designing gun skids to keep the artillery in proper position, and chasing a neighbor's cow out of the parade ground.[62] Following the Mexican War, Lee was assigned to oversee construction of a new fort, on an artificial foundation in the midst of Baltimore harbor. This was the Fort Carroll that Lee describes to Chief Engineer Totten in his detailed August 1852 letter. The exacting nature of the work is also evident here, from the careful alignment of the walls to the use of a "tremie"—an apparatus used to lay a cement foundation under water. Lee accompanied his reports with beautiful drawings of

the innovative equipment he used at Fort Carroll, and painstakingly detailed charts to show the exact number of blows—sometimes more than 150—it had taken to drive each foundation pile into the water. What is not as evident is the exasperation of these projects, which, like the river work at St. Louis, took place among gritty conditions of heat, mosquitoes, and mud, were constantly interrupted for lack of funding, and were stymied by the breakdown of equipment.[63]

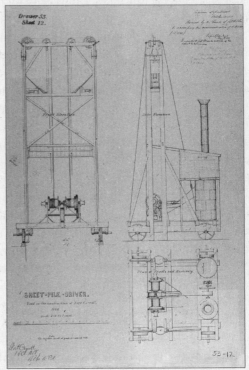

Lee was a competent engineer, and he knew how to do these jobs. As he began laying the underwater foundation at Fort Carroll, he told his son Custis that it was a "work of great trouble," but he saw his way clearly and thought he would "succeed in making as good a wall as if on dry land."[64]

A sheet pile driver used in the construction of Fort Carroll, designed under Lee's direction and signed by him.
NATIONAL ARCHIVES

He gave equally confident instructions on the best way to build a road in the wilderness and how to construct a transport and housing boat for use on the Mississippi. Later in life, when he was at Washington College, he designed the president's house, with a clever ventilation system that is still in use.[65] He was dedicated to these projects and uneasy when they were not complete. He once left a pleasant temporary assignment at West Point because of anxiety about Fort Carroll "inasmuch as it has never progressed to my satisfaction, & which I can endure no longer."[66]

Yet one gets the strong impression that Lee's soul was not wedded to the pursuit of technology. He spoke of himself as an "indifferent engineer" and grumbled continuously about the conditions and tedium of the work. The administrative part of the job, with its endless correspondence to Washington officials, left him in "perfect disgust" at the end of each day, anxious to forget it all by playing with the little Lees. After a particularly troublesome season at Fort Carroll, he would write to Markie Williams: "My thoughts are engrossed in the construction of cranes, Diving bells, Steam Pile drivers &c. . . . If it was not for my heart, Markie, I might as well be a pile of stone myself, laid quietly at the bottom of the river."[67] Lee lacked the imagination and passion of the most talented engineers, and he never rose above a conscientious proficiency in his work. While he was writing earnest descriptions of pile drivings, some of his colleagues were producing the most innovative engineering feats in the world. Chief Engineer Totten, himself a gifted chemist, successfully developed a cement that could withstand the ocean's powerful surf. Robert Parrott, who served with Lee at Fort Monroe, experimented with new kinds of rifles and cannon, and cast and constructed the hull for the first iron steamboat on the Great Lakes. The intrepid Montgomery Meigs, a fine architect as well as technician, was made chief engineer of the Capitol building in the 1850s, shaping the design of the House and Senate wings, the dome, and the acoustics. In 1859 Meigs planned the Washington aqueduct and the splendid Cabin John Bridge, in its day the world's largest stone masonry arch. More pedestrian in his abilities and ambitions, Lee would not reach this level of engineering.[68]

Despite his modest capabilities, the Corps of Engineers had a pronounced effect on Robert E. Lee. During his time it was developing from an experimental group, a mere handful of expert builders, into one of the most progressive agents of change in the nation. Though the physical realities of the work wore him down, in principle Lee liked this goal-oriented vocation, with its controlled risk taking. In the early years engineers also had a great deal of responsibility for their own projects, and this was appealing to a man of independent tastes and habits.[69] In addition, engineering gave him an identity, a prestigious association with men whose training and will to excel equaled his own. He knew it was a select brotherhood, so carefully chosen that for many years West Point did not add a single officer to the corps.[70] Lee was one of twenty-six engineers in the entire army the year he entered, most of them hardworking, high-minded men like himself. These were professionals who understood each other, preventing the kind of intellectual isolation that plagued many southern scientists in the early nineteenth century.[71] Lee appreciated the advantages of such a community and contributed to its vitality both through his correspondence and, on at least one occasion, an attempt to start a corps newsletter.[72] He collected an impressive library of books on engineering, and even after the Civil War was advising on the most useful treatises.[73] Moreover, the mechanical basis of engineering appealed to Lee's tidy, structured mind and reinforced his natural tendency to approach the world in a disciplined and productive fashion. Bright but not brilliant, curious but not questing, Lee had always preferred practical to theoretical science.[74]

Lee's association with engineering had another impact on him, one that may seem surprising: it encouraged him in ideals and assumptions that would today be called "middle class." The 1830s and '40s were a dynamic period, when attitudes were undergoing a profound transformation. The technological revolution helped lead to a growing belief that prosperity and progress were within the reach of all. Many strands of the society came to see potential rather than precedent as the impetus for action. The very work of the engineers was a reflection of a restless nation anxious to be on the move. An emphasis on individual initiative, on education as a basis for upward mobility, on future prospects, and on the invention—or reinvention—of the self all started to appear. Yet the rough-and-tumble of this changeable world left many with a search for predictability, and they sought it in stable employment, in the idealization of domestic pleasures, in child-centric households, and in the virtues of self-discipline. There was also a reaction against those who took too much advantage of the fluid society, and people began to assess each other by the conformity of their dress, their manner, and their speech. The paradox here is fascinating: at an important moment of liberation from preindustrial thought, many sought to standardize social principles in a way that mirrored the new mechanization. At the same time they wanted the chance to take full advantage of the seemingly unlimited prospects of the new era. If they were constrained in their dress and thought, they wanted no restrictions at all on their ambition.[75]

Lee had come from a background that reflected traditional standards of status and success: family lineage, large holdings of land and slaves, hospitality, and public service. To some extent he continued to identify with these patrician values. He once counseled a young colleague, for example, that he should never marry unless he could "do so into a family which will enable your children to feel proud of both sides of the house."[76] Lee's attitudes toward status and race also echoed the world of his forefathers, and it is here that his identification with a ruling class was the strongest. But Light-Horse Harry Lee had shown without a doubt that in America fortune's wheel could turn downward as well as up. The financial disaster and loss of prestige brought about by Lee's father and half brother more or less forced him to make his own way in the world. His relatives had stepped in with a fine-mesh safety net at some critical points, but essentially Lee had had to prove himself by performance. Sylvanus Thayer's adamant refusal to rank cadets on any standard other than achievement was an early reinforcement of this reality, and a foretaste of the meritocracy that Americans increasingly venerated. Lee would echo it during his own superintendence of the academy when he tried to create an inspirational collection in the library that would contain stories of men who had acquired distinction through initiative.[77] It may seem startling to call Lee a self-made man, but even his nephew noted that "no one knew better than he that in a republic . . . a man's ancestry could not help him, but that place and promotion depended on individual merit."[78] Lee had strengthened his ties to the old aristocratic values by wedding Mary Custis, but in assuming the progressive life of an engineer he adopted the future orientation, the belief in advancement, and the credo of duty and discipline that became hallmarks of evolving mainstream thought.

In myriad ways Lee reflected these values. To begin with, he had steady work and earned a predictable wage in a day when most men were still self-employed, often precariously so. However meager it seemed to him, his salary placed him more or less in the middle of the professional range, roughly corresponding to the pay of a top government clerk.[79] Lee's attitudes toward money—which embraced living within his means and saving for his children's education—also tracked with the values of the population at large.[80] Interestingly, the army that gave him this measure of stability also provided him with the mobility—physical and professional—so prized by those navigating the new era. It compelled him to live all over the country, with much of his time being spent in the burgeoning cities of the North and West. Though the formation of the new ideals of work, discipline, and aspiration were not exclusive to these areas—even yeoman farmers of the South embraced them—the attitudes were most clearly forming in places such as St. Louis, Baltimore, and New York, where Lee passed more than a decade of his career.[81] The necessity of separation from his family sparked a corresponding idealization of the domestic hearth and fueled the ambivalence Lee felt about continuing his military career.[82] He cared a great deal for proper dress and meeting expected social standards, was himself fastidious at all times, and showed frustration and even anger at his wife's slovenliness. When the establishment of a parlor became the way to show material success and respectability, Lee personally had such a room put together at Arlington.[83] Though it is hard to imagine that he ever read one of the manuals of deportment so popular during the era, he intimately understood the uses of politesse in an uncertain world, and personally embodied the rules of gentility and sincerity preached by these books. Lee had so internalized the popular principles of self-restraint, hard work, and perseverance that he was given to proselytizing on their virtues and by the end of his life had become more than a little strident on the subject.[84] Perhaps most tellingly, when he inherited some valuable land from his family, he chose not to tie himself to the old concepts of seignorial patrimony, but to sell the property and buy bonds and railroad stock.[85]

All of these attitudes and more placed Lee in the ranks of the professional classes, who had to work, but not with their hands, and who sought approbation from society while they looked for ways to advance. If he ever showed any consciousness of this "middle class" association, he does not mention the fact. But he must have been aware that his outlook differed from that of his wife, father-in-law, and two eldest brothers. George Washington Parke Custis and his daughter, with their huge landholdings and their association with Mount Vernon, *were* aristocracy: there was no one in the country with a higher status than those who were connected to the first president. They had nothing to prove, and cared little about outward trappings for the sake of conforming to societal expectations. G. W. P. Custis was charming but undirected, passing over responsible management of his estates to indulge his changeable temperament and artistic hobbies. Mary Custis Lee was gracious and intelligent, but said, did, and wore exactly what she pleased. Popular concepts of standardized behavior or self-denial had no resonance with her. Interestingly, Robert Lee's two eldest brothers, who had experienced the balmier days at Stratford, were also carefree dilettantes, living in a world they had lost, unapologetic for their outsize schemes or personal misfortunes. Robert and Smith, who experienced less of Light-Horse Harry directly and more of his aftermath, seem to have felt that they existed somewhat precariously in society, that they needed to be all things to all people to maintain a good reputation. This may be one explanation of Robert Lee's propensity for elaborate explanations whenever he tried to disentangle himself from responsibilities to his friends and family. Mary Lee involved herself when and where she liked, without apology. Her husband took care to make lengthy excuses, all of which were designed to show him in a respectable light.

The three letters that open this chapter might at first glance seem easy for a historian to pass over, yet they are a distillation of Robert E. Lee's professional personality, an extract of his bonhomie, his uninspired diligence, his frustrated ambition. Lee's education and experience as an army engineer would have a pronounced imprint on his personal thought as well as his approach to soldiering. The technological culture's emphasis on facts, on exactitude, on anticipation of pressures and weaknesses and the measures needed to fortify them, encouraged the sometimes formulaic approach he had to child-rearing, cadet-educating, and God-fearing. At the same time, engineering led him to appreciate innovation—to honor what had gone before, but build on past practices and make them his own. These attributes would significantly influence his success in battle, be it at Cerro Gordo or Chancellorsville. To all of these contests he would bring engineering principles—not simply in the sense of accounting for terrain or fortifications—but by planning for the unexpected and juggling a diverse set of variables while creating bold new designs. Moreover, Lee's most tragic moments are to be found when he neglected these scientific lessons. Whether in overzealous admonitions to his children or on the battlefield at Gettysburg, his disappointments would stem from miscalculation, overextension, and unstable buttressing, all violations of engineering's most fundamental principles.

Chapter Twelve

Black-Eyed Fancies

Cockspur, Wednesday 13th, 1831

What a convenient little memory you have got Miss Catherine. 'As I promised'! Do you mean to keep it? Well then I will keep it. Recollect you have been owing me a drawing (And some other things too) for a long time. So you cannot blame me if I take advantage of my good fortune. But if you are particularly anxious to have this one, I will exchange.

I will not distress you any longer Miss C. by the thought of keeping me from my 'soft repose' (of Manner).

So good night and yours truly RE Lee[1]

. . .

Fort Hamilton N.Y.
27 Nov 1845

The tenor of the law my beautiful Jule has wrested from the iron grip of the P.O. your letter of the 11 Inst.

What a blessed memory you have! That trip across the mountains I shall never forget. But take your memory a little farther. Did you not say when you were married it should be to your old Uncle? You can't deny it Juli & as you named your wedding day without mentioning the other party it is clear to my mind that I am to be the happy man! And this is the very day & I am chained to Fort Hamilton! Bound by a chain less yielding than one of iron, every link of which encompasses my heart. It is impossible then for me to be present & you know how disturbing my absence will be to me. Distance however will not prevent my seeing you in all your brightness and beauty nor can the wishes of all present for your future welfare exceed mine in earnestness sincerity or affection. May you enjoy every happiness—be always loved & cherished as now. To none can you be dearer than to your old Uncle.

RE Lee

Mrs. Lee begs me to express her regrets at being unable to accept your invitation & to offer her sincere congratulations & wishes for your happiness.

Miss Julia Gratiot[2]

. . .

Lexington Va: 21 Mar '66

My dear Mrs Chouteau

I have just rec^d your note of the 6 Inst which has been kindly forwarded by Dr Miller. As there is nothing you can ask which I will not grant, so it is with much pleasure that I send the autograph you desire. I also enclose the last photograph of me. I have nine taken in uniform, but they are all alike & tempt me almost to deny myself. Do you recognize your old Uncle? You will ever live in my memory as my "beautiful Jule," and I require nothing to recall you to my recollection. You stand before me now, as you then appeared, in the broad sunlight of youth & joy, undimmed by a single shadow of the intervening years.

I regret very much that I did not see Miss K. Eveleth when in Washington. I wished much to do so, but my stay was very short, (Saturday & Sunday) & time entirely occupied. Besides I am considered such a reprobate that I hesitate to darken the doors of those whom I regard, lest I should bring upon them some disaster. But I hope some day that I may again see you & that your little children may not learn to abhor me.

Praying that the blessing of Heaven may attend you & yours

> *I am with great respect*
> *Most truly yours*
> *RE Lee*

Mrs. Julia G. Chouteau[3]

⤐━◆━○━◆━━◄

Robert Lee spent thousands of hours writing personal letters, but none are more endearing than those he penned to the women he loved. Enormously attached to his wife, he nonetheless carried on a lifelong affair of the heart with ladies young and old. He adored them all: little girls in pantalets; beautiful young cousins with flashing eyes; soft, lavender-clad matrons. As we see in these three brief notes, he is relaxed and playful in their company, by turns saucy, joking, and tender. Nothing—not marriage, or war, or advancing age—kept him from acting the beau. Lee's undisguised interest in pretty women is particularly fascinating given the reticence of his day and his own otherwise reserved nature. Neither prurient nor a prude, he charted a course that was simultaneously safe and daring.

Amid hundreds of conflicting characterizations of Robert E. Lee, there is a single point of unanimity: he was an extraordinarily handsome man. He looked more like a Carter than a Lee, with his mother's dark hair and high coloring and the long, lean build of her brothers and father. Friends remarked on his pleasing animation, "bright eyes," and graceful carriage.[4] The earliest portrait we have of him was painted when he was about thirty, and it is a compelling, beautiful image. The artist, William E. West, captured Lee's classic features, but also something more—a wonderful liveliness in the eyes that shines from the canvas.[5] As he matured he became even more attractive, and few met him who did not comment on his impressive physicality. Not only were the features regular and the stature elegant, but "his face lighted up all over in the sunshine of his smile."[6] Even his army brethren were effusive. An officer serving with Lee in Mexico told his wife that he was "in the very prime of manhood, of remarkable presence and address, perhaps the most manly and striking officer in the service, of great grace of manner and great personal beauty."[7]

Lee was aware of his good looks and could be both self-conscious and vain about them. From the time he was sixteen he was his own barber, cutting hair, moustache, and beard with tiny snips each day so that he always looked the same—that is to say, perfect.[8] When he began to grow bald at an early age, he took to combing his wispy side hair up over the exposed forehead, and retained the habit until his death.[9] He was a bit of a dandy—he cared about fashion, and his portraits over the years show him sporting George IV curls, bushy sideburns, a matinee-idol moustache, and the war-era beard as soon as they came into style.[10] One of his most fascinating pictures is a postwar group shot of old heroes and northern tycoons, in which he wears a four-in-hand tie, the latest fashion.[11] Some of his friends teased him about this, "abusing" him, for example, when he showed up with long side whiskers as soon as they came into vogue.[12] But none of it ever seems to have gone to his head, perhaps because, good-looking as he was, he was not considered the handsomest of his family. That prize went to luscious, laughing Smith, who was described as having the "interesting character of an Adonis" and whose picture was in such demand that brother Carter considered selling copies to the local girls.[13] During the Civil War, catty Mary Chesnut wrote two lengthy diary entries on Smith Lee's superior looks.[14] Robert was perfectly aware of Smith's appeal and in his fifties would sigh that "no charming women have insisted on taking care of me, as they are always doing of him."[15]

Robert may have honed his social skills in compensation, for his arresting presence was enhanced by an unassuming, affable personality that itself was captivating. At West Point they recalled his fondness for witty conversation and self-deprecating stories, and even in the midst of war's tribulations a newspaper reporter stated that "when he smiles, and on the still rarer occasions when he laughs heartily, disclosing a fine unbroken row of white, firm set teeth, the confidence and sympathy which he inspires are irresistible."[16] One of the most delightful accounts of Lee's companionable nature was written by his friend Hugh Mercer, who had run into him on the streets of Savannah in 1849, and excitedly told his wife: "Bob Lee . . . looks remarkably well, and as young as ever he did, except that his hair is getting pretty well grizzled—I do not find him at all changed—he runs on just as he used to do—he made me laugh very heartily at some of his stories and laughed himself until the tears ran down his face."[17] As neighbor Elizabeth Lomax could attest, he was "handsome, yes, but not like marble. Colonel Lee is very human. . . ."[18]

Lee as he appeared in the 1850s. The photograph was taken by Mathew Brady.

ARLINGTON HOUSE, THE ROBERT E. LEE
MEMORIAL, NATIONAL PARK SERVICE

The ladies noticed Lee, and he was definitely looking back. "I have met them in no place, in no garb, in no situation that I did not feel my heart open to them like, like the flower to the sun," he wrote while praising the girls of St. Louis to his buddy Jack Mackay.[19] He became enamored of Mackay's five sisters on his first posting near their hometown of Savannah, and it was hard to tell whether he was more smitten by Eliza or Margaret or Miss Catherine, to whom he wrote such tempting little notes. Tell them, he told Jack, "I am famishing for a sight of them. The idea alone thrusts through my heart, like the neigh of my blooded stallion."[20] Some have speculated that he was in love with more than one of the Mackay girls and offered himself in marriage, but was rebuffed.[21] He took care to reassure Mary that his interest was based solely on lighthearted friendship, however, and that being with the Mackay girls only made his heart long for her. "Or do you suppose that because I sometimes *see* others, it is them I think of, even when with them," he challenged, "& that it does not make me more lament my hard fortune in being so far away?"[22]

Nonetheless, his was an expansive heart, and he rarely limited himself to just one flirtation. "As for the daughters of Eve in this country," Lee told Jack the year after he left Savannah, "they are formed in the very poetry of nature, and would make your lips water and fingers tingle."[23] He liked to watch the young women uncover their limbs for sea bathing and was much taken by the short skirts of the Mexican girls he met during the war.[24] He had a clear preference for brunettes, and all of his sweethearts boasted the dark eyes and hair of his wife—and mother. "Her eyes were as dark as India's sun and just as warm," Lee sang, admitting that his fancy ran to ladies of high complexion.[25] He also liked them fleshy. He consistently urged his favorites, including his intended wife, to plump up. "Oh if I could but see you in your dress of 133 Avoirdupois," he wrote shortly before their wedding. "But Mercy, that is very little. I thought 144 was your mark."[26] Even when he was devastated and ill after his 1865 defeat, Lee still found his eye roving to the belles. "I rode over to see Miss Anna Logan &c," he confessed that summer. "She looked killing & acted as bad. I took with me four beaux. They pretended to be overcome by the heat of the ride, but I knew from what they were suffering."[27]

He loved to flirt. Addressing his darlings with the flatteringly possessive "my beautiful," he easily launched into teasing repartee. "I wish you were here for I am all alone . . . ," Lee wrote to "My beautiful Tasy," the daughter of his St. Louis colleague William Beaumont, proceeding to tell her that he had caught his son creeping into a young lady's bed. "You must have taught him these tricks, Tasy," he impudently concluded, "for he never learnt them from his father."[28] With his "Beautiful Talcott," the stunning wife of his superior officer, Lee hinted at the tragic miscarriage of an "Affaire du Coeur," obliquely implying that he might be the father of her new daughter.[29] He simply wasted no opportunity to indulge in coquetry. In 1851 his old flame Eliza Mackay Stiles was amused to find him competing with fourteen-year-old Rooney to see who could "make the finest speeches" to her pretty teenage daughter.[30] At Smith's wedding he wandered out of sight of his wife and, in buoyant spirits, passed himself off to the girls as the younger brother of the bride. "Sweet innocent things," he boasted, "they concluded I was single and I have not had such soft looks and tender pressure of the hand for many years."[31] One New Year's Day he attended a series of receptions in St. Louis, where the French settlers were notoriously open in their affections, just so he could "obtain some of the favors they are said to permit." He apparently returned disappointed, "tho' they gave him some sweet thrills & an abundance of cake & wine."[32] "I hope you will keep your eye on him," Mrs. Lee wrote to the "beautiful Tasy" when Lee returned to St. Louis without her, "& not allow him to pass himself off for a gay young widower."[33]

With men Lee could be frank about his lusty thoughts, as he makes clear in his honeymoon letter to Talcott: "I *actually* could not find *time* before I left the District for anything but——."³⁴ However, it was an age when sexuality was not spoken of openly between unmarried men and women but left to the imagination, or communicated by glances and insinuation. In the South this was said to be particularly true, with heavy cultural curtains drawn between the sexes and intimate subjects veiled by either softly romantic or highly obscured terms.³⁵ One of the most interesting aspects of Lee's interaction with women is that he seems to have broken through these restrictive customs, seizing opportunities to express his sensuality. Consciously or not, he used language that in this post-Freudian age seems highly suggestive. In his seven-line postscript to Catherine Mackay he manages to hint at some things she *owes* him, allude to taking advantage of her, and mention going to bed. Tasy was also directed to think of beds, and told that he hoped a mutual friend would back away from her full-bearded lover, for "I should hate her sweet face to be hid by such briars unless they were—mine."³⁶ The "beautiful Misses Mason" were treated to a description of an old man and his younger bride, with Lee's expression of mock astonishment that the groom was still able to relish the joys of married life. "I am afraid at seventy they will prove too exhausting to his veteran frame."³⁷ Master of the double entendre, he heartily thanked one lithesome cousin for some new underdrawers she had made him, saying that the imprint of her hands would "impart to them I am sure additional warmth."³⁸ Another young lady was told that he had roamed the streets of New York to find her, that he longed to "*join* you & attend to *my part* of the transaction," and that he finally had resigned himself to staying in a hotel next to her so that he could "be near you at night—"³⁹ He was even less coy when he told his much-fancied Eliza Mackay that a letter from her had arrived that aroused him. "See what a temptation to sin you will give me," he wrote; and then, referring to a nineteenth-century autoerotic euphemism: "Do spare me the blame of its commission."⁴⁰ Then he wrote to Eliza on her wedding night, admitting that he envied her new husband and wondered about all that was taking place in Savannah. "And how did you deport yourself My child," he wrote quite blatantly. "Did you go off well, like a torpedo cracker on Christmas morning? Do regulate me thereon in your next."⁴¹

Just to make it that much more titillating, Mary Lee was party to it all. The openly sexual comments Robert Lee penned to blushing Eliza Mackay were followed on the same page by a demure congratulatory note from Mary. He told his wife jestingly that she had better stay by his side if she did not want to see him "turned out a Beau again," strutting down the street "with one hand on my whiskers & the other elevating my coat tail!"[42] He sent messages through her to inform his favorites that he was longing to kiss them and told her how he had cultivated a relationship with a prominent Mexican solely because his daughter was considered the prettiest girl in the region.[43] He described in detail the way attractive women used their eyes "unconcernedly & freely" in his presence, and in one extraordinary letter detailed a scene of would-be seduction in Texas where a "strong-minded" woman led him into her garden "to see her corn & potatoes by *star* light."[44] Used to Robert's flirtations, and to a parade of women approaching her at parties to "pour their flatteries into my ears," Mary Lee took it with her usual bemused confidence.[45] It would be interesting to know whether or not some of Lee's banter was meant to elicit a response from his wife—whose more reticent expression of affection, refusal to remove herself from the nurturing haven of her parents, and strong sense of self often gave her the emotional upper hand. If that was Lee's unconscious intent, he was disappointed. Recognizing that no one enjoyed the company of ladies more than her husband, Mary calmly called it the "greatest recreation in his toilsome life."[46]

Perhaps Mary Lee was simply secure in Robert's fidelity. In fact she had little grounds for worry, for his linguistic sparks never appear to have ignited a flame. This is intriguing, for Lee was not a prude, nor was he living in an atmosphere devoid of temptation. Army officers, who were often isolated or away from family, commanded the admiration of women for their gallantry and their bearing, and were allowed a good deal of social latitude in their associations. Some garrisons went so far as to hold "contact and friction" parties, during which they rushed into the arms of local girls just to enjoy the physical intimacy. The men seemed to think they had a particular license toward Indian and Mexican women, whom they believed to be inferior. Relations with them were common. At one fort it was reported that all but two of the officers kept Indian mistresses.[47] Lee's groomsman Dick Tilghman was one who retained a squaw, and in 1850s Texas Lee helped his friend "Shanks" Evans illicitly transport his "woman" into Camp Cooper. The mistress of another of Lee's subordinates in Texas lived openly with her lieutenant and gave birth in camp. Lee tolerated all of this without judgment, just as he did his cousins' adventures or the misuse of drink among the men. If he partook himself, no one ever whispered about it.[48]

Why Lee restrained himself in this permissive masculine world is unclear. He once told his assistant Henry Kayser that he did not believe in leading women into indiscretions. Wherever he had drawn this imaginary line for himself, it seems to have remained fixed.[49] He had before him the specter of his father and brother Henry, who had paid dearly for their self-indulgence, and whose actions had nearly lost him his Mary. Perhaps he took his cue from Winfield Scott, whom he greatly admired, and who had domestic arrangements as difficult as his own. Scott would suffer from time to time from the same bouts of depression that Lee did—what Scott called his "grief and seclusion"—but chose to master "the mutinous appetites" of the flesh rather than seek tawdry comfort in another's arms.[50] Self-denial was part of the soldier ethic Lee had enthusiastically internalized.[51] Moralists and health mongers of the day also strongly favored a behavioral code in which individual will triumphed over base or instinctual feelings, and saw sexual control as beneficial both to the spirit and to the conservation of strength.[52] But much of Lee's abstemiousness seemed to come also from a personal delicacy that recoiled at slovenliness, or contact with people he did not know well. The same repugnance he showed at dirt, unkempt children, and strange company restrained any casual familiarity with women.[53] At a White House reception in the 1850s, he complained the guests were packed so closely that "for a scrupulous man who dislikes his apparel to be brought into such intimate contact with the female dress, it is quite embarrassing."[54] In New York he once enjoyed a ride down Broadway in a crowded omnibus sleigh with a hilarious crowd of schoolgirls who were piled onto the gentlemen's laps. He admitted that it had stoked his fantasies and joked about it later—"Think of a man of my forbidding countenance John Mackay having such an offer"—but he also got up and left the party, despite the taunts of other passengers, who pronounced him a "curmudgeon." Upon reflection, he told Jack, he believed he had done right: "I thought it would not sound well if repeated in the latitude of Wash[n] that I had been riding down B.W. with a strange woman in my lap."[55] In Texas when he found that he was uncomfortably distracted by watching the Mexican women swim in their chemises, he started going to the riverbank very early or late so that he would not encounter them.[56] As he remarked to the coquette who had tried to arouse his interest through moonlight horticulture: "she had waked up the wrong passenger."[57]

In one instance it is hard to imagine that Lee did not come close to overstepping his sexual code of conduct. This was with Markie Williams, a cousin of his wife, and, in the complicated Tidewater tables of genealogy, probably his relative as well. She spent a good deal of time at Arlington, and, along with brothers Laurence and Orton, became an intimate family member. Another dark-eyed beauty, and of a sweet temperament, she and Cousin Robert developed a close and sympathetic relationship. Over time their letters, and Markie's diary entries, became increasingly sensual, often filled with sentiments that surpassed the bounds of close cousinly affection. "Oh Markie, Markie, when will you ripen?" Lee wrote to her when she was just fifteen; and then two weeks later in thanking her for a letter: "I have thought upon it, slept upon it, dwelt upon it (pretty long you will say) & have not done with it yet. I only wish you had brought it on yourself. . . ."[58] A decade later the language remains ardent. Lee begged Markie to write to him, say-ing that just the sight of it would soothe his sore eyes, pronounced his heart dead to all but a thought of her, and sent her a dried flower called heartsease, with the message "I wish it to last as long as my recollection of you, & that will be as long as memory lives—"[59] Markie's journals are more overt. She had a his-tory of being interested in unavailable men, and she found herself vulnerable to the handsome Lee. One day in the 1850s, when he appeared unexpectedly at Arlington, she recorded a scene that was "*quite over-powering*. What *extasy* to meet one so much loved after so long an absence. My love for Cousin Robert is perfectly *unique*."[60] What transpired af-ter this is unclear, for she tore out the di-ary entries for the next ten days. When the chronicle begins again, Lee has re-turned to West Point, and she is waiting to hear from him: "To-day I had hoped to

Martha Custis Williams, "Cousin Markie," who inspired Lee's effusive letters.

have received a letter from Cousin Robert—but, as is the fate of many of my hopes, it ended in disappointment. How I long for that letter."[61] Two days later, and still no letter, she exclaimed: "What can have caused this delay? My mind is filled with anxiety. I know not why."[62] Perhaps most telling was the fact that the servants picked up on their strong mutual attraction. In the quarters they laughed, imitating "Miss Martha Williams and the way she rolled her eyes . . . [and] used to come downstairs in the morning with her skirts billowing out and say to General Lee 'Good morning Cousin Rob-bie.' "[63] Human instincts are so very sharply attuned on such matters.

Any further speculation would degenerate into historical gossip, for, despite a powerful, lingering affection, there it probably ended. As al-ways, Lee gave mixed signals, with the words outpacing—and sometimes misrepresenting—any intended action. He continued to send what must have been leading messages to Markie. At the same time he teased her about her beaux, advised her to marry, and kept at kissing-cousin distance.[64] In 1869 he was still sending her bouquets of violets with the hope "when you inhale their sweet perfume that it may remind you of days that are gone & that their breath may speak the words that I would utter if within your reach."[65] During the pressures of wartime, while sorrowing over the nation's tragedies and his own personal losses, Lee penned lines that, unwitting or not, expressed the truth of their verbally passionate interaction: "We will have to resign ourselves to non-intercourse. . . ."[66]

One of the secrets of Lee's appeal for the ladies was this very duality—provocative talk coupled with gentlemanly action. Sly as his words could be, his public acts were consistently courteous and gallant. Lee had always liked women as much as he desired them, and his thoughtful gestures, just as real as his suggestive banter, lent a grace note to the lives of so many that he was never accused of impropriety. When Eliza Mackay Stiles, now a matron, unexpectedly met him on the streets of Washington, he accompanied her on her calls and bought her a book she had happened to mention.[67] He had learned to enjoy marketing during his boyhood, and when this chore fell to him, he sometimes offered to go along on shopping trips with ladies of his acquaintance. One family friend recalled running into him and hearing him whisper in her ear: "Going to buy your little beefsteak, Mrs—so am I, and you will allow me to offer you my arm?"[68] His daughters treasured memories of the roses he put round the breakfast table, each girl receiving a special flower, buds for the little ones and fuller blooms for the older girls.[69] He was interested in the intrigue and play-acting of flirtation and the sometimes ludicrous antics of newlyweds, and he was not above interfering when it pleased him to do so. When he could, he always invited newly married couples to a supper or breakfast at his home, and enjoyed a few mild jokes at their expense.[70] He wrote an unimaginably lovely letter to his prospective daughter-in-law, filled with striking, poetic expressions of tenderness. "I never thought my dear Charlotte when I held you a girl in my arms . . . that you would ever be nearer or dearer to me than then," it began:

> I feel very sensibly your kindness in consenting to enter our family. I fear you will find us rough soldiers. But I trust you will never have cause to doubt our affection. To me you will be as dear as my own daughter, & if you will allow me I will guard & watch over you with the care of a father.[71]

A male cousin remarked that Lee's charm was due to his rare combination of strength and gentleness, of refinement, tenderness, and manly resolve. From this, we would not want to omit sensuality.[72] Linger a moment on a porch in wartime Richmond and savor this image of Robert E. Lee, throwing his military cape round his shoulders as he prepares to leave two lady friends. "As he swept off his hat for a second and final farewell, he bent down and kissed me as he often did the girls he had known from their childhood. . . . We felt, as he left us and walked off up the quiet leafy street in the moonlight, that we had been honored as by more than royalty."[73]

Cautious or coy, in all these situations Lee worked to surround himself with admiring women. Officers and friends noted that in any parlor he always headed first for the ladies and children, and on his rare absences from camp he sought the companionship of his female friends. After the war a young woman visiting the Virginia springs reported that every evening he gathered together a group of girls, basking in their attentions, teasing them and enjoying their merriment, and intimidating any of their more likely potential partners. He "seemed to test them with an Ithuriel spear," she recalled, "and they were inclined to shrink from the lofty standards he maintained."[74] This may have been the technique that discouraged his daughters' beaux as well, though that is a more complex situation. There is no question that Lee was possessive of the young ladies, liking their ministrations and their company and thwarting their suitors. As teenagers his daughters were sent to a boarding school that Agnes frankly thought contrived to keep them "from the other sex as if they were roaring lions to devour [us]," and even when they were grown women, Annie complained they were "guarded from the *young gentlemen* as if we were gold."[75] After the war Lee pressed his daughters to remain home, playing the abandoned father whenever they traveled, telling them not to absorb any romantic notions at the local weddings, and feigning distaste for the match if one of his favorites proved herself indifferent to his overtures. "I cannot eat the wedding cake in any pleasure," he protested.[76] Daughter Mary ignored his demands, but Agnes and Mildred found it harder to defy them. When Agnes insisted on going to one wedding, he wrote three long letters on the matter, in a crescendo of parental authority: "I was in hopes she had made up her mind to eschew weddings & stick to her Papa—," he wrote irritably to his wife.[77] He avidly embraced Rooney's two wives and encouraged them to join the feminine world around him. At the same time, he pressed Rob and Custis to find partners, even arranging meetings for them with the circle of belles he had cultivated. On a trip to the Pamunkey estates he told Rooney that he was thinking "of catching up Rob

& marrying him to some of my sweethearts while I am down, so as to prevent the necessity of going down again."[78]

There is little question that Lee discouraged his daughters from marrying, though there were other influences at play. The situation was made more difficult by the dearth of available men after the war. One-quarter of all white men in their twenties were dead, and in Virginia alone there were 15,000 more white women than men. "There is but few men at home and what there is I reckon has declined the idea of marriage," wrote one forthright Virginian, and Mrs. Lee also remarked that "beaux are exceedingly scarce."[79] The Lee girls did have a social life after the war, sleigh riding, and going to the Virginia Military Institute's cadet hops with some courageous suitors, and were even thought quite bold because they ice-skated and went out without chaperones. Agnes, at least, was considered a catch, and Mary was reported to have abundant suitors.[80] The young women themselves appear to have been difficult to please: Mary jealously guarded her independence; Agnes was still in shock from the war's losses; Mildred idolized her father. Their mother was not anxious for them to leave either, but admitted, "the girls . . . seem to be in the position of 'poor Betty Martin' who you know the song said, could never find a husband to suit her mind."[81] Lee did not always stand in the way, but neither did he help—as he did with his sons—and in the end the right men never did appear. "Oh! Lucy, enjoy yourself while you can," Mildred wrote to a friend when she was nineteen. "When you get [to] *my age*, when your heart & hopes have been withered as mine have been, when where your heart once *was, there* remains only a *heap of ashes, then* . . . will you believe that life is all 'vanity and vexation of spirit.'"[82]

Attempts to scrutinize Lee's motives toward women have ranged from repugnance at his "foxy paternalism" to lengthy studies of his pent-up sexual frustration, said by some to have been released only on the battlefield.[83] Perhaps, as modern analysis would likely tell us, his choice of darlings—all dark-eyed beauties, and all cousins or sisters or wives of close friends—was a manifestation of his frustrated desire to have a fully completed relationship with his equally dependent, doe-eyed, and unavailable mother. His preference for the company of women and daring overtures to otherwise delicate ladies has also been apologetically characterized as a "slip-knot" from his matrimonial bonds.[84] Lee never showed the slightest inclination to abandon his marriage, but it may be he was unconsciously looking for a response that he failed to get from his underawed wife. Perhaps lacking the attention he desired, he created a stimulating but safe little harem of relatives or young girls, who teased and pampered him and allowed him to play the perpetual courtier. In this fantasy world he could feign indignation at the announcement of every engagement, but easily escape when real possibilities presented themselves. Mary Chesnut, in her usual unvarnished fashion, thought the motive behind such games quite straightforward: "It begins in vanity—it ends in vanity. . . . Flattery—battledore and shuttlecock—how in this game flattery is dashed backward and forward. It is so soothing to self-conceit."[85] Mary Lee could clearly hold her own in the game. The lightheartedness seems more in question when one encounters Markie's vulnerable soul—for she was clearly confused and hurt—or those "innocent creatures" at Smith Lee's wedding with whom his brother so gleefully toyed. A fellow officer remarked crisply that when the fun was over, Lee never allowed women to get in his way, and in Richmond the gossips observed that despite his furtive hand-kissing, "Cousin Robert holds all admiring females at arm's length."[86]

There is something nagging here that makes Lee's predilections seem a bit more than harmless flirtation. Women and children and animals were his favorite companions, all unquestionably subordinate to men. He could be so familiar and flattering with them because in the end they were not going to challenge him. His preference for their company helps us understand that he may have been more competitive than we thought. Lee had always been a striver, but had not achieved the recognition he longed for, and in the face of disappointment he carefully honed an air of detachment from ambition. It may be that he disliked the more aggressive world of male discourse, with its skepticism, cutthroat repartee, and pressure to live up to a preconceived image of success. Lee instead withdrew to a gentler world, through which he could navigate with ease.[87] In addition there are those mischievous letters, which for his day were quite provocative, and perhaps indicative of a need to reinforce his manhood by displaying sexual sophistication.[88]

Whatever was involved, it never seems to have veered onto a really muddy verge. His dedication to wife and family were not in question, and for the most part it appears the flirtations were pursued without malicious intent. "Of course he liked the ladies," one granddaughter would say with spirit. "Why shouldn't he?"[89] In the end one is rather glad he had this sensual edge to tempt him, and tease him, and return him to high spirits. "Such things keep us alive!" he retorted at the end of that devastating war when a lady friend accused him of playing with the tender feelings of his admirers. Pointing to a freshly picked hyacinth, attached to a card that read, "For General Lee, with a kiss!" he thumped his breast and announced: "I have here my hyacinth and my card—*and I mean to find my kiss!*"[90]

Chapter Thirteen

The Headache Bag

Baltimore 22 June 1850

My dearest Mother

Since I rec^d your letter I have been on to West Point with Custis. The indis-position of Dr Woods son I feared might detain him too long in Washington, & I therefore thought it best not to wait for his escort, which he had kindly ten-dered, & which would have otherwise been very agreeable to me, had the D^r been able to have gone on the first of June as he had intended.

After waiting ten days & having been disapp^d on some occasions appointed by the D^r to go on, I one mor^g while dressing determined to accompany him myself, & at 9 A.M. we were in the cars on our way. I took great pleasure in go-ing on with him, as it seemed to be a great comfort to him to have me along, & lightened considerably the pain of leaving home.

That night we reached New York, & next mor^g after an early breakfast went up to the Point. I had offered to spend a day in N.Y. if Custis desired it, which would have enabled him to have visited the Narrows, but he favored going on, & on reaching the Point I proposed to him not to report for duty till the after-noon, that he might walk about & look in, but he said he would rather go & have it over at once. After installing him however, I got permission for him to return to the Hotel at 1 P.M. & remain with me till 5 o'clock which he did. The next mor^g I went over to the Barrack to take leave of him. He had just returned from his first lesson in Squad drill. Said he had slept well during the night &c, but when I bid him adieu, he seemed for the first time to realize the full force of his separation from all of us, & the convulsion of his countenance indicated the grief at his heart. I returned to New York & arrived here the next day. I yester-day rec^d a letter from him, dated the 17th. He said he was very comfortable & every one was very kind to him. That it was not the dreadful place it had been represented to be, so that although he knew it was harder to him then than it would be subsequently, it was very agreeable to him. He had been promoted up

to the 1st drill square & liked his drill master very much. He particularized
Jerome Bonaparte, Laurence Williams, John Schaff, & Roger Jones as having
bestowed in kind attentions.

I saw all the cadets he has mentioned while there. They were all very well. I
fear Laurence will not receive a furlough this summer, which the rest of his class
will enjoy. According to the Regulations, a cadet whose number of demerits ex-
ceeds 150 in the year loses his furlough. Laurence poor fellow has exceeded that
number by 4, which he thought was so near the mark that it would make no difference, but the Sup^t seemed to think that he would be obliged to deny his application, which he regretted very much, but as a matter of principle the established
rule could not be departed from. L. thought he could get some of them excused,
but I fear he has not succeeded in this as Jerome Bonaparte arrived last night
without L. & he was to have accompanied him, & have come to see us. Bonaparte
said the class left with him & that L. was left behind. I am very sorry for it, as it
will be a great disappointment to him & his sisters. Perhaps he may come on yet.

I rec^d a letter from Dr Wood dated Monday, who is there on the medical
board, saying that he had seen Custis several times & that he was very well &
cheerful. Robt Wood was in the same room with him & they were getting along
very well. Custis drilled so much better than those who had come on about the
same time, that they had promoted him up to a higher squad. I suppose this is
the result of Mr Lee's tuition at Mr Graiths. I expect by Monday to hear the result of the examination for admittance, & although I apprehend nothing unpleasant from that, still I shall feel more at ease when he has regularly entered.

We are all very well but it is excessively hot here now which renders my trips
to Sollers anything but pleasant. The bath is in constant requisition & gives occasional relief. How is my Annie, & Wig, & when are you all coming on? Do not
get sick at A. Mother, but come on to your children. Tell the major we have
quantities of eggs, chickens, which I hope will supply the place of the winter
luxuries. But really it is so hot now that we eat nothing but vegetables & fruits.
Strawberries are in great abundance & cherries are now becoming plenty. New
potatoes, peas, cymblins, snaps, beets &c are to be had at all times.

I am delighted to hear such fine accounts of the rye grass &c at A.—I hope
this hot weather has brought forward the corn & that all is as flourishing as we
could wish. If he can once improve the land, I hope he will never be again annoyed by a scarcity. I hope you will both make arrangements to pay us a long
visit & will come on as soon as you can. A letter from Smith this mor^g. Says they
are all well. He is to be relieved from duty at Annapolis the 1 July, in consequence of having been promoted to Commander. He does not know yet where
he will establish himself. Anne is tolerable, nothing has been heard of M. since
he sailed. M. says she has nothing to send but her love, in which she is joined by

Mary, Rooney & the little ones. I am very sorry to hear of Mr Lloyd's indisposi-
tion. M. rec^d a letter within a day or two from Martha Wm^s. She reports M^{rs} L.
as being comfortable. I fear dear Lady she will scarcely be much better. From
what I hear from Mr Wm Harrison I think it very doubtful whether M^{rs} B will
come on this summer. Goodbye my dear Mother. May God guard & preserve
you all. Your affectionate son RE Lee

Love to all[1]

>⊷⊶⊶○⊷⊶⊰

THE LETTER Robert E. Lee wrote to his mother-in-law just after he had
delivered Custis to West Point is a kind of connecting tissue between
phases of his association with the U.S. Military Academy. It is wonderful to
see Lee here, released from the marble tombs of our imagination, musing
while he gets dressed and deciding to accompany his son; then reliving his
own arrival at West Point a quarter century earlier and bragging a bit about
his son's first days on the parade ground. He is also nervous, trying to control everyone's movements as he passes through an emotional moment. It is
evident that his concerns went beyond family separation. For Lee the anxiety was based on firsthand knowledge of what Custis would encounter; a
sharp remembrance of all that had to be achieved and suffered at West Point
in order to succeed.

Over the years Lee, like most graduates, maintained a connection with
the academy, serving from time to time on courts-martial or special visitation boards. But it is clear that he did not like to get too close to the institution. In 1839 he was offered a position as instructor of mathematics, and he
begged to be excused, saying that he had already "experienced the *disagreement* attending the duties of an Instructor" and that he knew "the character
of Cadets well enough to be convinced that it is not easy matter to make the
labour of mind & body pleasant to them."[2] He consistently discouraged his
sons, nephews, and other relatives from pursing a military education and
anguished over their experiences when they chose to ignore his advice. "I
turned from West Point on thursday with a heavy heart at leaving you behind me," he told Custis in 1851, "and had anxious thoughts concerning you
all the way home."[3] He did consent to serve on the Board of Visitors in 1844,
where he was responsible for assessing the "Moral, religious, Scientific and
Literary Instruction of the Academy." He enjoyed it, mainly for the company
of fellow board members Jack Mackay and Erasmus Keyes, and for the opportunity to work with Winfield Scott, who was the chairman.[4] When Jeffer-

son Davis, then secretary of war, ordered him in 1852 to become superintendent, Lee again tried to decline. This time he was not successful, though
he sent three letters requesting a different assignment.[5] When it appeared he
would have to follow the orders, he wrote an uncharacteristically whining
letter to his old comrade, P. G. T. Beauregard. He called it an "ill wind . . .
that is driving me toward W.P.," and lamented "the thanklessness of the
duty, and the impossibility of either giving or receiving satisfaction. I have
been behind the scenes too long. I know exactly how it works. The Sup^t can
do nothing right and must father every wrong." Having vented his irritation, he ended with the vow to "take it as we find it Beaur^y" and to do his best
despite the unsavory posting.[6]

"I do not now believe there are three persons in the country who could fill
his place," a member of the Board of Visitors had written of Sylvanus Thayer
in 1826. "No, no man would be indiscreet enough to take the place after
Thayer; it would be as bad as being President of the Royal Society after Newton."[7] No doubt this was among the pressures Lee felt as he installed himself
in the white clapboard superintendent's house on September 1, 1852. West
Point had changed little since his time as a cadet. Thayer's successor, Richard
Delafield, was a builder, and the north and south barracks were gone, replaced by crenellated stone structures in the style now associated with the
academy. Yet it was all so familiar. The old parade ground on the plain remained the focal point; the daily drill and tight gray uniform were largely
identical. Most of the same professors reigned over the classrooms. Bugle
calls sounded the hours of recitation; the food remained foul. Summer encampment retained its mixture of physical exertion and outdoor license.
After-hours visitors were still amused to watch the cadets gyrating amid
rows of candles with "a fervor and vivacity outdoing an Indian war dance."[8]
Benny Haven's continued to sound its siren call.[9] The cadets noted that
Colonel Lee had arrived, and waited to see what he would do.[10]

In fact he adopted Thayer's model as his own and did little that was innovative. The "Father of the Military Academy" had been more or less dismissed in 1833 by Andrew Jackson, who had pronounced him a "tyrant" and
moved to halt the progress of the professional military he mistrusted.
Thayer was followed by able but unimaginative men; as one observer noted,
he "left to his successors little to do, save rightly to administer that which his
mind had conceived and almost fully developed."[11] Here and there Lee saw a
need and sought to fill it. He felt the inadequacy of the riding facilities, and,
with the cavalry gaining importance, effectively lobbied for the construction of a larger stable and practice ring. He may have designed these himself,

*Lee as superintendent of West Point, painted
by Robert W. Weir around 1855.*

for the new building looked remarkably like the stable at Arlington.[12] He also improved the course in cavalry tactics. Cadet J. E. B. Stuart was one who remembered the new drill of "cutting with our sabers at artificial heads while going full speed."[13] Lee showed foresight here, for he trained some of the greatest cavalrymen in American history: Phil Sheridan, Fitz Lee, Joseph Wheeler, and, of course, Stuart. With the eye of an engineer Lee also upgraded the water supply and brought in gas lighting. Lee waged a long battle to have the cadet hospital revamped—which he finally won.[14] He was less successful in redesigning the cadet uniforms, which the academy doctor complained were so constricting that "a mechanical obstacle is presented to the free play of the thoracic and abdominal organs." The dress cap was also inadequate. Its black patent leather visor caused chafing, and its weight was excessively hot. Lee sketched a handsome new design, but the War Department, apparently favoring tradition over health and comfort, rejected all of the proposals, and the uniform was not changed during Lee's tenure.[15]

For the most part Lee also left the curriculum alone. He retained the system of deferring to professors on academic matters, and sought their advice within the same committee structure Thayer had developed. He seconded a few recommendations—that Spanish be taught, for example—but the course his cadets followed was remarkably similar to the instruction he had received. Lee had a lifelong interest in the English language and encouraged several boards to recommend that it be included in the curriculum, something that was finally achieved in 1854. The stringent system of oral examination was left untouched, and the young soldiers suffered the same anguish each January and June that Lee had endured. "Loud groans were heard at dead of night," ran an irreverent poem about the dread of January examinations. "And plebicants howled in mild affright / While dreaming of Geometry."[16] Lee worried about the stress of the heavy academic load and concurred with one Board of Visitors when it recommended that the course be lengthened from four to five years, though the idea was not original to him. The extension of the program was perceived by some as a sign of Lee's flexibility and creative approach to problem-solving. However, it had the opposite effect from that intended, adding a nearly intolerable extra year to the already grueling cadet experience. Greatly unpopular, it was rescinded after three years.[17]

Most of Lee's time as superintendent was taken up with worry about the cadets. Thayer had insisted that the government of West Point "is & ought to be paternal," and in this, as in other things, Lee followed his predecessor's lead.[18] Cadet Joseph Wheeler remembered how he would join the boys in their quarters every Sunday morning: "He would bow and say, 'Good Morning, young gentlemen,' and then glance around the room, and sometimes make kindly enquiries . . . especially when one of the occupants had been ill."[19] Mary Lee also took a motherly interest in the young men. She made a point of inviting cadets to their residence, occasionally serving them with the Washington tableware.[20] Others recalled how Lee visited them in the hospital or included them in gatherings when they were snubbed by the more exclusive cadet cliques.[21] Lee tried to follow each cadet's ongoing progress as Thayer had, offering little corrections and encouragements as the course advanced. The superintendent wrote supportive notes to those who did not do well, and also became adept at diplomatically enlisting the help of parents and friends to put pressure on underperforming cadets. He permitted all but the most egregious wrongdoers to resign rather than be expelled from the academy. "I hope . . . you will not let your son be discouraged at his failure," Lee wrote to one father. "If he has made an honest effort to succeed, as I have no doubt he has, he is entitled to as much credit as though he had."[22] Small boys, neighborhood ladies, and the Boards of Visitors noted his courtesy and the fine example he set for the young men. A reporter who visited the Point in the last year of his posting concluded, "It has never been our fortune to know a more noble-souled, high-toned, considerate and scrupulous man than Colonel Lee."[23]

One of the internal conflicts Lee faced at West Point was that he was a man of both principle and compassion, and while he felt sympathy toward the cadets, he was also unbending in his adherence to duty. For Lee, army regulations were nearly an extension of his own controlled personality, and he had great trouble understanding the inability or unwillingness of his charges to adhere to these rigid behavioral expectations. He sincerely believed that "all difficulties can be overcome by labour and perseverance" and that self-control was not only necessary for a successful life but a gratifying exercise in itself. Publicly he declared that "nothing turns [the cadets] from their labours or aspirations," yet discipline remained a very real problem. Boys were shooting rats out of the barracks windows, smoking cigars, and rowing across the Hudson to meet girls. Several were involved in serious debauchery. Among the offenders was Lee's nephew Fitz, who arrived at West Point a "wild, careless and inexperienced youth," with all the high spirits that would one day make him a dashing cavalry officer. He was nearly dismissed after two episodes of absence without leave, involving midnight rambles and bottles of whiskey, but was allowed to graduate after Lee bargained on his behalf with General Totten.[24]

Some of Lee's charges broke the rules out of forgetfulness, others for the thrill of defying authority. "I went to the Hotel this evening without any permit and enjoyed myself very much dancing," wrote cadet Ruben Ross about the time Lee arrived, "though my pleasure was great it was heightened by the fear of being detected, which acted as a seasoning to it as the danger renders hunting with animals delightful."[25] At Christmas 1854 things got out of hand in a way that was all too reminiscent of the Eggnog Riot. Cadet George Cushing told his father that "Benny Havens . . . drove a great trade that day, if I judge by the effects; the scene at the Mess Hall was rich,—one cadet jumped on his table and sang and danced and finished by kicking all the eatables off." New Year's Day was equally celebratory: "knives were used, and several first classmen were stabbed. . . . another will be dismissed because he knocked down the officer of the Day—one man stripped off his coat and shirt and fought desperately with a big carving knife in his hand." That evening at parade severe reprimands were read out: "two more Cadet officers (Capts) have been broke—"[26]

"Breaking"—or demoting—the corps officers was not the only punishment Lee imposed. He tried to use public rebuke as an alternative to

stronger actions, admonishing the young men to understand that "shrinking from duty" was "so contrary to the spirit of the true soldier."[27] This tactic was not adequate, however, and he moved swiftly to strengthen the
penalties for infractions. Only two days after Lee's arrival, the daring Ruben
Ross found to his dismay that he was in danger of a court-martial for a flip-

*"Christmas comes but once a year," a sketch made by James McNeill Whistler
while a cadet under Superintendent Lee.*
SPECIAL COLLECTIONS, UNITED STATES MILITARY ACADEMY

pant remark about absence from drill.[28] Cadets were stunned to find demerits being given for chairs that were not placed at a given angle or for neatly
folded clothes whose edges were not exactly flush with the edge of the shelf.[29]
Another boy wrote home that the principal news "about the Point are the
new administration which has lately come in to power and is now busying itself in tightening the chains which bind and shackel the freedom of Cadets."[30]
Lee rewrote the 1839 cadet regulations to require "self-incrimination," appointed two strict disciplinarians as commandants, and demanded exacting
performance under all conditions. He also changed the demerit system so
that dismissal was required for anyone who reached 100 demerits in a six-
month period. Under Thayer's program the limit had been set at 200 per
year, but Lee, believing that cadets only began to behave when they were up
against the prescribed limit, thought a tighter control would promote restraint.[31] He told General Totten that he could not "overlook the evil that

may result, at any excuse or justification on my part of the slightest departure of any Cadet from the plain path of uprightness & honor."[32] Lee also
heightened standards in drill to the point that his overzealousness caused
public comment. A visitor watching the invigorated riding classes, which
required hard trotting with crossed stirrups for hours before breakfast,
thought the scene gave him "an insight into the purgatorial mysteries" of
Lee's institution, and just stopped short of accusing the academy of cruelty.[33]
Once when Secretary Jefferson Davis was visiting, Lee insisted on keeping
the corps at attention in a ferocious storm, though the cadets "presented but
a sorry spectacle . . . plumes looking like drowned roosters." Dismayed,
Davis overruled Lee, finally calling a halt to the sad display.[34] At the end of his
tenure in 1855, his aggravation nearly complete, Lee wrote an impassioned
1,200-word letter to Chief Engineer Joseph Totten, extolling his inflexible
requirements as an example to would-be miscreants, and asking that his
tough disciplinary actions be retained.[35]

Totten doubted the wisdom of these stringent measures, and their effectiveness remains questionable today. In the face of expectations they
thought ridiculous, some cadets gave up and simply assumed there would
be black marks on their accounts. "The demerit business under the new
Command is carried to such an extent that it is a moral impossibility to
avoid them," complained one cadet, who likened Lee's administration to the
reign of Nero.[36] The actual number of recorded violations went up, not
down. In 1850, sixteen cadets graduated without receiving any demerit. During the two and a half years of Lee's superintendence, only one cadet left
with a perfect record.[37] At the end of Lee's posting, his own daughters
thought the cadets were more undisciplined than ever, calling them "excessively rowdy and ill-behaved."[38] Lee never did conquer his disciplinary problems, and his rigid administration was understandably unpopular.

"The cadets are fortunate to have a superintendent to whom they can look
up to with whole hearted admiration and respect—that means a great deal to
youth," stated the mother of one cadet.[39] Except for his fine presence, however,
it appears many cadets did not overly admire their superintendent. They
laughed at his fussy soirees, and even Lee admitted the events fell flat. "Was at
a Party at Col Lee's the other night girls neither pretty nor pumpkins—supper
very good—the affair a bore," was one upperclassman's assessment.[40] In addition, the cadets blamed Lee's reinforced system of discipline—not their own
behavior—for the increasing number of demerits. There is an interesting
discrepancy between those who wrote grand reminiscences of their superintendent, based on appreciative memory and the glow of Lee's wartime triumphs, and what they expressed at the time. When a request to visit a sick

brother was overturned in 1854, one offended family wrote that Lee had "about as much heart as an Iron Ram Rod." Another, who was denied permission to receive a Christmas box from home, acknowledged that the superintendent had "made me so angry that I do not know what to do."[41] The cadets hated the system of casting lots to determine quarters, which Lee had instituted in the name of fairness, for it broke up their old friendships. They derided a new type of French drilling that he introduced, claiming that it had them charging all over the field at 45-degree angles in a most painful and undignified fashion.[42] They released their frustrations by "roasting" the authorities at evening entertainments during summer encampment, in full view of visitors. The plain was "crowded with ladies and gentlemen to see the revels," wrote one

The "Shanghai Drill" as sketched by Cadet George Cushing. The movement, introduced by Lee, was much ridiculed by the corps.
SPECIAL COLLECTIONS, UNITED STATES MILITARY ACADEMY

of the players. "Songs were sung—decrying the merits of Old Bob Lee—and stating his cruelties to Cadets—how he 'skinned' a furlough man for wearing long hair, &c."[43] Some of this was the natural resentment young people felt for any constraining authority, but it is notable that few contemporary cadet letters show any affection for Colonel Lee.

Lee wrestled with the disciplinary problems of Phil Sheridan, J. E. B. Stuart, the grandson of Henry Clay, and his own son and nephew, but no case gained more fame than that of James McNeill Whistler.[44] "Jimmy" was the son of George Whistler, a celebrated West Point engineer who had been instrumental in developing railroads in both America and Russia. The younger Whistler had come to the academy surrounded by high expectations, but from the start he showed an amused contempt for discipline that flaunted every rule devised.[45] At the same time his brilliant artistic ability was undeniably evident—as was his need to express it. He doodled all the time—on tent flaps and camp stools, in the margins of official documents, and in the autograph books of friends. "In the recitation-room, at church, and almost everywhere," recalled a classmate, "the ridiculous incidents of a situation would strike him, and he would sketch, in a second or two, cartoons full of character and displaying the utmost nicety of appreciation of its ludicrous points."[46] Other friends remembered how he copied models with extraordinary agility, drawing face, feet, and clothing in a disjointed fashion until it all came together in splendid unity. Robert Weir, the drawing instructor, and himself a fine artist, recognized Whistler's talent, excused his insubordination, and offered him instruction beyond the usual classes in topography. Lee's concern showed in the careful letters he penned to Whistler's soon-to-be-immortal mother and his constant trimming of demerits to keep the cadet afloat.[47] Whistler seems to have been almost intent on punishment, however. There was no constraining his indolence, his irreverence, or his glossy black curls. He received demerits for not carrying his musket properly; for wearing his cap, shoes, and belt out of uniform; for being late at inspection and drill; for laughing and wildly swinging his arms while marching; for inattention in class and chapel; and for unsatisfactory haircuts.[48] He loved telling West Point stories on himself in after years, amusing his listeners with an incident when he forgot the date of the battle of Buena Vista. Asked what he would do if the question came up at a dinner party, Whistler replied: "Do? Why, I should refuse to associate with people who could talk of such things at dinner."[49]

The mounting demerits and a final cheeky performance during examinations ultimately put him beyond anyone's help. Standing before the Board of Visitors in 1854, Cadet Whistler was asked: "What is silicon?" "Silicon, sir," he replied, "is a gas." It was too much even for Lee to excuse. "I can therefore do nothing more in his behalf," wrote the superintendent, "nor do I know of anything entitling him to further indulgence. I can only regret that one so capable of doing well should so have neglected himself & must now suffer the penalty."[50] Whistler may have purposely thrown the exam to relieve himself of a restrictive obligation to the army, but at the last hour he tried to salvage the situation by appealing directly to the secretary of war. Davis was taken by his charm and, perhaps remembering his own demerit-prone cadet days, came close to accepting the young man's delightful reassurance that should he "be reinstated at West Point . . . silicon should remain a metal."[51] At Lee's insistence, however, Davis held firm. Whistler would later quip: "If silicon had been a gas, I would have been a major general."[52]

Lee's administrative challenges left him with little time to develop martial theories or pursue professional skills. He taught no classes and provided the cadets with no personal expertise on the military arts. Engineering professor Dennis Hart Mahan was at West Point when Lee returned in 1852, by now a renowned figure whose works were considered classic adaptations of military theory to American conditions.[53] Mahan initiated a "Napoleon

Club" that the superintendent did attend from time to time. The group met in a room Lee provided, its walls covered in charts and maps, and there they indulged in the great sport of armchair strategizing, sometimes inviting a promising cadet to join them. Perhaps in preparation for these gatherings, Lee checked out a number of books from the West Point library on Napoleon, showing a particular interest in the French general's early battles and his Russian campaign, and a curiosity about the geographical influence in the wars. His library list also indicates he studied the American Revolution, including the battles involving his father.[54] It is tempting to think that these sessions, with Mahan expounding his theories of offensive strategy, mobility and flexible tactical systems, and the need for effective entrenchments and rapid pursuit, influenced Lee's later field movements.[55] Though Lee would adapt all of these methods to his own circumstances, his wartime tactics were dynamic rather than rule-laden, following conditions not precedents, and reflecting no one strategic formula.

Indeed, Lee's main intellectual acquisition during this time may have had less to do with theory than with exposure to men whose ideas and actions would shape the coming decade. John Bell Hood, J. E. B. Stuart, Fitz Lee, E. Porter Alexander, Stephen Dill Lee, John Pegram, W. D. Pender, Phil Sheridan, John B. McPherson, and O. O. Howard were all trained under his eye, and he must have had some sense of their technical and emotional capacities when he met them on war's more consequential stage. West Point's staff included Major Robert S. Garnett, who would accompany Lee in the first year of the conflict; and Majors George Thomas and Fitz John Porter, who would oppose him. Senators, cabinet officials, and notable figures in American science and letters such as astronomer William Mitchell and historian George Bancroft visited the academy while Lee was at its head. All of these personalities broadened his experience outside of a restrictive regional or local experience.[56]

Superintendent Lee's struggle with discipline may also have provided some valuable lessons. His difficulty with the young men at West Point is intriguing, since it stands in such contrast with the leadership style he would later develop. Despite his attempts at kindliness, the impression he gave was otherwise. Even those who excelled under him did not openly esteem him. Everyone did exclaim over his personal magnetism and nearly perfect physique, but at this period of his life these may actually have caused some intimidation. Oliver Otis Howard left a picture of a well-proportioned man whose hair was just beginning to turn gray, with a dashing moustache and "shapely head as fine as if chiseled by an expert."[57] Another cadet, Lindsay Lomax, styled Lee "the marble model," a moniker that has never really left him.[58] Even grown men found such extraordinary looks to be "oppressive,"

and they must have been less than reassuring to adolescent boys just growing into their manhood.[59] Coupled with his well-known Mexican War
record, they may well have presented an unattainable ideal, alienating rather
than inspiring. Cadet Howard, who appreciated Lee's visits to him in the
hospital and admired his commanding presence, nonetheless told himself,
"Colonel Lee is my friend, but I must never approach too near him; he is
gracious, but evidently condescending."[60] In addition to the sense of distance his appearance invoked, the cadets found his preachy ways just as irritating as did his children and mother-in-law. Though Lee had hoped to
temper discipline by promoting soldierly honor and invoking shame, his
public rebukes were resented.[61] Consciously or not, these off-putting elements were absent from Lee's interaction with the rank and file during the
Civil War. His looks altered radically in the early years of that conflict, giving him the fatherly white-haired image his soldiers loved, and he avoided
the sermonizing that appears to have been counterproductive at West Point.
Instead he ignored many breaches of discipline, focused on the key element
of his men's performance—fighting—and avoided humiliation, appealing
instead to bravery and pride.

Lee greatly disliked the job of superintendent. The work entailed endless
correspondence on trivial matters, the more fatiguing since his eyes were
failing.[62] His attempts to take measured decisions were frequently overturned by Washington politicians, who undermined his authority and hampered his plans.[63] There was the constant parade of visitors, especially
around examination time, ranging from ex-president Martin Van Buren to
Mrs. Amelia Bloomer and her pantaloon-clad daughters. General Scott arrived one night with an entourage of ten, and Lee had to feed them on the
modest fare that had been prepared for his solitary dinner.[64] Worst of all was
the need to dismiss those who failed the examinations—"the most unpleasant duty I am called on to perform," as he told Cousin Markie.[65] Jefferson
Davis had insisted on assigning him as superintendent because of his commitment to order and because he had observed Lee's fondness for young
people. What Davis failed to grasp until later was that this concern translated into a taxing personal responsibility.[66] His family was together—
"Mim," children, slaves, and horses—and he was pleased to be near Custis,
who made him enormously proud when he graduated first in the class of
1854. He enjoyed the antics of teenagers Annie and Agnes, who laughed at
the shy cadets and styled themselves "Queens supreme of the Superintendent's House," and he took pleasure in accompanying young Rob through
the wild luxury of West Point's hills. Everyone liked the sleigh riding, the

ice-skating, and the military pomp.[67] Unfortunately, it could not really compensate for the stress, which was starting to affect his health. One night, when the family went out to hear the fine academy band, they left the superintendent stretched out full length on the sofa, a headache bag on his brow, "too poorly to go out to the concert."[68] Even the climate, Lee grumbled, was "as harsh to me as my duties and neither gives me any pleasure."[69]

Perhaps worst of all, his exertions did not always achieve the outcomes he desired. Lee was a good solid superintendent at West Point: he adroitly managed the finances, enjoyed widespread confidence in political and military circles, and graduated some of the foremost military men of his day. But, personally, it was as if everything he believed in most fervently was destined to disappoint. His prized diligence did not ensure favorable results in the military's bureaucratic maze. Improved disciplinary procedures created a response that was the opposite of what he had hoped for. Fairness could not always trump favoritism. Devotion to duty certainly did not result in happiness, or even, it appears, satisfaction. Moreover, he was discovering that an administrative position, as attractive as it was, and closeness to his family, as charming as domestic life could be, could not offer him the independence and stimulation he craved. A year into his West Point assignment, Lee was already writing that he had "less heart for the work." Eighteen months later, he admitted that the sooner he got away from it the better. He began to complain openly, so much so that he had to backtrack a bit when his disaffection became the stuff of gossip.[70] In March 1855 Secretary Davis offered him a position in the newly created 2nd Cavalry, and he accepted with alacrity. Even fourteen-year-old Agnes was aware that this new duty would entail a good deal of hardship: "Papa is glad to leave here & of course likes promotion but doesn't like giving up the Eng. corps, in which he has been for more than twenty years, & then to break up & leave us for those western wilds. . . ."[71] General Totten pleaded with him to remain in the Corps of Engineers, but Lee believed his well-being and career interests were at stake.[72] The girls expressed nostalgia for the parades and concerts, and threw bouquets to the cadets as they serenaded the family with "Home Sweet Home," but Lee never looked back. He left West Point as soon as he could, clambering onto a boat at dawn in a drenching rainstorm to avoid staying a single extra day.[73]

Chapter Fourteen

Mutable Shield

Baltimore 8 July 1849

. . . Mr Johns delivered the best Sermon to day I ever heard him preach. Indeed it could not well have been [delivered] by anyone [but] him [unreadable] obedience to God's commandments, His great mercy, the necessity of worshipping him in the manner he prescribes. . . . only by conforming to God's commandments that we could escape every evil & calamity. No one can be more sensible of these facts than I am. But it is so difficult to regulate your conduct by them. Man's nature is so selfish so weak. Every feeling, every passion urging him to folly, excess & sin that I am sometimes disgusted with myself & sometimes with all the world. My efforts to improve are too feeble to succeed, & I fear I shall never be better. Even in my prayers I fail & my only hope is in my confidence, my trust in the mercy of God. . . .[1]

. . .

Richmond 2 May 1861

My dear Sir

I am extremely obliged to you for your friendly & Xtian letter of the 29 & I thank you sincerely for your kind interest in my behalf. I shall need all your good wishes & all your prayers for strength & guidance in the struggle in which we are engaged, & earnestly & humbly look for help to him alone who can save us, & who has permitted the dire calamity of this fratricidal war to impend over us. If we are not worthy that it should pass from us, may he in his great mercy shield us from its dire effects & save us from the calamity our sins have produced.

Conscious of my imperfection, the little claim I have to be classed among christians, I know the temptations & trials I shall have to pass through. May God enable me to perform my duty & not suffer me to be tempted beyond my strength.

*I am writing amid much interruption & with many things pressing on my
attention & cannot say all I desire.*
    *Wishing you every happiness & a speedy peace to our beloved country
               I remain very truly yours RE Lee*

Rev. C. Walker[2]

>─♦──○──♦─<

H IS FATHER was a Deist, who came to admire Quakerism. His mother
followed the rationalists, and believed that a virtuous life was the highest expression of piety. His older brothers embraced a classical and humanist
ideal of righteous living. Uncle Edmund Lee, who oversaw young Robert's
upbringing, was a High Church man, much concerned with the minutiae of
the vestry and with the personal conduct of Christ Church's parishioners.
Aunt Elizabeth Randolph, who nurtured the boy through school at Eastern
View, was an evangelical, having sworn herself to penitence, prayer, and proselytizing during the religious revivalism of the early nineteenth century.[3]
Perhaps because of these varied influences, Robert E. Lee came late to any
profession of religion. For more than half his adult life he dodged attempts
by the well-meaning to harness his soul. When he did finally accept a perva-
sive faith, it was expressed with the regularity and symmetry of an engineer
rather than the enthusiasm of a convert. Then the war came, and righteousness was bound up with political justification, until Lee himself became a
symbol of suffering and redemption for the entire South.

Robert E. Lee lived during a time of powerful societal transition, which
shaped his professional life, influenced the way he perceived his role as husband and father, and colored his understanding of class and hierarchy. Religion, too, was transformed by the expansive spirit that followed the
American Revolution. His parents' generation had seen a move away from
the strict Calvinist creed of early America, with its emphasis on predestina-
tion and outward signs of piety. In the latter part of the eighteenth century
the spiritual worldview was one of order and rationality, in which the existence of God could be proven through scientific observation and an appreciation of nature's marvelous intricacy. One of the books Lee inherited from
his father's library was John Ray's *The Wisdom of God Manifested in the
Works of the Creation*, a Baconian volume that portrayed God as the ultimate skilled technician—a practical deity who not only caused the wind to
blow but gave man the power to harness it, so that mills would turn and sails

would billow.[4] At West Point more of this philosophy would be apparent, through teachers who embraced Spinoza and his vision that godliness was seen in the orderly rhythms of the universe.[5] This was faith based on intellect and wonder, not on emotional surrender. Henry Lee and his older sons, like others of the revolutionary generation, had been classically educated, and they grafted this scientific Deism onto ancient philosophy and enlightenment principles to form a credo that celebrated knowledge and human progress. Carter Lee wrote that when he and his siblings were growing up there was a motto in the house that "Religion never was designed / To make our pleasures less—" Taking a cue from the pagans, Henry Lee saw divinity in every delight. Daily prayers stressed the Psalms' praise and gratitude, and the mealtime blessing Carter recalled was elegant in its simplicity: "God give us grateful hearts & supply the wants of others."[6]

Under the influence of Ann Lee, this happy liberality was expanded to include a belief that morality was the greatest expression of godliness. "Your dearest mother is singularly pious from love to Almighty God and love of virtue, which are synonymous," Henry Lee would tell his son Carter, "not from fear of hell—a low base influence. . . ."[7] One of Robert's earliest memories was of his mother reading aloud from Hugh Blair's sermons, "when I was too young to read them myself."[8] Blair was a Scots Presbyterian, whose immensely popular homilies stressed ethical rather than theological questions and advocated showing devotion through virtuous acts. Boswell quipped that Blair could "stop hounds by his eloquence," and he converted many with his appealing belief that the fundamental quality of righteousness was an "amiable and compassionate spirit." Whether Blair's wisdom was absorbed consciously or instinctively in Ann Lee's house is not clear, but her son would later espouse the everyday philosophy reflected in those comfortable sermons. "Let us remain persuaded that simple and moderate pleasures are always the best," counseled Blair, in words Lee would repeat many times to his children, "that virtue and a good conscience are the surest foundation of enjoyment." In another sermon, "On Tranquility," Blair advocated a behavioral philosophy that previewed Lee's personal code: keep a clear conscience; trust in divine mercy; improve the mind; embrace regular industry and regular rest; govern the passions; never expect too much.[9]

During the years of Lee's boyhood another influence was spreading across the nation, which would challenge this graceful cerebral design. A series of religious revivals, collectively called the Second Great Awakening, swept from New York and New England into Virginia around 1811. The movement preached the importance of an individual relationship with God, which was open to all who sought it. Instead of relying on intellectual

proof of a divine providence, the evangelicals stressed intuitive, emotive aspects of faith—the very "enthusiasm" ministers of the Enlightenment era
had warned against. Each convert was convinced that the base nature of his
soul—indeed, of all humankind—was so repugnant that he must continually atone, by suffering agonies of earthly disappointment and praying for
peace and absolution in the hereafter. Christ was accepted as a guide and intermediary, but a strict and rather Old Testament God dominated evangelical thought. This God was a controlling figure, an active participant in
human history, leaving mankind helpless to define its own destiny. He was
not particularly merciful—the standard belief was that God distributed
punishment in good measure for the betterment of sinners—and he required persistent courting. Believers saw every misfortune as a sign of God's
discipline, and each success as an indication of divine approval. For most
Protestants, the Bible became the single source of authority, though in the
Episcopalian Church, the Book of Common Prayer retained its special importance. Those who embraced this kind of relationship eschewed materi-
alism and espoused order, self-restraint, and an active role in converting
others. Typically they "renewed" their faith through revival meetings or
other charismatic forms of worship.[10] The central idea was that no justification or rationalization could serve as the basis of faith—only resignation to
God's will and the heart's sincere reception of Christ.

Though the evangelical movement sometimes appeared to have sprung
up spontaneously, in fact it was responding to a series of pressing social concerns. The American population was embracing more democratic ways of
living and governing. Many wanted to see these trends reflected in their
churches, to feel more directly involved in their religion, and to spurn the
rigid hierarchies that had characterized some sects. At the same time, the fluidity and enterprise of the early national period, which fueled the ambition
of many, left others deeply unsettled and longing for stability. Evangelicals,
with their emphasis on order and community, and their rejection of material
satisfaction, provided an antidote for the chaos and greed that were seen as a
product of rapid economic expansion. In regions such as the South, which
had a widely dispersed population and a striated society, evangelical religion
also proved to be a unifying force, forming a community of the like-minded.
The missionary spirit of the evangelicals also heralded the beginning of widespread concern with perfecting not just the self but the whole society, and
from the tide of revivals came the first flood of reform movements. In addition, health issues dominated domestic concerns in the early years of the nation, when child mortality, epidemics, and loss in childbirth were distressingly
common. Though faith in science had enjoyed brief popularity during the

late eighteenth century, it had proven unsustainable, and the hope that human knowledge could conquer sickness and thwart death was disappointed for many decades. Above everything else, salvation offered the promise of being reunited with loved ones in a better world. With its strong emphasis on the afterlife, revivalism soothed the spirits of those who could find no other comfort against the helplessness of arbitrary loss.[11]

The shimmer of Virginia's "blue-lights," as the evangelicals were called, did not shine into the Lee household while Robert was growing up. His brothers Henry and Carter actively mistrusted the evangelicals, preferring the looser structures of Deism, and Light-Horse Harry continued to approach spirituality from an intellectual rather than inspirational vantage point.[12] Nonetheless, as a young man Robert was surrounded by the influence of the revival movement. His Aunt Elizabeth Randolph, with whom he stayed for long periods, was fired by the evangelical spirit, seeing herself as God's instrument to save those around her. "O how ought we to love God . . . ," she exclaimed to her family, "let Him only be yr stay yr delight & yr Glory."[13] Conversation among Lee cousins gave way to the new theology, and Uncle Edmund, as Alexandria's mayor, imposed his own piety on the townspeople, requiring a strict observance of the Sabbath.[14] As a schoolboy Robert was also exposed to the teachings of William Meade, one of the most important figures in the reformation of the Episcopal Church in Virginia. Meade arrived in Alexandria about the time the Lees moved to town. From the pulpit of Christ Church he proclaimed a message of loving subservience to God and separation from the temptations of the world, seasoned with prayer and supplication. He journeyed throughout the Virginia countryside, becoming intimately acquainted with his flock, urging them to repentance, but denouncing the unconstrained emotional scenes that inspired many revival camps. Like Ann Lee he continued to believe in the importance of rectitude, and closely monitored the conduct of his parishioners, yet one of the appealing qualities of his ministry was its practicality and joyfulness. "This sublime religion as I construe it bids me to be happy and recommends cheerfulness as the way to happiness," he wrote to his confidante and cousin, Molly Fitzhugh Custis, who had convinced him to join the ministry.[15] Meade put together a little book of parables for boys and girls, written with a simplicity that made it easy to absorb, and Robert later nostalgically recalled reciting this catechism. The young clergyman took an interest in the four-year-old that continued for half a century. In 1862, with war raging around him, Lee deeply mourned Meade's passing. "Of all the men I have known, I consider him the purest," he wrote.[16]

Mary Fitzhugh Custis, "a woman in a thousand," who greatly influenced Robert Lee's life.

By far the greatest influence in Robert Lee's religious development, however, was the bright spirit of Mary Fitzhugh Custis. Her fortitude, humility, and simple piety were emblematic of the evangelical movement, which was the center of her life. Like her cousin William Meade she viewed devotion and joy as intertwined; indeed she believed that no true pleasure existed outside the love of God. What impressed those around her was the way she lived out the precepts of her faith, incorporating them into the fabric of each day, never separating word from deed. "You always seemed to me, my dear Molly to be one of the happiest Christians I ever knew; and I have always thought I would give worlds to resemble you," exclaimed one of her wide circle of religious associates.[17] Her correspondence bears out the impression of her friends: it is endlessly cheering, comforting, and kind. When acquaintances blundered, she gently advised those with wagging tongues to embrace Christian charity. "She is truly to be pitied . . . ," Mrs. Custis wrote of one who had stumbled. "I hope you will all try to, I am sure you *do* feel towards her as a fellow creature in distress and therefore needing sympathy, in error and therefore needing instruction or rather *light* which let us pray that she may obtain."[18] It was this attitude that kept Robert and his brothers in Cousin Molly's grace when Black-Horse Harry's exploits shocked the neighborhood. Not only the Lee boys, but acquaintances far and wide, considered her a surrogate mother.[19] Although G. W. P. Custis never embraced the faith that moved his wife, he indulged her in it, and Molly Custis turned Arlington into a haven of beneficence. Prayers were said morning and evening, and as one friend wrote, God "was her daily companion, study and guide."[20] Her favorite passage was Psalm 103, which extolled the bounty of the Lord and humbly acknowledged that "we are but dust." Seeing herself as a servant of God, she chose as her ministry the amelioration of slavery. This inspired her devotion to the American Colonization Society, and caused her to free her own slaves and entreat her husband to follow her lead. However controversial the society's policies and successes, for Molly Custis it was a sincere way to ease the suffering she saw around her. "What casual observer, what stranger, what child has not been instructed, felt his soul warmed by the manner, the fervor of her heart-penetrating devotion," eulogized one admirer. Another said simply: "she is a woman in a thousand."[21]

Molly Custis multiplied her influence through a wide net of female friends throughout Maryland and Virginia. Chief among these was Anna Maria Fitzhugh in nearby Fairfax County. Cousin Anna, as Robert called her, had suffered terribly at her husband's sudden demise in 1830 and came to view her religion through the prism of sickness and death. She found comfort in the prospect of an afterlife with those she loved and sought to save as many of their souls as possible, for only through their conversion could they count on a glorious eternity together. Anna Maria Fitzhugh had an unusual rapport with the Lee brothers, and in their confidential conversations she transmitted her concern for their deliverance.[22] The death of Fitzhugh's husband was also the event that led Mary Anna Randolph Custis to her lifelong religious pursuits. She adopted an ardent form of evangelicalism that led to painful remorse, often for unspecified sins, and sometimes simply for the sorry fallibility of human existence. Her diary is full of pleading and anguish—of begging God to forgive her for daily ingratitude, and beseeching him to send trials that would test her will. Penitence for Mary Custis Lee came through denial of worldly pleasures, resignation to God's will, and passionate proselytizing. During her engagement to Robert, she wrote not of her present bliss but of the "instability of all earthly blessings which may be snatched from us at any moment & the necessity of fixing our affections upon those things which are eternal." Whereas her mother saw example and subtlety as the chief tools of persuasion, Mary robustly implored others to seek God, distributed religious literature, and doggedly pursued the salvation of her husband, father, children, and servants. She longed for a useful outlet for her zeal. Finally during the Civil War she found fulfillment in cheerfully providing for others and patiently enduring the crippling pain of rheumatism.[23] In an era when religious fervor was one of the few ways females could express their personalities, all of these women embraced the chance to gain respect, exercise authority, lead others, and improve the world. And all of them saw in Robert Lee the opportunity to harvest a soul for the glory of God.[24]

Lee came slowly to the evangelical altar. His classical and scientific training gave him great respect for human progress, and he was reluctant to discard the structured logic of West Point for unquestioning acceptance of an inscrutable God. While he was still at the military academy, another lion of the evangelical field, Charles Pettit McIlvaine, became chaplain and slowly began to sway some of the cadets. Notable among these was Leonidas Polk, who would become both a bishop and Confederate general. Cadet Lee failed to be impressed.[25] When he received religious exhortations in response to the lusty notes with which he courted his fiancée, Lee implored her to let him proceed toward grace at his own pace, and in his own way. "I think I would rather hear from anyone else how wicked all men are in general, and I in particular," he told his beloved. "That there is not happiness for me in this world, and that I had nothing to do but die and go elsewhere. Is this natural?"[26] So intense was his bride's campaign that he finally complained to Molly Custis, proposing that if he was to be guided, it should be by her hand.[27] After his marriage he held on to his scientific questioning and boldly announced that he believed that one could "disrupt the 'Lord thy God' by going contrary to the dictates of the reason & judgement he has given to guide us in this world."[28] For years he quoted Falstaff's merry men, Don Quixote, or General Scott rather than the Bible to explain the mysteries of the universe.[29] He admitted to falling asleep in church, and his young wife complained that he showed "little respect for the preacher" when he was able to stay awake.[30] At the onset of the Mexican War Lee consigned his fate to the outrageous play of fortune, not the will of God. When he heard that Markie Williams's father had been killed on the battlefield, he tried to soften her grief by invoking the tangible and temporal, not the prospect of a reunion in eternity.[31]

Mary Lee confided to her mother that she thought it would take "that faith which can move mountains" to accomplish a change of heart in her husband, but over time Lee did come to accept much of the evangelical doctrine.[32] Perhaps the conversion stemmed from frustration with his inability to advance himself through personal effort; perhaps it was the accumulated disappointments of his life—the disadvantage of awkward family members; the capricious way that assignments and promotion were distributed in the army; the difficulties of guiding his children or conducting a relationship with his wife. Though he is reticent in his description of the horrors he witnessed during the Mexican War, the initial exposure to man-made carnage was a thought-provoking experience for most men. In his narrow escapes during the conflict Lee experienced firsthand the randomness with which death is distributed in wartime, by what narrow margin one is hit or spared, and this terrible knowledge may have made him more aware of a need to nurture his soul. He began to fear that his days had been idle and empty, and as he tried to thank God for sparing him during the battles of Vera Cruz and Cerro Gordo found himself "far short of my obligations" and "unworthy" to ask for further mercy. He lost his dear friend Jack Mackay in these years as well, to tuberculosis, a disease that in his day was cruel and inexplicable.[33] By 1849, when Lee heard the riveting sermon described in the opening of this chapter, he was disgusted with mankind's folly and his own inadequacies. Unable to account for either his luck or his misfortune, he appears to have sought refuge in the evangelical notion that man's perception is imperfect, his efforts at control doomed, and God's chastisement just.[34]

Twenty years of cumulative social pressure may have influenced Lee's desire to trust solely in the mercy of God, but there is strong evidence that his epiphany came at the death of Mary Fitzhugh Custis in April 1853. Just as the passing of William Henry Fitzhugh had launched Mary Lee on her religious journey, his mother-in-law's unexpected demise proved cathartic to Robert Lee. He called it "the most affecting calamity that has ever befallen us" and struggled to find comfort.[35] The swiftness of her departure—"one day in the garden with her flowers, the next with her God"—impressed him with an understanding that each moment was precious. "The blow was so sudden & crushing," he told his wife in sympathy, "that I yet shudder at the shock & feel as if I had been arrested in the course of life, & had no power to resume my onward march."[36] Markie Williams accompanied her cousin when he visited Mrs. Custis's grave a few months later and was startled to see him sobbing uncontrollably. "It was a scene for pity to behold," she confided to her diary, "to see that strong man weep so bitterly."[37] Lee advised Markie and his children that the best way to honor Molly Custis was to emulate her, and he appears to have determined to do so himself. "May God give me the necessary strength, & above all the power to live, that when I die, my last end may be like her," he prayed.[38] He told his nephew Edward Lee Childe that he had moved beyond that point in life when he could contemplate the future with joy and expectation; now looking ahead brought only "feelings of apprehension & resignation."[39] Accordingly, he made the serious decision to be confirmed in the Episcopal Church, and on the evening of July 17, 1853, with daughters Mary and Annie at his side, he knelt at the altar of Christ Church and took communion for the first time. In the congregation Agnes watched "breathless" as Bishop John Johns preached a compelling sermon, calling all to Christ.[40] But no one was more moved than Mary Custis Lee, whose years of supplication were finally gratified. "I had the inexpressible happiness a few weeks hence of seeing my two daughters Mary & Annie with their dear Father kneeling at the confirmation table," Mary wrote in her journal, "& today I knelt with my husband at the supper of our blessed Lord. Happiness long waited for yet it could only be expressed in silent tears of joy. . . ."[41]

For the next eight years Lee would repeat the rhythmic phrases of the evangelical church. He avowed the conviction that God ordered all things for the best, berated himself for his innate wickedness, and consistently alluded to the suffering he underwent as a consequence. As he left his family to go to Texas in 1855, he wrote that it was "a just punishment for my sins"; if he was overtaken by depression, he proclaimed that "should it not please God to grant our prayers or favour our efforts, we must not repine, but be resigned"; when he saw death and despair around him, Lee counseled his family to "bow with humble resignation to all the chastisements of our heavenly father & submit ourselves entirely to his will."[42] During the 1850s he repeated these phrases in scores of letters, struggling to conform the skepticism and testing of his scientific training with the impenetrability of God's design and the belief that only faith could prove the presence of an almighty spirit. In the end he settled on a formula that must have pleased the engineer's heart—a tried and sure syllogism that explained everything and left nothing to chance. No matter what he or the world suffered, no matter the nature of favor or misfortune, no matter the unknown factors that could justify or refute an event, the second half of the equation would always end the same way: a merciful providence would order all things for the best. And man's role in this dynamic was equally unchanging: "We are all in the hands of a kind God, who will do for us what is best, & more than we deserve, & we have only to endeavor to deserve more, & to do our duty to him and ourselves."[43]

It was like a Gregorian chant in its soothing repeated tones and underly-

Christ Church in Alexandria, a few years after Lee was confirmed at its altar.

ing expression of simple harmony. In describing his religious feelings during these years, Lee forsakes the vivid, sentimental language that characterizes so much of his correspondence in favor of the palliatives of the era. Though never insincere, the words often seem to lack inspiration. The fervor of Mary Lee, whose single most emotional letter to her husband was written in the ecstasy of seeing her children dedicate themselves to God; the joy his mother-in-law found in easing the burdens of those around her; the exaltation of his daughter Agnes as she found a "sweet peace stealing over me making me so very happy . . . a feeling of deep gratitude to my Father in Heaven," were more elusive for Lee.[44] Nor was his a questing spirit. While his colleague Ethan Allen Hitchcock was examining the need for salvation ("saved for what?") and pondering the definition of eternity, and his old West Point nemesis Charles Mason was questioning whether the clergy's platitudes could ever describe God as eloquently as did the infinitude of space, Lee was constricting his faith to an unwavering, incurious set of rules.[45] Man's role, he wrote, was not to wrestle with larger theological issues, but only to "prove your gratitude and love to him by keeping his commandments and offering him daily your service, thanks and heartfelt worship."[46] Order appealed to him, as it did to many men who followed the revivalists, and the evangelical teaching of obligation and self-restraint meshed neatly with parts of his character that had long been formed.[47]

It was during these years that Lee became increasingly fixated—some writers have used the word "obsessed"—with the need to respond to "duty," and particularly to instill that attitude into his children and other young people.[48] "I hope our other dear girls are well and enjoying the satisfaction & serenity of the consciousness of doing their duty," he told Mary. "That is the greatest happiness that any can enjoy in this world. . . ."[49] Though the famous phrase associated with him—"duty is the sublimest word in the language"— has long been known to be a hoax, it nonetheless reflects his unswerving faith in the principle.[50] "I only wish to obey his commandments, to neglect nothing on our part for the accomplishment of that which is plainly our duty," Lee told his wife, "& with earnest prayers for his mercy & deliverance to leave the result in his hands."[51] The other part of the equation, that despite right and proper exertion by man, only God could command results, played to his passivity and indecision, encouraging complacency. Both of these concepts bolstered the freedom from guilt that Lee sought. We know that he was thin-skinned about disapproval, and that much of his perfectionism, his tendency to overreach to the point that he became "broken down a little," stemmed from a desire to deflect criticism by placing himself in an unassailable position. From his childhood, when he gained his mother's favor by sacrificing pleasure to his filial responsibilities, there is a hint that this was how he controlled the reactions of those around him and garnered approval. If one did his duty, one could do no more in the eyes of both God and man. And if God bore the ultimate responsibility for outcomes, no one could attack the decisions he took.[52]

Somehow, as he embraced these precepts more firmly, however, the soft edge of Biblical tolerance was lost. The good-natured ease, which as a young man he used so effectively to tease his acquaintances into gentlemanly comportment, gave way to less sympathetic pronouncements. As Lee struggled with the vision of man's sinfulness and helplessness, his outlook became ever more judgmental, ever more rigid. Human worth became reduced to a diagram of obligation and futility, and Lee's bemused acceptance of others fell prey to a harsh rule of inflexible responsibility. This may have influenced his overbearing pursuit of perfection in West Point's young men. It probably also underlay his increasing alienation from others as he entered his fifties, and the desperation he experienced in the following years, when he suffered from profound depression while serving on the plains of Texas. Though meant to be a shield against the uncertainties of life, tragically Lee's convictions seem to have brought him little comfort or pleasure.

Just before the Civil War, Lee's pronouncements become less negative and more aligned to praise and thankfulness. He began to rejoice again in the sensory evidence of God and the wonder of nature, recapturing some of the teachings of his youth. When Mary made a trip to Canada, he regretted that Annie could not accompany her. He had wished, he told her, that the "sight of Niagara with the rush of its mighty waters, might give you pleasure & more impress you with the might & sublimity of the great creator, & fill your heart with deeper gratitude for all his benefits."[53] In the following years, as the hideousness of war bore down on him, he often expressed his gratitude for the earth's beauty and took pleasure in the small daily delights of clouds and sunshine, violets and green hills. Early in the war, from western Virginia, he told of how he had relished the mountain vistas—"The valleys so peaceful, the scenery so beautiful! What a glorious world Almighty God has given us!" From Culpeper, soon after the battle of Chancellorsville, he struck the same note. "What a beautiful world God in his loving kindness to his creatures has given us. What a shame that man endowed with reason & a knowledge of right should mar his gifts."[54] The last line is another clue to a change in Lee's outlook around this time, as he stops berating himself and begins to lay collective sin at the door of the larger community. It was mankind that was alienating God through selfishness and ingratitude, and all would suffer or benefit according to the actions of others. This attitude came to reflect an important part of Lee's philosophy during the war, as he struggled to trust that his merciful providence would order all things for the benefit of the Confederacy. "I hope God will at last crown our efforts with success," Lee intoned: "But the contest must be long & severe & the whole country has to go through much suffering. It is necessary we should be humbled & taught to be less boastful, less selfish & more devoted to right & justice to all the world."[55]

As Abraham Lincoln would poignantly observe in his second inaugural address, both sides prayed to the same God; both firmly believed that He would intervene on their behalf; both invoked His aid against the other. At the start of hostilities, William Meade could write with certainty that he was "persuaded that God is with us & will give us success." From Ohio, Charles McIlvaine, long a friend and collaborator of Meade, would give similar assurances of God's favor to the Union.[56] White Southerners especially viewed the contest as a moral and religious crusade, a test of the superiority of their devoutness and their culture. Lee, who was under no illusions about the difficulties facing the Confederacy, believed that it might indeed take divine approbation for the South to succeed. "I pray that our merciful father in heaven may protect & direct us," he would write. "In that case I fear no odds & no numbers."[57] The early successes in Virginia boosted Confederate morale and gave them a special feeling of being shielded from disaster by God's favor. Lee fell into this idea along with his men, ascribing specific victories, and even small advantages, to the working of the Lord. "God has been so merciful to us in so many ways that I cannot repine at whatever he does," Lee noted after the Federal troops retreated in confusion at Fredericksburg. "His discomfiture of our numerous foes & obliging them to recross the river was a signal interference in our behalf. . . ."[58]

As the Confederacy's fate became linked to moral worth, personal and national salvation became intertwined. One of Lee's artillerymen expressed a near-superstitious belief in the connection of humility and victory as he contemplated the announcement of Stonewall Jackson's death.

> No news of any importance . . . except the confirmation of the reported death of Lieut. Genl T.J. Jackson. One of the greatest heroes of the war has been called from us by an all-wise Providence, no doubt as a punishment for our ascribing to a mere man praises due to God for giving to us Jackson with the virtues and talents he possessed. May it be a warning to us in the future, to remember that every man is what he is, only through the power and will of God; and that if we have successful and apparently great generals defending our cause, the honor and praise are due to God, and not to the mere men who are thus blessed.[59]

Such hurtful losses inspired revivals and conversions. The same cannoneer who wrote of Jackson's death described a baptismal event at which thirty-one soldiers were immersed in the river—a solemn scene "not accompanied by the jeering that might very reasonably have been expected, where so many reckless men were present."[60] Waves of religiosity swelled through the camps, peaking before critical battles and after the defeat at Gettysburg. In the presence of fear and slaughter, many of those in Lee's army were prepared to embrace the evangelical view of human depravity and to commit themselves to God. Some analysts believe that the nearly superhuman efforts of Lee's men during the Wilderness campaign were sustained by the charismatic belief in God's protection.[61] Lee applauded the devotions, sometimes joining in them and setting an example through attendance at prayers and through orders "to inculcate lessons of morality and piety among the troops."[62] He was open-minded about differences of worship, as well, which is interesting given his strong anti-Catholic pronouncements. Just as he had permitted Catholic cadets at West Point to worship at off-campus churches, he approved, when practical, special leave for religious observance among the Jews in his army.[63] Along with Jefferson Davis, he fostered the religious spirit by calling for days of fasting and prayer. From the trenches he described a religious meeting in the summer of 1864: "Mr Platt held service again today under the trees near my camp. . . . During the service I constantly heard the shells crashing around the houses of Petersburg."[64]

When outcomes became uncertain, the intent of the Lord was more difficult to fathom. Some viewed the emotion-laden revivals with cynicism, particularly after the disappointments of late 1863. Everyone was excited about a proposed camp meeting in Richmond, wrote a government clerk, but he thought it "the Caesarian method of being born again, violating reason, and perhaps outraging nature."[65] A staff officer in the Army of Northern Virginia railed against God in the days after Gettysburg, when a prolonged drought added to the Confederacy's woes. "Can we believe in the justice of Providence, or must we conclude that we are after all wrong? Such visitations give me great bitterness of heart, & repinings at His decrees."[66] Some soldiers even questioned the fundamental premise of their struggle, and their right to bear arms, though this was not widespread. "Two nations of professed Christian people are thrusting bayonets at each others bosom, and the highest excellence answered by the great success in killing human beings . . . ," a Confederate soldier wrote disgustedly to his wife. "It is so horrible in nature that it seems rational creatures would never engage in it. But we are poor fallen, covetous & wicked creatures." A Texan called participation in battle "the most blasphemous thing perhaps on earth."[67] Another observed that the number of revivals was outpaced only by the number of desertions.[68] The contradiction between personal righteousness and national defeat became increasingly uncomfortable, and Southerners began to fear that the course of the war was a divine indictment. They scrutinized their catalog of sins, from avarice to vanity, and looked to the pulpits for reassurance. Preachers had a newfound prominence as leaders in the years of evangelicalism, and the anxious congregations hung on their words. Most were happy to soothe the fraying nerves of their flocks. Savannah's Bishop Stephen Elliott, for example, argued there was nothing in the Gospel that prohibited war as long as it was defensive—and this of course was just the perspective Confederates continued to hold.[69]

Lee too needed comfort as the string of difficulties became more and more ominous. One day, toward the end of the war, he sat down and began to cull heartening words from the Psalms, words that gave strength to the weak and evoked God's aid against his enemies. "Preserve me, O God: for in thee have I put my trust," he copied on a scrap of paper; then "O keep my soul & deliver me: let me not be confounded for I have put my trust in thee." And at the end of the list: "Oh hide not thy face from me, nor cast thy servant away in displeasure."[70] From the start Lee had been superstitious about invoking God's anger through hubris, or ingratitude, or vice, and whatever feelings he held in his heart, his outward expression was always deferential. Overall he thought the war was a sign that the country was paying a severe penance for its collective deletions. Any act that took the Lord's favor for granted would arouse divine displeasure.

He cautioned troops and populace to hew to righteousness, to sacrifice and pray continually, and he feared the "heavy punishment" he believed had been sent to them. At the same time Lee began backing away a bit from the idea of an all-powerful God, suggesting that human exertion was critical, no matter what the heavens ordained. He cautioned his wife to leave Richmond at an early date because prudence, not Providence, willed it. A merciful God might order all things for their good, he told her, "but we do not know what that is, or what he may determine, & it behooves us to use the perception & judgment he has given us for our guidance & well-being."[71] He concluded one order to J. E. B. Stuart by "Commending you to a Kind Providence & your own good judgement. . . ." In the face of desperation, Lee announced that *he* had determined to fight to the last, whatever God willed.[72] And when the end grew near, he, like so many other Southerners, realigned his arguments to justify defeat. God and the South had had a sacred relationship. It was because God esteemed Southerners that he had so chastised them. The special tie was not ruptured as long as they bore the affliction bravely, he concluded, "until he is graciously pleased to pardon our Sins."[73]

It would be easy to interpret these lines as an admission of guilt over the wrongs of human slavery or the denial of God's commandment not to kill. In the South such soul-searching was generally too painful to be broached, and the sins that were evoked—breaking the Sabbath, impatience and foolish quarrelling, sloth and opportunism—substituted for a societal confrontation with shame. Those who dared to approach the ethical questions of slavery couched it in terms of abuse within the system, not a condemnation of the institution itself. Slavery, they believed, had been part of God's compact with the South, a precious burden placed there so that whites could be sanctified by their responsibility, and Africans could be civilized through Christianity. Few doubted this: it gave them a mission and a purpose, as well as a justification for their continued reliance on the institution.[74] Mary

Chesnut recorded her astonishment when, late in the war, she heard from the pulpit a complete reversal of the righteous credo that had heralded the opening of the conflict. What she learned was that God did not condone slavery, and that agony had been visited on the South because of its acceptance of such practices. "And so we came away," she exclaimed, "shaken to the depths."[75] Even when military defeat was obviously inevitable, it was denied by many, for the retribution it implied. Some have called it a massive cognitive dissonance, a denial of reality that substituted trivialities for transgression. In the North, where there was a temptation to point an accusing finger at the South, the faithful were similarly shaken as they contemplated their own capacity for destruction and inhumanity.[76]

In the Confederacy civilian will was undermined not just by the steady declines in military success but by the suspicion that southern actions were perhaps not as virtuous as they had hoped. In some cases there was a real fear that the slave states had offended God. No one scrambled to publicly abandon the cause, but they did redefine it, often within the parameters of evangelical doctrine. If God chastened the very folk he called to himself; if he burnished the select—then not only did misfortune become favor, but misery became martyrdom. If victory had evaded the military forces, moral triumph rested with the people, who could demonstrate in their destitution that they were the meek, the unfortunate, the agonized of God, and therefore the special lambs of his flock. Some went so far as to question whether or not victory would have been a spiritual blessing, since it was sure to foster loathsome pride. One historian has written that while feeling "desperately insecure and standing under apparent condemnation by both God and man, Southern churchmen soon began to argue that their suffering was not really a curse—but a testament to their vindication in the court of divine justice."[77]

At the center of this triumphant morality stood General Lee. From the beginning of the war Lee had been heralded as the very personification of noble character—a man with traits to which others might aspire, but seldom achieve. As the war progressed, his qualities also became bound up with the idea that he was an agent of God. Divine Will and Lee and Victory became a kind of trinity. He did not seek this, but neither did he negate it, and one senses that at times his acceptance of this anointment led him to overzealousness and imprudence. As the sad ending drew nearer, there were those who questioned whether they had misplaced their faith. "We have depended too much on Gen Lee too little on God," wrote one devastated woman, "& I believe God has suffered his surrender to show us he can use other means than Gen Lee to affect his ends."[78] Most, however, retained a reverence for the general that denied either error on his part or any celestial displeasure. He became a trophy of gentlemanly sensibilities and martyrdom, the incarnation of the South's superior virtue. His dignity in defeat seemed to epitomize the righteousness of failure. More important, his unambitious code, which shunned worldly success as the end goal of existence, flew in the face of every stereotype about the Yankees. With Lee's innate integrity, the South could recapture the moral high ground from the North. Some began to see meaningful similarities between Lee and their traditional beliefs: a man betrayed by lesser men; humble in the face of superior power; a voice advocating forgiveness against the unpardonable; with a character "honed to perfection by pain."[79] Lee, to his credit, never indulged or encouraged this, but it crept through the last years of his life just the same. And so he came full circle into an emotional world of veneration and imagery. The reluctant convert who drew every inexplicable event into an equilateral relationship between God's will, man's acceptance, and ultimate good; the true believer in a secular faith of duty and diligence: Robert E. Lee had now become a sacred symbol of southern dogma.

Chapter Fifteen

Odyssey

San Antonio, Texas
1 March 1860

Albert M Lea Esqr
  Engineer
  Dear Sir

I am very much obliged to you for your friendly letters of the 24th, 25th & 26th Ulto. which arrived together by the last mail. I feel that I owe to your kindness rather than to my merit your recommendations to Govr Houston. I am aware of his ability, & first became acquainted with him upon my entrance into the Military Academy. He was President of the Board of Visitors that year & the impression he made has never been effaced. I have followed with interest his career since, & have admired his manly qualities & conservative principles. His last position in favour of the Constitution & Union elicits my cordial approbation.

Should military force be required to quiet our Mexican frontier, I have no doubt that arrangements will be made to maintain the rights & peace of Texas, & I hope in conformity to the Constitution & laws of the country. It will give me great pleasure to do all in my power to support both. The number of U.S. troops in the State is so small, that they afford but a feeble guard against marauders of every kind—The Indian frontier seems to be infested by predatory bands, of three, five, 7 & 12 &c who steal into the settlements on foot, do all the mischief they can, mount themselves, & make good their retreat before they can be discovered & overtaken. I had hoped that the removal of the indians beyond the borders of Texas, would have arrested these thieving incursions, but on the contrary, I have never known them more frequent. Scouts are kept constantly out from all the posts, & the trails are followed till the horses fall dead under their riders, so much are they worn down by constant & hard service. I hope however when the Regiments from Utah arrive things will be on a more favourable footing.

The horses you mention being at Ft Leavenworth I have heard were intended for the 1ˢᵗ Cavʸ, a portion of which is in Kansas, & the rest on the Arkansas & Wichita County. They were awaiting the advance of Spring, & a consequent supply of grass, before sending them to this latter detachment.

I am very much pleased to get your opinion of the facilities afforded by Aransas Bay, as a harbour &c. It has always seemed to me as the natural Port of this place & the country north of it. With more reason will it serve the convenience of the country South & the Rio Grande line above Laredo. I wish I could accept your invitation to visit it, but it is impossible for me to do so at this time. I am sufficiently aware of the advantages of its position without a personal inspection, & when your improvements are sufficiently developed to attach the trade to that place & to open communication with the Eastern Ports, I feel very confident [the] Govt will be happy to avail themselves of the privileges it will afford.

You may rely upon my not mentioning the plans, preparations or views of the compʸ until disclosed by themselves, & upon my remaining very truly yours RE Lee[1]

. . .

San Antonio, Texas
22 Febʸ 1860
My precious Annie
   By the last mail I wrote to your mother at the White House & to daughter, announcing my safe arrival. To day I will write to you, but have nothing to say, except to repeat my distress at parting with you all, & my longing desire to see you again. I know it is useless to indulge these feelings, yet they arise unbidden, & will not stay repressed. They steal on me in the business hours of the day & the waking hours of night, & seem to hover around me waking or sleeping. I have not much work to do, but many vexatious reports to listen to & small means to correct & improve. In addition to Indian alarms & depredations, we have the filibustering reports & Mexican aggressions to scrutinize & discuss. The latter come so thick & various, that it is difficult to sift the chaff from the grain. I hear that the Governor has made a report to the President, so I suppose we shall soon hear, what is to be done. The troops are so scattered that the line is very attenuated, & more force will have to be thrown into the country, if anything is accomplished. I have seen some of my former acquaintances here. All are well & have recᵈ me with their usual kindness. They wonder I did not bring you all out. They do not know your capacity, & as compressible as you are on the surface, what space is covered by your numbers. I hope the poor Mim is

well, & that you girls will help her & take care of her. I have of course heard
nothing of her since I left. I presume she is at the White House, & trust she is
well. I hope F. & C. are also well & that I will soon get letters informing me on
all these points. I see but little change in San Antonio. Some good houses have
been built in my absence but my former residence has lost for me all its charm.
In the beginning of this month, the river rose eight feet & carried away the bath
house, the only tenement in the lot I coveted. I do not know where to fix myself,
nor whether to fix myself at all. Things look so uncertain. I am trying to get ser-
vants & horses. Give much love to everybody & love

    Always your father
    RE Lee[2]

>⊶─○─⊷<

ROBERT E. LEE's appointment as lieutenant colonel of the 2nd Cavalry opened a difficult period of his life. As he diplomatically hinted to Governor Sam Houston's aide, his command responsibility, which included restraining rancorous Indians and marauding Mexicans, was difficult enough. It was made more frustrating by the lack of adequate resources to do the job. Lee spent endless days in the saddle, riding through a punishing environment, to little effect. His ability to successfully manage his post was frequently interrupted by court-martial duty, something he heartily disliked. Back in Virginia his wife was ill; his children were at an impressionable age; and he was too far removed to give them meaningful help. Public apprehension was also high, as the nation careened toward disunion, precipitating wrenching decisions of loyalty and obligation. Forced to face conflicts he had left unresolved for decades, he despondently told faithful Anna Maria Fitzhugh, "one is rent by a thousand anxieties, & the mind as well as body is worn & racked to pieces."[3]

Robert Lee's Texas odyssey began with high expectations. The creation of two new infantry and two new cavalry regiments, the first army expansion in decades, was a major event in military circles. Competition was keen for the regimental leadership positions, with their promise of fresh adventure and the rare opportunity for advancement. Secretary of War Jefferson Davis and General Winfield Scott handpicked the officers, ignoring seniority in their exhaustive search for the best men. Davis was notorious for selecting those he personally liked, but he also chose unusually capable men, lending an appointment in one of the new regiments the prestige of a merit promotion. Albert Sidney Johnston, whose quick thinking had saved Davis's life during the Mexican War, was put in charge of the 2nd Cavalry, with Lee as his next in command. President Franklin Pierce questioned the number of Southerners proposed for the post; later Davis would be accused of having used the regiments as a training ground for officers who would fight with the Confederacy. Whether or not the criticism was justified, Davis's eye for talent was exceptional. Of the forty-three officers who served in Texas, an impressive sixteen would become generals during the Civil War, ten of them for the South.[4]

With such a concentration of ability, the regiments started out on an optimistic footing. "I was young and buoyant in spirit," remembered John Bell Hood, who was a lieutenant on Lee's staff; "my men were mounted and all eager for a chase as well as a fray."[5] The new units had provoked a loud debate within the government, and Davis was anxious that no detail be omitted that would ensure their success. He sponsored a "recruitment" campaign to find the finest horses in Kentucky, and approved the design of a dashing new uniform that boasted shell jackets, an elegant plumed hat, and pantaloons emboldened by a yellow stripe down each side.[6] Morale was high when the regiments assembled near St. Louis to continue recruitment—this time of men—and prepare for the overland trip to Texas. Colonel Lee was not quite so caught up in the excitement as some of the others. He had left the Corps of Engineers with reluctance, and now he sorrowfully left his family as well. He was further irritated when the army interrupted his preparations by assigning him to four courts-martial in as many months.[7] Nor did he underestimate the difficulties of the operations in Texas. It was, he told brother Carter, "a distant & hazardous expedition, the result of which can of course be known to none."[8]

The pretext for expanding the army had been the recurrent problem of Indian attacks in the immense frontier that stretched from the Red River to the Rio Grande. Despite the government's repeated assurances to the native peoples, white settlers were making steady inroads on their grounds. The Indians responded with punishing raids on the white men's horses and cattle. Horses were particularly important in Comanche civilization, which predominated in the region. Vehicles for hunting and for making war, horses also were used as currency, and in lean times were eaten. Those lean times were ever more frequent as buffalo and other game were pushed out by white encroachment. Around the time of Lee's arrival, a young Indian man was not permitted to join the ranks of the braves unless he had stolen horses or mules or had won a scalp. Whites were not inclined to romanticize Native Americans; nor did they forget the very real horrors of mass slaughter at their hands. After Texas achieved statehood in 1845, the settlers demanded protection, and the army built a series of forts to serve as a stronghold in case of serious attack.[9] Yet the vast, uncharted prairie was nearly impossible to control. Frederick Law Olmsted, who traveled through the area around the time of Lee's arrival, thought the placement of a few soldiers in the wilderness was laughable—"Keeping a bull-dog to chase mosquitoes would be no greater nonsense than the stationing of six-pounders, bayonets, and dragoons for the pursuit of these red wolves." Albert Sidney Johnston, though confident of his men's abilities, was also under no illusions about the difficulty of subduing the Indians. There was "nothing in the nature of the country offering any obstacle to their movements," he wrote soon after the regiment was formed. "The country is as open as the ocean."[10]

Though they would have more direct contact with the Indians than any other white leadership group, most army officers did not admire the native peoples, whom they considered indolent, vengeful, and intellectually inferior. Lee's friends Jack Mackay and Ethan Allen Hitchcock were among the few who would show sympathy for the Indians and an appreciation of their culture, but Lee, who termed the natives "hideous" and maintained that the government's job was to "humanize" them, was more in line with the mainstream view.[11] Regulars also feared the Indians, and in that fear was a grudging admission of their skill. The Comanche were superior horsemen who fought with great ferocity, and with an intimate understanding of the terrain. Their "wonderful caution and subtlety" were such that on one occasion a few warriors stole twenty horses by silently leading them through a guard of 600 soldiers.[12] These were components of guerrilla warfare for which West Point graduates were not well trained. Within Comanche society a brave rose to chieftain through his natural ability to attract followers, and this also gave them certain advantages of leadership. When scalp-bedecked warriors appeared on the horizon, brandishing their red-painted lances and round buffalo-skin shields, the army men looked upon them with dread and detestation.[13]

In addition to protecting the settlers, the army's mission was to uphold native rights and keep peace among the various tribal factions. One of its main jobs was to guard two reservations, holding about 1,500 Indians, which had been established in 1854. One of these was located on the Brazos River near Camp Cooper, the early headquarters of Lee's 2nd Cavalry. The policy was one of containment—the idea was to keep the Indians in a supervised area—and the unspoken agenda was to "civilize" the Comanche by teaching them agriculture, and impressing on them the need to conform to the white man's advance. In the racial presumption of the day, native peoples were expected to embrace the "superior" ways of the white man with gratitude. If they did not do so by choice, indiscriminate killing was the accepted alternative. "It is a distressing state of things that requires the applications of such treatments, but it is the only corrective they understand, & the only way in which they can be taught to keep within their own limits," concluded Lee.[14]

And so began the disheartening pattern of broken promises and untenable pressures that ensured failure for most Indian policies.[15] Nonetheless, Catumseh, the chief of one of the larger Comanche groups, had recognized that the depletion of hunting grounds and interfactional strife jeopardized the ability of his people to survive. For two years Catumseh's people cultivated the barren area along the Brazos, with some initial success. Unfortunately, around the time of the 2nd Cavalry's arrival a drought destroyed the crops—as well as Comanche trust.[16] Lee was among those who were delegated to deal with Catumseh, and Fitzhugh Lee, who also served on the Texas border, recalled a meeting at which his uncle Robert intended to show the chief who was really in charge. Lee offered friendly relations as long as the tribe "deserved" them, but told Catumseh he "would meet him as an enemy the moment he failed to keep his word." Unimpressed by the government's avowed reverence for truth, Catumseh replied that he was an important chief with six wives and "would have more respect for Lee if he had followed his example." "They separated," noted Fitz Lee, "mutually convinced that the other was a cunning specimen who had to be watched." It is regrettable no meaningful dialogue was developed with Catumseh, for he was a man willing to consider a variety of options to preserve his people. Confronting real want, the Comanche increased their depredations, and reservations became little more than a jumping-off place for the exploits of the braves.[17]

In early spring 1856, after hearing of one particularly gruesome raid, Johnston dispatched Lee with two companies of men to impress the raiders with the full power of the U.S. Cavalry. They set off in late May, the younger officers full of excitement. Camp Cooper, with its scanty supplies and austere accommodations, its useless drills, harsh winds, and monotony, was a difficult post. The expedition was seen as a welcome relief from boredom and a chance to show off the army's skill. Hubris was high after the successes of the Mexican War, and it was a still common conceit that twenty army men should be able to beat twice their number in Indian braves.[18] The expedition turned out to be more a primer on the realities of the Texas wilderness than a chastisement of the Comanche. For weeks Lee and his men patrolled the desolate country, encountering only one small band of

Indians, half of whom they killed. The same drought that had burned up the Comanche crops had parched the countryside, and the expedition became obsessed with the search for grass and water. The weather changed in a flash from broiling heat to the piercing winds of a storm from the north.

Comanche Meeting the Dragoons, by George Catlin.
SMITHSONIAN AMERICAN ART MUSEUM / ART RESOURCES

"Norther!" Johnston would exclaim. "It makes me cold to write the word. I do not believe that any of the hyperborean explorers felt the cold more intensely than did my regiments."[19] The men battled "fleas by day & mosquitoes by night" and compared rattlesnake stories around the campfire. To Lee's distress the elegant, hand-selected horses did not thrive under these conditions; nor did the heavy army coats prove appropriate to the climate. Captain E. Kirby Smith, who accompanied Lee, drew the paradoxical conclusion: only by adopting the Indians' methods, dress, and manner could the cavalry operate successfully against them. After drifting for forty days in the Texas wilderness, Lee's company returned to Camp Cooper.[20] The 1,100-mile journey had been as much a penance for their pride as a display of authority. "Justice always comes lumbering one day behind the rogue," sneered one observer of the army. "Wherever posted they are the standing butt of the frontiersmen."[21]

It was the first episode in what Lee called his "wandering over the plains."[22] Each expedition would prove as futile as the first, the Indians elusive and the hardships unimaginable. On one trip he rode for twenty-seven days through "the most barren & least inviting country" he had ever seen, drinking filthy, tepid water that even the mules refused, all in order to reach a court-martial that he had no desire to attend. On another journey the weather was so hot that the candles melted in their stands.[23] It was the Wild West without its glamour, and Lee's letters from this time are filled with evocative imagery that helps us to picture him in the unwelcoming landscape. "The mud is indescribable to those not acquainted with the soil," he writes from one expedition, "& with breeches rolled up to the top of my boots I plunge through regardless of its depth."[24] He told his youngest daughter that he had built a chicken coop on the back of his wagon, and that he carefully sheltered the poultry from wolves, snakes, and storms. "Soldier hens, however," he remarked, "must learn not to mind rain."[25] He described driving four stakes into the ground and spreading his blanket over them to make a shelter one Fourth of July. "The sun was fiery hot, the atmosphere like a blast from a hot air furnace, the water salt," he said, "still my feelings for my country were as ardent, my faith in her future as true, and my hopes for her advancement as unabated as they would have been under better circumstances."[26] Many of his men shed their uniforms for more informal and appropriate clothing, but Colonel Lee appears to have ridden across the chaparral in full regalia, sometimes getting it mired by the elements. "I was detained one day on the road by high water—had to swim my mules and get the wagon over by hand," he wrote from his twenty-seven-day marathon. "My mare took me very comfortably, but all my wardrobe, from socks up to plume, was immersed in the muddy water, epaulets, sash, &c. . . ."[27]

These adventures were constantly interrupted by orders to be present at courts-martial. Perhaps this was a compliment to Lee's discretion—or maybe it bespoke the unfavorable ratio of senior officers to criminal delinquencies. In any case, he found the need to sit in judgment of fellow officers distasteful, and the closed sessions excruciating. Lee could be at his satiric best when portraying the court scenes, and he indulged himself in lampooning the process in letters to his camp confidant, Captain Nathan Evans. "I am in a Court that likes *long* justice," he complained when one proceeding, involving a gangly officer, dragged on for months. "*Tall* justice it has to administer; but when it will get to the *end* of it I cannot say."[28] He took the responsibility seriously, writing to cousins and colleagues for legal advice, and one Lee biographer believes that the tedious days in the courtroom gave him important exposure to the inner workings of army bureaucracy. It certainly underscored his belief that conditions like those in Texas often caused weak men to err. "Fighting is the easiest part of a soldier's duty," he wrote. "It is the watching, waiting, labouring, starving, freezing, wetting, exposure & privation that is so wearing to the body & trying to the mind. It is in this state that discipline tells; & attention night & day on the part of the off^r so necessary."[29] Whatever the professional advantages, Lee longed to be excused from this duty. "You may ask in your turn what I am doing here, & that will be hard for me to answer," he groused to Evans. "I can only say . . . that I am of no use here & that I ought not to be here."[30]

Of the many hardships suffered on the frontier, Lee most keenly felt the isolation from family and friends. Stuck in the "desert of dullness," as he told his wife, he became increasingly despondent.[31] He tried to convince Mary and the girls to visit, praising the plucky wives of A. S. Johnston and George Thomas, and pointing out the opportunity to paint exotic birds and wildflowers along the Rio Grande.[32] When pressed, Mary Lee confessed to her husband that her rheumatism had progressed so far that she was often unable to walk, telling him that "it is fortunate for you that you have not got me in your tent at present. . . ."[33] This, and the consistent need to change posts and confront the punishing terrain, finally convinced Lee that it was best that his family remain in Virginia. After sticking his finger on a plant called the "Spanish Bayonet," Lee wrote in resignation: "Every branch and leaf in this country nearly are armed with a point, and some seem to poison the flesh. What a blessing the children are not here!"[34] Still, the greater wound was in his heart. He tried to drive the lonely thoughts from his mind, but, as he admitted to Annie, "they rise unbidden, & will not stay repressed."[35]

Faced with the bleakness of the plains, deprivation, and disappointment, Lee drifted toward introspection. He withdrew as much as he could from company, avoiding society in San Antonio and the larger forts. He warned his sons against "annoying and entangling" friendships and rode in solitude on the prairies to look at the birds and snakes.[36] Often his only outlet for expression was through the mails. Lee's letters from the years in Texas are among the most vulnerable and dejected of his writings, a great outpouring of loneliness and frustration. Writing itself was taxing, as he told his daughter Mary: "the violence of the wind requires all my hands to hold the paper and . . . my writing materials as you may perceive have been immersed in turbid water, & the dust of the Rio Grande besides, destroying the fluidity of my ink & the elasticity of my pen. . . ."[37] It seems remarkable that letters were delivered at all on that forlorn frontier, but by a long passage of boat, rail, and mule train many of them did arrive. Lee calculated the time of delivery to be about five weeks between Texas and Arlington, though, as he observed, one had to be "prepared for miscarriages." He resolutely advised himself to wait, "patiently if I can, but at all events wait," and wrote home at least once a week, whether or not he had received any mail.[38]

He was living out some universal themes—of man's struggle against nature, and of the flawed interaction among human beings. Pitted against these classic challenges, Lee retreated into an odyssey of the mind, seeking transformation. In his anguish he again raised "the question, which I have staved off for 20 years, whether I am to continue in the Army all my life"—and arrived at the same impasse.[39] The conflict between home obligations and army duty had never seemed more acute, nor his indecision more grating. In irritation he railed against a profession that "debars all hope of domestic enjoyment" and tried to convince his young relatives that a military career was not so romantic as they imagined.[40] Then he would backtrack, saying it was not the difficulties of army service that discouraged him—"the vicissitudes of camp life are no hardship to me"—but simple lonesomeness.[41] Perhaps this flood of dissatisfaction rose from an uncomfortable sense that he had abandoned his family, much as his own father had left him in his formative years. Whatever the complex emotions, he was seemingly paralyzed by his options, and failed to take the steps necessary to change his situation.

Lee was also grieving over real personal losses at this time. He was still recovering from his mother-in-law's death when, in July 1856, he received a letter from Mary telling him of the unexpected loss of his sister Mildred. They had been close when growing up, the two youngest children of that troubled family, and Mildred, with her beauty, her music, and her laughter, had always been a source of joy to Robert. He was "little prepared for this sudden & harsh severance," he would write. "It has cut short my early wishes and daily yearnings, and so vividly does she live in my imagination and affection that I cannot realize she only exists in my memory."[42] He cherished a lock of Mildred's hair, sent by his brother-in-law, and wound it round a carefully saved strand of his mother's dark tresses.[43] Soon thereafter two small children in the garrison expired from the heat. When the families asked him to read the funeral service, he performed the painful official duty, but it propelled him into unhappy contemplation of earthly misery.[44] The death of George Washington Parke Custis in October 1857, the man who had been "all . . . a father could," increased his despair.[45] Even the animals he turned to for comfort disappeared. His favorite mare was "carried off" by a wild horse and never found. A wildcat he kept in a cage became so vicious that he had to let it go, and finally his pet rattlesnake, which he had carefully fed, "grew sick & would not eat his frogs &c & died one night."[46] He began to dwell on his own death, portraying himself as having but a few years left to live. He feared that he would seldom again see his sons, and felt he had urgent incentives to prepare for the hereafter. "Life with me is very uncertain & I am anxious to accomplish what has devolved upon me," he would write.[47]

Lee appears to have felt a powerful loss of control during this period. He had been sent to restrain the Indians, but they continued to be sly and dangerous. He was helpless against his wife's illness, his children's whims, the desertion of the troops, and the unforgiving Texas geography. When he returned to Arlington for a time to settle the complicated Custis estate, he found he could not manage the slaves or make the property solvent. This was a deeply disturbing experience, collapsing any fantasies he harbored about pursuing the life of a gentleman farmer.[48] The army and his family so competed for his loyalty that he had been rendered impotent in melding his personal and professional aspirations. Unable to make a clear-cut decision, Lee could find no route to resolution and personal peace. He had lost the ability to order his own destiny.

Lee's letters of this time are filled with moralizing, as if he could manage his soul's sickness by offering resolute advice. His beliefs were strongly evangelical in principle, stressing the need to accept circumstance rather than a desire to command events. He justified his own passivity by calling on God to assume responsibility for the direction and final outcome of his efforts, relegating man to the role of respondent. Lee had been expounding this credo for years, but he reinforced it now in nearly every note he sent. Sometimes he was able to express it with wisdom lightly dispensed, and with such deep affection that it transcends the pedantic. At other times he offers his opinions with a disquieting severity. He told one desperately homesick daughter at boarding school that she should stop pining for the family and be "satisfied in doing what was right & . . . perfecting yourself in all usefulness."[49] For years his eldest son had also been the recipient of such counsel, often in the form of staccato orders. "Do not *dream*," Lee told him.

It is too ideal, too imaginary. Dreaming by day I mean. Live in the world you inhabit. Look upon things as they are. Take them as you find them. Make the best of them. . . . Do not imagine things are to happen as you wish. Wish them to happen right. Then strive hard to make them so. . . . Sad thoughts I know will sometimes come over us. They are necessary and good for us. They cause us to reflect. They are the shadows to our picture.[50]

Above all, he preached self-restraint and eternal vigilance against any indulgence that might lead to "the chains of idleness and vice."[51]

He was braiding together several strands of influence here: his mother's
unflinching determination in the face of misfortune; codes of manliness
that were currently in vogue; the evangelical religion of his wife and
mother-in-law, with its acceptance of a destiny that he could never affect;
the rigorous discipline drilled into him at Sylvanus Thayer's West Point. In
middle age Lee seems to have lost some of the genial acceptance of human
foible that had made him so popular in his youth.[52] Now he sought behavioral absolutes, as unvarying as the mechanical rules of engineering. Indeed
it seems at times as if he were trying to find an exact formula that would apply to all the uncertainties of the human condition; as if there were precise
theorems of personal conduct as certain and unassailable as a moral Euclid.
"We must be made to do what is *right*," he emphatically told his mother-in-
law, as if that would be self-evident in every case.[53]

As wise as are many of Lee's observations, there is some discomfort in
reading them; something that suggests arrogance, a belief that he alone knew
the true path, and an uncomfortable sense that Lee is abdicating responsibility for his own inaction. And, sadly, his inflexible standards contained little scope for wonder, or spontaneity, or pleasurable caprice. The American
birthright to pursue happiness is not to be found here, nor is there any con-
cession to his children's capacity to intelligently and creatively respond to
life. What is disquieting about this code of conduct is not the relentless-
ness—that fits well with the mores of the time and with the disciplined military life to which Lee was accustomed—but the joylessness of it. Perhaps it
was his only way of assuaging the conflict he felt about his absence from the
family, and his fear that they might blame him for it. Tragically, the more Lee
followed his narrow interpretation, the more he constricted his scope of action and the more discontented he became. "But I will not, dear Cousin
Anna impose my sad thoughts on you," he sighed to his longtime confidante, "for a man may manifest & communicate his joy, but he should conceal
& smother his grief as much as possible."[54] He had, it seems, a prescription for
everything but his own despair.

"I can think of nothing that would interest you in this paradise of the Texans," Lee wrote sourly, as he thought of all he was missing at home.[55] In
the 1850s Arlington was a bustling, chaotic blend of children's activities,
Grandpa Custis's ceremonial and artistic pursuits, and the demands of five
dozen slaves. Prominent guests shared its special ambience with a series of

yellow-striped cats, always named Tom. One visitor noted about this time that Arlington was "not the least bit in order"; but the disarray was eclipsed by its charming vista and venerable associations.[56] By now the house had the air of "an old castle," and Markie Williams treasured the sight of it in the moonlight—"truly the old mansion and its surroundings could not be exceeded at least in our partial eyes."[57] The younger Lees roamed the woods, swinging on grapevines, trying to catch squirrels, cracking hickory nuts.[58] Cousin Markie and the girls "laughed uncontrollably" while Mary Lee read aloud from Charles Dickens's new novel, *Little Dorrit.*[59] Lieutenant Custis Lee trooped home with comrade J. E. B. Stuart, and Rooney arrived "as large as life" with Harvard classmate Henry Adams in tow.[60] During the 1850s G. W. P. Custis was called on to inaugurate the Smithsonian Institution's new lecture room; to help Titian and Rembrandt Peale correctly model Washington's features; and to aid Constantine Brumidi as he created the heroic murals that would adorn the Capitol dome. Sculptor Thomas Crawford came to pay his respects and stayed to smoke a "segar" with Custis.[61] Despite such distinguished company, the family was wonderfully unpretentious. President Franklin Pierce spontaneously called one October morning, only to find the master of the house unavailable, young Miss Mary "in somewhat negligent attire," and Mildred too busy studying her French to look up.[62] From the moment that he arrived in Texas, Lee fantasized about reentering these scenes, yet the reality was disappointing when he finally obtained a furlough after the death of George Washington Parke Custis in 1857. His fastidious ways did not always correspond to the general mood of the household, he had trouble managing the estate, and he felt a sense of alienation from his wife and children. After he went back to Texas in early 1860, Lee petulantly told Annie that it "was better . . . that I am here. You know I was much in the way of every body, & my tastes & pursuits did not coincide with the rest of the household. Now I hope everybody is happier."[63]

Nonetheless, Arlington's chaotic gaiety was a notable contrast to the windswept prairies, and Lee was filled with heightened emotion whenever he thought of it. The letters he left from this period greatly illuminate his evolving mindset and also contain some of his most sentimental prose. However burdensome his correspondence, it is clear that it awakened his feelings and gave them form. In his search for a way to strengthen his precious connections, he could be touching, wry, or trenchant by turns. His style at this time had matured; gone were the affected, flippant phrases of his youthful letters; now the technique was more subdued, more elegant. But his old love of literature continued to be evident in the tales he recounted of adventure in Texas. Join him, for example, as he encounters Catumseh one afternoon:

> I was called upon the other day to visit Ka tem a se, the head chief of the Southern Camanches who was reported quite sick, & wanted a big *medicine man.* His lodges are only 2 miles below us, & when I presented myself before them on my big horse Bald Eagle, attended by an orderly dragoon, the explosion among the curs, children & women was tremendous. The medicine men rushed at me & made significant signs that I must disrobe before presenting myself before the august patient. I patiently sat on my horse till I ascertained what garment they considered most inimical to the practice of the healing art, which I learned to be the cravat. Then alighting, unbuttoning my coat & stripping off the noxious article, I displayed to their admiring eyes a blue check shirt, & was greeted by a general approving *humph.* The charm was fully developed, & I walked boldly in. The lodge was carpeted with Buffaloe robes. The sick man was stretched on his couch with his wives & suitors around him. His shield, bow & quiver were suspended in the outside, near which stood his favourite horse ready to be slain, to bear the spirit of his master to the far hunting ground. I thought him labouring under an attack of pleurisy—administered a loaf of bread & some sugar, of which I knew him to be very fond & which I had carried with me, & told him, I would send a man to complete his cure.[64]

The scene is wonderful, by turns tense and amusing, and quite revealing of the white man's patronizing feelings. Lee relates it so vividly that he takes us right into the drama. It is full of details that bring it alive: the carpet of buffalo robes in Catumseh's lodge; the chief's horse made ready to take him to the hereafter; Lee stripping off his uniform coat to reveal—a blue checked shirt! No wonder he was known as an entertaining storyteller.

He is equally expressive as he describes his feelings of isolation, particularly at Christmas. The season had always been an exceptionally merry one at Arlington, rich in the traditional trappings, and laced with the closeness of Lee's kin. Something stirred Lee mightily in his absence at Christmas, and he expressed it with affecting sincerity. "The time is approaching when I trust many of you will be assembled around the family hearth at dear Arlington, to celebrate another Xmas," he wrote wistfully in 1856. "Though absent, my heart will be in the midst of you; & I shall enjoy in imagination & memory all that is going on. May nothing occur to mar or cloud the family fireside, &

may each be able to look back with pride & pleasure at their deeds of the past year & with confidence & hope to that in prospect."[65] A few days later he carried the thoughts further. "I have been recalling my dearest Mary the many happy Xmas' we have had together, the pleasure I have enjoyed with you, your dear parents & the children around me. I ought not therefore, to repine at an occasional separation from you but be grateful for what I have had & be prepared to keep this solitary & alone. . . . I hope nothing will be omitted that I could have done, to make each one happy. . . ."[66] This is writing of a high order. Over and over in his letters Lee captures the simple joys and sorrows that made up the transcript of his life. But here the prose soars. Perhaps only General Orders No. 9, in which he bids farewell to his troops at Appomattox, reaches this eloquence, and that moving text, though edited by him and genuinely reflective of his thoughts, was drafted by an aide.[67] Lee's historical prominence has ensured that his letters have lasting value, but even had he remained an obscure cavalryman, his beautiful words would still speak across generations.

On his return from Arlington, Lee found that some colorful campaigns against the Indians had been initiated by Major General David Twiggs, commander of the Department of Texas. Twiggs, who was determined to use aggressive action to cut down on the tribal raids, won some of these battles, but the victories had been costly.[68] The Indian troubles were compounded by incursions of "banditos" from across the Mexican border. The most serious sorties came from a remarkable figure named Juan Nepomuceno Cortinas. Depending on one's perspective, Cortinas was either a horse thief and murderous rogue or a local champion, who fought to defend the honor of the *tejanos,* who were routinely treated as inferiors. Robert Lee called him "that myth Cortinas," and one regional folklorist has styled him "the most powerful, the most insolent, and the most daring as well as the most elusive Mexican bandit, not even exempting Pancho Villa, that ever wet his horses in the Rio Grande." Cortinas's exploits were aided by sympathetic supporters on both sides of the border, many of whom considered him a hero.[69] In the fall of 1859, after hearing about a Mexican compatriot who had been abused by some Brownsville toughs, Cortinas rode into town and quickly expropriated liquor, weapons, and authority—though he stopped short of indiscriminate killing. He told Brownsville's terrified population that he considered the town "a perfidious inquisitorial lodge to persecute and rob us, without any cause, and for no other crime on our part than that of being of Mexican origin."[70] The ailing and distracted Twiggs somehow misunderstood and believed that

Brownsville had been terrorized by Indians. He abandoned Fort Brown, the chief defense of the town. By early 1860, fears that Cortinas would ravage the countryside were widespread.

Exasperated, Governor Sam Houston complained to Secretary of War John B. Floyd, and was promised that an officer of skill and discretion would be sent to oversee operations in the Department of Texas. Colonel Lee was the man assigned. He was armed with orders from Floyd that allowed him an unusual amount of leeway in handling what had by now become a sensitive international issue. The catch for Lee was that Twiggs was still in titular command of the department and that he had very few resources. In the unenviable position of having full responsibility without ultimate authority, Lee had to act with delicacy in everything he undertook. His March 1860 letter to Albert M. Lea, which opens this chapter, is a masterpiece of careful bureaucratic writing, agreeing with the powerful governor but setting boundaries on his own actions. When Houston tried to get Lee to absorb the Texas Rangers into his cavalry regiments, Lee gently demurred, though he allowed them to accompany his forces on a long march along the Rio Grande, designed to corner the Cortinas gang. Lee used similar tact with the Mexican government, warning them of the need to uphold their border agreements and advising that the apprehension of Cortinas would be taken as evidence of friendly relations between the American and Mexican governments. But he was nervous. He hated trying to negotiate in a foreign language, "which makes convenient to misunderstand the proposition & dodge the answer," and he disliked the rumors of war and the prominence of his name.[71] Despite repeated attempts to capture Cortinas, the banditos eluded the U.S. Army and continued to burn ranches and harass the Texans. Charismatic and handsome as well as audacious, Cortinas went on to enjoy a popular political career, and was ultimately elected governor of Tamaulipas Province.[72]

It was another period of demoralization for Lee. He did not succeed against Cortinas, and his diplomatic obligations taxed his abilities and his resources. He was beset, as always, by routine matters. Troop changes; cavalry horses that, "nearly worn out, sometimes drop dead on the trail"; military posts described as "wretched"; and perpetual disciplinary cases—all kept him working into the late hours of the night.[73] At one point he was put in charge of a group of camels, which Jefferson Davis had ordered sent to the Southwest. The idea was to use the beasts to transport materiel and water in the arid countryside, where mules and men languished. The camels did well on a trial run, but Lee, scientific training to the fore, demanded another test. "I hope they will not suffer," Lee worried, but the expedition nearly ended in the death of both the camels and their escorts. Conditions were not much better in San Antonio. There was no ice, he told Agnes, and the water was "strongly impregnated with lime, too." Searing temperatures made sleep impossible. It was an atmosphere of low morale and smothered ambition. Desertion—another of Lee's headaches—was a chronic problem.[74]

Whatever melancholy he suffered, he did not let it show. Those who recalled Lee from this time represent him as a man of dignity, striking in every way. "I never saw Lee but once, but he made an impression upon me I cannot forget," wrote one Texan. "He was standing upon the gallery of the government building in San Antonio, watching a squad of infantry that were being drilled by a lieutenant. His appearance was so impressive that I stopped to look at him and ask who he was."[75] Another who was with him in 1860 described him as "capable, diligent, faithful and universally trusted," though his "grave cold dignity of bearing . . . rather chilled over-early or over-much intimacy."[76] Despite his intimidating demeanor and tendency to withdraw, Lee had never been quite as friendless on the frontier as he portrayed himself. John Bell Hood remembered his sociable conversation as they rode together over the plains.[77] A. S. Johnston shared many interests with Lee, and before Johnston was sent to chase the Mormons, they enjoyed a companionable relationship.[78] Lee spent Christmas holidays with Major George H. Thomas and his wife, both fellow Virginians, who would soon face Lee's own formidable dilemma of loyalty and duty.[79] Captain Nathan "Shanks" Evans was a friend special enough to enjoy Lee's irreverence and to share indiscretions that few were allowed to witness. With Evans he smuggled whiskey into the garrison in his water barrel, confided his "fancy" for belles "neither white nor yellow," and once even used his official powers to transport Evans's "woman"—not wife—in a specially escorted wagon to Camp Cooper. "I hope you will have great comfort in her," Lee drily remarked.[80]

One of the fascinating things about these depictions is how often they are at odds with each other, or with the preconceived image of Lee. Such varied representations give some insight into the reason historians must take a journalistic approach to their craft, cross-checking sources and questioning even the seemingly unself-conscious words of the protagonists. If we take Lee's family letters in isolation, they can be misleading, giving little indication of either garrison companionship or the respect in which Lee clearly was held. Both the chronically lonely, despairing man who could not achieve his goals and the serene "pillar of state" described by the awestruck Texan are one-dimensional figures—and both are quite different from the whiskey-smuggling, judge-bashing, wench-transporting pal of Shanks Evans.

One wonders if Lee did not purposefully create some of the stereotypes that surround him, through a need to mask the inner man by controlling any outward show of expression. More interesting is the multifaceted person who emerges as the various scraps of evidence are stitched together. It is only by reading every kind of source and reflecting on all modes of expression that we can appreciate Lee as a man of many parts, as complex and contradictory as the Texas environment in which he found himself.

All of these relationships are more sobering when viewed against the backdrop of the worsening political situation. By the time Lee returned to Texas in 1860, soldiers talked of little but the possible dissolution of the United States. The military camaraderie was such that men from every section of the country spoke openly of the crisis. Georgia-born David Twiggs was known to be an ardent southern nationalist, but Lee still harbored hopes that the Union might be saved by political acumen. Soon after Lincoln's election in November 1860, however, he began to feel the urgency of the situation. His letter to Albert Lea sweeps us into the undercurrent, with its emphasis on the Constitution, law, and the importance of upholding the Union. Lee was still acting as chief of the Department of Texas when he was informed by local "commissioners" of their intention to secede, and thereafter appropriate the armaments and fortifications of the U.S. Army. They also pressured him personally to declare himself on the side of the South. The brother of Major Robert Anderson, who would gain fame defending Fort Sumter, recalled that Lee became really agitated at the idea he would be forced to resign under this kind of intimidation: "He said that after forty years of faithful duty to his whole country . . . to be thus maltreated by such a committee was beyond his patience to endure."[81] The encounter, however, forced Lee to formulate an official plan for defense of U.S. property. Evidently he decided that if Texas did leave the Union on his watch, he would take the cavalry into Cherokee Territory with as much matériel as possible. In any case, he informed a subordinate, he would "defend his post at all hazards."[82] Twiggs returned to Texas and took over the command in mid-December, and Lee was relieved of the immediate responsibility of negotiating with the secessionists. On the eve of Lee's departure, Twiggs, hampered by conflicting orders from Washington and determined to avoid a conflict at all costs, formally relinquished the army's assets to the rebellious Texans. Not bothering to disguise his solidarity with the South, Twiggs liberally distributed leave slips so that the arsenals would be incompletely manned.[83] "Has it come so soon as this?" an appalled Lee asked when he heard the news. The following month he and Samuel Heintzelman had a conversation at Arlington about the army's property in Texas. Lee told Heinzelman he had decided that under his command "they could not get the arms from the troops without fighting for them." Had he remained in charge of the Department of Texas a few weeks longer, and had the secessionists forced the issue, as they later did at Fort Sumter, the Civil War might have begun there. Commanding the defense of Union property against the rebels would have been Colonel Robert E. Lee.[84]

Chapter Sixteen

Theory Meets Reality

My Name is Wesley Norris; I was born a slave on the plantation of George Parke Custis; after the death of Mr. Custis, Gen. Lee, who had been made executor of the estate, assumed control of the slaves, in number about seventy; it was the general impression among the slaves of Mr. Custis that on his death they should be forever free; in fact this statement had been made to them by Mr. C. years before; at this death we were informed by Gen. Lee that by the conditions of the will we must remain slaves for five years; I remained with Gen. Lee about seventeen months, when my sister Mary, a cousin of ours, and I determined to run away, which we did in the year 1859; we had already reached Westminster, in Maryland, on our way to the North, when we were apprehended and thrown into prison, and Gen. Lee notified of our arrest; we remained in prison fifteen days, when we were sent back to Arlington; we were immediately taken before Gen. Lee, who demanded the reason why we ran away; we frankly told him that we considered ourselves free; he then told us he would teach us a lesson we never would forget; he then ordered us to the barn, where in his presence, we were tied firmly to posts by a Mr. Gwin, our overseer, who was ordered by Gen. Lee to strip us to the waist and give us fifty lashes each, excepting my sister, who received but twenty; we were accordingly stripped to the skin by the overseer, who, however, had sufficient humanity to decline whipping us; accordingly Dick Williams, a county constable was called in, who gave us the number of lashes ordered; Gen. Lee, in the meantime, stood by, and frequently enjoined Williams to "lay it on well," an injunction which he did not fail to heed; not satisfied with simply lacerating our naked flesh, Gen. Lee then ordered the overseer to thoroughly wash our backs with brine, which was done. After this my cousin and myself were sent to Hanover Court-House jail, my sister being sent to Richmond to an agent to be hired; we remained in jail about a week, when we were sent to Nelson county, where we were hired out by Gen. Lee's agent to work on the Orange and Alexander railroad; we re-

mained thus employed for about seven months, and were then sent to Al-
abama, and put to work on what was known as the Northeastern railroad; in
January 1863 we were sent to Richmond, from which place I finally made my es-
cape through the rebel lines to freedom; I have nothing further to say; what I
have stated is true in every particular, and I can at any time bring at least a
dozen witnesses, both white and black, to substantiate my statements; I am at
present employed by the Government, and am at work in the National Ceme-
tery on Arlington Heights, where I can be found by those who desire further
particulars; my sister referred to is at present employed by the French Minister
at Washington and will confirm my statements.[1]

>·◦·○·◦·◦·<

W ESLEY NORRIS's testament was given to an antislavery newspaper
in 1866 and is one of several accounts of this incident. The story created some uncomfortable negative publicity for Robert E. Lee when it first
surfaced in 1859 and continued to haunt him after the war. Its veracity has
been questioned by generations of Lee aficionados, and we might be
tempted to dismiss it as the exaggerated ranting of a bitter ex-slave. Except
for one thing: all of its facts are verifiable.

Lee's neat philosophy about the relations between master and slave
moved from theory to reality in a dramatic way with the death of George
Washington Parke Custis in 1857. Never a careful steward of his holdings,
Custis had particularly neglected them in his later years. When he died he
owned three estates, assorted other properties in the Chesapeake region,
and 196 slaves. Most of the land, including Arlington, was not very productive, a number of the properties listed in the will had uncertain boundaries
and titles, and Lee estimated that debts ran upward of $10,000, a mighty
sum at that time. By the terms of Custis's will, Lee was made executor of the
estate. When he heard the news of his father-in-law's death, he left his post
on the Texas frontier to join the mourners at Arlington.

Custis had provided for his kin in what he believed to be equitable and
even grand style. He left his daughter the Washington heirlooms and a life
interest in Arlington. These would revert to his eldest grandson upon Mary
Lee's death. The White House and Romancoke estates were given to his
other grandsons, and a $10,000 legacy to each of his four granddaughters.
The old man also freed his slaves, with the stipulation that the estate debts
and legacies were to be paid first and that the manumission was to take place
within five years. Custis had meant to be generous, but his scanty understanding of the state of his properties and a naïveté about the human reactions

such a will would cause made it extremely difficult to fulfill. "He has left me an unpleasant legacy," Lee would write.[2]

Lee arrived to find that "everything is in ruins and will have to be rebuilt."[3] Mills, slave dwellings, and mansion houses were leaky and dilapidated. Long-neglected lands were producing little, if any, cash crops. Some of the properties that Custis noted "I may own" did not have deeds or other legal certificates. To pay off the will's provisions would encumber Arlington, a property valued at $90,000, with a $50,000 debt. In addition, the instructions of the will were contradictory, and Lee thought they would require legal interpretation. Virginia law stipulated that freed slaves had to move out of the state, and that the former master must support any who were underage, old, or infirm, but no allowance for the newly freed blacks was specified in Custis's instructions. "There is *no* such provision nor indeed *any* for their maintenance which proceeded from his usual want of care in matters of business & I presume a belief that we should take care of them," wrote Mary Lee in exasperation. The situation was serious enough that Lee doubted he could really comply with Custis's intentions. "I can now see little prospect of fulfilling the provisions of your Grd father's will within the space of five years, which seems to be the time, within which he expected it to be accomplished & his people liberated," he told his eldest son.[4]

Lee put his own money into the effort and tackled the job with his customary conscientiousness. He rebuilt the outbuildings, changed the farming emphasis from livestock to wheat and vegetable production, experimented with fertilizers, and tried deep plowing to tap richer soils. He found progress slow, and the effort extremely frustrating. "Mr. Lee is with me," Mary Lee wrote to a friend, "but is so harassed with the cares and trouble he had in settling this large estate with very inadequate means, that I do not have the comfort that his presence might otherwise have afforded me." In the years that Lee managed the Custis estates, he revamped the labor system, upgraded buildings, purchased new tools, and opened virgin lands to cultivation. But he came nowhere near fulfilling the requirements of the will. "I succeed badly," he told Rooney.[5]

Lee had financial and legal headaches, and the emotional strains of a still-grieving family, but his greatest difficulties came from the estate's slaves. He understood that they were to be freed and had no intention of thwarting Mr. Custis's desire. Nonetheless, he took seriously the will's provision that the emancipation was to take place at the discretion of the executor. There is no evidence that Lee thought of slaves as property in the sense of a liquid asset, to be bred, bought, and sold for profit. But he did see the system in

terms that historians would later describe as that of a practical entre-
preneur. To Lee the blacks remained bondsmen, a workforce to be used
at the owner's will. It was his right to employ them where and how he
wanted, to increase the profits of the estate: "dispose of them at the end
of the year to the best advantage," Lee instructed one agent, who was to
handle a half dozen slaves he had wrenched away from Arlington and
lodged in a Richmond jail.[6] If he did not own their souls, Lee certainly
believed he owned their skills, their energy, and their time. The Lees could
not afford to support a large band of idle workers, and they felt they
could not free them immediately and still fulfill both the Virginia laws
and the Custis will. The labor of the slaves was the key to enhancing
productivity—and productivity was what Lee needed in order to make the
property solvent.[7]

In this, his first experience as master of a large labor force, he tried to use
the philosophy he had honed over the years. "I wish to make them as comfortable as I can," he told Custis Lee, and set the slaves to repairing their own
houses. His estate accounts show that he spent considerable sums for the
slaves' clothing, food, and medical care. "I desire to do what is right and best
for the people," he later wrote. But he also desired that the slaves should
work with a will. He told Arlington's heir that "while being fair & just you
must not neglect your interests," and as he looked for a new overseer, Lee
commented that he wanted an "energetic honest farmer, who while he will
be considerate & kind to the Negroes, will be firm & make them do their
duty."[8] The great challenge was to mesh his concept of responsibility with
the slaves' quite different sense of their obligations.

For slaves, the death of a master was a distressing event, one that threw
their world into uncertainty and apprehension. Since they did not control
their own future and had no idea what a new master might bring, they were
at their most vulnerable. Over the years George Washington Parke Custis
had grown more and more lax with his servants, particularly at Arlington.
Finally he had asked little of them but to cultivate their gardens and raise the
food they would eat.[9] Now they encountered a master who believed that it
was their *duty* to work and, moreover, was accustomed to the disciplined
structure of the army. From his arrival at Arlington, Lee found himself "endeavoring to urge unwilling hands to work" and trying to reorganize his
human resources in a rational fashion. Already disgruntled with the taxing
new demands, the slaves were further dismayed when Lee began hiring
hands to other plantations. With no means of communication, they had no
idea where they were being sent, how long they would be there, or what the
conditions would be. In addition, Lee rented out so many hands that the

black community at Arlington was badly fragmented. The youngest and strongest were chosen to be hired away because they brought in the greatest revenue. By 1859 old men and little boys were the only workers left at Arlington. Worst of all, Lee ruptured the Washington and Custis tradition of respecting slave families. By 1860 he had broken up every family but one on the estate, some of whom had been together since Mount Vernon days.[10] There was singular distress among the slaves, and the community's opinion that Lee was a "hard taskmaster" and "the worst man I ever see" was sharpened.[11] Their response was to withhold cooperation, and finally to protest openly.

Many of the slaves Lee hired away were extremely unhappy. They felt exiled from their friends and families at Arlington and thought the measure a degrading punishment. Three men who were hired off the estate returned after one day "on account of the work being too hard." Lee reprimanded them and sent them to work for an even more demanding master.[12] Some of the hiring does appear as a kind of punishment, calculated to give difficult workers the discipline of a seasoned overseer, or keep sullen blacks away from the Arlington workforce. This was the case for several slaves whom Lee "could not recommend for honesty"—he hired them in Richmond, where, he noted to Custis, they were "put to your service and mine and much to your mother's relief."[13] The next year, he advised his son, "it may be better to hire them all out. Their presence seems to be of no advantage." Even faced with a near epidemic of runaways, and with other resistance from the slaves, he turned a deaf ear. His wife, in denial about the social dislocation taking place at her home, could only complain: "The ingratitude & bad conduct of these slaves . . . has wounded me sorely, some of them now whom I least expected such conduct have done worst of all."[14] One of those Lee hired out against his will was Wesley Norris.[15]

The slaves were increasingly unsettled under Lee's control, and not just because of his theories of labor management. They believed they were already free.[16] Old Mr. Custis should have been aware of the possibility that his imprecise will would create this kind of discontent, since he had witnessed a similar situation at the Fitzhugh estate. William Henry Fitzhugh had left a will freeing his slaves in twenty years; but in the intervening time they were disgruntled and sullen—so unmanageable that Molly Fitzhugh Custis and her daughter gave up their interest in the property rather than become entangled in the difficult situation.[17] Mount Vernon had also witnessed similar problems. Washington freed his own slaves in his will, but the rest of the

Mount Vernon servants belonged to his wife and were not to be freed until she passed away. When news of Washington's will spread through the quarters, the remaining slaves became so restless that Martha Washington liberated them only a year later. Washington had foretold this, commenting to Mount Vernon tutor Tobias Lear that "the idea of freedom might be too great a temptation for them to resist. At any rate it might if they conceived they had a right to it, make them insolent in a State of Slavery."[18] At Arlington, this is exactly what happened. Speculation spread quickly through the slave ranks, heightened by promises Custis had purportedly made while he was alive. According to Wesley Norris's testament, "years before" Arlington's master had hinted that freedom would come with his death. Other servants recounted how on his deathbed George Washington Parke Custis had gathered them together to take his leave and tell them of their liberation.[19]

Among those who heard these tales were reporters for the abolitionist press. Northern newspapers—first the *Boston Traveller,* then the *New York Times* and the *New York Tribune*—all carried the story, which was printed with varying degrees of salaciousness. Wrote the *Boston Traveller* of the Custis slaves: "it is already whispered about town that foul play is in process in regard to those negroes on the Virginia plantations; that they are now being sold South; and that all of them will be consigned to hopeless Slavery unless something is done." Lee tried to answer the accusations, saying that the family had no knowledge of the deathbed scene, that the Custis will was available in the county courthouse for all to see, and that there was "no desire on the part of the heirs to prevent the execution of its provision in reference to the slaves."[20] Nevertheless rumors continued to circulate.

As it happens, the hearsay had a disturbing element of truth to it. From the outset Lee had interpreted the Custis will to mean that all the bequests must be paid before manumission. The will itself, however, actually called for land to be sold to pay the debts and legacies, and never states that these obligations should take precedence over freeing the slaves. Soon after he arrived at Arlington, Lee petitioned the courts to give him a ruling on the competing demands of the Custis will. In it he not only asked that "the emancipation of the slaves should be postponed till the said legacies are raised, and the debts of the estate are paid off," but hoped for a decision that would justify "removing the property of the testator, beyond the limits of the State." This petition was the servants' worst fear, and may have been the origin of newspaper gossip about the slaves being sold South. This request would not have actually allowed the slaves to be sold, but it would have permitted Lee to send them out of Virginia, far from their families and the benevolent oversight they had traditionally enjoyed at Arlington. When the court denied Lee's petition, he applied to the Supreme Court of Appeals of Virginia to have it overturned.[21]

There was thus some justification for the Custis slaves' fear that they were to be sent south. They had no way of communicating with those who had been hired as far away as Richmond, Hanover, and New Kent counties and did not know their fate. Most importantly, they did not understand why they all had not been immediately freed. Mary Lee indicates that the Lee family tried to explain the situation and motivate the workforce to put forth an effort so that they could be emancipated more quickly. She told a friend that "the servants here have been so long accustomed to do little or nothing that they cannot be convinced of the necessity now of exerting themselves to accomplish the conditions of the will which the sooner they do the sooner they will be entitled to their freedom. . . ."[22] Wesley Norris says that Lee "informed" the servants that they must remain slaves for five more years, a message that cannot but have been ill-received. Unfortunately, Lee was notoriously poor at what we would today call "cross-cultural communication." He did not identify with those outside his class and race, did not like to be familiar with them, and did not really take their side in issues of social justice. He had not been successful, for example, in his attempts to interact with the Comanche on the Texas plains. Lee's similar failure to communicate with the Custis slaves was to have dire results.

Almost immediately the slaves began to test Lee, and at an early stage he lost control of the situation. Only three months after he returned to Arlington, his wife wrote in some alarm that the slaves were uniting to demand their freedom and that only "the merciful Hand of Kind Providence & their own ineptness I suppose prevented an outbreak." Four months after that a number of the slaves did rise up against Lee. "I have had some trouble with some of the people," he wrote to Rooney in May 1858. "Reuben, Parks & Edward, in the beginning of the previous week, rebelled against my authority—refused to obey my orders, & said they were as free as I was, &c, &c—I succeeded in capturing them however, tied them and lodged them in jail. They resisted until overpowered & called upon the other people to rescue them." Lee kept the three in jail for two months, until they could be hired through a slave trader. He also specified that they were not to be sent back to Arlington at Christmastime, though it was customary for hired servants to be reunited with their families at this season.[23] Several other slaves tried to assert the freedom they believed to be theirs, and it appears from Mary Lee's diary that those who remained continued to resist their master, causing "constant trouble in our domestic affairs."[24] Lee had had to physically "overpower" the rebels, narrowly avoiding a dangerous revolt at Arlington, and he and the whole household were shaken. Soon thereafter, Wesley Norris, his sister Mary, and their cousin George Parks ran away.

Among the things the Lees seem to have misjudged was how much the Custis slaves wanted to be free. Their perspective was that the black people had led a nearly ideal life at Arlington, where a minimum of work was required and some trouble was taken to provide them a little education and maintain cordial relations. Markie Williams recorded a conversation with George Washington Parke Custis a few years before his death, during which he maintained that his slaves were much better off than the lower classes in England—a standard proslavery argument—and that no counterpart for the situations described in the recently published Uncle Tom's Cabin could be found at Arlington. "To eat & drink & sleep are the only duties with wh[ich] he has anything to do—with regard to most of them," Markie noted. "They have their comfortable homes, their families around them and nothing to do but to consult their own pleasure. Their eating & drinking & clothing is all provided for them. And truly in many instance[s] the master is the only slave."[25] Mrs. Lee echoed this opinion in her outrage that one of the runaways was her own chambermaid, who, she maintained, led a life equal to that of her daughters. The troublemakers, she fumed, were those "for whom I have ever since my earliest recollection done all I could." She asked God to forgive them for their presumption.[26] The condescension implicit in these statements, not to mention a flimsy knowledge of the actual conditions of slave life (Lee had found those "comfortable homes" to be nearly falling down) was a measure of the delusion under which slaveholders lived. The Custis and Lee families failed to read the longing in their servants' hearts, heard what they wanted to believe in professions of close ties between master and slave, and mistook obedience for fealty. They were not alone in this: a few years later plantation owners across the South were stunned by the "betrayal" of their "loyal" and "pampered" servants, who chose to leave at the first chance of freedom. "We wear the mask that grins and lies," wrote African-American poet Paul Laurence Dunbar of the way slaves protected themselves and manipulated their masters' perceptions. "It hides our cheeks and shades our eyes. . . . / Why should the world be overwise?"[27]

The slaves' feelings of injustice were heightened by the presence of abolitionists in the neighborhood. By the mid-nineteenth century, abolitionists had stepped up their antislavery campaign, moving from tracts and speeches to active intervention in border areas. Starting around 1830 they waged a consistent campaign in Washington, D.C., the purpose of which was to destroy slavery through a program of guerilla-like activities, including organizing blacks, embarrassing proslavery officials, and aiding runaways. The Lees had been exposed to their activities before, particularly when they lived in Baltimore, and had been concerned about the effect on the servants at that time. Lee wrote his wife that "the abolitionists are very active here & opportunities great. That is the experience of all that have brought their servants here."[28] This was not an idle fear. By 1855, the hated "Yankee emissaries" were so prevalent around the nation's capital that a special law was passed to prohibit hiring slaves there, lest they fall into the hands of abolitionists. Only a few weeks after the death of G. W. P. Custis, the Lees were upset by two men "constantly lurking about here tampering with the servants & telling them they had a right to their freedom *immediately* & that if they would unite & *demand* it they would obtain it."[29] When northern newspapers began writing articles about the situation, some based on hearsay and half-truths, the Lees were incensed. Lee chose to remain silent, but Mary Lee reacted violently, calling the stories "villainous attacks upon my husband by name and upon my father's memory in language I would not pollute my lips by repeating."[30]

One can picture Lee, face taut, contemplating the presence of antislavery activists at Arlington. He had a strong animosity to the abolitionists. Over the years Lee had denounced the "evil passions" of radical Northerners, finally declaring "that they contend for the ruin of the present American Church & the destruction of the present Union."[31] The Lees and their kin shared with other landed whites a belief that these were dangerous adventurers, who lacked a true understanding of the relation between master and slave. Having convinced themselves that their servants were content, slaveholders often blamed abolitionists for stirring up feelings of "disloyalty" that the slaves would not have felt on their own. They were outraged that antislavery groups felt they had a right to meddle in the affairs of the South and thought that they should be left alone to solve the problem. They did not see this as a national dilemma to be resolved jointly with the North. In fact, they believed that the abolitionists created a vicious circle by their interference, in which the slaves were worked up into an unnatural discontent, became less docile and more likely to rebel, and as a result had to be treated more harshly. If cruelty was to be found, it was because the abolitionists inspired it, not because they had uncovered it. Lee's cousin Hill Carter, who in 1834 had written a syrupy tract on the paternalistic management of slaves, became vehement when he spoke of abolitionists. No severity existed in the slave system as he knew it, Hill Carter wrote, and there would be no occasion for it "if the fanatics will only let us alone." Lee stated this in somewhat loftier terms: the slaves' emancipation would "sooner result from a mild and melting influence than the storms and contests of fiery controversy." He challenged the antislavery advocate to "leave the slave alone if he would not anger the master."[32]

It was the unequivocal condemnation of abolition in Franklin Pierce's December 1856 State of the Union address that caused Lee to write his oft-quoted political diatribe on the peculiar institution. Lee had gotten hold of a copy of the speech in some newspapers his wife sent him in Texas, and it seems to have had a galvanizing effect on him. Pierce had slammed the abolitionists, criticizing their extremism, condemning acts that facilitated the escape of slaves, and labeling them agitators. He blamed them for preparing the nation for civil war "by doing everything in their power to deprive the Constitution and the laws of moral authority and to undermine the fabric of the Union by appeals to passion and sectional prejudice, by indoctrinating its people with reciprocal hatred, and by educating them to stand face to face as enemies, rather than shoulder to shoulder as friends." It was a remarkable and reckless speech that could only have been delivered by a president such as Pierce, who had already been voted out. Lee agreed with it all. He called the president's views "truthfully and faithfully expressed" and criticized the abolitionist for "interference in what he has no concern." Antislavery zealots, Lee concluded, had "neither the right nor the power" to force a change in the South.[33] Usually a master at avoiding political debate and the controversies of his day, Lee had been provoked to take a stand.

Historians have questioned the degree to which abolitionists were responsible for slave escapes, noting that the African-Americans who did run were hardly passive recipients of white planning, often receiving as much help from fellow slaves and free blacks as from professional activists. Abolitionists were certainly present in the Lees' neighborhood, however, and it is clear from the ensuing newspaper articles that the Arlington slaves were exposed to them. It remains uncertain whether or not antislavery agitators inspired Wesley and Mary Norris and George Parks to run away, as the Lees believed. But run they did, in the late spring of 1859. We know that the incident took place, not only from the account by Norris but from Lee's own description, as well as court and newspaper records. As Lee describes it, the three "absconded some months ago, were captured in Maryland making their way to Pennsylvania, brought back and are now hired out in lower Virginia." Records from Westminster, Maryland, show that they were held there just as Norris relates, and that they may have added a guide or additional runaway to the party en route.[34] Exactly what happened after they were returned to

Arlington is more difficult to determine. The abolitionist press picked up on the story, probably recounted by the slaves, and immediately printed it in sensationalist style. Like Norris, they described a scene of punishment, with the runaways being taken to the barn and whipped. In the newspaper accounts, the events are more dramatic than those later described by Norris, with Lee himself taking the whip when the overseer refused to wield it against the girl, lashing the bare-breasted woman thirty-nine times. Another version, printed about the same time, also has Lee personally administering the blows.[35]

Did Robert E. Lee indulge in this kind of tyrannical behavior? Generations of Lee-revering biographers have rejected the idea. "It is needless to remark," said a typical curt commentary, "that while Lee on occasion was a firm disciplinarian, he was never brutal."[36] Historians have long used care in relying on the abolitionist press, geared as it was to passion and propaganda. There are also many questions about the credibility of slave narratives, which were often filtered through antislavery forces, or retold many years later through the subjective pens of white interviewers. The two contemporary versions in the *New York Tribune,* with a furious Lee seizing the black girl, do seem exaggerated. But Wesley Norris's more sober account rings true. He was, after all, one of the protagonists, and the tale, though told to an antislavery paper, was given straightforwardly, only a few years after the incident. Moreover, every detail of it can be verified, from the time he ran away (after seventeen months) and the number of slaves at Arlington, from the names of the jail and the overseer (Norris says "Mr. Gwin," a corruption of his actual name, "McQuinn") to the place they were taken after the punishment (Hanover County) and their subsequent employment after the war. We know a whipping post stood at Arlington. The added sting of washing the bloodied backs with brine is corroborated by another eyewitness, who also mentions that the whipping was done by the county constable.[37] Even the constable's name is right—Dick Williams. Lee's account book for June 1859 carries this item: "to Richard Williams, arrest, &c of fugitive slaves—$321.14." The sum, which did not include the transport of the slaves to Hanover County—Lee paid another $50.53 for that—is exceptionally large. We know that Lee's standard reward for returning runaways was ten dollars per slave. The previous year Lee's accounts show that he paid Williams only $57.25 to arrest and detain three other fugitives, and another $37.12 to transport them to Richmond. The costs for the earlier capture had also been inflated by the need to keep them in jail two months. The services rendered by Williams in relation to the Norris party must have been extraordinary to command a fee nearly six times as high as those paid the year before.[38]

The interior of the slave pen in Alexandria.
LIBRARY OF CONGRESS

Any trial lawyer will tell you that the witness who gives testimony that can be verified on every detail is likely to be considered believable on the whole. Although Wesley Norris's statement does not entirely fulfill the credibility wish list comprised by some historiographers (it was not, for example, recounted immediately and was almost certainly filtered through a white journalist), it was unquestionably predicated on facts. It does raise a question about why the statements of slaves should be considered any more biased as a source than those of their white contemporaries. Wesley Norris gave his interview after he was freed, when he had nothing to hide, gain, or fear; the fact that it was published in a northern newspaper does not necessarily make the information unbelievable, any more than Hill Carter's sentimentalized version of ideal slave management, obviously meant for the apologist press, must be taken as entirely insincere. Slave testimony, with all of its qualifications, constitutes a precious insight into the victims' side of a cruel system. It is no more manipulative than any other historical resource.

Indeed, the perfectly accurate source simply does not exist. There seems to be no obvious reason that Norris's description of his treatment, corroborated by five different witnesses, and substantiated by Lee's own records, should be discounted.[39]

Lee never completely denounced the story. "The New York Tribune has attacked me for my treatment of your grandfather's slaves," he told his son Custis a few days after the event, "but I shall not reply."[40] Years later (years more removed in time than Norris's statement, if that is our test of credibility), he told a friend that "the statement is not true; but I had not thought proper to publish a contradiction." And to the same correspondent: "There is not a word of truth in it. . . . No servant, soldier, or citizen that was ever employed by me can with truth charge me with bad treatment."[41] But there *was* more than a word of truth in the accounts: virtually all of it can be directly verified. What Lee may have objected to was the scene of his personally whipping the slave girl, the most doubtful part of the story. That does seem to stand against the class distinctions of the day, for constables such as Dick Williams, who had been paid such a lavish sum, existed precisely to do this kind of demeaning chore. But that he lost control of his famous temper, and demanded punishment as a hindrance to further mischief among the slaves, is entirely in keeping with his previous statements and indeed with his record of advocating punishment, whether for cadets or for slaves, as an exercise in deterrence.[42] It is doubtful that under the circumstances whipping would have, in his mind, constituted "bad treatment."[43]

Lee's method of directing operations at Arlington had been insensitive to the slaves' fears, longings, and attachments, and his entire history with the institution had been one of upholding the master's right to discipline the blacks. In addition, many of the slaves at Arlington had crossed an important psychological barrier, believing that they truly were free. Frederick Douglass and other African-Americans have described the critical moment when their spirits were liberated, even if they physically remained in bondage. After this point there was really no way to control them. Once this occurred at Arlington, Lee lost the power that came from an unspoken recognition of his right to command. If the blacks decided to challenge the master's prerogatives, he had little choice but to resort to physical force to maintain discipline. This, coupled with the need to make an example of those caught in flight, made whipping the preferred method of punishment. Fugitives seem to have been particularly irritating to masters, both for the trouble it caused to bring them back and for the direct affront to their authority. Whipping was the most common expression of the masters' frustration. Frank Bell, a slave on an estate near Arlington, gives us some insight into the situation when he tells how his master had never touched one of the plantation blacks, until he ran away one time too many. "Ole Marser was some kind of mad," Bell recalled. "Cost a lot of money, it did, when you go git a runaway slave. 'Hue and Cry' dey called it, you got to put notice in de papers, an' you got to pay a reward to whoever catches de runaway."[44] Fed up with the sullen, uncooperative servants he had been appointed to manage, and seemingly oblivious to their concerns, Lee may well have wanted, as Norris described it, to teach them a lesson they would never forget.

Of course Lee was well within his legal rights to apprehend and punish the runaways. Not only state but federal laws protected the slave owner's property. There had been laws to return fugitive slaves as early as 1793, though all of them contained loopholes. Throughout the antebellum period southern whites fought to strengthen those laws, especially as fears of abolitionists or insurrection took hold. The Fugitive Slave Act of 1850 was a piece of landmark legislation that theoretically ensured federal support for slaveholders who were trying to recover their property. One of the ironies of this hard-fought compromise is that it was so rarely invoked. The act allowed for a complicated procedure of petitions and warrants, involving federal judges or commissioners, formal determination of ownership, and several hearings before a slave was allowed to be repossessed. Many thought that it had been designed to be so complicated that it would not be used, and in practical terms this seems to have been the case. After nearly a decade of enforcement, only around 200 slaves were ever returned to their masters. Most planters, like Lee, appear to have resorted to private seizures, rather than go through the time-consuming process called for in the law. Whether or not they were in violation for not following the due process is an interesting question. In any case, legal historians maintain that there is no evidence that anyone was ever charged with violating the act because they failed to follow the procedures.[45]

Slaves were things; they had no rights under the law. The master determined the kind and amount of their labor, what they ate and wore, where they went, what they possessed, how they conducted themselves in public, whether or not they were to remain with their families. They could not hold property, be a witness against a white person, or change masters at will. The master was given considerable leeway in their discipline and punishment. Whipping slaves was not an offense; indeed, it was prescribed by law in Virginia and Maryland for everything from straying outside the plantation limits to keeping a dog, even for "beating up" the river to attract fish. The fugitive laws could not protect the owner sufficiently from those slaves who wanted to escape or those who refused to accept their authority. As a result, a complex penal code was established, meant to impress the slave with the master's sovereignty and to deter trouble. Whipping was not just allowed under the law; it was stipulated in cases of runaways. The owner might exercise some judgment in how his slaves were punished, and occasionally an overzealous master was arraigned for mistreating a slave. But it was the master's duty to enforce the law and carry out its provisions. If Wesley Norris and his compatriots were indeed whipped, as the evidence suggests, those of Lee's class and persuasion would hardly have considered it cruel, criminal, or even "bad treatment."[46]

Lee postponed returning to his military command in hopes of hearing the decision of the court, but after infinite delays rejoined his Texas regiment in 1860.[47] He largely abandoned the role of executor after this point, and the eruption of war the following year made any further efforts sporadic. As the five-year deadline for liberation approached, Lee discussed a number of schemes for fulfilling all aspects of the will, including keeping the servants indefinitely in bondage. In early 1862, however, the court finally ruled against Lee, stating that the black people were to be liberated with or without the payment of the other legacies, and that the will should be fulfilled by the sale of land as Custis had stipulated.[48] Lee bowed to this decision and took some trouble behind the Confederate lines to see that the slaves all had their manumission papers. Most were finally freed on January 1, 1863, the final day acceptable to the court. Coincidentally, it was also the day the Emancipation Proclamation took force—giving the Custis slaves a double liberation.[49] Determined to uphold his trust, Lee used his own funds and the sale of land to accomplish all of G. W. P. Custis's exacting requirements. He also tried to help some of the freed men hire their labor, and resisted attempts by the white community in the Pamunkey region to keep them in bondage.[50]

In all, Lee passed twenty-six months as executor of the Custis estate. It proved to be one of the most painful experiences of his prewar life. The carefully developed ideals he had tried to live by—of conscientiousness and hard work and a disciplined but just way of treating slaves—failed him when he met with the reality of being a master. He had wanted badly for this work to succeed, both from his sense of responsibility to his wife and late father-in-law, and because he knew that with his soldier's salary this was the only sizable inheritance his children would receive. It seems also to have shattered any dreams he cherished of leaving the army for the life of a planter; hereafter his fantasies centered on a simple rural existence with labor supplied by the family, not a host of black bondsmen.

Lee was unsuccessful as a master largely because he neglected to see the situation in human terms. He embraced the legal and economic aspects of the master-slave system without really grasping its complex underlying relationships. He never recognized the slaves' fundamental desire to change their condition; instead he tried to superimpose his sense of "duty" upon them. Moreover, by breaking up families and proposing to ship them far away from their community, he both denied the slaves' humanity and stepped beyond the genteel code of paternalism that even proslavery men professed. Lee could have freed the slaves immediately at the death of his father-in-law; as executor he had that ability. Virginia law made this difficult, but the law had been circumvented before at Arlington.[51] He could have freed them and rehired them to make the estates solvent, or worked with imported labor. Instead Lee took decisions that ultimately had to be upheld by force. The option he finally chose, of selling land to furnish money for the legacies, was what Custis had specified from the beginning. His failure to communicate on human terms and to see beyond self-interest caused him to mishandle a delicate situation. Lee never lost his legal rights over the slaves, but he did lose his moral authority. And that was because he continued to treat the African-Americans at Arlington as property, when they thought of themselves as free men.

Chapter Seventeen

"Upon a Fearful Summons"

Arlington 20 April 1861

My dear Cousin Roger

I only rec^d to day your letter of the 17th. Sympathizing with you in the troubles that are pressing so heavily upon our beloved country, & entirely agreeing with you in your notions of allegiance &c I have been unable to make up my mind to raise my hand against my native state, my relations, my children & my home. I have therefore resigned my commission in the Army & never desire again to draw my sword save in defence of my State.

I consider it useless to go into the reasons that influenced me. I can give no advice. I merely tell you what I have done that you may do better—.

Wishing you every happiness & prosperity.

I remain faithfully

Your kinsman RE Lee[1]

· · ·

Fort Columbia, Gover^s Island
NY Harbor
May 14, 1861

General Winfield Scott
Dear General
My reasons for writing this letter are:
1. To inform you why I wished to resign.
2. To assure you that Gen. Lee did not advise me to such a course & to explain my motives for not resigning before.
3. To explain the reason why I did not accept the kind offer to send me on some duty at a distance from the scene of active operations, but took the course I did.
4. To try to thank you for your great kindness to me & to beg that you will not accuse me of ingratitude.

I do not approve of the course of the South Generally, nor the way in which Virginia has acted as a state; but individual disapprobation of her conduct, will do as little towards bringing her back into the Union, on her former footing, as the marching of hostile armies into her Territory.

If the policy is, to conquer the seceded states by invading armies, they can only return to the government a[s] devastated provinces. Which under the present constitution, the US cannot legally hold. Consequently at the end of this unhappy war, either the South as a subjugated Territory or the North as Victors, will be under a military dictator or other form of consolidated military jurisdiction (and I incline strongly to the belief that this first is the more probable) or, there will be two governments each adapted to the customs and education of those over whom they will be established.

If the former of these two premises be true, I have to choose, whether I will be one of the oppressors of my kindsman or share with them the tyranny with which I otherwise might have helped to burden them.

Henceforth, there must be two peoples, Northerners and Southerners—the north must necessarily & will ultimately conquer the South—Napolean Bonepart[e] on one occasion remarks "The greatest number, always beats." Those who are not mad, in Virginia, know this. I have in prospective rank station and riches, but will be surrounded by friends who I may lose at any moment, by becoming uncongenial or incapable of serving them; while the blood of my Brethren [curses] unto me from the ground, for having been one of those, who instead of saying "wayward sisters go in peace"—have brought them to a degree of degradation, that even their conquerors did not first dream of.

On the other hand, if I espouse the cause of my relatives,—poverty, destitution and even actual want, to say nothing of that loss of independence of which every true man is proud, stare me in the face; this is indeed a hard fate, but becomes bearable when I recognize in my sympathizers the friends of my youth— those who are nearest and dearest to me. If the second hypothesis be true and I remain on the side of the north, I must become a stranger in a strange land— far from the sod under which my ancestors lie buried. I can never again revisit the scenes of my childhood without meeting at every step the ghosts of those who may well say—we deserved better things at your hands.

You can never tell the mental agony which I suffered, during the last three weeks of my sojourn in Washington. . . .

With sentiments of the most profound admiration I remain

Yours with greatest respect Orton Williams[2]

Two MEN FACE personal and national disaster. One response is terse, unwilling to advocate a cause or elaborate on private motives. The other is filled with passion and self-justification, emblematic of the moment. The men who wrote these were relatives—twenty-one-year-old Orton Williams was the brother of Cousin Markie, who had been part of the Arlington household for so long. Williams's language is not as sleek as Robert E. Lee's, but the document is remarkable in its reading of the war's probable outcome and for the way it fills the tense silence in Lee's epistle. Its timbre is richer for the fact that Williams wrote from a prison on Governor's Island, where he was jailed on suspicion of transferring information to the South as soon as he decided to resign from the staff of General Winfield Scott.

It is the very brusqueness of Lee's response that shows us the awful cost of his decision to resign from the U.S. Army. He was always publicly silent on matters that affected him deeply, and this decision pitted him against himself. Here was a man who had written only a few years earlier that his country "was the *whole* country. That its limits contained no North, no South, No East no west, but embraced the broad *Union*, in all its might & strength, present & future. On that subject my resolution is taken, & my mind fixed." Then, with underlined emphasis, he concluded: "I know no other Country, no other Government, than the *United States* & their *Constitution*."[3] Lee had disavowed this lifelong allegiance only hours before he wrote Roger Jones, who was another young cousin, and another West Point graduate with a divided heart. At this moment, on April 20, 1861, Lee knew that Virginia had seceded from the United States, but he did not yet know what her stance would be in the looming conflict. He was also unaware that the previous day Jones had defended the U.S. arsenal at Harper's Ferry against Virginia forces, finally burning the establishment to keep as much of its ordnance as possible out of rebel hands. He could not guess what Jones's choice would be; nor did he know what his own future held. Reeling from the consequences of his irreconcilable loyalties, Lee must have wondered how he and his family had reached this abyss.

October 17, 1859, was a bright fall day at Arlington. Robert E. Lee was absorbed in procuring winter clothes for the slaves and harvesting the late crops. He "wuz a-stanin' out whar de men was a-cuttin' a little rye," remembered Jim Parks, one of the slaves. "A mounted soldier cum up an' s'luted an' giv Cun'l Lee a note. He took hit an' read hit, den sent fo' he ker'idge driver."[4] The soldier who arrived so unexpectedly was Lieutenant J. E. B. Stuart, and the note he carried advised Lee to appear at the War Department immediately. Without changing clothes, Lee rode over to Washington and found himself in a meeting with President James Buchanan and several cabinet members. What they told him was disturbing: an insurrection had been reported near Harper's Ferry, Virginia, and a day-long contest between the insurgents and local militia had left the area in panic. According to some rumors as many as 3,000 men were marching on the town, and fears of a slave rebellion were widespread. Secretary of War John B. Floyd personally directed Lee to lead several companies of artillery and a detachment of marines that had been sent to restore calm. Stuart volunteered to accompany him, and Lee accepted his offer. The marines and artillery were already en route, so Floyd ordered a special locomotive for Lee and Stuart, who caught up with them about ten o'clock that night.[5]

On arrival the marine commander, Lieutenant Israel Green, gave a fuller account of the emergency. Instead of thousands of rebels, a group of eighteen armed men had attacked the federal arsenal at Harper's Ferry, easily overpowering the lone watchman, cutting the telegraph wires, halting trains, and taking both slave and white hostages. The alarmed citizenry had formed themselves into a loose militia force. Though disorganized, they had been able to contain the outbreak and trap the insurgents in a small brick engine house at the armory. In the ensuing skirmish several men had been killed on both sides. The first casualty was a mild-mannered freedman named Hayward Shepherd, and in the months and years that followed, his murder would be pointed to as an unsettling portent. There had been an attempt to negotiate with "Captain Smith," as the leader of the insurrectionary band styled himself, but he had refused to surrender, vowing he would not give up until safe passage was assured. Lee and the marines took stock of the disorderly militiamen and quickly relieved them of guard duty. Believing little more could be accomplished that night, Lee decided to confront the insurgents at dawn.[6]

By early the next morning Lee probably knew that the leader of the rebels was John Brown, the fiery abolitionist who had horrified the nation with his murderous rampage against the spread of slavery into Kansas Territory.[7] Lee was also aware that one of the captives was a distant relative, Colonel Lewis Washington, the great-grandnephew of the first president. Concerned for the safety of the hostages, Lee put together a neat plan that would afford Brown an opportunity to surrender. Lee had written out the terms the night before, and though he did not think they would be accepted, he instructed Stuart to offer them when told to do so.[8] The arrangement called for an immediate assault after Brown rejected the terms, so that he would be unable to push the hostages to the front of the engine house where they could be used as leverage against an attack. In addition, Lee took the precaution of ordering the troops to use only their bayonets so that no hostage would fall victim to a stray bullet.[9] Lee then offered the militia captains the honor of leading the attack, and when they declined, gave the responsibility to Lieutenant Green. About 7:00 A.M. the operation began.[10]

Stuart, wearing the same dashing chapeau that would distinguish him a few years later, approached the reinforced wooden doors of the engine house, waving a white flag. The door opened a crack, and Stuart saw a grizzled face and the nose of a carbine. He quickly recognized "Old Ossawattomie Brown," whom he had encountered on duty in Kansas Territory. Stuart presented Lee's terms, which, as expected, were rejected. The marines waited nervously while Brown indulged in a long "parlay" for counter terms, and the hostages cried out for release. When it was clear that Brown would not give up, Stuart waved his cap and the plan was carried out.[11] Lieutenant Green recalled that his forces attempted to smash the doors with sledgehammers, moving forward "like tigers, as a storming assault is not a playday sport." When this proved ineffective, Green grabbed a nearby ladder. Using it as a ramrod, the marines splintered the portal on the second blow. Green clamored through the opening, and Colonel Washington, who had moved to the door, pointed out Brown. Instantly Green slashed Brown with a saber, cutting through his scalp and knocking him out. In the three-minute skirmish that followed, one marine and two more insurgents, including one of Brown's sons, were killed. The hostages—"the sorriest lot of people" Green had ever seen—were released unharmed. Through it all Colonel Lee stood a dozen yards away, still in his civilian clothes, coolly giving orders.[12]

"Were you not enchanted to see . . . him [in] command of the troops sent to put down the John Brown rebellion," gushed one of Lee's friends from Savannah, "& did you read the accounts of how ingeniously he contrived & how cleverly his success was managed?"[13] And indeed, it was a model operation. Not only had Lee brought an uncertain situation under control within a few hours, he had captured Brown alive and with a minimum loss of life. Moreover, by using what might now be called police actions rather than military siege tactics, he had protected the hostages.[14] It was all done with admirable correctness. Brown was offered every inducement to peaceably surrender and given medical treatment and protection after the attack. Lee lavished official praise on the volunteers, despite their uneven performance, and mollified a superfluous group of Baltimore troops by sending them to find evidence at Brown's headquarters. With supreme tact he allowed the marines—who belonged to the navy—to take center stage.[15] President Buchanan was impressed enough to invite Lee to dinner.[16] Governor Henry Wise was impressed enough to try to take credit for the action by implying that he had formed the plan and given Lee instructions. Incensed, Stuart protested, praising Lee's *immense but quiet, service,*" which he thought deserving of "a gold medal from Virginia." In Lee's mind the chief achievement was that he had stifled fanaticism, a sub-

John Brown, on the floor at right, being interviewed after his capture.
The man third from left is almost certainly Lee, who was known to have
been in the room and wearing civilian clothes. He is carrying a sword,
possibly a sign of his military role at Harper's Ferry. If it is Lee,
this is the first known published image of him.
FRANK LESLIE'S ILLUSTRATED NEWS, COURTESY OF VIRGINIA HISTORICAL SOCIETY

ject increasingly on his mind after the troubled events at Arlington. It had been a strange and distasteful piece of work for regular troops. Thankfully men of reason were back in charge.[17]

As his subordinates would affirm, Lee viewed this as a minor skirmish, dispatched with an ease that had eluded him on the Indian frontiers. It is fascinating that he clung to this mindset as long as he did, for he was witness to some powerful cautionary events. Lee left for Arlington the day after the capture, but not before he had heard Brown speak for himself, in the most ominous terms. A few hours after he regained consciousness, his hair still matted with dirt and blood, Brown was questioned about his intentions by Governor Wise and a congressional delegation. Lee was present, as was a reporter for the *New York Herald*, who made a transcript of the interview. Brown, with quiet confidence, affirmed that his intent was to free the slaves; that he believed he was an instrument of God; and that he was not only willing to kill for what he believed, but to die for it too. "I wish to say furthermore," he stated toward the end of the meeting, "that you had better—all you people at the South—prepare yourselves for a settlement of that question that must come up for settlement sooner than you are prepared for it. . . . You may dispose of me very easily, I am nearly disposed of now; but this question is still to be settled—this negro question I mean—the end of that is not yet."[18]

If Lee was listening, he did not hear the message. Disdainful of Brown's poor effort at revolution, Lee dismissed it as "the attempt of a fanatic or a madman that could only end in failure."[19] Though his wife considered the events to be "an alarming crisis," Lee continued to underplay the danger, speaking lightly of it with his relatives and military colleagues. When he returned to western Virginia, ordered to forestall any disruption at Brown's execution, he jokingly told his comrades that he was fighting "the *Harper's Ferry war*" and would rather be back with the Comanche.[20] A few days after Brown was hanged, Lee characterized the scene in dialect, something he used when being facetious. "Poor fly he done buzz," was how he described Brown's demise. Never had his political antenna been so poorly attuned.[21]

For the buzz that Ossawattomie Brown began at Harper's Ferry would have an immense resonance. Early in the episode Brown had shown his theatricality by capturing Lewis Washington and some coveted Washington relics, notably a sword said to have been given to the general by Frederick the Great of Prussia. Brown understood the symbolism of holding this property, and he continued in the six weeks following his arrest to rivet the entire nation with the drama of his cause. If he was a poor anarchist, he was a brilliant self-publicist. Throughout his highly questionable trial he coupled stirring, apocalyptic words with an unruffled approach to death that roused his allies and terrified the South. Public figures in the North such as Ralph Waldo Emerson and Henry Thoreau fed the alarm by calling for Brown to die a martyr's death rather than be spared, and Brown readily slipped into the role.[22] He dismissed lawyers who tried to plead insanity on his behalf, and faced his jurors with a steely eye. "Now if it is deemed necessary that I should forfeit my life . . . ," he cautioned from a makeshift cot in the courtroom, "and mingle my blood . . . with the blood of millions in the slave country whose rights are disregarded . . . I say let it be done!"[23] The prosecutors denounced his "fearful crimes," "done in the darkness of a Sabbath night," but they could not erase Brown's righteousness from the public mind.[24] Before riding to the gallows on his own coffin, Brown had the final revelatory word. He slipped a little note to one of his jailers that read in part: "I, John Brown am now quite *certain* that the crimes of this *guilty, land:* will never be purged *away;* but with Blood."[25]

In retrospect the hanging of John Brown seems heavy with foreboding. Among those who stood with Lee to watch Brown's soul jolted away were Thomas J. (later Stonewall) Jackson, who was leading a group of Virginia Military Institute cadets; Edmund Ruffin, who would fire the first shot at Fort Sumter; and John Wilkes Booth, in a uniform borrowed for the military-only occasion.[26] It was as if they were witnessing the last convulsions of the old Union, for, just as Brown had predicted, his death was not the end but the beginning of events that would ultimately achieve his goal of emancipation. "Be of good cheer," a friend had written to him while he was in jail, "thee has loosened the wheel on its axel and it is now ready for action."[27] After an initial period of quiet, when Southerners comforted themselves with the idea of Brown's madness and the fact that only a few slaves had rallied to his side, a cycle of fear began, fueled by the discovery of maps, letters, and plans that indicated Brown had ambitions beyond the attack on Harper's Ferry, as well as powerful backing in the North. Henry Wise initiated checks at the borders of Virginia and augmented militia drills, calling on Lee to aid him in the task.[28] The slaves, who had their own excellent lines of communication, showed signs of heightened expectation—and long-quiescent farms and communities began to wonder and dread.[29] No one captured the growing malaise better than the Lees' friend and neighbor Constance Cary Harrison.

> The only association I have with my old home in Virginia that is not one of unmixed happiness relates to the time immediately succeeding the execution of John Brown at Harper's Ferry. Our homestead was in Fairfax, at a considerable distance from the theater of that tragic episode; and belonging as we did to a family among the first in the State to manumit slaves . . . there seemed to be no especial reason for us to share in the apprehension of an uprising by the blacks. But there was the fear . . . dark, boding, oppressive, and altogether hateful. I can remember taking it to bed with me at night, and awaking suddenly oftentimes to confront it through a vigil of nervous terror. . . . In the daytime it seemed impossible to associate suspicion with those familiar tawny or sable faces that surrounded us. . . . What subtle influence was at work that should transform them into tigers thirsting for our blood? The idea was preposterous. But when evening came again, and with it

the hour when the colored people . . . assembled themselves together for dance or prayer-meeting, the ghost that refused to be laid was again at one's elbow. Rusty bolts were drawn and rusty fire-arms loaded. A watch was set where never before had eye or ear been lent to such a service. Peace, in short, had flown from the borders of Virginia.[30]

In February 1860 Lee received orders to return to Texas. He left behind Virginia's anxieties, only to be faced with a mounting secession movement in the Lone Star State and the worried discussions of his fellow officers. The regular army was an unusually close-knit group, having forged common bonds at West Point and in the hardship of war. Most of the men knew each other, and some owed their lives to their colleagues. Moreover, it was an apolitical institution, which discouraged displays of partisan sentiment and muted any parochialism in its officers. At the military academy a cadet was "taught that he belongs no longer to section or party but, in his life and all his faculties, to his country."[31] At the same time there was a good deal of sympathy for the South, and slavery was generally tolerated in military circles. Lee was just one of many who brought black servants with him to post. In fact, the celebrated Dred Scott decision, which established the right of a master to keep his slaves in bondage while visiting a free state, had been argued over a slave who accompanied an army doctor.[32]

The divisive election of 1860, and the secession debate that followed, forced military men to face their competing allegiance to home, family, and nation. "The officers & men of the Regiment are much exercised as to their future," Lee told Agnes, describing a scene of increasing malaise.[33] He watched in despair as his closest friends began to resign from the army. Winfield Scott, himself a Virginian, tried to keep the forces together by mocking the secession movement. "I know your little South Carolina," he snorted. "I lived there once. It is about as big as Long Island, and two-thirds of the population are negroes. Are you mad?"[34] But others were touched by a different sensibility.

An officer's wife wrote that she would never forget the terrible months of 1860–61, when souls were "torn asunder by the conflicting passions." This was the crucible, the dreadful moment of truth, and the stories surrounding these days throb with anguish. Albert Sidney Johnston hoped he could sit out the war by remaining at his command in San Francisco, but was relieved of duty by suspicious authorities in Washington. He wandered overland to Texas in "a hopeless and desperate state of mind," and finally took up arms with the Confederacy. In 1862 he was killed at Shiloh.[35] Joe Johnston, weeping bitterly, was escorted in a state of collapse from the rooms of the secretary of war after his resignation.³⁶ In another wrenching scene Lewis Armistead—nephew of the general who had defended Fort McHenry on the night of the "Star-Spangled Banner"—tearfully grabbed his friend Winfield Scott Hancock by the shoulders. "Hancock, good-by," he choked out. "You can never know what this has cost me." Armistead was cut down by Hancock's men during Pickett's Charge.³⁷

Lee, shocked at the thought of dismantling the nation, maintained that disunion was "anarchy" and that "secession is nothing but revolution."³⁸ Exasperated with extremists both north and south, he decried equally the "aggressions" of the former and "selfish & dictatorial bearing" of the latter. Long after the "fire-eaters" were manipulating public emotion, he clung to the fantasy that secession could be peaceably reversed.³⁹ "I trust there is wisdom, patriotism enough in the Country to save them, for I cannot anticipate so great a calamity to the nation as a dissolution of the Union," he told one of his favorite nieces.⁴⁰ Lee's distress was so acute that it fractured the correct demeanor he normally cultivated. Not only did he startle his colleagues by exploding with rage when secessionists tried prematurely to force his resignation, he broke down when he heard that Texas had actually left the Union. "I shall never forget his look of astonishment . . . his lips trembling and his eyes full of tears," a friend wrote of that bleak February day.⁴¹

From the start of the crisis Lee knew that his destiny was to follow the fortunes of Virginia. If his state chose to stay in the Union, so would he; if it withdrew, his actions would follow suit. He was candid about this with everyone who asked him and never changed his conviction that this was the only respectable course. He hoped the crisis would abate, he explained to Markie, but acknowledged that if it continued he would "go back in sorrow to my people & share the misery of my native state & save in her defence there will be one soldier less in the world than now."⁴² As he left San Antonio, a fellow officer shouted after the ambulance he was riding in, "Colonel, do you intend to go South or remain North?" Lee stuck his head out and replied: "I shall never bear arms against the United States,—but it may be necessary for me to carry a musket in defence of my native State, Virginia, in which case I shall not prove recreant to my duty."⁴³

It is clear that the nation's emergency had imposed a personal crisis on Lee. He never wavered in his determination to link his actions to Virginia's, but he was less clear about his reasons for it. "While I wish to do what is right," he declared in a moment of supreme confliction, "I am unwilling to do what is not, either at the bidding of the South or North."⁴⁴ He told a friend, Charles Anderson, that even though he saw little justification for secession, he had been educated to believe that his "loyalty to Virginia ought to take precedence over that which is due to the Federal Government." Anderson, recalling the legacy of Lee's brother Henry, who had railed against the primacy of states' rights, and Light-Horse Harry's passionate belief in Washington's nationalist principles, recalled: "I sadly asked myself: *whence was this education?*"[45] Light-Horse Harry Lee had led an army to stymie the first challenge to federal authority during the Whiskey Rebellion, and though he was once heard to declare that Virginia was his "country"—which he felt bound to "obey"—he had ultimately concluded that "our happiness depends entirely on maintaining our union" and that "in point of right, no state can withdraw itself from the union."[46]

Another part of Robert Lee's dilemma was that although he was convinced that the framers of the Constitution had never intended the right of secession, he strongly agreed with the secessionists on virtually every other policy.[47] He believed in racial supremacy and could not envision an egalitarian society; he thought the nation had been founded on "perpetual union," but admitted that if the bond could "only be maintained by the sword and bayonet, instead of brotherly Love & friendship . . . its existence will lose all interest with me."[48] He spoke out for the Crittenden compromise, which would have guaranteed the permanent existence of slavery and permitted its extension into the territories, maintaining that this cornerstone of proslavery thought deserved "the support of every patriot."[49] Above all, Lee "resented" aggressive badgering by the North and feared southern political impotence under the rule of its majority population.[50]

The way Lee envisioned his own role in the conflict was particularly convoluted. Here his pronouncements often appear at odds not only with themselves but with realistic expectation. He could not raise his sword against the United States—but if called on to carry a musket for Virginia, he would not shirk. He would take to planting corn, and there would be one less soldier in the world—"save in defence of my native state." None of this seems plausible; yet it would not be the last time Lee retreated to a dream world of subsistence farming and revolutionary imagery. One of the more intricate steps in this psychic Virginia reel is the word "defence."[51] It appears Lee thought that if he stayed in the old army, he might be able to maintain a position that resisted offensive operations; and that if Virginia seceded, he could restrict himself to actions that checked aggression. Apparently this belief was bolstered by General Scott, who showed him cabinet papers that denounced war and maintained that any mobilization was solely for the protection of the capital. Indeed he clung to this vision of reactive defense until well after the first battle of Manassas.[52]

The only way out of this corner was for Virginia to remain in the Union so that Lee could both uphold the United States and defend his natal ground. Lee was open in his hope that this would be the case. "I am particularly anxious that Virginia should keep right," he advised Agnes, "as she was chiefly instrumental in the formation & inauguration of the Constitution, so I would wish that she might be able to maintain it, to save the union."[53] One of the haunting questions of these anxious months is why he did not use his influence to guide Virginia's decision. In this, the most critical moment of his life, it seems he fell back on his old passivity. Lee's name was not yet a household word, but his reputation from the Mexican War was widely appreciated, and his part in the peaceful termination of the John Brown affair was celebrated throughout the South. Neighbors and relatives waited to follow his lead: one recalled that "for some the question 'What will Colonel Lee do?' was only second in interest to 'What will Virginia do.'"[54] It was well known that he had the ear of General Scott and that his opinion might sway the lawmakers in Washington. Harper's Ferry had also given him special access in Richmond. His standing there was such that Confederate vice president Alexander Stephens admitted "a look, or even intonation of voice" by Lee at this time would have had enormous power.[55] Perhaps acting on his old dislike of politics and prominence, he chose not to shape the momentous events before him. Instead he linked his fate to the volatile public will, stating that he must wait patiently, relying on God to order all things for the good.[56] When he was begged by statesmen and relatives to lead in brokering a peace, he remained resolutely out of the discussions.[57]

In fact Lee almost got his wish that Virginia would remain with the Union. Pro-secession factions tried to force an early decision after South Carolina withdrew from the Union in December 1860, but through skillful diplomacy the choice was left to a statewide convention, which opened the following February. That the Old Dominion would secede was anything but a foregone conclusion. Thirty-one percent of its people were enslaved, the largest actual number of bondsmen of any state in the South. Yet in the 1850s Virginia had been heavily influenced by an influx of northern immigrants, the growth of railroads, and political reforms that were beginning to challenge the old seignorial class. With its diversified population and economy, it had more in common with Maryland, which remained with the Union, than it did with the Cotton States. Though there were some notably aggressive pro-secession personalities in the Old Dominion, overall there was no great leap to embrace the risky policies of South Carolina. Nowhere was this truer than in Lee's section of the state, where the economy was booming and the influence of slave culture waning. Union sentiment remained widespread in northern and western Virginia even as the final votes for secession were counted.[58]

During the early months of 1861 Virginia conducted an extraordinary public discussion of secession, unequaled elsewhere. This was not a debate about war: as Henry Adams would observe, few in America expected or wanted the horrors that rocked the land from 1861 to 1865.[59] Instead it was a sober attempt to resolve a conflict of incompatible regional differences, constitutional rights, and factional politicians. Secessionists tried to exploit the emotional aftershock of Lincoln's election, but in these early months they were overridden by those who still thought the Union offered the best guarantee of liberty and prosperity. Only one-third of the delegates to the state convention favored secession, and their arguments were not holding the day. Lee had legitimate grounds to hope that his home state and his country were at least feebly reconciled when he returned to Washington, at Scott's behest, on March 1, 1861.[60]

He found the atmosphere alive with tension. Washington was filled with edgy troops, called in for Lincoln's inauguration. Many, like Mary Lee, thought the lanky westerner should have resigned for the sake of the country rather than take the oath of office.[61] Though Lincoln tried to appear conciliatory, saying that he would not interfere with slavery where it existed, he also made clear that he recognized no independent states and intended to protect federal property. Lee's colleague Samuel Heintzelman attended the March 4 inauguration and thought the address a prescription for war. When he saw Lee at Scott's office the next day, Lee also expressed concern.[62] Lee's movements for the next month appear to have been low-key and cautious. In theory Scott had recalled him to sit on a board revising the army's regulations, and while the board was being formed, he remained at Arlington without official duties.[63] Lincoln was starting to put his administration together, making appointments and reassigning troops, and Lee's capabilities—and his allegiance—were under discussion. Lincoln had appointed Simon Cameron as secretary of war, and one aide recalled a meeting between Cameron and Scott that focused on Lee. "The Secretary asked the General if he had full confidence in Lee's loyalty, to which the General replied, 'Entire confidence, sir. He is true as steel, sir, true as steel!'"[64] In full dress uniform Lee attended a reception given at the White House on March 13 for seventy-eight military officers. It was probably the only time he met Lincoln.[65] A week later the new president promoted Lee to full colonel of the 1st Regiment of Cavalry—a coveted position that Lee was confident enough to accept immediately.[66]

But the tenuous chance for peaceful resolution was quickly shattered. In early April Lincoln made the difficult decision to resupply Fort Sumter, which was holding out against a rebel blockade in Charleston harbor. He apprised southern officials of his intention and essentially gave them an alternative: Would their response be peace or war? They chose war, firing at the fort on April 12. In the ensuing panic Lincoln made another fateful choice, this time calling for 75,000 soldiers to defend U.S. property. These two actions galvanized both sides, as the North feared wholesale revolution and Southerners believed Lincoln was preparing to invade their homes. Those who had so dexterously crafted a fragile peace in Virginia were caught in the fury, their months of compromise overturned. A woman who tried to defend the February decision against secession was told by Senator R. M. T. Hunter, "My dear lady you may place your little hand against Niagara with more certainty of staying the torrent than you can oppose this movement."[67] On April 17 the question was again put to the convention in Richmond. This time they chose secession.[68]

"Events crowd so fast I cannot write them in my diary," exclaimed the Lees' friend Elizabeth Lomax. "Virginia *has* seceded!! Heaven help us!"[69] The verdict was not yet finalized—that would depend on a popular referendum scheduled for May 23—but few doubted the outcome. At Arlington, Lee learned with dismay of the convention's impending vote—probably on April 16, when the rumors first reached Washington. According to one family story he dined that night with his brother Smith and cousin Phillips Lee, both U.S. naval officers. His two companions bantered awhile about how Cousin Phil, who intended to stay with the Union, would be bombarded by Smith Lee's Confederate forces, after which the two would discuss the contest over an amiable toast. During this levity Robert remained miserable and mute. Believing that his silence was born of indecision, Phillips Lee hastily told federal government officials that if they were to sway his cousin they must act quickly.[70] The next day a note was dispatched to Arlington, calling Lee to the offices of Francis Preston Blair, one of Lincoln's closest advisers, along with another message that requested his presence in General Scott's headquarters. At the meeting with Blair, Lee was told that Lincoln intended to offer him command of the forces being called up to defend the Union. The two talked for a long time, Blair "very wily and keen," playing on Lee's sense of responsibility and ambition. Lee declined on the spot. He saw nothing but "anarchy & ruin" in secession, he told Blair, yet he could not bring himself to raise his sword against his Virginia home and heritage.[71] From Blair's office Lee marched straight to see Scott, in such agitation that

he dispensed with his usual courtesies and insisted on being admitted to
the general's office. Lee and Scott, bound for so long in mutual admiration, talked candidly for several hours.[72] What can be pieced together
from the available accounts is that Scott tried to persuade Lee that any
forces amassed by the Union would be so vast they would stifle the
South's will to rebel, making offensive
action unnecessary. When Lee said he
was convinced aggression was inevitable, and he could not lead an invasion of the South, Scott brusquely
rejoined: "If you propose to resign it is
proper that you should do so at once;
your present attitude is equivocal."
Now there was nothing left to say. A
journalist was told the two men stood
grasping each other's hands, "too full
of feeling to find utterance for one
word. . . ."[73]

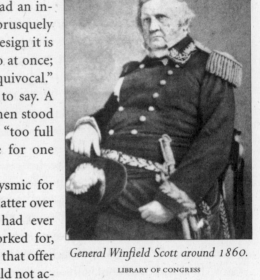

General Winfield Scott around 1860.
LIBRARY OF CONGRESS

The day had been cataclysmic for
Lee, and he went to talk the matter over
with Smith. Everything he had ever
been, everything he had worked for,
seemed to have culminated in that offer
of command, and now he could not accept it. He did not want his state to
secede, but had felt powerless to halt the course he believed would be so
destructive. That night came reports that Virginia troops had seized the
armory at Harper's Ferry, the same arsenal he had so recently defended
against wild, prophetic John Brown, and he must have known that all
chance of peaceful redress was over. He had wanted to hang on to his hopes,
as well as his commission, until the May 23 referendum made secession irrevocable in Virginia. But Scott's pressure forced him to contemplate the loss of not only his job but his credibility within army circles.[74]
Those who met him and his family in Alexandria noted the sharp contrast in their deep depression with the general exhilaration in the town.
The people had "lost their senses," Rooney remarked in dismay.[75] Agnes
would write quietly to Mildred that nothing at Arlington was "talked or
thought of except our troubles . . . our poor Father & brothers need all
our prayers. . . ."[76]

For two terrible days Lee contemplated the matter. His wife, as torn as he was, told him that she would support whatever decision he made.[77] The slaves watched as their master "walked backwa'd and fo'ward on de po'ch steddyin'," noting that he "didn't cahr to go. No . . . he didn't cahr to go."[78] A little boy who was visiting the family also remembered seeing Lee pacing in the garden and hearing the floors creak as he knelt and prayed in his upstairs bedroom.[79] Arlington felt "as if there had been a death in it," said Agnes, "for the army was to him home and country."[80] At midnight the house was still ablaze with lights, as the family gathered with miserable anticipation in the parlor. Finally Lee bowed his head and wrote his resignation, as well as a short explanatory letter to General Scott. Then he slowly walked down the long staircase and handed the letters to his wife. "Mary," he said, "your husband is no longer an officer of the United States Army."[81]

Lee's most renowned biographer called it the "answer he was born to make." Another writer stated that "it was not that the anguished man had any choice."[82] Yet everything we know indicates that the decision was, in his wife's words, "the severest struggle of his life."[83] This poignant moment, when a strong, steadfast man paced and prayed in despair, is a scene worthy of Shakespeare precisely because it so palpably exposes the contradiction in his heart. Why, if he believed all he said, did he come to this point? Lee's explanation was the spare, elegantly worded one he gave to his cousin Roger Jones and repeated nearly verbatim to each person who asked: "With all my devotion to the Union and the feeling of loyalty and duty of an American citizen, I have not been able to make up my mind to raise my hand against my relatives, my children, my home."[84] Yet even his formulaic language gives an impression quite the opposite from banal inevitability. In later years he confessed he held on to his resignation letter for a day before sending it, the moment was so painful.[85] Lee would later concoct elaborate constitutional theories to explain his decision, but they belied the words he spoke at the moment of crisis. His reticence speaks to his distress, and suggests he knew he must hold on to his conviction and avoid expressing its contradictions, lest he second-guess his own actions.

For in reality there were numerous options available to him, options that others in his situation did choose. Winfield Scott was a Virginian, and he knew that his path lay with the Union. When he was approached by state officials, he dismissed as an insult any suggestion that he would renege on his solemn oath of loyalty. So did George Thomas, with whom Lee had companionably ridden over the Texas desert. Both Thomas and Scott would suffer the social ostracism that Orton Williams prophesized in his resignation letter. " 'Fuss and Feathers' has distinguished himself," one prominent Virginian critically remarked. "You ought to hear how he is spoken of by his family and State."[86] Thomas's family never again communicated with him except to ask him to change his name.[87] A young Virginian, just out of West Point, acknowledged that by retaining his commission he had been shunned by all of his southern associates; yet still he derided those who would hold their obligations so lightly as to abandon the nation when it most needed them.[88] In all, about two-fifths of the officers from Virginia stayed in the U.S. Army after their state seceded, enduring varying degrees of censure for their stance.[89] Others opted not to fight on any side. West Point's Dennis Hart Mahan, another proud Virginian, chose not to uphold a cause he believed unworthy and sat out the war.[90] North Carolinian Alfred Mordecai resigned his commission, but rejected an offer to lead either the Confederate ordinance service or engineer department. He spent the war years teaching mathematics in Philadelphia.[91]

Lee had hoped to avoid pitting himself against his family, but that desire would also remain unfulfilled. In fact his decision was controversial in his innermost circles. "I feel no exalted respect for a man who takes part in a movement in which he can see nothing but 'anarchy & ruin' . . . and yet that very utterance scarce passed Robt Lees lips . . . when he starts off with delegates to treat with Traitors," was one response from his family. A young relative began a school fight when he was asked whether his father—a Unionist—was "the Rebel traitor Lee."[92] Roger Jones, whom Lee declined to advise, finally decided to fight for the Union. A bevy of relations in the army and navy followed suit. Phillips Lee never wavered from his Union loyalties, serving through the war with distinction. His younger brother John Fitzgerald Lee, an 1834 West Point graduate, retained his position as judge advocate of the Union army. Cousin John H. Upshur also resisted "tremendous pressure" in order to remain with the Union.[93] Orton Williams, of course, did resign; but his brother Laurence fought on the side of the North, serving at one point as an aide-de-camp to General McClellan.[94] Philip Fendall, whose family had done so much for Robert Lee's mother, never wavered from his Union loyalties.[95] Sister Anne was also not in agreement with Robert, and her son, Louis Marshall, fought with General John Pope against his uncle. No one in that family ever spoke to Lee again.[96] With great reluctance Smith Lee became a Confederate naval officer, where he served without enthusiasm, and as late as September 1863 still "pitched into" those responsible for "getting us into this snarl." Saying that both the Lees and his in-laws in the Mason family had pressured him with ideas that Virginia came first, he grumbled, "South Carolina be hanged. . . . How I did want to stay in the old navy!"[97] His wife tried to reverse their son Fitz Lee's pro-South decision and herself held "to the north end of the Long Bridge" until she was "dragged away from Washington . . . kicking."[98] In early 1861 Mary Lee was also conflicted, and her daughters teased her about her staunch Unionist talk. Though she sympathized with some of the South's complaints, she wrote, "for my part, I would rather endure the ills we know, than rush madly into greater evils & what could be greater than the Division of our glorious Republic into petty states, each seeking its private interests & unmindful of the whole."[99] Lee's sons joined the Confederate forces, but only after their father had declared his intentions. There is a strong chance that if Lee's decision had been different they would have followed his lead.[100] Had Robert Lee taken the part of the Union, he still would have faced confrontation within his border-state family, many of whom sided with the South. But his assertion that he was acting in simple solidarity with a like-minded group of relatives would never be borne out.

In describing his decision, Lee rarely uses the word *honor*. In January 1861 he tells Markie there is no sacrifice he is unwilling to make for the Union "save that of honour"; he makes a similar comment to Rooney about the same time. Later he has the "honor" of tendering his resignation from the army.[101] It is a weighty word, and its multiple meanings in Lee's situation may have made it too painful a choice for his pen. In southern society honor was bound up with family connections and local reputation and a desire to avoid public shame. For those who felt it keenly, the individual consideration of honor could take precedence over civic order or personal welfare—even culminating in violence—the cult of the duel being a notable illustration. Lee may have been influenced by this, though the split in his family makes the question of private loyalties a problematic one. There was no linear path to rectitude in Lee's case, and every avenue was strewn with irreconcilable principles. For example, one of the concerns that pressed Lee to resign quickly was the worry that he might be ordered by the army to undertake aggressive duty against the South; in military circles it was "dishonorable" to resign because of unwelcome orders. Lee acted on this definition of honor at the very time he was "dishonoring" vows of thirty years.[102] The concern that seems to have motivated him was the bullying of the North, which he had been complaining about since the 1830s.[103] It was not just his distaste for abolitionists or the fear of an increasingly powerful northern majority so much as the horror of lost self-esteem, the rage of not being able to defend oneself in the face of mounting humiliations. Secession became the most "honorable" option to Southerners because it showed independence and a

spirit of self-protection. Many of those who chose to fight for the South gave
this as the reason for their fierce determination, and throughout the war the
reaction against "subjugation" was a strong motivating force. It had nothing
to do with the inherent principles in their cause; more accurately it could be
called "pride," that second cousin of honor. In Lee's case this likely colored
not only his decision to leave the U.S. Army, but his strongly aggressive performance on the battlefield.[104]

Lee sat on his decision for a day and then dispatched his letters to General
Scott. Orton Williams, who had not yet left Scott's staff, reported that the
resignation had been approved and that the whole army was "in a stir over
it."[105] While Arlington's inhabitants were still in shock at the thought of having arrayed themselves against the flag of their country, Lee was contacted
by Judge John Robertson, who Governor John Letcher had dispatched to assess his availability for service with Virginia. It must have been an agonizing
afternoon, for Robertson was detained by a lengthy, unpleasant interview
with Scott, and never arrived for Lee's appointment.[106] The next day, a Sunday, Lee was seen earnestly conferring with some strangers, probably
Robertson and other representatives from Richmond, on the grounds of
Christ Church. Several relatives stood with Agnes Lee and watched them,
remembering that "the vibrations in the air were intense" and that Lee's face
showed "a mortal struggle . . . much more terrible than any known to the
din of battle." After a long conversation, Lee agreed to meet Judge Robertson
the following morning on a train bound for Richmond. One family member thought he had gone to confer about peace; others believed that he was
simply weighing his options.[107]

   Much has been made about Lee's whirlwind transformation in those few
April days, for outside the heightened moment it seems his transition from
a loyal United States officer to a committed rebel was just a little too quick.
Whether or not he was cagily playing both sides for the greatest advantage
has been the subject of some debate.[108] Lee had indeed been approached by
southern leaders as early as mid-March, but if he responded, the correspondence has yet to be found.[109] Certainly he was assessing every possibility, for
it would have been unwise not to, given his beliefs and the precarious political climate. There is no indication, however, that he proffered his services,
or ever sought information about receiving a commission in any southern
army before his resignation. When he was finally offered the leadership of
Virginia's forces, state officials took some trouble to avoid soliciting him before he had resigned his commission, feeling that it would be "dishonorable" to pressure anyone still under oath to defend the United States.[110] His

cousins, always the sounding board of his soul, believed his preference was to outwait the crisis at Arlington, and Lee also mentioned that this was his intention.[111] Yet excitement and opportunity were in the air, and there was a good deal of discussion among resigning officers about who would pluck the limited number of plum positions with the southern forces. Lee may have succumbed, as did J. E. B. Stuart, to the urgency to act before "the southern army will all be drawn and you will have the place of the laggard."[112]

According to Judge Robertson, Lee did not know that he was to be offered any command until he boarded the train. He may have been interested in going to Richmond just to assess the situation; he later said, rather questionably, that he went to look at the Pamunkey estates. It seems unlikely that so cautious a man would have made the journey without a strong understanding of its purpose. Others had certainly caught wind of the state's intentions, and along the rail route Lee was excitedly cheered.[113] By the time he reached Richmond, the state convention had voted him commander in chief of all forces. Before he had much time to ruminate, he found himself being presented with George Washington's sword, and hailed a hero in a powerful tribute by the president of the convention. Was he caught unawares and forced to react too quickly, or was this really the very spot where he most longed to be? Was this finally the recognition Lee sought—the culmination of his skill and his self-discipline? It is hard to say, for Lee fell back on the accepted, courteous platitudes of his era, expressing surprise at the praise and protesting his inadequacy for the job. But it pleased him enough that a newspaper account of this triumph was found in his pocket diary at his death.[114]

The quick turnaround was probably entirely logical in Lee's heart, for he had said from the first that he would link his fate to Virginia's. As can be imagined, however, few outside the South believed the decision reflected the noble principles he invoked to explain it. Honor was in the eye of the beholder in 1861, and from the beginning Lee's motives were criticized. Technically Lee had acted correctly by resigning when he felt that he could no longer uphold his vows to defend "the United States paramount to any and all allegiance . . . to any State" or "against all enemies or opposers."[115] The skeptics, however, believed that those who swore easy oaths in fine times, and then abandoned them, not only shamefully betrayed the country but had no honor. When she heard from Mary Lee that Robert had spent two prayerful days in decision, a cousin remarked acidly: "I wish he had read over his commission as well as his prayers."[116] At West Point someone drew a picture of Lee with his head attached to the body of an insect. Lincoln would use Lee's "deceitful" dealings as a justification for his suspension of habeas corpus.[117] The reaction of former army friends was just as sharp. "Robert Lee is commander in chief of the forces of the Commonwealth—'O Lucifer son of the morning star how art thou fallen,'" was the response of one colleague's family. The phrase echoed words that Light-Horse Harry's beloved Nathanael Greene had used to condemn Benedict Arnold.[118]

While still in frontier Texas, Lee had recognized that his decision would be based on intangibles. "I know you think and feel very differently, but I can't help it," he had told esteemed northern colleagues. In the end it mattered not that Henry Lee believed "the good of the state is entwined with the good of the Union," or that his son's fortunes might prosper by following another course.[119] Solemn oaths and Unionist relatives ultimately could not override the pull of what Lee's cousin Anna Maria Fitzhugh called "a sweet binding to this spot of earth, this soil of Virginia that is irresistible."[120] Lee tried to disavow private interests in his statements, but in fact it was the intense personal quality of his struggle that made it emblematic of the nation's torment.[121] His decision came to represent more than a divided country, or divided regional fidelity; it went beyond a divisive vote on secession or a splintered family. It strikes a timeless chord because it evokes that lowest of all miseries: the nightmare of a divided soul.

A cartoon made of Lee at West Point after he decided to fight for the South.

SPECIAL COLLECTIONS, UNITED STATES
MILITARY ACADEMY

That pensive, disciplined Robert E. Lee made an emotional decision affects each of us every day. One of the most trenchant "what-ifs" of the Civil War is the question of how Lee's stance shaped the course of the nation. We sense that history would have been altered if the options presented to Lee—resignation; leadership of the Union troops; acceptance of high command in Virginia—had been decided differently. We do not know exactly how this would have developed, but intuitively we know it to be true. Lee's dilemma was not simply a historic wrestling match between right and wrong, patriotism or treachery. It stands as a critical moment in our nation's pageant because it forces us to consider some very basic questions. What is patriotism?

Who commands our first loyalty? Can loyalty be divided and still be true? And who defines truth anyway? It is the excruciating gray area that makes these questions universal. Lee tells us that the answer to each is highly subjective. By taking a stand and never turning back, Lee also teaches us that they must be faced by every individual at the moment they are summoned, no matter how unsure or unprepared, and that the grandest theories in the world fall away at the moment of heightened instinct. And then his decision tells us something more: that following the heart's truth may lead to censure, or agonizing defeat—and yet be honored in itself.[122]

Chapter Eighteen

Field of Honor

Richmond 30th April 1861

My dear Mary

On going to my room last night I found my trunk & sword there & opening it this morning discovered the package of letters, & was very glad [to] learn you were all well & as yet peaceful. I fear the latter state will not continue long, not that I think Virginia is going to make war but if the Federal Government should be disposed to peace there is now such a mass of ——— in Washington such a pressure from the north, & such fury manifested against the South that it may not be in the power of the authorities to restrain them—Then again among such a mass of all slanders it might be considered a smart thing to cross into Va & rob, plunder, &c especially when it is known to be the residence of one of the Rebel leaders—I think therefore you had better prepare all things for removal that is the plate pictures &c. & be prepared at any moment—<u>where</u> to go is the difficulty—when the war commences no place will be exempt in my opinion, & indeed all the avenues into the State will be the scene of Military operations—Tell Custis to consider the question He is a discreet person & prudent & advise what had better be done—I wrote to Robert that I could not consent to take boys from their school & young men from their colleges & put them in the ranks at the beginning of the war when they are not wanted & where there were men enough for the purpose—The war may last 10 years where are our ranks to be filled from then? I was willing for his company, to continue at their studies, to keep up its organization & to perfect themselves in their military exercises & to perform duty at the College but not to be called into the field—I therefore wished him to remain—If the exercises at the College are suspended he can then come home. I do not wish any more socks or shirts at this time. I forgot to take from the old uniform coat I left for the servants the eyes or hooks from the shoulders that confined the epaulettes—will you cut them out & also the loops at the collar—you will have to rip the coat & take them out If

you will then wrap them up carefully & send them to Mr. John G or Mr Dan-
gerfield directed to the Spottswood House there are persons coming on every
day by whom they can be forwarded I was much interested in Mary Childe's
letter—My poor Anne how she must have suffered—I have not time to write to
her—There is no prospect or intention of the government to propose a truce—
Do not be deceived by it—Custis must exercise his judgement about sending to
the Alexa market—It is your only chance—Give much love to all my dear chil-
dren & Helen   Tell them I want to see them very much—May God preserve
you all & bring peace to our distracted country   Truly yrs

RE Lee[1]

⊱━◆━○━◆━⊰

A CENTURY AND A HALF have passed since this urgent, distracted letter
was written, yet it still has the power to rivet our attention. Like the audience at a Greek drama, we know the outcome of this story, but cannot resist hearing the whole tragic tale once more. The letter also impressed Mary
Lee, and when the little note deteriorated to the point that it was unreadable, she made this copy, full of spelling errors and repeated words that
would have been uncharacteristic of her husband. Her carefully preserved
transcript makes it clear that she understood exactly what this message
meant. In its simplest terms it signaled the end of the Lees' life at Arlington.
But in the hasty, broken sentences and casual asides Robert Lee also presages
most of the terrible reality of 1861, a reality that few wanted to admit at this
early date. The hope for peace was gone; the long season of posturing and
threats would now turn to protracted violence. Young men like his son Rob
would be snatched in all their promise, many to be marched to merciless
death. Order as they understood it would be painfully altered. Of this we
need no greater witness than Lee's stunning admission that he had given his
slaves the heavy blue U.S. Army coats he had worn so proudly for thirty-four
years.

Now the lines between public and personal life were also becoming
blurred, and Lee began to realize that his words were no longer his own, that
his privacy would be an early victim of the war. It had been but ten days
since his resignation from the U.S. Army, and he had traveled only a hundred miles to Richmond. Yet these figures belie the immensity of the journey he had taken. Lee had been an ordinary citizen, respected and liked, but
safe in his obscurity. Now he was becoming a kind of civic property, open to
scrutiny, a lightning rod for hope, for emulation—and for censure. During

the next few months he took on the appearance generations after would associate with him, growing a beard, his hair becoming prematurely white.
(Whether a nod to the fashion he always courted, or to avoid shaving in the
field, it was to his family's horror that the beard appeared.) His very name
was recast about this time, with the popular press calling him "Robert E.
Lee," a formulation not used by himself or his family, and with which he
never identified. His wife's home was no longer a private sanctuary; it was
now a potential artillery position. The unsettling shift from a life of privileged anonymity to public expectation was part of the general confusion
that reigned in those early days of mingled exaltation and apprehension.
Nowhere is this more evident than in the last line of his letter, where Lee
calls on God to "bring peace to our distracted country." The problem is, we
do not quite know to which country he is referring.[2]

The spectacular view from Arlington's front portico had charmed visitors
for nearly six decades. It was one of the chief glories of the place, remarked
on by everyone from Lafayette to the young Henry Adams. Arlington had a
prospect that took in a dozen miles in three directions, including the water
approaches to Washington and the old ports of Georgetown and Alexandria. The Capitol was just over three miles away; the White House even
closer. The best artillery could now reach targets three or four miles distant.
"It is not hard to imagine what would have happened if Confederate cannon
had found lodgement on the plateau . . . ," wrote one observer, "and had
started practicing artillery fire with the White House as a target." Once Virginia had seceded, both sides knew that control of these heights was a tactical necessity.[3]

The arrival of thousands of untrained Yankee troops in the nation's capital did nothing to dispel this conviction. The area was strongly divided
about the conflict. In Washington, and across the river in Alexandria and
Fairfax County, powerful Union sympathies coexisted with Confederate
zeal.[4] The streets were as full of rumor as they were of laughing, loafing, and
drilling soldiers. The poet Charles Russell Lowell wrote to his mother on
May 13 that the northern troops "parade here and the crowds stare at
them—in Alexandria . . . the Virginia troops parade and crowds gape at
them—as to fancying any hostile relation between them, it is almost impossible, and yet I firmly believe there will be a collision within three weeks."[5]
The newspapers joined in the intrigue by speculating on everything from
imminent southern invasion to the price of wheat. Fretfully awaiting credible news at Arlington, Mary Lee thought the papers of both sides "below

contempt" and fumed that their "falsehoods & surmises would be amusing if they were not on such a serious subject." No one knew whom to trust, nor did the troops make them feel particularly safe. In the Senate chamber, at the White House and War Department, nervous officials began to make plans to reinforce the capital's defenses.[6]

Robert Lee was under no illusions about what this meant at Arlington. He had admired the estate's vista since boyhood, but in 1861 he gazed out from Arlington Heights as a professional engineer who had spent his career building defensive fortifications. He was only too aware of the strategic value of this site, and assumed that the property would be appropriated for military use.[7] His son Custis, who opposed secession but nonetheless resigned from the U.S. Army shortly after his father, put it quite clearly. He told a cousin that "were he able to dictate proceedings he would call [secession] revolution and order at once the seizing and fortifying of Arlington Heights."[8] Military advantage aside, Lee also sensed that personal animosity was to come. "In reference to the action of the U.S. Govt, you had better make up your mind to expect all the injury they can do us," he told Mary. "They look upon us as their most bitter enemies & will treat us as such to the extent of their power."[9]

Lee's foreboding made him anxious for the family to leave Arlington as soon as possible. He wrote on the subject every few days that spring, with increasing concern. He wanted to be assured that his wife and daughters were in a place beyond the reach of danger, but, as he told Mary on April 30, he did not really know where that might be.[10] Mrs. Lee did at length send Agnes and Annie to the old Fitzhugh property, Ravensworth, along with the Mount Vernon silver and family portraits, but as her husband grew more nervous, she continued to linger on at Arlington. She clung to every report of possible peace, and proposed that the whole question might be resolved by stationing a guard on the grounds.[11] The thought of leaving was made more wrenching by one of the loveliest spring seasons in memory, the hillside covered with roses, the air heavily perfumed with yellow jasmine.[12] Mary Lee found a dozen reasons to tarry and at times became defiant. "I would not stir from this house even if the whole Northern Army were to surround it," she declared to Mildred.[13]

In the tense weeks that followed, Mary Lee would chide her daughters and Custis for ignoring their family's danger, but seemed unable to grasp the situation herself. She was aroused to fury when Mildred complained about a bonnet "at a time when her Father's life is in peril, her home in danger of being trampled over by a lawless foe, if not leveled to the ground," yet she too seems to have been caught in profound denial. Her days were spent directing the servants, working in the burgeoning garden, copying a portrait of Rob.[14] The pain of abandoning her home was simply too much to accept: "altho' warned to prepare for the worst," she later admitted, "I could not realize the actual state of affairs."[15] Arlington, as she sorrowfully noted, "was a place dearer to me than my life, the home of every memory of that life whether for joy or sorrow, the birth place of my children, where I was wedded, & where I hoped to die & be laid under those noble oaks by the side of my parents to whom as an only child I had been an object of absorbing & tender love—The idea of leaving this home could scarcely be endured. . . ." She bowed to the inevitable only when cousin Orton Williams, who still worked in the office of General Winfield Scott, appeared anxiously one early morning to announce that plans were going forward for the immediate takeover of Arlington Heights.[16]

Then she worked with speed to fold away Martha Washington's silk curtains and fine carpets, to take pictures from the walls and remove wine and other valuables from the premises. She packed up the lovely china that had been presented to the Washingtons, and the famous punch bowl, and placed them in the cellar. She was so distraught at leaving that she hastily stored many valuables, putting General Washington's war tent in open sight in the garret, and fine clocks and engravings in unlocked rooms. Plans were finalized for the servants to be supported by selling produce from the estate in local markets. Mrs. Lee thought she had "a reprieve from execution" when Orton returned to say he thought the occupation had been postponed, but it soon became clear that only a few days might be gained, and that she must depart. On May 19, with the ratification vote on Virginia secession only four days away, she joined her daughters at Ravensworth. She told General Lee that her only consolation was that the war would be soon over and she would be back in a few weeks. In fact, Mary Anna Randolph Custis Lee had left Arlington forever.[17]

As Orton Williams had known, the Union's initial intention was to take control of Arlington as soon as Virginia made its declaration of secession. On May 3 General Scott, determined "not to lose a moment in anticipating the enemy," had directed the Department of Washington to occupy the heights and construct enough fortifications to hold them. Part of the pressure came from persistent speculation about Virginia troops on or near the property.[18] Mrs. Lee had hoped, of course, that this is exactly what might take place. However, despite the bravado of some young Confederate officers, who claimed that forces protecting Manassas Gap Junction could arrive in time to prevent a seizure, Arlington remained in Federal hands throughout the war.[19] Many could not understand why southern officials had not moved swiftly to control the position. Ironically, Lee himself fed the reticence by ordering Virginia operations to be defensive as long as possible. Indeed, the first official message in his hand after accepting Virginia's command directs a subordinate to proceed quietly, and to take care so "that conflict be not provoked before we are ready."[20] But in Washington the worst was believed, and preparations for a ring of defensive forts went forward. Long before plans were finalized, northern papers began speaking confidently of "the cool airy rooms & cool commanding position for summer quartering on 'Arlington heights.'"[21]

In the end, Virginian Winfield Scott waited for the formal ratification of secession before he directed troops to cross the worn old Long Bridge. But once he heard the jubilant cheers from the southern bank of the Potomac, he wasted no time in making his move. On May 23, just hours after the decision, the orders were given. Soldiers who had been sleeping on their arms in preparation for the advance began to snake across the river. It was a memorable moonlit night, and one volunteer, at the head of the column of eight thousand men, wrote that "the moonbeams glittered brightly on the flashing muskets as the regiment silently advanced across the bridge." A slave watching from Arlington saw a different image: to him it "look lak bees a-comin'."[22] A smaller column crossed the Aqueduct Bridge above the capital city, while a regiment of Zoaves was dispatched downstream to Alexandria. The action was completed with just a few isolated exchanges of fire. The gravity of the unfolding conflict was soon apparent, however, as an irate citizen shot dead the Zoaves' commander, a popular Chicagoan named Elmer Ellsworth, for removing a Confederate flag from the roof of his Alexandria hotel.[23]

At Arlington the Union men immediately began to throw up fortifications that could protect the bridgeheads and establish points of support for troops in the field. Charles Russell Lowell, who talked his way into the camps the day after the crossing, saw that earthworks were already well begun. Construction continued the next day, despite the fact that it was Sunday, and even the chaplains pitched in to help. Within forty-eight hours tents started to arrive, many of them relics of the Mexican War, and stores were sent over to supply surgeons and a hospital.[24]

General Irwin McDowell, an acquaintance of the Lees, was put in charge of the encampment. He chose to make his headquarters outside the mansion rather than occupy the family's property. For a brief time it looked as if all might be as cordial as possible under the circumstances. Mary Lee had written a farewell letter to General Scott, "in sadness and sorrow," declaring that it was only for her husband's sake that she had left Arlington: "Were it not that I would not add one feather to his load of care, nothing would induce me to abandon my home."[25] Scott had given orders that everything possible was to be done to protect Arlington and its unique historical possessions. A number of former colleagues in the U.S. Army visited the Heights and expressed general unhappiness over the predicament of the country, and relief that the house and its contents had not been disturbed. In these early days, hope for a miraculous resolution to the worsening crisis was still alive.[26]

It appears that a genuine attempt was made by Union leaders in the first months to treat the occupation as temporary, and to respect the property. With the establishment of a defensive stronghold and the encampment of thousands of soldiers, however, came an inevitable deterioration of the estate. Wood was needed for buildings and fuel, and the great forests began to be cut down. The day after the assault, one New York outfit "proceeded to level to the ground a fine peach orchard of three hundred trees." "Cherish these forest trees around your mansion," Lafayette had once told Molly Custis.[27] Now, despite a few efforts to place cautionary placards on some particularly fine oaks, by summer's end the landscape was scarred with huge stumps.[28] Three days after his march across the Long Bridge to Arlington, Edward A. Pierson, a surgeon's mate in the 1st Regiment, New Jersey Brigade, wrote to his aunt that "Frank Price says he will show me where to steal chicke[n]s & other Poultry—also where to steal secession Strawberries."[29] Bored, hungry, or vengeful soldiers shot the overseer's chickens and rabbits, and then threatened his life. When they tired of shooting animals, the soldiers aimed bullets at buildings, trees, and each other, with such regularity that Confederate troops in the vicinity complained of the noise.[30] The riverbank pavilion that had once welcomed merry picnic parties became a location for smuggling goods to the regiments in Virginia. A captain in the 15th Connecticut Volunteer Infantry described coffins filled with lager and bolognas in boxes labeled quinine, and called the operations at Arlington an "eyeopener to the wiles of human nature."[31]

The necessity of Arlington's fortifications became clear with the first battle of Manassas, on July 21, 1861. In an unexpected rout, overconfident Union forces were left scrambling back to Washington—to the derision of many, including Mrs. Lee.[32] Yankee arrogance was replaced by real fear and a realization of the seriousness of the crisis. As the remnants of McDowell's

Union soldiers at Arlington, 1864.

troops scattered in retreat, the Army of Northern Virginia might have had a chance to retake its leader's home. By pushing the rear Union guard back against the Potomac and occupying Arlington Heights—just as Federal officials feared they might—the Virginia forces could arguably have made a strong political as well as military stand. However, Jefferson Davis and General P. G. T. Beauregard thought the Confederate boys too weary, and, paradoxically, too demoralized by the victory, to make the pursuit. "To *that* disorganization and *that* demoralization the safety of Washington was due," one Union officer later stated.[33] When the rebel forces did not seize the initiative, the northern army hardened its position overlooking the capital. It also hardened its spirit of animosity toward the South.

One result of the battle was the dismissal of General McDowell, and with the appointment of a new Union commander, George B. McClellan, Arlington became a larger, more animated encampment. Thousands of drilling soldiers trampled the gardens, and officers now took over the rooms of the house. It was a messy place, with tents of many varieties stretching across the horizon, no latrines, and a stale odor of tobacco, damp fires, and crudely cooked rations.[34] About this time the property also began to be labeled as the home of a traitor, and the Lees' possessions started to disappear into the pockets of souvenir hunters and angry veterans of the battlefield. They picked up trinkets at first, but soon the soldiers found a way to transport items as large as sofas and grandfather clocks. They walked off with the children's portraits, Mary Custis's girlhood school notebook, custard cups, and the venerable Custis Bible. The family dog was stolen and sold to a sailor from Canada. By January 1862 the Mount Vernon treasures were also in jeopardy. Martha Washington's damask curtains were lost, Washington's tents carted off, and the grand punch bowl disappeared. "It is better to make up our minds to a general loss," Lee wrote philosophically at Christmas 1861. He was to be proven right. By the end of the war, when they had stripped the house of everything else, the boys in blue even took the iron door latch.[35]

Pillaging and vandalism have been persistent problems since armies first took the field. Union authorities anticipated this and had given some thought to curbing the activity. In his initial call for troops Abraham Lincoln set the tone by asserting that the "utmost care" would be taken to avoid any destruction or disturbance of civilian life. General Scott was also convinced that "hard war" policies were counterproductive, and had pioneered conciliatory practices during the Mexican War. In the spring of 1861 he bullied his general staff to uphold the president's decision.[36] Several historians have analyzed official northern attitudes toward civilian property, postulating that in the early stages of the Civil War a "rosewater" policy emerged, which sought to enlist the loyalty of border-state Southerners by protecting their rights and using courteous behavior in their presence. Policies of calculated harshness, meant to place doubt on the Confederacy's ability to safeguard its citizens, appeared only later.[37]

Arlington and the neighboring Virginia counties seem to have been exempt from any such grace period. Serious plunder, insulting behavior, wanton destruction, and what one Union cavalryman termed "almost daily acts of high-handed robbery" began immediately after the arrival of Federal troops.[38] One inhabitant called the conduct "vile, abusive, scurrilous, blasphemy" and accused the Yankees of plunging the citizenry into "the greatest state of anxiety and excitement."[39] The foraging campaigns were not necessarily planned, but it is clear that officers knew about the raids and even participated in them. Men in the ranks came to rationalize foraging as an act of righteous vengeance, or confused random destruction with military need. According to Henry W. Halleck, who in 1861 essentially wrote the rules regulating interstate relations in wartime, private property was fair game if seized as a penalty for military offenses or taken directly from the field of battle. It could also be confiscated if it was needed to support the army or used to defray the expense of maintaining order. The latitude implied was obvious.[40]

Though Robert E. Lee probably would not have overtly expressed these views, he doubtless understood the concept. Northern Virginia's citizens were not at all exempt from the degradations of their own forces. A Fairfax County citizen recalled that her family's property had held enough timber to last "for hundreds of years" until Virginia troops "cut down every last bit of it."[41] Confederate general Earl Van Dorn expressed regret that he had to call attention to previous directives "to those in & around Fairfax Co to uphold civilian rights." Lee also had to remind his officers of "the necessity of preventing troops from all interference with the rights and property of the citizens of the State."[42] Union generals delivered the same commands, with similar dismay at having to repeat their orders.[43] When a journalist mentioned to General Scott in July 1861 that he had seen farmhouses near the Washington aqueduct completely sacked, "the General merely said, 'It is deplorable!'" and literally threw up his hands in defeat.[44]

Mary Custis Lee knew of the devastation and disdainfully pronounced the Yankees "those cow thieves who will plunder & destroy everything."[45] She was well aware of the situation in Fairfax County, but the knowledge that she was not alone in her losses did nothing to mitigate her outrage. She was incensed when she found she was required to have a pass to visit her old home after its occupation, and refused to request it.[46] That she was the heiress of Mount Vernon's traditions heightened her indignation. When, in 1862, Union forces driving forward on the Peninsula campaign forced her to flee the White House estate, now the property of Rooney, she pinned an angry note to the door of the house: "Northern soldiers who profess to reverence Washington, forbear to desecrate the house of his first married life, the property of his wife, now owned by her descendants," signed, "A granddaughter of Mrs. Washington." She was further stunned about this time to learn from the newspapers that the Washington memorabilia, including the blanket under which the first president had died, had been removed from Arlington and put on public display.[47] Her husband, more resigned to the destruction that accompanied armies in the field, counseled acceptance, advising that "even if the enemy had wished to preserve it, it would have been almost impossible." Yet he too could be roused to bitterness at the thought of Arlington's desecration. "I should have preferred it to have been wiped from the earth," Lee told a daughter, "its beautiful hill sunk, and its sacred trees buried, rather than to have been degraded by the presence of those who revel in the ill they do for their own selfish purposes."[48]

It is hard to overstate the effect the seizure of Arlington had on the Lees.

Every member of the family expressed sorrow, anger, and despair, with an eloquence that rings through the centuries. Lee thought the blow so devastating that it must be a sign of divine displeasure, a punishment for his inadequate appreciation of the home they had shared together.[49] As the Lees began to understand that they might never return, the loss radicalized them with a power far beyond political rhetoric. They had been reluctant, borderline secessionists—anguished over the conflict at its commencement and still heartsick about the turn of events well after hostilities had begun.[50] Prior to the war the family was associated with the United States to an unusual degree. Their ancestors had conceived the very idea of the Union, had forged its structures and fostered its growth, and they were surrounded by the mementos of that glorious history. The capital city, and all the promise it held, was in daily view from their doorstep. Robert Lee had defended the nation for thirty-four years in the U.S. Army, seeing the country from northern New England to the Rio Grande, far more aware of America's vast splendor than most of his contemporaries. But the seizure of Arlington had exiled the Lees, and impressed upon them an awful truth: that former friends and colleagues, even those long received as family, were now enemies. They cared little whether the destruction was ordered or accidental, whether it was termed requisition or robbery. It was an act of personal violation and as such invoked a personal vengeance. In Mary Custis Lee this response was particularly strong, and for the rest of her life she would reserve her most heated words for the men who "without honour or pity" had carried "tyranny & despotism . . . to a height I could not imagine possible, it only wants the guillotine to complete it."[51] Their house sacked and their most cherished political principles questioned, Mrs. Lee stoutly declared that "our duty is *plain*, to resist unto death. . . ."[52] With the occupation of Arlington, the Lees finally became rebels. From this time forward their identification with the fate of the South never wavered.

While the Lees were agonizing over the destruction of their past, events were taking place that presaged the future. It was not all mud and plunder at Arlington. William Tecumseh Sherman was among a group of officers who gathered in the large parlor—now the office of the adjutant-general— "trembling" to hear their fate in the wake of the disaster at Manassas. "Every mother's son of you will be cashiered!" predicted Lee's former colleague Samuel Heintzelman. To their surprise, an aide entered the room waving a list of promotions, and there at Arlington Sherman was given his general's command.[53] The promotions were a key part of Lincoln's plan to rally his army at this critical moment. The president also drove over to Arlington to address the foot soldiers. Standing awkwardly in an open carriage, speaking in his simple, homey way, he talked of "our late disaster at Bull Run, the high duties that still devolved on us, and the brighter days to come." Sherman, who accompanied Lincoln, called it "one of the neatest, best and most feeling addresses I ever listened to."[54]

Other visitors to Arlington found inspiration in the great mass of men and their dedication to the precepts of the Union. One day a middle-aged woman traveled through the tent cities, her carriage surrounded by boys of the 6th Wisconsin, all singing the irreverent marching song "John Brown's Body." Her mind filled with the soldiers' endless tramping, Arlington's "hundred circling camps" and "burnished rows of steel," she went into her rooms at Willard's Hotel, and late that night wrote out a new lyric. "I returned to bed and fell asleep, saying to myself, 'I like this better than most things that I have written,'" remembered Julia Ward Howe. She had just composed "The Battle Hymn of the Republic."[55]

Some programs were established at Arlington that also pointed to the future dynamism of the nation. Among the most famous was McDowell's decision to test the military value of gas-filled balloons for reconnaissance. Almost daily excursions were made above the hills of northern Virginia, proving that they could be guided accurately and that telegraph equipment could be attached to them to relay information. Though not widely adopted, the balloons signaled the importance of air operations in warfare and the beginning of experimental flight.[56] The property also became the site of a far-reaching project for educating the newly freed slaves. "Freedman's Village" was the outgrowth of the Union Army's attempts to care for Arlington's black people and a response to the needs of thousands of runaways who arrived in Washington. In 1863 the Department of Washington directed that inhabitants of the "contraband" camps be consolidated at Arlington, and at one point up to two thousand people lived and worked in the rows of whitewashed buildings on the southern corner of the estate. Schooling was arranged, a hospital was erected, and a farm was developed. To complete the village, a cemetery was created in one corner of the grounds. The experiment was not without its challenges for officials as well as inhabitants. One of the Yankee soldiers who was living at Arlington in 1862 wrote in his diary that the residents "sing dance play cards and get drunk and are a nuisance. . . . they get plenty to eat from the government and don't care to work for *now* they are 'free niggers.'"[57] Nonetheless Freedman's Village did educate and protect many former slaves, providing an important stepping stone in the transition from bondage to freedom. The message implied by the establishment of a community of freed blacks on land belonging to a leading family of the proslavery Confederacy was not lost on most observers, and indeed may have been one motivation for its location.[58]

It was well that the Lees did not know all that was happening at Arlington, for it would have been harsh intelligence during a difficult time. Lee's early days with the Virginia forces were not easy, filled as they were with the work of creating a viable military structure and the need to juggle a bevy of difficult egos. By June 1861, in the turmoil resulting from the transfer of Virginia forces to the Confederate army and his own temporarily uncertain status, he even talked of resignation. When Bishop Meade gingerly inquired what his position in the Confederate army actually was, Lee replied that he did not know. Lee wrote that he was "mortified" when he was kept from participation in the first battle of Manassas. He again used the word "mortification" to describe his failed campaign at Cheat Mountain in September 1861, a bungled opportunity that was made more dreadful by the death of a young cousin whose skill he had admired and whose company he had enjoyed.[59] He had trouble, as well, in closing his accounts with the U.S. Army, was short of cash, and may have feared that his long career had been capped by a dishonorable discharge.[60] Though Lee wanted Rob and young men like him to remain in college, he had had to relent when he found that his son was of age to make his own decision about joining the army.[61] Worst of all, by Christmas Mary Custis Lee was nearly totally crippled by rheumatism. "I cannot walk a single step without crutches & very few with them," she told a daughter, explaining that she was trying a new cure, this one based on molasses and whiskey. Her life was now that of "a Southern refugee," as one friend put it. In the first year of the war she changed location a dozen times and was twice caught behind enemy lines. Her infirmity made the constant moving from place to place as painful as the cruel exile from her home.[62]

To compound matters, the Lees continued to have trouble collecting their assets and paying taxes in the United States. The situation became critical when a direct tax on property in the "insurrectionary districts" was levied in 1862, which the owners were required to pay in person. In the case of default, a group of commissioners was to determine the disposition of the property. The amount held against Arlington was not exorbitant—$92.07 plus a late penalty—but it had to be tendered by Mrs. Lee herself, in Alexandria, which was under Union occupation. In the summer of 1863 the property was confiscated, though the final deadline for the payment was January 1, 1864.[63] Physically unable to travel, and fearful that she might be captured, Mary Lee tried to send a cousin with the payment, but the money was refused.[64] A land sale was held less than a week later. "The first property sold was—No. 1—Arlington estate, lately occupied and owned by Gen. R.E. Lee," stated the *National Republican* on January 12, 1864, adding, "at times the bidding was quite spirited and the prices were considered good." The price for the 1,100-acre Arlington estate, however, was anything but good and was possibly fixed. The sole bidder was the Federal government, which paid only $26,800 for the property, though it had been valued at $34,100. The Custis mills, with 500 acres of land, went for $4,100, also considerably below value. They did not yet know it, but the heirs of George Washington Parke Custis no longer owned Arlington.[65]

Quartermaster General Montgomery C. Meigs of the Union army.

Certainly the appropriation of Arlington had been a dubious procedure, even in wartime, as the Supreme Court would determine twenty years later. But in 1864 the Federal government assumed it held title to the property and moved to expand its military use. The house was now a barracks, and a huge remount stable was erected on the grounds. The great battles of spring 1864, however, ultimately determined the future of the property. As the campaign of General Ulysses S. Grant unfolded, from the Wilderness and Spotsylvania through Cold Harbor to the trenches of Petersburg, a shocking number of dead and wounded began to arrive in Washington. Over the course of this military season some 65,000 casualties were registered on the Union side alone. The nation had no context for understanding such a number of fatalities. It also had no facilities for their burial.[66]

The Union officer in charge of such necessities was the quartermaster general, Montgomery C. Meigs. Fascinating and irascible, from childhood Meigs had been "a regular warrior in the nursery" and an inveterate master builder. It was the same Meigs who had shared adventures with Lee on the Mississippi River in 1837, and the two had retained their friendly contacts in after years. When Meigs was assigned to Washington to supervise the expansion of the Capitol and the construction of its great dome, he and his wife sometimes visited the Lees at Arlington. Meigs's enthusiasms were intense: they ranged from his love of milk toast with cucumbers and French dressing for breakfast to his obsession with designing an early home sauna. With the outbreak of the war, one of his passions became the Union army and the assurance of its success. As quartermaster general he took a personal interest in facilitating the supply, comfort, and movement of these troops, often at the scene of battle. By all accounts he did it brilliantly.[67]

Meigs was hardly a moderate. From the start he assigned blame to the proslavery factions and censored anyone who chose to serve the Confederacy. As he watched from a window on the May night when columns of blue-clad soldiers crossed the Long Bridge, he thought bitterly that "they were going to suffer for the ambition and villainy of these . . . politicians of the South."[68] He became more radical as the war went on, especially once he saw the terrors of Libby Prison and witnessed the slaughter in the "Titanic Struggle" of the Wilderness. He blamed his old friend Lee both for abandoning the United States and for "almost alone" prolonging the conflict in 1864.[69] By the end of the war, his cherished son killed and his army diminished, Meigs was advocating executions for Confederate leaders and punitive measures that included reapportionment of property to the freedmen and denial of civil rights to southern whites. Noted a granddaughter: "He had great contempt for the South."[70]

If Meigs had hatred in his heart in May 1864, he also had a burden of necessity upon his shoulders. Hundreds of ill and wounded soldiers were dying in the Washington hospitals, and the numbers were increasing as the weeks of dreadful fighting wore on. He saw that the city's burial grounds were filled, and he also saw caustic newspaper accounts claiming callous treatment of the honored dead by Federal authorities.[71] It is clear that he was under considerable pressure, but less clear is what aroused his interest in Arlington.[72] The Meigs family story stated that President Lincoln, who admired his quartermaster general, asked him what should be done with the property. It concerned Lincoln that Lee was still alive, and that no just outcome seemed clear. "Mr. President, why not make it a field of honor?" Meigs was said to reply. "The ancients filled their enemies fields with salt and made them useless forever but we are a Christian nation, why not make it a field of honor." Lincoln reportedly adopted the idea immediately.[73] In fact, interments had already begun, mostly near the cemetery at Freedman's Village. On June 15, 1864, Meigs wrote a memorandum to Secretary of War Edwin M. Stanton—himself a believer in "hard war" policies—suggesting that "the land surrounding the Arlington Mansion, now understood to be the property of the United States, be appropriated as a

National Military Cemetery." The grounds around the stately home, added Meigs, were "admirably adapted to such a use." Stanton approved the plan the same day, and the first official burials, both Union and Confederate, followed quickly. By the end of June, some 2,600 soldiers lay at Arlington.[74]

Only two days after Stanton's decision, the northern press commented on the action, applauding the creation of a "Great National Cemetery" and calling the juxtaposition of Union dead on property associated with one of the rebel leaders "a happy thought." Stanton was given full credit for the farsighted move; later Mrs. Lee would also ferociously lay the responsibility at his door.[75] Yet Meigs remained the driving force. He was dedicated to the idea that the cemetery would be in the immediate vicinity of Arlington House—"encircling" was the word he used—and personally selected the site just behind Mrs. Custis's gardens for a mass grave of unknown soldiers from the first battle of Manassas. When Meigs found that some subordinates were circumventing his plans to place Union dead around the house, he reiterated the orders, and when on a second visit he found that still no burials had taken place, he personally paced off the graves, had several coffins disinterred, and "caused the officers to be buried around the garden. . . ." Mary Custis Lee ascribed the act to pure malice. "They are planted up to the very door," she seethed when she knew of the burials, "without any regard to common decency."[76]

In 1892, a few months after Meigs's death, a pamphlet was published that accused him of plotting to prevent the Lees from returning to Arlington. Though no source was cited, the story that Meigs orchestrated the estate sale and declared that "the arch-rebel shall never again enjoy the possession of these estates" came to be so often repeated that it took on the quality of fact. Given the circumstantial evidence, it is tempting to believe this interpretation. The document that would authenticate the assertion has yet to be found, however, and Meigs's alleged statement that if Lee returned to Arlington he would be sleeping "among ghosts" stops short of proving a deliberately vindictive action.[77] There is a risk here, as well, of concluding that Meigs's plan was made for one reason alone, or that it could not simultaneously embrace rational and emotional elements.[78] We know that Meigs regarded the South with hostility, but we also know he was under strong political pressure to find an appropriate place for the dead. Despite some rough early moments in the burial procedures, sober commentary generally lauded the decision to find a respectable resting place for those sacrificed on both sides.[79] In addition, a persuasive argument could be made for a third and powerful impetus for Arlington's designation as a national landmark.

Meigs was, above all, a designer. He sketched arches and cupolas on nap-kins, and was proud of being one of the foremost contributors to the grandeur of the federal city. He was recruited to oversee the Capitol improve-ments when Washington was a sad, unrealized dream: "an overgrown water-ing place," as one observer described it, "and the pigs you see grubbing in the

Fresh graves at Arlington, including a tomb for unknown dead from the first battle of Manassas, placed in the center of the family flower garden.
HARPER'S WEEKLY, COURTESY OF VIRGINIA HISTORICAL SOCIETY

main thoroughfares seem in keeping with the place."[80] Meigs had a strong sense of the theatrical and was one of those who could foresee what the capi-tal would become. He wrote in triumphal terms of the "Great Review" of Union troops down Pennsylvania Avenue in 1865 and translated this elation into his plan for the Pension Building by placing a line of eternally march-ing soldiers on its terra-cotta frieze. For the remainder of his days he "was constantly interested in the expansion and security of the city and the beauty of it."[81] This artist's eye had not failed to see the grand sweep from the Capitol dome to the hills of Virginia. It was, ironically, altogether in keeping with the prescient way George Washington Parke Custis had situated his house and chosen a design that so flawlessly reflected the mood and monu-mentality of the new Republic. The desire to create a sanctuary on the promontory, in full sight of the nation's most sacred structures, rather than on an obscure and swampy corner of the property, fits with many of Meigs's assertions that Arlington was a fitting monument to the nation's heroes.[82]

Pragmatism, aesthetics, or malevolence? Meigs does not tell us, and we may never be able to draw a certain conclusion. We do know that his conscience did not trouble him, and that he chose to associate himself forever with this deed. Meigs had his name affixed to one of the cemetery's avenues, inscribed it on a memorial arch, and chose Arlington for the resting place of his son, his wife, and himself. They were buried within sight of the mansion, surrounded by other veterans of the Union Army. In perfect engineer's language he instructed those building his tomb to make it of hydraulic cement, tempered with water to avoid any fissures caused by swelling. "Replace the lid . . . ," he concluded, "and leave me to await the Resurrection."[83]

The emotion that Arlington National Cemetery evokes today—of sorrow and sacrifice, of misty, faded grandeur, of mingled anger and pride—were evident from the first. The day after Federal troops crossed the Long Bridge, a visitor remarked, "I suppose today it is occupied, and in spite of its importance and of its owner's treason, I cannot think of it with much pleasure."[84] Just at the end of the war Benson Lossing, a family confidant and coeditor with Mary Custis Lee of her father's *Recollections and Private Memoirs of Washington,* visited the estate. Prodded by Mrs. Lee to condemn the injustice done to her and her family, he wrote a passionate response, which he wisely never sent. In it he mourned the loss of the noble trees, and paid homage to the grave of his longtime friend George Washington Parke Custis. But, he noted with scarcely disguised ire, all of that was erased when he thought of the prisons at Belle Isle and Richmond and "the fresh graves of seven thousand of our countrymen—many of them the flower of our youth—who had nobly fallen in the defence of the *Government* established by Washington."[85] Perhaps most evocative of all are the words of a young Englishman who had written a smug account of his travels in the United States, full of sophomoric humor. When he reached Arlington, a few months after it was made into a cemetery, his witticisms seemed to leave him. Walking among solemn regiments of gravestones, he saw markers with the sole word REBEL interspersed with graves carrying Yankee names, and was shocked by the magnitude of the nation's loss.

> None of the crippled forms I had seen in the streets, none of the bleeding wounds that I had met with in the cars, not even the ghastly look of a poor fellow whose leg had just been summarily amputated at a railway station, turned me so sick and sorrowful as the sight of that soldier's burial ground. And then to see the home of Robert Lee sacked and made into a cemetery, and to fancy the thoughts that would fill that

great heart to behold the work of devastation going on, and to feel one-self actually in the presence of war with all its attendant horrors, and in the midst of people blinded to them by the blunting experience of four years' bloodshed. All these thoughts, and others like them, were so strange to me, and in their strangeness so painful, that I doubt whether I ever had a sadder walk than that visit to the heights of Arlington.[86]

Chapter Nineteen

"A *General* . . . Is a Rare Product"

<u>Confidential</u>

H^dQrs: Near Richmon<u>d</u>
5 June '62

His Exc^y
    President Davis

    After much reflection I think if it was possible to reinforce Jackson strongly it would change the character of the war. This can only be done by the troops in Georgia, S.C. & N.C. Jackson could in that event cross Maryland into Penn^a. It would call all the enemy from our Southern Coast & liberate those states. If these States will give up their troops I think it can be done. McClellan will make this a battle of Posts. He will take position from position, under cover of his heavy guns, & we cannot get at him without storming his works, which with our new troops is extremely hazardous. You witnessed the experiment Saturday. It will require 100,000 men to resist the regular siege of Richmond, which perhaps would only prolong not save it—

    I am preparing a line that I can hold with part of our forces in front, while with the rest I will endeavor to make a division to bring McClellan out. He sticks under his batteries & is working day & night. He is obliged to adhere to the R.R. unless he can reach James river to provision his Army. I am endeavoring to block his progress on the R.R. & have written up to see if I can get made an iron battery on tracks with a heavy gun to sweep the country in our front. The enemy cannot move his heavy guns except in the R.R. You have seen nothing like the roads in the Chick[ahominy] bottom. Our people are opposed to work. Our troops, officers, community & press. All ridicule & resist it. It is the very means by which McClellan has & is advancing. Why should we leave to him the whole advantage of labour. Combined with valour fortitude & boldness, of which we have our fair proportion, it should lead us to success. What carried the Roman soldiers into all countries, but this happy combination. The

indices of their labour last to this day. There is nothing so military as labour, &
nothing so important to an army as to save the lives of its soldiers.

I enclose a letter I have recd from Genl D.H. Hill, for your own perusal. Please
return it to me. I had taken means to arrest stragglers—I hope he is mistaken
about his Brigadiers—I fear not in Rains case. Of Featherston I know nothing. I
thought you ought to know it. Our position requires you should know everything
& you must excuse my troubling you. The firing in our front has ceased. I believe
it was the enemys shell practice. Col: Long &c went down early this mor^g to keep
me advised, but as I hear nothing from them, I assume it is unimportant.

Very resp^{ty} & truly RE Lee^1

. . .

H^{d}qrs 20 Sept '64

Genl

It is very important that I should know what force the enemy has at
Williamsburg & vicinity, or in & about Warwick CtHouse. What is the proba-
bility of a party of men getting below Williamsburg without discover & what
force the enemy could bring to oppose their return. Is there any force in Charles
City County & of what character? I wish you would send trusty *scouts* secretly
in both directions & let me know the true state of things.

Very Resp^y your obtSert

RE Lee
Genl

Genl Gary
Commd^g &c^2

⤐⬦○⬦⬅

R ARELY DO DOCUMENTS reveal the essentials of a leader's thinking as
clearly as do these two short messages from Robert E. Lee's headquarters. Lee wrote the first, to Jefferson Davis, just five days after accepting field
command. In it he candidly expresses his thoughts on a great range of issues, some of which came to characterize his generalship. He discusses his
anxieties about being held in a siege and his preference for fighting in the
open; he previews his desire to "change the character of the war" by launching an invasion of Maryland and Pennsylvania; he vents his frustration
about the army's reluctance to work diligently, and reiterates his own absolute commitment to the task at hand. He also takes some initial steps to
crack down on straggling, which would plague his army to the last, and at
the same time tries to gain approval for drawing troops from other theaters

to augment his own forces. The importance of transportation—railroads and the slick red mud of the notorious roads near the Chickahominy River—is touched on too. The second note was scribbled as the Confederate command tried to anticipate Grant's movements during the battle of Petersburg. It typifies Lee's thirst for information, and his preference for quiet operations led by a few men he trusted. The letters even inadvertently crack the old myth that he was too much of a gentleman to refer to the Federal forces as "the enemy." Of course he did so, countless times, though the longevity of that particular fable is impressive.[3]

Lee's renown comes from his much-heralded prowess on the battlefield. This is why we trouble to know him; this is the context by which he must be judged. That he did much with little is accepted wisdom. He has so kindled imaginations that the risk-defying feats of the Army of Northern Virginia often seem to outweigh the ultimate failure of his mission. Unlike Grant, Lee was not undefeated, but his men never knew it, and among the resolute the will to fight did not die. For some, including many who served under Lee, there was an uncomfortable sense that his successes were won through the wanton sacrifice of hundreds of thousands of lives, justified by unsustainable hope. Nonetheless, Lee snatched popular victory from the South's destruction, leaving generations of military buffs with daring tactics, ingenious maneuvers, and inspiring leadership to pleasurably dissect. In many eyes his mode of generalship still defines the term.

When Robert Lee was offered command of Virginia's forces in April 1861, he accepted with the apology that he "would have preferred had your choice fallen on an abler man."[4] The phrasing reflects the niceties of the era and Lee's desire to portray himself modestly, but in this instance there was a ring of truth to the words. Lee's battlefield experience was limited to reconnaissance and engineering staff work during the Mexican War. His only field command was the largely administrative one in Texas, with action restricted to small, inconclusive raids against the Indians and Mexicans. His fine reputation within the U.S. Army stemmed largely from Scott's patronage and his nonconfrontational collegiality, not from his leadership of large units of men. Indeed, Lee's most valuable experience in handling subordinates may have been at West Point, where he struggled to develop a firm but fair style. He did not perfect it until the war years, although when he did, it was remarkably effective. No military leader, North or South, was fully prepared for the cataclysm that followed the events of early 1861, but Lee actually had fewer qualifications than many of his professional counterparts.[5]

Sometimes a genius appears out of thin air, so suddenly that it seems the talent lay there all along, needing no development, only expression. Such was the case of Thomas J. Jackson, who quickly morphed from an awkward, even incoherent, instructor at the Virginia Military Institute to the irrepressible Stonewall. Lee's history was not like this. In the first months of the war he was set to creating a national military structure from scratch, a hugely challenging job, but one that kept him from early engagements and oppressed him with the desk work he abhorred. Jefferson Davis finally ordered him to western Virginia in September 1861, but Lee faltered in his campaign to dislodge Union troops under General William Rosecrans. There were many excuses for what Lee called his "mortifying" defeat, including abysmal weather, untried troops, and poor maps, but two critical elements presaged flaws that would remain with him to the end. The first was a failure to coordinate movements effectively among the various components of his army. The second was an inability either to issue clear orders to his subordinates or replace those who hesitated in carrying out instructions.[6] After this disappointment Davis sent him to command coastal defenses in the Carolinas, then brought him back to Richmond as a senior adviser on his staff. Some thought this showed a lack of confidence in Lee's field ability. It certainly asked less of him than he thought he had to give. As Davis' adviser Lee spent much of his time interacting with Generals Joe Johnston and Stonewall Jackson, learning not only their personal quirks and strengths but those of the commander in chief. In Richmond's inner circles he began to gain a reputation for measured talk and military sagacity, but probably the most important outcome of the experience was the firsthand knowledge he acquired about Davis, his various generals, and other key officials in the Confederate government.[7]

Early estimations of Lee's leadership ability were divided. Many heralded him as a legatee of the revolutionary generation or a man of unsurpassed character.[8] Jackson, drilling cadets at the Virginia Military Institute, thought the state had gotten an officer "of more value to us than Gen. Scott could render as commander."[9] Others were more skeptical, especially after the embarrassment of Cheat Mountain, a battle at which the Confederates were so uncoordinated that the attack had to be called off. Fiery Edmund Ruffin remarked to his diary that "Genl Lee . . . though reputed to be an accomplished & great officer (deemed the best in the U.S. Army, before he resigned) is, I fear, too much of a red-tapist to be an effective commander in the field."[10] Soldiers in service felt the same way. Thomas Goree, who served as General James Longstreet's aide-de-camp, remarked disparagingly that Lee was a "great military man in theory, but he has never had any practice," and correctly predicted that Rosecrans would outmaneuver him. "Beautiful state of affairs!" exclaimed a Maryland artillerist. "This army . . . has gotten it in shape to whip the enemy, now to be given to a failure."[11] There were suspicions that Lee was not 100 percent behind the southern cause, and accusations of both overcautiousness and parade-ground preening. After his recommendations for fortifying South Carolina proved inadequate to the threatening Yankee force, Mary Boykin Chesnut registered her disdain. "Preux chevalier," she sniffed. "Booted and bridled and gallant rade he. So far his bonnie face has only brought us ill luck."[12]

Circumstances gave Lee a second chance to prove himself. Throughout the spring of 1862, Union forces crept toward Richmond, which McClellan expected to take with a concentrated siege, using heavy artillery. This was the emotional heart of the Confederacy, and the citizenry waited with apprehension as bluecoats "spread around our devoted City, with their eyes like hawks, gloating over the chickens he intends to destroy."[13] When commanding officer Joe Johnston was severely wounded at the battle of Seven Pines on May 31, Jefferson Davis temporarily replaced him with Lee, who was near to hand. Lee quickly devised a mixed defensive and offensive strategy that combined extensive earthworks—which would allow a small force to hold a line against attack—with bold field maneuvers meant to disrupt the enemy's supply lines, forcing his withdrawal. Large entrenchments were still a rarity in the war, and many of the rank and file were disgruntled to find themselves armed with spades instead of rifles. Lee personally rode through the lines to encourage them and, largely through his effective use, such field fortifications would become a significant feature of Civil War engagments. In the meantime he sent the intrepid J. E. B. Stuart to scout out the position and weaknesses of McClellan's army. With his hat plumes dancing in the wind, Stuart took 1,200 cavalrymen on an astonishing dash around the northeast side of the Union troops. When it appeared outlying Federal units might attack him if he turned back, Stuart kept on riding to complete an entire circuit around the northern army. It was one of the great cavalry feats of the war, as romantic as it was critical to Lee's intelligence.[14]

In possession of the information he needed, Lee called up Stonewall Jackson from the Shenandoah Valley, where he had already gained a reputation for brilliant tactics and unshakable dedication. The plan was for Jackson to augment the tired forces under James Longstreet, so that Lee could carry out several actions at once. For seven days in late June, at local landmarks such as Mechanicsville, Gaines' Mill, Frayser's Farm, and Malvern Hill, Confederate forces tried to use unpredictable movements and persistent pressure to dislodge the Yankees. Lee's plan showed the detailed prep-

aration and measured risk of a master engineer, but he ran into trouble
when he tried to adapt it for major offensive assaults. His strategy required
clockwork timing and close coordination among his generals that he was
never able to achieve. Plagued by overly complex tactics, unfamiliarity with
his generals in the field, and poor communications between his headquar-

Destruction of the Locomotives on the Bridge over the Chickahominy,
*sketch by Alfred Waud, 1862. The severing of McClellan's transportation lines
helped Lee gain a strategic victory during the Seven Days battles.*
LIBRARY OF CONGRESS

ters and the various commands, Lee ceded virtually every one of the battles
to the Union army. Yet the Yankees were exhausted by the severed supply
lines and the ferocity of the fighting, causing them, just as Lee had hoped, to
give up their siege operation and make a difficult retreat through swamps
and thickets. The capital had been saved, but the price was a bloodletting
unlike anything yet seen in the war. Confederate losses far surpassed those
of the Union. At Gaines' Mill, the only tactical southern victory, Lee's forces
suffered nine thousand casualties in six hours. The battle of Malvern Hill
was characterized by bungled orders that sent rebel units forward piece-
meal, in a horrible procession of extermination. One of Lee's generals,
Daniel Harvey ("D. H.") Hill, later said it "was not war—it was murder."[15]

Officers like D. H. Hill sharply criticized the faulty execution as well as
the shocking loss of troops, and bemoaned the vanished opportunity to

fully defeat McClellan. "Lee was far below the occasion," observed Brigadier General Robert Toombs, a famous grumbler. "If we had had a general in command we could easily have taken McClellan's whole command and baggage."[16] Lee's defenders placed the blame on disobeyed orders and lackluster will among subordinate officers. Soldiers in the fight were simply elated to see the backs of their adversaries, even if agreeing that the follow-up was disappointing. "I am afraid Gen Lee will lose much of the advantage he has already gained by allowing [McClellan] to rest . . . Lee ought to drive him into James River," wrote one enlisted man. Nonetheless, he allowed, "there never has been such a fierce struggle on this continent—All voices are singing with the praises of General Lee for planning the battle." Everybody agreed that Lee had showed remarkable combativeness, seeking opportunities for confrontation, driving and pounding his foe, and ignoring staggering casualty figures in his quest for a victory. That determination rubbed off on the men. "One thing it has accomplished," wrote a Mississippian who was wounded at Malvern Hill, "it has imbued every man of ours with a determination to fight like demons."[17]

The warrior Lee is an interesting contrast to the courteous, calm, and sometimes passive private man. Both sides of his personality existed simultaneously, and in his lifetime people sometimes found it hard to reconcile his polarized character. "He had the combative instinct in him as strongly developed as any man living," was an artillery chief's assessment.[18] Guerrilla fighter John S. Mosby, himself no shrinking violet, concurred, calling Lee the "most aggressive man I met in the war, and was always ready for any enterprise."[19] He liked, as an aide noted, "to move out, to manoeuvre, to concentrate, and to fight."[20] After his resounding triumph at Fredericksburg in December 1862—and the near slaughter of Federal troops—Lee wrote to his wife that his opponents had "suffered heavily as far as the battle went, but it did not go far enough to satisfy me."[21] This bellicosity, even joy in the battle, was evident in the Mexican War, where daring feats exhilarated Lee. From the beginning of his command of the Army of Northern Virginia, Lee demonstrated a policy of aggressive defiance, marked by unshakable self-assurance, and a willingness to stake all on his belief in the superiority of his army. Such a compulsion to fight, and the courage that sustained it, is a badge of fine generalship and one that exacted swift concessions from more timorous opponents such as McClellan or Joseph Hooker.

What inspired him is a larger question. Theorists have proposed that Lee's aggression stemmed from pent-up sexual frustration, anger from his difficult childhood, or the release of a long repressed personality. Others have seen it as a need to experience the thrilling rush of adrenaline.[22] Perhaps if family traits are one explanation, it coursed through his blood as a legacy from Light-Horse Harry, described by one of Lee's brothers as "unharmed by the battle, and gay in its rage."[23] Robert E. Lee exhibited some of his father's battlefield inclinations: his ability to develop esprit in his troops; his liking for movement, action, and bravado. Like his father, he would command his forces more through personality and morale than strict discipline, and he preferred to control the field rather than embrace a free flow of ideas among his top command. Light-Horse Harry would have been fixed hauntingly in Lee's mind during part of the war, for sometime around 1863 an acquaintance gave him the daybook Henry Lee had kept during his exile in the Caribbean. The book is a terrible and moving document, containing the ramblings of a soul nearly deranged by lament. Desperate to console himself with grand thoughts, Henry Lee scribbled down disjointed pieces of wisdom from the Aztecs, the Vedas, and Shakespeare, interspersed with lofty advice to future generations. More an ode to a pitifully squandered life than an inspiring exhortation, it may nonetheless have spurred Lee to recapture his family's pride on the field.[24]

Other men have also been linked to Lee's forceful martial style. He is often compared to George Washington, though the analogies are imperfect. Both exhibited sangfroid in battle; both fought wars against predominant powers with vastly superior resources; both had an instinctive desire to attack. Lee, like Washington, was sometimes at his most agile on the retreat. But a year into the Revolution Washington listened to his advisers and chose a war of attrition, ceding major cities and substantial victories to the British, yet menacing their forces until he had completely frustrated imperial patience. A year into the southern rebellion Lee chose the opposite strategy—an aggressive policy that sought to break northern will through military annihilation. Both men inspired great loyalty among their men, though Washington's interaction with the rank and file was driven more by awe than by the kind of paternalistic rapport Lee was able to develop. More interesting is the tradition of leadership that Washington's era imparted. It was understood in Lee's world that the whole sway of history could be altered by one's personal conviction—and that self-sacrifice and perseverance could have not only breathtaking consequences, but deep meaning in the psyche of a nation. This is what Lee is driving at in his letter to Jefferson Davis when he rails against those who will not work. It is not just laziness or arrogance that frustrates him; it is the need for common goals and commonweal, the hallmark of Washington's era.[25]

Whatever Lee thought about his father, or the father of his country, they were shadowy figures, not reality. The most concrete experience Lee had with exceptional generalship was under Winfield Scott in Mexico. Lee was open in his admiration of this man, and if ever he had a hero, this is the only one he publicly claimed. To his brother he lauded Scott's "stout heart," his "bold self-reliance," and his "indomitable courage, as well as his admirable ability to maintain discipline in a foreign country rife with "the temptations to disorders."[26] Lee enthused in a similar fashion to Jack Mackay, calling his commander "our great reliance" and a "great man on great occasions."[27] Days before his surrender at Appomattox Lee was reading Scott's *Memoirs,* which he sent to his wife with a recommendation that she would benefit from the "bold sagacious truthful man as he is—"[28] What was it Lee absorbed from this mentor? Certainly the understanding that leadership can transform the improbable into the inevitable; and that force of character is needed to overcome political as well as military setbacks. Moral courage, decisiveness, and attention to detail all helped Scott command events. Scott also taught Lee the possibility of conquering superior forces by "head-work" and that unorthodox movements, executed with fervor, could be a winning formula. Lee's personal experience of the Mexican campaigns convinced him of the advantage of flanking maneuvers, which would become his battlefield signature, and that political nerve centers could hold the key to ultimate victory. But there were also things Lee did not fully learn from his experiences with Scott: the effective use of staff consultation, or the need at times to let cautious professionalism override zeal. Perhaps most importantly, Scott left Lee a model of unshakable personal assurance that kindled reciprocal confidence in his men. It was a trait Lee would hone to perfection.[29]

We do not know if Lee consciously emulated anyone or even if he strove to fulfill a particular ideal. There was something of many different men in his command style: his father's dash and daring; Washington's cool capability under pressure; Sylvanus Thayer's intense discipline; Napoleonic theories of force concentration and the need to conquer armies to gain territorial objectives; Winfield Scott's grandeur of presence and cerebral gambling. But was it by copying old masters that he became an artist himself? Whatever he took from others, the uniqueness of Lee's generalship rests with his own instincts and judgments. Its lasting influence lies not in imitation, but in originality.

In the aftermath of the Seven Days battles, Lee reorganized his forces while McClellan withdrew to Washington. In his stead Lincoln placed General John Pope in charge of a new Army of Virginia. Pope, who had won respect in the western theater, quickly became anathema to the Confederacy because of his hard policies toward civilians and encouragement of runaway slaves.[30] Lee was among those who viewed Pope with contempt.[31] In addition, he feared that McClellan would refresh his troops, link the two Federal armies, and force him into a showdown. Lee wanted Pope "to be suppressed," and under his orders Jackson narrowly beat Union field commander Nathaniel P. Banks at Cedar Mountain in early August. He failed to drive the Federals out of northern Virginia, however. Determined to face Pope on a field of his own choosing, Lee again sent J. E. B. Stuart on a breathless raid, this time behind the Union lines toward their supply depot at Catlett's Station. As so often happened, luck followed Stuart's showy movements. Stuart lost his flamboyant hat during this campaign, but he exchanged it for 300 prisoners, $350,000, and Pope's dispatch book. The captured orders proved that Lee's concern about a reunification of Federal forces was justified, and he determined to take the initiative before Pope could be reinforced.[32] Lee rightly gauged Pope's overconfidence as well as his gullibility and devised an intricate plan that ran against conventional military wisdom. Dangerously dividing his army, Lee proposed to trick Pope into chasing Jackson, who feigned a retreat. Jackson made a heroic march toward Manassas Junction to effect this ruse, luring Pope's army into a fierce battle on August 28. This time Lee's corps commanders, General James Longstreet and Jackson, managed a delicate synchronization. Longstreet arrived the next morning to rejoin the two forces in the heat of fighting, an immensely difficult battlefield maneuver that is still widely regarded as a martial tour de force. Attacking Pope's vulnerable flank the next afternoon, August 30, he rolled up the Union left, and the Army of Northern Virginia chased the panicked bluecoats to the horizon. The undulating territory and broad vistas made it an epic military tableau. A foot soldier told the story this way: "we charge them and run them one mile. we slade sevral hundred and on the 30 the biggest battle was fought that has bin fought in this campaine."[33] John Bell Hood, whose Texas Brigade formed the hinge between Jackson and Longstreet, called it "the most beautiful battle scene I have ever beheld."[34]

Critics complained that Lee took too many unnecessary risks on the campaign; that luck and Pope's ineptitude rather than Confederate skill held it together, and that in strategic terms it failed either to crush the Union army or move it out of Virginia. In addition, as Jackson delicately noted, the days were "sanguinary"—though northern losses outnumbered those of the South. Yet second Manassas was one of the few battles that Lee viewed with satisfaction. In three short months he had moved from a precarious defense of Richmond to the tactical offensive and shifted the theater of action to the outskirts of Washington. The rebel lads were exhausted and begrimed from constant marching and fighting—artillerist Robert E. Lee Jr. recalled having to be introduced to his father on this field when the general failed to recognize him under the bluish powder-sweat and ragged clothes—but everyone was delighted to be whipping the Yanks again on their old Manassas battleground. Morale soared.[35]

The elation of the troops was infectious, and Lee wanted to keep his momentum. Now, he felt, was the time to implement the plan to invade Maryland and Pennsylvania. His support for this movement showed how his thinking had evolved since the previous year. Not only had Lee declared he would never raise his sword save in defensive actions, he had rebuffed all attempts to pursue an offensive war. Both popular opinion and some persuasive generals wanted it otherwise, including Stonewall Jackson, who lobbied for a punishing campaign into northern territory as early as May 1861. From his desk in Richmond, Lee had deterred Jackson. His change of heart just a year later indicated not only how Arlington's loss and the destruction in Virginia had radicalized him, but the degree to which he disliked the idea of waiting passively to respond to Union attacks. Finally he became persuaded that there were important political as well as military reasons for an incursion northward.[36]

He had no territorial point he hoped to capture, and he did not see his army as a conquering legion. He presented the plan instead as an expanded raiding party. One of his goals was to capture the Baltimore & Ohio Railroad and destroy the Pennsylvania line, thereby undermining the North's transportation advantage. Publicly he said he wanted to feed his regiments on Maryland's greener pastures and to make the adversary scramble away from Virginia to protect his own territory. The constant movement of his army also made the Federals hustle to keep up with him, and scattered their forces. This was part of his strategy for preventing a concentrated buildup of the enemy that might corner him, forcing him to fight on their terms. He hoped his presence would demoralize the Unionists and bolster secessionists in the border state.[37] Privately he was riding on the same tide of high spirits as his men and aimed to win a victory in the North that would galvanize European support. After the war he would admit: "I went into Maryland to give battle."[38]

Much has been written about Lee's purported circumvention of the authorities in Richmond during the planning of this campaign, although, as his June 5 letter to Davis shows, he had been open about the strategy from his earliest days in command. Moreover, Davis shared his taste for the offensive, albeit with perhaps a bit more caution. As early as 1861 the president was

A rare photo of the Army of Northern Virginia on the march. The shot was captured by a citizen of Frederick, Maryland, a few days before the battle at Sharpsburg.

advocating robust actions, and the following spring he chastised the Confederate Congress for falling into "the not uncommon mistake of supposing that I have chosen to carry on the war upon a 'purely defensive' system." A few months later he was more specific: "There could be no difference of opinion as to the advantage of invading over being invaded . . . My early declared purpose and continued hope was to feed upon the enemy and teach them the blessings of peace by making them feel in its most tangible form the evils of war."[39] Indeed, at the same time Lee was snaking his columns toward Federal soil, Davis approved similar strategic offensives into Kentucky. Lee *was* cautious in his information to Davis, advising him of the Potomac crossing, only after the feat was accomplished. But Davis, as buoyant as the troops at the idea of a northward excursion, had wanted to ride at the head of his army. Lee hoped to avoid the honor of his presence, which demanded tedious protocolary detail and would likely interfere with his independent authority. He may also have shunned any too-precise correspondence because he feared his plans might be intercepted, as in fact they later were.[40]

Davis's concern was timing and calculation, and Lee might well have heeded this caution. He admitted to his commander in chief that the Army of Northern Virginia was poorly prepared for such an invasion. "It lacks much of the material of war, is feeble in transportation, clothes and in thousands of instances are destitute of shoes."[41] He kept on marching, however, spurred by the public popularity of an expedition to "relieve" sympathizing Southerners trapped in Union territory. Ladies in towns along the way fluttered their handkerchiefs, the bands played "Maryland, My Maryland," and one soldier watched J. E. B. Stuart kiss "Old Line State" soil after crossing the river in early September.[42] Nonetheless, one day after Lee promoted his plan to Davis he had to send round an order against straggling, which became a chronic problem in the hungry, overmarched columns. After ten days, it is estimated he had lost more than 20 percent of his troops.[43] Problems with the invasion increased as it became clear that two-thirds of Maryland's population sided with the North, and that the atmosphere above the Potomac was sullen, if not openly hostile. "People are kind enough generally, but they fear us with a mortal terror," wrote a Virginia cavalry officer; "many of them seem to think us Goths and Vandals and Huns; they tremble sometimes when spoken to. . . ."[44] A comrade concurred, observing that even sick and wounded Rebs were turned away from the Marylanders' doors. "It is true, as we passed along we would meet a Secesh family here and there but they were scarce," one of the invaders wrote. "I don't want to stop in Maryland five minutes longer than I can help."[45]

The campaign was hampered by Lee's tendency to underestimate the Union's capacity and to overextend his army. The march into Maryland was a grueling one, during which the dazed troops subsisted on little but pride. Once across the Potomac, Lee divided his sorely diminished army by sending Jackson's corps to Harper's Ferry on a rumor of Federal threats to his supply base there. It was a gutsy gamble—dividing his forces under McClellan's very nose—but he assumed his opponent would be too slow or too cautious to pursue him and that he could parry his inferior numbers through agility and surprise.[46] What he could not know was that a mislaid—or intercepted—copy of his battle orders had been found wrapped around three cigars and was delivered to McClellan's hands. Apprised of Lee's intentions, McClellan attacked him on September 17, in a day-long series of assaults along Antietam Creek, near the town of Sharpsburg. The Federals fought with passion, forcing Lee to thwart defeat by nimbly shifting forces to meet each challenge. It was not a coordinated battle but a series of violent skirmishes, in which Lee was always the underdog. "I never saw Genl Lee so anxious as he was at Sharpsburg during the battle," wrote an artillery man. "The center gave way & but for four or five batterys there would have been a route & with no infantry we held for hours . . . Genl Lee exposed himself entirely too much. He got down & endeavored to rally W.R. Jones men but in vain—They ran like hounds." The situation was so desperate that Longstreet, renowned as a fierce fighter, personally manned the guns at a battery that had been decimated by Yankee fire, saving one collapsing line.[47] The "route" was avoided by McClellan's underemployment of available Union forces and by the timely arrival of General Ambrose Powell ("A. P.") Hill's men, who had made a near running march to Sharpsburg after their success at

Alfred Waud's sketch of a near hand-to-hand skirmish between the Brooklyn 14th Infantry and three hundred rebel cavalrymen along Antietam Creek. Waud's drawings were made directly on the battlefield.
LIBRARY OF CONGRESS

Harper's Ferry. A private observed that when Lee saw the men, his "worried look left him as he noticed the enthusiasm of Hill's Division. He raised his hat to salute each passing regiment."[48] Though McClellan was unable to destroy the Army of Northern Virginia, he brought Lee to an exhausted stalemate and forced him to prematurely recross the river. Losses were again numbing. One Union commander reported that "every stalk of corn in the . . . field was cut as closely as with a knife, and the slain lay in rows precisely as they had stood in their ranks a few minutes before." On this, the bloodiest day in American history, some 23,000 men were killed or wounded.[49]

Lee narrowly staved off disaster by ably handling the tricky retreat to Virginia. But the Maryland campaign would have serious ramifications. Around the campfires, company and regimental officers criticized Lee's conduct, especially the division of the army. The campaign failed, observed a lieutenant colonel, "because our Army fought the enemy in detail while the [enemy] was concentrated. If Gen Lee had had his whole force at Boonsboro instead of scattered at Hagerstown & other places McClellan never would have known what hurt him."[50] The rank and file were also demoralized by what they had experienced north of the Potomac. Much of the South styled the episode a victory, but the army knew better. "I have been a party to one of the most disgraceful circumstances of the war, the invasion of Maryland," a Mississippi volunteer wrote hotly. "Our papers will probably say that we whipped the Yankees, this will be false, too." Obliged to fall back in a half-starved condition, they suffered as well from the knowledge that their self-satisfied campaign had accomplished nothing. Desertions reached a high point after the campaign and conscription laws to replace the losses were unpopular. Lee struggled to retain his strength for the rest of the war. One of the army's brigadiers recorded that of 19,000 men in his corps, only 5,000 reported for duty after Sharpsburg.[51] The rebels had seen little sympathy for their cause, and had watched the bluecoats fight aggressively, for once having the advantage of home turf. A Georgian remarked, "I never want to go to Maryland any more, for . . . the Yankees fought us hearder than they every did before." A compatriot from Alabama expressed to his brother the men's distress after the experience. "I have been in marylan an come back. in hope that we will go over there no more for it is dangerous over ther teritry. Mat I am Bothered so I cain write. Our boys is all cut to peaces."[52] Evidently Lee too was dazed by the affair, for more than one officer recalled that in the days after the battle he seemed confused. "I have never seen him exhibit such indecision and embarrassment," stated D. H. Hill.[53]

Worse than dejection and fatigue was to come, however. Lee's ambitious objectives were not only unrealized, they were completely overturned by a political offensive from Lincoln. At Jefferson Davis's insistence, Lee had entered Maryland by making a proclamation to its people, sympathizing with the "wrongs and outrages" suffered under a "foreign yoke." Lee admitted that he had found few willing to join his cause or his army, however, and, unable to operate with the ease he had in Virginia, tasted some of the disadvantages of the intruder. Bringing the war north did not demoralize the local population to the point of rebellion; rather, it galvanized their territorial instincts and fighting spirit. Back in the Confederate capital some congressmen were spitting mad about the whole escapade. This "rash and inexcusable invasion of Maryland deprives us of the great advantages which we had gained in the last two months," wrote a member of the foreign affairs committee, adding that he thought all chances for European recognition had now collapsed. "The North will be re-energized . . . inspired by the idea that we have become the invaders, and that the war, on their part, is no longer

one of one-sided subjugation, but of necessity and defence." Lincoln capitalized on just this spirit by declaring victory and issuing the Emancipation
Proclamation, which articulated a high purpose for the Union. In Maryland
Lee had hoped to triumph in a way that would allow the Confederate states
to negotiate for peace on their terms. Instead Lincoln took away the moral
imperative, changing the nature of the contest. Back in Virginia, Lee's adjutant admitted that when band members now struck up "Maryland, My
Maryland," they were "prevented from proceeding by the groans & hisses of
the soldiers."[54]

Privates were not the only disheartened members of Lee's army. After the
Maryland campaign there was active disgruntlement within the senior
command. The majority were Virginians—with notable exceptions such as
James Longstreet and D. H. Hill. Those closest to him included Longstreet,
whom the army called the "old war horse"—a fine corps commander who
was beloved by his troops for his bravery and his care for their comforts. He
was a stolid man, sometimes stubborn in consultation and slow to take action, but a ferocious fighter, as Lee found during the Seven Days battles.[55]
From his West Point years and the John Brown raid Lee was acquainted with
genial J. E. B. Stuart, who traveled with an African-American banjo player
and always interpreted his cavalry orders to their outer limits.[56] Intense, remote Jackson was Lee's closest associate. Although Jackson, from fatigue or
religious fanaticism, had let Lee down at Frayser's Farm, he had the most
compatible operational viewpoint, innately understanding Lee's desire to
use the army forcefully. It was with Jackson that Lee shared his plans, consulting frequently, and trusting absolutely.[57] On the next rung were A. P. Hill,
who was often ill, but always fiercely aggressive; Richard Ewell, a curious-
looking and flighty man, but much admired by his men, who honored him
with acceptance when he took over the irreplaceable Stonewall's position;
Jubal Early, an irascible Virginian, whom Lee called his "Bad Old Man" and
probably overtrusted; John Bell Hood, an old colleague from Texas, whose
personal charisma inspired his troops to extraordinary loyalty and daring;
and D. H. Hill, who was mercurial, but exceptionally courageous and not
afraid to speak his opinions plainly.[58]

Lee knew what he wanted from these officers. He called the ideal general
"attentive, industrious & brave"; "prompt, quick and bold"; and "cheerful
under all circumstances."[59] He did not always make it easy for them to fulfill
these expectations. Though unparalleled in his dedication, and usually careful not to take credit for others' work, Lee could be stern and unbending. He

sometimes left officers as senior as Longstreet out of his plans, and gave discretionary orders that could cut a subordinate two ways. His instructions frequently pushed officers to take responsibility and initiative, but this flexibility also left the orders open to misinterpretation. At the same time he expected unquestioning obedience, and grew sarcastic if his generals made even small diversions from what he thought was his clear intent.[60] One of Lee's men remembered this kind of tricky instruction. "General Lee . . . said he wanted me to reconnoiter along the enemy's left and return as soon as possible . . . and left me only that knowledge of what he wanted which I had obtained after long service with him, and that was that he wanted me to consider every contingency which might arise."[61]

Lee did not like to get involved with interpersonal frictions among his high level officers and tried to stay away from their jealousies and ambitions. That such feelings existed was natural, if unfortunate. His subordinates were proud, strong-willed men, with drive and aspiration, dedicated to a violent profession. Enemies were seen in camp as well as on the battlefield. As Lee took over the Army of Northern Virginia, D. H. Hill and General Robert Toombs were engaged in a dispute over pointed remarks Hill had made about Toombs's whereabouts at Malvern Hill, and their mutual animosity threatened to deteriorate into a duel. Jackson and Longstreet sparred over the allocation of guns and their competing access to Lee. Jackson was famous for his feuds with subordinates A. P. Hill and Richard B. Garnett, and took official actions against both of them, which remained unresolved until his death.[62] Lee hated such squabbles—he once railed at General Jubal Early for making remarks to fellow officers that were "improper & uncalled for"—but did try to intervene in the case of A. P. Hill and Jackson, for he could not afford such dissension in his 2nd corps. Hill rejected his attempt at reconciliation, and vented his feelings instead, in a colorful note to J. E. B. Stuart.

> I suppose I am to vegetate here all the winter under that crazy old Presbyterian fool—I am like the porcupine all bristles, and all sticking out, too, so I know we shall have a smash up before long. . . . The Almighty will get tired of helping Jackson after a while, and then he'll get the d——nest thrashing—and the shoe pinches, for I shall get my share and probably all the blame, for the people never blame Stonewall for any disaster.[63]

A. P. Hill also had grievances with Lee's strategy: "I think a fatal error has been committed, providing the Yanks have sense of take advantage of it . . . ," he wrote after the Maryland campaign.[64] Longstreet was disgruntled, as well, for he had warned Lee not to divide the army before Harper's Ferry and had been ignored. He sent a remarkable letter to Joe Johnston a few weeks after Sharpsburg, in which he nearly begged Johnston to take over his corps. "I command the 1st Corps in this Army," Longstreet wrote, after casting some aspersions on Lee's leadership; "if you will take it you are more than welcome to it, and I have no doubt but the command of the entire Army will fall to you before Spring."[65] D. H. Hill, too, was sullen, feeling that his efforts at South Mountain, near Harper's Ferry, had been underappreciated, and that Lee had passed him over for promotion in fall 1862—which indeed he had. He later attempted to resign, but stayed in the Confederate army when he was moved away from Lee. Tension existed between the two for the remainder of the war.[66] Even Jackson was cross. He resented Lee's attempt to reapportion the heavy guns in his corps, and he thought Longstreet was receiving superior troops, blankets, and rations. D. H. Hill later stated that Jackson told him he had also advised Lee against dividing the army during the Maryland campaign, but had been overruled.[67]

Such personnel issues have always been the bane of high command. Lee had seen them all too clearly during the last days of the Mexican War. He kept open office warfare from sullying his operation, but otherwise stayed away from the rivalries, often sending his staff to deal with such problems. Had he wanted to replace these men, Lee did not have unlimited choices. Neither did he make spotting and promoting talent a priority—a major mistake in the eyes of those who believed astute casting was a vital component of success. Nor did he scrupulously remove underperformers, though occasionally he did so, usually by having them quietly transferred to the western front. He did not use his authority to reinforce weak points or check excess in his subordinates, even when he was clearly aware of officers who were faltering. His relationship with Ewell, a man he thought hindered by "quick alternations from elation to despondency" and "want of decision," was a case in point. Despite his awareness of Ewell's shortcomings, Lee neither shored him up nor chewed him out.[68] A tradition arose that this laissez-faire management style was proof of Lee's exceptional character—an aide thought it stemmed from noble generosity—but even these defenders also acknowledged that inattention to his command structure was not "compatible with the generally accepted notions of perfection in a revolutionary leader."[69] Some thought he was also slow to see superior potential or to marry assignments with ability. After the devastating battle of Cedar Creek in 1864, an observant company officer remarked that General John Gordon, who had talent but needed coaching on reliability, would have been a better commander than Early, who had retreated into a kind of personal fog of war on the field.[70] A thoughtful officer in Longstreet's corps also criticized Lee for never looking beyond the ranks of professionally trained soldiers for promising leadership.

> Leaders like Napoleon could and he did see the greatest cavalry leader of the age in the stable boy Murat . . . and a host of others whose only learning came to them in the experience of the campaign and the lessons of numerous battles, but General Lee never did and was resolutely set against going outside the regular grades to find men who might have been very Sampsons to help him multiply his scant resources. He never discovered or encouraged a [Nathan Bedford] Forrest and many a man far more fit than his leaders went to his death trying to win against the incompetency of men who should have been brushed out of the way when they failed.[71]

Lee's inconsistent record in fostering talent, and promoting unity among his senior officers, would haunt him at Gettysburg, in the Shenandoah Valley, and in the final campaigns of 1864–65.

Lee was also wearied by the need to manage the unwieldy, unpredictable, and imperfectly supplied army under him. The vast operational problems taxed his stamina as well as his ingenuity. On any given day he might be writing to Richmond about increasing the number of conscripts, worrying how to cross the Potomac with a minimum of transport, anticipating Union troop movements in the Shenandoah Valley, or cautioning against plunder as the boys tramped through Maryland. He established courts of inquiry, wooed governors to increase forces from their states, complained about arms smuggled through North Carolina, and advocated certain kinds of potted meat as rations.[72] Military management that is pragmatic, highly organized, and well prepared is essential for the functioning of a large army, and men of ability in this capacity can often protect their forces against uncertainty and misfortune. In certain ways Lee's exacting methods were well suited for logistical matters, and he had certainly learned its science from the master of all operational generals, Winfield Scott. But it annoyed rather than buoyed him; he preferred the grand style of heroic leadership, with its mixture of tradition, courage, and inspiration. The very best generals combined both, of course—Scott was one, and Napoleon another—or had an officer of organizing genius under them to anticipate and relieve these needs. Given Lee's self-proclaimed greatest challenge—"overwhelming numbers and resources"—perhaps this was the lieutenant he should have zealously sought.[73]

Jackson was still irritated at the close of 1862. In December Lee again faced a Union army that was anxious to seize the initiative against the smaller but more aggressive Army of Northern Virginia. Now under the command of General Ambrose Burnside, the Federals decided to feign a movement in central Virginia, while actually concentrating forces at Fredericksburg where they would cross the Rappahannock River and move quickly on Richmond. Lee did not cooperate, of course. Though he never completely understood Burnside's plan, he brought Jackson back from the Shenandoah Valley to avoid being attacked with only half his army present, and entrenched himself among the hills and stone walls near Fredericksburg. The one-sided battle that ensued on December 13 showed the advantage of defensive positions for the technology of the day. The improved range and accuracy of rifled muskets and guns meant any attacking force could be handily repelled—or slaughtered, as at Marye's Heights on this particular field—if the defenders were well protected. The rebel commanders again showed dexterity in choosing their positions and coordinating their movements, and Lee wisely simply allowed the dazed Federal forces to run into his fire rather than launch a counterassault. Fredericksburg "was but a frolic for our men, being the first that they had ever had the pleasure of being entrenched and await the enemy," noted a soldier in Lee's army.[74] The northern losses rocked an already shaken Union. Clara Barton, who had ministered to the fallen of both sides on many fields, stood aghast at the carnage and later wrote that when she left one hospital room, "I wrung the blood from the bottom of my clothing, before I could step, for the weight about my feet."[75] It was at this battle Lee is said to have made his famous remark: "It is well this is so terrible! We should grow too fond of it!" Despite a clear-cut win, however, many saw it as a victory empty in all but the demoralization of the North.[76] Lee believed he could maximize his gains on the following day, but his cowed opponent slunk away and the Federals remained camped in the vicinity for the rest of the winter. In Washington, Lincoln shook his tired head and declared, "If there is a worse place than Hell, I am in it." Despite such pronouncements, and the jubilation of the South, Lee was depressed by the outcome, which "had really accomplished nothing."[77] Jackson was highly irritated at having to come in rapidly from the Shenandoah Valley for what he considered a useless battle. "I am opposed to fighting here, we will whip the enemy but gain no fruits of victory," he told D. H. Hill, saying that he preferred to confront the Federal army farther south. "I have advised the line of the North Anna [River], but have been over-ruled."

Irked by this episode, and his continued belief that Lee showed favoritism to Longstreet, he too was said to have threatened to resign.[78]

What strikes one most about Lee's generalship in the latter half of 1862 is not the perfection of it—for there were glaring management faults, and major tactical as well as strategic errors—but its intensity, its variety, and its initiative. From the time Lee took the command of the Army of Northern Virginia, he seized control of the military arena, forcing the Union to respond to him, and even transforming their offensive drives into desperate defensive stands. He was on the move, evading superior forces, agilely repositioning, and frustrating his adversaries by the difficulty of pinning him down. Lee pioneered the use of entrenchments, but was quick to exploit opportunities to gain the upper hand through surprise, innovation and sheer bravura. He experimented with tactics, too, staging assaults, invasions, and counter-offensive movements as well as maneuvers that combined both defense and offense elements. Though he faltered in his attempts to exploit victory, he did not relinquish the momentum. All over the South, and certainly within his army, he raised expectations as well as morale by the very dynamic he created. And the fighting spirit he encouraged in his soldiers set a standard for combat performance that the North was compelled to meet. By Christmas 1862, Lee was forcing every combatant to wage the war on his terms.

Chapter Twenty

Apogee/Perigee

Camp Fred^g 24 March '63

My dear brother Carter

 I have recd your letter of the 18th will endeavour to forward the enclosure to Mrs. Taylor. I do not know where she is now. When last at her house on the Rapp^k the enemy seemed to be preparing to cross very near it. Whether it was a feint or a reality I could not tell, but recomm^d they should make arrangements to evacuate if necessary & I have heard they proposed going to their country house in the forest. Genl Jackson is quite near me & her residence is not near him. The weather has been very unfavorable to those exposed to it & the roads are nearly impassable. Genl Hooker seems to be prepared for a move somewhere, & this day week the indications were he was coming over. He threw his cav^y over Kellys ford & brought his inf^y to the U.S. ford & just below the mouth of Rapidan, but the former was so roughly handled by your nephew Fitz that it had to retire at night, & the latter stuck to their position.

 The reports from within their lines are that the Cav^y was to have swept around to the Central & Fred^g R R.s. Burn our depots & cut us up generally, under cover of which their inf^y was to cross, but that we had forestalled them &c & they changed their minds. I presume it will be repeated in some shape the next fine day. As far as I learn Fitz Lee & his Brigade behaved admirably, & though greatly outnumbered stuck to the enemy with a tenacity that could not be shaken off. The report of our scouts north of the Rapp^k placed their strength at 7000, Stuart does not put it so high. While Fitz did not have with him more than 800. But I grieve over our noble dead! I do not know how I can replace the gallant Pelham. So young so true so brave—Though stricken down in the dawn of manhood his is the glory of duty done! Fitz had his horse shot under him but is safe. The news from the west is favourable & at the south the blow is still impending on Charleston. When it falls it will be heavy, but if we do our duty I trust we shall not be crushed. Through God we shall do great acts & it is He that shall tread down our enemies. Give much love to Sis Lucy, "Mildred & them"— Tell them I wish I could get there. You must take them all out in the fields & raise us quantities of corn. We are in great need both man & beast. Set all the farmers to work. If they do not do better I shall have to call forward our glorious women—I was glad to have seen George in Richmond. He has become a fine boy. Your affec^{te} brother RE Lee[1]

Notes passed between generals Longstreet and Pickett and Colonel Alexander as they prepared for Pickett's Charge.

Hd Qrs ~~~~~ July 3d '63

Colonel

If the Artillery
fire does not have the
effect to drive off the enemy
or greatly demoralize him
So as to make our effort
pretty ~~~~~~~ certain
I would prefer that you
Should not advise Gen
Pickett to make the charge
I shall rely a great deal upon
your good judgment to
determine the matter, And

Reply to it

Near Gettysburg July
Lieut Genl Longstreet Comdg

General I will
be able to judge of the effect
of our fire on the enemy by his
return fire as his infantry
is but little exposed to view
& the smoke will obscure the
whole field. If ~~~~~~~
~~~~~~~~~ there is any
alternative to this attack
it should be carefully
considered before opening
our fire, for it will take
all the arty ammunition we
have left to test this one
thoroughly & if the result is
unfavorable we will have
none left for another effort
& even if this is entirely
successful it can only be
or at a very bloody cost
Very respy yours
E P Alexander
Colo Arty.

[AE 5189]

Shall expect you to
let Genl Pickett know
when the moment offers

I Sl Mt Respk

I Longstreet.

Lt Gen Com

Col E P Alexander
Arty

⊱—⊷—○—⊶—⊰

THE NATURE OF HISTORIC DOCUMENTS has fundamentally altered during the last hundred years. Historiography of the twentieth and twenty-first centuries will differ significantly from the way we evaluate evidence from earlier times. Lengthy evocative letters like the ones Lee and his marvelously eloquent soldiers penned are rare now. Our feel for the temporal has also radically changed. Nineteenth-century writers took the *time* to be expressive; they knew their letters would require *time* to arrive; and they expected they would be carefully kept as *timeless* momentos. The invention of photography and sound recording has given us much more immediate information about events and people. Instead of reading descriptions of long-gone scenes, now we can see and assess them for ourselves, play them over and over, hear the tone of voice, watch the response of the crowd. Journal keeping may also have made a reappearance, with bloggers registering their reactions just as spontaneously—if not as secretly—as diarists always have. No one form of communications is superior to any other: who would want to give up the powerfully unself-conscious words of the Civil War private—and, by the same token, who would relinquish the chance to *hear* Martin Luther King Jr.'s indescribable clarion tones? Each source has its advantages and its flaws. What we often lack in early records is the sense of being personally present at a historic moment, which modern playback culture now affords us. For this reason the documents above are in elegant contrast. One is a particularly nice combination of Lee-the-general's ability to see around corners in the campaigns of 1863 and Lee-the-brother's affection for his family—but it is a traditional descriptive account of events. The other group is a rare, nearly real-time depiction of impending tragedy.[2] This is a series of notes passed back and forth on the battlefield of Gettysburg between Generals James Longstreet and George Pickett and Colonel E. Porter Alexander as they prepared to launch Pickett's Charge. Alexander, who had a profound sense of the historic, managed to save them, and taken together they make chilling reading. The notes put us right in the midst of battle, sharing the nervousness, feeling their despair at the waning supplies of ammunition. The anxious give-and-take makes us hope that each notation will halt the attack; yet we are powerless to arrest the flow of history. The doom that hangs on every word sends a shiver through the centuries.

———————

During the frigid winter following the battle of Fredericksburg, Lee kept Jackson in close consultation. They had a new challenger to face. Burnside had been relieved in the aftermath of his "blunder" at Fredericksburg. Major General Joseph "Fighting Joe" Hooker, a veteran of the Peninsula campaign and the battle at Sharpsburg, was now in command of the Army of the Potomac. Perhaps to offset Lee's growing aura of invincibility, Hooker took command with great show, declaring that the "Confederate Army is now the legitimate property of the Army of the Potomac. They may as well pack up their haversacks and make for Richmond, and I shall be after them."[3] Actually Hooker was building up his combat effectiveness, and Lee was concerned. He told his wife he wished his forces were not so scattered and that his fodder and provisions were better. He also wired Richmond for the return of Longstreet's corps, which was on a foraging campaign in southern Virginia. The request was refused. Still, Lee was sanguine of victory and thought if only he could "baffle" the enemy for a few more months, it would demoralize the North into suing for peace.[4] Lee was right about his unfavorable position; Hooker had twice his men and a clever plan that sought to envelop Lee's army with forces coming from several sides simultaneously. By late April Hooker had positioned himself so well upstream that Lee considered retiring to Richmond, if only to protect his supply lines. "The enemy," Hooker bragged from a crossroads called Chancellorsville, "must either ingloriously fly, or come out from behind his defences and give battle on our own ground where certain destruction awaits him."[5]

Lee called his bluff. Leaving only a small force to protect his rear, where he believed Hooker would send one prong of the attack, Lee defied conventional wisdom and struck from a disadvantage, giving battle when Hooker had anticipated retreat. He further offset the numerical discrepancy by fighting ferociously in the area's scrub woods, where the thick undergrowth gave his men cover. Unfamiliar with the terrain, the Union forces were bewildered and could not effectively use their superior numbers. Lee further handicapped them by taking full advantage of their flawed leadership.[6]

On the night of May 1–2, Lee and Jackson devised a plan to confound the enemy by splitting their forces and marching the larger portion under Jackson around Hooker's flank to surprise his rear, while Lee distracted and pinned him down with a smaller force in front. Fitz Lee provided invaluable intelligence that spotted the weakness of Hooker's entire right side; Jubal Early kept Hooker's other wing occupied; Stuart protected Jackson's columns from enemy detection. Jackson's march and the subsequent Confederate rout of the bluecoats was one of the boldest feats in military history, daring in concept and implementation and requiring immense speed and stealth. It was also a model of synchronization, with each general understanding and expertly playing his part. In the aftermath, Lee was aided by the intervention of a cannonball, which hit a porch column at Hooker's headquarters, knocking the commanding general senseless. The resulting timidity of Union leadership allowed the rebels to stun their foe, just as Lee had hoped. The following day, fighting on two fronts and seizing on every Yankee weakness, Lee was able to reunite the two halves of his army, capture the most favorable artillery position, then launch a devastating barrage. He pressed the attack until Hooker pulled his men back to their innermost position. The superb maneuvering had allowed the Army of Northern Virginia to move from a defensive position of great vulnerability to a winning tactical offense. "Hooker, the great braggart . . . has been crushed, ruined and must now give place to some other man," exalted one of Lee's soldiers. "Meanwhile our own great Lee continues to grow in the confidence and esteem of our soldiers and people."[7] At the end of the battle, when Lee rode through his men, his fine form silhouetted against the blazing ruins of the Chancellor tavern, he was greeted with the frenzied enthusiasm reserved for history's great chieftains. "I wish you could have seen and heard the boys cheer him as he rode down our thinned ranks after the battle was over," a Virginia infantryman exclaimed to his mother. "Even a number of Yankee prisoners were constrained to cheer him so grand and majestic was his appearance."[8]

How did Lee realize this extraordinary victory? Like so many dazzling feats, it had as much to do with painstaking decision-making and judicious management as it did with bravura. During the days leading up to the battle Lee expertly sized up the terrain—even making some personal reconnaissance, reminiscent of his Mexican War scouting. He was also assessing the psychological factors that would impel Hooker's movements. He rightly guessed that the Union commander would not move in a way that would leave Washington vulnerable and that he had little familiarity with the tangled Virginia terrain. He also sensed that his opponent's confidence might falter when faced with unanticipated, intimidating aggression. Lee capitalized on surprise by assertively fighting when Hooker, believing he had cornered the Army of Northern Virginia, expected an inglorious retreat. And he was directly involved in all aspects of the battle, from planning to leading attacks, a very real presence that stood out in his officers' minds. In so doing Lee captured the moment and made it his own. He also had his most sympathetic and enterprising generals around him—Jackson, Stuart, Fitz Lee, A. P. Hill—all of whom could be counted on for derring-do. Though he chafed at the absence of Longstreet's two divisions, the more plodding gait of the Old War Horse might not have been helpful in this fight. Jackson's twelve-mile march around Hooker's forces and attack on his right are the stuff of military legend, of course. But the success of the maneuver was due

General Robert E. Lee in 1863, photographed at the studio of Minnis and Cowell in Richmond.
VIRGINIA HISTORICAL SOCIETY

as much to shrewd understanding of the troops' enthusiasm, utilization of local roads and resources, and the Federals' susceptibility as it was to glamorous martial tricks. A good deal of ink has been expended in speculating about who originated the brilliant tactic. Jackson's mapmaker, who is among the most credible sources, implied that it was his chief. Lee later went to rather elaborate efforts to give himself the credit. What is more important is the fact that it showed a near-perfect collaboration in design, timing, and execution between the two men—a symmetry that was missing on too many other occasions among senior leaders in the Army of Northern Virginia.[9] Ultimately everything worked at Chancellorsville because it was infinitely prepared and precisely implemented; and because the very audacity of the movements flabbergasted the Yankees and undermined their fighting spirit. That demoralization carried over from this field, leaving a lingering disquiet about what Lee and his army were capable of doing.

Lee's imposing appearance before the flaming Chancellor tavern was a classic moment, his showpiece, the triumph that more than any other gave him a place among the great generals. The laurels were again won at dreadful cost, however. While attempting to follow up his devastating flank attack on May 2, Stonewall Jackson was accidentally shot by his own men, wounded in the left arm and right hand. The arm was amputated, and it was at first thought that Jackson would recover; but in his weakness he contracted pneumonia and died a week later. Distraught, Lee said he wished it had been him instead of his lieutenant, and told his wife: "Any victory would be dear at such a price."[10] Unfortunately, Jackson's death was only emblematic of the fearsome toll at Chancellorsville. Despite its success, Lee's army counted nearly as many killed and wounded as did Hooker. Proportionally it was an appalling loss, by some estimates nearly a quarter of the participating army.[11] Listen, as a private and an officer describe the aftershock of such violent death. "I have been on the battle field eight days," Mississippian John Berryman Crawford wrote, clearly still traumatized:

> the sight I saw I cant pen it down it is a slaughter pen it is enough to make old master weep the dead the diying the wounded they was straad for ten lines in ever direction oh what a sight what a sight to behold the loss on boath sides I cant tel but it look like enough to make a wourld.[12]

A brigadier nearly matched Crawford's eloquence:

> There are periods in every man's life when all the concentrated sorrow and bitterness of years seem gathered in one short day or night. Such was the case with myself as I lay under an oak the second night, black with smut and smoke, and reckoned the frightful cost of that complete victory and reflected that in less than thirty-six hours one-third of my command had been swept away; one field officer only left for duty out of the thirteen carried into action—the rest all killed or wounded and most of them my warmest friends; my boy brother who had been on my staff, lay dead on the field, and Stonewall Jackson . . . whom as my general, I then loved, was lying wounded; and probably dying, shot by my own gallant brigade. . . .[13]

It was hard to question success, of course, but when victory was more elusive, this expenditure of life could seem wanton. From the beginning Lee had determined to use whatever he needed to thwart the enemy. Some had been quickly taken aback at the casualty figures coming out of the Seven Days fight. In just one modest example, an aide to Longstreet was stunned to find that the Palmetto Sharpshooters, a crack unit of 375, had lost 44 killed and 210 wounded.[14] Some of Lee's most loyal officers also questioned his determination to give battle when it could be avoided. Jackson had thought Fredericksburg an expensive, empty exercise, and E. Porter Alexander, Longstreet's artillerist, believed Antietam was fought "where he had nothing to make & everything to lose—which a general should not do." Alexander then went on to worry that Lee would provoke another unnecessary bloodletting in the days after Chancellorsville.[15] Lee also expressed horror at the high casualty rates and marginal gains, saying that though the public was "wild with delight," he was depressed after Chancellorsville from the severe loss and the fact that again "we had gained not an inch of ground and the enemy could not be pursued."[16] But he never changed his preference for furious offensive actions, even during 1864, when defensive operations were the more realistic and fruitful option. Lee's expenditure of life often left his army so weak that he was not able to follow up on an advantage to deal a final blow. It also added to the problems of desertion and straggling, as he began to have a reputation as "a Great Gambler in human life."[17] Some men grew concerned that they were being sacrificed for grand amorphous glory, when other, less costly approaches might be found. Johnston was praised for protecting his men; they were "not allowed to be butchered . . . to have his name and a battle fought . . . to go back to Richmond for his own glory."[18] Lee did not view the loss of life frivolously, and he certainly had victory as well as glory in mind as he waged his battles, but the almost unrestrained use of his men seems worth contemplating. If, as he so persistently claimed, his ultimate defeat had been due to the North's superior numbers, why did he not guard his most precious resource, expending it only when necessary or when he knew he could reap a strategic benefit? Perhaps it was the pulse-raising thrill that he clearly got from his contests; perhaps it was his belief that a knockout blow was needed to quickly end the war.[19]

Lee felt from the first that the best chance for the Confederacy's survival was to decisively defeat the Union army, and he held to this belief until the end of the war. "If we can defeat or drive the armies of the enemy from the field, we shall have peace," he would write. "All our efforts & energies should be devoted to that object."[20] The idea of achieving victory through the annihilation of an opponent's armed forces rather than conquering territory was an old one. During the American Revolution it influenced Washington and others, who chose to cede key locations but keep their armies intact, and was also advocated by military theorists who had fought with Napoleon. Lee believed that quick, crippling victories would so devastate northern morale that the will to oppose the South would collapse. He also responded to southern public opinion that soared on news of big victories, bolstering popular support in spite of the increasing difficulties of daily life. As a result he continued to seek aggressive action, always hoping for a chance to "entirely break up," "suppress," or "ruin" the Federal forces. From Lee's perspective each battle might be decisive; therefore each required maximum resources and unconstrained effort if it would be the determinant encounter.

Practically, however, the changed military technology of the Civil War era made it difficult to actually destroy an army through the large-scale field operations he preferred: as one historian observed, Lee and his generals "won the kind of battles which were not to decide this kind of war."[21] Improved transportation allowed for rapid resupply, directional change, and regrouping of forces. More flexible unit and command structures, also pioneered by Napoleon, allowed generals to change fronts and mass troops more effectively. The use of accurate, long-range rifled muskets and artillery meant that infantry was rarely overwhelmed by cavalry attacks, and indeed, if well entrenched, was largely impervious to frontal assaults of any kind.[22] Lee had experienced firsthand the defensive advantage at Fredericksburg, and was certainly abreast of current military technology, yet he actually became more vocal about his desire for a crushing, definitive blow as the war progressed. In 1864, when slow erosion by partisan operations might well have sapped northern esprit prior to the critical presidential election, and the Confederate public was willing to accept a more defensive posture, Lee was still openly insisting that his men must "strike them a blow!" or "unite upon [the Army of the Potomac] and endeavor to crush it."[23]

It was with this mindset that Lee determined to move north again after Chancellorsville. The public was jubilant, and he was frustrated and anxious to finish the job. Moreover, the Army of Northern Virginia was at the pinnacle of self-assurance, believing itself fully equal to anything it might encounter and nearly unbeatable under Lee's leadership. "We looked forward to victory under him as confidently as to successive sunrises," recalled one officer.[24] Lee convinced Davis that the moment was propitious for reinvasion, and Secretary of War James A. Seddon reluctantly gave up his opposition, though he was later to regret it greatly. But given the lessons of the previous year's Maryland campaign, they were now more hesitant about the prospects for a northern incursion. The timing was also unfortunate, since it was a critical moment at Vicksburg and they had actually thought to borrow a piece of Lee's army for western support. Lee finessed the power structure in Richmond, retained his troops and his political backing, but failed to get additional forces for the invasion. "A far as I can judge there is nothing to be gained by this army remaining quietly on the defensive," he told Seddon, adding that he believed unless the Army of the Potomac could be drawn away from northern Virginia it would simply wait, regain strength, and concentrate for an attack.[25] For a time it all seemed to go as smoothly as Lee had planned. He and his men crossed the Potomac without incident, to the dismay of Lincoln and skeptical northern editorialists. The Confederates' unchallenged tramp through southeastern Pennsylvania also resurrected talk of diplomatic recognition by foreign governments, and in parlors from Paris to Pittsburgh everybody waited to see just what Lee's actions would bring.[26]

There is no leader who proceeds without a misstep, but the timing and nature of that misstep can have great consequence. In the Gettysburg campaign the unsure footing of northern soil was complicated by innate risk—in numbers, in intelligence, in political support. There were those who wished Lee's magnificent army would remain on the alert before Richmond, and saw no reason to provoke the powers at Washington to greater energy and determination. Lee had bet on the flip side of this coin—Union demoralization and fatigue—in which there was some validity. Lee went into Pennsylvania, as he had Maryland, to meet the enemy on his soil, to beat him there in a show of will and superior skill, and thereby to consign him to defeat. He glossed over this objective in his later years, stating that he wanted just to forage, to draw his opponent out of Virginia, to "baffle and break up their plans," denying any intention to take offensive actions except to defend himself.[27] But more than one senior officer wrote a contemporary description of Lee's plan for a battle that would "come off near Frederick City or Gettysburg," and Lee even candidly told Jefferson Davis that his idea was to lure the enemy "out into a position to be assailed."[28]

Unfortunately, he was obstinately clinging to an old structural design, one that had proven to be unstable the previous year—and that was something his engineer's education had taught him not to do. Once north of the Potomac he encountered much the same atmosphere he had in Maryland. He made another gesture toward peace with the local population, but found, in the words of one of his men, their "hostility to us is strong & open & [they] are furious at the invasion."[29] The ambience was not enhanced by the extensive official foraging that was done by his army. Lee had sent round orders, commanding his men to exhibit their superior civility by refraining from poaching on the local population. The orders were tacitly ignored by many unit commanders, "who paid not more attention to them than they would to the cries of a screech owl."[30] At least one of Lee's senior generals, Lafayette McLaws, thought the nonpillaging policy was actually unfortunate since the men were hungry to avenge the devastation at home and the Federals gave way any time their adversaries "even threatened retaliation."[31] The regulations required that Confederate currency or vouchers be exchanged for food or animals, but these were unredeemable in Pennsylvania and, indeed, nearly worthless in points south. The policy resulted in such scenes as Lieutenant John Hampden Chamberlayne entering a Sunday-morning church service, holding the congregation at gunpoint, and distributing vouchers while his men appropriated all the horses tethered in the churchyard.[32] Overall there was little direct violence against civilians, but plenty of chickens went missing.

Worse was the sight of Confederates kidnapping blacks who lived in the vicinity. It appears that several hundred African-Americans were dragged from their homes, and some sold again into slavery. According to witnesses, small children were roped to the front of rebel wagons and "driven just like we would drive cattle," sometimes guarded by the company chaplain. This was not a set of random acts, but a willful policy of abduction. Infuriated at the Yankee destruction of southern property, and alarmed and insulted by the induction of African-Americans into the Union army, the Confederate Congress passed a proclamation in May 1863 that authorized Jefferson Davis to take "full and ample" retaliatory measures, including the apprehension of free black people and their return to the slave states. The policy showed a deep-seated need to demonstrate the continuity of slaveholding culture, and denial that the Emancipation Proclamation, or any other aspect of the two-year war, had altered the fundamental right to own human property. Evidence links virtually every infantry and cavalry unit in Lee's army with the activity, under the supervision of senior officers. "I do not think our Generals intend[ed] to invade except to get some of our Negros back which the Yankees have stolen and to let them know something about the war," noted one of Jubal Early's sergeants. Longstreet reminded his division commander, George Pickett, that "the captured contraband had better be brought along with you for further disposition." General Robert E. Rodes was said to have personally threatened to burn down a town after its citizens tried to rescue one convoy of captured African-Americans. Since the activity was so wide-spread, Lee must have known of the abductions and condoned them, though in general he had tried to stay away from retaliatory policies, which he thought counterproductive.[33] None of this was conducive to either amity or capitulation on the part of the North. One of Lee's major miscalculations on this trip into Federal Territory, as on his previous excursion, was the belief that the presence of his army would deflate the Union's will to defend itself, rather than prod it into self-protection. "Lee is playing a bold and desperate game . . . ," warned a soldier in the Army of the Potomac, "Lee's advance northward may prove the advance of his army to capture or destruction."[34]

A first principle of engineering is to build on accumulated knowledge: to guide a project by experience and base innovation on solid past precedent. Lee had already ignored this scientific training when he copied a campaign that had previously failed. Throughout the excursion into Pennsylvania he seemed to leave behind the precise mental tools of an engineer. It is doubtful that Lee could have wandered for long north of the Mason-Dixon line without being challenged in the field, yet he left his supply lines behind, which precluded remaining for a prolonged time in any one spot. Although situated at the hub of five roads that made for ease of reinforcement, geographically Gettysburg was a difficult spot for the kind of aggressive actions he preferred. The town was located between creviced ridges and boulder-strewn hills, the geological aftermath of retreating glaciers. George Meade, who was put in charge of the Army of the Potomac in late June, was himself a first-rate engineer; he had sent his most trusted subordinates to scope out the area and wanted to avoid battle there.[35]

It was also an awkward time operationally for Lee's army to execute any highly coordinated or delicate maneuvers. Jackson's death was a serious blow to the Army of Northern Virginia. Despite their differences, Lee and Jackson had viewed operations from a similar perspective, and Lee had come to regard Stonewall's corps as the most reliable at his command. Lee had reorganized after Chancellorsville, carving three corps out of the original two, and placing Longstreet, A. P. Hill, and Richard Ewell in charge. Longstreet was greatly experienced, but the others were new to the job, which involved considerably more managerial expertise and strategic judgment than their previous division assignments. An essential part of a top commander's job is to ensure a smooth transition during such personnel changes, but there seems to have been little priority given to coordinating the new team, or managing weak points, like Ewell's indecision or Hill's fitful aggression. Stuart was off harassing Yankee supply lines to the west, following discretionary orders from Lee to do just that. Lee, a stickler for precise information, was handicapped by his absence, and indeed seems not to have known exactly where Stuart was. As a result, Lee entered the battlefield without knowing the landscape, the size of the Union's force, or the ability of his top generals to perform under pressure. As questioning James Longstreet would write: "The army . . . moved forward, as a man might walk over strange ground with his eyes shut."[36]

Gettysburg could have been a successful one-day contest for Lee, before positions were drawn and while the Confederates outnumbered the Yankees. In fact, on July 1, when advance troops from A. P. Hill's corps unexpectedly met two brigades of Union cavalry, they opened the contest with a near rout of the bluecoats. General John Reynolds, one of the most highly esteemed corps commanders in the Federal army, fell in defense of his native Pennsylvania, and the Northerners were driven through the town, with more than 4,000 taken prisoner. "It was a terrible battle yesterday," wrote a Union officer from the field. "We were completely overwhelmed by superiority in numbers, were flanked by the enemy, exposed to an enfilade fire, and it looked as if we would all be 'bagged.'"[37] The only bright spot for the Northerners was the shrewd fallback arrangement they had made to regroup on Culp's Hill and Cemetery Ridge, high ground southeast of the town. Meade's engineers had done a reconnaissance of the area and determined that the ridges, which offered superb visibility and abundant natural cover, were strongly defensible. Confederates later regretted that Lee did not recognize this sooner and take the positions early in the battle, when "it would have been a comparatively easy matter . . . to have brought more troops into action . . . and captured the key-point of the position."[38] By the time Lee directed Ewell's corps to take Culp's Hill "if practicable" on the evening of July 1, the commanding general felt he could not spare additional men to buttress the assault. Ewell, receiving mixed signals—a conditional order without the support he needed to carry it through—called off the attack as night fell. Some of the top men, notably Longstreet, warned Lee that the enemy's position was "very formidable" and would likely be reinforced during the night, and that to continue an attack at that spot would have a questionable outcome. Longstreet believed that the Army of Northern Virginia should do a flank march around the Federal troops, placing itself between Meade and Washington. He thought Meade would be forced to attack, which would give the rebels the advantage of a strategic defensive position. Others thought the Southerners should at least outwait Meade and see if he either retreated or launched an assault, which could be defended from their position on another piece of high ground, Seminary Ridge.[39]

To Longstreet's intense dismay, Lee did not accept the advice. "If the enemy is there to-morrow," he insisted, "we must attack him." Later that night Longstreet's concerns were reiterated by all of Lee's other senior men.

Longstreet would attest that Lee seemed in a state of controlled excitement, which often characterized him when "the hunt was up," and was unmovable as to his plan. Why this was so has never been fully explained. Lee later hinted at the difficulties of withdrawal from the field, and foraging in that vicinity, now a necessity with his supply lines cut.[40] Fresh from the day's unqualified victory, confidence in his forces was high. He may also have shared his men's open disdain for the fighting ability of the Union army and assumed they would be beaten.[41] But the explanation seems to lie more in Lee's character than in military logic. In his wartime experiences he had always liked to make opportunities rather than be forced into a responsive posture. He also had a tendency to overreach, to push himself and those around him to fulfill nearly unachievable expectations, whether it was hurling himself across the inky Pedregal or demanding that his untalented daughters learn to sing. Cartographer Jedediah Hotchkiss heard him give this explanation a few weeks after the events: "He said our army had not been defeated, but had been asked to do an impossible thing and had not done it."[42] There is also another trait that appears to have come into play. Lee could be stubborn as a bulldog when he had determined to do something. A line from a letter penned many years before, when he was courting his wife, seems apt as the drama of Gettysburg unfolds. Writing about setting their wedding date, Lee insisted: "But if you do *fix* it, do not *change* it. For I am so in the habit of considering an event that I have once determined upon as *done,* & want so readily for its accomplishment, that it is sometimes hard to recall me, & worse, to efface the effects of my commencement."[43]

On July 2, Lee hoped for an early coordinated attack by Ewell's forces at Culp's Hill and Longstreet's on the Union left that would split the northern defenses. Mixed orders and willful foot-dragging from his unenthusiastic generals meant that he was never able to get the creative, forceful cooperation he desired. Longstreet, whom Lee put in charge of the primary assault, despite knowing of his reluctance, has generally been blamed for tardiness, which kept his men off the field until late afternoon and foiled the plan. Yet a rebel officer attested that "about noon I remember that Lee and Longstreet rode up together and sat for half an hour on the very spot where my guns opened up the fight at 4 P.M. and at that time the infantry was [with]in a quarter of a mile of the position where they began fighting . . . and I have never understood why, if General Lee wanted the fight to begin, what delayed it then. Surely he could have begun it if he so desired."[44] Meanwhile Lee was donating precious hours to the Federal cause—just at a point when, as one southern officer noted, "Time, it seemed to us, was everything."[45]

While Lee was trying to push his men forward, Meade was carefully engineering his defense. The Union army had been reinforced strongly during the night. Meade arranged his troops in an ingenious fishhook-shaped formation that covered weak spots in the line, and allowed for quick support from the inward curve of the "hook" should it be needed. His chief engineer, General Gouverneur Warren, rode out along the ridge and reported back that although strong for defense, it was not an appropriate field to launch an attack. In consultation with his corps leaders the Union commander determined to await movement from Lee. In addition, he recognized that one key to his success would be retaining command of the impressive natural fortifications—Culp's and Cemetery Hills, and Little Round Top, a scraggy, rocky promontory that proved critical to dominating the field. Southern troops had also surveyed the little mountain, but recognized its importance too late, for minutes earlier Warren had ordered its reinforcement.[46]

The blue-clad men battled valiantly to protect these positions. Over the next two days, the Confederate army would learn just how badly it had misgauged its adversary's capabilities. "The Army of the Potomac was no band of school girls," as one Yankee would drily put it.[47] Southern scorn of the Union men had never been really justified; the Army of the Potomac had generally fought bravely, the more so since their top command rarely did them credit. At Culp's Hill, they showed their mettle by staving off a near victory for the South. Using well-designed entrenchments that multiplied the effect of their force by three, the Yankees held the ground even when some of their comrades were siphoned off to meet Longstreet's offensive, as Lee had calculated. The famous contest over Little Round Top, fought in some places with bayonets, was won for the Union by sheer grit.[48] Though the southern forces came within yards of dislodging the Yankees, and ended the day with the taste of victory still in their mouths, the Federals had retained control of every advantageous position on the field.

On the night of July 2, Meade felt confident enough to hold a council of war and obtain concurrence from his commanders to remain on the field; Lee again faced serious dissent among his generals for continuing his assault. Meade, still in scientific mode, planned no attack, but recognized that his strength lay in his superior defensive position. Since the Confederates had failed on July 2 to break his line on either side, or, in the words of Lee's aide, "to drive the Yankees from their Gibraltar," Meade anticipated Lee would try a massive assault, probably on the center.[49] Officers under him, who had recently clashed with the irrepressible J. E. B. Stuart at Brandy Station, believed also that Lee would try to ride round the Federal army to attack vulnerable points on the flank or in the rear. Recognizing the formula that had proven so devastating at Manassas and Chancellorsville, this time the Union Army was forearmed, dispatching a cavalry force on the roads that curved round the right of the fishhook to open ground behind Meade's guns.[50]

Meade also borrowed Lee's tactics of deception. The Union guns joined a cacophonous two-hour artillery battle in the early afternoon of July 3, the greatest of the war, but ended their fire before the ammunition was spent, giving the impression of capitulation.[51] Fooled, Lee ordered two of A. P. Hill's divisions to join George Pickett's men in a three-quarter-mile march across open fields and into the massive force of the supposedly damaged Federal army. Then Meade unexpectedly renewed the fiery storm, mowing down the lines, to the horrified awe of those watching. As Longstreet and Alexander's urgent battlefield notes tell us, the Confederates had nearly run out of artillery shot and were unable to provide cover for their men. In addition, their officers were uncoordinated: General Lewis Armistead's brigade, for example, should have reinforced the units on his right, but "owing to mismanagement" was out of position and advanced in the wrong direction, into the "mingled mass" of the center lines. A few of the 12,500 rebels reached the Federal lines, but more than half were slaughtered, including two-thirds of Pickett's division. Leaderless and terrified, those remaining broke ranks and retreated in disarray. From the top of Little Round Top the Union boys "sat on the rocks and laughed at them."[52]

Confederate officers, including Lee, tried to encase it all in nobility: courageous men launching themselves into the forces of an oppressive power, charging with unflinching valor into superior fire. It was a scene, as one rebel wrote, "that will be the theme of the poet, painter and historian of all ages."[53] Yet a participant in the charge recorded something different that day, as he sat next to a friend whose skull had been blown apart, and gazed on comrades who were "actually *fainting*" from dread. "I tell you there is no romance in making one of these charges. . . . I tell you the enthusiasm of ardent breasts in many cases *ain't there*," he soberly testified. "Virginia's bravest noblest sons have perished here today and perished all in vain!"[54] Lee appears to have again ignored the overall management of his battle, dismissing the counsel of his generals; unaware that his side really was out of ammunition; failing to firmly press some of his orders; forcing through others, even when his own countenance "did not look as bright as tho' he were certain of success."[55]

There is, at least, compelling evidence that Pickett's charge was not the foolhardy throwback to eighteenth-century assault tactics it sometimes appears, but part of a larger plan, which Meade's men thwarted. Lee seems to have decided to follow his winning pattern of attacking on several fronts.

Pickett's showy advance was to be made in tandem with cavalry action to the Union rear, while Ewell again assailed Culp's Hill. After seven hours of brutal fighting, however, Ewell's men were beaten back from their trenches by the reinforced Federal 12th Corps, ending Lee's chances to pierce Meade's right line while assaulting his center.[56] In the meantime, J. E. B. Stuart, who had finally rejoined Lee on July 2, was sent with all available horse units to ride around the fishhook with orders to launch an unexpected, debilitating strike at the rear, which would compel the Yankees to fight on multiple fronts. But Stuart's horsemen were anticipated by three Union cavalry brigades, one led by George Armstrong Custer, who had days before been brevetted from first lieutenant to brigadier general. On July 3 he earned his promotion. Surprised by the interception, Stuart made a desperate charge, which turned into a vicious revolver-and-saber contest between dismounted units. Persuading forces in the vicinity to join him, and rallying the 1st Michigan Cavalry with cries of "Come on you Wolverines!" Custer's improvised unit held the ground until they were reinforced, fighting with an intensity that matched their comrades on Little Round Top.[57] Despite inferior numbers, they foiled Stuart's intentions, allowing the Federal army to concentrate all of its power against the awful procession of Pickett's exposed men.

"I still think that if things had worked together [victory] would have been accomplished," Lee sadly told Jefferson Davis a few weeks later. His strategy might have succeeded had he built it on a less boggy foundation. The Union's ability to fight with boldness and heart had been laughingly dismissed, and Lee's penchant for secrecy excluded his chief officers, who understandably failed to coordinate on a battle plan about which they knew nothing.[58] As night fell, this time the Union boys had an opportunity to cheer. "The wave has rolled upon the rock," wrote one Yankee, "and the rock has smashed it. Let us shout too!"[59]

It was an awful hour for Lee, seeing his troops slashed and panicked: the remnants of regiments, the sole survivors of once-proud companies, all running rearward to Confederate lines.[60] The sight seems to have jolted him back into his inspiring generalship. It was perhaps his most terrible moment, but also among his most magnanimous. A witness called Lee's presence "sublime" as he rode among the men, calming them, his face showing nothing but encouragement, his voice even and cheerful. "All this will come right in the end; we'll talk it over afterwards; but in the meantime all good men must rally," he told them. To a devastated brigade commander he intoned, "Never mind, general, never mind. It is all my fault, and you young men must help me out the best you can."[61] The following day he made plans for a retreat, and led his men through one of their worst ordeals—a race

Confederate dead at Gettysburg, photographed by Alexander Gardner.
LIBRARY OF CONGRESS

against the Union's menacing pursuit, in torrential rains and amid the screams of the wounded, who accompanied them by the wagon-load. The men had eaten nothing for days; the commanders fished dead horses from the river to salvage their shoes. Yankee skirmishers knocked off men and horses with stones and gun butts. His dexterity reestablished, Lee then accomplished a master feat: conducting his army across the swollen Potomac with great skill, saving them from near destruction at the hands of the Federals.[62] The army returned to northern Virginia, and Lee continued to take the blame for Gettysburg, publicly and privately. He wrote disjointed, mistake-strewn notes to his family, and letters of resignation to Jefferson Davis.[63] The Confederate president, unable to afford the loss of this general, dismissed them, and rode with him through Richmond. No one cheered. The next day Lee suffered what appears to have been a coronary-related attack.[64]

Though it is widely seen as the turning point of the Civil War, Gettysburg was not the decisive battle. The conflict continued for twenty-one months after this date, even though Vicksburg had also fallen to the Union on July 4.

The most devastating encounters were still to come. The battles of spring 1864, with Grant's steamroller determination and the exhaustion of the Confederacy, would prove more conclusive.[65] Nor did the Army of Northern Virginia think itself vanquished. Morale suffered, and the men accepted the situation as a major setback, but Lee did a laudable job of bolstering their hope and recovery. "The truth about Gettysburg," judged a graycoat, "is that we were *repulsed* at the *final* position of the enemy, & that the want of success was a *terrible calamity* but we were not *defeated.*"[66] In the North, though victory was loudly proclaimed, neither Lee nor his army completely lost their mystique. "That rebel army fights so hard that every time it is touched it is like touching a hot iron," complained General Montgomery Meigs. "Whoever touches it gets hurt."[67] Seven months later the U.S. general in chief, Henry Halleck, remarked that only a monumental legion could defeat Lee.[68]

What went wrong for the South at Gettysburg? It was not superior numbers, for the contest was one of the most equally balanced in the eastern theater.[69] Nor was it a want of courage among the rebels, who fought as gallantly as ever. Richard Ewell is said to have confessed that "it took a dozen blunders to lose Gettysburg, and he had committed a good many of them."[70] Lee's generals have traditionally been blamed for the failure, and to be sure, there was considerable inadequacy among them, although through the prism of hindsight much of their reluctance may have shown good sense. Lee later remarked that the battle would have been won if Jackson had been there. But at the time he knew he had lost that card and must play with the hand he held.[71] Ultimately it was up to Lee to maximize his situation; to direct the strategic flow of his forces; to massage here, and admonish there; to make certain not only that his commands were carried out, but that they were understood, and that resources were provided to do so. That, in essence, is the role of the commanding general.[72] Absent was the discerning touch he needed to finesse details, foster communication, and win support for his plans. Lee's justifiable pride in his army was also leaning dangerously toward hubris, so often a harbinger of defeat. "The truth is we had too much confidence," is how one of his men assessed the situation. "Had we been more cautious and circumspect, the result might have been different."[73]

Another fundamental error in Lee's strategy is that it presupposed a collapse of northern morale in the face of Confederate invasion, rather than a fierce resistance to it. Far from demoralizing the Yankees, Lee's invasion energized them to protect their territory and their homes—the very taproot of military spirit. "Men will not fight with so much good will in the Enemys own country as they will in their own," one Virginian concluded after the battle. A Georgian concurred: "I think they fight harder in their own Country, than they do in Virginia, I had rather to fight them in Virginia then here."[74] One can imagine that had Lee actually won at Gettysburg, the protective impulse would only have been strengthened. It may have brought about a swifter end to the war, galvanizing Union will to resist him, quickly marshaling the resources he always feared would be brought to bear. Against this he might easily have been trapped away from his sources of supply, for despite the heady expectations of some of Lee's staff, he had no ability to occupy Union territory or besiege major cities.[75] Moreover, by 1863 the political stakes had changed. Debate was still sharp in the North about war aims and gains; but after the Emancipation Proclamation there was little possibility of a negotiation that might either award the South independence or return the nation to the status quo ante. Nor did the invasion diminish the Union's ability to fight in the west. Not one soldier was transferred to the eastern theater as Lee marched through Pennsylvania, and the Union captured an important victory at Vicksburg just as Gettysburg was won. On the field, Lee's judgment was equally problematical. He undervalued territory and timing; he was either overbearing or undersupportive with those who had to carry out his ideas; and he provided neither the blueprint nor the resources to complete his vision. In simple terms, at Gettysburg Lee was out-engineered, out-generaled, and out-fought.

How then are we to assess the famous military prowess of Robert E. Lee? There were sublime moments—and not all of them were delivered at the hands of inferior generals. He stands out for his daring, physical and intellectual, which challenged his opponents into near intimidation. When he allowed his rational training to supersede instinct he was capable of devising some of the most ingenious tactical plans in the history of warfare. Lee's sway over his troops is unsurpassed in military annals. Yet he never resolved the fundamental difficulty facing him—that is, manpower and matériel—and indeed on many occasions he reacted as if these resources were unlimited. In terms of grand strategy, more questions must be asked. His forays into the North were not only operationally unsuccessful, but politically naive. His penchant for aggression, attack, and the near-impossible annihilation of the Union army may have cost him the war. Many believe that had he remained on the defensive, which the technology of the day favored, he could have conserved his scarce resources and outlasted the ennui of the Yankees. Extended guerilla-type warfare, so admirably executed by his father during the struggle for independence, was another option. It has been the classic tool of revolutionaries for centuries, and in terrain and temperament the South was well suited to it—if the tenacity of the populace could be tapped. Loyal E. Porter Alexander was among those who came to believe this would have been the most fruitful approach. "We could not hope to *conquer* her," he wrote of the Union. "Our one chance was to wear her down."[76] Twentieth- and twenty-first-century Americans will appreciate how quickly superior strength can be sapped by unremitting, targeted, and occasionally heinous attacks against a supposedly unbeatable power.[77] But all of this carries us into the "what-ifs" and the "if-onlys" that sometimes threaten to make Civil War history a kind of science fiction. Let us allow Lee to set the benchmark for fine generalship. In 1847 he wrote a letter to his friend Jack Mackay, exuberantly describing the qualities he admired in Winfield Scott. "Our Genl. is our great reliance . . . ," he told Mackay. "Never turns from his object. Confident in his powers & resources, his judgment is as sound as his heart is bold and daring. Careful of his men, he never exposes them but for a worthy object & then gives them the advantage of every circumstance in his power."[78] Later, he added to this the importance of "producing effective *results.*"[79] We can only guess how Lee measured himself against these standards.

Chapter Twenty-one

Overwhelmed

Richmond 3 Nov '62

My Precious Child

Since we parted a great affliction has overwhelmed us. May God in his mercy turn it to our benefit & cause us to be prepared for the summons to his presence. Now that your dear Sister has been taken from you consider her character with affection. If you find in it any thing to admire try & imitate it. If any thing to condemn, avoid it. Thus her death may prove of as much advantage to you as her life. I can not tell you how much I lament her loss. How much I grieve over her early death. Yet I know it is well, & the heavy blow that has been dealt to us, was sent in mercy & kindness to her—I feel that she is now safe & far removed from all harm & danger—. But as those dear to me are diminished I cling more anxiously to those who remain. To you my dear child my heart yearns with intense affection & I long to see you. Look closely to your conduct & course & may we yet meet in happiness—I pray constantly for you & think of you constantly—With great love & affection your devoted father   RE Lee

Miss Mildred C Lee[1]

. . .

My very dear cousin—

I received your letter of the 16th last night & hasten to reply to it. Indeed I thought of writing you an account of the cruel capture of our dear Gen: when it happened. It was so fully discussed in the papers immediately, that I thought it unnecessary. He had been with us from the day after he was wounded (Charlotte being with us at the time.) His Mother and sisters Agnes & Mildred had joined him here, Robbie coming with him. We were such a happy family party! We females secretly rejoicing in the wound which kept him away from the dreadful battles going on. Corse's brigade close to us, with a promise to give us *timely notice of any advance from the White House. We had no fear or thought of danger, when the alarm was given by a breathless boy "the Yankees are in the lane." Robbie was ordered to save himself and Moses to save the Gen's horses. In ten minutes the barbarians were galloping across the lawn. Still I was not alarmed. I was <u>used to such things.</u> They would surely parole him. Entirely helpless from his wound it is impossible such an outrage can be committed as the taking him off will be! But ah! that Lieutenant and that Surgeon—wicked monsters—so elated at the prize they had in their power—the son of Gen. R.E. Lee—nothing could soften or turn them from their savage purpose and three or four of them bore him from his bed to the carriage. Many of the men when they saw he had to be brought out in that way, expressed their disapprobation aloud. Fitzhugh went through the whole with perfect calmness and dignity, and dear Charlotte, poor dear child—she bore up wonderfully, collecting and packing up such things as he required, looking deathly pale. When it was all over and he was gone, she gave way in a burst of feeling that must have softened the hearts even of those two dreadful officers had they witnessed it. You may imagine how sad and cast down our household was. It was painful to see dear Charlottes grief and her anxiety about Fitzhughs sufferings. She was cheered very much by hearing favorable accounts from time to time. Her health is exceedingly deli-cate. She left us yesterday morning for the Rockbridge Allum [Springs]. Dear Cousin Mary and her daughter left us two days before for the Hot Springs. Poor cousin Mary is a great sufferer from rheumatism. She can scarcely move and has to be lifted about. Her spirits are excellent & she is a most delightful com-panion. We miss the whole party greatly & shall be most happy to see them back. Mildred returns to Raleigh to school. Mary recently arrived from King George in fine health & spirits. Margaret Stuart came with her—has been to see us & we are much pleased with her. Having accomplished the great object of their visit here, the Yankees were so well satisfied, that we are astonished at their moderation in the damage done ourselves knowing that they "fear not God nor regard man" & that we were completely in their power for Mr. Wickham was in Richmond. But our Heavenly Father watched over & protected us. They broke open the Smoke House, but helped themselves very moderately. Two of them made me give them brandy by threatening to get it themselves. It was on an-other visit that they went into the Wine cellar & helped themselves very freely to Brandy & moderately to wine being satisfied with two or three bottles apiece. They took the carriage horses—the buggy horse—Mr W's and Mr Priddy's rid-ing horses & two beautiful brown mares. But these are all trifles for the girls had more <u>fun</u> in a few wagon rides than a year's use of a carriage could have af-forded them. Between 30 and 40 of our people have gone—our most efficient hands—young men mostly. I was <u>right brave</u> in the day, but the constant ap-*

prehension of an alarm in the night, & once we were aroused a little after day break by the most violent knocking at my chamber entry, the stamp of horses and clanking of swords—the memory of those sounds make me tremble still. Dear Uncle—they dealt hardly with him, taking all his spirit & wine— breaking open his locks & searching his house & threatening to strike him if he attempted to withhold the meat. More than twenty mules they stole from him. I am not able to give you any information from Horn Quarter, having heard only that very few people were remaining there. Remember Luce & myself most affectionately to your Lucy, Mrs. Tayloe Nannie & Bettie—We wish we could have the pleasure of seeing them again. Dear Carter I am almost ashamed to send you this long letter which perhaps you may find difficult to decypher—— Always remember that I am your devoted cousin Anne Wickham

Mr. C. Carter Lee
Fine Creek Mills
Powhatan[2]

. . .

My dear Sister
Do not believe that I am a spy—with my dying breath I deny the charge— I hope you will not grieve too much for me—I believe in "Jesus Christ who came into the world to save sinners"—although I die a horrid death, I will meet my fate with the fortitude becoming the son of a man whose last words to his children were—"Tell them I fell at the head of the column." I remain with love to my sisters, brothers & relatives your devoted brother

Lawrence W. Orton[3]

⤖⬦⭘⬦⭤

O NE COULD READ through this procession of mournful letters, written during a single nightmarish year, and know without further commentary that the Lees suffered devastating loss during the war. In 1862 and 1863 Robert E. Lee was performing some of the most impressive military feats of his career, becoming an American Caesar in the opinion of many. The triumphs, however, were as expensive personally as they had been in battlefield blood. The cherished circle of kin was broken—then smashed and broken again. Events were moving Arlington from them forever. Loss and devastation brought on the specter of financial ruin; too many deaths and too much sorrow shocked and finally shattered the more fragile members of the family. For Lee there would be no unconditional glory. Instead it was increasingly eclipsed by a private devastation that struck at his conscience and seared his soul. "In the quiet hours of the night, when there is nothing to lighten the full weight of my grief," he admitted to his eldest daughter, "I feel as if I should be overwhelmed."[4]

In early July 1862, just as General Lee was testing his spurs as commander of the Army of Northern Virginia, a series of family disasters began to throw a shadow over the bright expectation of military victory. That month the initially benevolent occupiers of Arlington strengthened their hold on the property, with officers moving into the house and possessions disappearing in the night.[5] At the same time, Rooney's two-year-old boy, the namesake of Robert E. Lee, "a most lovely little fellow," caught cold and died. His grandparents, who had escaped the heartbreak of childhood death, were deeply saddened, and Rooney, completely devastated, tortured himself with remorse, citing his "many & daily sins" as the cause of death. "It almost makes me feel that I am the murderer of my boy," he told his wife.[6] While they were still recovering from this sorrow, McClellan's forces seized and burned the White House plantation that Rooney had inherited. Mrs. Lee had believed the historic associations of the White House—the site of George and Martha Washington's wedding—would be enough to save it, but it was thoroughly pillaged, the slaves taken as contraband, the house and barns left a pile of smoldering ashes. "I trust I may live to see the day of retribution," snapped Mary Lee, who was daily becoming more radicalized.[7] Annie Lee, who was with her mother when they were driven from the White House, echoed the spirited sentiments. "Indeed I really wish from the bottom of my heart that the Yankees were all in the infernal regions," "gentle Annie" told Agnes.[8]

Like her mother and sisters, Annie was a refugee, living among friends, with no fixed home during these years. On a trip to the Virginia springs in August 1862 she contracted what appears to have been a case of typhoid fever, and with Agnes moved to Jones Springs, North Carolina, which they thought more healthful. Symptoms of headache, dizziness, and intestinal troubles still discomfited her, but she told her mother she thought it was just "a little bilious attack, so I have been persuaded to take your favorite, a *blue pill* for the last two nights."[9] That pharmaceutical reference is ominous, for blue pills, or blue mass, a common prescriptive of the day, contained large doses of mercury, within the more benign casing of licorice root, honey, and rose petals. In even small doses mercury could cause aggression, depression, and chronic fatigue; in larger amounts it resulted in nerve damage and death.[10] For several weeks Annie remained ill, though everyone expected she would recover. Typhoid fever was a serious illness in the nineteenth century, causing high temperatures and weakness, but if left to natural healing powers many patients got well.[11]

Yet Annie grew more listless, then began to have violent fevers, palpitations, debilitating diarrhea, deafness. Now the doctors augmented her regimen with an hourly dose of brandy, cream, and morphine. Alarmed, Mrs. Lee with difficulty traveled to North Carolina to nurse her. Agnes ministered during the day, and her mother took over at night, sleeping by the sickbed, wiping the alternately flushed and chilled brow. Annie slipped into a coma. The disease and the combination of poisonous medicines proved more than her system could support. Mary Lee proclaimed her to be "in the hands of God who will do all things well for her," and Agnes crawled into her bed to try to keep her warm. Annie only vaguely regained consciousness, once asking for a hymnbook, later murmuring "I am ready to rise." At seven o'clock on the morning of October 20, 1862, Anne Carter Lee expired, her frigid hands sheltered in her mother's bosom for warmth. She was twenty-three years old.[12]

In shock the two women laid out Annie "with her black hair braided over her marble brow" and covered her with flowers from the neighborhood. "My darling Annie I never had expected to weave a funeral wreath for her," mourned Mary Lee, as she sent the sad news to her eldest daughter.[13] The scattered family members were stunned, for no one had anticipated this calamitous event. "I never even heard of poor Annie's illness until I heard she was dead," exclaimed Rob from his artillery camp.[14] His father was also taken by surprise. An aide handed him his personal mail, not knowing the intelligence it contained. The two spent several minutes discussing routine army matters, and the aide left. When he unexpectedly returned, entering Lee's tent without ceremony, he was startled "to see him overcome with grief, an open letter in his hand."[15] "To know that I shall never see her again on earth, that her place in our circle which I always hope one day to rejoin is forever vacant, is agonizing in the extreme," Lee told Mary.[16] The blow was cruelest for Agnes. She and Annie had been like "twin roses on one stem," as a sympathetic cousin put it, and Agnes was so distraught that she was unable to rouse herself from depression.[17] Her parents comforted themselves with faith that glorified an afterlife and looked on misfortune as evidence of divine mystery. "He has taken the purest & best," Lee wrote to Mary. "May you be able to join me in saying His will be done!"[18] And, later, more darkly: "I know affliction has been sent me by a merciful God for my own good."[19]

The family was just beginning to accept their loss when affliction visited them again. Rooney's wife, affectionately called "Chass," gave birth that autumn to a baby girl, but this second child succumbed to a lung infection and died before she could be named. In deep sorrow Lee sympathized with his daughter-in-law, conjuring up visions of "sweet angels in heaven," but to his wife he expressed despair. "I have grieved over the death of that little child of so many hopes & so much affection, & in whose life so much of the future was centered," he brooded. "I feel much for the father & mother. . . ."[20]

"Old age & sorrow is wearing me away & constant anxiety & labour day & night leaves me but little repose," Lee wrote as he prepared for the spring campaigns in 1863.[21] His troops, coming out of the doldrums of winter and on the heels of their successes of the previous year, were feeling feisty, but Lee was ill, suffering from chest pains and chronic lung problems severe enough to force him into bed. The attacks marked the onset of coronary complaints that appeared intermittently during the course of the war, eroding his stamina.[22] Then, only weeks later, Lee's immediate family suffered its first casualty. On June 9, 1863, Rooney, aka "Fitzhugh" or W. H. F. Lee, now a major general in the cavalry, was shot in the thigh at Brandy Station, where his horsemen arrived late in the action to save the day for J. E. B. Stuart. His father saw him on the night after the battle, as they were bringing him from the field. Though distressed that his son "would so soon be sent to the rear disabled," he was optimistic. Neither bone nor artery had been shattered, and Rooney was young and strong: he would soon rally. His own home destroyed, Rooney, accompanied by Rob, was taken to convalesce at Hickory Hill, his wife's family home.[23]

There, with sisters Agnes and Mildred and his mother in attendance, Federal troops raided the estate and took him prisoner. No one could tell the story with more dramatic verve than Anne Wickham does in the animated letter to Carter Lee that opens this chapter. The Yankees wreaked comparatively minor havoc for those days—some horses and hams were taken and the brandy casks opened, but Rob dodged capture, and the ladies were treated with courtesy. All thought that Rooney's wound would protect him from mistreatment, but to the horror of the family he was laid on a bed and carted away. "I can't conceive greater hardness of heart than it required to resist the entreaties of that beautiful young wife and infirm mother," protested one of the Lees' friends.[24] Devastated, Charlotte broke down completely. A month later, her father-in-law, himself in anguish, and now facing the grim aftermath of Gettysburg, could do little to comfort her. "Nothing would do [Fitzhugh] more harm than to learn that you were sick & sad," he cajoled, urging her to "cheer up & prove your fortitude & patriotism."[25]

Rooney's capture began a torturous period of waiting, and scheming through the bureaucracy for his release. He was initially taken to Fort Monroe, where the Union kept a prison under the command of General Benjamin Butler. Returned prisoners reported that he was well treated, that his leg was mending, and that the local ladies, who were all loyal Virginians, brought him a basket of delicacies each week.[26] But the process of obtaining release or even getting accurate information was slow and labyrinthine. The Confederate government was besieged with anxious families trying to locate their missing relatives, and not everyone had sympathy for the sons of the well-connected. "Why not?" queried one when she heard of Rooney's capture. "[He] was within the enemies lines." The best course was to proceed quietly, Lee cautioned his wife.[27] The Federal authorities were resisting exchanges, which they thought to the advantage of the personnel-poor southern army, and, as Anne Wickham had foreseen, Rooney's status was an excellent trump card in their hand.[28] When Rooney was transferred to Fort Lafayette in New York Harbor, Custis was said to have offered to take his place, so that his brother could be with his failing wife.[29] This too was denied, and Lee was daily more anxious. "His detention is very grievous to me, & I besides want his services," he told Mary.[30]

Worn down by grief and disappointment, Chass never rallied in strength or spirit, and despite all ministrations, she slipped out of life around Christmas 1863. This death placed another weight on Lee, who had been especially fond of her since she was a girl. "I grieve for our lost darling as a father only can grieve for a daughter, and my sorrow is heightened by the thought of the anguish her death will cause our dear son and the poignancy it will give to the bars of his prison," he wrote in a Christmas letter, markedly different in tone from the Santa-and-fruitcake-laden missives he had penned a dozen years earlier.[31] Rooney was finally released in March 1864, under circumstances that are not clear. He returned to Richmond to find his wife dead, his home still under occupation, and the Confederacy's social fabric badly frayed. Ever-jovial Uncle Smith Lee thought he would soon get over it, since Richmond was notoriously filled with merry widows and widowers. "How I wish glass could be as easily mended as widowers' hearts," Smith laughingly told Mary Chesnut. "Then I would not be left with only three glass tumblers."[32] His brother did not share the lighthearted sentiments. Too choked with emotion to express his relief on seeing Rooney, Robert Lee told Mary, "my heart was so full I could say but little."[33]

Refugees were a staple of the wartime South, and the Lees had been among the very first to fly before the Union army. In the early months of the conflict they moved among their cousins' estates in something of an extended, if despondent, house party. When the White House was burned, however,

Mary Lee decided to live in Richmond. After doing penance in a series of unsatisfactory quarters, she and her daughters moved into a house at 707 Franklin Street that Custis had rented with his messmates. Custis was an aide-de-camp to Jefferson Davis, a role he detested since it kept him far from the action, but one that his father found convenient for a number of reasons. Not only did Custis serve as an unofficial intermediary between the general and the president's office, he acted as his father's surrogate on everything from legal matters to tailor's model. His presence also relieved Lee's mind about the family's safety. He was not easy while they were in Richmond, and never ceased begging his wife to move to a location farther from the maelstrom. However, one of the difficulties for women during the war was isolation from their menfolk, and Mrs. Lee, placed so that she could see Custis daily and Rob, Rooney, and her husband occasionally, ignored the general's commands and remained at "the Mess."[34] From there she watched the progress of her sons—Custis at the president's office, Rooney rising to major general of cavalry, and Rob, who first became an officer of artillery and later fought with his cousin Fitz Lee's cavalry unit. "I think camp life agrees with them," she confided to one of their cousins, "for they all look well & handsome."[35] There was some rolling of the eyes in Richmond parlors at the quickness of their promotions, and Lee's staff referred to them as the "royal family," but in fact they all acquitted themselves proudly. Custis finally got into the fight during the last battle of the war, and Rooney and Rob proved themselves implacable under fire at Second Manassas, Antietam, and the Wilderness.[36]

For Mary Lee, who eagerly monitored the war news and the whereabouts of her family, Richmond was a good, if uncomfortable, perch. The city was like a swollen sponge, seeping refugees. With the arrival of the Confederate government and thousands of persons fleeing from real or perceived Yankee atrocities, the population doubled in the first year of the war. The huge internal migration was one of the Confederacy's most difficult social problems, adding to the desperation of its defense and the difficulties of morale. The number of refugees actually increased during the war, and with it the growing problem of food production and distribution, as well as internal cohesion.[37] As the war progressed, Richmond saw prices rise until even the well-heeled were reduced to scavenging. The twin specters of "demon avarice" and "the gaunt form of wretched famine" haunted one War Department clerk, and he chronicled in detail the growing want. "Such is the scarcity of provisions that rats and mice have mostly disappeared, and the cats can hardly be kept off the table," he recorded on December 21, 1863.[38] Clothes were stolen from laundry lines; women stooped to pick up pins. The worst part was that the farmers seemed to be producing well; more than one distressed citizen noted that they were starving in the midst of plenty.[39] After the poorer citizens rioted in early 1863, Jefferson Davis made modest efforts to curb speculation by regulating prices and controlling distribution. Unfortunately, these measures were inadequate and, in some cases, counterproductive. When the government tried to impress foodstuffs for both soldiers and citizens, they ran into a states' rights philosophy that blocked their ability to act as a national entity. A 10 percent "tithe" of crops met with huge popular resentment, as did an unrealistic attempt to divert precious grain from the distilleries.[40] By April 1864, Robert E. Lee had become so alarmed about the famine looming in Richmond that he was said to advocate forcibly removing 20,000 people to the countryside to ease the insufficiencies.[41]

As if to ward off reality, the Confederate capital also embraced a frenzied social life. Many of the leading families of the South took up residence there, and partied away their sorrows. Balls, fancy weddings, and soirees glistened in defiance of bad news, and receptions at the president's mansion still boasted an elegant company in revamped finery.[42] The grande dame of the city was said to have spent $30,000 on entertainment during the inflationary last year of the war. Richmond boasted the courtiers and intrigues of all capital cities, and it resounded with the delicious buzz of political gossip. General Josiah Gorgas, the chief of ordinance, acknowledged that "we listen to and feel here every rumor. . . ."[43] For the less fortunate—or more committed— "starvation" parties, where few or no refreshments were expected, offered a social outlet without the diminution of pocketbook or patriotism. The city also hosted a huge contingent of military men, anxious to throw off the horror or ennui of the field. The popular romantic image of the day showed "valor courting beauty," and belles such as Constance Cary found themselves thrilled with scores of gallant beaux. Miss Cary, styling herself "La Refugiata," accepted tributes from General Beauregard, held hands with R. E. Lee, and planned assignations with his nephew Fitz, all while carving out a literary career based on upbeat dispatches from the cramped city.[44] The Lees' own Miss Mary also attracted a good deal of attention—her brother Rob saw her in passing one day, "so surrounded by old city beaux, with eye glasses, spies, squints etc, & lameness that I hardly could say a word to her."[45] Even grieving Agnes caught the attention of dashing J. E. B. Stuart, who begged that she allow him to get her "anything on land or sea which you desire. . . ."[46]

Mrs. Lee was a firm fixture of the Richmond elite, acknowledged by all rungs of society. She shunned frivolity, especially as her health restricted her

movement, and the family was in mourning. "I wonder how people can enjoy such things in these troublesome times," she quietly noted.[47] As a result
the Lees participated in few of the capital's glamorous gatherings. Indeed
their home became known for its
austerity, which acted as linchpin between divergent social worlds. The
girls wore homespun, and their
mother, never a fashion plate, was
satisfied with country cotton. One
old friend remarked a little cattily
that Mary Lee, in her "*mussed,* bright
yellow calico dress," had "a cracker
appearance generally."[48] The Lees
were never in actual want, for
friends, admirers, and the commissary department took care that they
were looked after, but their life was
simple and devoted to work for the
war effort. A dinner in summer 1864
consisted of dried Indian peas, rice,
and salt pork. From camp General
Lee worried about how they subsisted on daily rations of a quarter
pound of bacon and a pint and a half

Mary Custis Lee as she appeared
during the war.
ARLINGTON HOUSE, THE ROBERT E. LEE
MEMORIAL, NATIONAL PARK SERVICE

of meal per person. He evidently missed the irony that this was very nearly
the allotment slaves had traditionally been given.[49]

Mary Lee wanted to be in Richmond for reasons beyond family proximity.
Like many women of her era, she sought an outlet for her energized emotions, yearning to join the cause and play a part in the victories. "To be idle
in wartime is torture," one Virginia lady wrote, and the Lee women set out
to prove themselves equal to the challenges before them.[50] They knitted hundreds of socks and gloves, made soldiers' shirts, and distilled blackberry
cordial for the sick wards. Although hospital aid was not their main contribution, occasionally they braved the stench and "bloated, disfigured counte-
nances" to deliver supplies and encourage the men. One suffering volunteer
remembered that Mrs. Lee "spoke a cheerful word to each sick, or wounded
soldier, which pleased them, & gave them something to talk of for hours after."[51] The wartime ethic called for women to be optimistic, brave, and patriotic; to endure death notices, dashed hopes, and everyday hardship with stoic

strength. Many did so, and one visitor to the Confederacy during this time concluded that "the South will owe her independence eventually very much to the fiery enthusiasm of her own daughters."⁵² General Lee overtly encouraged this, but it was his wife who gave life to the credo. "No. 707 became a common meeting place," recalled a neighbor.

> People came to talk of victory or sorrow; they could stay here if they had nowhere else to go; they gathered here to work, the disheartened came for comfort from the tender, loving wife of the commander-in-chief, whose nature was sympathetic, who was intelligent, agreeable and brave, who listened, and strengthened, and smiled. . . . The brightness of her nature amidst uncertainty and pain, was wonderful.⁵³

For years Mary Lee had been praying to God for a purpose, a way to use her faith actively and to test her commitment. Her mother had been dedicated to the American Colonization Society, but it had never really been Mary's calling. Now she had found a mission and an identity that built on the Mount Vernon–based nobility with which she had been raised. It was her moment, and she triumphed in it. In photographs from the war years she appears serenely regal, quietly commanding from her rolling chair, with a determined twinkle in her eye. She not only complemented her husband's dignity, she lent real material aid to the Confederate cause, and became its most loyal political supporter. Rising above self-pity, she reflected instead on the larger tragedy around her. "In these times we must all 'in patience possess our souls,'" she counseled.⁵⁴ She took both success and misfortune in her stride, checking those who swaggered in the days of triumph by remaining quiet in victory and calm in defeat. Only once did anyone record that she was truly rattled, and that was after J. E. B. Stuart was killed at Yellow Tavern in 1864. "Jackson is dead," she is quoted as saying, "and now Stuart is gone. What will become of us?"⁵⁵ As the retreating Confederate government torched Richmond in April 1865, the fire sweeping over St. Paul's Church and across Capitol Square to Franklin Street, she sat knitting, a picture of defiant dignity. Told a few days later that her husband had surrendered the Army of Northern Virginia, she remarked: "General Lee is not the Confederacy."⁵⁶

Nothing daunted Mary Custis Lee—not bereavement, nor crippling disease, nor her husband's defeat. But her outlook did change during these years. The Civil War was a personal revelation for many women, North and South. Accustomed to being told they were frail, they found they were resilient. Used to leaning on a man's judgment, as well as his escorting arm, they found that they had a moral as well as physical backbone. Uncertain of

their voice, they wrote powerful words in diaries and letters that still shape
our understanding of their era. Mary Lee and her daughters were part of this;
their concept of "normal" changed to include independent travel and exerting real political influence—and no matter that it was whispered in the ear of
an official rather than registered at the ballot box.[57] Subject to enemy capture,
house arrest, days of uncertainty, and the loss of a heartbreaking number of
family members, the Lee ladies did not flinch. Yet in a most intriguing turnabout, Mary Lee came to identify herself more and more with her husband
during this period. She continued to ignore his dictates, of course, and did
just what she pleased, but she began to link her status and destiny to his success. Hers had been the greater ancestry, the unassailable legacy, the centerpiece of family tradition. Now he had established a name that rivaled all she
had been taught to revere. For the first time she boasted about him, proud of
her association, pleased to defer to his reputation—if not his advice. This was
particularly marked after the war, when she spent hours coloring little photos of the general and dwelling on the underappreciation of his merits. Once
she had proudly identified herself as the granddaughter of Martha Washington. Now she was Mrs. General Lee.

Of the Lee children, the one who suffered most during this time was Agnes.
She had not easily recovered from her sister's death, and now another shock
wave crashed through her life. Among the Lees' close-knit circle was Orton
Williams, Markie's brother, who had warned Mary Lee of the impending
occupation of Arlington. He had been orphaned at an early age, and had
grown up to be a bright but somewhat wild and unpredictable young man.
Robert E. Lee watched him with concern, tried to discourage his interest in
a military career, and tried even harder to dampen his interest in Agnes.
Nevertheless, a shared love of horses, and Orton's charismatic spirit, kept
the two conspired in romance for years. Markie once reminisced that at Arlington "it was always—where are Agnes & Orton?—Those Forest shades
could tell."[58] With a bit of reluctant help from his cousin Robert, Orton had
wrangled a place on General Scott's staff, but stayed only sixty days before
writing his emotional letter of resignation and joining the Confederate
army.[59] There he was considered smart, polished, and volatile. Promoted to
captain, Orton distinguished himself at the battle of Shiloh, leading an important charge and lending invaluable support to General Braxton Bragg.
Still, he continued to be reckless—"he was not a sound man," wrote a comrade. In one instance he ran his sword through a private who refused to
salute him.[60] At Christmas 1862 he made an unannounced visit to Hickory
Hill, where Agnes, in deep mourning for Annie, was staying. According to

a relative who was present, the small children viewed them as a dashing Prince Charming and his lady, and everyone expected the pair to become engaged. They were disappointed: "after a long session in the parlor . . . he came out, bade the family goodbye and rode away alone." Whether Agnes was overwhelmed by family loss, or heeding her father's caution, is unclear. Nor is it certain that Orton proposed. His record from this point becomes as convoluted as his cousins' fanciful fairy stories.[61]

The first strange occurrence was that Orton changed his name from William Orton Williams to Lawrence William Orton, a variation of his brother's name. No explanation was given, though some surmised that he may have been trying to overcome the reputation he had sustained since slicing his subordinate to death. He then appears to have met a "widow" whom he married, or at least offered marriage, though it was later revealed that her husband was actually alive.[62] When he next surfaced it was on the front pages of the *Richmond Examiner* for June 13, 1863, which announced that he, along with a Lieutenant Dunlop, had been hung as a spy by the Federal army on June 9. When Lee saw the article, he was incensed. "I read in the papers yesterday an account of the death of Orton Williams, which I can hardly believe. . . . I see no necessity for his death except to gratify the evil passions of those whom he offended by leaving Genl. Scott."[63] The explanation for Orton Williams's death, however, was far murkier than simple retribution.

On the evening of June 8, Colonel Lawrence William Orton and Major George Dunlop appeared at Fort Granger near Franklin, Tennessee. They were dressed in Federal uniforms, including hats covered with crisp new havelocks—an item used to shield the head and neck from excessive sun. Dunlop was in reality another relative, Walter Gibson Peter. "Gip" had spent his life trailing his exciting cousin Orton, and had evidently been talked into this excursion as well. The two introduced themselves as an inspection team from Washington, and told how they had been attacked and robbed by rebel pickets. Their papers seemed to be in order, and when they asked for a loan to continue their journey, the post commander, Colonel John P. Baird, advanced it. After they left, several officers at the fort began to question their story. Something seemed odd: the havelocks, for example, had been used at the beginning of the war, but they had long since been discarded. Orton was also calling himself "Auton," and it seemed wrong that they would have been attacked and still escaped with their horses. The Union officers were also worried about the presence of rebel partisan Nathan Bedford Forrest in the neighborhood and anxious to protect their position. Finally the two were followed and brought back to the camp, where they were placed under guard while frantic telegrams were sent to verify their identities, "as they can given no consistent account of their conduct." At length word came back from General James A. Garfield—who ostensibly had signed the bogus inspection team's orders—that there were "no such men . . . in this army, nor in any army so far as we know." On searching the two more closely, Baird found that Dunlop's sword carried the inscription "Lt. W. G. Peters, C.S.A.," and that each man had his real name on the band of the headgear they had artfully covered with the havelocks.[64]

Baird contacted Washington again and was instructed to conduct a quick court-martial and, if found guilty, to hang the men immediately. The drumhead court-martial, among the most chilling of wartime events, took place in a dark tent, lit by rows of candles along the edge of a long table. One of those present remembered that the "tiny flames threw garish shimmers of light on side-arms and brass buttons," casting a fearful glow over the proceeding.[65] When pressed, Williams and Peter confessed that they were Confederate soldiers, but denied repeatedly that they were spies. Williams alluded to a larger mission, vaguely mentioned something about France or Canada, but would divulge no details. The prize, he said, "fully justified the fearful hazard he had made to gain it." In short order the two were pronounced guilty and sentenced to death.[66] As the gallows were erected and coffins prepared, Williams and Peter talked with a chaplain and wrote their last letters, including the one to Markie and another that the minister described as being "to a daughter of Genl Lee, stating . . . that if he had been successful they would have been married & on their way to Europe in a month."[67] At nine a.m., three hours after the execution was to have started, the company assembled, and the two men marched to the gallows. When Walter Peter began to whimper, Orton announced: "Let us die like men!" Then the wagon on which they were perched was driven from under them, their bodies left dangling in the air.[68] According to newspaper accounts, neither died instantly. Gip struggled almost two minutes, and Orton, grabbing the rope with both hands, strangled for five minutes or longer. The chaplain and others present were greatly impressed by their dignity and youth and bravery. Baird, who initially had told Garfield that his bile was stirred, "and some hanging would do me good," was sorry in the end that "the trial was not more deliberate." The "rudest" soldiers present, wrote the chaplain, "gave evidence of painful emotion."[69]

Just what Walter Peter and Orton Williams were actually doing has remained a mystery. If they were indeed on an official mission, they played their final roles very well, for their secret has never been discovered. Neither the North nor the South had a coordinated intelligence network during the war. Though various branches of the Confederate government—the War Department, Signal Corps, and State Department, for example—all used intelligence operatives, chiefly they relied on their ability to penetrate the telegraph offices or other official information sources of the Union, or on ad hoc agents, who maneuvered independently. The actions of Williams and Peter, who shunned the opportunity to linger in a Union camp, do not really mesh with this kind of operation.[70] Markie came to believe that they had embarked on an ill-advised lark, testing their courage and luck as they had together as boys. Lee, absolutely infuriated by the incident, also thought the men were off on an adventure and that their execution had been "ordered from a spirit of malignant vindictiveness, common in a cowardly people."[71] Part of Lee's ire may have sprung from the fact that he had not been consulted about any proposed mission, and had been given no chance to advise on the young men's suitability. Williams's and Peter's well-forged documents and genuine Federal uniforms seem too authentic to have been rigged up informally, and their poised insistence that they were traveling officially impressed all of their interlocutors as genuine.

Orton Williams, seated, and Walter Gibson Peter in Confederate officers' uniform.
TUDOR PLACE HOUSE AND GARDEN, WASHINGTON, D.C.

Such missions did take place, and stood apart from the work of spies, who infiltrated the enemy, passing intelligence covertly, or of scouts, who rode out on reconnaissance, but always openly represented their own side. The Confederate government, for example, waged an active publicity campaign in Europe, sending numerous agents to win hearts and minds. The most famous of these was Rose O'Neal Greenhow, who slipped through the blockade on an English man-o'-war, was received by Napoleon III and Queen Victoria, and spent two years charming people into political support for the Confederacy. In August 1863 a War Department clerk recorded meeting with Professor Albert Taylor Bledsoe, who was about to embark on a government ship for London to publish his apologetic treatise *Liberty and Slavery*. "I think it probable he has a mission from the President, as well as his book to publish," noted the clerk.[72] Since Canada was also a staging ground for Confederate operations and a departure point for those looking to circumvent the blockade, operatives also frequently worked their way north to link with units there. Nor is it unlikely that the general's relatives would have been chosen for such a mission. Robert E. Lee's cousin Cassius Lee, who moved over to the Confederate cause after the first year of war, worked unofficially in Canada, acting as a clearinghouse for information and aiding transiting agents. In suspicious times kith and kin were considered the most trustworthy messengers.[73]

The execution of Orton Williams had a severe effect on the family. It is said that Orton's sister Kate never recovered from the news, finally dying from her sorrow. Markie, previously torn in her loyalties, became a confirmed Southern sympathizer after Orton's death, and brother Laurence, who had showed great promise as an aide-de-camp to McClellan, deserted from the Union army later that year.[74] Agnes was perhaps the worst hit. Whatever had transpired between them, she and Orton had been close since childhood, and he was intertwined with every pleasant memory of her life. One of her relatives stated that the "terrible death of Orton Williams was a shock to Agnes from which she never recovered. She became very quiet and pensive in after life. I do not recall hearing her laugh, and when she smiled it seemed to me she was looking beyond."[75] In a photograph taken after the war she is still lovely, but dressed in mourning, and caught in just the lost expression her cousin described. Like the plunder of civilian homes, the incident politicized the Lee clan, giving them a reason for hatred that was more immediate than abstract notions of states' rights. Lee was only too familiar with the excesses of war, but he speaks harshly of this one, stating that only God—not he—could forgive it, and even years later remarking: "I cannot trust my pen or tongue to utter my feelings."[76]

The Lees' personal losses were now mounting at a horrific rate. Bishop Meade, who had heard Robert say his catechism as a toddler, died in 1862, clutching Lee in his last hours with a "cold and pulseless" hand. "'I ne'er shall look on his like again,'" paraphrased Lee, recalling the bishop's kindness to him.[77] A few months after Chass died, while Lee was still in heightened anxiety about Rooney's imprisonment, Anne Lee Marshall breathed her last. A Union sympathizer to the end, she had never reestablished contact with her brother, though it was said that in her Baltimore home she often bragged that none of the Federals "can whip Robert."[78] Growing ever more despondent, Lee tried to comfort himself with his evangelical formulations, but he could not hide his depression. When Mary Childe, the niece he adored, passed away in the last months of the war he grieved as he had at Annie's death, anguished that he had now been left without a link to his father, mother, or sisters.[79] Worse yet was the carnage of the battlefield, with its horror and waste, and haunting sense of responsibility. Even in the bright days of anticipation after Chancellorsville, Lee wrote that he was tired of the conflict, sick at heart over the calamity to the country, and tormented by the pain he saw in so many households. "Every day is marked with sorrow," he told Agnes, "& every field has its grief, the death of some brave man!"[80]

Caught in the dual prisons of accountability and suffering, Lee found an outlet in the letters he wrote to his family. He was distracted and exhausted, his burdens nearly overwhelming and the mail routes precarious, yet he faithfully corresponded in all but the most heated moments. He told his wife not to expect to hear from him very often, but hardly a day went by when he did not pen a letter to some family member throughout the war.[81] The letters are shot through with wartime vignettes, but most are like chatty everyday conversation, with talk of rain, of the great general's increasingly tatty underdrawers, and teasing little jokes to ease the inner anguish. "I send you Mrs. Lee a likeness of your husband that has come from beyond the big water," Lee wrote from camp before the 1863 campaigns. "He is a hard favoured man & has a very rickety position on his pins. I hope his beard will please you, for the artist seems to have laid himself out on that."[82] Lee took care in what he wrote because of his concern that messages might be intercepted, but for the most part he desired to capture the ordinary rhythms, the dear familiar human aspects of life, that make up a family's shared moments. Letters became the substance of the Lees' relationships during the war years, just as they did for countless boys in blue and gray who yearned to give their thoughts expression and to keep fast their strongest human ties. "Can't you conceive how delightful it is to hear from home when one is in camp, how pleasant it is to recognize the handwriting on the back, how delightful to open & imagine yourself talking with . . . sister or mother, notice all the time little peculiarities in expression & thought which brings them more forcibly before the reader," wrote a homesick Virginia cavalryman from a dismal winter camp in 1865. That young rebel was Robert E. Lee Jr., who vividly shared his father's feelings.[83]

Not every letter arrived at its destination, and this worried Lee. He had a well-developed loathing for the public spyglass, and he did not want his adversaries to pinpoint either his location or that of his family. Though led by the able Texan John Henninger Reagan, the Confederate postal system was a cameo of every dislocation in the awkward Richmond government. The War Department quarreled with it over use of the railroads; Congress demanded that stamps be purchased with specie—an almost unknown item—and when inflation plagued the Confederate monetary system, stamps themselves became small-change currency, with nothing left to paste on envelopes. In addition, the post office lacked forms, twine, and mailbags. Its agents, theoretically exempt from military duty, were conscripted, and the various states wrangled over the most lucrative routes.[84] Lee actually compounded the situation by claiming that the exemption of postmasters from the army was "more than it could bear," and demanded the carriers be released to fill his depleted ranks.[85] "I have not the most remote idea how you will get this letter," Markie once wrote the family; but receive it they did, despite complaints that the "mails are deranged every where."[86] Generally the Lees sent their messages by friends or military couriers, but Lee was nervous about this as well. "I can only hold oral communication with your sister," he advised Agnes after trying to contact daughter Mary. "I have received one letter from her, but have forbidden the scouts to bring any writing. . . . If caught it would compromise them."[87] The messages Lee received were torn up. "I must thank you for the letter you wrote to me while at Fredericksburg," Lee told Chass. "I kept it by me till preparing for the battle-field, when, fearing it might reach the eyes of General Hooker, I destroyed it. We can carry with us only our recollections."[88]

Whether regarded as patriots or traitors, perpetrators or protectors, the Lees suffered every calamity the war held. Their homes were ravaged: as Lee advised his son, "the negroes have been liberated, every thing swept off them, houses, fences &c all gone. The land alone remains a waste."[89] Their relatives were killed or alienated, their future balanced on precarious underpinnings. With no time to follow personal matters, with courts and currency uncertain, Lee worried about the settlement of the Custis estate and about his finances, which were rapidly diminishing. "I have no time to think of my private affairs," Lee remarked to his wife. "I expect to die a pauper, & I see no way of preventing it."[90] He was not exaggerating. In 1863 he was too poor to pay his taxes and asked Custis whether a way could be found. He listed his holdings: some Virginia and North Carolina bonds he thought largely worthless; assets in the United States whose value was uncertain and which he could not then touch; and "3 horses, a watch, my apparel & camp equipment."[91] This was all he possessed. Caught in the doom of Petersburg's trenches, left nothing save his family's affection, he longingly told his wife, "I trust there is some peace, some quiet & some comfort in store for us, that the evening of our lives may be cheerful & happy together. . . . God bless you my dear Mary & may he guard & protect you now & ever."[92]

The Political Animal

Head Quarters ANV^a
April 25th 1864

Res. returned to his Excellency the President. The best way for the citizens of the
Northern Neck to save their cattle grain bacon &c. from these marauding parties, is to send them across the Rapp^k and sell them to the Confederate government. To keep their produce stored in large quantities is but to invite the enemy.
A proper corroboration & energy on the part of the citizens with what aid government agents can give would in this way save a great deal for the Army & the
people. Much has been accomplished by this means in the past winter. There are
no companies which I can well detach for duty in this region—If the members
of the two companies spoken of by Mr. Newton are liable to conscription they
should be in the Army—If not then they form very good material for protection
against raiding parties being thoroughly acquainted with the country. If they act
with the boldness & spirit which should characterize men who are protecting
their families from insult & their houses from desolation they would give the enemy a wholesome fear of coming into the country.   RE Lee Genl^l

. . .

H^d Q^{rs} CS Armies
30th March 1865

Lt. Gen RS Ewell
Comman^g re:
General,
General Lee directs me to acknowledge the receipt of your letter of the 29th
inst: and to say that he regrets very much to learn that owners refuse to allow
their slaves to enlist. He deems it of great moment that some of this force should
be put in the field as soon as possible, believing that they will remove all doubts
as the expediency of the measure. He regrets it the more in the case of the own-

ers about Richmond, inasmuch as the example would be extremely valuable, and the present posture of military affairs renders it almost certain that if we do not get these men, they will soon be in arms against us, and perhaps relieving white Federal soldiers from guard duty in Richmond. He desires you to press this view upon the owners.

He says that he regards it as very important that immediate steps be taken to put the recruiting in operation, and has so advised the Department. He desires to have you placed in general charge of it, if agreeable to you, as he thinks nothing can be accomplished without energetic and intelligent effort by someone who fully appreciates the vital importance of the duty. He has written to the Dept to that effect, and also requesting compliance with your suggestion with reference to Col. Otey & Adg^t [unreadable]. He thinks that if the conscript be fit to command, it would be well to accept the offer of the 200 men. He will recommend any suitable persons to be employed on recruiting duty that you may name, who can be spared, and thinks they should be sent out at once. He expects greater results if suitable persons be authorized to raise companies, battalions & even regiments, than from mere recruiting officers, as contemplated in Gen. Order No. 14.

Prompt action is all important, and the general only waits to receive your suggestion.

Very resp^y
Your ob^t serv^t
Charles Marshall
Lt Col & AAG[2]

▷·◁▷·○·◁▷·◁

R OBERT E. LEE had disdained politics and politicians since young manhood. He saw it as a dangerous arena of parochial self-interest, where the actors lacked both deep understanding of the issues and social subtlety. As an officer in the U.S. Army he had watched as his superiors were ensnared in losing situations that thwarted and sometimes entirely undermined their military accomplishments. He left the only job he ever held at Washington headquarters because of "*dis-g-u-st*" at what he observed in its corridors, and sidestepped political issues as neatly as he could thereafter. During the Civil War he found to his sorrow that the job of commanding general carries with it more than the glorious duties of a field marshal. In a democracy a military leader must respond to civil authority, and to gain logistic and strategic support he must wheedle when he cannot persuade. In these two letters we see Lee's approach to interaction with his government.

It was a multilayered style that combined flattery, suggestion, and exhortation. His underlying political goal was to secure the full commitment of every citizen to the cause at hand, using just enough official intervention to bring along the laggards. Despite his personal prestige, it was an imperfect success. Lee never lost the confidence of some very tricky political masters, but neither did he get all of the backing he sought.

Confederate political philosophy evolved from the proposition that individual and communal interests overrode national authority. Southerners hoped to create a sort of clarified republicanism, from which the nasty scum of political factions and the tyranny of an unwelcome majority had been skimmed. In this cleansed system their special society would be protected by the primacy of "free and independent" states. This ideology was elaborately and sometimes eloquently justified, but its practical application proved challenging. Once the Southerners decided to multiply their strength by forming a confederacy, they were faced with a paradox: how to sustain a compact between states whose very motivation for departing the Union was their objection to federal authority.[3] Creating a cohesive nation under these circumstances was a difficult task, which only grew harder as the struggle moved from political independence to physical survival. Moreover, there was little consensus about what form a new southern political culture should take. Ruptures were frequent among the various factions. Some eschewed political parties and fought demagoguery; others favored autonomy over unity and mistrusted patronage. Governmental institutions were suspect, as were individuals who greedily sought power, and few leaders or political entities gained legitimacy during the brief life of the Confederacy. As economic circumstances changed from 1861 to 1865, it also became harder to balance the prudent with the philosophically pure. Ironically, the very movement that had broken the chains of centralized "repression" moved increasingly toward absolutist politics. By early 1863 a thoughtful Confederate congressman found that the "idea begins to prevail that popular Government is in failure, and that states to be permanent must necessarily have a centralizing tyranny. . . ."[4]

The only thing that was clear was what the secessionists were against— the old Union and the insulting behavior that today we might call northern "hegemony." This was one of the ligaments that connected the disparate southern communities; another was the excitement of the moment, when bands and booming cannons quickened emotions. In the absence of a cohesive ideology, Confederates began to develop symbols that helped them define themselves: heroes who stood for their definition of liberty; distinctive songs and flags that sparked their allegiance. But these signs too were problematic. George Washington was claimed as the political and emotional founder of nations on both sides of the Mason-Dixon line. In the South, as in the North, patriotic banners were composed of stripes and stars, and were colored red, white, and blue. The new constitution was remarkably similar to the one they had just rejected: it made a nod toward the subordination of political parties, but its main difference was the legitimization of secession and slavery. Alabama representative William Russell Smith acknowledged this: "there is nothing *original* in this movement, not the building up of a new government, but a mere transfer of principles and a change of rulers and boundaries." If, as most Southerners believed, their revolution was essentially conservative, preserving continuity rather than fomenting radical change, how was one to explain the disruption of ties with the United States, which, after all, did not preclude dialogue and had taken no legal measures to overturn southern institutions?[5]

One important unifying element of the southern cause was the widespread belief that theirs was a unique social system, which had successfully retained a delicate balance within a diverse population. Much of the South was rough frontier, on the fringes of civilization, and the population was made up of what a Lee cousin called "*all sorts & shades.*"[6] Social stratification was managed at least in part by understanding one's place in it. Slavery was at the heart of this system, even for many who thought the institution unfortunate. Its retention had to do not only with protection of property rights among the wealthier classes, but with the establishment of social order. All whites, from squires to squatters, could identify with each other because of what they were not: black. And blacks, who were considered a dangerous public menace if not under strict management, were effectively controlled. The moral issues were carried away on a sea of reassuring rhetoric and self-delusion, in which the slaves themselves were frequently participants. The intimate understanding of this social structure lent a sense of identity to divergent southern communities, a kind of cultural familiarity that did not need to be explained or internally rationalized. The feelings of commonality were heightened during wartime by the idea that Southerners of all castes were united in their fight against abolition and northern tyranny; that theirs was a classless revolution.

Still to be achieved, however, was any cohesive sense of nationhood. Many states chose to follow a quasi-independent stance, viewing every act of the central government as a presumption, no matter how pragmatic. State courts assumed jurisdiction that legitimately belonged to Richmond, obstructing the execution of laws so blatantly that an exasperated cabinet official protested that he was not accustomed to recognizing "the eccentric opinion of local judges" as the Confederacy's highest authority. Strong governors, such as Joseph E. Brown of Georgia or Zebulon B. Vance of North Carolina, did not hesitate to interfere in every aspect of national governance, be it control of the army, taxation, or management of the railroads.

The head of the Bureau of War in Richmond described a "querulous" letter from Vance, complaining that North Carolina's rivers and ports were undefended, that South Carolina was receiving an unfair share of support, and that Lee's troops were deserting because the states had declared the conscription law unconstitutional. Private citizens often saw their aspirations in small terms as well—and promoted provincial concerns over national interests. This tension would prevail throughout the war, undermining effective policy making and sapping the will to sacrifice.[7]

For many it came down to making a personal peace with their divergent loyalties. Lee seems to have been more effective at this than many of his countrymen. He had always been comfort-

The cover sheet to a piece of patriotic Confederate music.
LIBRARY OF CONGRESS

able with a high degree of ambiguity, and now he unapologetically joined his dedication to Virginia with a larger cause that could possibly subordinate state interests. The words "our people" and "our country" came easily to him, and just weeks into the conflict he told his wife that "all my thoughts & strength are given to the cause to which my life be it long or short will be devoted."[8] Two years later he had not lost his dedication and maintained that he would be content to eat cornbread for the rest of his life if only independence could be won.[9] Yet he also held unswervingly to the belief that his highest duty was to Virginia; and indeed took little interest in battles that were not waged in defense of his state.

Lee had more of an opportunity to understand the complexities of creating true unity than did most of his military counterparts. In the earliest days of the conflict he was tasked with organizing and outfitting an army that had not even hooks enough to attach shoulder insignia to its uniforms.[10]

From this vantage point, and his later perspective as chief military adviser to Jefferson Davis, he witnessed the immense political problems that slowed the ability of the Confederate government to make and implement lasting decisions. Richmond was as much a magnet for ambition and special interests as any other capital, and the poorly defined lines of authority in the weak central government made the political jockeying especially rough. The congress began scheming to gain ascendance over the president; military officers fought for place; office seekers loudly hawked their personal skills. Pride and what James Hammond of South Carolina called "*Big-man-me-ism*" took the place of cooperation and a steady pull at the oar.[11] Not only was loud criticism of Jefferson Davis and the new government heard in statehouses and salons, it was echoed from sometimes reckless southern presses. One historian has likened the self-defeating demagogues of the South to "crazed cannibals" who in their "frenzy of blood thirst" devoured themselves along with their nascent country.[12] There was a considerable display of bombastic rhetoric in the early days as well, which deflected attention from the real issues at hand. A shrewd contemporary observer noted that few except Lee "have been able to shut their eyes and what is harder still, their mouths and give their whole minds and bodies to doing the best they could with such means as they had and against the difficulties thrown in their way by those who would wear the lion skin before the beast was slain."[13]

Despite the proximity to power, Lee did not want these advisory jobs, which he thought devoid of either advantage or pleasure. He hated the counterproductive finagling and stayed out of the intramural wrestling, particularly when it had to do with rivalries among military officers. "He dreaded [the quarrels]," Secretary of the Navy Stephen R. Mallory observed, "and kept his interests tied tightly to his responsibilities."[14] He equally disliked lengthy bureaucratic meetings, and told a trusted assistant after one tedious session with the president "that he had lost a good deal of time in fruitless talk."[15] Lee's circumspection helped him gain a reputation for being "sensible and soldierly," but he could not avoid the demanding personalities that filled the war and state departments.[16] He had to deal with a parade of cabinet officers, some chosen more for their political bloodlines than their skill, and all subject to Davis's mercurial temper. Lee reported to four secretaries of war in the first eighteen months of hostilities. One, George Randolph, handed him so much authority that aides in the department gossiped about how Lee had turned the secretary of war into "a mere clerk."[17] Lee had to change his profile in November 1862 when Randolph was replaced by James A. Seddon, who was a capable and pragmatic man, despite a chronic illness that made him "resemble an exhumed corpse after a month's interment."[18] In reality

Seddon and his ideas were very much alive, and his thoughts frequently differed from those of Lee, particularly on the importance of the war's western front. Though they developed a professional way of interacting, and Seddon eventually deferred to Lee's military expertise, theirs was not a close relationship. Lee never harbored any political aspirations, but as the conflict went on, and his reputation grew, many looked to him for possible civil leadership. There were rumors in 1862 and 1865 that he would be made secretary of war, or be given even greater executive powers. Popular sentiment seems to have been favorable to this as well. An artillerist wrote in July 1864: "In fact I should like to see him as King or Dictator. He is one of the few great men who ever lived, who could be trusted."[19] Despite the rumors, Lee never showed the slightest interest in political office. Since Davis jealously guarded his powers and rarely allowed others to make a decision, this was just as well. In the end, the absence of rivalry with Davis or other senior officials probably increased Lee's influence.[20]

Of the delicate relationships Lee had to manage, none was as critical as his interaction with President Jefferson Davis. Lee and Davis had known each other since cadet days, and had cordial, if not warm, dealings when Davis was U.S. secretary of war. The Confederate president's interest in technical military affairs was keen, and his belief in his superior strategic insights equally so. Indeed his record from both the Mexican War and the War Department was a fine one. He took seriously both the idea of civilian control of the military and his role as commander in chief; nonetheless Davis's propensity to get lost in minutiae irritated his generals and wasted valuable time. He had an uneasy personality: insecure, overbearing, stubborn, vain. He was less interested in interchange than deference and apparently lacking in some of the most fundamental qualities of diplomacy. "Oh, for a man like William of Orange, a man of steadfast calm temper, heroic character and genius, a man fertile in resources, equal to emergencies," wrote a Confederate government official. "This, it is quite evident, Mr. Davis is not."[21] Yet he was an intelligent man, dedicated and willing to defend painfully unpopular stands. A contemporary summed up the situation this way: "I credit President Davis, and his advisors at Richmond with the utmost zeal and much intelligence; but none of them with great practical, constructive statesmanship."[22]

Davis trusted only a handful of people and he had particular trouble with his generals. Despite the vaunted reputation of southern military tradition, few stars shone in the top command. Joseph Johnston proved himself peevish, disrespectful, and immovable. P. G. T. Beauregard was all flash; he failed to inspire lasting confidence and aired his grievances publicly, which was anathema to Davis. Braxton Bragg caused dissention among his officers and men and was, like Johnston, reluctant to make the bold move. Albert Sidney Johnston, whom Davis idolized, was killed before he could prove his worth. Davis saw Lee as "standing alone among the Confederate soldiers in military capacity," remarked Secretary of the Navy Mallory.[23] Not only did Lee fight with a will; he subordinated his personal interests to the larger political goals and never vied for power. Lee was the only military adviser to claim a seat in cabinet meetings. At least occasionally Davis actually deferred to him in affairs of war. During the Seven Days battles Davis liked to ride out to watch the show, sometimes exposing himself to danger, other times interfering with the army's onerous task. In a memorable scene Lee challenged Davis and his large entourage at the battle of Mechanicsville, which was going badly. "Who are all this army of people, and what are they doing here?" Lee is said to have asked the president, staring him down until he meekly left the field.[24] Acceding to Lee's request for reinforcements during the Second Manassas campaign a month later, despite the fact that it left the capital underdefended, Davis said: "Confidence in you overcomes the view which would otherwise be taken of the exposed condition of Richmond. . . ."[25]

This kind of trust was earned by hard work on Lee's part. Davis never quite felt he was informed enough or respected enough, and Lee took the trouble to offer him both endless reports and near total fealty. From the time he took over the Army of Northern Virginia, Lee regaled his commander in chief with a running account of matters large and small, always couched in the most obsequious terms. When he ventured a suggestion, it was quickly followed by a phrase such as "I hope Your Excellency will not suppose that I am offering any obstacles to any measure you may think necessary."[26] He sent newspaper clippings, details of terrain, tidbits gleaned by scouts—a veritable flood of information that kept Davis placated. In one fine example Lee rambled through a list of men who might be promoted and the need to teach disciplinary habits to commanding officers, then described his attempts to find out if the Yankees were constructing a canal, the quality of an assault on Union lines, and his constant frustration with deserters.[27]

Such letters were among the most important that Lee would ever write, as they were the key to his influence with the government and ability to advocate for his army. His aide Charles Marshall recalled that their composition was laborious and they still read as if the words are carefully weighed. They have the air of dispassion, but in fact are among Lee's most artful writing. The thread that runs through them is the looming threat of an overwhelming foe, and his need for additional forces and supplies. It is the agenda of nearly every letter, and Lee effectively uses the power of suggestion as well as straightforward statements to reinforce his point. Sometimes he doctors figures either to show his need or underscore his success. He also omits details, especially when he feared Davis or Seddon might disapprove of his actions. After reading a report of the Gettysburg retreat that euphemistically characterized a bloody skirmish as an "unfortunate round-up of stragglers," a cousin sighed: "Robert is sensitive & less exact than one was once disposed to think; I have heard that from some of his former fondest Engineer corps friends—" The war department also questioned the veracity of some of his accounts. "General Lee's report of the Pennsylvania campaign . . . is as jejune and unsatisfactory a document as I have ever read," fussed a Richmond official.[28]

Despite the enlightened self-interest of his messages, Lee was not entirely successful in his advocacy—Davis did not always lend him the troops he demanded, and Lee was never completely able to block attempts to siphon off parts of his army.[29] But he had established enough interdependence that the president at least listened to his pleas. Lee balked when Davis tried to send him to the faltering western command, and was able ultimately to avoid the transfer.[30] He was less successful in getting his army supplied, and has been criticized for not showing enough force to obtain what he needed. Instead, points out one analyst, he described the suffering of his men as if it were sublime and wrote ineffective requests that "one would scarcely expect from a junior clerk."[31] It is true that Lee's exchanges with Davis do not show a fighting spirit that equaled his temperament on the field, and that he never was able to get Davis to use his political authority robustly to manage the sluggish Confederate production, rampant speculation, and transportation difficulties that undermined military supply. Unfortunately, neither did Lee form a coalition with Secretary of War Seddon, who shared his outrage at the ineptitude of the subsistence bureau. Even had Lee boxed and bellowed, however, it is uncertain, given the poisonous political scene, whether the Confederate president could have commanded all he needed. Ultimately the self-effacing style Lee employed may have been the price of keeping his army largely under his own control and avoiding presidential dictates that might undermine his intentions.[32]

Lee's success in retaining his independence became more important as his overarching views diverged from those of Jefferson Davis. From the outset Davis and Lee were in agreement that the key to victory was to sap the morale of the North. In this politico-strategic view they never wavered, but in its operational application they sometimes differed. Though he kept tight control of military movements, Davis never really articulated a unified national strategy.[33] Neither did Lee, though the major tenets of his philosophy are clear throughout his letters. His strategy rested on five pillars: the desire that every southern community and citizen be fully committed to an all-out war effort; a belief that encouraging northern ambivalence about the conflict could lead the public to demand an end to the hostilities; a desire to "strike a blow" that would destroy either the Federal army or northern public support; an instinctual sense that a threat to the nervous hub of Washington might intimidate the Federal government into a negotiated peace; a hope that outside support might bolster the Confederacy's position. He was less wedded to the latter proposition than was Davis, but nonetheless cognizant of the advantages European assistance could bring.

What is noteworthy about this game plan was the degree to which popular support was a determining factor. Clearly Lee saw the aggressive annihilation of resolve as an effective antidote to technological might. The South could overcome its disadvantages by sheer will; the North would not fully employ its advantage without the will to do so. This was an old philosophy, going back to the fifth century B.C., when Sun Tzu's *Book of War* proposed that success was best achieved by the destruction of the enemy's spirit to resist.[34] Lee's approach was to do it forthrightly, if possible by a spectacular defeat of his opponent's army. Although from the beginning he had envisioned a protracted war, as he increasingly observed the erosion of southern commitment he was anxious to bring the struggle to an end. In addition, he linked military victory to political leverage and hoped to avoid negotiating from a disadvantageous position.

Davis did not disagree with this, though he may have felt that wearing the North down by harassment and rebuffing techniques could achieve the same effect. And whereas Lee had only to worry about his army, Davis had other matters of a national nature to consider. Every state was clamoring for protection of its borders—a vast order, since the Confederate frontier was as large and convoluted as Europe's. Each state also wanted to maintain troops sufficient to protect itself and at the same time demanded that southern forces be dispatched to augment their own. Western operations were being undermined by the poverty of leadership in the Army of Tennessee and the president was not adept at either motivation or finding new talent. Davis also felt the pressure of being directly accountable for the malaise of the populace which increasingly feared they would be overrun.[35] On none of these critical issues—including the importance of the western theater of war—was Davis able to harness Lee's support, nor does it appear he was willing to force it. All evidence indicates that he approved every one of Lee's actions, and ultimately coerced the more reluctant Seddon to do so too.

Whether Lee's reluctance to take a truly national view of strategy was due to parochialism or sound judgment is a debate unlikely to be resolved. Lee had legitimate reasons as a commander in Virginia to center his attention there and resist weakening his increasingly thin forces. This was his operational mandate; it was his job to uphold it. One cannot criticize him simultaneously for failing to succor the Army of Northern Virginia and refusing to diminish it. There were also good reasons to keep a concentration of troops in the area, since the public and governmental eyes of both sides were focused there. (On the other hand, it is clear that Lee had little enthusiasm for war service away from the Army of Northern Virginia. Had he accepted the urging of Seddon and David early in the spring of 1863 to take a command in the west, leaving Jackson to defend Richmond, or had he willingly sent his men to reinforce Vicksburg rather than marching them to Gettysburg, subsequent campaigns, if not the war's outcome, might have developed differently, and Lee himself might be remembered as a brilliant supreme commander rather than the leader of a single army.) Lee and Davis most clearly broke in their strategic thinking after Appomattox, when, stunned at his general in chief's capitulation, Davis still saw hope in an irregular resistance in the country's interior. Southern territory was unusually well adapted to this kind of warfare; still it is impossible to know whether the more reptilian approach of remaining low, unpredictable, and dangerous would have attracted the popular support needed to finally achieve Confederate independence.[36]

Lee and Davis understood the necessity of deflating the North's will to fight, but they also recognized the importance of keeping southern esprit aloft. Aside from Lee's own exhilaration in battle, both men saw great field contests as morale boosters. As the war progressed, the southern population identified increasingly with their armies, particularly the Army of Northern Virginia, with its intrepid marches and rousing string of successes. The national mood reflected victory or defeat; it played off the notion of invincibility and at the same time augmented it. The war was as close to a national experience as Southerners would have. Their suffering defined them as a people, and as loved ones tramped off to distant regions of the Confederacy they expanded their concept of local loyalty to embrace a broader country. With the Confederate government faltering in its ability to protect and provide for its people, the army became the nation's rallying point; its hope; its unifying theme. Moreover, it gave Southerners a mission that justified its existence. "The Army of Northern Virginia alone, as the last hope of the South . . . will sooner or later by its own unaided power win the independence of the Confederacy," proclaimed a captain in the Georgia Infantry in

1864.[37] As the weaknesses in Jefferson Davis's leadership—his inability to inspire, his high-handed political actions, his failure to control the economy—became more grating, the expectations from Lee rose in proportion. "[We] are full of hope," wrote a woman from Tennessee, who had endured two years of Yankee occupation. "We are expecting a great deal from Lee."[38] Walter Taylor noted that Lee was so popular, it was quite trying to accompany his chief in public: "Everybody crowds the way and stops on the pavement to have a look."[39] After Lee reluctantly accepted the largely empty title of general in chief of the Confederate armies in February 1865, there was even greater anticipation of a turnaround. "Providence raises up the man for the time, and a man for this occasion, we believe, has been raised up in Robert E. Lee, the Washington of the second American Revolution," editorialized the *Richmond Times-Dispatch*.[40] For his part Lee mistrusted the popularity and the way it artificially reinforced a national mood of indomitability. "More I think is to be dreaded from the too sanguine & feverish expectations of the community & the clamour of the press, which may drive commanders into imprudence not to say rashness from which disasters are sure to follow," he told brother Carter.[41]

Though the citizenry loudly cheered his army, Lee was never able or willing to use his popularity to influence civic actions, and his writing shows continual frustration with the Confederate public's lackluster embrace of the war effort. From the beginning of the conflict, he had believed that the South would have to support itself in its efforts. "You must not build your hopes on peace on account of the United States going into a war with England," he advised his wife. "She will be very loath to do that, notwithstanding the bluster of the Northern papers. . . . We must make up our minds to fight our battles & win our independence alone."[42] Part of his strategic vision was a total civic commitment, something akin to the mobilization of the entire population that took place in the United States during World War II. He felt that agricultural production, manufacturing, and all other economic activity should be directed to the cause; that austerity and uncommon exertion should become the norm; and that reverses should be bravely borne and turned to advantage.[43] Like other Confederate officials, however, he found the populace largely oblivious to the urgency of the situation and slow to embrace real sacrifice. "Va is almost asleep," complained the navy secretary, "& one could hardly believe that the foe is upon her soil to judge from the conduct of her people."[44] Lee too complained at every chance. "The victories of the enemy increase & consequently the necessity of increased energy & activity on our part," he grumbled to Custis. "Our men do not seem to realize this & the same supineness & carelessness of their duties continue."[45] He was also annoyed at what he considered the frivolous life of some of his daughters—"What they do I do not know"—and admonished them to "be working at some good result, sewing, weaving, knitting, &c, for the poor soldiers."[46] Carter Lee, who was too old for military service, was pressed into activity as well by both of his brothers. Charm ever to the fore, Smith Lee regaled him with stories of living on cornbread and water, then badgered him to increase his farm production.

> I mention these things to show you the necessity of planting everything and anything—Put in the potatoes & vegetables—cover the face of the land you own in something—work yourself, and make the boys work. This is no time to play gentleman, as far as work is concerned. Make Miss Pet Mildred go to the spring, sweep and clean, lend out the servants to work by night and keep no cats as the saying goes, but what catch mice.[47]

The much-revered Lee brothers never rallied the populace with such language, however, and though capable, the South failed to sustain itself. Railroad owners refused to cooperate on routes and rates; speculators jacked up the prices until life inside refugee-bloated cities became nearly impossible; farmers hoarded grain to capitalize on the meteoric price rise or sold foodstuffs to the Yankees in occupied areas for ready cash. The congress and the government seemed oblivious of the suffering. "There is a sullen *deadness* here to the conditions of the country," a representative wrote in disgust from the Capitol chambers. As Lee suggested in the 1864 note to Davis that opens this chapter, if the government and people could have "corroborated" to compensate the farmers for desperately needed rations and find a way of quickly transporting them, it might have done much to alleviate several problems. Not everyone was indolent or greedy, of course, and many individuals gave an all-out effort for their cause. Yet the Confederate population never pulled together in the kind of total effort that would save Stalingrad, for example, eighty years later. Many believe that it was this lack of unity and will that led to their defeat.[48] "All of the patriotism is in the army, out of it the demon avarice rages supreme . . . ," cried a Richmonder. "Was it not thus in the trying times of the Revolution? If so, why can we not bear privation as well as our forefathers did? We must!"[49]

There are many reasons why they did not. One was their over-reaching self-confidence. Secessionists had started out with a great burst of enthusiasm and pride. "I am neither a prophet, nor the son of a prophet, yet I predict that in less than sixty days the flag of the Confederacy will be waving over the

White House," boasted one orator the day after Virginians voted to leave the Union.[50] "Subjugate or *bring* to *terms* such a people!" crowed one of the Tyler family, "little do you *dream* at the North of what stuff they are made."[51] After the rout at Manassas in July 1861, they believed it all would be short and splendid and, given their disdain of the Yankees, nearly effortless. Many sat back and awaited recognition by outside powers. As long as there were fine victories, they were easily able to compartmentalize the war effort as something that others would take care of. Only when the inadequacies of the government, reverses in the West, and a series of misguided conscription policies confused and demoralized the nation did Confederate morale begin to erode. After 1862 there was an uncomfortable realization that Confederate attempts to overturn British ambivalence had ended in an empty campaign, just like the Maryland invasion that was meant to solidify foreign support.[52]

The consolidation of power in Richmond was disconcerting as well. An act suspending habeas corpus and increasingly strict regulations on conscription gave Davis a disconcertingly consolidated authority. "Now the President is clothed with DICTATORICAL POWERS, to all intents and purposes, so far as the war is concerned," wrote one troubled Confederate.[53] It might have been fine had the government been able to use the increased powers to relieve both the army and the citizens from wartime excesses. But the effect was one of license without accountability. Horror stories of impressment—"a capital word," remarked a cabinet member, "& one covering a multitude of sins"—also undermined confidence in the Confederacy's integrity. Men and animals were driven off, "often taken from the plow, at work in the field," without the niceties of official permit. Lee too was infuriated with the inadequacy of the authorities in Richmond. "Well Mr. Custis, I have been up to see the Congress," he told his son in March 1865, as he prepared to evacuate his lines at Petersburg; "and they do not seem to be able to do anything except to eat peanuts and chew tobacco while my army is starving."[54] Added to this was the relentless burden of occupying armies—both Union and Confederate—which sapped resilience and precious resources. Exasperated at the constant forays of John S. Mosby's raiders throughout northern Virginia, one of Lee's cousins fumed: "if all the army are as self indulgent & inefficient as this part it is not to be wondered at the sad condition of the confederacy . . . the county is praying that Mosby's command may be removed & if it is not the people will have to leave here."[55] Then there was the faith that Providence or Fate or Luck or Lee would pull them through. And of course they hoped—"You know how we live on hope," Lee had written.[56] As things grew more desperate, every hour was just that darkest moment before daylight.

The loss of the protecting and providing male population also fed anxiety. Four out of five white men of military age spent some time in the Confederate service. Women and children who did not have steady help were often left destitute for want of labor, or vulnerable to Yankees or unscrupulous neighbors.[57] Worries about the enslaved population also fueled discontent. Key to the southern social model was the control of blacks, and with unprecedented numbers of white males away from the fields and factories, there were fears of insurrection or massive defections. In areas occupied by Union forces, particularly after the Emancipation Proclamation, a great many former slaves did run away, or were enticed to do so. Lee's cousin Hill Carter, for example, recorded in his daybook that virtually all of his prime male hands, some thirty-three in total, had run away.[58] The government tried to manage the issue by passing what became known as the "20 Nigger" law, a corollary to the conscription act that exempted any male who oversaw twenty blacks. Though perhaps a practical solution to a vexing complaint, it was widely regarded as favoring the upper classes, pointing up the contradictions in the South's supposedly egalitarian rebellion. The first real wave of desertion followed its passage.[59]

This was only one of the mis-starts that Confederate conscription policy underwent. An 1862 act to require duty for all men between the ages of eighteen and thirty-five was resented because it coerced men who preferred to believe that service was a noble personal act. Every loophole, from the enlightened exemption for men with key skills to the provisions for substitution, seemed to be equally offensive. Haphazard enforcement made things worse. Subsequent conscription laws were more stringent, and equally resented, causing the army to suffer an uneasy mix of proud volunteers and sullen draftees.[60] One Richmond man observed conscripts being conducted in chains through the city's streets in April 1864: "It made a chill shoot through my breast."[61] Even when the draft was expanded to include old men and foreigners, the manpower shortage was never eliminated. "We must have *more* men," wrote an aide to Longstreet as Grant's forces pressed their lines at Petersburg.[62] Lee concurred. "It is a matter of great moment that the recruits for this army should reach it in full time for the coming campaign," he told Davis in the wake of 1863's disappointing campaigns, "and whatever is to be done to bring them out should be done without delay."[63] From the outset he had been in favor of turning the entire nation into a fighting machine, with soldiers recruited for the duration and producers dedicated to its sustenance, and one of the first tasks he assigned Charles Marshall was to draft a proposal that, with some unfortunate alterations by the congress, became the basis for the first Confederate conscription act.[64] Since the size of his fighting forces was chief among Lee's concerns, so did his vexations center on desertions and draft evaders and waning public enthusiasm.[65] In his desperation for men, he ultimately advocated a blanket amnesty for deserters who returned to the army, a reversal of his earlier, strongly worded opinion, which called for the "rigid enforcement of the death penalty."[66]

The anxiety about manpower was starkly aired in late 1864 when a debate began on using slaves in the fighting forces. Blacks had always been part of the Confederate army, working in menial capacities. Officers like Lee had personal servants, and slaves were employed making bricks, driving wagons, and constructing fortifications. But arming black men, and expecting them to stand and defend individual whites and southern principles, was another matter. The Union army had gingerly begun forming black regiments by 1862, and one of the defining aspects of the Army of Northern Virginia was that it had stood in combat against these troops. The fierce reaction to this by the southern troops underscored the fundamental fear they had of armed blacks, fighting for their freedom. The most notable encounter was at the Crater in July 1864, when Federal forces blasted a huge hole in the rebel fortifications around Pe-

An African-American soldier in the Union army, drawn by Alfred Waud.
LIBRARY OF CONGRESS

tersburg. They initially overwhelmed the Southerners, but were themselves trapped in the bowl-shaped depression as Lee furiously ordered reinforcement of the defenses. African-American soldiers were predominant among the bluecoats, and as on other occasions when they came face-to-face with black troops, the Confederates murdered a good number rather than allow them to surrender.[67] Fighting against black men was greatly unsettling; fighting against brave and competent African-Americans challenged every underlying tenet of southern society. For many it sharpened the will to resist all that the Union was trying to impose on them. "A few of our men were wounded by the negroes, which exasperated them very much . . . ," admitted a Virginia artillerist who fought at the Crater. "It seems cruel to murder them in cold blood, but I think the men who did it had a very good cause for doing so. . . . I have always said that I wished the enemy would bring some negroes against this army. I am convinced since Saturday's fight, that it has a splendid effect on the men."[68]

The political debate about the use of slaves in the army heightened in late 1864, and ultimately filtered down into the army. Lee was behind this. He, like Davis, had sidestepped the issue when it was first raised by General Patrick Cleburne of the Army of Tennessee earlier in the year, and he had not changed his mind about his preference for keeping the blacks subjugated.[69] In his definitive letter on the subject, Lee reiterated his belief that the "relation of master and slave . . . is the best that can exist between the white and black races while intermingled as at present in this country. . . ." But he tempered this by saying that he could only be persuaded to relinquish the relationship "to avert a great calamity." He now had to think in raw survival terms. His chief concern was that the slaves would have small incentive to fight on his side. To countermand this, Lee believed they must be promised freedom.[70] After reluctantly embracing the idea, he persuaded Davis to float it among southern leaders, while he instituted a remarkable democratic discussion within his army.

It was an explosive issue that hit at the most fundamental assumptions of the South's rebellion. Within Lee's ranks there was dissension, and discomfort at the idea of soldiering in equal partnership with persons they had long considered inferior. Lee's wisdom in calling for a debate and vote deflected much of the tension, however. Most men reluctantly went along with the idea, in large measure because their general endorsed it, but also because they recognized the precariousness of their position. Virginian Silas Chandler decided that since "Gen Lee is in favor of it I shall cast my vote for it I am in favor of giving him any thing that he wants in the way of gaining our independence." A South Carolinian concurred with an interesting nuance, saying there was "some talk of our leading men putting negro troops in the field but I don't think that will doo well there is a great many men that would not fight aney more but I say aney thing before subjugation."[71] Those who did protest made clear their position. "I did not volunteer my services to fight for a free negroes country but to fight for A free white man's free country," wrote a North Carolina enlisted man, "and I do not think I love my country well enough to fight with black soldiers."[72] The discussion among politicians and editorial writers was equally heated, and in many ways articulated the South's defining motives and social conventions more candidly than ever before. Howell Cobb, a general who had been speaker and president pro tempore of the Provisional Confederate Congress in 1861–62, called the enlistment of black soldiers "the most pernicious idea that has been suggested since the war began." A fellow Georgian mused, "Whenever we establish the fact that they are a military race, we destroy our whole theory that they are unfit to be free." John Daniel, an editor for the *Richmond Examiner,* pointed out the illogic in offering freedom as a "reward" when the foundation of slavery's justification was that African-Americans were occupying the position that was "best" for their race.[73] Citizens were also concerned by the implications this had for their belief that God had ordained the peculiar institution and thereby exonerated them from guilt about slave-owning. They were quick to see a paradox in the idea of slaves fighting for a system that kept their brethren in bondage. Military considerations finally prevailed, however, with most accepting the cold logic that independence without slavery was better than suppression by the North.[74]

A limited form of black conscription was established in March 1865, but only a handful of African-American soldiers were ever mustered in. Reluctance on the part of both masters and slaves seems to have been the reason. This was the cause for Lee's emphatic letter to Richard Ewell on March 30, and his frantic efforts to expedite the augmentation of his troops, now seriously depleted by desertion. One of Lee's officers wrote to his wife that he was disgusted at farmers who "cheerfully give up their sons & brothers to go to death & when it is reached they seem to bear it with marvelous fortitude as the fate of war, but only suggest the necessity of taking a cuffee or two or some other property & what a storm is aroused."[75] Nonetheless, the bridge had been crossed. By opening the debate, Southerners had been forced to realign their understanding of what they were protecting and to recognize the contradictions in their carefully honed rationalization. Some would still staunchly defend it; others would adopt the ostrich's honored posture. But many understood only too well that they had already surrendered.

Robert E. Lee had read Machiavelli as a cadet at West Point, but he had never warmed to political manipulation. As he once reportedly told a Richmond politician, he thought the civil and military spheres distinct, and that he was not competent to make political pronouncements. "I shall endeavor to take care of the army," he told his interlocutor, "and you must make the laws and control the Government."[76] He was a battlefield warrior, not a bureaucratic infighter. He certainly never executed a brilliant maneuver in Richmond's marble corridors that would rival his shining victories on fields such as Chancellorsville. However, his overall strategy of circumventing the petty ambition that trapped most of his fellow generals, and consciously retaining the loyalty of his commander in chief, was sound, if not inspired. He retained his favor at court; whether he gained what he needed to survive in camp is a different question. Lee consistently claimed that his defeat was a political one—the gallantry of his men had been undermined by lack of resources, which only the government and populace could deliver. If this was truly the source of his failure, then his political strategy looks less successful. It was not his place to give rousing speeches to the citizenry and finesse delicate issues between the administration and congress, but he was never able to harness those whose job it was to work these critical support lines. His army became the most unifying symbol of national spirit to be found in Dixie, yet he shied away from using it to impress Southerners with the sacrifice needed to win their cause. If he must share the blame for the political inadequacies that characterized the Confederate nation, he also deserves sympathy for the near impossibility of meeting his needs under its haphazard structures. From the outset Lee had thought the South's outsize dreams nearly impossible to realize. At the same time, however, he had always felt some value in pursing those dreams, even if their completion was uncertain. The struggle, to Robert E. Lee, was as important as the victory. And that is one of the most telling facts of his generalship.

Chapter Twenty-three

Ragged Individualists

H^{d}qrs: 8 Aug '62

Good bye my dear Col: May every happiness & success attend you. I am glad that Genl Jackson will have the benefit of your presence, & yet regret your loss to the good Govr—I thank you sincerely for your advice—The latter part is good. I have regretted my inability to see more of the troops. I have never had time to be with them except at their duties—Their parades &c I have been unable to attend. I visit their camps & their lines &c but as I have had to keep them so constantly at use, so much has to be done, & so much is yet to be done, that I have felt I ought not to take them from it & engross their time with reviews &c for my gratification. You know how we live on hope. I have always hoped that a better time was coming.

Now I must give you some advice. Take care of yourself & I know that the great God above us will take care of you. To him I trust you & confidently rely upon his goodness in all that may occur. I pray that you may soon be returned to us, bringing in your footsteps the blessings of peace—Think sometimes of your friend: RE Lee

Col: S. Bassett French[1]

. . .

Camp Fred^g 21 May 1863

My dear Sir

I cordially thank you for the kind sentiments expressed in your note of the 9th Inst: & heartily unite in your commendation of this army. The country cannot overestimate its worth. There never were such men—in any army before, & there never can be better in any army again. If properly led they will go anywhere & never falter at the work before them. Since it has pleased Almighty

God to take from us the good & great Jackson, may he inspire our commanders with his unselfish devoted & intrepid spirit, & diffuse his indomitable energy through our ranks. Then indeed we shall be invincible & our country safe——

Wishing you every happiness & prosperity

I remain very truly yours

RE Lee

Honb^le Wm C. Rives
Castle Hill[2]

. . .

From the diary of Edward Richardson Crockett, 3rd Sergeant, Company F, 4th Texas Infantry

[May] The 6th [1864] ere the dawn of day we were again on the march. The Sun rose clear & bright. soon the sound of cannon in front admonished that the foe was near, our whole corps moved forward in quick time, in double column. rapidly we neared the battle-field, & louder & louder grew the din & roar of the conflict. soon we meet the retreating columns of A.P. Hill's corps followed by the elated hosts of Grant. a few minutes more & Hoods old Division was in line of battle. The Texas brigade & Hoods old brigade, in front, with Genl Lee close in rear & cheering them on to deeds of desperate daring. He said that Texans had always driven the foe. soon the command passed along the lines. forward, guide center: (the harbinger of Death) one minute more. The Texas brigade is moving to the charge Genl Lee following them closely. soon the balls are whizzing by us and our rifles in fierce defiance are belching forth storms of leaden hail on the hated foe. (now some one seizes the Genl Lee's bridle & says he must go no farther. he stops & to our great relief turns back.) we carry the yankee works & force them back some distance but our brigade is terribly cut up, our men have fallen 'Like the leaves of the forest when Autumn hath blown' in support on the right & left—with fresh & heavy lines hurled upon us we gradually give way, soon reinforcements pass us & the Yankees are driven still farther back. we fall back a short distance, reform, and go in again at another point, drive the yanks back once more. loose nearly all our men. are relieved & fight no more till late in the evening when we drive in a line of skirmishers. so ends our fighting for the day. The Slaughter of to-day is terrible. the day is ours though hundreds of our bravest & best are sleeping to wake no more on earth. The Sun goes down on a field of blood & all is quiet again, save the groans & piteous cries of mangled ones. Oh! that god would grant us victory & peace.[3]

>━┤━◆━┤━<

I N C IVIL W AR ANNALS General Robert E. Lee and his Army of Northern Virginia are nearly synonymous. Mutual trust cemented the bond between Lee and his "strange army of ragged individualists," forming it into one of the great unions of American history.⁴ "There never were such men," Lee tells Confederate congressman William Rives, with a simplicity that needs no icing. "If properly led they will go anywhere. . . ." Infantryman Edward Crockett proves the point, as he and his company heed Lee's cry to hold a fragile line in the Wilderness of Virginia, and are cut to ribbons in the process. Men and officers of this army became legends by sleeping in the snow, subsisting on parched corn, and staring down stupendous odds. Who inspired whom? In the end the question became irrelevant. By 1865 the true-hearts and their chieftain moved as with one motion. When there was no Confederacy left to defend, they fought for each other.

One day in autumn 1863, when hope was thin but not yet worn through, a group of Richmond grandees stood at a turnpike intersection and watched ten thousand soldiers file by. They were somewhat stunned, for their idea of fighting men was formed in the early days of the conflict, when bright eyes and gold braid flashed from every passing parade. Now they saw "rags and tags—nothing alike—most garments and arms taken from the enemy—such shoes! . . . Such tin pans and pots tied to their waists—bread or bacon stuck on the ends of their bayonets." One of the spectators uttered a wail on behalf of the brave boys; but they seemed oblivious, and continued their whooping laughter as they marched along. Only the men skulking behind the ladies caught their attention, and they taunted them with crude jeers about shirking and cowardice.⁵ For many these tough veterans still represent the greatest army that has ever fought on this continent. Who they were, and how they mocked deprivation and danger is a fascinating story.

The Army of Northern Virginia officially came together in late spring 1862 during a consolidation of Confederate military departments. Though the name had been used as early as January of that year, when Joseph E. Johnston was in command, its identification with Robert E. Lee would be lasting. When Johnston was wounded at the battle of Seven Pines, Davis quickly put Lee in charge of the veteran troops. The appointment was made on June 1, 1862, and despite the grumblings of Johnston and other contenders for the position, Lee did not relinquish it until his surrender at Appomattox.⁶

Over the course of four years, between 35,000 and 85,000 men fought at any one time for the Army of Northern Virginia. They were a diverse lot. The soil they defended was mainly in the Old Dominion, but they came from every state in the Confederacy.⁷ One study showed the soldiers' average age to be around twenty-two; about half were married. Only a minority owned slaves, though data on this is difficult to find and measure. Many were students, and there were also professional men, skilled laborers, and merchants. The majority hailed from farms or plantations, but the Army of Northern Virginia knew the whole range of southern landscapes, from bayous to green mountain valleys, from

Alfred Woodsworth Thompson's drawing, Irregular Troops of Virginia Riflemen, *gives a sense of the rough-and-ready quality of Lee's men.*
VIRGINIA HISTORICAL SOCIETY

Tidewater coast to Texas hills.[8] They laughed at the wide variation in regional speech patterns, and even in the beginning had no defining uniform. They were meant to be equipped by their states, but clothing for most was a matter of homegrown trial and error—or expediency. By the time they met Richmond's gentry at that crossroads, a large share of veterans sported Yankee uniforms, appropriated from captured commissary wagons or the dead. "I regret to state that in some instances our men stripped the dead bodies of the enemy stark naked," confessed an enlisted man in the 3rd Virginia Infantry regiment, "and in other instances dug up bodies of those that had been buried to get their clothes."[9] As the war progressed, Lee himself found clothing scarce and sent home for his old U.S. cavalry pants.[10] One observer recorded that the Confederate soldier had no ambition to look like a regular army man—"he looks the genuine rebel; but in spite of his bare feet, his ragged clothes, his old rug, and tooth-brush stuck like a rose in his button-hole, he has a sort of devil-may-care, reckless, self-confident look, which is decidedly taking."[11]

Their reasons for fighting were as varied as their uniforms. Money, which they thought motivated the North, was never an issue: a southern soldier earned eleven Confederate dollars a month—when he was paid. Few talked of "rights" of any sort, but many wrote of their fear of subjugation and the need to defend themselves against northern aggression. Others joined the army to be with their friends, to avoid shame in their community, or to taste adventure. Few admitted to being conscripts, though their numbers were large during the final phases of the conflict.[12] Honor and duty, and its relationship to their notions of manhood, were motivating factors as well, though these were flexible terms, whose meaning changed as the war progressed.[13] Protection of slavery was rarely mentioned overtly, though the language is powerful when it is. "I never want to see the day when a negro is put on an equality with a white person," a Louisiana artilleryman protested. "There is too many free niggers . . . now to suit me, let along having four millions."[14] The fighting men did often refer to their foes as "the Abolitionists," revealing how closely they connected the conflict with racial issues. "I am heartily sick of [the war]," admitted a captain in Lee's forces. "Yet am still willing to suffer any and every hardship rather than submit to the abolitionists who are now invading our soil. . . ."[15] Toward the end of the conflict slavery and subservience in the army's rigid structure, or possible submission to the hated Yankee, were nervously linked. Below the Stars and Bars on a Virginian's notepaper was a motto that spoke of their fear of bondage:

> Far better to perish with honor,
> Far better to go to the grave.
> And better to die as a freeman,
> Than to live as a Northerner's slave.[16]

Ultimately this potpourri of motives and anxieties came together in the simple desire to fight rather than submit, and the process of resistance became as important psychologically as its results. It was this that struck a visitor to General Lee's headquarters in 1864. While he noted the contrast between dirt farmers and highly educated aristocrats among his troops, what impressed him most was their unity of purpose: "there was but one feeling paramount with them—a settled & determined resolve not to lay down their arms until they were either killed in battle or . . . the Yankees have been driven from the soil."[17]

They prized individualism, they honed it and flaunted it, yet they became one of the most cohesive fighting units in history. A variety of factors helped form the Army of Northern Virginia's unique identity. The first was the association with Virginia itself. The Commonwealth was not only the most populous state in the Confederacy, it had the most developed industrial economy and was the site of the Confederate capital. In addition, it had a long history of fostering statesmanship and military genius, and leading the nation in political philosophy. There was a little grumbling about Virginians' lofty airs, or alienation from their home states, but most men were proud of the connection to this cradle of democracy. The proximity to Richmond and Washington also meant that there was an urgency in their actions, and corresponding attention paid to them in the Confederate White House and bureaucratic halls.[18] In addition, the army defined itself by its perceived differences from the enemy, whose culture and commitment they thought vastly inferior to their own. Though there were more thoughtful analyses, most viewed northern soldiers with contempt and loathing, convinced they were a cowardly, pampered club, largely intent on plunder, who lived in a world of brandy, preserved fruit, and whole shoes.[19] "Pope's men by all accounts are a dastard set," concluded one Virginian in 1862.[20] All this helped bolster the men's sense of righteousness and collective self-worth, as well as their courage under fire.

Battlefield experience was probably the most unifying of all factors in every rank. Lee's army had literally been born under fire and knew severe struggle in the first weeks of its existence during the Seven Days battles. That campaign had set the tone for what was to come, both in terms of action and appalling losses. What men saw on that field, and the terrors they would undergo in the next three years, linked them together with a chain of unutterable experience.[21] In the face of stupefying danger, bravery and stamina fostered company and regimental pride, but valor also transcended provincial interests to instill esprit in the army as a whole. As the full catalog of horrors was faced together, men became protective of themselves and one another, understanding instinctively that they were brothers in survival. Ghastly memories such as this one from 1864 bound comrades together in revulsion and endurance.

> I struck the Cold Harbour Road, traveling across the battlefield some weeks ago. As we neared the fortification what a horrible sight. Had to move ten or twelve bodies, hogs had routed them in to the road, the stench is so fearful, the horses will hardly pass. Their clothes were good, but some heads had rotted from the bodies and rolled down into the road. Had to open the road for the gun and caisson to pass through. Our finer feelings are blunted, we hear jokes over this awful scene.[22]

The war was not a set of idiosyncratic events but a shared experience, and it was this, as well as common ideals and cultural similarity, that made a devoted army.

In his first campaign with the army Lee made many tactical errors, suffering from his overly ambitious plans and the limitations of his generals. Nonetheless, the strategic success of the Seven Days battles associated the Army of Northern Virginia with victory in a way that never left them. For three more years his men admitted only to drawn battles, never defeat, and the heartiest among them got up from disaster and attacked anew. Viscount Wolseley, an English military officer who visited the ANVa headquarters on more than one occasion, observed that their early strategic triumph had bred a self-confidence that was "in fact, the twin brother of success."[23] If they were not invincible, the Army of Northern Virginia's soldiers *thought* they were. They had particular peaks of confidence in the spring of 1863 and just prior to the beginning of the Overland Campaign the following year, but in general it was a self-assured group that looked on tempests and was rarely shaken. As Virginian Micajah Woods mused, "there is something glorious in belonging to the army of Northern Virginia, whose pathway has only been strewn with victory, which has literally been achieved by the valor and prowess of its heroes in the deadly fray."[24]

Lee managed this huge assembly of men through echelons of officers, from corps commanders to company sergeants. No army, on either side, had a depth of experience equal to the enormous challenges of 1861–65, but the Army of Northern Virginia was richer than most in leadership ability. About two-fifths of the West Point men who joined the southern cause came from Virginia, and the Virginia Military Institute augmented that expertise. Militia officers were more uneven, but there were some excellent ones, and they had enough knowledge about tactics, discipline, and armaments to give confidence to their units. Taken altogether the Army of Northern Virginia had more organizational experience than its Confederate counterparts. Company officers were more of a problem. These men had day-to-day control of their units, and played the crucial role in actually leading the men into battle. One of the war's best commanders, William Tecumseh Sherman, acknowledged that good corporals, sergeants, lieutenants, and captains were "far more important than good generals."[25] The Confederate forces suffered from a system that allowed each company to elect these officers, frequently with a nod toward popularity instead of skill. In Lee's army this led to command confusion, and overturned the officer structure at crucial moments—in the Peninsula campaign, for example, some men actually voted in the trenches while in battle. Worse, it negated the possibility of promotion for valor. Lee thought the line officers should all come from the gentry; it pained him "to see young men like [Beverley Tucker], of education & standing from all the old & respected families in the state serving in the ranks." He hated the electoral system, but never convinced Richmond to change it.[26] Giving the men a choice over their company commanders at least assured their willing compliance, for the men were apt to resent those who exercised direct power over them, and did not always recognize supervision they thought unworthy. Often they complained that they were treated like the slaves they disdained. One soldier declared that "when such upstarts get authority as we have among us, I feel no inclination to place my carcass at their disposal and shall be apt to look before I leap next time."[27]

Lee administered this and myriad other operational complexities with a stripped-down personal staff and mobile headquarters. Within days of beginning his service in 1861, he made it clear that his staff would be small and professional.[28] He did not like favoritism, and turned away nephews who hoped to accompany him, as well as his son Rob.[29] Nonetheless, the personal staff he created was a cozy Virginia clique. For most of Lee's three years with the Army of Northern Virginia it consisted of Assistant Adjutant General Walter H. Taylor; a military secretary—first Armistead L. Long, then Charles Marshall; and several aides-de-camp, notably Charles Venable and engineer T. M. R. Talcott, the son of his old boss Andrew Talcott.[30] Together they accomplished a wide array of tasks, which included writing reports, processing dispatches, interrogating prisoners, setting up camp, and protecting their general from unwelcome visitors. Lee has been criticized for underdeveloping his staff, and indeed he never gave it priority. His austere headquarters has been held responsible for poor communications among the branches of his army and ineffectual supply from the quartermaster department. Some have gone so far as to blame the confusion over official orders at battles such as Seven Days and Gettysburg on the inadequacy of staff work.[31] Lee's desire for a streamlined headquarters probably stemmed from his personal inclination toward solitude, as well as his experience with Scott in Mexico, who had agilely handled a massive army with a handful of aides. Lee was less disposed than Scott to bellow or buck the bureaucracy when nicely appointed staff work failed, however, and as a result, many of his intentions were not fully carried out. His administration was better in 1865 than it had been three years earlier, but overall it failed to support his strategy as robustly as it should have.[32]

The staff was overworked and huddled two or three in a tent, in camps that were devoid of either comfort or military trapping. "The Chief," as his aides dubbed him, generally refused to make headquarters in a nearby house, even when the occupants insisted that the honor would be theirs. Once when the camp was located on a bare prominence facing a cutting northern wind, Lee declined to let the staff stay in comfortable quarters that had been offered. "*We* knew he would," remarked Taylor, seeing it as proof of his earlier assessment that Lee was "never so uncomfortable as when comfortable."[33] In addition to overwork and bleak surroundings, the staff suffered Lee's difficult temperament, with some audible sighs. He was quick to censure and slow to praise or recommend his team for promotion, causing several aides to cast around for better opportunities. Lee's indifference to staff recognition was not quite as pronounced as they maintained, but their feeling of undervaluation is revealing.[34] He also still had difficulty in accepting personal blame and sometimes rebuked aides for his own shortcomings. Once, when Lee lost control during an interview, he berated Venable: "Why did you permit that man to come to my tent and make me show my temper?"[35] After quarreling with his subordinates he sulked and snubbed them for days, and, unable to apologize, finally tried to make amends by offering a glass of buttermilk or a peach.[36]

An uninitiated staff member found that everyone around the general was afraid of him, and though the newcomer had known Lee socially before the war, he soon felt the same way. Some of it was Lee's unpredictable temper, the fear of seeing "the flush . . . over that grand forehead and the temple veins swell"; but it was also the way Lee constantly tested the men against his impossible standards and ridiculed them on sensitive points, joking not with them, but at their expense.[37] Lee may have been trying out his old army banter on the boys, but verbal jousting between second lieutenants is not the same as a general's mocking tease. Lee knew this instinctively: "The young men have no fondness for the society of the old Genl," he told his wife; and he admitted to Agnes that he was "so cross now that I am not worth seeing anywhere."[38] A good deal of this irascibility was simply the pressure and proximity of camp, especially the winter following the disappointment at Gettysburg. This the staff understood, and most left Lee's service with lasting respect, if not affection.[39] Yet somehow he could not keep his scolding or his sarcasm in check, and it caused the disaffection of some of those he relied on most. "The Grand Tycoon," Taylor styled him, "the cruel old Chief." Venable threatened to leave the staff because he and Lee were too high-tempered to tolerate each other. When Taylor asked Lee for a furlough to get married and was treated to a cutting joke, Taylor cautioned: "He cannot, must not deny me this. It will impair my usefulness if he does. . . ."[40]

Some of the austerity of Lee's camp life stemmed from his desire to share hardship with the men, and to eschew any trappings that might create distance between the ranks. In October 1861, Lee was already writing that his troops "barely get bread from day to day," and the situation would steadily worsen.[41] By 1863, Lee found the insufficient clothing and forage to be more than a discomfort—it was an obstacle to military success. He could not pursue Meade's army in the Bristoe campaign in October 1863, he claimed, because "thousands were *barefooted*, thousands with fragments of shoes, & all without overcoats, blankets or warm clothing—I could not bear to expose them to certain suffering, or an uncertain issue—"[42] One of these men wrote to his wife that the boys had "got pretty hungry and eat acorns like rip. . . . Cout, I hope you may never feel the keen aching, raving pangs of hunger."[43] A Virginia artilleryman in the Shenandoah Valley in 1864 jotted these entries in his diary for the week of August 17, 1864:

> August 17, 1864: My horses literally starved.
> August 20, 1864: My horse could no longer be ridden to do any good.
> August 24, 1864: We then went on to Winchester. . . . Here we expected to get rations, but there were none to be had. There was no chance to get anything to eat in the country.[44]

From Petersburg a few months later a foot soldier asked his wife to send soap since the ration was one teaspoonful every two weeks, and "There is some men out hear that has not had on a clean Shirt sense the first of August last. . . ." The bread ration was not much better: "we get Corn Bread now in place of wheat Bread it is Baked in town and it looks like a pile of cow dung Baked in the sun I could knock down a cow with apone of it."[45] Writing home, cavalryman Robert E. Lee Jr. referred to himself as "your poor ragged hungry brother who sits disconsolate in the wilderness. . . ."[46]

The splendid descriptive quality of these letters gives us an insider's understanding of the deprivation suffered by the Army of Northern Virginia. Lee was far more comfortable than his tattered soldiers, of course—he was sent turkeys and venison, and "box after box" of pound cake, jellies, sweet potatoes, and other precious vegetables.[47] He neither sought nor solicited these luxuries, and was all too aware of the want among his men. "We are enjoying ice water in abundance," Lee feebly joked in January 1865, "our neighbors also possess the same luxury." When his thoughts turned to the meanly clad men, his words were more sober: "Up to our knees in mud & what is worse on short rations for men & beasts. This keeps me miserable. I am willing to starve myself, but cannot bear my men or horse to be pinched."[48] Many have analyzed the reasons for the inadequate supply in the

Confederate army, since for most of the war there should have been food and fodder to spare. "Horses starving in the midst of cornfields ready for gathering, Alas, what mismanagement," exclaimed a Confederate War Department clerk after he had received a notice that Lee's cavalry was expiring for want of forage.[49] Lack of initiative among the farming population, the poor distribution system, the greed of scalpers and speculators, and Lee's ineffectual requests to Jefferson Davis have all been blamed.[50] Whatever the reason, in the face of want those modest tents pitched on an uncomfortable prominence were reassuring.

Lee did not succeed in keeping his men supplied, but he did fight against preference and privilege in the distribution of rations. When some of his subordinates, including Longstreet and his artillery chief E. Porter Alexander, petitioned Lee to allow officers a larger ration than the enlisted men, Lee disapproved the request. "I do not think it would be advantageous to issue one ration to the soldier & another to the officer, nor would it conform to the regulations of the law," he wrote, and he convinced Richmond of the same.[51] He knew in the prickly subservience of army hierarchy the enlisted men resented those who lived well and stayed well away from bullets too, and he fought partiality, not only on positions and rations, but for furloughs and family visits. An officer in the "bombproof" quartermaster's department told his wife that his chances for a furlough were slim since "Genl Lee thinks . . . that men in the ranks who are subjected to all the dangers and hardships of the service should have greater indulgence than others."[52] Lee told his son Rooney that if his wife were to appear in camp, "she must talk quick to you . . . the soldiers complain of officers wives visiting them & theirs cannot."[53] Through it all, Lee expressed pride in the uncomplaining fortitude of men who lived without blankets and shoes and stifled their grumbles when rations were cut to the bone. "I will trust R.E. Lee to provide for all such," declared a Virginian who had just returned after a detail with the Army of Tennessee, "for when [I] was under him before we was well card for in every respect. And I am glad we are under him agane."[54]

Lee was sincerely concerned about his men, but his exertions were also a curb against the lax discipline that plagued his army. Desertion, straggling, and plunder against their own countrymen were all conspicuous problems, described in detail by privates as well as generals. A dedicated foot soldier wrote in disgust of some comrades at Chancellorsville who "acted very bad . . . they fell to the rear and plundered while the battle was going on."[55] Jubal Early's artillery chief placed the responsibility for 1864 failures in the Shenandoah Valley on an army that had "dwindled down to a mere handful by straggling & they run at the sound of their horses hoofs."[56] Alarmed at the numbers dropping from the ranks, particularly during and after the Maryland campaign, Lee tried to check the flow by placing sharpshooters at the rear of the columns "with orders to shoot every one who fell to the rear, unless wounded." The designated shooters were reluctant to target their own comrades, however, and the plan did not fix the problem.[57] Lee complained to Richmond of the increasing numbers of deserters in every year of his command, stating that he could not advance as he hoped because his army was drifting away, and begging for policies that would induce men to stay in the army.[58] Part of the difficulty in controlling desertion was that it was a highly personal decision, made for a wide variety of reasons. Men lost heart from insufficient rations, the relentless marches, and terrifying battles. Others heard of the fear or poverty of their homefolks and chose to protect them in person. "We are so tired of this war," wrote an artillery officer during the still heady days of 1862, "nothing but blood blood & absence from . . . all that is precious to us," and in nearly the same breath complained that twenty-five men had disappeared from the last two companies he had trained.[59] Toward the end, desertion reflected a lack of confidence in the outcome of the conflict and became for some a political statement. By then the numbers of deserting men was crippling the army. A brigade commander reported to Lee in 1865 that he had only 70 men in one regiment—"eight went off last night led by an officer"—and in the brigade as a whole 1,157 enlisted men were absent without leave.[60] In Richmond, cynics noted that Lee's army was "melting like a Scotch mist."[61]

Pillaging was the other chronic temptation for the underfed soldiers. After the war there was a conspiracy of silence about Confederate looting, but the evidence of it is abundant. One of Lee's brigadiers called the army "little better than an armed mobb," then continued, "the wanton destruction of private property by our army is a shame & a reproach, when our army marches & camps desolation follows."[62] Lee's relatives at Kinloch were repeatedly harassed by Ranger Mosby's men, who not only "impressed" food from the local population but incited the nearby Federal troops to further destruction.[63] An open-eyed Confederate wrote his wife that "you will be pesterde by our own soldiers . . . stealing your chickens, etc. I had almost as leave have Yanks around my hous as our own men, except they will not insult ladies."[64] On Christmas day 1863 Governor Zebulon Vance of North Carolina complained to Richmond that the outrages perpetrated by some cavalrymen were "worse than any of the plagues of Egypt" and that if no remedy was found he would "collect his militia and levy war against the Confederate States troops."[65] Lee was well aware of all of this. He teased John

Bell Hood that the "chickens have to roost mighty high" when his Texans came around; and despite his order not to pillage en route to Gettysburg, a South Carolinian described how Lee looked on as a shrieking woman saw the family gobbler appropriated: "Thus you see that even our Commander-in-Chief sanctioned their marauding expeditions."[66] His own table was evidently also served in this manner. When Mosby dined with the general a few months before the surrender, he reportedly found the fare sparse, except for a nice leg of mutton, which, Lee remarked without humor, "some of his staff-members must have stolen."[67]

Lee wanted badly to contain all of these delinquencies, not only because they offended his sensibilities but because they exhausted his army and undermined its morale. From the desktop perspective of 1862 Richmond he had thought the Confederate army should be able to control both friendly and enemy pillaging, but when he took field command he found out just how hard this was.[68] He tried several methods, all without success. He penned admirable orders calling the troops to restraint and invoking their pride. He was not given to making speeches, and the orders were the most vital way Lee had to communicate with men who only infrequently spoke with him. The writing is intriguingly similar to the letters he had sent to his distant children, by turns heartening, affectionate, or instructive. "Stragglers are those usually who desert their comrades in perril such characters are better absent from the army on such momentous occasions as those about to be entered upon," was the message on the road to Sharpsburg, when desertion threatened to undermine the army.[69] After that shockingly expensive draw, he sent out General Orders No. 116, a heroic commendation of the army's bravery under fire, and a not entirely accurate ode to the nobility of retreat. "Achievements such as these, demanded much valor and patriotism," Lee concluded, shrewdly bolstering his forces at a moment of uncomfortable doubt.[70] When his army was nearly starving in the winter of 1864, he distributed an inspirational order that recalled the sacrifice of patriots during the American Revolution and recommended the spiritual nourishment of high resolve. A surgeon told his wife that though the men had been desperate for full rations, "since that beautiful order of Genl. Lee's they do not mourn & will endure anything for the cause."[71]

Lee also requested that Richmond supply better rations, change conscription policies or give amnesty to past deserters and start anew. He experimented with a furlough procedure that allowed enlisted men leave for exceptional service, and another that granted a thirty-day furlough for bringing in a new recruit.[72] None did more than modestly stem the tide. The lack of an established regular army, poor training, individualism, and incompetent or indifferent subordinate officers—all worked against rigorous order in the army. In military tradition it was discipline itself that created morale, and in its absence Lee had to fall back on other methods of keeping the fighting spirit aloft.[73] He was disinclined to be too tough on the common soldier; it pained him in the face of their obvious sacrifice and denied the benevolent persona he carefully crafted. The description of a visit Lee made to a guardhouse near Savannah in 1862, though undoubtedly embellished by a postwar pen, is consistent with his commonsense approach to the hardship of camp life. When a veteran, jailed for absence without leave, revealed he had slipped out at night and swum fifteen miles to see his dying wife, finally returning to camp, Lee held up his hand. "Turn him out, Corporal," he said, "turn him out, and send him back to his command; he will do better service there."[74]

The enlisted men heard of such actions through the long tentacles of the army grapevine and believed Lee to be fair as well as caring. "No matter what it is if Genl. Lee says do it it is all right," wrote a Virginia infantryman. "The commonest private can always have justice done him . . . he always gives them a fair hearing."[75] Other gestures also fueled their respect and love. They believed he kept his headquarters open to them, and enough privates told tales of being received graciously by the general that it became part of their inspirational folklore. One enlisted man who arrived hot and dusty to deliver a message at headquarters described how Lee personally offered him a cup of cool water; another was shown a chair with the deference due an honored guest.[76] Like the sagas of Lee's hardtack dinners, facts were not entirely consistent with cherished myth. (Walter Taylor spent much of his day deflecting visitors great and small from Lee's tent.) But it mattered not if the stories were half-truths or, in some cases, near parables. The understanding was that Lee was accessible, and there was enough reality in the perception to give it genuine value. Far removed from day-to-day interaction with a gruffer and more harassed Lee, the soldiers could safely idealize him. And this part was certainly right: Lee, who genuinely respected his men, cultivated a manner of speaking with them that recognized the dignity of each individual. He seems never to have talked down to them, never showed the arrogance of position or appeared to hurriedly pass them off to his staff. One wise Virginian told a newly minted captain that he should never shun even the roughest soldier. "Treat them kindly and respectfully without exception. . . . Kind words will unman the best of them and make them your servants forever."[77] Lee either innately understood, or observed well, that for the hierarchically minded Confederate soldier, gentlemanly gestures instilled respect.

It was pure southern paternalism, of course, its classist tone barely covered by a dulcet accent. Lee would use this traditional combination of sympathetic expression and authority to great advantage. Far from feeling any manipulation, his army was convinced that he gave them the careful protection and guidance of a father and frequently spoke of him in paternal terms. "Our father, Lee, was scarcely ever out of sight when there was danger," a Louisianian jotted in his journal on the retreat from Gettysburg. "We could not feel gloomy when we saw his old gray head uncovered as he would pass us on the march." Another soldier wrote home before the battle of the Wilderness about the pride Lee showed his army, calling them "his children, his pets."[78] Lee deftly reassured his men with language and actions that were parental. Join a nervous lieutenant as he enters a tent where the general, ill and in bed, is awaiting news of impending action. "I thought I heard firing," remarked Lee, "but I was waiting for some one to come and tell me, and you are a good boy for telling me."[79] The trademark white hair and beard seemed also to comfort all who met him, civilians and soldiers alike. His appearance, though impressive, was now eroded by care, and it gave him a soothing demeanor that softened the formidable magnificence of his person. In 1861, when the jutting chin was clean-shaven and he still sported a bristling black moustache, an awed private thought he had "the sternest expression of countenance I ever saw."[80] Two years later another Virginian would write: "Dear old General! How I've always admired and loved him, but what a filial reverence mingles with that feeling now and how much more the father than the general he seems. How his hair is silvered and his brow marked with thought and care, yet what a noble, benevolent spirit looks forth from his brown eyes."[81] His men called him "Old Pap" and "Uncle Bob," expressing the same unquestioning trust that a child feels for his parents. One soldier facing Grant's legions left these unpolished but heartfelt words: "we are not a frade of the yankes while we have old Generel Lee to lead us in the fites."[82]

The nature of leadership is a mystery, a fascinating compound of talent and mystique that makes a body of people want to follow the direction of a specific individual. Leadership is not a single quality, or even a single style. Some lead by oratory, expounding ideals through inspirational rhetoric; others by patient, workmanlike translation of those ideals into solid governance. Patrick Henry and James Madison come to mind here; both worked brilliantly to create a functional new nation, yet their contributions differed greatly. Leadership qualities that work in one situation can be also counterproductive in another. Light-Horse Harry Lee is the classic example of a daring battlefield warrior who found brinksmanship to be foolhardy in peacetime. Nor is leadership always inherently obvious. Before the Civil War, Robert E. Lee's mixture of traits had caused him to be almost instantly *recognized* as a leader, yet he was not always tapped for leading roles. Sometimes he had trouble exercising authority, as at West Point, and in the delicate situation with his father-in-law's slaves. At other times, as at the capture of John Brown, he showed a near-perfect instinct for command. His leadership of the Army of Northern Virginia was an amalgam of intuition and experience, and to a very large degree the product of a remarkable power of personal projection.[83]

Lee's soldiers loved him for characteristics they could observe: the way he gave orders "calm as a summer cloud"; his concern for their welfare; his seeming lack of interest in personal advantage; and the fact that he consistently guided them into victory or out of trouble. Others were grateful that in a crisis he dispelled rather than caused alarm. An artillery officer recounted an incident when Lee was absent, and Generals Chilton and Jackson overreacted to a scare, which proved to be "all bosh." Lee "is never stampeded," the man wrote in comparison, "& when he draws up a line of battle there is a fight on hand."[84] The quality that appears to have most profoundly affected the Army of Northern Virginia, however, was Lee's majestic presence. Only a few in his dedicated army actually knew him, and most rarely saw him.[85] When they did, it never failed to make an impression. Admiration for his fine physique and noble bearing is nearly ubiquitous whenever Lee is mentioned, be it in victory or defeat. The simple eloquence of Georgian colonel James Cooper Nisbet spoke for hundreds who tried to capture the spellbinding force of Lee's persona: "The manly grandeur of his appearance is beyond my powers of portraiture. He is ineffaceable."[86] Like leadership itself, this ability to project an imposing aura is both unmistakable and subtle, more easily recognized than defined. Lee looked like a great man, and the obvious corollary was that he *was* a great man. The Army of Northern Virginia had good reasons to trust and admire Lee, but they largely followed him by instinct, recognizing something compelling in his commanding presence. Today it is still that inspiring, formidable, used and abused *image* that most powerfully forms our collective perception of Lee.

One of the hallmarks of such charisma is that it really cannot be effectively learned; it is innate rather than studied. Nevertheless Lee was increasingly aware of the effect his appearance had on men living on the edge of deprivation. Lee had little time for mingling, but he took Colonel Bassett French's point about creating an effective command personality. He cultivated the unpretentious style that overrode fears of the "awful presence of the commander-in-chief," which could intimidate even the daring Mosby.[87]

At the same time Lee took some trouble to stand before his men in martial splendor. He reportedly told General Grant at Appomattox that he always wore his sword—the symbol of his authority—whenever he moved among the troops.[88] He attended frequent parades and reviews, with great displays of music and regimental colors, and spirits soared as high as the banners. Many recalled him on these days, a figure of easy elegance, yet full of force and fire. A Virginian emotively told his wife of one splendid review, held near Orange Court House in September 1863:

> Gen. Lee, attended by Lieut. Gen. Hill and their aids, also each Maj. Gen. as they came to their Divisions, rode in front and rear of each line in a spirited gallop. Gen. Lee is the best rider I ever saw. He was mounted on a fine gray horse. I cannot look at him with his gray hair and beard only with feelings of awe and almost devotion. The General then took their position on an elevated place and we all passed them in columns of companies. . . . We had excellent music and all passed off finely.[89]

As victory stopped being a certainty, such rallies became vital for raising morale and reinforcing commitment among the ragged men. When Lee appeared, for a grand moment the war was not about lice and gore and half-baked bread; it symbolized something larger than themselves; something they dreamed of, but could not articulate.

Reverence for Lee increased after the death of Jackson, for "Old Stonewall" had also stirred the soldiers mightily. Many had given Jackson the edge in field direction, praising his technique, timing, doggedness, and ability to court luck. A favorite campfire sport was to compare the two leaders. Despite his quirky, inscrutable personality, which did not invite familiarity, the men admired Jackson's implacable determination in a fight and nearly blind belief in their abilities. A good number sensed he inspired more enthusiasm than did Lee. One of his men admitted that Stonewall looked like "an old fox hunter but I tell you he knows how to hunt yanks his men almost worship him. . . ."[90] On reflection some soldiers thought that Jackson, for all his exceptional skill as corps commander, did not have the stuff to be a general in chief, and gave Lee the leafier palm. Others thought the two generals' skills to be complementary. An aide from the quartermaster's corps weighed their strengths in a letter to his sister: "Yes, you all who have had Stonewall with you awhile give him the credit for all of the Victories but never think of the Planning of the glorious RE Lee. . . . I admit that Stonewall is a splendid fighter but he cant plan like Lee, and I expect Lee can

plan better than he can fight but take the two together Genl Lee is far superior." A cannoneer in Jackson's corps compared the generals by saying one
was "the expression of military strength and dignity and power; the other of
military sagacity and genius."[91] Perhaps most telling was the way each general was saluted. When Jackson passed, the men wildly huzzahed, cheering
themselves and their odds-off successes as much as the general. When Lee
rode by, wrote one of his men, "the boys never cheer him, but pull of their
hats and worship."[92]

In the aftermath of Gettysburg, Lee's leadership became less remote, his role
at times resembling that of a regimental commander. By fall 1863 the Army
of Northern Virginia was anxious to recoup both its reputation and its momentum. But the campaigns of that season showed Meade to be more elusive and skillful than Lee had anticipated. In October, at Bristoe Station, two
cleverly entrenched Union corps mauled two of A. P. Hill's brigades, capturing a battery of artillery. Three weeks later at Rappahannock Station and
Kelly's Ford, the Federal troops sneaked over the river, taking 1,200 of Jubal
Early's men and several more precious guns in the process. The mistakes
had been almost painfully simple: advancing without good intelligence; too
much eagerness to be aggressive. Lee's fall campaign had failed, and, as a
perceptive southern officer observed, worse than the army's matériel damage was the "lost prestige & confidence in its leaders." No one was comfortable blaming Lee, but army chatter exonerated the brigadiers, who were
only following orders, and ultimately the responsibility lay with the chief
and his chosen lieutenants.[93] Stung, Lee planned to attack Meade on the
night of December 1, paying personal attention to the works and the line,
"directing important changes here & there, endeavoring to impress the officers with the importance of success in the impending engagement and presenting a fine example of untiring energy and zest." After a day or two of
inconclusive skirmishing, however, Meade wisely determined that the rebels
were too strong to oppose and slipped away in the night, much to Lee's chagrin. "I am too old to command this army," he told his staff; "we should
never have permitted those people to get away."[94]

    In this mood the Army of Northern Virginia faced the campaigns of
1864. The men felt far from defeated: "Lee's Army has never in a Single in-
stanse been *whiped* . . . & it is still invincible," declared a Georgian.[95] Spirits
were buoyant and everyone was itching for a fight, the general included. Recovering from one of his rheumatic, possibly heart-related illnesses, he told
his adjutant that "we have got to whip them, we must whip them, and it has
already made me better to think of it."[96] Ominously, such bold pronounce-

ments came simultaneously with the admission that his forces were less than he hoped and he had neither the cavalry nor the artillery to drive the Federals from the Rappahannock.[97] Lee knew that Ulysses S. Grant had been made general in chief of the Union forces, but he did not know him personally, and appears to have underestimated both Grant's willpower and the size of his resources. Supposing that the Federal army was impaired by the close of their three-year enlistment terms, Lee publicly told associates that he hoped to wipe out the army on their next encounter.[98] Grant himself was derided: "He has been much over-rated," stated Walter Taylor, "and in my opinion I am sorry to say, owes more of his reputation to Genl [John] Pemberton's bad management than to his own sagacity & ability. He will find, I trust, that General Lee is a very different man . . ."[99] Grant did some undervaluing himself, believing Lee's army was close to desperation. He and Union general in chief Henry Halleck made a confident plan to "stop cutting the toenails of our enemy instead of grasping his throat."[100]

What ensued was the Overland Campaign—some seven weeks of relentless, brutal fighting unlike battles seen previously in any theater. It was characterized by horrific and costly skirmishes, in which both sides claimed victory but clear-cut advantage was difficult to gauge; extensive use of entrenchments, as the forces tried to minimize their vulnerability to massed attack; and hand-to-hand fighting of a viciousness unequaled in the war. A Union officer described it as "a raging storm of lead and iron," and some of its most dramatic moments have become synonymous with the horror of combat. The opening days in the Wilderness found men grappling with each other in the dense, impenetrable scrublands, and when night fell, ammunition set fire to the underbrush and the wounded lay screaming as they were burned alive. A week later at Spotsylvania the armies fought with wild frenzy along a Confederate breastworks called the Mule Shoe, men jumping on top of the parapets and shooting or throwing rifles with bayonets affixed into the trenches until they themselves fell. It had rained nonstop for days, guns and ammunition were ruined, and the earthworks became a slimy mass of mud, blood, and human debris, the dead smothering the wounded, the blue and gray coats hideously tangled together. Some saw individual acts of heroism in the battle; others viewed the fight with numbing disbelief. In yet another cameo of warfare-most-terrible, in early June Grant flung his troops against a zigzag line of Confederate defenses at Cold Harbor, losing 7,000 men in a few hours—another fruitless frontal attack that was likened to murder. This was grinding, ceaseless combat, fundamentally different from the occasional set-piece battles, followed by a respite, of the previous year. Citizens North and South looked on with dismay at the incredible list

of casualties: 44,000 Federals and 25,000 Confederates lost among the lau-
rel blossoms of Virginia's woods. It was beyond all precedent.[101]

For Lee and Grant it became a contest in anticipation and maneuver, as
each tried to check the movements of the other. Neither had yet faced an enemy of such skill and ferocity, and each was forced to learn his opponent on

"Wounded escaping from the burning woods of the Wilderness," by Alfred Waud.
LIBRARY OF CONGRESS

the march. When the Army of Northern Virginia pushed back Grant, Lee assumed that the Federal army would follow its old pattern of withdrawing after a rebuff. Instead they pressed forward, thrilled to continue the offensive.
Grant vastly undervalued the resilience and determination of the Confederates, and the easy roll-up he had foreseen turned into a prolonged, frustrating campaign. "I propose to fight it out on this line if it takes all summer," he
famously remarked, but after Cold Harbor he admitted to his wife that "this
is likely to prove a very tedious job."[102] There was much miscalculation on
both sides; and luck, or unintentional blunders, saved each army as frequently as did prescience. Grant's plan was to hold Lee—if he could not be
defeated outright—so that Sherman could subdue the southeastern states
and move through the Carolinas to link with the Army of the Potomac. Instead of chasing Lee, Grant decided to flank and outmarch him, beating him
twice across crucial rivers and shrewdly bypassing a direct attack on Richmond in favor of cutting key communications at Petersburg to the south. It
was an inspired strategic plan, executed with innovation and tenacity. It

changed the dynamic of the conflict, taking the initiative from Lee, forcing him to react to Grant's relentless push forward. Nonetheless Grant found it far harder going than he anticipated. Lee's agility at responding to untenable situations, often turning disaster to his own advantage, kept his army and the Confederacy together, though he watched with exasperation as Grant inched his way south and bottled up the rebel forces in trenches before Petersburg. Commissary officer Thomas Claybrook Elder gave a revealing account of the point/counterpoint of the two generals as they faced off at that city during nine long months. "[Grant] moves a heavy body of troops to the north side of James river and pretends that he is going to advance on Richmond from that direction: Genl Lee is obliged to move a force over there too: because if Grant should find the way imperfectly guarded he would actually dart into Richmond. This being done, Grant casts his eye around Petersburg and finding a weak point, he assaults it and takes [it]; and Genl Lee cannot afford to lose the number of men it would require to recapture the lost position."[103] But Lee, convinced that "we must strike them a blow—we must never let them pass us again—we must strike them a blow!" was biding his time, still waiting for the right moment to attack.[104] Equally stubborn, Grant insisted, "I will work this thing all right yet." Then he paid a tribute to the Army of Northern Virginia. "To lose this battle they lose their cause. As bad as it is they have fought for it with a gallantry worthy of a better."[105]

Why did that skeletal army fight with such valor? It is one of the classic questions of the war, for the clashes were so protracted and bestial that many of the men were stunned from shock and exhaustion. "Never has such fighting been known before," a Georgian told his wife. "They have locked bayonets time and again and fought with the buts of their guns."[106] A company officer from the 4th Texas Infantry noted in his diary in early June that "we have quit sleeping almost entirely."[107] Abandoning his usual understatement, Lee admitted that Grant had been repulsed "with great slaughter."[108] Part of the reason for the high Confederate morale was the conviction that they were winning. Many of the clashes of this campaign were inconclusive, assessed in casualty figures or by which side left the field first.[109] When the Federals withdrew, the southern side viewed it as retreat, not always knowing or understanding that the bluecoats were moving forward—southward—not creeping back to their Washington defenses. On the same day Grant informed his wife that the "enemy were really whipped yesterday," a rangy Texan shouted with jubilation: "Thousand upon Thousands of yankee slain cover the battlefields. We have resisted Grant for eight days with great success. hurrah! Hurrah! For the Southern Confederacy."[110] In October 1864, despite the enervation and choking dust of the trenches, and disgust at eating bacon "that outranks Gen. Lee," huge numbers of the army were sanguine of eventual victory and convinced that the war was still being fought on their terms.[111]

Grant thought this élan was fueled by the desperation of their situation: they *had* to win, else all would be lost. Much of the stamina and fighting spirit, however, was injected by Lee personally. He was more present and available during these months than any other time of the war, and the confidence between him and his men was a striking feature of the 1864 campaigns. Lee had worked among his troops before, energizing them as they irritably dug fortifications before the Seven Days battles; vainly seeking to rally infantrymen who "ran like hounds" when his center broke at Sharpsburg; directing a small detached force at Chancellorsville while Jackson executed his beautiful flanking maneuver.[112] In 1864 he was almost forced to take a more active field role, for Longstreet was wounded at the Wilderness, Ewell buckled under the pressure, and A. P. Hill seemed unable to inspire his men to daring. None of these commanders had pleased Lee at Gettysburg, where he had stayed a safe distance from danger, and, as if to belatedly fill that gap, he now placed himself in it. The stakes were very high from the Wilderness to Petersburg, and Lee personalized the contest, exerting his forceful character to its maximum extent, taking each victory or setback with open emotion. He was thrown into a fury when A. P. Hill failed to hold back Grant at the North Anna River; he lost his temper again when Grant outmaneuvered him at the James; he personally ran after stragglers and skulkers, once berating a man in the rear whose head wound was hidden under his cap—and was pitifully unable, as always, to apologize afterward. He was often seen riding alone along the breastworks, saluting and animating the soldiers.[113] The most famous instance of Lee's motivating force is the one Texan Edward Crockett recorded when the general rode among A. P. Hill's routed men, personally attempting to lead a charge. "Go back, Genl. Lee, go back!" the boys shouted, and then moved on to win the assault. On other occasions the troops remembered how he looked "with the light of battle on his face," or when he simply reassured them by his mere presence. At the Mule Shoe, Lee exposed himself to the booming cannon, fixing his image indelibly on the mind of a Virginia artilleryman. "Old Mas' Bob rode out of the smoke on Traveller, amid the loud shouts of A.P. Hill's Corps. . . . The expression on his face as he rode out of that smoke has always remained firmly vised in my memory."[114]

This was the stuff of legend, and indeed, it was just such memories that created the first idolization of Lee. Historical hagiographers of the late nineteenth century would develop elaborate mythologies and instill (with remarkably lasting success) a regionwide hero worship, but the aura already existed for the Army of Northern Virginia. Officers might whisper that Lee was perhaps no longer the right leader for their cause—he was "too slow, too retiring for these times"—but the privates believed to the last that their general possessed unmatched skill, integrity, and simple humanity.[115] "Gen lee has 60,000 of the best soldiers in the world and they have unbounded confidence in him," wrote a member of Lee's staff on the last Christmas of the war, "they know he will not tell them to go, when there is no necessity and when he says the word—we will storm Grant in his breastworks if they were twice as strong, and take them too—or die trying."[116] As the numbing weeks in Petersburg's trenches wore on, and even indigestible bread gave out, some of course lost heart, deserting to the enemy in such numbers that a Yankee officer recorded the sad sight of old veterans defecting by squads. The staunchest and the bravest stayed with Lee to the last, until a breakdown of supplies and the failure of an eleventh-hour assault against the Union stronghold at Fort Stedman, and the defeat at the battle of Five Forks forced them down the dismal road to Appomattox. Lee himself might now be fighting only because it was "proper that we should prepare to resist [the Federals] to the extent of our abilities," but his men still caught a whiff of glory and they followed him by habit.[117] To the end the Army of Northern Virginia was fueled by the power of Lee's example. The men believed he would never let them down; they could not imagine leaving his side. "You are the country to these men," Henry Wise is said to have remarked the morning of Lee's surrender. "They have fought for you." Though the incident has never been corroborated, the sentiment rings unmistakably true.[118]

When Confederates heard of the surrender, they simply could not believe it. An adjutant commented a few days afterward that it had fallen like a clap of thunder on the men, and that even those who had feared and expected it were "astonished, even stupefied, at the terrible news." A soldier fighting in the Shenandoah Valley said that in "their wildest conjectures" they had never thought of such an explanation for the last march.[119] A member of Jefferson Davis's cabinet noted that the president was wholly unprepared for Lee's capitulation.[120] In the civilian population the shock was no less great. "News has come that Lee's army has surrendered!" exclaimed Margaret Junkin Preston from the ravaged town of Lexington. "We are struck dumb with astonishment!"[121] Lee had placed his trust in God's ability to order events to his advantage; but the southern people had put their faith in General Lee, and they believed in him as if in a miracle worker. When the devastating news came, many took the time to record their bleak thoughts, and it is worth reading them, for they help us to understand what it was like for Southerners to have experienced social upheaval, to have sacrificed and lived on hope, and be left with naught but bitter draughts to slake their thirst for a better future. "Why then all these four years of suffering—of separation—of horror—of blood—of havoc—of awful bereavement!" Margaret Junkin Preston wailed into her diary the day after the surrender. "Why these ruined homes—these broken family circles—these scenes of terror that must scathe the brain of those who witnessed them till their dying day! Why is our own dear Willy in his uncoffined grave? Why poor Frank to go through this life with one arm?"[122] In a field, not far away, artillerist Milton Wylie Humphreys described the last night with his comrades, camped after a march that had "seemed like a funeral procession, and now we were in the graveyard."

> The life of the soldier in war is considered disagreeable in the extreme. He is exposed to great peril on the battle-field; he is exposed to the inclemency of the weather; he is fatigued on the march; he suffers for want of food and often even for want of water. He is deprived of all the pleasures of society, and of all the endearments of home. But never in my life did I feel so oppressed with sorrow and sadness as I did when the time arrived which was to end all these discomforts and annoyances. I had been camping, marching and fighting side by side with some of my comrades for three years, others two, others one, and others for a less period. I had no kinsman in the Battalian; but many of its members were as brothers or more than brothers. Now I was parting from these men, not only never again to camp with them, or see them all together again, but never again to see the most of them at all—Very many shed tears, and some . . . wept as little children.[123]

Everyone in the South had a theory about why the war had been lost: foolish politicians, bad distribution of supplies, lack of enterprise among the populace, or the favorite, the inevitable dominance of northern resources. One angry Alabama private maintained it was due to "Skulkers, Cowards, Extortioners and Deserters not the Yankees that makes it worse."[124] But in the parlay no one ever denigrated the Army of Northern Virginia's battlefield mettle, or the leader who aroused it. "I fought the enemy at every step," Lee would tell a confidant. "I faced him and . . . I believe I got out of [my army] all they could do or all any men could do." It is an assessment that stands today.[125]

What he gave them in return was peace with honor. The idea of submission was debasing to men who believed so proudly in their superior manhood and their fighting ability. Lee was determined not to subject his army to conditions that would belittle them or endanger their future. As he and Grant began to correspond on the possibility of an end to hostilities, Lee gingerly probed Union intentions. It was a final last maneuver between the two military giants, with Lee hoping that a dignified ceasefire could be established and Grant, in skillful diplomatic language, stating that he had no authority to treat on anything but surrender. But Grant, mirroring Lincoln's plea to "let 'em up easy," also made clear that the terms would be generous: there would be no unconditional terms, no retribution or imprisonment, the Southerners could simply go home. And Lee, knowing he could ask no more, surrendered as much to Lincoln's goodness as he did to Grant's armies.[126]

So after the recognition of futility; after fantasies of dashing to join Joe Johnston's forces had been squashed by Grant's aggressive pursuit; after Lee had remarked on the ease of choosing liberating suicide in front of his lines; after he had donned his finest uniform and sat waiting in a bare parlor for the end of the world; after small talk about the Mexican War and large talk about an agreement that would foster reconciliation; after the famished had been promised rations—after all this Lee walked out the door of Wilmer McLean's house at Appomattox Court House and prepared to face his heroes.[127] He had shown very little emotion on that Palm Sunday, the day of martyrs, only a stubborn refusal to word his acceptance of surrender terms with the nearly pro forma phrase "I have the honor . . ." "Say I accept," he told his aide.[128] But an officer waiting on the steps outside caught the twitch and flush of Lee's neck as he left the house; heard his voice break as he called for his horse; saw him pound his fist into his hand as he waited to ride away. And then all was silent as the Union officers in the courtyard raised their hats in respect.[129]

He rode among his proud, loyal, ragged men, head bowed. E. Porter Alexander had lined them up along the road, instructing them to show quiet respect.[130] Sensing the dreaded rumors were true, the men spontaneously broke ranks and crowded around their old commander, clambering onto the backs of horses and wagons to catch a glimpse, shouting their fealty, grasping his hand. Still no orator, Lee could not find words to express his feelings, but choked out a few simple phrases; and then the whole gathering dissolved in the overwhelming emotion of the moment. For once the accounts do not seem gift-wrapped in nineteenth-century sentiment; that tears streamed down Lee's cheeks and the faces of his veterans is not only well documented, but wholly believable.[131] And at that moment, when privates and generals cried in each other's presence, the army and its commander were as one, rankless, seamless, woven together with glorious memories and dashed dreams.[132] At that hour cheers of a different sort began to be heard from the Union camps: men beside themselves with relief and joy, "perfectly wild," throwing shoes, hats, rifles, and comrades in the air, weeping and laughing, wrestling each other in the frenzy of the moment. "You may paint, draw, write and talk over it and about it," a Union officer told his wife that night, "and you have but a faint idea of what it was."[133] Grant, who later wrote he had approached the McLean house with intense sadness, called off the celebrations, stating that the rebels were now their countrymen, and the noise of jubilation was not the order of the day. A few spoke to their former adversaries, and one of Lee's staff long held the memory of a Union soldier saying "If I were you, I would be the proudest man in the world. When I rode into your lines this morning and saw the poor remnant of the army which had baffled us so long, I was ashamed of myself."[134] Then the talk was hushed, and a Northerner wrote home that "a dead silence reigned in the night—many seemed stunned. . . . The unarted stillness was awful even. . . . Yes, the War was over."[135]

Lee and aide Charles Marshall, sketched by Alfred Waud as they left the McLean house just after the surrender.

LIBRARY OF CONGRESS

In a moment of searing intensity, Lee's men would have a final acknowledgment from their adversaries. As the defeated troops marched through ranks of blue-clad men in the formal surrender proceedings on April 12, yielding up their rifles and cherished battle flags and submitting to the unbearable loss of identity and pride, the Union forces were called to attention by General Joshua Chamberlain, who had viciously fought on Little Round Top. Hearing the order to "carry arms," the Federals raised their rifles to the shoulder, acknowledging the valor of their former enemies in a sign of military respect.[136] Lee declined to be present on this day, yet he left his men with a lasting tribute. Expressing in writing what he could not convey in

speech, he released a heartfelt message to his troops. In it Lee praised the devotion, the gallantry, and the "unsurpassed courage and fortitude" of the
survivors of so many hard-fought battles. More than "Dixie" or the "strange
wild cry of the rebel yell," his General Orders No. 9 would be a permanent
expression of the bond between Lee and the Army of Northern Virginia,
and the common drama they had experienced. Whatever strength the men
had taken from the indomitable will of their commander, Lee had been
doubly inspired by their own. With this in mind he prepared to wage perhaps his greatest campaign, as he led his defeated men into a future without
humiliation.[137]

A Leap in the Dark

Richmond 16ᵗʰ April

My dear Louisa

I cannot tell you how much I was affected by your kind letter the first I have received from any friend since our terrible calamity & your offering us an asylum in your hospitable home when I know with your large family you must find it very difficult to maintain them—Should we never be in a situation to reward your kindness God will not forget you & your store like the widows cheese will never fail. We have passed thro' a terrible ordeal the last 10 days. Our gallant army greatly reduced by starvation & constant exposure during the whole winter to a foe which outnumbered them so greatly, discouraged by the knowledge that their homes were desolated their families suffering—became demoralized—25 thousand threw down their arms & the 8 thousand 5 hundred who alone restrained them, after several days of hard fighting without any food save a few ears of corn nor rest day nor night cut off from all their provisions altho' they told Genl Lee they would follow him any where & they had decided if Grant had <u>required</u> an <u>unconditional</u> surrender to sacrifice their lives & cut their way thro' the enemy, yet when the terms he offered were so honourable Genl Lee told them he did not think it right to sacrifice the lives of so many brave men when nothing could be gained by it & they surrendered honourably, & were treated with great consideration. My husband & 2 sons got here yesterday & Rob I believe is safe tho he has not appeared yet—There are accounts of all this in the Herald so falsified that you would have a very incorrect idea of the whole affair, one thing is certain that the enemy have succeeded in their cruel & cowardly design <u>openly</u> <u>avowed</u> for more than a year past of starving out those whom they could not subdue in any honourable way—

It would take volumes to record the savage cruelty which has produced this state of things of the houses burned over the heads of the inhabitants even in the depth of winter the last morsels taken from helpless women & chil-

dren even the bedclothes that covered them, the mills & all implements of agriculture destroyed, the watches torn from the bosoms of our refined & gentle ladies the rings from their fingers & ears, & insulted & even knocked down by these wretches & often by negro soldiers & yet we are expected to return with joy into the union with such a people & to forget the desolation they have wrought upon our fair land & our people. Future generations may forget but we never can & there is many a foul deed committed upon isolated & unprotected dwellings that can never be recorded—I wish you could have witnessed Lincoln's triumphal entry into Richmond. He was surrounded by a crowd of blacks whooping & cheering like so many demons there was not a single respectable person to be seen & one kerchief was waved from the window of the Spotswood Hotel by a Yankee woman—we must submit to the will of Heaven but this is a bitter pill for the South to swallow May God overrule it all for their eternal Good & let us all see that in mercy we have been so afflicted & humiliated—

The girls & Nannie Lee who is staying with me unite in much love to you & yours & all our old friends in Alex[a]

Genl Lee begs his special regards to you & yours & tells you how much he appreciates your kindness. We are all unsettled now & know not what our future may be. I will write again when our plans are arranged—There is a report here today that Lincoln & Seward are assassinated but I cannot believe there is any truth in it. I should be glad to hear from you, can you tell me anything of Arlington

> *Yours most affec'ly*
> *MC Lee[1]*

. . .

Lexington, Va.
Nov. 22, 1865
Genl J.A. Early
My dear General:
I received last night your letter of the 30th ult., which gave me the first authentic information of you I had received since the cessation of hostilities, and relieved the anxiety I had felt on your account. I am very glad to hear of your health and safety; but regret your absence from the country, though I fully understand your feelings on the subject. I think the South requires the presence of all her sons now more than at any period of her history; and I determined, at the outset of her difficulties to share the fate of my people.

I wish you every happiness and prosperity wherever you may go, and in compliance with your request, enclose a statement of your services, which I hope may answer your purpose. You will always be present to my recollections. I desire, if not prevented, to write a history of the campaigns in Virginia.

All my records, books, orders &c were destroyed in the conflagration, and retreat from Richmond. Only such of my reports as were printed, are preserved. Your operations in 1864, 65 were among those destroyed. Can not you repeat them and send me copies of such letters, orders &c of mine (including that last letter to which you refer) and particularly give your recollection of our affective strength at the principal battles? My only object is to transmit, if possible, the truth to posterity, and do justice to our brave soldiers.

Most truly your friend RE Lee[2]

>-+-◆>-○-◆+-<

A FRATRICIDAL CONFLICT is the most horrific event that can befall a nation. Every death is as morally grotesque as it is shocking to the senses. Bloodshed, however, is not the greatest calamity of civil war. What lingers is the gaping fissure in confidence; the collapse of old understandings and easy interaction. By the end of the war Robert E. Lee personified the guts and glory of the battlefield, winning national respect for his ability despite his defeat. In the months following Appomattox he would offer inspiration of another kind. As Mary Lee so richly relates, the South was staggering under a weight of shock and mortification. In her husband Southerners found a guide to recovery. He had led their last desperate attempt to support an unsustainable culture. Now he offered the means of relinquishing that past and beginning a different future.

THE END roared the headline in the *New York Herald* announcing Lee's surrender.[3] The banner celebrated the conclusion of hostilities, but for many Southerners it had a graver meaning. This was the end of more than the terrible, draining conflict. It was the end of a long-cherished civilization; the end of pride and validation; the end of their dreams. A friend of the Lees penned words of disbelief as she watched the Confederate flag "dragged down" from the Richmond capitol: "Was it to this end . . . that the wives and children of many a dear and gallant friend were husbandless and fatherless . . . that our homes were in ruins, our State devastated?"[4] A Confederate Navy veteran expressed the same dispair as he surveyed "this shipwreck of country kinsman & friends."[5] Agnes Lee, trying to fathom the swift change from springtime expectation to utter devastation, would write despondently: "Ah, how long four weeks have been, and yet too short to bury our Confederacy."[6]

No one was more traumatized than General Robert E. Lee. He arrived in Richmond on April 15, riding faithful Traveller, accompanied by Custis and Rooney and a few aides. The sad troop was followed by a couple of ambulances, so dilapidated that a worn quilt had been used to patch up the canvas wagon cover. People quietly began to gather as he picked his way through Richmond's smoking ruins, and the throng swelled as word spread of his arrival. They stood in silent respect, or quietly raised their hats, and there were cheers as well, including some from those clad in blue. The man who acknowledged them was still wearing a mud-spattered uniform, his head bowed, his face "ridged in self-respecting grief." The crowd thickened as he reached "The Mess," and at the gate some of his old soldiers caught Traveller's bridle as he dismounted. One woman who was present saw he was so overcome that he had trouble controlling his physical actions and could not easily get off his horse. Then he gave "a courtly bow to the multitude," entered the house, and left behind forever the remnants of his old world.[7]

For weeks Lee remained in semi-isolation in that house. The shutters were drawn and his sons kept the string of visitors at bay. He slept for long hours. Anxious to avoid attention, he paced on the back veranda for exercise. At night he shuffled through the darkened streets, sometimes accompanied by Mildred, sometimes alone. Lee was wrenched by the sight of his tattered men, by the requests for help from boys still in Libby Prison, by the adulation he attracted. A U.S. Army guard, placed in front of the house for protection, was appreciated, but it had its own painful connotations. When Mathew Brady, the celebrated photographer, pressed the family to persuade Lee to pose for a historic picture, the general reluctantly agreed, and the camera caught his fabled wrath, coursing through the neck and blazing from his eyes. Sometimes he let in girls who asked for autographs and tried to cheer him up. One young neighbor, struck with the depth of his anguish, asked him: "Why will you look so heart broken?" "Why shouldn't I?" Lee replied, "my cause is dead! I am homeless—I have nothing on earth."[8]

Technically he was a prisoner of war; worse, he was a prisoner of his thoughts.[9] He was under no illusions about extending the fight and felt only relief when Joe Johnston surrendered on April 26. But Jefferson Davis was still at large, and his own fate was quite uncertain. On the day of his surrender, Lee had been vilified in many northern newspapers, some of them calling for his head. Though he publicly deplored Lincoln's assassination, rumors that the murder had been plotted by southern leaders were spread thickly among the horrified public. The new president, Andrew Johnson, was said to believe that "a good way to disenfranchise the [rebels] is to break

Robert E. Lee, as photographed by Mathew Brady a few days after Appomattox.

their necks!"[10] In these early days of uncertainty, it became clear to Lee that he would have a public role, whether or not he sought one.

He was not a natural politician, and was unaccustomed to being the voice of a people. And so it seems he faltered in his first foray into the public arena. A reporter from the *New York Herald* named Thomas Cook asked to interview him. He assented, apparently believing that he could mold public opinion toward the South in a way that would minimize punishment and foster goodwill. According to the resulting story, Lee took care to present himself as confident, robust, and anxious for reconciliation. He was quick to point out, however, that "should arbitrary, or vindictive, or revengeful policies be adopted, the end was not yet." He stated that the issue of states' rights had been decided by military power, not philosophical justice, then trivialized the entire conflict as a difference of political opinion—hardly grounds for accusations of treason. He excused Jefferson Davis's actions and proposed that Davis should be shown leniency because he had been a late and reluctant convert to secession. He explained his own actions in the same way. Lee further stated that the "best men of the South" were pleased to see the end of slavery, and they had only continued the institution because of their Christian concern for black people. According to the reporter, Lee then showed his hand a bit more and said: "The negroes must be disposed of, and if their disposition can be marked out, the matter of freeing them is at once settled," suggesting that without such a "disposal" the former Confederate states would work to undermine emancipation. Lee's main message, however, was that the South had waged a "half earnest" rebellion, that every Southerner had overcome his moment of passion, and that no one should "be judged harshly for contending for that which he honestly believed to be right." Above all, Lee argued that the former Confederate states be treated with moderation so that the sons who were the country's "bone and sinew, its intelligence and enterprise" might stay and work for its future.[11]

Lee seems to have underestimated the result of such an interview, given only three days after the final end of the war. Still reacting to the initial overture of peace, he failed to feel the mood of the North. The Yankees were as devastated in their way as was the South, and were anxious to see some signs of contrition for the carnage they were still struggling to comprehend. "Beware the People weeping," Herman Melville whispered in poetic warning, as the full meaning of Lincoln's death began to sink in: "They have killed him, the Forgiver / The Avenger takes his place. . . ."[12] Not once during the interview did Lee show regret for the slaughter that had occurred over a "disagreement on political questions." Nowhere was the South's responsibility for its actions discussed, nor its role in reconciliation delineated. Instead it read like a series of demands to the victors: they should be lenient; they should "dispose" of the freed slaves; they should forget the destruction of the last years and "pacify" the Southerners. Though it may have been naive to grant the interview, in fact it candidly expressed the prevailing mood in much of the South, and previewed the way many events would transpire.[13] Not surprisingly, the piece was met with derision among Unionists, particularly over Lee's characterization of the South's noble disinterest in slavery. "Indeed we cannot discover that our correspondent has extracted from General Lee a single idea of any practical value," ran a scathing editorial, "except as illuminating the shallow pretences upon which he entered into the services of Jefferson Davis, and the impossible concessions . . . to treason in behalf of peace."[14]

The historian's omniscient view, with its certainty of what will come, is useful in many ways. It can lend perspective, or encourage the examination of numerous sources over many years, giving breadth to issues that seemed illusive or transitory in their own time. Foreknowledge can also be a handicap, however, when it tempts us to assume too much and forget the slow pace of events, or the uncertainty under which decisions and ideas are developed. The devastating months after Appomattox are just such a time. We know that Robert E. Lee was not tried for treason. We know that he was fortunate enough to keep his life and his liberty and to escape the historical gallows as well. But in those raw spring weeks he did not know what he would face, or whether on any given day the temper of the country might turn against him. "Our masters are thirsting for our blood," contended one of Lee's officers, expressing the prevailing fear, "and you may be sure that they will have it, and that too in copious streams."[15] Lee's uncharacteristic interview with the *Herald* gives us some insight into both his continuing rebellion and the anxiety that must have filled his mind during the "intolerable uncertainty" of the first days of peace.[16] Viewed from a distance, it seems an act of near panic, a clumsy attempt not only to justify himself but to argue away the threat of retribution. Among the things that Lee told Thomas Cook was that "he would have been pleased had his life been taken in any of the numerous battle fields on which he had fought during the war."[17] Here was despair, as well as defiance.

Lee did not repeat this mistake of publicly defending the South's actions. Instead he cautiously endured what must have been excruciating weeks, watching with distress as Jefferson Davis was apprehended and thrown in prison, and the level of rhetoric in both sections of the country escalated.[18] His wife was among the most outspoken of partisans and recklessly voiced her bitterness. "Virginia will rue the day that so many of her people laid down their arms," she told a longtime friend, "and tho' starvation is a cruel thing to contend with even that might have been endured for a time to accomplish their independence." The future, she told another, "seems so dark now, that we are almost tempted to think God has forsaken us."[19] Lee neither disavowed nor agreed with such statements, but when General George Meade and others approached him about making special application to the president for the return of his citizenship, he initially demurred, saying that he did not intend to take any oath of allegiance until he saw how the South would be treated.[20] Having read the first of many wobbly decisions on amnesty, Lee knew that he was excluded from the general provisions on two grounds: first for having been a leader of the Confederacy; second, for having broken previous oaths to the United States. Then, on June 7, Lee learned that Judge John C. Underwood in Norfolk had recommended that a jury indict him for treason, along with Custis, Rooncy, and Fitz Lee. Lee tried to calm those around him and refused to attempt an escape from the bitterness and repercussion that faced him. When a band of ragged Confederates tried to persuade him to hide in their mountain passes, he quietly told them that they would lose all pride in their commander if he ran away and that he must stay and meet his fate.[21] "I shall avoid no prosecution the government thinks proper to institute," he told Cousin Markie. "I am aware of having done nothing wrong, and can not flee."[22] He did reassess his political standing, however, and the advantages of inclusion in the amnesty President Johnson declared on May 29, which granted full rights to those who swore an oath of allegiance to the United States. On June 13 he sent a letter to General Grant expressing confusion over the new conditions of amnesty and how they related to assurances given at Appomattox, which he understood to protect him from prosecution. He took the precaution of enclosing an application for the amnesty, but failed, whether inadvertently or in a final protest, actually to take the oath of allegiance. Then he continued to wait, anxious and uncertain. "I can do nothing until I learn what decision in my case is made at Washington," he told Rob.[23]

He could do nothing, but he was formulating a plan that would have tremendous consequences for the Confederate veterans he so revered, as well as for his own safety. It was less a set of actions than an attitude, a paradigm, that would greatly impress observers both North and South. The editors of the New York Herald were not quite right when they declared that Lee had not "a single idea of any practical value," for his concern that the South's young men must be kept in the country to work for a better future was eminently farsighted. From the time of Appomattox Lee had been en-

couraging his former soldiers to lay down their arms, reject hostility, and return to their communities. When an ex-cavalry scout met him on a late-night
walk in Richmond and asked what he should do, Lee had told him to "go
home, all you boys who fought with me and help build up the shattered fortunes of our old state."[24] He expanded the idea over the next several months,
finally persuading Confederate veterans to take the oath of allegiance, dis-
suading officers who contemplated moving to Mexico or Brazil, encouraging everyone to work and wait patiently for better times. Now he turned the
notion into one of the formulas he liked to develop and repeat; a standard
expression of his opinion, which was underscored with each reiteration. His
example was as important as his words, and he let it be known that he would
not leave the country, and that he would apply for amnesty. On the back of
his application to the president, his son Custis penned a little note: "when
Gen[l] Lee requested me to make a copy of this letter to Pres[dt] Johnson, he remarked: It was but right for him to set an example of making formal submission to the Civil Authorities, and that he thought, by so doing he might
possibly be in a better position to be of use to the Confederates, who were
not protected by military paroles, especially Mr. Davis."[25]

"The coward looks back, the brave ahead," Lee had once told Rooney,
and now he began to act earnestly on this philosophy.[26] There would be no
more public explanations, no exodus from the country. He applauded General P. G. T. Beauregard's decision to remain and serve the South, and he told
Fitz Lee that their obligation now was "not to keep open the sores of civil
war but to follow the examples of those nations who endeavored to obliterate its marks."[27] He advised a former captain of the Army of Northern Virginia that "the questions at issue between them and the Northern States
having been decided, I believe it to be the duty of every one to unite in the
restoration of the country, and the reestablishment of peace and harmony."[28] To a businessman in Petersburg he gave his doctrine in full:

> It should be the object of all to avoid controversy, to allay passion, give full
> scope to reason and every kindly feeling. By doing this and encouraging
> our citizens to engage in the duties of life with all their heart & mind, with
> a determination not to be turned aside by thoughts of the past & fears of
> the future, our country will not only be restored in material prosperity,
> but will be advanced in science, in virtue, and in religion.[29]

Though his political views would calcify as reconstruction policies became harsher, for the remainder of his life Lee outwardly professed this philosophy. It was to be a great balm on the bruised Southern sensibility, but it

had a practical effect on countless individuals as well. A colonel recalled that at the end of the war he and his men were disgusted with their "humiliation and persecution" and wanted to express their feelings violently. Visiting General Lee in Richmond, they made the case for continued hostility, a perpetual war against capitulation. Lee turned their desperation aside, saying that it was their duty to remain and share the fate of their people, to rebuild the wasted places and care for their families. "Great as I had held him as a military chieftain," said the colonel, "my admiration of him in this trying hour . . . was even grander than when I had seen him at the head of invincible legions."[30] Another old soldier recorded the effect of Lee's policy on some of the boys in Mississippi. "Your great and wise example of retirement and peace, obedience to government and law we are all pursuing and following. . . . All your old men here are peacefully at work trying to build up their shattered fortunes, and the Country, its peace and prosperity."[31]

He had led them in war, and now he would show the way through an unendurable peace. Three-quarters of eligible white men had fought for a least a time with the Confederacy. They thought they knew what manhood was, and what liberty and loyalty meant.[32] Now they had to redefine these terms, and General Lee helped them to do it. He showed them a way to carry on with self-respect, to find hope against deprivation and domination. If this man could rise above defeat, they could follow him, just as they had intuitively followed him against the deadly odds of combat. It was an act of spiritual fortitude, as audacious in its way as anything he had ever performed on the battlefield. Through it he held up courage and dignity as the only path through a frightening and unfathomable wilderness. In this moment of personal bravery, Lee transcended his own violent emotions and showed himself superior to misfortune.[33]

"I expect now to have to be always poor," Mildred Lee wrote to a friend soon after the surrender, and indeed, earning a living was one of her father's dilemmas.[34] The family was not entirely destitute, for Lee had a few northern railroad bonds he thought might still be worth something, and he quietly began to look into redeeming them.[35] The Custis lands on the Pamunkey, though ravaged, were also clear in title, and Rooney and Rob began to work them. Lee thought he would like to find a little farm of his own, something modest and far removed from the swirl of events, and in June 1865 a family friend lent them a dilapidated house not far from Richmond, named Derwent. In a way Lee was happy there. He enjoyed reviving the garden and took rides on Traveller, and Mildred remembered that he was "enthusiastic about a home life, however humble, after those five years in a tent."[36] At fifty-eight, he had no way to earn a living, and despite rumored proposals from around the world, there is scanty evidence that he received requests for his services in these first postwar months. The situation was so peculiar that Lee's outspoken daughter Mary announced at a party in Staunton that "the people of the South are offering my father everything but work; and work is the only thing he will accept at their hands."[37] It appears this conversation was overheard by a trustee of Washington College, a small, nearly ruined school in the mountains of southwestern Virginia. The information was reported back to the other school administrators, who determined to take the extraordinary step of asking the great General Lee if he would serve as its president. A few weeks later, borrowing the one decent suit owned by the trustees, Judge John Brockenbrough called at Derwent to make the proposal. He played heavily to the thoughts forming in Lee's mind: the need to help the young men who had borne the burden of the war; the importance of education, with its focus on the future; the desire to be of service to Virginia. Lee was reluctant at first, for he questioned his qualifications, and his political status was precarious. Still, it seemed a felicitous convergence of needs, and, as he told a clergyman, it might appear ungrateful to look further when this was the door God had opened for him. In mid-September Lee mounted Traveller and, wearing his old uniform, with insignia removed, rode alone through the steep green peaks to the southwest, sleeping one night under the stars. Four days later he reached the dilapidated school.[38]

The public viewed Lee's new role as just the splendid gesture they needed to inspire them. "And now that grand old Chieftain . . . betakes him to as noble a work as ever engaged the attention of men," the *Richmond Whig* wrote loftily.[39] For Lee as well it offered a new articulation of purpose. "I have a self-imposed task, which I must accomplish," an admirer quoted him as saying. "I have led the young men of the South in battle; I have seen many of them fall under my standard. I shall devote my life now to training young men to do their duty in life."[40] It would prove to be a challenge. The college had respectable roots, being the successor to Liberty Hall, which had claimed George Washington as a benefactor. Its symmetrical red-brick edifice and Ionic columns bespoke a long reverence for classical learning. But when Lee arrived, Washington College had been ransacked by General David Hunter's forces and was reduced to forty students. The faculty had not been paid in years, and the school was perilously in debt. Lee knew that he was chiefly expected to lend prestige to the college, to be a great guiding spirit rather than a day-to-day administrator, but to the surprise of the trustees, the town, and the students, he immediately immersed himself in the details as well as the image of the institution. Within weeks he had proposed a modernized curriculum, established an honor system, and installed a number of managerial policies reminiscent of West Point. Lee adopted Sylvanus Thayer's commitment to knowing the standing and character of

Washington College in 1867.
WASHINGTON AND LEE UNIVERSITY

every student, as well as his reliance on the faculty to advise on instructional matters. Academic excellence was considered essential. Lee himself participated in many of the examinations, which were held biannually—again on the West Point model—and he took pride in showcasing the best students. Those who would not or could not perform were simply sent home. He not only oversaw the repair of the damaged buildings, he personally laid out the grounds. He took a holistic approach to academic preparations, fighting for the construction of a gymnasium, encouraging attendance at chapel, interesting himself in the health of the students. Nor did he neglect his responsibility as a magnet for the college. Under his influence the number of students rose to 410, hailing from twenty-two states, and Lee managed to scrape together funds for those lacking tuition. Within a year Lee had also attracted enough money to begin paying the college debts. By the end of his five years as president, donors like Cyrus McCormick and George Peabody had given the school so much support that its endowment was double the prewar size.[41]

Educational reform was not Lee's specialty, and he did not enjoy the work. That he performed it conscientiously is not in question. What is more remarkable is that he developed an innovative approach with far-reaching applications. Feeling that the old classical studies still had merit, but that science and more practical branches of knowledge were best suited to changing conditions, he grafted modern languages, chemistry, advanced mathematics, natural history, and mining engineering onto the curriculum.

Then he steadily lobbied his patrons for means to establish essential profes-
sorships and acquire the right apparatus. He put top men in the new positions.[42] He wrote strongly worded treatises about the role of the teacher and
the key elements of children's formation, holding that example and personal integrity were as important as academic expertise, and reflecting
many of the opinions about child development he had devised while raising
his sons and daughters. Always he emphasized the intrinsic importance of
learning. Providing young people with a good education, he told his cousin
Robert Beverely, "in my opinion, no matter what pursuit they may take in
life, is the greatest benefit you can bestow upon them."[43]

Lee also attached Judge Brockenbrough's private law academy to the college and, in a prescient move, tried to establish a school of journalism, perhaps the earliest of its kind. Some of these experiments fared better than
others—the journalism school, for example, did not survive long after Lee's
death—but all of them heralded a fresh approach to the needs of southern
society. A year before his death Lee proposed an embellishment of his original plans, which called for agricultural and technical training as a way to
sharpen the skills of working men. "The great object of the whole plan,"
wrote Lee, "is to provide the facilities required by the large class of our
young men, who looking forward to an early entrance into the practical
pursuits of life, need a more direct training to this end than the usual literary courses." The plan would not totally escape criticism—some thought
Lee's innovations "over-reaching" for the abilities of such a small college—
yet it foreshadowed the region's needs and was a notable alternative to the
imposed policies of northern politicians or businessmen. Indeed, Washington College was one of the few southern institutions not under the control
of carpetbaggers during this period. In its way, it was a self-imposed reconstruction, which looked to inner resources and long-term investment for
revitalization. "The boldness of the step was astounding," wrote one commentator. "It was a leap in the dark, with a prayer and a hope."[44]

One of the most interesting aspects of this period is that Lee left such a variety of impressions with the students. A large proportion were Confederate
veterans, for whom the general was as much legend as man, and, clad in his
old army coat, his was indeed an éminence grise on campus. No one questioned his absolute authority, though he had taken care to abandon any
structured military discipline. "His spirit overshadowed everything about
the college and community," wrote one former student. "General Lee's
slightest wish was law."[45] One year, when he determined that everyone
should work through Christmas holidays, just as the cadets had always done

at West Point, the Washington College students decided to write a petition in protest. Hearing of the scheme, Lee held firm, announcing that "any student whose name appears on that paper would be sent home; and that if every student signed it, the college would be closed and the key to door placed in his pocket."[46] He knew each student by name as well as class rank and reputation, which heartened some and worried others. He liked to invite the new students to his home, where Mrs. Lee gave them a motherly welcome and Mildred served "cold tea"—a euphemistic name for sherry cobbler, which was strong enough to send one unsuspecting young man reeling out onto the porch.[47] Many found him to be genial and kind, with a personal interest in their well-being. Though he hated doing it, he signed literally thousands of little photographic *cartes de visite* for the boys to give away or sell to support their social clubs.[48] One student wrote home that no one could "help liking Gen. Lee he is so polite and gentlemanly. He talks to a boy just as if he were his own son."[49]

Others chose to keep their distance. Lee was known for his "fierce and violent temper, prone to intense expression," and his administrative staff, as well as the students and faculty, learned to be wary, especially as the explosion often carried over to those not responsible for annoying the president.[50] Some were concerned that nothing seemed to impress him; that he never apologized when clearly in error; that he had a way of testing the youths and their teachers to prove his superiority. Milton Humphreys, one of the brightest pupils in the school, who later became a professor at the college, was upbraided one day for asking for Lee's editorial comments on a new college catalog.[51] Several former students wrote that the old general "grappled their souls 'with hooks of steel'" or that they generally viewed him with "fear and distance," and one remembered actually hiding behind a column when he saw Lee pass.[52] No one longed to receive a note from Lewis, the African-American janitor who passed around appointment requests each Monday morning. The summons itself was generally bad news—"that meant a lecture for some misfeasance or malfeasance"—but the worst was that Lee did not make a distinction between those two words.[53] Errant students had no idea whether they would meet the gentleman or the tiger behind that office door, and Lee, who disliked these interviews as much as the boys did, had perfected the art of conducting them to his own advantage. Generally he killed the students with kindness, invoking the importance of education or the disappointment their parents would feel at their progress. Recalled one miscreant: "I wished he had whipped me but he talked to me about my mother and the sacrifices she is making to send me to college . . . the first thing I knew I was blubbering like a baby."[54] After a few years, when Lee grew feebler and more familiar and fewer of the scholars had followed him into battle, he lost some of his mystique. No one ever publicly or privately said a jesting word about him, but it is clear that they were no longer in awe. One student wrote to his mother about a Latin examination at which the college president participated: "Gen. Lee was sitting right by me. The old fellow had a book looking on, and tried to look wise but I flattered myself that he did not know much about it."[55] With wonderful irreverence, another student summed it up: "Gen. R.E. Lee is President of this concern & has performed his duties very well considering his age."[56]

Lee's family joined him in Lexington in early 1866. During their years in the town they occupied two different houses, both comfortable, the second of which Lee helped to design so that it would accommodate his wife's wheelchair. Despite Mildred's predictions of destitution and her father's fears, they lived well amid the scarcity. In addition to the use of the house, Lee was making $3,000 a year by 1867, quite a comfortable sum in the postwar South.[57] Custis got a teaching job nearby at the Virginia Military Institute. Rob and Rooney visited occasionally, and both married during these years, with a good deal of encouragement from their father.[58] Smith and Carter Lee sent their sons to the college, and the young nephews added some zest to the family meals. Daughter Mary continued to distance herself; Agnes was quiet and sad; Precious Life took on the housekeeping duties with a good deal of authority, which greatly amused her father. "Mildred . . . considers herself now a great character," he told one of his new daughters-in-law. "She rules her brother & nephews with an iron rod & scatters her advice broadcast among the young men of the college. I hope it may yield an abundant harvest."[59] Romantic encounters for the girls, however, were rare. Beaux were scarce in the South at that time: so many young men had been killed, and those who remained were too poor or too distracted to don their wooing clothes.[60] The general did not encourage suitors, and though some hardy gentlemen braved Lee's intimidating house, finding his daughters "splendid and lively" if not beautiful, few measured up to his or the young ladies' expectations.[61] "I am dreadfully lonely," Mildred confided to one of her friends. "The number of old maids here quite appall me—my fate was decided from the first moment I put my foot on shore."[62] Instead of moonlight walks the Lee girls skated and rode horseback together, entertained students, took part in church activities, read aloud from Thackeray and Dickens. For Lee it was a congenial domestic life, and he was possessive of his clan.[63] But, as Mary Lee continually noted in her letters, Lexington was an "isolated spot," with a judgmental Protestant morality, and the family was

not really happy. One Washington College student described the townspeople as "severe to the point of simplicity; intense in their religious fervor . . . loving and possessing education, yet often narrow-minded," and
sighed that even the hedges were trimmed in prim Presbyterian style.[64] In
Lexington the Lees struggled, as did all of their southern brethren, to make
a new life for themselves. It was a beginning; it was a blessing; but it was not
home.

The dignified relinquishment of command is among the most ennobling of
American traditions. The United States borrowed it from earlier democra-
cies, reinforcing the belief that authority rests outside the will of any individual. George Washington's withdrawal from an adoring world in 1796 was
a precedent-making exercise in the peaceful transition of power. John
Quincy Adams, who contentedly returned to the House of Representatives
after knowing presidential might, and Harry Truman, who declared on leaving the White House that by rejoining the citizenry he had been promoted,
are two more stirring instances of this attitude. Robert E. Lee's actions just
after the Civil War are a proud example of that tradition. His courageous
military restraint in 1865 and his early words of reconciliation were more
than a face-saving final bow from the stage. They offered a model for a great
and proud army that felt itself humiliated; a salve for a devastated citizenry;
a running start toward reconciliation. Some may be disappointed that Lee
was not perfectly noble in every word and deed during the postwar period.
Yet his tremendous forbearance under pressure of prosecution, public criticism, and personal ostracism is notable. Lee knew that he and his culture
were caught as if in parentheses between what had happened and what they
wished had happened. Three-quarters of a century later another American,
T. S. Eliot, would exactly express the reality of that moment: "Time past and
time future / What might have been and what has been / Point to one end,
which is always present."[65] In the first two years after Appomattox, Lee consciously lived in that present tense. All he could do was to rise to each day
and try to grace it. By the accumulation of these hard-won moments, he
would construct something concrete and optimistic. By this he could—and
did—raise a beacon against bewilderment and despair.

Chapter Twenty-five

Blurred Vision

Lexington Va*
9 July 1866

My dear Sir

silence &

I was truly glad to receive your friendly letter, after so many years of ^

I ~~was~~ rejoiced *~~the~~ expression* *same*

separation, & ^to find ~~that you still retained~~ ^ *the ^ feelings of*

intercourse

kindness & friendship that marked our ^~~acquaintance more than~~ in early

both

life—I assure you these feelings are cordially reciprocated ^ by myself &

~~respond with pleasure~~ *numerous acts [of]*

Mrs Lee, & we shall ^never forget the ^~~substantial~~ kindness extended to us
by you

give you my

^ during our ~~whole~~ sojourn in the West. But I ^ ~~am under~~ special

thanks *doing me the justice in*

^ ~~obligations to you~~ for ^ believing that my conduct during the last eventful

five *governed*

^ years, has been ^ ~~dictated~~ by my ~~a consciencious~~ sense of duty. I had no

Nor had I seen *~~defence~~*

other guide.^ & no other object than the ^ maintenance of those principles

~~according to~~

of American liberty, ^ upon which the Constitutions of the several states, & of

originally founded *they are strictly rigidly*

the U. States were ^~~formed based~~ & which unless ^ *preserved I fear there*

to

will be an end ^ ~~of~~ Republican Govt. in this country.

---

*Lee used superscript numbers to mark where he wanted to move lines or para-
graphs in this draft letter. He seems to have intended, for example, that the number 2, in brackets, be moved to the spot that the second number 2 appears.

But I ^will not ~~take up~~ your time in ~~arguing~~ ^ the matter. I have never
~~do not intend to~~ occupy   ~~refuting~~ discussing ~~such~~

taken part in the ^political questions ~~of the country, & it is not proper for me~~
      ~~discussion of~~

~~to do so now~~ but I felt in common with every American citizen, the

importance of a well regulated government. The assertion of the ~~reserved~~

rights of the states, & that state interposition as a means of protection against

the misuse of powers beyond the meaning of the Constitution ~~the states~~
       Govt
is by no means new in the history of the ^ country—In the convention which

adopted the Constitution of the U. States, it was admitted that the State

Governments were invested with complete sovereignty, & the proposition

"that Congress should have the power to call forth the force of the Union

against a refractory state" was indefinitely postponed. [2][The right of State
   interpretation
^ interposition, as a means of protection against the exercise of powers
                asserted   many north & south
beyond the meaning of the Constitution, has been ^ ~~declared~~ by ^ ~~several~~

~~northern~~ states.] [1][Pennsylvania in the resolution adopted by her Legislature

in 1811, declared that the Union was to all intents & purposes a treaty between

Soverign States-] The state of Ohio in the proceedings of her Legislature in

1820, to prevent the establishment of the U.S. Banks within her limits,

recognized & approved the doctrines asserted by the Legislatures of

Virginia & Kentucky in their resolutions of 1798 & 1800, which asserted an

equal right by the states to interpret the Constitution for themselves when
                interference of the
their Sovereign rights were involved. The ^ State of New York ~~in 1824~~ was

invoked in 1824, ~~by~~ in certain resolutions offered in her Legislature, with

regard to the right of Congress to demand tonnage on boats navigating

the
^ *canals of the State, & Mr Van Buren subsequently in the Senate of the*

U.S. gave notice that New York "ought & would resist." [2] *[& ~~the House of~~*

~~Repr~~ of the State of Maine in Jany 1831 ~~in a reference to the N.E. boundary~~,

resolved that the Constitution of the U. States ~~did~~ conferred only a special &
                                                                          by
modified sovereignty ^ to the Genl Govt: without authority to cede any
                                                                  her
portion of territory belonging to a State without ^ ~~its~~ consent, & that
Maine
^ *~~they~~ would not consent to relinquish any portion of her territory. [In Feb^y*
                                              act of
1830, the State of Massachusetts, ~~led~~ by ^ her Legislature, declared the treaty

of the Genl Govt with Great Britain relative to the Northeastern boundary

"null and void & in no way obligatory"—]. Several of the southern states

have at different periods, by acts of their Legislatures declared, that a State
should
^ *might of right refuse obedience to any measure of the Genl Govt manifestly*

against, & in violation of the Constitution; & the ~~general~~ opinion has
generally
^ *~~hitherto~~ prevailed that resistance to the Genl Govt was ~~not only a right but~~*

~~a duty~~, when acting beyond the limitations of the Constitution, was not only

a right but a duty. [~~But I will not occupy your time with these questions~~]
                                          withdrawal
[2] *[I never encouraged or approved the ^ ~~separation~~ of Virg^a from the Union,*
                                                  people
but when in a convention of her ^ ~~citizens~~, ~~after~~ she decided that ~~it was~~ her
        required her   ~~nothing left but to~~
duty ^ to do so, I had ^ ~~either~~ but to remain with her to whom my
              I believed   it was intended that
allegiance ^ was first due.] [1] *[Inasmuch as ^ the authority of the soverign*

states should resist encroachments by the Genl Govts: as well as that the power

of the latter should resist the aggression of the states & that thus the Genl &

States Governments would reciprocally check the usurpations of each other.][1]

>-+-<>--O--<>-+-<

ROBERT E. LEE's field glass rests today at Arlington, on a desk he used to plan forward-thinking defensive structures in Baltimore harbor. The glass is a beautiful instrument, the best to be had in the 1850s, brass fitted, and of wood gleaming with the patina of loving hands. He used it well into the war, though its ocular properties were becoming a little blurred, and the lens no longer possessed the range and clarity of newer advances. The spyglass comes to mind when thinking about Lee in the years after his defeat, for its structure and its limitations recall his political thinking during this time. Lee's progressive stance toward education, and his belief that Southerners should stay with their homes as they faced uncertain prospects, was an exceptional moment of foresight—justly admired and still resonant after fifteen decades. This long-range outlook, however, seems to have been relegated to one compartment of his mind. Lee's political precepts, as well as his effort to accept the tragic events of the war (and his part in them), would be far more myopic. As the uncompleted letter above illustrates, he planted himself in his favorite aggressively defensive position, denying any positive outcome to the conflict and balking at social change. His struggle is quickly visible in this draft, for Lee stumbles over nearly every word, trying to reformulate his thoughts in a genteelly defiant fashion. He is anxious to state his opinion on the war's outcome, and do a little revisionist history on the reasons for his participation in it. He hesitates just as he launches forth, however, and it appears the letter was never finished. Lee did not exactly look backward, but neither did he use either his charismatic authority or his old problem-solving skills to create political innovations that would allow the South to change comfortably. Like his handsome field glass, Lee's old ideas had been impeccably maintained, indeed polished to satin perfection. Unfortunately, their craftsmanship bespoke the limitations of a bygone era.

As Mildred Lee fretted about becoming a mildewed specimen of a vanished world, her mother was suffering from spiritual starvation of a different sort.[2] She was truly crippled now, and her summer sojourns to Virginia's healing springs made little difference in the progress of her disease. Her interest in life had always been caught up in the fine-meshed network of her relatives and their lilac-scented homes. Of all the devastations of the war, the loss of this world was the cruelest blow. "I long for old scenes & old haunts," she moaned to a cousin in Clarke County. "I feel caged here in every sense of the word my infirmy confines me almost entirely to my chair & the house & I cannot even see out of my window anything but the few trees in the yard . . . . I cannot take root in a new soil—I am too old for that."³ The loss of Arlington and its precious Washington artifacts deeply wounded her. Nearly every letter sent by Mary Lee during the postwar years was a veritable beating of the breast, a long wail of loss and injustice—and open hatred for those who had robbed her. "I cannot write with any composure on . . . my own cherished Arlington," Mary told a friend. "Even *savages* would have spared that place for the sake of the former associations & my Father's uniform & *special* kindness to the *Northern people,* yet they have done every thing to *debase* & *execrate* it."⁴ She knew that a shroud was now thrown over her old home, but she declared that the graves could be moved, the ex-slaves dispersed and that she would "never rest until it is restored nor will I *ever* relinquish my claim to it."⁵

Her husband was more cautious, reluctant to press any claim until his political status was clearer. He made some quiet enquiries through his lawyer and his brother Smith, and did try to settle his father-in-law's estate, selling property and finalizing deeds. In 1869, however, Lee admitted that he still had not taken any steps to recover Arlington "under the belief that at present I could accomplish no good."⁶ He counseled his wife to accept God's will in this as in all things, saying it would never matter in a hundred years who owned the property, then adding a little political barb about how he hoped the presence of the Washington mementos in the nation's capital would remind the Yankees of the founding fathers' principles.⁷ His wife would not be placated. Lacking Robert's caution, and "*maddened* daily," she sent a petition to Andrew Johnson, and continued to express her outrage to all who would listen.⁸ In words she admitted were "too *bitter* & *agonizing* for the public," she told Benson Lossing, her former historical collaborator, of the way she had conspired to keep Washington's papers from General David Hunter's "Vandals," and how they had been destroyed as a result.⁹ Lossing was stunned that the nation's irreplaceable artifacts had been handled in such a cavalier manner. He advised Senator Henry Wilson that the Congress, which was considering a return of the Washington treasures, should under no conditions allow Mrs. Lee to repossess them. "I *know* her to be utterly unworthy of such a trust, and believe her motives to be wholly mercenary," he declared passionately. Congress tabled its motion to restore the relics to the Lee family, and they did not recover them until the turn of the century.¹⁰

Until the end of her life Mrs. Lee mourned the loss of her home. In 1873, unable to resist her desire to revisit it, she suffered great pain to travel to Arlington. Friends drove her up through the decimated forests, through the acres of graves, past the familiar, much-loved haunts of her childhood that were "so changed it seemed but a dream of the past."[11] Hobbling out of the carriage, she took a drink from the stone-banked well, then turned away in anguish. She died three months later. Mildred remembered that in her last hours her mind wandered—and once again Mary Custis Lee was a young lady at Arlington, gathering violets, her babes in her arms.[12]

Mary Lee's connections to her family seat were particularly strong, but her feelings were not unique. The cornerstone of southern society was the home, the site of safety and identity. From it sprang a style of patriotism that was linked to place, something that had more to do with the smell of mist rising from fragrant earth or a face framed in candleshine than it did with the complexities of states' rights.[13] The Civil War was a catastrophe for southern families, who had sacrificed not only dear sons and brothers, but the rootstock of their lives as well. Though the cruelty of marauders and the suspicion that the sacred hearth could not be defended by either the army or government had eroded Confederate commitment during the war, para-doxically, in the end the appalling destruction served to create a unity among Southerners that was more solid than it had been at the outset. To-gether with the abolition of slavery, the devastation was viewed as a crude northern attempt to overthrow a culture, a deliberately insulting act of per-sonal dispossession. The outrage of this formed an important basis for mutual sympathy, a rallying point for resistance—passive or otherwise—against the victorious North. It connected people to a past they could not retrieve, and blinded them to the opportunity inherent in their painful chaos. "Let us leave our land and emigrate to any desert spot of earth rather than return to the Union, even as it Was!" exclaimed one southern woman. Home ways threatened had begun the war; home ways destroyed would retard the peace.[14]

The overturned economic structure added to the emotional havoc. Southern gentry moved uncertainly from their familiar stratified life to a postfeudal world they had difficulty imagining. Questions of labor and land were practical realities rather than the stuff of high philosophy to these people. If they still controlled one-half of the dynamic—land—they found to their consternation they could not command the other. Not only were so-cial assumptions aggressively challenged by the freedmen and their protec-tors, but $2 billion in slave property had been lost. The socioeconomic base had been destroyed, and cutthroat competition arose.[15] In addition, the half decade after the war was a political roller coaster for the South, particularly for prominent Confederates. The lenient policies of Grant and Lincoln were unevenly voiced by President Johnson, and his indecision opened the way for those with more radical views. The North was aghast at Lincoln's assassination, and they had grievances against the South as heartfelt as those expressed by Mary Lee. Northerners believed the "flower of their youth," some 360,000 men, had been butchered in a useless, immoral war begun by undisciplined hotspurs.[16] They read with revulsion of seemingly crass inhumanity at Andersonville, Belle Isle, and other southern prisons. The tales told by former slaves did not lead one to admire too much the South's fallen paternalism. One could argue endlessly—people still do—about whose views were correct: the salient feature in the late 1860s was that the North had the power to act legally on its horrified feelings. As a result there were vicious debates about black political rights, about the conditions under which the southern states should be readmitted to the Union, and about punishment for men like Lee. In Virginia alone, amnesty policies changed three times in as many years, with confusion and political finagling increasing toward the end of the decade.[17]

Incensed by the loss of Arlington and the stormy political winds, Mary Lee voiced her convictions with unconstrained spirit. "Nothing occurs except the heaping up of *tyranny* & insult from Washington by the *meanest* most *cowardly* & unprincipled lot of men ever assembled together to curse any people," she wrote as, "up to her eyes in newspapers," she followed the debates on Reconstruction.[18] She was particularly aggrieved at the favoritism she thought was shown toward the freed people. The Lees had minimal contact with their former slaves, some of whom had had the temerity to aid the Union or to leave at the first opportunity, and Mary Lee was convinced that they could not have been so "ungrateful" had they not been "beguiled off by the Yankees."[19] She was shocked when Congress appropriated millions of dollars for the education of the blacks—money denied to destitute white Southerners—and concluded that had the Confederates known how much they were to endure, they would never have relaxed their efforts toward independence. Having already experienced the malice of the Yankees, she believed her people were now exposed to "a set of *lazy idle negroes* who roam about by day *marking* what they may steal at night & are kept attending political harangues of which they understand about as much as *the African Gorilla.*" She hoped the freedmen would all be forced to emigrate to Africa or the North, "as it is hard that we at the South who have already done so much for them more than their labor has ever repayed should be tormented with them the rest of our lives—" She begged the recipient of this letter to pardon her political commentary, but, she noted, "it is so hard to refrain."[20]

Whether Lee listened to these speeches, or tried to restrain them in any way, is not clear. His education and temperament had made him a good deal more adaptable than many of his contemporaries. He did not necessarily disagree with his wife, however. His style was quite different, of course, and the stakes were also higher for him. To begin with, his civil status remained unclear for some time. The treason charges had been dropped, and he had taken the amnesty oath in hopes that it would provide a positive example to the Washington College community. Notwithstanding Grant's "earnest recommendation" that his full rights be restored, no official action was ever taken, and he regained his civil liberties only under Andrew Johnson's blanket pardon of Christmas Day 1868. Even this excluded him from holding office, for the proclamation denied that privilege to anyone who had broken a previously sworn loyalty oath to the United States.[21] Despite this, his name was raised both in connection with the governorship of Virginia and as candidate for president of the United States in 1868. Lee was personally disinclined toward political office, but also thought such a move would be provocative, and ultimately injurious to the South.[22] In fact, his overall philosophy was to avoid publicity, saying that it was "extremely unpleasant to me . . . that my name should be unnecessarily brought before the public; and I do not see that any good can result from it."[23] The instinct was underscored when he hit a wall of vituperation during his campaign to raise funds for Washington College. One pro-Republican newspaper was shocked to see "the arch traitor Lee placed over [students] to instruct them in more treason." Another called Washington College "a great center of Southern training in hate of the North and of the Union." Much of this was inflated election-year rhetoric, but it reinforced Lee's instinctive hesitancy.[24]

Cautious, yet himself increasingly politicized, Lee developed a policy of public reticence and private advocacy. He repeatedly maintained that he "avoided all discussion of political questions" and had "a great reluctance to obtrude [his] political opinions upon the public," announcing to one friend that "as I am anxious to do as little harm as possible, I deem it wisest for me to remain silent."[25] In early 1866 he was summoned before the congressional Joint Committee on Reconstruction, and here too he pleaded near total ignorance of political conditions and local debate, saying that he had been living "very retired" and had no knowledge of general opinions. The testimony cannot have been easy: it took place in the Capitol—still draped with captured rebel war flags and overlooking the ghostly mausoleum of Arlington—and before men who had summoned him largely for voyeuristic reasons. Lee's performance was a masterpiece of reticence. His "briefly straightforward, coldly clear" answers may have been technically accurate, but they stopped short of the whole truth.[26] Notwithstanding his statement that he "had but little communication with politicians," he was in discreet contact with many public figures.[27] He followed both the northern and southern press—though he publicly denied that he read any newspapers—and had strongly formed views about the actions needed to rebuild his region.[28] Some of these views were remarkably advanced, as his innovations at Washington College indicated, and his support for enhanced technology, education, and industrial reform presaged many aspects of the "new" South.[29] In the main, though, he was staunchly conservative. Most of his opinions sought to justify the preeminence of states' rights, and he expressed an overt dislike—even fear—of majority politics and strong federal government. He wrote candidly to his nephew that the "tendency seems to be to one vast Government, sure to become aggressive abroad & despotic at home" and longed to "bring things back to the principles of the old Constitution."[30] In relation to his former adversaries he publicly took a much-respected high road. He reportedly told some young women he met at the Virginia springs that he had "never known one moment of bitterness or resentment," advising them that it "was unworthy of them . . . to cherish feelings of resentment against the North."[31] In private he penned political treatises that throb with controlled rage, containing harsh words about "a national civilization which rots the life of a people to the core"; "the gaol to which our progress in civilization is guiding us"; or "unprincipled men who look for nothing but the retention of place & power in their hands." This and several other draft essays he wrote were never published, but their cross-hatched and unfinished pages are like the smoke from a roiling volcano.[32]

Lee's growing ire paralleled a political shift away from the comparatively moderate politics of Andrew Johnson's reconstruction, when Southerners had thought they might be able to arrange their own affairs, and a realistic and adaptive attitude was cautiously advanced. Radical Republicans gained political ground, enacting policies that put the old Confederate states under brief military rule, appointing hardliners to governorships, and ramming through constitutional amendments that enfranchised African-Americans. Even the most sanguine southern leaders realized that cooperation and patience could soothe their distraught population or advance reconciliation.[33] Lee was among those who became alarmed. "The avowed objects of the war, 'the restoration of the Union with all the dignity, equality & rights of the States *unimpaired*,' have not been fulfilled . . . ," he wrote hotly. "The certain part seems to be that though the war has ended, peace is not restored to the country."[34] Surprisingly, his solution was for the individual southern states to show less independence. He would have them reunite, he told a niece, "not only for their own protection, but for the destruction of this grand

scheme of centralization of power in the hands of one branch of the Gov^t."[35]
He balked at all attempts to keep moderates in power at the convention
called to discuss Virginia statehood, including a move to form a coalition
among those seeking a middle path between the status quo ante and the
policies of the radicals. He also declined to align himself with those who
thought influencing the Republicans by
participating with them might soften
their policies.[36] In public he magisteri-
ally proclaimed that all "should vote for
the most intelligent, honest and conscientious men elligible to office, irrespec-
tive of former party opinions, who will
endeavor to make the new Constitutions . . . as beneficial as possible to the
true interests prosperity and liberty
of all classes and conditions of the
people."[37] Privately he appears to have
advocated restrictions on franchise
rights that would exclude a great number of blacks as well as some whites
from the polls.[38] Finally, in the election
of 1868 he openly backed the rightist
policies of the Democratic Party, sponsoring a meeting of former generals and
other conservative southern leaders at
the White Sulphur Springs. The group

Lee in the late 1860s.

ARLINGTON HOUSE, THE ROBERT E. LEE
MEMORIAL, NATIONAL PARK SERVICE

wrote a manifesto that called for an end to "oppressive misrule," dismissed
legitimate power-sharing with the blacks, and proposed a return to the
"kindness and humanity" of their former social system.[39] The letter was addressed to William Rosecrans, the former Union general who had outfoxed
Lee in western Virginia during the campaigns of 1861, and was now one of
the managers of the Democratic national campaign. It was the familiar paternalism, vintage 1860, clumsily offered under a new label. The men involved seem to have ignored the justification it would give to the radicals;
they meant it for publication. Lee must have been aware of the enormous
influence the affixture of his name carried. Now safe from the threat of
prosecution, he allowed his alignments to be made clear. The tract was
widely reprinted throughout the South. Popularly he still styled himself the
disinterested private man. ("But I must not wander into politics," he cau-

tioned a friend just after the White Sulphur paper was published, "a subject I carefully avoid . . . ."[40]) In private he allowed himself to exhibit his true feelings about the "vindictiveness and malignity of the Yankees, of which he had no conception before the war."[41]

Among the most vexing questions was the changed status of African-Americans. Lee had never been comfortable with the idea of intermingling

Lee and southern leaders at White Sulphur Springs.
VIRGINIA HISTORICAL SOCIETY

with blacks, and the issue of race and power was one that seemed to jar his most fundamental assumptions. Lee had consistently stated that he did not approve of slavery, that he "had always been in favor of emancipation—gradual emancipation." Since he believed the system unworkable, and detrimental to the interests of whites, there is no reason to question his sincerity on this point.[42] This, however, did not mean that he could accept anything that approached egalitarianism. Like others of his region, he persisted in truly believing that blacks were incapable of functioning on their own, that they had no inclination to work, and aspired to nothing beyond daily comfort and amusement. Such attitudes not only justified the adherence to slavery in the first place, they calmed the unspeakable worry that the freed blacks might succeed, thereby becoming a threat to status, economy, and pride.[43] Lee's worldview was still strongly hierarchical—even within his enlightened vision of widespread education, he could not see beyond offering only as much "knowledge & high mental culture as the limited means of the humble can command."[44] From the end of the war he took care to distance himself from the ex-slaves as much as possible, maintaining his control by

aloofness. He tried to employ white rather than black servants in his household, though in the end the family acquiesced to hiring three or four "tolerable . . . respectable, but not energetic" freedmen.[45] As before the war, his
expectations fulfilled long-honed stereotypes. He told Congress he thought
the ex-slaves less able than whites to acquire knowledge and inclined only to
work sporadically on "very short jobs . . . they like their ease and comfort,
and I think, look more to their present than to their future condition."[46] He
advised his planter friends to shun black labor, for he felt the freedmen
would work against their former owners and destroy property values. "I
have always observed that wherever you find the negro, everything is going
down around him," he told one cousin, "and wherever you find the white
man, you see everything around him improving."[47] Although he did not always state it so starkly, he continued to think, as he had told the *Herald,* that
the blacks had best be "disposed of" and endorsed the idea of importing European workers to replace them. Lee particularly hoped that English immigration could be increased so that the South would benefit from "good
citizens whose interests & feelings would be in unison with our own."[48]

The promotion of European immigration was a popular plan in the
early postwar years, which embraced not only the elimination of black
workers but a return to an idyllic preindustrial world of small farms and rural pleasures. It never worked out exactly as envisioned in the southern
imagination—indeed the evidence indicates that, like the doomed American Colonization Society, the attempt to force such demographic change
turned into something of a charade.[49] Lee's vision did not include granting African-Americans the same option of productive citizenship that he
wished to offer to immigrants. He explained to the Joint Committee on Reconstruction that "at this time, they cannot vote intelligently" and that he
opposed black enfranchisement on the grounds that it would "excite un-
friendly feelings between the two races . . . ."[50] He was also concerned about
the educational opportunities being provided to the blacks by the Freedmen's Bureau and private northern charities, preferring they be taught
by white Southerners, who were "acquainted with their characters and
wants."[51] Most of all he feared that blacks might procure enough political
leverage to offset white control. The blacks lacked the capacity "necessary to
make them safe depositories of political power," stated Lee and his compatriots. Therefore, "in common with a large majority of the people of the
North and West," the White Sulphur Springs group was "inflexibly opposed
to any system of laws that would place the political power of the country in
the hands of the negro race."[52] It was all couched delicately, but the alarm is
barely disguised.

The White Sulphur paper went out of its way to claim that there was "no enmity" toward the freedmen, and in outward gestures Lee strove to uphold
this. He wrote a polite letter to an ex-slave from Arlington, and told her and
others he wished them well, though no aid to them was ever forthcoming.[53]
In one famous incident it was reported that Lee knelt next to an old black
man at St. Paul's Church in Richmond and took communion, while the rest
of the congregation remained frozen in place. There is only one source for
the story, and it was written forty years after its supposed occurrence, but it
is not entirely improbable. Lee had worshiped next to slaves all his life at
the little Arlington chapel; such a move would not have overwhelmed him.
As the document is written, however, Lee kneels some distance from the
black man, underscoring the established custom of the Lord's table—"even
there—black, white, and brown, separate according to caste." Likewise Lee
simply ignores the man's presence, signaling more that the new order could
not sway him from the rituals of his life than that there has been a shift in
social expectations.[54]

He took a similar detached stance from the racial malaise that reigned in
Lexington, though there the immediate risks were far greater. Once the local Freedmen's Bureau opened, the directors found that, despite its pride in
education, the town was far from enlightened. In their first report they observed that "General Lee's Boys" would make it "a *hard* place for 'Nigger
Teachers.'" Incidents proved them right.[55] The local paper carried panicky
stories about allowing blacks in first-class cars and opening universities to
them, and called out rallies of all "who believe that white men should rule in
the land of Washington, Jefferson, Lee and Jackson."[56] Lee certainly did not
attend such meetings, though he opposed universal education of blacks, especially if superimposed by the North. Washington College students, along
with their cadet cohorts from the Virginia Military Institute, threw stones at
the freedmen's school windows, loudly sang rebel songs during spontaneous evening rallies, and harassed teachers. Northern women working
with the Freedmen's Bureau reported that they were spat upon in the
streets. One was habitually greeted with the call: "Damn Yankee bitch of a
nigger teacher."[57] When they wrote their stories to the *New York Independent*
and other northern papers, there was a strong backlash, which may have
contributed to editorial harangues that same year against the "traitorous"
Lee and the practices he was encouraging.[58]

Lexington Freedmen's Bureau agents and teachers at the African-
American schools reported also that the college boys were consistent sexual predators against black women, citing several attempts "to abduct . . .

unwilling colored girls [for] readily divined purposes."[59] The students at Lee's college appear to have formed a chapter of the Ku Klux Klan, scaring blacks and whites alike with notices depicting skeletons, coffins, and black crape.[60] This behavior was unacceptable enough, but the activities escalated into at least two dangerous incidents involving Washington College students. One concerned a provocation made by some army officers who were investigating town actions against the Freedmen's Bureau. One afternoon during a skating party, reciprocal insults were exchanged, weapons were brandished, and the pleasant scene nearly turned into a lynching. Lee and others tried to downplay the event, but it was grave enough that the bureau agent called on the army to send troops from Lynchburg. When the threatened man, E. C. Johnston, sent an account of the episode to the northern papers, it created more negative publicity for Lee and his school. Lee apparently dismissed the worst offenders, but the provocations did not end.[61]

More serious was an incident in which Judge Brockenbrough's son was shot after he attacked an African-American who had not stepped into the gutter when his mother passed. The students sent out a vigilante committee to find the black man and nearly perpetrated another lynching when he was caught. Some of the collegians threatened to storm the jail and "shoot the negro." "It has quite a wholesome effect for some of the students to shoot one occasionally," opined a Washington College student who was involved, adding that the blacks were "incited to their impudence by a trifling Bureau agent here."[62] Both army and Freedmen's Bureau officials warned Lee (as well as Virginia Military Institute head Francis Smith) that such "rambunctious" behavior needed to be curtailed. Lee had sent out advisories forbidding his students to take part in these activities, and in both instances Lee promised army and city officials that those participating would be penalized. The incidents did nothing to help Washington College or Virginia's ability to shed northern supervision, and Lee undoubtedly hoped to forestall future mischief. But at best, he gave out ambiguous signals. The number of accusations against Washington College boys indicates that he either punished the racial harassment more laxly than other misdemeanors, or turned a blind eye to it. "It was reported that the Gen. had dismissed some of the boys," a student told his parents, "but I have not known of any leaving."[63] Certainly he did not exercise the near imperial control he had at the school, as he did for more trivial matters, such as when the boys threatened to take unofficial Christmas holidays. Given the hardened attitudes and quick resentments among the men, many of whom were well used to violence, it is perhaps less surprising that the unfortunate actions took place than that there were not more of them. Still, it is hard to reconcile the situation with Lee's statement to Congress that everyone "expresses kind feelings toward the freedmen. They wish to see them get on in the world."[64]

Although slow to show outward chagrin, Lee was nonetheless suffering from the same social dislocation as his veteran-students. The contradiction between his smooth glide forward on educational reform and the clumsy sideways steps on political and racial issues is illustrative of his deep malaise during this time. It is difficult to imagine the total readjustment of assumptions and status that white Southerners faced after the Civil War. Even a man like Lee, who had fought family misfortune and earned much of his success by diligent application, had been given a jump start in life by his race and his sex. The change away from a social structure that had associated white males with prerogative and prestige might be ethically commendable—it might even be recognized by some as beneficial—but it was nonetheless cataclysmic. "The surface of society, like a great ocean, is upheaved, and all the relations of life are disturbed and out of joint," wrote a reporter for the *Montgomery Daily Advertiser*. Lee's soul felt the turbulence.[65]

His disquiet was evident in a number of ways. He began writing little treatises on the "complete sovereignty" of the states that were in sharp contrast to his thinking in 1861, when "secession is nothing but revolution" was his watchword. That they remained in draft like his other political essays, laboriously reworked, but unread by others, underscores the conflict he felt.[66] Lee claimed that the war had settled nothing: it had merely decided by the sword that which negotiation had been unable to resolve. "Looking at the late war from this point of view, it is difficult to find results which justify the conflict," Lee maintained. "Political quarrels were the motive of the war, but what difficulties in the way of the development of the country have been removed by it?"[67] Anxious to reassert the moral authority of the South, he told his cousin Cassius Lee that it was imperative to mold "the opinion which posterity may form of the motives which governed the South in their late struggle for the maintenance of the principles of the Constitution."[68] He could see nothing but threat in clarification of one of those principles—majority rule—and he especially balked at the idea that the war had been fought over slavery. He remained unmoved by the assertions of P. G. T. Beauregard and his aide Charles Marshall that this was exactly what had been at issue, nor was he persuaded by the proud words of former Arlington slave William Burke. "The affliction caused by the war . . . has been very great," wrote Burke, "yet we cannot but regard it as the means employed by God to break the strong hand of Slavery. . . . Who can fight against the great God!"[69]

Who indeed? Just how Lee viewed defeat in his heart is another sobering question. It was one thing to have lost the political objective, but to confront the staggering cost of his various decisions was nearly unbearable. If, as he had proclaimed throughout the years of battle, God would determine the outcome, had he been wrong to believe that God favored the South? If God's favor lay elsewhere, as Union victory seemed to indicate, had he defied God's will by defending the Confederacy and all it stood for? Lee staunchly maintained that his men had never let him down—and if this was true, and God had cheered their cause, it must have been he, as he said at the close of the battle of Gettysburg, who had let down both God and man. Evangelical theology had given Southerners a convenient way out of the corner by claiming that God loved best those whom he chastised. Self-blame was limited to small failings of pride and ingratitude rather than a breach of the most sacred commandments. To this Lee added the old comfort of God's inscrutability. "We failed," he wrote in sorrow, "but in the good provenance of God apparent failure often proves a blessing. I trust it will eventuate so in this instance."[70] Nonetheless, it is clear that something pricked him, something he needed to set right in his mind, as well as in the opinion of the world. When John S. Mosby met with him in later years, he found him terribly "oppressed by the great memories" and pacifist in his conversation. Lee also repudiated war to nephew Edward Childe and a Washington College patron, refusing to applaud the course of the Franco-Prussian conflict then looming.[71] He was so disturbed by past events, he told a journalist, that he had been unable to read a single word about the war.[72] Though this assertion was not strictly true, it starkly revealed the anguish of the moment.

Faced with enormous consequences in blood and integrity, and far from serene, he began to struggle with a justification for his own actions. He now wrote that his determination to side with the South had been based on constitutional principles, and embraced the notion of a southern right to independence, reversing his formerly stated opposition to secession. He sought to validate his decision by invoking other historic changes of heart. "I need not tell you that true patriotism sometimes requires of men to act contrary, at one period, to that which it does at another," Lee suggested to Beauregard, "and the motive which impels them—the desire to do right—is precisely the same. The circumstances which govern their actions change, and their conduct must conform to the new order of things."[73] He tried to realign Light-Horse Harry's opinions, and even his father's leading part in the Federal repression of the Whiskey Rebellion, to make them conform to his new states' rights stance.[74] He did a little historical boasting and rewriting, subtly staking a claim to each fine success and revising some embarrassing moments.[75] He considered airing his version of events by writing his memoirs, but was handicapped by a lack of records and time. Though he wrote repeatedly to his comrades in search of recollections and official materials, he finally discarded the project, believing that his version of the story would not "bring forth a good result" and in the end admitting that he "was too interested and might be biased."[76] He may have been right. Historians have long lamented his abandonment of the book, but the notes left by Lee were strongly geared to an explanation of defeat by overwhelming resources or inaction by subordinates, rather than a forthright assessment of triumph and failure.[77]

He was like an old caged lion, cuffing at every threat, but shackled and silenced by his political captivity. Any public justification of his motives and actions would be seen as more than normal self-defense; his silence endorsed judgments he felt to be false. Lee partially removed his muzzle by having conversations with select associates at Washington College, some of them former comrades to whom he complained loudly about the avalanche of postwar reassessments. Their notes give a fascinating replay of some elements of the wartime action, but they also make for sad reading. Like the snippets he jotted for his memoirs, Lee's words are long on self-vindication and show no ability to accept fault, or acknowledge personal error. He may have announced to the world after Gettysburg that it was "all my fault," but privately he pointed the finger at J. E. B. Stuart, at Ewell, at the absence of Jackson, and even tried to make the intriguing case that he had in fact whipped the Yankees in Pennsylvania. These notes are far from the brisk and candid assessment penned by E. Porter Alexander, or Grant's forthright chronicle of his accomplishments and blunders. Eavesdropping on these conversations through the notes of Lee's interlocutors, we hear the voice of a disappointed man, growing taut and hard as we listen.[78]

Political concerns and family problems provided the backbeat to Lee's growing dissatisfaction in his later years. The work of the college annoyed him at best. Despite the reputation the school was earning, after a short time in Lexington he told Rooney he wanted to leave, and he still dreamed of having a little farm. As his health grew steadily more fragile, however, it became difficult to make any changes.[79] He took no pleasure in the adulation of the southern public, and ignored the admiration expressed by much of the North. He turned down all of his numerous invitations to speak, and hated to have his picture taken. When his wife pressed him to sit for the celebrated Virginia sculptor Edward Valentine, he acquiesced and said the artist could come at his convenience—"All times will be irksome to me."[80] Though Lee steadfastly maintained his outward manifestations of piety, working in the church, and lecturing the students on the importance of moral values, it appears he had also lost some of his confidence in the evangelicals' ordered world. No one can truly fathom another's heart, but the writings he left from this time rarely commend his loved ones to God's care, and gone are the old psalmist exhortations about the wonders of creation or assurance that a divine providence will arrange everything felicitously. With few outlets for his grief or his questioning, the frustration and depression grew. He spoke of himself as being "stiff & crabbed" or "grave & melancholy" and found his only pleasure in riding Traveller through the verdant Virginia mountains each afternoon.[81] In company he always tried to keep a cheerful demeanor, and his brother Smith's boy, who stayed with the Lees during these years, remembered his gentle whimsy and courtly manner.[82] Personal friends also remarked that Lee tried his best to bring back the old-time courtesy and gaiety, and that everyone in the town received his pleasant salutation, especially the children. "He kept his suffering locked up in his great heart and it did not show in his face," wrote daughter Mildred.[83] Yet here and there the anguish did seep through the genteel facade. "Life is indeed gliding away & I have nothing of good to show for mine," he once wrote to his wife. On another occasion he said that his challenge was to bear silently each day's disappointment "as I have all the others."[84] Visitors noted that he was depressed, "pale and haggard," with eyes that were often moist—not "the Apollo . . . known in the army."[85] The outbursts with students probably stemmed as well from this inner turmoil; and once, to the astonishment of Mildred, he even furiously beat poor old Traveller.[86]

His eyes hurt so badly that he could often see only dimly. The firm, elegant handwriting began to trail off uncertainly. He told his friends he was an old man bound to what had been, unenthusiastic about new prospects.[87] At sixty he was tired of life, and he began to speak of death with envious words. Thinking of Annie, he remarked, "her quiet & innocent repose I much covet."[88]

"If Vanquished, I Am Still Victorious"

7th October

My dear Carter

Our first mail for more than 8 days arrived this morning & brought with it your hurried letter to Robert. As it may be very long ere he will either read or write another, I will answer at once lest you should be needlessly alarmed with the newspaper accounts. He is better today than he has been since his seizure & Dr. Madison assures me there are no symptoms of Paralysis in his case nor of apoplexy, that he thinks it is over tension of the nerves of the brain with some connexion with his late illness & that he may possibly be in better health when relieved. He is improving slowly, but steadily each day & though he does not seem inclined to talk occasionally utters a sentence very distinctly we feel much encouraged about him tho' still anxious & I know it will be long ere he can resume at all the immense correspondence that annoys him so much & which no one seems able to carry on to his satisfaction. I will now give you a detailed account of the whole attack. On Wednesday 29th Septr He rose earlier than usual & was always rather in a hurry to get his breakfast & get the girls off to Chapel which has been his fancy lately thinking if the ladies would patronize it that the students would be more interested in going then he went to College & remained there the whole time till half past one oclock or later, which he has but done recently generally coming home during the morning & taking a little walk or ride. ate as usual a plate of grapes before dinner & then his ordinary dinner about half past 2 a very slight one for we had nothing but a poor pair of chickens. after dinner he took his usual snooze in his chair & went over to church after which there was a prolonged & anxious vestry meeting about which I knew he had been troubled at 7 oclock our tea came in & he had not come so I sat down with my sewing & Custis on the sofa about half past I heard him come in the front door & take off his hat & cloak & deposit them in his room & as he entered the dining room I said "where have you been all this time, we have been waiting for you" He stood up at the foot of the table as if to say grace but ut-

tered no sound & then sank back in his chair. I said you look very tired let me give you a cup of tea. He tried to reply but uttered something unintelligible. I looked up & his countenance alarmed me Custis came to him & asked him what was the matter but he did not speak but continued sitting in the chair we sent off for the Doctors who had both been at the same vestry meeting & had not reached home & they both arrived in less than 10 minutes applied cold cloths to his head & hot baths to his feet & then got off his clothes & lifted him in to a bed which was brought down into the dining room & where he has been ever since. He slept almost continuously for two days & nights the Drs thinking entire rest might restore him but finding that it did nothing cupped him & have been giving him medicines since & he is now much more aroused tho' he still sleeps a good deal, seems to enjoy what food is offered him tho' rarely asks for anything I trust that a life so important to his family & country may be longer spared & that I may soon be enabled to report him to you much better. Tell my dear little Mildred I have not time now to write to her as I am very tired having been writing nearly all day [letter ends abruptly][1]

. . .

Lexington Dec 27th 1870

My Dear Lizzie,

Thank you for yr kind sympathizing letter. I was glad to hear of you again and had thought of writing to you during the summer. I have not felt as if I could write since even now it is so hard to speak of what my heart is so full, and so hard to speak of anything else. You and all who loved and admired his character can realize partly how much we have had to give up, but the daily companionship, the mutual dependence, which increased with his advancing years, so our quiet life here is only known to our longing, empty hearts.

But we have been given so much! And love can be strong enough to wish rather the happiness of the beloved than our own. He has left his children such a blessed inheritance of honour and nobility of character, we are still rich in ennobling and happy memories of him. Especially this past year I had been so much with Papa. Had felt so anxious from his first serious attack more than a year ago. Had had such a beautiful journey South with him last Spring, saw him improving all the time, and only in Sept he felt himself so well my fears were lulled. But God was very good to him. The thing he seemed to dread— failing strength—he was not to suffer long. In the midst of his energy and usefulness God took him. I have written so much to you dear Lizzie, because I like to think of you as one of my real friends, as the links of life lesson, I like to hold to those that were formed in earlier lighter days and believe them as strong as ever. I enclose a photograph of my father for my little namesake.

Agnes Lee[2]

>─┤◂▸─○─◂▸┤─◂

M Y CHILD," said General Lee to one of his young lady friends in the
summer of 1869, "I think I am the very oldest man you have ever
seen."³ It might have been a gentle quip, but his listener did not think he was
joking. It was a moving recognition of spiritual loss rather than a reckoning
of accumulated years. He was only sixty-two, just eight years past the days
when he had appeared striking—splendid—a robust man. For some time
he had been telling friends and family that life with him was "very uncertain" and cousins spoke in shocked undertones about his physical deterioration since the opening of the war.⁴

On the morning of September 28, 1870, Lee arose as usual, determined to
step firmly through the day. He wrote a genial note to Samuel Tagart, who
had met him the previous year and wanted to "inveigle" a better acquaintance. It was to be the very last of his thousands of letters, and with its pretty,
old-fashioned courtesies and talk of friendship, it seems a sentimental finale
to his literary life. He wife chronicles his day: the general did his office work;
enjoyed some late grapes; then took a short snooze—little things that taken
together add up to a life. But a student who saw Lee that morning said he
looked "bent and broken" and another noticed the deep lines on his face—
formed, he thought, more by grief than disease. By evening, Robert Edward
Lee would be changing worlds.⁵

Though he had courageously envisioned a new purpose for his life, and was
viewed as a symbol of hope by millions, Lee seemed in his last years to woo
death. He told his wife that he looked forward with joy to the time that he
would lie down and rest, and to Markie he admitted, "My interest in time &
its concerns is daily fading away & I try to keep my eyes & thoughts fixed on
those eternal shores to which I am fast hastening."⁶ He had been ill since the
spring of 1863 when he suffered severe chest pains as the army camped near
Fredericksburg. Though he sloughed it off as a cold, and cheerily complained that the doctors were "tapping me all over like an old steam boiler
before condemning it," he also admitted to paroxysms that were quite
sharp.⁷ The severity of the condition increased through the years until he
was "in terrific anguish" and could not walk from his home to the college
without acute discomfort.⁸ Doctors disagree on the diagnosis, but it was
probably angina pectoris—painful spasms caused by insufficient oxygen
to the heart—the result of atherosclerosis. He had rallied after a trip with
Agnes to the balmier climate of the Carolinas the previous year. There he
had visited his father's grave, pondering perhaps who this man had been,

and what of him survived in his own person. The pilgrimage also led to Annie's final resting place in North Carolina. When his beloved brother Smith died in July 1869, he returned to Alexandria. Visiting his boyhood home on Oronoco Street, he lingered silently in his mother's old room.[9] He passed several days with Britannia Peter, who had been a bridesmaid in his wedding, and evenly told her he had wanted to stay once more at Tudor Place before he died.[10] He was exhausted and crotchety, with little zeal for anything, even annoyed by the excited girls who stood in line to kiss him after services at Christ Church. "The general is failing," whispered his hosts. In sadness Lee departed for Lexington.[11]

He sat for a long time near the window that afternoon of September 28, watching as a terrible storm approached, and gently chiding Precious Life when she magnified the gloom by playing the Funeral March on the piano. He was irritated that he had to attend a difficult vestry meeting and told her in his gentle, jesting way that he wished he "did not have to go & listen to all that pow wow." But he went over to the chapel and sat on the cold pews before starting the meeting, hugging his military cape about himself and chatting amiably of his boyhood acquaintance with John Marshall. As he had predicted, it was a long and anxious meeting, and when he could find no consensus on raising funds for a new steeple, he put an end to it all by writing the fifty-five-dollar check himself. Then he walked home to tea, but as his wife relates, when he rose to say grace the words came incoherently. Unable to walk, he sank into his armchair, and then was laid on his camp cot, set up in the dining room.[12]

There he hovered for two weeks, somewhere between Earth and eternity. The storm that had threatened arrived with torrential rain—"as if," wrote Mary Lee, "the very elements were in convulsive thrusts weeping with us." Then the weather changed to bright, golden October light, and the mood of the family raced between the same points of despair and hope.[13] He could move a little and seemed to understand what was said to him, and over the course of weeks spoke three or four sentences. But what haunted Mildred for the rest of her life was the silence of those days. "He would lay straight & motionless, gasping, with that solemn unutterable look into the flames that played on the hearth—& . . . the words seemed frozen in all our mouths. He was speechless—and so were we." Agnes was there, rubbing his hands in the way he had loved when she was a child. Custis took over the direction of the household and helped with the nursing; Mary Lee sat at her husband's side, fanning him and moistening his lips.[14] She told one friend a few weeks later that several times he spoke excitedly, "his mind wandering back to those dreadful battlefields," and informed another caller that he had once uttered the words "let the tent be struck."[15] The physicians, more optimistic than expert, thought he only needed rest. They prescribed standard medicines for the day, including turpentine, strychnine, and morphine. Their patient ate a little, but showed no interest in the struggle for life. When he rallied for a moment the doctors cheerily encouraged him to think of taking a ride on Traveller, but he only shook his head and waved them away.[16] On October 10 his condition worsened, and Precious Life watched in horror as "he tried to speak—looked so beseechingly at us . . . always those glorious dark eyes from the little bed, speaking with imploring, heart-rending tones!" Then on the morning of October 12, with Mary holding his wet, perspiring hand, he made two painful gasps, and with a little sigh his "breath seemed to pass away gently."[17]

The Lees knew of course that their anguish was a public one—a "common sorrow," Mrs. Lee called it.[18] About 9:40—ten minutes after the general's death—college classes were suspended, and Lexington, Richmond, and other southern towns began to put on their mourning garb. A correspondent for the *New York Tribune* arrived the same day to find Lexington "overwhelmed with grief." Stores were shuttered; prayer meetings were packed with mourners; tremulous streamers of crepe draped from windows, columns, and hatbands. In the state capital a day of mourning was declared.[19] Many people commented on the strangely subdued atmosphere that took hold in the days following Lee's death. The quietude was heightened by the terrific storms that had flooded the area and cut off the town. The only sound seemed to be the tolling of bells.[20] "You never saw such unaffected grief," acknowledged Margaret Junkin Preston, a friend of the family. "I sat with Mrs. Lee for some time, a few days since. Her noble fortitude and Christian resignation are touching in the extreme. She said—her eyes filmed with quiet tears—'God saw he was *so* tired, and needed rest—and it was best he should go. I never imagined that *I* was the one who should be left behind—' "[21]

Mary Custis Lee had always been a strong pillar in times of trouble, bringing a calmness and clarity of vision to those who were overwhelmed.[22] Now she spoke with acceptance of her loss, and pride in her celebrated husband. But she could not bring herself to attend the funeral on October 15, and sat at home instead, reading through his dear, expressive letters. Outside there was a crowd of thousands. Townspeople, Lee's doctors, adoring veterans, and the students of Washington College marched in step to muffled drums behind a hearse decorated with greens and flowers. Old bewildered Traveller brought up the rear, but Robert E. Lee was not part of this procession: the hearse was empty. His body remained in the chapel, where it had lain in state since his death, guarded by students from the college and the Virginia Military Institute. It was just as well, for although the tribute was unquestionably genuine, it was the kind of display Lee detested. He would have abhorred the open coffin, as well as the stunned expressions of the curious as a cloth was lifted from his face to reveal his shrunken remains.[23]

Death mask of Robert E. Lee.
VIRGINIA HISTORICAL SOCIETY

The funeral service was more in keeping with the man: his children in the front pew, heavily veiled, stifling their sobs; a simple reading of the beautiful Episcopal Order for the Burial of the Dead; the solemn placing of his body in the crypt of the chapel; his favorite hymn, "How Firm a Foundation Ye Saints of the Lord," with its promise that the "rivers of woe shall not thee overflow." Then the people of the South were left to contemplate his steady gaze and self-contained composure; his easy hand with horses, and girls, and tricky situations; the way he had embodied their dreams. His family went home and longed for "the Light, the soul, the mind, the joy of our lives," picturing him waiting with Traveller after an exhilarating ride, "his eyes sparkling with fun."[24]

The biblical passages read at Robert E. Lee's funeral called on the congregation to "Mark the perfect man and behold the upright," then advised: "The law of God was in his heart"; therefore did "none of his steps slide."[25] It was not the first instance of lavish praise about Lee, for during the Civil War his leonine qualities had been generously described. In a famous article in *Blackwood's Magazine* in 1863 Viscount Wolseley had proclaimed Lee "the most perfect man I ever met," and the image had fixed itself in the southern mind.[26] He was revered not only for his military ability but for his fine personal character—and just as much for his supposed or superimposed qualities. He was humble, he was bold; he was indefatigable; he was audacious. He never used the word "enemy"; his fare was spartan; no double entendre had ever passed his lips; no drop of alcohol had ever stained his breath. Some of this was even true, though much more was exaggeration, verging on folklore. Lee may have fostered—or come to believe—some of this publicity during the war, for he was well aware of the power of image. After Appomattox, however, he ridiculed such adulation. One visitor to Lexington recalled how he showed her an elaborate saddlecloth embroidered with the words "To Our Deliverer," holding it up with a "tender, humorous smile" and saying: "They thought I would ride through the city with that on my horse."[27] Despite his refreshing irreverence, Lee was nevertheless held in some awe. Students sometimes feared coming face to face with the general, thinking he was "a kind of superman," unapproachable in life as well as in example.[28] One newspaper had gone so far as to declare that in Lee's "composition original sin seemed omitted."[29] The adjectives outstripped the facts, but the authenticity of the admiration was never in question. Now, with Lee's death, it was as if an open season of adoration had been declared.

Just weeks after the burial, Mary Lee set the tone for what was to come, by terming her husband "the Hero of a lost cause," whose "Martyr" blood was shed for his country. The religious imagery, as well as the concept that there was glory in failure, would be echoed for more than a century.[30] Those who attempted dispassionate analysis of Lee's performance as a general were dismissed. Catastrophic events such as the Gettysburg campaign were recast as a draw, for which Lee's "only fault was the generous fault of overconfidence."[31] The rector of Christ Church in Alexandria tried to talk about the boy his congregation had known, recalling his diligence, friendliness, and genuine modesty. However, he too finally succumbed to the temptation to put Lee on a higher plane, where disappointment begat greatness. Lee, he wrote was "foredoomed by Fate to fail in his Titanic effort to establish the Southern Confederacy, but in spite of failure—yes by reason of his failure, rising to a height of moral grandeur never reached by any other American."[32]

As old soldiers and men of God sought to establish Lee's significance in the public record, the words became ever more superlative, the images more sublime. Admirers spoke of a mystical aurora that had appeared at his death. His office was kept untouched as a sacred memorial, and some began to refer to Lexington, with its twin graves of Jackson and Lee, as "Mecca." "The glory and pathos of his life are like the sun as it rises and sets," wrote Charles Francis Adams Jr., a consummate Yankee. "The historian and writer have tried to describe him, and have found that he is beyond description."[33] Lee was compared to Washington, to Napoleon, to Caesar, even to Ulysses S. Grant.[34] Some came perilously close to blasphemy, adorning Lee with the vision of prophets, the qualities of Christ, the power of a "divine example."[35] It all survived well until the late twentieth century, when a popular painting placed Lee at the right hand of Christ, in a triptych whose other secular saint was Elvis Presley.

Perhaps the pinnacle of veneration was reached in the 1930s by Douglas Southall Freeman. Though a meticulous chronologer, Freeman was hardly an objective biographer, openly revering his subject and at one stage making multiple-columned lists of superlative qualities he supposed Lee to possess.[36] In several undocumented passages he proposed that Lee's greatness was a culmination of centuries of good breeding choices among the Virginia gentry—a triumph of eugenics. The examples he used, however, are either mistaken or strange. Freeman claimed, for example, that Lee inherited his good looks from his paternal grandmother, Lucy Grymes. Yet no pictures of her exist, nor any description beyond an assertion that she *may* have once been called "the lowland beauty." He also asserts that Lee came by his impressive physique from his father, though Light-Horse Harry Lee was described by his contemporaries as "a man of light and weakly form." Deftly and persistently Freeman promoted his tidy, unidimensional Lee: man raised to god by intermarriage, duty, and defeat.

This was more than simple scholarly adulation. Lee's example continued to have important political resonance, and admiration for him was a powerful healing agent for the wounded southern psyche. There was still a huge gulf between the teaching that God intervened in human affairs, with results dictated by his pleasure, and the fact that the South had not only lost the war but seen their proud civilization shredded, physically and philosophically. Evangelical ministers had done their best to bridge the chasm by proclaiming that God punished those he best loved, and that postwar suffering was but a honing of the South's spiritual mettle. Doubts lingered, however, and the community spirit seemed still to need a rationale and a route back to recovery. In the years following Lee's death there was a revival of southern literature, much of which emphasized an idyllic world of splendid plantations and patriarchal benevolence. Novelists John Esten Cooke and Thomas Nelson Page were two leaders of this romantic movement in Virginia, but private individuals were also recording their nostalgic recollections. One of Lee's young lady friends, Christiana Bond, wrote a description of the dreadful days of 1861 in the border states, when brothers chose to fight each other, and communities were wrenched apart. Despite the fact that she well re-

Trinity—Elvis, Jesus and Robert E. Lee *by Clyde Broadway—a modern interpretation of the esteem in which Lee has been held.*
COURTESY OF THE ARTIST AND THE OGDEN MUSEUM OF SOUTHERN ART

membered the family divisions and the "wreck and ruin and shattered illusions," she chose to look away. In her words: "Emotions had been too intense, interests too vital, hatreds too cruel, sorrows too keen." In her hands the web was woven instead with "youthful romance" and "a delicious sense of lurking peril." Carter Lee perfectly entwined these emotions in a postwar reminiscence that paired charming childhood memories with unbridled diatribes against the Yankees' crass destruction of his perfect world. In such stories the slaves were content; secession was an issue of jurisprudence; resources had determined the war's outcome; and "jessamine" perfumed the air.[37]

Reverence for Lee was part of this effort to idealize the past and resist reality. His presence, courage, and fealty to his state were not simply portrayed as patriotic moral qualities, but as an example of white supremacy, a validation of secession, and a rejection of the need for postwar societal change.[38] Such notions persisted not only because they justified the old culture, but because the actual truth was so painful. Southerners were not the only ones, of course, to shield themselves from full acceptance of the callous bloodbath that was the Civil War, nor the way that it had left rifts and uncertainties in the society. Northerners also chose to emphasize pathos and heroism, or linger sentimentally in an unreal past, creating a mystical mood that still evokes a popular response. Many in the North also romanticized Lee and his men, painting them as underdogs or epic warriors, until Grant actually complained, and Frederick Douglass noted sourly: "We can scarcely take up a newspaper that is not filled with *nauseating* flatteries of the late Robert E. Lee. . . . It would seem from this that the soldier who kills the most men in battle, even in a bad cause, is the greatest Christian."[39]

Part of this southern offensive was the surge of memoirs by soldiers and sailors who had served the Confederacy. Many of these sprang up spontaneously, and some were candid accounts of the trials and elations of the war years. During the 1870s a movement also arose that more or less openly began to channel the reminiscences into a collective historical viewpoint. This celebrated the spirited rebels, reinforcing the idea that only superior numbers had—or could have—overtaken the Confederate forces. Lee himself played into this trend with his search for materials that would bolster the "overwhelming numbers and resources" thesis in his projected memoirs, and in his painstaking reversal on the legitimacy of secession, which he had so unequivocally condemned in 1861. The campaign was sustained by Jubal Early's untiring efforts, over twenty-five years, to elevate Lee above other Civil War chieftains, and to promote the idea that the South had not been defeated, only compelled to surrender to overwhelming odds.[40] In addition, soon after Lee's death, one of his first biographers, a Baptist minister named J. William Jones, introduced the idea of Lee as a quasi-religious, inspirational figure. Jones led in the formation of the Southern Historical Society, and acted as its secretary for a decade. The society was dedicated to the revivification of regional honor and was controlled for nearly half a century by Lee admirers. Those, such as James Longstreet, who dared to question Lee's judgment, or propose that faulty Confederate leadership, lack of popular will, or military mistakes could have contributed to defeat, were shut out. The legend of Lee's invincibility was essential to the society's goals. Through well-placed monuments, well-written battlefield drama and well-manufactured popular perceptions they succeeded in elevating Lee's already considerable reputation.[41] It was exactly the kind of aggressive defense Robert E. Lee had liked: victory snatched from the supposition of defeat.

Added to this were Lee's real and impressive character traits, always a lightning rod for southern pride. In the end national politicians would try

to requisition this image, and use it as a conduit to countrywide reunification. Those who took the lead in this movement were unassailable personalities with strong ties to the North. Charles Francis Adams Jr.—who had
once dined at Arlington, and whose father was instrumental in keeping
Great Britain from recognizing the Confederacy—gave Lee entire credit for
the decision to disband peaceably at Appomattox, and proposed that, far
from being a traitor, responsible for hundreds of thousands of deaths, Lee
was the founder of peace. Woodrow Wilson, a Virginian, and a wartime
president who had won the Nobel Peace Prize for his efforts at international
reconciliation, recast Lee as a "celebrated *American* general in the Confederate service"; a "culmination" of soldierly resolve and genteel temperament.[42]
The South, however, took care to hold on to Lee, as its own savior and symbol. This fine man, with superb personal qualities—not to mention a charm
that could never be achieved by a Yankee—this man, who chose integrity
against his own self-interest, fighting magnificently, even miraculously,
without the resources to do it; this kindly, noble warrior, as fabulous in defeat as in victory; *this* was what the South was about, and *this* is what the barbarous Grants and Shermans had destroyed. As the *London Standard* would
conclude: "A country which has given birth to such a man as Robert E. Lee
may look the proudest nation in the most chivalric period of history . . .
fearlessly in the face."[43]

In time many of the myths would become self-perpetuating, repeated so often that they became common knowledge, difficult to overturn from the
sheer certitude of their acceptance. The disturbing point about this is not
that Lee was portrayed in such an idealized light, but that so much was lost
as man was turned into monument. He needed no publicists; they only diminished him, reducing a complex person to a stone icon. By denying Lee's
common follies and foibles, his devotees removed him from us, setting him
apart, so that his true ability to inspire was obscured. The truth is, Lee lived
an all too human existence, fraught with dilemmas and decisions that would
challenge the sturdiest soul. He handled some of these situations well, others with disastrous error. Never did he turn away, however, and even his
sharpest critics never questioned his steadfastness. This is where our sympathy with him lies; here and in the heart-rending way that he strove, but
failed, to achieve his dreams—number two at West Point by fractions of a
point; perennially disrupted in the home life he coveted; denied professional recognition until he stood on the very brink of national disaster; defeated when he had so confidently felt the capacity for victory. Through all
this he was brave and tenacious, and set no limits on what he would give or

try to accomplish. Yet Lee, who could be as self-serving as any of us, was not intrinsically more virtuous than others. He simply harnessed his fine points—notably persistence and self-control—to ovecome failings within and around him. The greatest honor we can give Lee is to admire him for who he actually was, rather than as an imaginary creature, which only insults him by implying that the reality was inadequate.

Lee the underdog might quicken our empathy, but it is important to recognize that he was never a victim of fate. His story, in fact, forces us to confront the weight of one person's decisions in a free society. Like all tragic figures, Lee's life was a product of his own will. He was dealt a problematic hand as a young person, but every other aspect of his life was of his own creation. He cajoled his mother into allowing him to attend West Point. He made a love match with Mary Custis, a difficult, if ultimately inspired, choice. He declined to pursue clever intrigues for advancement in the army—or to resign—leaving himself in a professional and personal stalemate. Those choices had private consequences, which only he was qualified to assess. When he followed his heart in 1861, however, his decision had larger ramifications. One can only guess where the rebellion might have gone if Lee, an unusually able Virginian, had stood at the head of the Union army. Would 620,000 military men and countless civilians have died? What of his strategy in the following years, when he led his armies northward, a twice-told failure, which not only ended or scarred the lives of nearly 75,000 men but galvanized the Union into taking measures so harsh that it destroyed the southern landscape he loved, and the institutions he sought to defend?[44] What if he had gone west to join the defense of Vicksburg instead? Would he have become the true savior of the South? Had Lee not chosen to be a model of quiet, nonconfrontational citizenship in the days after Appomattox, would Virginia have devolved into anarchy, provoking the Union to establish martial law? The crystal ball is as clouded in hindsight as it is in premonition, but it is hard not to conclude that Lee's inclinations and actions had powerful consequences. The point here is not whether they were right or wrong. Rather, it is to remind us how strong is the potential power of one individual in a truly democratic society, and therefore how great the burden of responsibility.

The persistent adulation of Lee is also important for what it says about our thirst for idols. Heroism is a slippery, subjective term. Heroes are created out of needs, reflecting standards a society reveres, rather than an absolute and eternal set of qualities. At heart a hero must speak to our hunches as well as our highest aspirations; we feel heroism more easily than we define it. During the Civil War, Lee put his life on the line for a set of principles he and others believed in, even when the decision was contrary to his own ambitions, and success was against the odds. He fought as he felt he should, and put his best into the effort. This is what constituted valor in the South, and still renders him a shining knight in that region. By the same token, these actions deny Lee heroic recognition everywhere, for they represented local, not universal truths. The fealty that is hugged to the bosom in Virginia cuts to the quick at West Point. Lee produced some undoubtedly spectacular movements in battle. But if we take care to avoid ennobling or sentimentalizing aggression, granting it validity only when it leads to societal progress, his military legacy becomes unclear. Although he led a series of thrilling feats, any timeless achievement seems elusive, for he could neither make his cause last, nor give it enduring meaning. Lee helps us understand that heroism can be local and transitory; something quite strong, yet limited in audience and meaning; indeed, something that for all its power stops short of universal significance.

Lee's story continues to have dramatic power, as well as relevance, because it prods us to consider what constitutes genuine greatness. Say it lies in noble efforts and loyalty; in supreme composure, perseverance, and quiet suffering; in local sensibilities and courtly gestures—all this strikes an appealing note. Say it also comprises an uncommon capacity to inspire men to act beyond normal expectations and endure prolonged privation, an ability that is highly admired by those assessing leadership. Lee's influence extended beyond the battlefield to motivate his former soldiers to lay down their hatred as well as their guns, and step with confidence into a postwar world. All of these were laudable qualities, superior, in fact, if taken in isolation. Lee's unswerving devotion to his region, and his willingness to fight— to really fight—for it are probably enough for him to be forever idolized south of the Potomac. Assessing his *contribution* is more problematic. We want him to be great because he had elements of greatness in him. To be timeless and true, however, greatness must rest on two pillars. It must create something that not only benefits the world each day but endures, and can continue to be positively interpreted or expanded. The Bill of Rights is a classic example; so is the discovery of a polio vaccine. Then greatness must embody a farsightedness that reaches beyond the complacency of one's narrow experience. It must rise above convention, and clearly advance a larger set of truths than those commonly held. It is hard to see such transcendent importance in Lee because his actions were tied to questionable mores, which were already largely rejected in his day, and were neither morally defensible nor sustainable over time. The tragedy is that he allowed his essentially noble spirit to founder in the ignobility of his era's easy assumptions. Even had he won the war, and helped to carve out a new nation with a unique political structure, its foundation inevitably would have collapsed under the global condemnation of human slavery—which Lee himself admitted. He came closest to real greatness in the enlightened decisions he took to foster peace and rebuild the South in the early aftermath of war. This was his grand visionary moment. After this he anchored himself firmly to old prejudices, resisting the currents of change and expanded freedom as they flowed swiftly beyond him.[45] What gives Robert E. Lee his poignancy is that rarely have such conundrums—of heritage and potential, of judgment and outcome, of loyalty and betrayal—been so starkly embodied in one person.

Aside from the remarkable success of his publicists, what then has drawn us to Robert E. Lee for nearly a century and a half? What is it that we want this man to tell us? Perhaps in a society so compulsively fixed on achievement, his message is that it is possible to fail and yet not be a failure. That every endeavor carries pride in its execution as well as its accomplishment. That there is very little to counter disappointment in this life save acceptance, and the courage to keep trying. That in everything that is won, something is lost as well, and our ability to label those terms is sadly imperfect. To some, Lee demonstrates the pain of unrewarded gallantry, while another beholder sees only that a good man can make bad decisions. Both of these views are particularly provocative, because they fly in the face of fundamental American beliefs. Duty and diligence—Lee's personal credo, but also the cornerstone of nineteenth-century aspiration—brought him neither success nor happiness. His own American dream devolved into a retreat from the world, where he could live on cornbread and bacon and watch his daughters weave homespun—the antithesis of the spirit of progress that characterized his age, as it does ours.[46] That he remained a revered figure despite defeat is an astounding exception to American tradition. And this may be what fundamentally inspires us about Lee: the reassurance that the worst will not destroy us, that there is a possibility of redemption.

We still recognize importance in Lee because he has left us an enduring example of personal courage against the vagaries of human existence. This is what makes Lee worth knowing—not the flash of the saber, but his handling of the everyday tribulations of this world. The difficulties he faced in a life both greatly blessed, and unfairly cursed, remind us how fleeting are wisdom, optimism, and control. Like all of us, Lee was often misguided, and his words did not always match his deeds. Though he did not fulfill his dreams, or live up to his own elevated standards, he was tireless in the attempt to do so. One of the greatest ironies of the manufactured Lee is its dependence on artifice, for there were few men who hated pretense more than he. His example lies not in superhuman virtue but in human determination; not in battlefield glory but in triumph amid life's unexpected skirmishes. The truth he leaves with us is the one he learned from his own literary heroes, be it Don Quixote or Hamlet: that the quest is as important as the outcome—and that in the end, if you are left with nothing more, you must know that you have been faithful to yourself. Lee beckons us not to attain some impossible height of moral righteousness, but to be fabulous in our fallibility, to face unflinchingly all of the vicissitudes of life, and in so doing to transcend them.

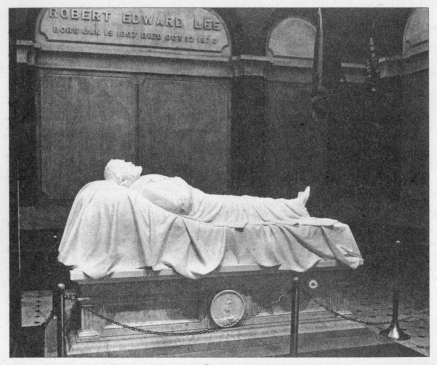

Recumbent statue of Lee, by Edward Valentine.

ARLINGTON HOUSE, THE ROBERT E. LEE MEMORIAL, NATIONAL PARK SERVICE

Acknowledgments

ONE OF THE PLEASURES of writing this book was the immense support I received from professional colleagues and from friends.

I am especially indebted to the Lee descendants, who shared with me their papers, their insights, and their enthusiasm. Several of them, notably Robert E. L. deButts Jr., Susan Vogel, and Anne Carter Zimmer, have themselves done important research on their family. Mrs. Zimmer's wonderful *Robert E. Lee Family Cooking and Housekeeping Book,* which used homely kitchen concoctions to explain important transformations in society, especially inspired me. The family made recently discovered documents available to me and embraced my research with an open spirit. It must be very difficult having a parade of historians pick apart one's personal history, and I marveled at the Lee family's generous encouragement of new scholarship.

The Virginia Historical Society deserves special praise for their assistance. Not only did they support me as a Mellon Fellow two years running, but their unequaled collection of Lee materials and marvelous staff became the backbone of my research. I will always be very proud of my association with this fine institution.

I would also like to thank the Episcopal Women's History Project for awarding me a grant to research the formative influence women had on Lee's spiritual life.

The skilled archivists and librarians I encountered expanded my knowledge, conspired with me to ferret out elusive documents, and made everyday research a pleasure. I met with helpful assistance virtually everywhere I went, but I am particularly indebted to the staffs of the Library of Congress Manuscript Division; the Georgia Historical Society; Stratford Plantation; and the special collections divisions at the Alexandria Public Library, Duke University, Tulane University, the U.S. Army Military History

Institute, the U.S. Military Academy, the University of Virginia, and Washington and Lee University.

Arlington House remained my inspirational home, and I greatly benefited from the expertise of the National Park Service's first-rate historians, curators, and rangers. Indeed I must tip my hat to the National Park Service professionals at all of the battlefield and historic sites associated with Robert E. Lee. Like Lee himself they are chronically undersupported, and like the general they do a great deal with very little.

Neal Anderson, Walter Kaiser, and Catherine Freedberg all pushed me forward when no one else could think of a good reason to write another book about Robert E. Lee. Frances Hardin became something of an unofficial publicist and introduced me to a number of helpful people, including my agent. Beverly Louise Brown, Drew Faust, Matthew Furbush, Randy Hackenburg, Scott Hartwig, Judy Hynson, Nelson Lankford, Robert Muller, Frances Pollard, William Rasmussen, Charles Rosenberg, Patrick Schroeder, Richard Sommers, Barbara Stephenson, and Janet Tighe all read and commented on chapters of the book. I benefited from their excellent critical advice. Ray Wanner was especially courageous, consistently working through raw text and offering moral support as well as spot-on suggestions. I also appreciated the many friends who indulged my single-mindedness and offered valuable ideas, respite, and glasses of wine.

Deborah Grosvenor, my agent, proved to be extremely skillful in every professional interaction, as well as adept at sustaining my enthusiasm. Paul Slovak, my editor at Viking, has been equally so. Both showed unusual patience in dealing with my many persnickety notions about the book.

To each of you, my sincere thanks.

Notes

Nineteenth-century grammar was less uniform than modern usage; however, no attempt has been made to "streamline" either Lee's words or those of his contemporaries. "*Sic*" has rarely been employed; readers should assume that any discrepancies are in the original documents and enjoy the variety of expression. Only the dates have been standardized to the present familiar form. Abbreviations used are as follows.

ACH	Alexandria, Virginia Courthouse
AHA	Arlington House Archives, National Park Service
ANB	*American National Biography*, eds. John A. Garraty, Mark C. Carnes, 24 vols. (New York: Oxford University Press, 1999).
B & L	*Battles and Leaders of the Civil War* (Century Co., 1887)
BLA	Kate Waller Barrett Library, Alexandria, Virginia
BLC	Bancroft Library, University of California at Berkeley
CCL	Charles Carter Lee Papers
CD	Records of the Society of the Colonial Dames
CL	Custis and Lee Family Papers
DE	DeButts-Ely Papers (all items in collection are photostats)
DSF	Douglas Southall Freeman Papers
DU	Special Collections, Duke University
EA-LC	Ethel Armes Papers, Library of Congress
GBL	George Bolling Lee Papers
GHS	Georgia Historical Society
GU	Special Collections, Georgetown University
HL	Henry E. Huntington Library
LC	Library of Congress
LFP	Lee Family Papers
LJF	Lee-Jackson Foundation Papers
LoV	Library of Virginia
MCL	Mary Custis Lee Papers
MoHS	Missouri Historical Society
ML	Morgan Library
MOC	Eleanor S. Brockenbrough Library, Museum of the Confederacy
NARA	National Archives and Records Administration

NYHS   New-York Historical Society
OR   *The War of the Rebellion: Compilation of Official Records*
REL   Robert E. Lee Papers
RL   Rockefeller Library, Colonial Williamsburg Foundation
SH   Jessie Ball duPont Library, Stratford Hall Plantation
SHC   Southern Historical Collection, University of North Carolina
SPP   Shirley Plantation Papers
TPA   Tudor Place Archives
TU   Tulane University Archives
USAMHI   U.S. Army Military History Institute
USMA   Special Collections, U.S. Military Academy
UT   Special Collections, University of Texas
UTA   Special Collections, University of Texas at Arlington
UVa   Albert and Shirley Small Special Collections Library, University of Virginia
VHS   Virginia Historical Society
VMHB   *Virginia Magazine of History and Biography*
WL   Special Collections, Leyburn Library, Washington and Lee University

Correspondents
ACL   Anne Carter Lee (daughter)
CCL   Charles Carter Lee
EAL   Eleanor "Agnes" Lee
EPCL   Eleanor Parke Custis Lewis
GWCL   George Washington "Custis" Lee
GWPC   George Washington Parke Custis
MARC   Mary Anna Randolph Custis [MCL prior to marriage]
MCL   Mary Custis Lee
MCL(d)   Mary Custis Lee (daughter)
MCW   Martha Custis Williams ("Markie")
MFC   Mary Lee Fitzhugh Custis
MiCL   Mildred Childe Lee
REL   Robert E. Lee
REL Jr.   Robert E. Lee Jr.
WHFL   William Henry Fitzhugh Lee ("Rooney")

Preface

1. Mary Boykin Chesnut, *Mary Chesnut's Civil War,* ed. C. Van Woodward (New Haven: Yale University Press, 1981), pp. 115–16.

2. Stephen Vincent Benét, *John Brown's Body* (New York: Holt, Rinehart, and Winston, 1928), pp. 171–74.

3. Ann Carter Lee to Sydney Smith Lee, April 10, [1827], photostat, EA-LC. Ironically, Ann Lee was also a poor correspondent and risked the loss of more than one friend through a failure to answer her letters. Nor did Smith Lee change his ways. Smith's brothers Robert and Carter, both of them diligent correspondents, and several cousins, continually complained about his unresponsiveness. See Ann Carter Lee to Mrs. Richard Bland Lee, February 18, 1799, May 10, 1803, December 20, 1804, and January 11, 1807, all CL-LC; Anna Maria Fitzhugh to CCL, November 12, [1831 or 1832], photostat, EA-LC; and REL to CCL, Old Point, October 12, 1831, REL-UVa.

4. For conditions in early-nineteenth-century America, see James M. McPherson, *Battle Cry of Freedom* (New York: Ballantine, 1988), pp. 6–46; literacy statistics pp. 19–20; Paul Starr, *The Creation of the Media* (New York: Basic Books, 2004), p. 88; Daniel Boorstin, *The Americans: The National Experience* (New York: Vintage, 1965); and Jack Larkin, *The Reshaping of Everyday Life, 1790–1840* (New York: Harper and Row, 1988); also Wayne E. Fuller, *The American Mail: Enlarger of American Life* (Chicago: University of Chicago Press, 1972), pp. 51–71; and Lyman Horace Weeks, *A History of Paper-Manufacturing in the United States, 1690–1916* (New York: Lockwood, 1916), pp. 170–81.

5. John Custis of Williamsburg quoted in James B. Lynch, *The Custis Chronicles: The Virginia Generations* (Penobscot, Maine: Picton Press, 1997), p. 74.

6. Ibid.; Starr, *Media,* p. 96; and Fuller, *American Mail,* pp. 51–72.

7. For a discussion of intimate correspondence, see Karen Lystra, *Searching the Heart: Women, Men, and Romantic Love in Nineteenth Century America* (New York: Oxford University Press, 1989), pp. 14–20.

8. Diary of George Washington, June 19, 1773, and letter to Burwell Bassett, Mount Vernon, June 20, 1773, can be found at http://memory.loc.gov/ammem/gwhtm/2qwintro.html. Washington's diaries are published in Donald Jackson and Dorothy Twohig, eds., *The Diaries of George Washington,* 6 vols. (Charlottesville: University Press of Virginia, 1976–79).

9. REL to "Precious Life" (MiCL), March 22, [1857], DE-LC.

10. REL to [George] Cullum, Wash., May 18, 1837, LFP-WL.

11. Benson Lossing to GWPC, December 7, 1852, TPA.

12. Diary of Martha Custis Williams (hereafter cited as MCW Diary), June 5, 1858, AHA.

13. REL to Major U. S. Rives, March 26, 1863, photostat, CL-LC. This is a theme that Lee repeated many times: for example, REL to CCL, City of Mexico, March 18, 1848, and May 15, 1848, both REL-UVa; and REL to MCL, Camp at Valley Mt., September 9, 1861, DE-LC.

14. Clara Barton to Elvira Stone, "Headquarters 2nd Division, Army of the Potomac, Camp near Falmouth, Va.," December 12, 1862, Clara Barton Papers, LC.

15. As he was so often on the move, Lee's traveling desk was an important part of his personal kit. See MCL to Mrs. A. Talcott, St. Louis, January 1, 1839, Talcott Family Papers, VHS. His laptop desk from the 1850s is at Arlington House; a similar one from the postwar years is at VHS.

16. REL to "dearest Mother" (MFC), Baltimore, March 17, 1852, DE-LC.

17. Dard Hunter, *Papermaking in Pioneer America* (Philadelphia: University of Pennsylvania Press, 1952), p. 11.

18. See REL to MCW, September 2, 1844, and September 17, 1844 [?], in Robert E. Lee, *"To Markie": The Letters of Robert E. Lee to Martha Custis Williams,* ed. Avery O. Craven (Cambridge, Mass.: Harvard University Press, 1933), pp. 3, 5.

19. Stamps became available around 1847, and prepayment of postage was mandatory after 1854. Early postal charges were based on the number of sheets in the letter and the distance it had to travel. REL paid $1.64 to send a two-page letter in the late 1840s, just as postage stamps were becoming available. See Starr, *Media,* p. 142; Fuller, *American Mail,* p. 67; Richard Bland Lee to William Price, Fairfax Co., October 21, 1805, Brock Collection, HL; and REL to "My dear Welcher" [George Lewis Welcher], n.d. [April 25–May 24, 1846–1848], photostat, HL. Also REL to MCL, Fort

Mason, March 28, 1856, DE-LC; and REL to "My dearest Mr. Boo" [GWCL], Baltimore, September 14, 1851, in J. William Jones, *Life and Letters of Robert Edward Lee, Soldier and Man* (repro, Harrisonville, Va.: Sprinkle, 1986), pp. 75–76.

20. Fitzhugh Lee, *General Lee* (New York: D. Appleton, 1898), p. 72.

21. See, for example, REL to MCL, St. Louis, August 21, 1837, REL-UVa.

22. REL to "My dear Cousin Anna". [Maria Fitzhugh], San Antonio, Texas, June 6, 1860, MoC.

23. MCW Diary, November 19, 1853, AHA.

24. Ann Carter Lee to Sydney Smith Lee, April 10, [1827], photostat, EA-LC.

25. REL to MARC, CockSpur Island, January 10, 1831, in Robert E. L. deButts Jr., ed., "'Yours Forever': R. E. Lee's Engagement Letters to Mary Custis, 1830–31," *VMHB*, forthcoming; and MCL to Gen. R. H. Chilton, Lexington, December 12, 1870, MoC.

26. Quotation in Catherine Clinton, *The Plantation Mistress* (New York: Pantheon, 1982), p. 174.

27. For Lee's editing of his father's letters, see Henry Lee, *The Revolutionary War Memoirs of General Henry Lee,* ed. Robert E. Lee (repr., New York: Da Capo Press, 1998); and Paul C. Nagel, *Lees of Virginia,* (New York: Oxford University Press, 1990), pp. 294–96.

28. MCW Diary, January 9, 1854, AHA.

29. Ibid., March 5, 1858.

30. Robert Knox Sneden Diary (hereafter cited as Sneden Diary), n.d. [c. October 1862], p. 735, Robert Knox Sneden Papers, VHS.

31. H. L. Wright to MCL(d), "Darter Putman Co Ind," June 23, 1884; Ro[bert] Ould to Lt. Col Jno E. Mulford, Richmond, December 17, 1864; Chas Albright to Capt. Chas. J. Wickersham, Hd. Qrs., Fairfax Station, Va., January 26, 1865; S. J. Turner to MCL(d), Kinloch, January 17, [1865]; and C. B. Winn to MCL(d), Russellville, June 19, 1884, all MCL-VHS.

32. MCL to "My dear Gertrude," January 31, [1873], photostat, CL-LC; note in hand of MCL on Lydia H. Sigorney, to MCL, Hartford, January 17, 1860, copy in hand of MCL, DE-LC; MCL quoted in Benson J. Lossing to MCL, unsent draft letter, Poughkeepsie, N.Y., March 2, 1866, Benson J. Lossing Papers, HL; and in Benson J. Lossing to Henry Wilson, "The Ridge," Dover, N.Y., July 19, 1870, Henry Wilson Papers, LC; Anne Carter Zimmer, ed., *The Robert E. Lee Family Cooking and Housekeeping Book* (Chapel Hill: University of North Carolina Press, 1997), p. 43; and "Remarks of Mrs. P. R. Alger," Annapolis, Md., 1957, Montgomery C. Meigs Papers, LC (hereafter cited MCM-LC).

33. MCW to MCL, n.d. [July 1861], fragment, DE-LC.

34. Sneden Diary, n.d. [c. October 1862].

35. Ro[bert] Ould to Lt. Col Jno E. Mulford, Richmond, December 17, 1865; Chas. Albright to Capt. Chas. J. Wickersham, Fairfax Station, Va., January 26, 1865; H. L. Wright to MCL(d), Darter Putnam Co., April 21, 1884; and William H. Hawkins to MCL(d), Springfield, Mass., July 21, 1913, all MCL-VHS.

36. See Linda Wheeler, "In a Dusty Vault, an Abundance of Lee Family Relics," *Washington Post,* November 27, 2002.

37. Lee lamented the loss of his private as well as public papers on many occasions. A sample: REL to General [P.] G. T. Beauregard, Lexington, Va., October 3, 1865; REL to Edward A. Pollard, Lexington, Va., September 26, 1866; and REL to Wm. A. Bryan, Lexington, Va., February 12, 1870, all LFP-VHS.

38. Anne Carter Zimmer to the author, January 13, 2004.

39. Benét, *John Brown's Body*, p. 171; Marietta Minnigerode Andrews, a cousin of the Lees, used this phrase in her memoir *Scraps of Paper* (New York: E. P. Dutton, 1929).

CHAPTER ONE: Torn to Pieces

1. [Samuel Appleton Storrow] to "Sister," September 6, 1821, EA-LC.

2. See William Shippen to Henry Lee, August 25, 1770, quoted in Lee, *General Lee*, p. 8; and William Lee to Henry Lee, 1770, quoted in Cazenove Gardner Lee Jr., *Lee Chronicle* (New York: Vantage Press, 1997), pp. 86–87.

3. Margaret Sanborn, *Robert E. Lee: A Portrait* (Philadelphia: J. B. Lippincott, 1966), p. 4; and Thomas Boyd, *Light-horse Harry Lee* (New York: Charles Scribner's Sons, 1931), pp. 8–9.

4. Henry Lee Jr. quoted in Ethel Armes, *Stratford Hall: The Great House of the Lees* (Richmond, Va.: Garrett and Massie, 1936), p. 228.

5. Philip Vickers Fithian, *Journal & Letters of Philip Vickers Fithian*, ed. Hunter Dickinson Farish (Williamsburg, Va.: Colonial Williamsburg, 1965), p. 62; and Harry Lee quoted in Boyd, *Light-horse Harry Lee*, p. 2.

6. John Morgan Dederer, "In Search of the Unknown Soldier: A Critique of 'The Mystery in the Coffin,'" *VMHB* 103, no. 1 (January 1995): 106; and Lee, *General Lee*, p. 8. Harry Lee was well aware of what caught Washington's eye, and just before his first appearance at Morristown begged to receive special supplies before his unit appeared before the General. Edmund Jennings Lee, *Lee of Virginia* (Baltimore: Genealogical Publishing, 1974), p. 330.

7. Washington quoted in Charles Royster, *Light-Horse Harry Lee and the Legacy of the American Revolution* (New York: Alfred A. Knopf, 1981), p. 21; and William Johnson, *Sketches of the Life and Correspondence of Nathanael Greene*, 2 vols. (repr., New York: Da Capo Press, 1973), 2:305.

8. The dashing reputation of Lee's Legion also attracted volunteers from the countryside, increasing its flexibility and access to vital information. John Morgan Dederer, *Making Bricks without Straw: Nathanael Greene's Southern Campaign and Mao Tse-Tung's Mobile War* (Manhattan, Kans.: Sunflower University Press, 1983); Royster, *Light-Horse Harry Lee*, pp. 17, 44; and Boyd, *Light-horse Harry Lee*, pp. 24–25, 61.

9. Henry Banks quoted in Royster, *Light-Horse Harry Lee*, p. 19.

10. For Washington's collaboration with Lee on the plan to surprise the garrison, see George Washington to Henry Lee, West Point, September 1, 1779, Edmund Jennings Lee Collection, SH. Congress awarded only eight such medals, and Lee was the youngest of the recipients.

11. Johnson, *Nathanael Greene*, 1:406, 2:36–37, 100–103; Greene quoted on the "wonders" performed by Lee's Legions in Richard M. Ketchum, *Victory at Yorktown* (New York: Henry Holt, 2004), p. 130.

12. Dederer, *Making Bricks without Straw*, pp. 20–21, 40, 47. Nathanael Greene quoted in Royster, *Light-Horse Harry Lee*, p. 63.

13. Marquis de Lafayette to Major Henry Lee, Light Camp, October 16, 1780, CCL-LoV.

14. General Charles Lee was not related to the Virginia Lees, though in later life, Charles Carter Lee would try to establish a connection. Charles Lee quoted in Royster, *Light-Horse Harry Lee*, p. 14.

15. Ibid., p. 40.

16. George Washington to Major Henry Lee, Head Quarters, New Windsor, July 9, 1779, in George Washington, *The Writings of George Washington*, ed. John C. Fitzpatrick, 39 vols. (Washington, D.C.: GPO, 1936), 15:388.

17. Royster, *Light-Horse Harry Lee*, pp. 36–37; Henry Lee's account of the action is in Lee, *Revolutionary War Memoirs*, pp. 258–59. Robert E. Lee, in editing this memoir, tries to defend the action as well, but it continued to be criticized for four decades. See Johnson, *Nathanael Greene*, 1:453–55.

18. Henry Lee to Nathanael Greene, February 13, 1782, typescript, EA-LC; and Henry Lee to Nathanael Greene, "18th Feb., etc.," HL.

19. Harry and Matilda must have arranged to be married the previous autumn, when Lee supposedly caught a glimpse of his cousin during the Yorktown campaign, for they wed in April 1782, soon after Harry's return, Armes, *Stratford Hall*, pp. 225–26.

20. Lee, *Lee Chronicle*, pp. 91–92; and Lee, *Lee of Virginia*, p. 336.

21. Joseph Ellis called the atmosphere of the early national period a "nearly scatological political culture." *Founding Brothers* (New York: Alfred A. Knopf, 2000), p. 186.

22. Boyd, *Light-horse Harry Lee*, pp. 159, 168–78; and Minutes of the Virginia Convention, June 5 and 9, 1788, printed in Armes, *Stratford Hall*, pp. 255–56. Lee had to use all of his persuasive powers to secure ratification. The final vote was 89–79.

23. See Ellis, *Founding Brothers*, p. 186; Boyd, *Light-horse Harry Lee*, pp. 159–60, 216, 218–21; Royster, *Light-Horse Harry Lee*, pp. 133–35; quotation, James Branch Giles to James Madison, April 12, 1795, James Madison Papers, LC.

24. George Lee quoted in J. Anderson Thomson Jr. and Carlos Michael Santos, "The Mystery in the Coffin: Another View of Lee's Visit to His Father's Grave," *VMBH* 103, no. 1 (January 1995): 87–88; Arthur Lee quoted in Armes, *Stratford Hall*, p. 252.

25. Armes, ibid., pp. 259–60; Henry Lee to James Madison, n.d., quoted p. 266. Several biographers, notably Nagel, *Lees of Virginia*, p. 176, and Emory M. Thomas, *Robert E. Lee* (New York: W. W. Norton, 1995), p. 25, have stated that Henry's eldest son, Philip Ludwell Lee, died after Henry's marriage to Ann Carter. Lee's letter to Madison indicates that the tragedy occurred the previous year.

26. Henry Lee to George Washington, April 29, 1793, quoted in Armes, *Stratford Hall*, p. 276; George Washington to Henry Lee, n.d., quoted p. 277.

27. Henry Lee to Alexander Hamilton quoted in Boyd, *Light-horse Harry Lee*, p. 203.

28. Henry Lee to Alexander Hamilton, May 6, 1793, quoted in Royster, *Light-Horse Harry Lee*, p. 66; and Charles Royster, *The Fabulous History of the Dismal Swamp Company* (New York: Alfred A. Knopf, 1999), p. 352.

29. Charles Carter to Henry Lee, Shirley, May 20, 1793, photostat, CCL-LoV.

30. For the hot weather on Lee's wedding day, see Henry Lee to Charles Carter Lee, June 18, 1817, CCL-LoV; also *Virginia Gazette and General Advertiser*, June 26, 1793; George Washington to Henry Lee, n.d., quoted in Lee, *Lee of Virginia*, p. 341; and Boyd, *Light-horse Harry Lee*, p. 216.

31. Henry Lee to Charles Carter Lee, June 18, 1817, and Charles Carter to Henry Lee, May 20, 1793, both CCL-LoV.

32. Armes, *Stratford Hall*, p. 271–74, 276; musical interests are highlighted in Tom Shippen to Betsey Farley Shippen, Nesting, November 9, 1791, p. 273. For riding horseback, see Ann Lee to Mrs. Richard Bland Lee, Stratford, May 13, 1797; and Ann

Lee to Mrs. Richard Bland Lee, February 18, 1799, both CL-LC; for the presence and dignity of Ann Lee, see Ann Stuart Robinson to Elizabeth Lee, February [?], 1807, in Alice Coyle Torbert, *Eleanor Calvert and Her Circle* (New York: William Frederick Press, 1950), p. 121; and Diary of Henry Heth June 20, 1793, William Heth Papers, LC.

33. Ann Carter Lee to Elizabeth Collins Lee, n.d. [Autumn 1800], quoted in Boyd, *Light-horse Harry Lee*, p. 280.

34. Heth Diary, June 20, 1793.

35. Charles Carter Lee was born in 1798. An elder son, Algernon Sidney Lee, was born in 1795, but died in infancy. Carter Lee's memories of his parents are found in CCL-LoV.

36. Henry Lee's address in H[enry] Lee IV, *Observations on the Writings of Thomas Jefferson with Particular Reference to the Attack they Contain on the Memory of the Late Gen. Henry Lee; in a Series of Letters* (Philadelphia: J. Dobson, 1839), pp. 171–72.

37. Lee's tribute to Patrick Henry quoted in Sanborn, *Portrait*, p. 9.

38. Major General [Henry] Lee, *A Funeral Oration on the Death of General Washington* (Philadelphia: John Ormand, 1800); clipping "Familiar Quotations," in REL Memorandum Book, 1855–61, LFP-VHS. John Marshall was asked to deliver the original address, written by Lee, and for many years he was confused with the author. Others came forward to claim credit for the speech, and Henry Lee's eldest sons, Henry IV and Carter, waged long battles to prove that their father had coined the phrase. Eyewitness accounts and the original printing confirm his authorship.

39. Among those joining Henry Lee in land speculation were Thomas Welling, the president of the Bank of the United States; Patrick Henry; Thomas Law, the husband of one of Martha Washington's grandchildren; groups of Dutch bankers who were buying up millions of acres in western New York State and Pennsylvania; Robert Morris, the major financier of the American Revolution, who would be bankrupted by his efforts; James Madison; and, of course, George Washington, who acknowledged that large landholdings were the key to wealth, and that most were acquired "by taking up and purchasing at very low rates the rich black lands which were thought nothing." See Rosalie Stier Calvert, *Mistress of Riversdale: The Plantation Letter of Rosalie Stier Calvert*, ed. Margaret Law Calcott (Baltimore: Johns Hopkins University Press, 1991), p. 3. George Washington quoted in Henry Wiencek, *An Imperfect God: George Washington, His Slaves, and the Creation of America* (New York: Farrar, Straus and Giroux, 2003), p. 27; Ellis, *Founding Brothers*, pp. 63, 71, 133. For a taste of the complicated players and intricate dealings, see Royster, *Dismal Swamp Company*.

40. Lee, *Observations on the Writings of Thomas Jefferson*, p. 179.

41. For financial dealings with Robert Morris, see "Henry Lee's Schedule," [1808], additional notes, 1810, Brock Collection, HL; and Henry Lee to "dear Sir," Alexandria, February 27, 1804, HL.

42. Richard Bland Lee to the president of the United States, Washington, January 31, 1815, CL-LC. By 1821, Richard Bland Lee noted in desperation that his family was "actually starving." [Richard Bland Lee] to "My dear Philip" [Fendall], Washington, May 9, 1821, Fendall Papers, LC; and Robert S. Gamble, *Sully: The Biography of a House* (Chantilly, Va.: Sully Foundation, 1973), pp. 51–52. For further debts of Henry Lee to his brother Charles, see Ledger of Charles Lee, 1800–1815, and Daybook of Charles Lee, 1808–15, both CL-LC. In 1808 Henry's debt to Charles was $24,000.

43. Will of Arthur Lee, Recorded in County Court, Middlesex County, December 24, 1792, typescript, EA-LC; Henry Lee to ?, Stratford, November 8, 1800, HL.

44. George Washington quoted in T. Michael Miller, "An Analysis of Light Horse Harry Lee's Financial and Real Estate Transactions," unpublished MS, copy SH; and Henry Lee to Thomas Jefferson, Occoquan, February 24, 1806, Papers of Thomas Jefferson, LC.

45. Henry Lee will, probated in Prince William County, Va., October 1, 1787, in Lee, *Lee of Virginia*, pp. 295–97; Deed of Trust between Matilda Lee and Henry Lee, August 10, 1790, in Armes, *Stratford Hall*, p. 259; Will of Charles Carter, 1803, in Boyd, *Light-horse Harry Lee*, p. 284–85. Ann Lee's sister would also choose to leave her estate to the increasingly impoverished family, "free from the controul of her husband General Lee." See Will of Mildred Lee, quoted in Boyd, *Light-horse Harry Lee*, p. 287.

46. Albert H. Tillson Jr., "Friendship and Commerce: The Conflict and Co-Existence of Values on Virginia's Northern Neck in the Revolutionary Era," *VMHB* 111, no. 3 (Summer 2003): 224–60; and Bertram Wyatt-Brown, *Southern Honor* (New York: Oxford University Press, 1982), pp. 345–46.

47. Royster, *Light-Horse Harry Lee*, p. 78.

48. See, for example, Deposition of Randsdell Piece, April 28, 1807, *Lee vs. Rowand*, photocopy, SH.

49. *Thomas Rowand vs. Henry Lee*, January 1, 1806, Westmoreland County Court Papers, Box 70–1809 Bundle, LoV.

50. Elizabeth Collins Lee quoted in Gamble, *Sully*, p. 51. A typical correspondence on Lee's debts, from the letterbooks of his in-laws, is found in the Stephen Collins & Son Papers, LC; one of his classic replies is Henry Lee to ?, Stratford, November 8, 1800, HL; quotation Henry Lee to Mr. R. B. Lee, New York, November 11, 1786, CCL-LoV; and George Washington to Henry Lee, January 1798, quoted in Royster, *Light-Horse Harry Lee*, p. 177.

51. N. Pendleton to Col. G. Doneale, Alexandria, July 18, 1805, Richard Bland Lee Papers, VHS, typescript, SH; and Nagel, *Lees of Virginia*, p. 181.

52. "Testament of John Mayo, Jno Pendleton & Wm Fowler to the General Court," Richmond, June 23, 1795, certificate in HL.

53. For Ann Lee's ill health, see Henry Lee to Patrick Henry, Shirley, April 22, 1795, Patrick Henry Papers, LC; Jn Walker to Genl Henry Lee, March 28, 1805, Thomas Jefferson Papers, LC.

54. For Henry's absence, see, for example, Ann Carter Lee to Elizabeth Collins Lee, Stratford, February 18, 1799, CL-LC. Stratford was also filled with the memories of Matilda, whose clothes still hung in the wardrobe, and whose ancestors gazed from the walls. Henry persisted in keeping her memory alive by talking of her to his children. Sanborn, *Portrait*, p. 15; Boyd, *Light-horse Harry Lee*, pp. 102–4.

55. Ann Lee to Richard Bland Lee, Stratford, March 12, 1807; and Ann Lee to Elizabeth Collins Lee, Stratford, February 18, 1799, both CL-LC.

56. Ann Lee to Elizabeth Collins Lee, Shirley, May 10, 1803; Ann Lee to Elizabeth Collins Lee, Stratford, January 11, 1807; and Ann Lee to Richard Bland Lee, Stratford, March 12, 1807, all CL-LC.

57. Storrow says in particular that Lucy "proved to be everything that was abominable . . ." Lucy evidently did not get along with her stepmother, and it was said that she married Ann Carter Lee's brother Bernard Carter—"the handsomest man I ever saw, but what a fool!"—simply for spite. When Bernard would not move to Philadel-

phia with her, it was said that she burned down their house, Woodstock, which had been a wedding present from Charles Carter. She lived for most of her life alone—in Philadelphia. Armes, *Stratford Hall,* pp. 293–94.

58. Ann Lee to Henry Lee, Shirley, July 6, 1806 in Armes, *Stratford Hall,* pp. 306–7.

59. Family tradition is that Robert Edward Lee was born in the same room as two cousins, Francis Lightfoot Lee and Richard Henry Lee, both of whom had signed the Declaration of Independence. Armes, *Stratford Hall,* pp. 308–9; also Henry Lee to Thomas Jefferson, Berkeley County, January 17, 1807; and Thomas Jefferson to Henry Lee, February 1, 1807, both Thomas Jefferson Papers, LC. Lee had in fact voted for Burr in 1800, though it seems less certain that he supported his later duels, rants, and traitorous expeditions.

60. Arrest warrant for Henry Lee, July 18, 1808, quoted in full in Boyd, *Light-horse Harry Lee,* p. 295; see also pp. 297–99. Henry Lee quoted in Royster, *Light-Horse Harry Lee,* pp. 82, 175.

61. The Morris estate denied any further claim, except for some lots thought to be worth about $90. Indenture papers show that Morris transferred two 45,000-acre tracts of land to Lee in 1800 and 1802 and that they were still in the family in 1840. Indenture between William and Beulah Craig and Charles Carter Lee and Bernard F. Carter, September 17, 1839, and December 30, 1840, both in CCL-LoV.

62. A compilation of Henry Lee's debts and double-deals from 1783 to his death, made in the early nineteenth century, ran to 56 pages, with 50 specific exhibits. A careful examination of this, and the final reckoning of his 1810 "schedule," shows that even had Morris's estate paid additional monies, Lee's remaining obligations would have been overwhelming. "Complaint of William Tibbs to Judge John Brown," Chancery Court, Baltimore, n.d. [post 1818], CCL-LoV; "Henry Lee's Schedule," 1810, Brock Collection, HL; "Indenture between Henry Lee and Henry Lee Jr. [*sic*]," January 22, 1810, CCL-LoV. See also Thomson and Santos, "Mystery in the Coffin," p. 89.

63. Boyd, *Light-horse Harry Lee,* pp. 300–301; the veterans' reminiscences of the Revolution, sent to Henry Lee in jail, are in CCL-LoV; for questions about the book's objectivity see Johnson, *Nathanael Greene,* 1:406, 2:36, 100–103, 144, 233. Quotation in Custis, *Memoirs of Washington,* pp. 361–62.

64. Ann Stuart Robinson to Elizabeth Lee, February ?, 1807, in Torbert, *Eleanor Calvert,* p. 121; for Ann Lee's sorrowful letter about the death of her sister and "heavy calamities with which I have been sorely oppressed for the last sixteen months," see Ann H. Lee to Richard Bland Lee, March, n.d., 1807, in Boyd, *Light-horse Harry Lee,* p. 287; for offers of sanctuary and determination to establish her own home, see Ann Lee to Dr. Carter Berkeley, Stratford, November 26, 1809, EA-LC.

65. Wyatt-Brown, *Southern Honor,* pp. 345–46.

66. W. R. Davie to Henry Lee, Catacuba, [S.C.], April 20, 1810, Brock Collection, HL; Boyd, *Light-horse Harry Lee,* pp. 305–6, 330. For Lee's unfortunate reputation, see Nagel, *Lees of Virginia,* p. 166; *American Watchman and Delaware Republican,* August 5, 1812; Ann Lee to Philip Fendall, Eastern View, September 21, 1811; and [Richard Bland Lee] to Philip Fendall, Washington, May 7, 1821, both Fendall Papers, LC; Richard Bland Lee to James Monroe, January 31, 1815, CL-LC; and Eliza[beth] Collins Lee to Dolley Madison, Washington, March 4, 1817, in Dolley Payne Madison, *The Selected Letters of Dolley Payne Madison,* ed. David B. Mattern and Holly C. Shulman (Charlottesville: University of Virginia Press, 2003), p. 215.

67. Lee, *Revolutionary War Memoirs,* pp. 298–99; John Walker to Henry Lee,

March 28, 1805; and Henry Lee to Thomas Jefferson, Belvoir, September 8, 1806, both Thomas Jefferson Papers, LC. The feud would continue nearly to Jefferson's deathbed, with Lee's son Henry writing poisonous tirades against Jefferson to defend his now-dead father. See Charles Royster, "A Battle of Memoirs: Light-Horse Harry Lee and Thomas Jefferson," *Virginia Cavalcade* 31, no. 2 (Autumn 1981): 112–27, quotation p. 127.

68. For accounts of the Baltimore riot, see Armes, *Stratford Hall,* pp. 335–42; Boyd, *Light-horse Harry Lee,* pp. 307–27. Lee's own version of the story is in Henry Lee, *A Correct Account of the Conduct of the Baltimore Mob . . .* (Winchester, Va., 1814); and Richard Bland Lee to John Jay, n.d. [1812], CL-LC.

69. John Jay to Richard Bland Lee, Bedford, Westchester Co., September 7, 1812, CL-LC; and Boyd, *Light-horse Harry Lee,* pp. 304–5.

70. Edmund Jennings Lee to Luther Martin, Alexandria, May 14, 1813, Brock Collection, HL.

CHAPTER TWO: **Perplexity**

1. Henry Lee to Sydney Smith Lee, n.d. [Nassau, c. 1817], GBL-VHS.

2. Ann H. Lee to Charles Carter Lee, Alexandria, July 17, 1816, EA-LC.

3. Henry Lee to [Nicholas] Fish, Nassau, [November] 4, 1816, LC. Nicholas Fish was a soldier in the American Revolution and a leading Federalist, closely aligned with Alexander Hamilton.

4. A. C. R[obertson] to MFC, Sudley, March 4, 1821, MCL-VHS.

5. For more on Lee's siblings, see Lee, *General Lee,* pp. 17–19; MCL to MFC, Fort Hamilton, September 9, [c. 1841], MCL-VHS; quotations CCL, "Autobiographical Sketch," MS, n.d. [c. 1865–70], CCL-LoV; A. C. Stier to ?, "Sunday Morning," n.d. [c. 1814], REL-DU.

6. Henry Lee to James Madison, Barbadoes, August 4, 1813, CCL-LoV.

7. Edmund Jennings Lee to Luther Martin, Alexandria, May 14, 1813, Brock Collection, HL.

8. Henry Lee to William Yeats, Bridgetown, Barbadoes, August 14 [1814], CCL-LoV; and Narrative of James H. Causten, c. 1865, typescript, VHS.

9. Henry Lee to William Yeats, Bridgetown, Barbados, August 14, [1814], CCL-LoV; James H. Causten to Ann Hill Lee, Baltimore, April 11, 1818, copy VHS; and Causten Narrative, VHS.

10. See, for example, Henry Lee to "my dear son" [Henry Lee IV and Charles Carter Lee], Barbados, September 3, 1813, CCL-LoV. Other examples are found in Lee, *Revolutionary War Memoirs,* pp. 61–78.

11. Henry Lee to "my dear son" [Henry Lee IV and Charles Carter Lee], Barbados, September 3, 1813, CCL-LoV.

12. CCL to Henry Lee [IV], New York, July 21, 1831, CCL-LoV.

13. See, for example, Henry Lee IV's monumentally antagonistic *Observations on the Writings of Thomas Jefferson;* and Royster, "Battle of Memoirs," pp. 112–27.

14. CCL, "My Boyhood," MS, n.d. [c. 1865–70], CCL-LoV.

15. CCL, "Poetry Cong Strat," 1817, and "Recollections of Stratford," n.d., both EA-LC. For a description of a Lee family banquet, see Cornelia Lee to Eliza Lee, Alexandria, July 11, 1801, typescript, EA-LC.

16. See L. P. W. Balch to P. R. Fendall Jr., Leesburg, June 14, 1827, and Frederick, July 18, 1827, both Fendall Papers, LC.

17. Henry Lee to Ann Lee, Nassau, N. Providence, May 6, 1817, GBL-VHS; and Henry Lee to [Nicholas] Fish, Nassau, [November] 4, 1816, LC. Though in his letter to Fish Lee talks of "the impossibility of communicating with my own home from hence, no vessel ever having gone since I have been here to the Chesapeake," other correspondence shows he was in touch with his family before this time. See e.g., Henry Lee to CCL, Port-au-Prince, St. Domingo, June 26, 1816, in Lee, *Revolutionary War Memoirs,* p. 57.

18. CCL, "My Boyhood," CCL-LoV.

19. Ann Lee to Dr. Carter Berkeley, Stratford, November 26, 1809, photostat, EA-LC; A. L. Long, *Memoirs of Robert E. Lee* (repr., Secaucus, N.J.: Blue and Gray Press, 1983), p. 24; and Ann H. Lee to Philip Fendall, Eastern View, September 21, 1811, Fendall Papers, LC.

20. Mary Louisa Slacum Benham, *Recollections of Old Alexandria and Other Memories,* ed. Elizabeth Jane Stark (Starkville, Miss.: privately published, 1978), p. 27. Mrs. Benham, who was born in Alexandria a few years before Robert Lee, was close to his immediate family and large circle of cousins.

21. For the family's move, see Lee, *Lee of Virginia,* p. 412; Armes, *Stratford Hall,* p. 331; and T. Michael Miller, "The Lees as Landowners in Old Town Alexandria," May 1980, unpublished MS, BLA. Descriptions of Alexandria are found in James Craik, "Boyhood Memories," ed. Mary Craik Morris, *VMHB* 46, no. 2 (April 1938): 135–37; Elijah Fletcher to "Dear Sir," Alexandria, October 1, 1810, in Elijah Fletcher, *The Letters of Elijah Fletcher,* ed. Martha von Brieson (Charlottesville: University Press of Virginia, 1965), pp. 18; and George G. Kundahl, *Alexandria Goes to War: Beyond Robert E. Lee* (Knoxville: University of Tennessee Press, 2004), pp. 2–7.

22. Alexandria City Tax Records show Henry or Ann Lee occupying 607 Oronoco Street from 1812 to 1816 and again in 1821–25. Family histories have the Lees moving in during 1811, and this would mesh with the tax data, which was recorded only in the spring. *Potts-Fitzhugh House Historic Structures Report,* September 1, 2000; Gay Montague Moore, *Seaport in Virginia: George Washington's Alexandria* (Richmond: Garrett and Massie, 1949), pp. 206–8, claims that Robert E. Lee's bedroom was just below his mother's, but the architectural analysis of the house showed that no such room existed in the Lees' time. For recollections of the snowball bushes, see Jones, *Life and Letters,* p. 26; also Benjamin Hallowell, *Autobiography* (Philadelphia: Friends' Book Association, 1883), p. 104; and *Alexandria Gazette,* October 2, 1818.

23. Horace Binney was a Philadelphia lawyer and judge whom Ann Hill Lee had met when her husband was a congressman and she was living in Philadelphia. During the time that he befriended young Robert, Binney was writing his classic six-volume work on the decisions of the Supreme Court of Pennsylvania, still considered a nearly perfect model of legal reporting. CCL, "My Boyhood," CCL-LoV.

24. Edward V. Valentine, "Reminiscences of General Lee," *Outlook* 84, no. 17 (December 22, 1906): 966; CCL, "My Boyhood," CCL-LoV; and REL to "My Darling Daughters," Savannah, November 22, 1861, SH.

25. CCL, "My Boyhood," CCL-LoV; and REL draft letter to Rt. Rev. John Johns, Lexington, Va., March 7, 1866, REL Letterbook #3, LFP-VHS.

26. Marguerite Du Pont Lee, *Virginia Ghosts* (Berryville: Virginia Book Company, 1966), p. 156; Freeman, *R. E. Lee,* 1:30–31; T. Michael Miller, "A Profile of John Lloyd, Alexandria Merchant," unpublished MS, copy in John Lloyd Papers, LC; REL to William B. Leary, Lexington, Va., December 15, 1866, REL Letterbook #4, LFP-VHS;

Cassius Lee quoted in Long, *Memoirs,* pp. 25–26; and REL to "Sir," [John C. Calhoun] Alex[a], February 28, 1824, facsimile in the *San Francisco Post,* February 18, 1886.

27. Hallowell, *Autobiography,* pp. 82–83; 96; 101–3; and Benjamin Hallowell quoted in Long, *Memoirs,* pp. 27–28.

28. CCL, "My Boyhood," CCL-LoV; and REL to MCL, C[ity of Me]xico, damaged letter, March 24, 1848, DE-LC.

29. CCL, "My Boyhood," CCL-LoV.

30. Benham, *Recollections of Old Alexandria,* p. 28.

31. P. G. T. Beauregard, Joseph Johnston, and Philip St. George Cocke, contemporaries who served with Lee in the U.S. and Confederate armies, recalled similar childhood pastimes. See John Hope Franklin, *The Militant South* (Urbana: University of Illinois Press, 2002), pp. 14–16. For more on the way boys were raised in the early national period, see E. Anthony Rotundo, "Boy Culture: Middle-Class Boyhood in Nineteenth-Century America," in Mark C. Carnes and Clyde Griffen, eds., *Meanings for Manhood: Constructions of Masculinity in Victorian America* (Chicago: University of Chicago Press, 1990), pp. 16–36.

32. CCL, "My Boyhood," CCL-LoV; and CCL to mother, Cambridge, January 31, 1819, AHA.

33. CCL, "My Boyhood," CCL-LoV; and S. S. Lee to CCL, Camp Bluff, March 28, 1863, Fitzhugh Lee Papers, UVa.

34. For laudatory notes on Ann Lee, see Armes, *Stratford Hall,* p. 276; Lee, *Lee of Virginia,* p. 412; and Sally Lee to MCL, Gordonsville, November 10, [1870], DE-LC.

35. Ann Hill Lee to Sydney Smith Lee, April 10, [1827], photostat, EA-LC; Elizabeth Randolph to Mary B. Carter, E[astern] V[iew], August 3, 1829, Shirley Plantation Papers, RL; and Carter Berkeley to Ann Hill Lee, Edgewood, November 26, 1811, AHA.

36. See, for example, Henry Gilmour to Henry Lee IV, Belmont, June 5, 1816, CCL-LoV; MFC to MCL, n.d., quoted in Rose Mortimer Ellzey MacDonald, *Mrs. Robert E. Lee* (repr., Arlington, Va.: Robert B. Poisal, 1973), p. 38; CCL, "My Boyhood," CCL-LoV; S. S. Lee to CCL, Camp Bluff, March 28, 1863, Fitzhugh Lee Papers, UVa; and REL to Edward Childe, Ringgold Barracks, Texas, November 1, 1856, SH.

37. REL to MCL, June 25, 1857, in Jones, *Life and Letters,* p. 86; Sally Lee to MCL, Gordonsville, October 27, [1870], DE-LC; and Cassius Lee to MCL, Menoken, November 8, 1870, DE-LC.

38. Sally Lee to MCL, Gordonsville, October 27, [1870], DE-LC.

39. Gamaliel Bradford, *Lee the American* (Boston: Houghton Mifflin, 1912), p. 6. Some analysts have maintained that Robert's devoted care of his mother was indicative of an Oedipus complex, a desperate wish to supplant his father in his mother's affections. The double liability of this condition is that those who have a measure of success in their quest feel abnormal guilt as adults. See Thomson and Santos, "Mystery in the Coffin." Role reversals between parents and children can also cause confusion and excessive striving for achievement and perfection. See Janice L. Krupnick and Frederic Solomon, "Death of a Parent or Sibling during Childhood," in Jonathan Bloom-Feshbach and Sally Bloom-Feshbach, eds., *The Psychology of Separation and Loss* (San Francisco: Jossey-Bass, 1987), pp. 345–71.

40. RB Lee to "Mrs. Anne H. Lee," Warrenton, April 7, 1818, GBL-VHS.

41. Henry Lee IV to Mrs. A. H. Lee, Westm[nd], April 7, 1818, GBL-VHS.

42. Causten Narrative, VHS.

43. Henry Lee IV to Mrs. A. H. Lee, Westm[nd], April 7, 1818, GBL-VHS; Causten

Narrative, VHS; James H. Causten to Ann Hill Lee, Baltimore, April 11, 1818, copy in VHS; also Charles C. Jones Jr., *Reminiscences of the Last Days, Death and Burial of General Henry Lee* (Albany, N.Y.: Joel Munsell, 1870), pp. 18–20, 23–31; and "Mrs. Greene," "General Harry Lee's Funeral at Cumberland Island Georgia, March 1818," in CL-LC. For descriptions of Dungeness see REL to MCL, Coosawhatchie, S.C., January 18, 1862, DE-LC; and Frederick A. Ober, "Dungeness, General Greene's Sea-Island Plantation," *Lippincott's Magazine of Popular Literature and Science* 31, no. 8 (August 1880).

44. Henry Lee to Ann Lee, Nassau, N. Providence, May 6, 1817, GBL-VHS; family story in Armes, *Stratford Hall,* p. 347.

45. Ann Lee to CCL, Alexandria, February 17, 1817, EA-LC; Causten Narrative, VHS. Some doubt has been cast on the objectivity of this narrative, which was written around 1865, and which expresses great disdain for Robert E. Lee and his decision to fight for the Confederacy. But Causten also wrote to Ann Lee—in more diplomatic terms, of course—a few days after Henry Lee's death, with much the same information, and his brother's presence on one of the ships off Cumberland Island and the temper and tone of the final days can all be corroborated. See James H. Causten to Ann Hill Lee, Baltimore, April 11, 1818, copy in VHS; Causten Family Papers, Special Collections, Georgetown University; and Jones, *Reminiscences of the Last Days.*

46. CCL to Ann Hill Lee, Cambridge, January 31, 1819, AHA.

47. MCL to CCL, Lexington, August 1, 1870, EA-LC. We know that at least one person wrote to Ann Lee of Henry's state in his final weeks; see James H. Causten to Ann Hill Lee, Baltimore, April 11, 1818, copy in VHS.

48. Those wishing to explore the trauma of childhood loss will find interesting Sigmund Freud, "Mourning and Melancholia" (1917), in James Strachey, ed., *The Standard Edition of the Complete Psychological Works of Sigmund Freud,* 24 vols. (London: Hogarth Press, 1953–74), 14:239–58; George H. Pollock, "Mourning and Adaptation," *International Journal of Psycho-Analysis* 42 (1961); Alicia F. Lieberman, "Separation in Infancy and Early Childhood: Contributions of Attachment Theory and Psychoanalysis," and Krupnick and Solomon, "Death of a Parent or Sibling during Childhood," both in Bloom-Feshbach and Bloom-Feshbach, *Psychology of Separation and Loss*; and John Bowlby, *The Making and Breaking of Affectional Bonds* (London: Tavistock, 1979). They postulate that such loss can cause a boy to cling to and yet try to dominate the surviving parent; that sharp fears of dependence on any person may be absorbed; that during mourning young children may reproach themselves, believing they contributed to the death; and that guilty feelings may arise from this; that there may be rage or despair in the face of abandonment; that those who internalize these feelings may later suffer either depression, feelings of inadequacy, or physical illness, sometimes masked by an outer shell of equanimity.

49. Benham, *Recollections of Old Alexandria,* p. 34; and Roy Blount, *Robert E. Lee* (New York: Viking, 2003), p. 15.

50. Thomas L. Connelly, *The Marble Man* (Baton Rouge: Louisiana State University Press, 1977), pp. 5–6, 176–80; Michael Fellman, *The Making of Robert E. Lee* (New York: Random House, 2000), pp. 3–39; Blount, *Robert E. Lee,* pp. 167–84; Thomson and Santos, "Mystery in the Coffin"; Dederer, "In Search of the Unknown Soldier"; and Alan T. Nolan, "Grave Thoughts," *VMHB* 103, no. 1 (January 1995).

51. Andrew Jackson, quoted in Michael Paul Rogin, *Fathers and Children: Andrew Jackson and the Subjugation of the American Indian* (New York: Alfred A. Knopf, 1975), p. 40.

52. REL to CCL, City of Mexico, March 18, 1848, and REL to CCL, City of Mexico, May 15, 1848, both REL-UVa.

53. Henry Adams, *The Education of Henry Adams* (repr., New York: Oxford University Press, 1999), p. 23.

54. The pistols were apparently acquired by Henry Lee under questionable circumstances. During the Civil War General Fitz Lee wrote to one of REL's daughters that he had heard from a man named Massie that Henry Lee had offered to buy them but that he had never paid. Robert E. Lee later returned them to the owner's descendants. Fitzhugh Lee to MiCL, Head Quarters, Cavalry Corps, Army of Valley, February 4, 1865; and REL to Thos. Jas. Massie, Lexington, Va., June 1, 1866, REL Letterbook #3, both LFP-VHS.

55. Lee family friend William Slacum was among those who as a young boy wanted to fight the British occupying his hometown. Benham, *Recollections of Old Alexandria*, pp. 91–92; and REL to Albert Sidney Johnston, October 25, 1957, quoted in Marilyn McAdams Sibley, ed., "Robert E. Lee to Albert Sidney Johnston, 1857," *Journal of Southern History* 29, no. 1 (February 1963): 104.

56. Robert himself said that she tried to talk him out of a military life and opposed his going to West Point. REL to Mary Anna Randolph Custis, May 13, 1831, in deButts, "Yours Forever." Dederer, "In Search of the Unknown Soldier," pp. 89–90; and Freeman, *R. E. Lee*, 1:23.

57. REL to "My dear Sir," Lexington, Va., November 20, 1865, in REL Letterbook, #3, LFP-VHS.

58. The William E. West copy of Gilbert Stuart's portrait is at Washington and Lee University.

59. Much has been made of these visits to Cumberland Island, including the question of why Lee did not visit his father's grave during the time he was stationed at Cockspur Island. For the grand debate, see *VMHB* 103, no. 1 (January 1995). It is doubtful that he did so at that time, since he spent the year in agony over whether his father and brother's deletions would stand in the way of his proposed marriage to Mary Anna Randolph Custis. His letters also indicate he barely had time to visit Savannah, let alone Dungeness, a considerable journey. See chapter 5, "Long to Be Remembered." For an account of Lee's final, peaceful visit to the grave, see REL to CCL, Savannah, Ga., April 18, 1870, photostat, LFP-WL.

60. For evidence of ancestral pride, see REL to "My dear Sir," Lexington, Va., November 20, 1865, in Jones, *Life and Letters*, pp. 22–23; and Joseph E. Johnston quoted in Long, *Memoirs*, p. 71.

61. REL to Sir [John C. Calhoun, Secretary of War], Alexa[a], February 28, 1824, facsimile in the *San Francisco Post*, February 18, 1886.

62. James Longstreet, *From Manassas to Appomattox; Memoirs of the Civil War in America* (repr., New York: Da Capo Press, 1992), p. 287.

63. REL to MCL, City of Mexico, December 23, 1847, GBL-VHS.

64. REL to MARC, CockSpur Island, April 3, 1831, and May 13, 1831, in deButts, "Yours Forever."

65. REL to MCL, Camp near Agua Nueva, November 26, 1846, LFP-VHS.

66. For Mrs. Lee's recollection of his "*exactness* in all financial matters," see MCL to "My dear Mr. B.," Lexington, December 11, 1870, REL-DU. In REL to MCL, Ringgold Barracks, Texas, October 13, 1856, LFP-VHS, he lectured his wife on the necessity of

keeping minute track of the finances, writing, "it is unpleasant to give checks in Banks & not have the funds to meet them. People may think I am endeavoring to *swindle*."

67. Fitzhugh Lee to MiCL, Head Quarters, Cavalry Corps, Army of Valley, February 4, 1865, DE-LC.

68. REL to WHFL, Ringgold Barracks, Texas, April 2, 1860, DE-LC; in REL to ?, fragment, n.d. [post-1865] CL-LC, Lee directs an unknown youngster to "study hard & do something for the Lee name in the next generation."

69. Among Carter Lee's other projects was the defense of General Charles Lee, an eccentric Irishman who fought with the patriots during the Revolutionary War, but who was no relation to the American Lees. He disobeyed Washington's orders during the battle of Monmouth, and was court-martialed and dismissed. His fame grew when he indulged in some spectacularly imprudent remarks about Washington. See CCL to REL, Fine Creek, Powhatan County, July 25, 1866, DE-LC; CCL to Richard Henry Lee, March 21, 1860, EA-LC; and "Charles Lee," in *Dictionary of American Biography*, 10 vols. (New York: Charles Scribner's Sons, 1933), 6:98–99.

70. Robert E. Lee's letters show clearly that he undertook the introductory sketch to humor Carter and get him off his back, though he has been credited with far loftier goals. One biographer portrayed it as part of a conscious and continual search for his father; another believes he wrote the preface to remind citizens in both sections of the newly reunited country that Southerners, including the Lees, had been instrumental in forming the nation. The latter assertion seems unlikely, given Lee's adamant words to his brother about not raising anything of a political or controversial nature in the book. See REL to CCL, Lexington, Va., March 14, 1867, and July 8, 1869, both LFP-WL; R. E. Lee, "Preface," June 1, 1869, and Charles Royster, "Introduction," both in Lee, *Revolutionary War Memoirs;* also Thomas, *Robert E. Lee*, pp. 400–401.

71. See for example, Harry's advice to "love virtue & abhor lying," in Lee, *Revolutionary War Memoirs*, pp. 57–78. All of the original letters have not been found; those available are in CCL-LoV, EA-LC, and photostats at SH. The letters are also quoted, as edited by Robert E. Lee, in Lee, *Lee of Virginia*. For Lee's concerns that he create a benign image, see REL to CCL, Lexington, Va., March 14, 1867, MoC. For the kind of cribbing Lee did, see his description of his father's literary ability: "a surprising quickness and talent, a genius sudden, dazzling, and always at command, with an eloquence which seemed to flow unbidden." The words are an unattributed quote from his father-in-law's pen portrait of Light-Horse Harry. Lee, *Revolutionary War Memoirs*, pp. 51–52; Custis, *Memoirs of Washington*, pp. 361–62.

72. Valentine, "Reminiscences of General Lee," p. 966; Thomson and Santos, "Mystery in the Coffin," p. 89; REL quoted in REL to CCL, Camp, August 12, 1864, LFP-WL.

73. Henry Lee to Mrs. A. H. Lee, Nassau nr. Providence, May 6th [18]17, GBL-VHS; T. Michael Miller, "The Lees as Landowners in Old Town Alexandria," BLA. For Meade hearing young Lee's catechism, see REL to MCL, Richmond, March 14, 1862, DE-LC; also Bishop William Meade, *Old Churches, Ministers and Families of Virginia*, 2 vols. (repr., Baltimore: Genealogical Publishing, 1995), 2:269.

74. Elijah Fletcher to [Father], Alexandria, Va., October 31, 1810, in *Letters of Elijah Fletcher*, pp. 20–21; CCL, "Recollections," EA-LC; "Recollections of Matilda Lee Love," in Lee, *Lee Chronicle*, pp. 288–89.

75. See for example, REL to CCL, Camp, August 12, 1864, LFP-VHS; and REL to Mary Tabb Bolling Lee, Lexington, Va., May 29, 1868, GBL-VHS.

76. Much has been written about the social bonds of extended southern families. See, for example, Joan E. Cashin, "The Structure of Antebellum Families: 'The Ties That Bound us Was Strong,'" *Journal of Southern History* 56, no. 1 (February 1990): 55–70; Bruce Collins, *White Society in the Antebellum South* (London: Longman Group, 1985), pp. 125–31; Moore, *Seaport in Virginia*, pp. 203–4; Clinton, *Plantation Mistress*, pp. 37, 58; Jean E. Friedman, *The Enclosed Garden: Women and Community in the Evangelical South, 1830–1900* (Chapel Hill: University of North Carolina Press, 1985), pp. 10–11.

77. Thomas Lee quoted in Nagel, *Lees of Virginia*, p. 38.

78. William Cabell Bruce quoted in Zimmer, ed., *Housekeeping Book*, p. 21.

79. Miller, "Lees as Landowners"; Armes, *Stratford Hall*, pp. 220–22, 293; "Genealogical Notes," EA-LC; and "Tudor Place Genealogy," TPA. For the full list of Lee intermarriages through the nineteenth century, see Lee, *Lee of Virginia*.

80. REL to CCL, Old Point, May 26, 1831, REL-UVa.

81. Some examples of the intricate interactions of Lee's extended family are found in REL to Z. C. Lee, St. Louis, January 12, 1839; REL to Wm. L. Marshall, Washington, January 20, 1840; REL to Thomas Biddle, Fort Hamilton, N.Y., May 31, 1842, REL Letterbook #1; REL to John F. Lee, Fort Brown, Tex., December 11, 1856; REL to MCL, San Antonio, Texas, June 3, 1860; and REL to EAL, San Antonio, Texas, June 8, 1860, all DE-LC. The part played by Lee's relatives in securing his appointment to West Point is in Freeman, *R. E. Lee*, 1:37–44.

82. CCL to Henry Lee (IV), New York, October 8, 1831, CCL-LoV.

83. Armes, *Stratford Hall*, p. 367; and Petition "To the Electors of the Congressional District Composed of the Counties of Stafford, King-George, Westmoreland, Richmond, Northumberland and Lancaster," October 28, 1816, Fitzhugh Lee Papers, UVa.

84. F. W. Gilmer to Henry Lee, Winchester, April 16, 1816; and Richmond, June 10, 1818, both CCL-LoV.

85. H. Lee to Philip Fendall, June 13, 1818, Fendall Papers, LC.

86. [Samuel Appleton Storrow] to "Sister," September 6, 1821, EA-LC.

87. H. Lee to Philip R. Fendall, August 1, 1818, Fendall Papers, LC; Armes, *Stratford Hall*, pp. 372–73; *Alexandria Gazette*, October 2, 1818.

88. Fourth Decennial Census of the United States (1820), Westmoreland County, Virginia, NARA.

89. Armes, *Stratford Hall*, pp. 222, 374.

90. Ibid., pp. 373–75; Helen Gilmour to Henry Lee, Belmont, June 5, 1816, CCL-LoV; and A. C. R[obertson] to MFC, Sudley, March 4, 1821, MCL-VHS.

91. Eleanor Parke Custis Lewis to Elizabeth Bordley Gibson, Woodlawn, March 22, 1821, in Nelly Custis Lewis, *George Washington's Beautiful Nelly: The Letters of Eleanor Parke Custis Lewis to Elizabeth Bordley Gibson, 1794–1851*, ed. Patricia Brady (Columbia: University of South Carolina Press, 1991), p. 107.

92. Elizabeth McCarty to Dr. Richard Stuart, "Tuesday Evening," n.d. [c. 1821], Stuart Family Papers, UVa.

93. Armes, *Stratford Hall*, p. 375; and M. and Ann Rose to Ann McCarty Lee, Montrose, September 26, 1825, SH.

94. E. H. R[andolph] to Mary B. Carter, E[astern] V[iew], March 5, 1821, SPP-RL.

95. Eleanor Parke Custis Lewis to Elizabeth Bordley Gibson, Woodlawn, March 22, 1821, and April 23, 1821, in Lewis, *George Washington's Beautiful Nelly*, pp. 107, 110.

96. Bennett Knight to Richard Stuart, September 1821, Stuart Family Papers, UVa.; and Armes, *Stratford Hall*, p. 375.

97. See Richard F. Brown to Henry Lee, Windsor, September 5, 1825; and William B Hodgson, Consulate General of the U. States, Algiers, July 11, 1827, both CCL-LoV.

98. Maj. Henry Lee to John Tyler, Paris, August 24, 1833, typescript, EA-LC.

99. CCL to Henry Lee, The Spring Camp, April 21, 1833; and July 15, 1835; and CCL to Henry Lee, Geotown, August 5, 1829, all CCL-LoV. Carter Lee's continuing concern with his brother's finances can be found in CCL to Henry Lee, City Hall, August 12, 1829; CCL to Henry Lee, Washington, October 7, 1829; CCL to Henry Lee, Spring Camp, November 9, 1833; and CCL to Henry Lee, Spring Camp, September 25, 1835, all CCL-LoV. Carter Lee finally sold the family slaves to make ends meet, taking a loss and bucking popular prejudice against such sales as he did so.

100. Quotation CCL to Henry Lee (IV), Geotown, August 5, 1829, CCL-LoV. For a sad string of letters in which Carter berates Black-Horse Harry for continuing to place the family in debt, see CCL to Henry Lee (IV), City Hall, August 12, 1829; CCL to Henry Lee (IV), New York, July 21, 1831; CCL to Henry Lee (IV), Broad Neck near Hanover C[ourt] H[ouse], January 23, 1832; and CCL to Henry Lee (IV), Spring Camp, November 9, 1833, all CCL-LoV.

101. See REL to Mary Anna Randolph Custis, CockSpur Island, October 30, 1830, April 3, 1831, and May 13, 1831, all in deButts, "Yours Forever."

CHAPTER THREE: **The Torchbearers**

1. R. R. Gurley to Mary L. Custis, September 7, 1825, MCL-VHS. Ralph Randolph Gurley was a clergyman and one-time chaplain of the U.S. House of Representatives, and the chief agent of the American Colonization Society, which hoped to end slavery by freeing blacks and sending them to Africa to settle the colony of Liberia. Mary and George Washington Parke Custis became Robert E. Lee's parents-in-law. The U.S. *Brandywine* was christened in June of 1825 and outfitted to take General Lafayette to France in September of that year. Robert Waln Jr.'s *Life of the Marquis de Lafayette* appeared in 1825.

2. J. Bennett Nolan, *Lafayette in America Day by Day* (Baltimore: Johns Hopkins Press, 1934), p. 305; and Harlow Giles Unger, *Lafayette* (Hoboken, N.J.: John Wiley and Sons, 2002), pp. 359–60. Nolan, though an extremely useful source, is not completely accurate. For example, he states that Lafayette was in Washington on December 14, 1824; however, diaries by those accompanying the general, and the *Alexandria Gazette,* indicate that he was at Mount Vernon and Alexandria during much of that day. Nolan is in agreement with contemporary accounts that on September 6, 1825, Lafayette stayed late at the White House while the president broke with protocol to offer lengthy toasts. Lafayette's party then went on to Arlington House, where there was an "illumination" in his honor.

3. "Genl. La Fayette's Visit to Arlington House," n.d. [1825], TPA. The author of the document is not known. Its heroic style and artistic liberties are reminiscent of the essays written by George Washington Parke Custis; however, it is not in his handwriting. Though this document at first appears to be a firsthand description of Lafayette's visit to Arlington on September 6, 1825, it seems more likely that it is actually a composite of several excursions the marquis made to the Custises' home. It claims, for example, that Mary Lee Custis and her daughter were at the scene—whereas, as Gurley's letter shows, they were not present—and makes other errors of assumption and detail.

4. Unger, *Lafayette,* pp. 349, 351.

5. Ibid., pp. 350–58; Dolley Madison to John G. Jackson, November 27, 1824, in *The Selected Letters of Dolley Payne Madison,* p. 257.

6. For extensive information and photos of the memorabilia surrounding the visit, see Marian Klamkin, *The Return of Lafayette, 1824–25* (New York: Charles Scribner's Sons, 1975); poem in Hallowell, *Autobiography,* p. 99.

7. John Quincy Adams quoted in Unger, *Lafayette,* p. 360. Lafayette was actually present in the House of Representatives for the debate on the four-way electoral tie in the 1824 presidential election and used his prestige to calm some of the contentious actors. Margaret Bayard Smith, *The First Forty Years of Washington Society,* ed. Gaillard Hunt (New York: Frederick Ungar, 1965), p. 189.

8. Barry Schwartz, *George Washington: The Making of an American Symbol* (New York: Free Press, 1987); John Adams quoted p. 194.

9. MCL and REL to GWPC, [St. Louis], August 25, 1837 [*sic* 1838], REL-UVa.

10. *Alexandria Gazette,* October 19, 1824; Robert D. Ward, *An Account of General La Fayette's Visit to Virginia in the Years 1824–'25* (Richmond: West, Johnston, 1881), pp. 10–12; Moore, *Seaport in Virginia,* pp. 49, 110, 176, 239–42; Nelligan, "Old Arlington," p. 166; and MacDonald, *Mrs. Robert E. Lee,* pp. 22–23.

11. Hallowell, *Autobiography,* pp. 99, 101; and *Alexandria Gazette,* December 16, 1824. In the language of the day, "dinner" would have been an afternoon meal. Remembering the visit many years later, Hallowell errs in his dates, stating that Lafayette came to Alexandria on October 14, rather than October 16. A local historian, T. Michael Miller, believes that Hallowell erred completely, that the only visit to the Lees was on December 14, and that Hallowell may have exaggerated to place the visit closer to the date of his wedding, which took place on October 13. T. Michael Miller, "When Did General Lafayette Visit the Boyhood Home of Robert E. Lee?" unpublished research paper, April 22, 1990, copy BLA.

12. Unger, *Lafayette,* pp. 121, 159; and Lee, *Revolutionary War Memoirs,* pp. 512–13. *Ultimo ratio,* literally translated, means "final argument," but in terms of war it had come to signify the last accounting between belligerents.

13. George Washington Parke Custis's father died when he was six months old. His mother, Eleanor Calvert Custis, was overwhelmed by her four orphaned children, and it was for this reason that the Washingtons chose to raise the youngest two at Mount Vernon. Nelligan, "Old Arlington," pp. 1–57; *The Custis Chronicles,* 2:204–5. Lafayette quoted in undated clipping, Mildred Lee Scrapbook, Ross Family Papers, UVa.

14. GWPC quoted in Zimmer, ed., *Housekeeping Book,* p. 14.

15. Benson J. Lossing, "Arlington House, the Seat of G.W.P. Custis, Esq.," *Harper's New Monthly Magazine* 7, no. 40 (September 1853): 435.

16. Torbert, *Eleanor Calvert and Her Circle,* p. 101.

17. Rosalie Stier Calvert to Mme. H. J. Stier, Riversdale, December 29, 1803, in Calvert, *Mistress of Riversdale,* p. 70.

18. The Greek style symbolized the classical love of democracy to which Custis was committed, but he also made the house an extension of the Potomac landscape of his youth. The core of the house was constructed of local timber and the bricks fired from red Virginia clay, which were covered over with plaster made of oyster shells from the riverbeds and horsehair from his stables. The labor was also local, a large part of it supplied by slaves inherited from Martha Washington. Lossing, "Ar-

lington House," p. 436; Nelligan, "Old Arlington," pp. 70–75. GWPC to "Dearest Wife and Daughter," September 10, 1839, CL-TPA.

19. REL to MCL, Old Point, April 24, 1832, GBL-VHS.

20. Rosalie Stier Calvert to Mme H. J. Stier, Riversdale, May 12, 1804, in Calvert, *Mistress of Riversdale*, p. 82; Nelligan, "Old Arlington," p. 81; and *Potts-Fitzhugh House Historic Structures Report*, September 1, 2000, p. 6.

21. The original portrait hung for many years at Arlington, and is now in the Virginia Museum of Fine Arts.

22. MCL to ?, Lexington, December 22, 1869, typescript, AHA; for an example of the enthusiastic descriptions of Arlington's gardens, see Elizabeth Randolph Calvert, "Childhood Days at Arlington, Mixed with After Memories," unpublished MS, AHA.

23. The encomiums are innumerable, but see, for example, M. F. Powell to "My dear Nannie" [Lee], Oakly, July 18, 1886, quoted in Andrews, *Scraps of Paper*, p. 200; Mary Anna Randolph Custis [Lee] Diary (hereafter cited as MCL Diary), May 20, 1853; Eleanor Parke Custis Lewis to Elizabeth Bordley, Woodlawn, December 4, 1804, quoted in Lewis, *George Washington's Beautiful Nelly*, p. 66; and Rosalie Stier Calvert to Isabella van Havre, Riversdale, July 15, 1811, in Calvert, *Mistress of Riversdale*, p. 240.

24. Mary L[ee] F[itzhugh] to GWPC, n.d. [c. 1803–4], AHA; letter to the editor of the *National Intelligencer*, Savannah, May 16, 1853, quoted in Mary Custis Lee, preface to Custis, *Memoirs of Washington*, pp. 53–54.

25. See Elizabeth Randolph to Mary B. Carter, E[astern] V[iew], June 25, 1822, and Ladonia Randolph to Mary B. Carter, E[astern] View, November 5, 1830, both SPP-RL.

26. Henry S. Foote, *Casket of Reminiscences* (repr., New York: Negro Universities Press, 1968), p. 16.

27. George Washington quoted in Torbert, *Eleanor Calvert and Her Circle*, pp. 66–67; also Wiencek, *Imperfect God*, p. 342; for Custis's concern with carriages and livery, see his own story told in MCW Diary, April 7, 1854; and Sara B. Bearss, "The Farmer of Arlington," *Virginia Cavalcade* 38, no. 3 (Winter 1989): 124.

28. Lynch, *Custis Chronicles*; Washington's views on GWPC's father Jacky Custis are on pp. 137–38.

29. MCL quoted in preface to Custis, *Memoirs of Washington*, p. 72.

30. John Hill Hewitt, *Shadows on the Wall; or, Glimpses of the Past* (Baltimore: Turnbull Brothers, 1877), pp. 90–93.

31. Calvert, "Childhood Days" AHA; Hewitt, *Shadows on the Wall*, pp. 90–93; and Lossing, "Arlington House," pp. 436–37.

32. R. R. Gurley to MCL, Washington, October 6, 1858, quoted in MCL, preface to Custis, *Memoirs of Washington*, pp. 11–12.

33. The "Stewarts" were probably the family of David Stuart, Washington Custis's stepfather, who had an impressive number of children. Custis's mother, Eleanor Custis Calvert Stuart, had died in 1811.

34. Carter Lee, who was something of an amateur bard, enclosed a poem with his rosebush alluding to Mrs. Custis's talent for cultivating both plants and friends. See "To Mrs Mary L. Custis with a Moss Rose Bush," n.d. (c. 1825); and M. L. Custis to C. C. Lee, Arlington, March 17, 1825, photostats, EA-LC.

35. CCL to Henry Lee, April 20, 1831, CCL-LoV.

36. CCL to Henry Lee, New York, January 14, 1831, CCL-LoV; Sally Nelson Robbins, "Mrs. Lee during the War—Something about 'The Mess' and its Occupants," in

Robert Alonzo Brock, ed., *Gen. Robert Edward Lee: Soldier, Citizen and Christian Patriot* (Richmond, Va.: B. F. Johnson, 1897), p. 323.

37. M. F. Powell to "My dear Nannie" [Lee], Oakly, July 18, 1886, quoted in Andrews, *Scraps of Paper,* p. 200. For one of many examples of Lee's agony at the death of Mary Fitzhugh Custis, see REL to MCW, West Point, September 9, 1853, in Lee, *"To Markie,"* p. 33.

38. REL to MCW, West Point, January 2, 1854, in Lee, *"To Markie,"* p. 39.

39. Diary of Mrs. William Thornton, August 24, 1814, in W. B. Bryan, ed., "Diary of Mrs. William Thornton: Capture of Washington by the British," *Records of the Columbia Historical Society* 19 (1916): 175.

40. Lossing, "Arlington House."

41. Ibid. *National Intelligencer,* September 4, 1824; and Clayton Torrence, "Arlington and Mount Vernon, 1856, as Described in a Letter of Augusta Blanche Berard," *VMHB* 57, no. 2 (April 1949): 140–75.

42. Custis's emancipation plan called for the slaves to be freed after sixteen years, but required that they work one day a week for Custis to repay his economic loss, and that they agree to emigrate to Liberia. He never put his plan into effect, something lamented by the visitors for practical as well as philosophical reasons. "If Mr. Custis, instead of the great number of indolent slaves who devour his produce, and leave his roads in a bad condition, would employ a dozen free laborers," wrote a member of Lafayette's entourage after a visit on December 7, 1824, "I am sure he would soon triple his revenues, and have one of the most delight properties, not only on the District of Columbia, but of all Virginia." Nelligan, "Old Arlington," pp. 168–70; and A[uguste] Levasseur, *Lafayette in America in 1824 and 1825,* 2 vols. (Philadelphia: Carey and Lea, 1829), 2:12.

43. In 1854 Custis noted that, though infirm, nothing would keep him from the Washington birthday celebration, the sixty-third he had attended. GWPC to Anna Maria Fitzhugh, Arlington House, [February] 22, 1854, GBL-VHS; for a description of his appearance at the annual Alexandria Fourth of July celebration, see Mary Gregory Powell, "Reminiscences of Our Childhood," MS, n.d. [c. 1920], BLA; and Nelligan, "Old Arlington," pp. 178–79.

44. Nelligan, "Old Arlington," pp. 177–81, *Alexandria Gazette,* February 15, 1825, May 12, 1825, September 22, 1825, and October 13, 1825.

45. Nelligan, "Old Arlington," pp. 84–89; Rosalie Stier Calvert to H. J. Stier, Riversdale, June 6, 1809, in Calvert, *Mistress of Riversdale,* p. 206; GWPC to MFC, Arlington House, September 16, 1839, photostat, AHA; and Bearss, "The Farmer of Arlington."

46. See Murray H. Nelligan, "American Nationalism on the Stage: The Plays of George Washington Parke Custis," unpublished MS, 1949, copy at AHA; Lynch, *Custis Chronicles,* 2:251; Jared Sparks to GWPC, Cambridge, January 11, 1855, and Rembrandt Peale to GWPC, Philadelphia, August 20, 1857, both TPA; and Agnes Lee Journal, entry for February 16, 1853, DE-LC.

47. Several of the paintings, including the huge *Battle of Monmouth,* can be seen at Arlington House, NPS; *Washington at Yorktown* is in the Masonic Temple at Alexandria. Residents of Alexandria also recalled that Custis painted murals for the Washington birthday celebrations. Lossing, "Arlington House," pp. 445–54; and Mary Custis Lee quoted in MCL, preface to Custis, *Memoirs of Washington,* p. 68; Mary G. Powell, *The History of Old Alexandria* (Richmond, Va.: William Byrd Press, 1928), p. 243; and CCL to Henry Lee, Spring Camp, May 23, 1836, CCL-LoV.

48. *The Spirit of Seventy-Six,* May 10, 1811.

49. Unidentified newspaper obituary, 1857, clipping, AHA.

50. Bearss, "Farmer of Arlington," p. 128.

51. REL to CCL, Engineer Department, Washington, May 2, 1835, REL-UVa; and CCL to Henry Lee, Spring Camp, May 23, 1836, CCL-LoV.

52. CCL to Henry Lee, New York, April 19, 1831; Ravensworth April 15, 1832; and Spring Camp, May 23, 1836, all CCL-LoV; REL to CCL, Fort Monroe, April 14, 1834, photostat, EA-LC; and REL to CCL, Engineer Department, Washington, May 2, 1835, REL-UVa.

53. Lee and Washington were dissimilar in many ways, including Washington's more direct skill and involvement in politics, more overt interest in acquiring wealth, and more open ambition—or at least greater willingness to directly pursue it. Washington's style as a general differed significantly from Lee's as well; the differences would later be used to criticize Lee in assessments of his Civil War strategy. The two men's reflections on slavery, though similarly labyrinthine, ended in different places. An overview of the historiographical assumptions about bonds between Lee and Washington is found in Richard B. McCaslin, *Lee in the Shadow of Washington* (Baton Rouge: Louisiana State University Press, 2001), pp. 225–33. For Washington's character I found most helpful James Thomas Flexner, *Washington: The Indispensable Man* (New York: New American Library, 1974); and Joseph J. Ellis, *His Excellency, George Washington* (New York: Vintage Books, 2004).

54. REL to MFC, Baltimore, March 17, 1852; and REL to MCL, January 23, 1861, DE-LC; and REL to MCW, Lexington, Va., February 22, 1869, in Lee, *"To Markie,"* p. 84.

55. CCL, "Autobiographical Sketch," LoV.

56. REL to [P.] G. T. Beauregard, Lexington, Va., October 3, 1865, in REL Letterbook #3, LFP-VHS.

57. REL to MCL, January 23, 1861, typescript, DSF-LC.

58. McCaslin, *Lee in the Shadow of Washington,* pp. 2, 23.

59. Lee, *General Lee,* p. 22.

60. McCaslin, *Lee in the Shadow of Washington,* p. 21. McCaslin cites Henry Lee's paternal guidance, but the letters quoted never mention Washington, and none of them were addressed to Robert; nor is there any evidence that he saw them. Indeed many of them never arrived until the younger Lees were grown men. He quotes Henry Lee on the nobility of Washington, but the quotation is from his memoirs, not in correspondence to his children. Though it might be supposed that Robert saw the memoirs, there is no evidence of this until well after the Civil War, and certainly no indication of any effect they may have had on him.

61. Adams, *Education of Henry Adams,* pp. 9–24.

62. Freeman, *R. E. Lee,* 1:453. Other examples of extrapolation are found in McCaslin, *Lee in the Shadow of Washington.* To cite a few of many assumptions: On page 47: Lee's happiest moment during the opening days of the Mexican War was "when he embellished a Christmas feast with 'Revolutionary knives & forks' used by Washington." Lee did take a knife and fork to Mexico and laid them out at this feast, but never refers to this as "his happiest moment." In the description cited he shows equal delight in the centerpiece—"three bottles of the genuine anchor brand." Page 51: "In the army he had become the 'living legacy' of Washington." Lee's role in the Mexican War—largely as a scout, working solo—was justly heralded, but there is not one comparison of him to Washington at this time; such encomiums were rightly reserved for General Scott. Page 60: "He continued to remodel Arlington, providing

display space for relics." Lee did pay to remodel a large parlor in 1855, but he filled it with Lee family portraits, the carved Victorian furniture he had himself purchased at West Point, and his daughters' piano; detailed descriptions of the new parlor mention only one Mount Vernon tea cup in the room. Agnes Mullins, "Furnishings Plan for Arlington House the Robert E. Lee Memorial" (National Park Service, 1978), pp. 67–85.

63. See for example, REL to Jack Mackay, Fort Hamilton, N.Y. June 21, 1846, typescript in Mackay Family Papers, SHC-UNC; REL to Jack Mackay, National Palace, City of Mexico, October 2, 1847, USAMHI; REL to Smith Lee, City of Mexico, March 4, 1848, SH; and REL to MCL, Petersburg, March 28, 1865, DE-LC.

64. Calvert, "Childhood Days," AHA; and M. E. W. Sherwood, "Washington before the War," *Lippincott's Monthly Magazine* 45, no. 8 (August 1894): 261.

65. "MCG" to MCL, Myrtle Grove, May 26, [1853], DE-LC.

66. Lee, *General Lee*, pp. 26–27.

67. REL to MCW, West Point, March 11 and March 15, 1854, in Lee, *"To Markie,"* pp. 42–43.

CHAPTER FOUR: **The Long Gray Line**

1. REL to Sir [John C. Calhoun, Secretary of War], Alex[a], February 28, 1824, facsimile in the *San Francisco Post*, February 18, 1886. The handwriting in the letter has been compared by the Virginia Historical Society with a letter written three months later, and is virtually identical. The letter, which is missing from the file of Lee's application papers at the National Archives, is mentioned as an enclosure with one sent by Lee's older brother Carter of the same date. Carter Lee's letter, as well as those written by Congressman R. S. Garnett and Lee's teacher William Leary, are printed in Freeman, *R. E. Lee*, 1:40–43.

2. The discrepancy between the dates given in this letter for Lee's birth and the traditional date of January 19, 1807, raises some interesting questions. Though Lee may have boosted his age a little, thinking it would give his application an advantage, there is also intriguing evidence that he may actually have been born in 1806—the family Bible, for example, says his birth occurred on January 19, 1806, with the final number crossed out at a later date. West Point records also imply that Lee was born in 1806, and a cousin corroborates the information. It seems that the family at least thought for a time this was the correct date, and changed it for unknown reasons. Lee Family Bible, LFP-VHS; W. H. Fitzhugh to John C. Calhoun, Ravensworth, 7 Feb. 1824, RG 94, NARA; George W. Cullum, *Biographical Register of the Officers and Graduates of the U.S. Military Academy at West Point, N.Y.*, 3 vols. (Boston, 1891), 1:420-21; for Lee's mother-in-law's scolding about his moralizing, see MFC to MCL, "Wednesday night," n.d. [c. autumn 1831], MCL-VHS; for his children's frustration, see chapter 16, "Odyssey"; for staff aides' comments, see Walter H. Taylor to "My dear Bet[tie Saunders]," Camp at Violet Bank, August 15, 1864; Petersburg, Va., November 7, 1864; and Edge Hill, December 18, 1864, both in Walter Herron Taylor, *Lee's Adjutant: The Wartime Letters of Colonel Walter Herron Taylor, 1862–1865*, ed. R. Lockwood Tower (Columbia: University of South Carolina Press, 1995), pp. 182, 203, 212.

3. U.S. Military Academy, West Point, N.Y., *Register of Merit*, Record Group 404, ser. 198, NARA; and Merit Rolls for the Class, 1826, 1827, 1828, and 1829, copies at USMA.

4. All of Lee's advocates stressed his conscientiousness, "amiable disposition,"

and the Revolutionary War service of his father, all good qualifications, but as Lee would find as superintendent, it took political connections to secure the appointment. Sally Lee to MCL, Gordonsville, October 27, 1870, DE-LC.

5. Copies of Lee's letters of introduction and his response are in Freeman, *R. E. Lee,* 1:39–44.

6. REL to MARC, Old Point Comfort, Virginia, May 13, 1831, in deButts, "Yours Forever," Freeman, *R. E. Lee,* 1:38; Cassius Lee to MCL, Menoken, November 8, 1870; and Sally Lee to MCL, Gordonsville, October 27, 1870, both DE-LC; and REL to Albert Sidney Johnston, October 25, 1857, in Sibley, ed., "Lee to Albert Sidney Johnston," p. 104.

7. See the reference to Robert's letters in Ann Carter Lee to Sydney Smith Lee, April 10, [1827], photostat, EA-LC. George Pappas speaks familiarly of a letter from Cadet Lee to his family, but gives no citation and could not confirm the document to the author when he was contacted. An examination of contemporary documents revealed a letter by Leoindas Polk that was written during the same period and covers precisely the same issues that Pappas attributes to the Lee letter. See George S. Pappas, *To the Point: The United States Military Academy, 1802–1902* (Westport, Conn.: Praeger, 1993), p. 215; and William M. Polk, *Leonidas Polk: Bishop and General,* 2 vols. (New York: Longmans, Green, 1915), 1:80.

8. Albert E. Church, *Personal Reminiscences of the Military Academy from 1824 to 1831* (West Point: USMA Press, 1879), pp. 6–13; F. A. Mitchel, *Ormsby MacKnight Mitchel: Astronomer and General* (Boston: Houghton, Mifflin, 1887), p. 21; and Diary of Samuel P. Heintzelman (hereafter cited as Heintzelman Diary), June 26–28, 1825, Samuel P. Heintzelman Papers, LC.

9. Pappas, *To the Point,* pp. 115; Thomas Jefferson Cram, Extracts from "Recollections . . . as a Cadet . . . and an Officer," MS memoir, USMA. For years it was thought that the traditional gray uniform was designed to commemorate the 1814 Battle of Chippewa, at which the brave Chippewa Indians, clad in gray, had sided with the Americans against the British. Actually gray uniforms were adopted because they were cheap and functional. Allan Peskin, *Winfield Scott and the Profession of Arms* (Kent, Ohio: Kent State University Press, 2003), pp. 46–47.

10. Pappas, *To the Point,* p. 150.

11. Abner R. Hetzel to Father, June 17, 1823, quoted in Sidney Forman, *West Point: A History of the United States Military Academy* (New York: Columbia University Press, 1950), pp. 91–92.

12. Church, *Personal Reminiscences,* p. 12; and Edward L. Hartz to Father, Military Academy, West Point, January 30, 1853, Edward L. Hartz Papers, LC.

13. Heintzelman Diary, September 3, 1825; oath quoted in U.S. War Department, *General Regulations for the Army; or Military Institutes* (Washington, D.C.: Davis and Force, 1825), p. 410.

14. Washington later came out in favor of the militia, when he found it politically prudent to do so, but his use of a national army rather than the militia during the Whiskey Rebellion signaled his ambivalence. Russell F. Weigley, *Towards an American Army* (New York: Columbia University Press, 1962), pp. 12–19; Francis Paul Prucha, *Broadax and Bayonet: The Role of the United States Army in the Development of the Northwest, 1815–1860* (repr., Lincoln: University of Nebraska Press, 1995), pp. 29–30; and Edward M. Coffman, *The Old Army: A Portrait of the American Army in Peacetime, 1784–1898* (New York: Oxford University Press, 1986), pp. 38–40.

15. William B. Skelton, *An American Profession of Arms* (Lawrence: University Press of Kansas, 1992), pp. 168–71, Thayer quoted p. 170.

16. Charles Mason, "Life and Letters of Judge Charles Mason of Iowa," c. 1836, typescript in Charles Mason Remey Papers, LC; Walter Creigh Preston, *Lee: West Point and Lexington* (Yellow Springs, Ohio: Antioch Press, 1934), p. 11.

17. "Report of the Committee of the Board of Visitors on the General Condition of the Military Academy," June 1826; *Register of Merit*, NARA; and *Official Register*, 1826, 1827, 1828, 1829, all USMA. Lee would later recall that he particularly enjoyed the study of astronomy: "I think it afforded me more pleasure than any other branch of study." REL to MCL, HdQrts, Fredericksburg, March 27, 1863, LFP-VHS.

18. Jefferson Davis, "Robert E. Lee," *North American Review* 150 (January 1890): 56. In addition to being diligent, Lee probably benefited from the extra year's tutorial he had had with Benjamin Hallowell. One of the cadets during Lee's superintendence wrote to his sister that "where all study, and study with the assiduity which characterizes the Cadet, success depends also upon something else—either previous preparation or good mental endowments." Edward L. Hartz to "Dear Jenny," Military Academy, West Point, N.Y., March [?], 1853, Hartz Papers, LC.

19. Thomas Jefferson Cram, "Recollections."

20. Mason, "Life and Letters of Judge Charles Mason."

21. Church, *Personal Reminiscences*, pp. 42–44.

22. REL to GWCL, Baltimore, April 13, 1851, DE-LC.

23. Leonidas Polk to father, November 16, 1823, in Polk, *Leonidas Polk*, 1:72–73.

24. Diary of Charles Mason, June 19, 1864, typescript, Charles Mason Remey Papers, LC. In the end, Mason, who was not in favor of the war and sat it out in somewhat sullen copperhead sympathy, concluded that he could not have continued his military career with integrity. "I have at the same time a feeling of self-respect," he wrote, "a consciousness that I have not violated my sense of right and justice which I might have done if I had engaged in this civil war."

25. Polk, *Leonidas Polk*, 1:80; Cram, "Recollections."

26. Report of the Board of Visitors to the U.S. Military Academy, West Point, 1827, USMA.

27. Pappas, *To the Point*, pp. 136, 214–17; Cram, "Recollections"; Report of the Board of Visitors to the U.S. Military Academy, West Point, 1827 and 1829, MS at USMA; quotation George Tickner, "West Point in 1826," in *The Annual Reunion of the Association of Graduates* (West Point: USMA Press, 1886), p. 3.

28. Sylvanus Thayer to George Cullum, 1855, quoted in Pappas, *To the Point*, p. 161.

29. On the "dogish life" of a cadet officer, see Edward L. Hartz to Father, Military Academy, West Point, N.Y., March 24, 1855, Hartz Papers, LC; and REL to GWCL, copy in hand of GWCL, Baltimore, January 12, 1852, LFP-VHS.

30. See for example the pen portrait of Thayer written by Ethan Allen Hitchcock, who was the commandant of cadets and instructor of tactics in the 1820s, which is nearly identical to later descriptions of Lee. Ethan Allen Hitchcock, *Fifty Years in Camp and Field*, ed. W. A. Croffut (New York: Freeport, 1909), p. 49. One historian cites a letter from Lee as a cadet that is actively critical of Thayer, his methods of "espionage," and his austerity. As per 3n, the author believes this letter was written by Leonidas Polk.

31. Church, *Personal Reminiscences*, p. 17; and Pappas, *To the Point*, p. 153; Polk, *Leonidas Polk*, 1:72–73, 80.

32. Ruben Ross Diary (hereafter cited as Ross Diary), October 30, 1852, typescript, USMA. Other versions of "Benny Havens O" are found in [George C. Strong], *Cadet Life at West Point* (Boston: T.O.H.P. Burnham, 1862), pp. 302–3. The song is still sung today, with creative new verses added each year.

33. Report of the Board of Visitors, MS, June 1828, USMA.

34. Heintzelman Diary, January 1, 1825, November 4, 1825, December 24, 1825, December 25, 1825, and June 25, 1826.

35. Davis, "Robert E. Lee," p. 56.

36. Notes on Douglas Southall Freeman in Robert E. Lee Vertical File, April 24, 1941, USMA.

37. Preston, *West Point and Lexington*, pp. 8–9. Preston concludes that Davis and the West Point historians are wrong; but cites only the 1826 report. Archivists at West Point believe that the delinquency books were begun only after the initial "plebe" year—hence the absence of a record for Lee in 1825—and were maintained throughout a cadet's years, so that the 1826 record would be the only one referring to Lee.

38. Heintzelman Diary, July 4, 1825; Pappas, *To the Point*, p. 160.

39. Heintzelman Diary, December 25, 1825; quotation Church, *Personal Reminiscences*, pp. 7–8.

40. Pappas, *To the Point*, pp. 169–73; John Quincy Adams quoted p. 173. Records of the official investigation are in USMA. Jefferson Davis was evidently pained by the memory of this incident for the rest of his life. See William C. Davis, *Jefferson Davis: The Man and His Hour* (New York: HarperCollins, 1991), pp. 35–37. A detailed, but semi-fictionalized account is found in James B. Agnew, *Eggnog Riot* (San Rafael, Calif.: Presidio Press, 1979).

41. Joseph E. Johnston quoted in Long, *Memoirs*, p. 71.

42. Craig L. Symonds, *Joseph E. Johnston: A Civil War Biography* (New York: W. W. Norton, 1992), pp. 10, 18–19; Preston, *West Point and Lexington*, p. 11; Ewell quoted in "General Lee's Birthday," address of D. Gardiner Tyler, January 19, 1911, in *Tyler's Quarterly Historical and Genealogical Magazine* 10, (1929): 252.

43. Emily Mason quoted in Long, *Memoirs*, p. 30.

44. Ibid.; Johnston quoted in Symonds, *Joseph E. Johnston*, p. 18.

45. John Mackay to "My dear Mother," West Point, June 15, 1829, typescript, Mackay-McQueen Papers, GHS.

46. Heintzelman Diary, "Thursday 15th June," [1826].

47. John Mackay to "My dear Mother," June 26, 1829, Mackay-McQueen Papers, GHS.

48. Charles Mason, "Valedictory Delivered before the Dialectic Society, United States Military Academy, West Point," 1829, typescript, Charles Mason Remey Papers, LC.

49. REL to MCL, C[ity of Me]xico, damaged letter, March 24, 1848, DE-LC.

50. Mason, "Life and Letters of Judge Charles Mason"; O. O. Howard, *Autobiography of Oliver Otis Howard*, 2 vols. (repr., Freeport, N.Y.: Books for Libraries Press, 1971), 1:59–60; and Church, *Personal Reminiscences*, pp. 22–26.

51. J. Mackay to "My dear Mother" [Eliza Anna McQueen Mackay], New York, October 4, 1829, Eliza Anna Mackay Papers, DU.

52. Stephen E. Ambrose, *Duty, Honor, Country: A History of West Point* (Baltimore: Johns Hopkins University Press, 1966), pp. 130–31; Edward L. Hartz to "Jenny," Military Academy, West Point, April 6, 1853, Hartz Papers, LC.

53. Edward L. Hartz to Father, Military Academy, West Point, N.Y., March 24, 1855, Hartz Papers, LC.

54. Lee evidently made this statement to Washington College professor Milton Wylie Humphreys. See M. W. Humphreys, "Reminiscences of General Lee as President of Washington College," in Franklin L. Riley, ed., *General Lee After Appomattox* (New York: 1922), p. 38. Humphreys was adamant about Lee's remark, underscoring his story by saying "he certainly used the above quoted words."

55. Peter S. Onuf, "Introduction," and Samuel G. Watson, "Developing 'Republican Machines': West Point and the Struggle to Render the Officer Corps Safe for America, 1802–33," in Robert M. S. McDonald, *Thomas Jefferson's Military Academy: Founding West Point* (Charlottesville: University of Virginia Press, 2004).

56. Church, *Personal Reminiscences*, pp. 50–56; Weigley, *Towards an American Army*, pp. 38–53; Skelton, *American Profession of Arms*, pp. 247, 258; also Brigadier General Eben Swift, "The Military Education of Robert E. Lee," *VMHB* 35, no. 2 (April 1927): 97–157. This article is outdated but it does point out several interesting highlights from textbooks used at West Point.

57. Church, *Personal Reminiscences*, p. 52.

58. For a list of books Lee checked out from the West Point library during a three-month period, see Freeman, *R. E. Lee*, 1:72–73.

59. Church, *Personal Reminiscences*, pp. 46–47; the adjectives describing Hitchcock and Worth are from Mason, "Life and Letters of Judge Charles Mason."

60. For more on the lessons learned during the Mexican War, see chapter 9, "Adrenaline."

61. Preston, *West Point and Lexington*, pp. 13–15; Freeman, *R. E. Lee*, 1:78–79. For Lee's comments, see Jones, *Reminiscences*, p. 218; and "War," essay fragment in REL hand, n.d. [c. 1868], MCL-VHS.

CHAPTER FIVE: **Long to Be Remembered**

1. REL to Captain Andrew Talcott, Ravensworth, July 13, 1831, LFP-VHS. Talcott was Lee's superior officer while he was stationed at Fort Monroe, Virginia. He struck up an intense friendship with Talcott and his wife, which lasted throughout their lives. General Charles Gratiot was the chief of the Corps of Engineers. The "Ingham Affair" was a scandal in Andrew Jackson's cabinet. When Secretary of War John Henry Easton married a woman of notorious reputation, several members of the cabinet, including Secretary of the Treasury Samuel Ingham, resigned rather than have to socialize with her.

2. John Mackay to "My dear Mother" [Eliza Mackay], June 26, 1829, Mackay-McQueen Papers, GHS.

3. Sanborn, *Portrait*, p. 66; and Edmund Jennings Lee, "The Character of General Lee," in Brock, ed., *Gen. Robert Edward Lee*, p. 383.

4. CCL to REL, [August 1829], CCL-LoV. Ann Lee's sister, Elizabeth Randolph, also spoke of the "feelings of the Heart that presses on us" at her death and how melancholy Ann's children were. Elizabeth Randolph to Mary B. Carter, E[astern] V[iew], August 3, 1829, SPP-RL.

5. Nagel, *Lees of Virginia*, pp. 215–17; and Armes, *Stratford Hall*, pp. 385–86. In a poetic irony, the purchaser of Stratford was Elizabeth Storke, neé McCarty, the very girl Black-Horse Harry had so cruelly misused. She lived at Stratford through the

Civil War, attempting to redeem her name and valiantly defending the property against the intrusions of Yankee soldiers.

6. CCL to Henry Lee, March 28, 1830, CCL-LoV; Armes, *Stratford Hall,* pp. 392–98; and Nagel, *Lees of Virginia,* pp. 214–19.

7. On the Mackays, see Sanborn, *Portrait,* pp. 68, 72; Fellman, *Making of Robert E. Lee,* pp. 31–32; and REL to CCL, CockSpur Island, May 8, 1830, REL-UVa. It has been intimated that Lee hoped to marry one of the Mackay women, but early letters show that he was already interested in Mary Custis by the time he arrived in Savannah, and that he thought of the Mackays only as teasing, bantering friends who had generously adopted him into their family. See Mildred Lee to MARC, West River, August 22, 1829, GBL-VHS; and REL to MARC, CockSpur Island, December 1 and 28, 1830; April 11 and 20, 1831; all deButts, "Yours Forever."

8. Fitzhugh's portrait is now in the Lee Chapel Museum, Washington and Lee University. Mary Custis thought that her uncle had fallen from his horse, but Fitzhugh's father-in-law, who was with him when he died, told the story of sudden illness and wordless death. One fears Fitzhugh may have been the victim of medical ignorance, for many popular medicines of the day contained mercury and other poisonous substances. See Elizabeth Randolph to Mary B. Carter, E[astern] View, May 26 and 28, 1830, SSP-RL.

9. Fitzhugh's tombstone gives the date of his death as May 21, 1830. Obituary in the *National Intelligencer,* August 14, 1830; and MCL Diary, July 22, 1830, and May 20, 1853, LFP-VHS.

10. MCL Diary for 1830–31.

11. MiCL, "Reminiscences of Mother," December 11, 1894, DE-LC; and MCL to Sarah Beaumont, Fort Hamilton, July 6, 1841, LFP-BLC.

12. R. R. Gurley to MFC, Norfolk, June 27, 1824, MCL-VHS; Mary A. R. Custis copybook, February 1823, CL-LC; and MiCL, "Reminiscences of Mother."

13. There are few surviving documents that give any indication of Mary Custis Lee's relationship with her father; certainly he loved her dearly, but this author has found nothing to indicate "incessant attentions," and Connelly does not cite his source for this assertion. Connelly, *Marble Man,* p. 7; and Emory M. Thomas, "The Lee Marriage," in Carol K. Bleser and Lesley J. Gordon, eds., *Intimate Strategies of the Civil War* (New York: Oxford University Press, 2001), p. 36. Additional undocumented negative comments about Mary Custis Lee can be found in Blount, *Robert E. Lee,* pp. 174–75; and Charles Bracelen Flood, *Lee: The Last Years* (Boston: Houghton Mifflin, 1998), pp. 137–40.

14. See Charles Cocke Turner to MARC, Toulouse, March 9, 1830, GBL-VHS; and Foote, *Casket of Reminiscences,* p. 16.

15. Auguste Hervieu painted a flattering picture of Mary Custis in the months prior to the wedding, emphasizing her bright eyes and a serene smile. We also know from Hervieu's correspondence that he hoped to please the Custis family, whose status he thought would aid his artistic career. And Mary herself seemed to think the portrait "superior to the original." See Aug[us]t[e] Hervieu to MFC, n.d. [prior to September 1830], Custis Family Papers, VHS; and REL to MARC, CockSpur Island, February 1, 1831, in deButts, "Yours Forever." The portrait is on loan to Arlington House, NPS.

16. Eleanor Parke Custis Lewis to Elizabeth Bordley Gibson, Woodlawn, December 2, 1823, in Lewis, *George Washington's Beautiful Nelly,* p. 138. The Randolph family agreed with Nelly Custis Lewis. "What a sweet young Girl she is," wrote one. "O! what

a blessing is a sweet temper—such as hers!" Elizabeth Randolph to Mary B. Carter, E[astern] V[iew], June 25, 1822 and Ladonia Randolph to Mary B Carter, E[astern] View, November 5, 1830, SSP-RL.

17. Mildred Lee to MARC, West River, November 4, 1829, GBL-VHS.

18. MEA Lewis to Charles M. Conrad, November 16, 1834, quoted in Nelligan, "Old Arlington," p. 231.

19. R[osalie] Stuart to Mary Anna Randolph Custis, Cedar Grove, July 26, 1825, LFP-WL. Evidently Carter, Smith and Robert all showed an interest in Mary Custis.

20. Carter Lee's suit went so far that at one point they were thought to be engaged. However, Mary evidently dismissed both Smith and Carter rather summarily, for Robert later chided her for failing to turn "them off in such a way as to make them friends for life." REL to MARC, Cockspur Island, December 28, 1830 and March 8, 1831, in deButts, "Yours Forever"; Elizabeth Randolph Turner to MARC, Kinloch, December 26, n.d. [c. 1828–1830], GBL-VHS; Elizabeth Randolph Turner to Mary B Carter, E[astern] V[iew], August 3, 1829, SSP-RL.

21. Mildred Lee to MARC, West River, November 4, 1829, GBL-VHS; and MCL Diary, [July] 15, 1830.

22. Eleanor Parke Custis Lewis to Elizabeth Bordley Gibson, Woodlawn, June 24, 1827, in Lewis, *George Washington's Beautiful Nelly*, p. 191. Aunt Lewis was in fact scheming for Mary Custis to marry her son. See Eleanor Parke Custis Lewis to Elizabeth Bordley Gibson, April 15, 1824, in ibid., pp. 146–47.

23. Mildred Lee to MARC, West River, November 4, 1829; and December 23, 1829, both GBL-VHS.

24. Mary A. R. Custis to Mrs. Eliza P. Custis, Peter Grove, n.d. [c. 1826], Lafayette–Eliza Custis Law Papers, Maryland Historical Society; and MCL Diary, July 4, 1830.

25. Unidentified commentary in Long, *Memoirs*, pp. 30–31.

26. CCL to Hill Carter, March 10, 1824, SPP-RL.

27. Mildred Lee to MARC, West River, August 22, 1829, GBL-VHS; CCL, "Robert to Miss Polly" and "Miss Polly's Answer," n.d., CCL-LoV. The poem might possibly have been written for Carter's cousin Robert Randolph, who married Mary Buckner Thurston Magill—another potential Polly—though the circumstances fit those of Robert Lee and Mary Custis. Polly was also the name of a parrot—the Custis family symbol—fitting with Carter's love of double entendre.

28. REL to CCL, CockSpur Island, May 8, 1830, REL-UVa.

29. MCL Diary, [July] 5, 1830; "Arlington and Its Proprietors," undated newspaper clipping in Mildred Lee Scrapbook, Ross Family Papers, UVa; Robbins, "Mrs. Lee during the War," p. 323; REL to MARC, CockSpur Island, December 1, 1830, in deButts, "Yours Forever." One story states that Lee remembered courting his wife under the shade of the stately trees at Chatham, and sentimentally recounted the tale to a fellow officer as he looked at the house through a spyglass during the battle of Fredericksburg. The story is attributed to Betty Churchill Lacy's "Memories of a Long Life," which can be found at http://homepages.rootsweb.com/~elacey/chatham.htm, but there is no evidence that Lee was in the neighborhood of Chatham during the period of his courtship, and no other corroborating data has been found. See Ronald W. Johnson, "Preliminary Historic Resource Study: Chatham," Fredericksburg and Spotsylvania Country Battlefields Memorial, National Military Park, National Park Service, pp. 160–64.

30. Robbins, "Mrs. Lee during the War," p. 323.

31. Mary A. R. Custis to Hortensia Moore, October 14, 1830, AHA.

32. REL to CCL, Arlington, September 22, 1830, REL-UVa.

33. Mary also seems to have given Lee a portrait of herself; see REL to MARC, Baltimore, October 30, 1830; and REL to MARC, Cock-Spur Island, November 11, 1830, in deButts, "Yours Forever."

34. MARC to REL, Arlington, September 20, 1830, LFP-VHS.

35. Lee's letters are in MCL-VHS, and will be published in their entirety in deButts, "Yours Forever." I am indebted to Mr. deButts for allowing me to read and quote from them before their publication.

36. MARC to REL, September 20, [1830], LFP-VHS.

37. Mary A. R. Custis to Hortensia Moore, October 14, 1830, AHA; and REL to CCL, Arlington, September 30, 1830, REL-UVa.

38. REL to MARC, CockSpur Island, March 8, 1831, in deButts, "Yours Forever."

39. REL quoted in Almira Russell Hancock, *Reminiscences of Winfield Scott Hancock* (New York: Charles L. Webster, 1887), pp. 46–47.

40. Lynch, *Custis Chronicles*, 2:218.

41. Marcus Cunliffe, *Soldiers and Civilians: The Martial Spirit in America, 1775–1865* (Boston: Little, Brown, 1968); Peskin, *Winfield Scott*, p. 66; and [Varina Howell Davis], *Jefferson Davis: A Memoir by His Wife*, 2 vols. (New York: Belford, 1890), 1:95, 161–62.

42. REL to CCL, Arlington, September 30, REL-UVa.

43. REL to MARC, Old Point Comfort, May 13, 1831, in deButts, "Yours Forever."

44. Henry Lee to CCL, Paris, February 16, 1831, CCL-LoV; and REL to MARC, CockSpur Island, March 8, 1831, in deButts, "Yours Forever."

45. REL to MARC, CockSpur Island, April 3, 1831, in deButts, "Yours Forever."

46. CCL to Henry Lee quoted in Sanborn, *Portrait*, p. 76; and Nagel, *Lees of Virginia*, p. 237.

47. Henry Lee to CCL, Paris, February 16, 1831, CCL–LoV.

48. Cornelia Lee Hopkins quoted in Nagel, *Lees of Virginia*, p. 236; and Mary Meade to MFC, Lucky Mt., July 12, 1808, MCL-VHS. Census records also list her birth date in the same year as Robert's. See for example, Eighth Decennial Census of the United States, Alexandria County, Va., NARA.

49. MEA Lewis to CM Conrad, Arlington, March 14, 1835, typescript, AHA.

50. Alexis de Tocqueville quoted in Michael Kimmel, *Manhood in America* (New York: Free Press, 1996), pp. 51–52.

51. For studies of female attitudes toward matrimony, see Melinda S. Buza, "'Pledges of Our Love': Friendship, Love, and Marriage among the Virginia Gentry, 1800–1825," in Edward L. Ayers and John C. Willis, eds., *The Edge of the South: Life in Nineteenth Century Virginia* (Charlottesville: University Press of Virginia, 1991), pp. 9–36; Anya Jabour, "Albums of Affection: Female Friendship and Coming of Age in Antebellum Virginia," *VMHB* 107, no. 2 (Spring 1999): 125–58; Barbara Welter, *Dimity Convictions: The American Woman in the Nineteenth Century* (Athens: Ohio University Press, 1976), pp. 12–15; and Stephen M. Frank, *Life with Father: Parenthood and Masculinity in the Nineteenth Century American North* (Baltimore: Johns Hopkins University Press, 1998), pp. 86–88. The hazards of childbirth will be discussed in greater depth in chapter 6, "Seven Arias."

52. Mildred Lee to MARC, West River, November 4, 1829, GBL-VHS; and MCL to a daughter, n.p., n.d. [c. 1857], in DE-LC.

53. MCL to MFC, April 11, [1834], DE-LC.

54. See REL to MARC, CockSpur Island, December 28, 1830; and January 10, February 14, and March 8, 1831, all in deButts, "Yours Forever."

55. MCL Diary, June 12, 1831.

56. REL to MARC, [Old Point Comfort], June 12, 1831, in deButts, "Yours Forever."

57. REL to CCL, Old Point, May 26, 1831; quotation REL to CCL, June 15, 1831, both REL-UVa.

58. REL to MARC, Cockspur Island, April 3, April 20; and Old Point Comfort, June 3, 1831, all in deButts, "Yours Forever."

59. R. R. Gurley to MFC, Office of the Col. Society, Washington, June 23, 1831, MCL-VHS; REL to MARC, [Old Point Comfort], June 3, 1831, in deButts, "Yours Forever"; Sanborn, *Portrait,* p. 83; and REL to CCL, Old Point, May 26, 1831, REL-UVa.

60. The wedding party consisted of Catherine Mason of Analostan Island, Mary Goldsborough and Julia Calvert of Maryland, Angela Lewis from Woodlawn, Britannia Peter from Tudor Place, Marietta Turner of Kinloch; and Smith Lee, Thomas Turner from Kinloch, and Lieutenants John P. Kennedy, James A. Chambers, Richard Tilghman, and James H. Prentiss. Nelligan, "Old Arlington," p. 205; REL quoted in REL to CCL, Old Point, June 15, 1831, REL-UVa.

61. "Arlington and Its Proprietors," undated newspaper clipping in Mildred Lee Scrapbook, Ross Family Papers, UVa.

62. Joseph Packard, *Recollections of a Long Life* (Washington, D.C.: B. S. Adams, 1902), p. 157.

63. Nelligan, "Old Arlington," pp. 206–7; Marietta Turner Powell to "My dear Nannie," Oakley, July 17, 1886, quoted in Andrews, *Scraps of Paper,* pp. 202–3; and U.S. Quartermaster Corps, *Arlington House and Its Associations* (Washington, D.C.: GPO, 1932), p. 3. Much of the information in the latter document came from early-twentieth-century interviews with former Arlington slaves.

64. REL to Captain Andrew Talcott, Ravensworth, July 13, 1831, LFP-VHS; and Marietta Minnigerode Andrews, *Memoirs of a Poor Relation* (New York: E. P. Dutton 1927), p. 91.

65. Dolley Madison quoted in Lucia B. Cutts, ed., *Memoirs and Letters of Dolly Madison* (Port Washington, N.Y., Kennicat Press, 1866), p. 51.

66. MEA Lewis to Mrs. S. H. Conrad, Alexandria, July 27, 1831, typescript, AHA; and Andrews, *Poor Relation,* pp. 89–90.

67. In time Virginia's wedding parties became nearly legendary. A story was popularly related of one young couple who started on their wedding tour and continued their round of visits until they had nine children. Lucy Lee Pleasants, ed., *Old Virginia Days and Ways: Reminiscences of Mrs. Sally McCarty Pleasants* (Menasha, Wis.: George Banta, 1916), p. 35. For the story of Smith Lee's wedding party, see Long, *Memoirs,* p. 38n; REL to John Macomb or Dick Tilghman, quoted in part in Freeman, *R. E. Lee,* 1:133; EP Lewis to C. M. Conrad, March 1 [1835], typescript, AHA; and REL to Jack Mackay, Washington, D.C., February [1835], typescript, Mackay-McQueen Papers, GHS.

68. The etched-glass decanters are at Arlington House, NPS; and Marietta Turner Powell to "My dear Nannie," Oakley, July 17, 1886, quoted in Andrews, *Scraps of Paper,* p. 203.

69. Zaccheus Collins Lee to CCL, July 6, 1831, photostat, EA-LC.

70. On nineteenth-century ideals of marriage, see Buza, "'Pledges of Our Love,'" pp. 9–36; and Lystra, *Searching the Heart,* pp. 28–42, 193–95. Among those who paint a picture of southern marriage as based on starkly separate "spheres," see Clinton, *Plantation Mistress;* Wyatt-Brown, *Southern Honor;* and Anne Frior Scott, *The Southern Lady: From Pedestal to Politics, 1830–1930* (Chicago: University of Chicago Press, 1970); also Carroll Smith-Rosenberg, "The Female World of Love and Ritual: Relations between Women in Nineteenth-Century America," *Signs* 1 (Autumn 1975). The Lees' marriage seems more to fit the pattern of loving, striving, and committed partnership described in Elizabeth Fox-Genovese, "Family and Female Identity in the Antebellum South: Sarah Gayle and Her Family," in Carol Bleser, ed., *In Joy and in Sorrow: Women, Family and Marriage in the Victorian South* (New York: Oxford University Press, 1991); and Fox-Genovese, *Within the Plantation Household: Black and White Women of the Old South* (Chapel Hill: University of North Carolina Press, 1988).

71. REL to Jack Mackay, Fort Monroe, February 27, 1834, typescript, AHA. Lee's words are a paraphrase of *Hamlet,* act 1, scene 1.

72. Buza, "'Pledges of Our Love,'" p. 24; Lystra, *Searching the Heart,* p. 195.

73. Steven M. Stowe, "Growing Up Female in the Planter Class," *Helicon Nine,* no. 17/18 (Spring 1987): 195–205.

74. See MCL Diary, July 3, 1831; for examples of the continuing tension between spiritual issues and the distractions of marriage, see also entries for January 8 and February 14, 1836, and May 20, 1853.

75. Zimmer, ed., *Housekeeping Book,* p. 32; Lynch, *Custis Chronicles,* p. 3; Mildred Lee to MARC, West River, November 4, 1829, GBL-VHS; and Elizabeth Lindsay Lomax, *Leaves from an Old Washington Diary* (New York: E. P. Dutton, 1943), pp. 85–86. Elizabeth Lomax, who was a close friend of Mary Custis Lee, held roundtable discussions on the need to provide women with higher education. Freeman trivializes Mary Lee's political commentary, but in many cases it is more knowledgeable than her husband's. See Freeman, *R. E. Lee,* 1:108; and MCL to Sarah Beaumont, Arlington, June 12, [1839 or 1840], LFP-BLC; and MCL to MiCL [February] 19th, [1861], DE-LC.

76. For Mary's handling of the finances, see for example, REL to MCL, City of Mexico, March 15, 1848; MCL to REL, Arlington, August 12, 1856; MCL to REL, September 2, 1856; REL to MCL, San Antonio, Texas, April 7, 1857; and REL to MCL, Camp Cooper, Texas, June 1, 1857, all DE-LC. Quotation MCL to REL, Arlington, September 6, [1856], DE-LC.

77. MCL to Sarah Beaumont, Arlington, December 17, 1839, LFP-BLC.

78. See chapter 6, "Seven Arias."

79. Robbins, "Mrs. Lee during the War," p. 378; MCW Diary, May 10, 1857; "Reminiscences of Mrs. Harriet S. Turner," n.d. [c. 1892], George Washington Campbell Papers, LC.

80. REL to Capt. A. Talcott, Wash[ington, D.C.], November 25, 1835, Talcott Family Papers, VHS.

81. REL to Captain A[ndrew] Talcott, Corps of Engineers, Fort M[onroe], April 10, 1834, and MCL to MFC, "Saturday," n.d. [c. 1831], both REL-VHS. Another complaint about her housekeeping ability is found in REL to MARC, Fortress Monroe, May 24, 1831, in deButts, "Yours Forever."

82. MCL to MFC, "Saturday," n.d. [c. 1831], REL-VHS; MFC to MCL, "Wednesday

night," n.d. [c. Autumn 1831], MCL-VHS; REL to John Mackay, Arlington, January 23, 1833, LFP-WL; and MCL to Sarah Beaumont, May 31, [1839], LFP-BLC.

83. REL to Hill Carter, Fort Hamilton, January 22, 1842, REL Letterbook #1, LFP-VHS.

84. See MCL to MFC, Fort Hamilton, August 17 [1844], MCL-VHS; and REL to MCL, Fort Monroe, November 27, 1833, quoted in Norma B. Cuthbert, "To Molly: Five Early Letters from Robert E. Lee to His Wife, 1832–1835," *Huntington Library Quarterly* 15, no. 3 (May 1952): 267.

85. Lee Jr., *Recollections*, p. 12.

86. REL to MARC, Old Point, June 21, 1831, in deButts, "Yours Forever"; REL to MCL, April 24 and May 14, 1832, DE-LC; and REL and MCL to Eliza Mackay Stiles, January 4, 1832, typescript, Lee Papers, GHS.

87. REL to MCL, Old Point, May 14, 1832, LFP-VHS.

88. Ibid.

89. MFC to MCL, "Wednesday night," n.d. [c. Autumn 1831], and Eleanor Parke Custis Lewis to MCL, Audley, October 3, 1832, both MCL-VHS.

90. Margaret J. Preston to Paul Hamilton Hayne, Lexington, Va., November 2, [1870], Paul Hamilton Hayne Papers, DU.

91. Mary Custis Lee again disproves expectations in Clinton, *Plantation Mistress,* p. 69; Stephen V. Ash, *When the Yankees Came: Conflict and Chaos in the Occupied South* (Chapel Hill: University of North Carolina Press, 1995), pp. 6–7; Jacquelyn Dowd Hall, "Partial Truths: Writing Southern Women's History," in Virginia Bernhard et al., eds., *Southern Women: Histories and Identities* (Columbia: University of Missouri Press, 1992), p. 3; and Jabour, "Albums of Affection," p. 148. The recommendations of MCL's grandmother are in "The Advice of My Dearest Aunt Fitzhugh to Her Daughters," n.d. [prior to 1793], GBL-VHS.

92. Lee quoted in W. G. Bean, ed., "Memoranda of Conversations between General Robert E. Lee and William Preston Johnston, May 7, 1868 and March 18, 1870," *VMHB* 73, no. 4 (October 1965): 477.

93. REL to MCL, St. Louis, November 3, 1839, AHA.

94. REL quoted in Hancock, *Reminiscences of Winfield Scott Hancock,* pp. 46–47.

95. For MCL's dislike of moving and difficulty in making friends, see MCL to Mrs. A. Talcott, St. Louis, January 1, 1839, Talcott Papers, VHS; and MCL to Sarah Beaumont, Fort Hamilton, July 6, 1841; and MCL to Sarah Beaumont, Arlington, October 18 [1847?], both LFP-BLC.

96. There is much back-and-forth in the Lees' letters about whether or not to stay at Arlington, as well as evidence of the great draw it had for them both. A sampling: REL to MCL, Old Point, April 24, 1832; REL to MCL, St. Louis, November 7, 1839; REL Letterbook #1, which shows that he traveled constantly to Arlington even while posted to Fort Hamilton, N.Y., 1841–44; E. C. Turner to MCL, n.d. [1853]; MCL to REL, Arlington, May 22 [1857]; REL to ACL, San Antonio, Texas, August 27, 1860; and MCL to "My dear child" [December] 5, [1860], all DE-LC.

97. REL to WHFL, San Antonio, Texas, September 7, 1860, GBL-VHS; quotation MCL to MFC, n.d. [c. 1849–52], MCL-VHS.

98. For her belief in Robert's "excellent judgment," see "Will of MC Lee, copy in her hand," November 3, 1857, GBL-VHS.

99. REL to MCL, Camp Petersburg, June 30, 1864; REL to MCL, South Bend, Sep-

tember 2, 1835, HL; REL to MCL, September 10, 1837; REL to MCL, Key West, February 22, 1849; and REL to MCL, March 3, 1860, all DE-LC.

100. MCL Diary, March 3, 1836.

101. MCL to Edward Turner, December 6, 1870, LFP-VHS.

CHAPTER SIX: **Seven Arias**

1. REL to MFC, Fort Hamilton, N.Y., October 31, 1843, GBL-VHS. The letter is to his parents-in-law, whom he habitually called "Mother" and "the Major." Hill Carter was his first cousin; Uncle Williams was Williams Carter, his mother's brother.

2. REL to WHFL, Ringgold Barracks, Texas, November 1, 1856, REL Letterbook #1, LFP-VHS. The original document did not have paragraph divisions; these have been inserted for reader's convenience.

3. Ella Carter in William Franklin Chaney, *Duty Most Sublime: The Life of Robert E. Lee as Told Through the Carter Letters* (Baltimore: Gateway Press, 1996), pp. 128–130; Cousin George Upshur in George Lyttleton Upshur, *As I Recall Them: Memories of Crowded Years* (New York: Wilson-Erickson, 1936), p. 14; REL to MCL, St. Louis, September 4, 1840, EA-LC; "The Southern Confederacy," *Times* (of London), December 30, 1862; and Robbins, "Mrs. Lee during the War," p. 332.

4. REL to CCL, September 18, 1832, LFP-VHS.

5. REL to MCL, St. Louis, September 10, 1837, DE-LC; and REL to MCL, April 18, 1841, REL-UVa.

6. REL to MFC, St. Louis, July 26, 1839, DE-LC.

7. See, for example, MCL to MFC, May 23 [1833]; MCL and REL to MFC, Fort Hamilton, May 1, 1844, both GBL-VHS; MCL to MFC, April 11 [1834], DE-LC; and REL to A[ndrew] Talcott, Arlington, May 5, 1836, LFP-VHS. For Lee's feelings about Mildred, see REL to "Precious Life," Fort Brown, Texas, January 2, 1857, DE-LC: "for you are truly precious to me, more than life."

8. REL to MFC, Fort Monroe, May 20, 1833, DE-LC.

9. Lee Jr., *Recollections*, p. 9.

10. REL to MCL, Fort Hamilton, N.Y., March 24, 1846; quotation REL to MCL, "On Board Ship Massachusetts, Off Lobos Isd.," February 22, 1847, all DE-LC.

11. REL and MCL to MFC, Fort Hamilton, May 1, 1844, GBL-VHS.

12. Lee Jr., *Recollections*, p. 9; and REL to MCL, Fort Hamilton, N.Y., February 1846, DE-LC.

13. For examples of calling Annie and Agnes "the hussies," see REL to MCL, Fort Hamilton, N.Y., February 5, 1846, and REL to MCL, Soller's Point, June 23, 1849, both DE-LC; on Mildred's chickens, see REL to "My dear dear Son" [GWCL], Arlington, May 17, 1858, REL-DU.

14. Lee Jr., *Recollections*, p. 10; and REL to MFC, Fort Hamilton, N.Y., April 13 [1844], GBL-VHS.

15. Lee Jr., *Recollections*, pp. 9–10; Harriotte Hopkins Lee Taliaferro, "Reminiscences of Robert E. Lee," typescript, BLA; and MiCL, "My Recollections of My Father's Death," August 21, 1888, typescript, LFP-WL.

16. "Story Told by General Lee to His Son Robert," n.d., typescript, EA-LC.

17. For these and other pastimes of the children, see MCL to Sarah Beaumont, May 31, [1839]; and June 12 [c. 1840], LFP-BLC; and MiCL, "Recollections" in ALJ, Lexington, July 20, 1890, DE-LC. A cousin who spent a good deal of time with the

Lees also remembered their childhood pastimes, the girls spending as much time outdoors as the boys. "Our pleasures were of a simple sort: long walks on the hills, flower-picking, skating in winter, and sledding over 'jumps' on the snow-clad heights above our home.... I was out-of-doors, scouring the woods, climbing trees, riding horses to water, wading streams, and picking wild flowers." Mrs. Burton Harrison, *Recollections Grave and Gay* (New York: Charles Scribner's Sons, 1912), pp. 12, 23.

18. MCL to Sarah Beaumont, Arlington, January 28, [1844]; January 29, [1845]; and June 12 [?], all BLC; MCL to MFC, December 25, [1845], DE-LC; and REL to Jack Mackay, Arlington, March 18, 1841, Gilder-Lehrman Collection, NYHS.

19. REL to MCL, White Sulphur Springs, W.Va., August 4, 1840, DE-LC; and Edward Carter Turner Diary entry for July 27, 1839, quoted in MacDonald, *Mrs. Robert E. Lee,* p. 80.

20. This complete reordering of attitudes toward children, and indeed toward all of domestic life, was one of the great themes of nineteenth-century social history. For in-depth discussions of this, see John Demos, "The Changing Face of Fatherhood," *Past, Present and Personal: The Family and the Life Course in American History* (New York: Oxford University Press, 1986); Bernard Wishy, *The Child and the Republic* (Philadelphia: University of Pennsylvania Press, 1968); James Reed, *From Private Vice to Public Virtue: The Birth Control Movement and American Society since 1830* (New York: Basic Books, 1978), p. 21; Sally G. McMillen, *Motherhood in the Old South: Pregnancy, Childbirth, and Infant Rearing* (Baton Rouge: Louisiana State University Press, 1990), pp. 3–6, 181–83; Philip I. Greven, *The Protestant Temperament: Patterns of Child-Rearing, Religious Experience, and the Self in Early America* (New York: Alfred A. Knopf, 1977), pp. 266–274; and Jan Lewis, *The Pursuit of Happiness: Family and Values in Jefferson's Virginia* (New York: Cambridge University Press, 1983). The descriptions of hoops and paper "babies" are found in REL to GWCL, Fort Hamilton, N.Y., June 1, 1844; and MFC to "My dear Grandson," December 5, 1851, both DE-LC.

21. REL to MCL, St. Louis, October 16, 1837, DE-LC.

22. Thomas, *Robert E. Lee,* has a discussion of Lee's criticism of his wife's mothering, pp. 103–4.

23. Demos, *Past, Present and Personal,* pp. 57–60; McMillen, *Motherhood in the Old South,* pp. 181–83; Wishy, *Child and the Republic,* pp. 4–5, 21; and Frank, *Life with Father,* pp. 23–33. Lydia Sigourney, who was a friend of the Lees, wrote a book called *Letters to Mothers,* which counseled women, not men, to take charge of young children's discipline. For Lee's thoughts on these "text-books," see REL to MCL, St. Louis, October 16, 1837, in Jones, *Reminiscences,* pp. 368–69.

24. Mary Custis DeButts quoted in Zimmer, ed., *Housekeeping Book,* p. 28.

25. MCL to Sarah Beaumont, Arlington, October 28, 1839, LFP-BLC.

26. MCL [c.1848] quoted in Mary P. Coulling, *The Lee Girls* (Winston-Salem, N.C.: John F. Blair, 1987), p. 27.

27. MCL to Sarah Beaumont, Arlington, June 12, [c. 1840], LFP-BLC.

28. MCL Diary, October 8, 1833.

29. This too was a change from earlier centuries, when fathers were thought to be the best providers of ethical guidance. Lee again tried to keep his influence alive on moral issues, but the children's recollection was that most of this guidance came from their mother and grandmother. See "Story Told by General Lee to His Son Robert"; quotation MCL to REL, March 17, 1857, DE-LC; see also entries in MCL Diary for April 5, 1856, and March 1, 1857.

30. Jan Lewis and Kenneth A. Lockridge, "'Sally Has Been Sick': Pregnancy and Family Limitation among Virginia Gentry Women, 1780–1830," *Journal of Social History* 22, no. 1 (Fall 1988): 9–12; and Friedman, *Enclosed Garden,* pp. 5–6. Robert Dale Owens's classic *Moral Physiology; or, A Brief and Plain Treatise on the Population Question* was published in 1831, and after this time birth control became something of a private crusade in bourgeois southern society. Reed, *Private Vice to Public Virtue,* pp. 6–7; and Clinton, *Plantation Mistress,* p. 205.

31. REL to MFC, Fort Hamilton, N.Y., February 14, 1846, DE-LC.

32. McMillen, *Motherhood in the Old South,* p. 107.

33. Eleanor Custis Calvert Stuart, mother of George Washington Parke Custis, bore twenty children, eleven of whom lived; Charles Carter fathered twenty-two children in addition to Ann, who married Light-Horse Harry Lee; Mary Carter of Shirley Plantation gave birth to seventeen offspring between 1818 and 1844; and Rosalie Calvert finally took measures at birth control after nine pregnancies in her first twelve years of marriage. See Lynch, *Custis Chronicles,* 2:161; Calvert, *Mistress of Riversdale,* pp. 169, 216, 233n; and Shirley Plantation Book for 1828, frontispiece; and Carter Family Bible, both SPP-RL.

34. Anna M. Fitzhugh to CCL, Alexandria, July 28, [1844], copy in EA-LC.

35. REL to MCL, Fort Hamilton, N.Y., March 17, 1846; quotation REL to MFC, Fort Hamilton, N.Y., February 14, 1846, both DE-LC.

36. Intervals for the births, starting with the Lees' wedding night, were 14½ months, 34 months, 22½ months, 24½ months, 20½ months, 32 months, 27½ months. Entries in the Custis Family Bible, Custis Family Papers, VHS.

37. Condoms, contraceptive sponges, and chemical douching were also known and available in New York, Baltimore, and Alexandria, where Mary Lee spent many of her later childbearing years. Like coitus interruptus, another oft-mentioned method, these were imperfect, however, and sometimes associated with brothels or other illicit sexual activities. Lewis and Lockridge, "'Sally Has Been Sick,'" pp. 9–12; Reed, *Private Vice to Public Virtue,* pp. 6–13; Calvert, *Mistress of Riversdale,* p. 216; and Kimmel, *Manhood in America,* pp. 45–47.

38. Of course, unless a couple were physically separated, abstinence had a way of being abandoned, as Mary's cousin Rosalie found. "It is one of those decisions a moment of folly can do in," she confided when she asked her sister how she managed to avoid pregnancy. "I shall never again take a trip—each one unfailingly results in a baby." Isabelle van Havre to Rosalie Stier Calvert, [Spring 1812], in Calvert, *Mistress of Riversdale,* p. 233n; also McMillen, *Motherhood in the Old South,* pp. 107–8; Lewis and Lockridge, "'Sally Has Been Sick,'" pp. 9–12; REL to CCL, 1836, quoted in Nagel, *Lees of Virginia,* p. 241; Thomas, "The Lee Marriage"; REL to MFC, Fort Hamilton, N.Y., February 14 and March 17, 1846, DE-LC; and Lystra, *Searching the Heart,* chapters 3 and 4.

39. MCL and REL to MFC, August 15 and September 17, 1832, CL-LC.

40. McMillen, *Motherhood in the Old South,* p. 81 and appendix I, table 3.

41. MCL to REL, Arlington, July 14 [1857], DE-LC.

42. MFC to Mary Meade, Ravensworth, August 9, [c. 1840], Jones Family Papers, VHS; see also McMillen, *Motherhood in the Old South,* pp. 5, 60; Larkin, *The Reshaping of Everyday Life,* pp. 94–97. It is unclear whether Mrs. Lee had a doctor after her first confinement, or if she ever used a midwife. It is also unclear whether any of the slave women at Arlington assisted at the births. Lee implies that on at least one occasion she was attended by a black nurse, possibly Eleanor Harris ("Old Nurse"), of

whom Mary Lee was particularly fond, but we have insufficient evidence to judge what role she or any other servant might have played. REL to MFC, Fort Hamilton, N.Y., October 31, 1843, GBL-VHS.

43. Men attended the birth of a child in increasing numbers during the years that Mary and Robert Lee were producing children. Many wanted to be there, and women frequently voiced a desire for their support. Even those who did not attend the birth generally tried to be at home. Doctors, who liked to control the birth chamber, preferred to labor alone, without the presence of husband, mother or midwife. See Clinton, *Plantation Mistress,* p. 153; and Steven M. Stowe, *Doctoring the South* (Chapel Hill: University of North Carolina Press, 2004), pp. 170–71. For an example of Mary's desire for Robert's presence, see REL to MCL, Fort Hamilton, N.Y., March 17, 1846, DE-LC, in which he mentions impatiently that he understands that she is anxious for him, since "you so frequently have alluded to the subject."

44. McMillen, *Motherhood in the Old South,* pp. 85, 99, 107. A sample of allusions to Mary's ill health: REL to MCW, Fort Hamilton, September 2, and September 17, 1844, in Lee, *"To Markie,"* pp. 3, 5–6; and MCL to Sarah Beaumont, Arlington, June 1, 1846, LFP-BLC.

45. REL to MFC, Fort Hamilton, N.Y., October 31, 1843, GBL-VHS.

46. CCL to Henry Lee, Spring Camp, August 9, 1836, CCL-LoV.

47. Nelligan, "Old Arlington," pp. 239–40; MCL Diary, January 8 and February 14, 1836.

48. REL to MCL, Detroit, August 21, 1835, HL.

49. Marietta Turner Powell quoted in Long, *Memoirs,* p. 31.

50. For discussion of the evolving role of fathers, see Robert L. Griswold, *Fatherhood in America: A History* (New York: Basic Books, 1993); Frank, *Life with Father;* Wishy, *Child and the Republic;* and Lewis, *Pursuit of Happiness.* The patriarchal model given by Bertram Wyatt-Brown in *Southern Honor,* pp. 121–22, does not seem to pertain to Lee.

51. REL to GWCL, Fort Hamilton, N.Y., November 30, 1845; REL to MCL, West Point, May 5, 1853; and REL to MCL, Jefferson Barracks, Mo., September 3, 1855, all DE-LC; and REL to MCL, City of Mexico, December 23, 1847, GBL-VHS.

52. As nineteenth-century society developed, it was no longer enough to train up a child to be obedient and beholden, or to view them as a hedge against incapacitation and old age. Now the goal was to produce loving companions, who through industry, strong character, and good citizenship would reflect the virtues of the parents and guarantee the fortunes of the family—and of the republic. See Wishy, *Child and the Republic,* pp. 31–33; and Lewis, *Pursuit of Happiness,* pp. 118–22, 152–54, 179–84.

53. There are dozens of letters in which Lee describes his aspirations for his children. Some examples are REL to MCL(d), City of Mexico, December 8, 1847, MCL-VHS; REL to GWCL, Baltimore, May 4, 1851, in Jones, *Life and Letters,* pp. 71–72; REL to MCL, Jefferson Barracks, Mo., September 3, 1855; REL to MCL, Fort Riley, Kansas Territory, November 5, 1855; REL to MCL, San Antonio, Texas, June 3, 1860; and REL to MCL, San Antonio, Texas, June 18, 1860, all DE-LC. For the courses taken by Annie and Agnes, see Coulling, *Lee Girls,* p. 54.

54. REL to WHFL, Ringgold Barracks, Texas, November 1, 1856, REL Letterbook #1, LFP-VHS. Lee's concern with education, and the continuation of his own professional status through his sons, was once again reflective of the times. See Frank, *Life with Father,* pp. 154–56.

55. REL to MCL, On Board S.B. from Charleston to Savannah, September 4, 1846, DE-LC.

56. REL to MCL, St. Louis, October 16, 1837, DE-LC; and REL, "On Education," in REL Diary, LFP-VHS.

57. See Brenda E. Stevenson, *Life in Black and White: Family and Community in the Slave South* (New York: Oxford University Press, 1996), pp. 108–18; Wishy, *Child and the Republic*, p. 44, 54–61; Demos, *Past, Present and Personal*, p. 46; and Griswold, *Fatherhood in America*, p. 18.

58. Although he feared there would be laxity when he was away from home, Lee's authority may actually have increased with absence—his formal power and prestige being more formidable than the familiar, easygoing supervision of their mother. Quotation Lee Jr., *Recollections*, p. 9.

59. REL to GWCL, Baltimore, February 1, 1852; and REL to MFC, Baltimore, March 17, 1852, DE-LC; and REL Letterbook #1, both LFP-VHS.

60. REL to MCL, Fort Riley, Kansas Territory, November 5, 1855, DE-LC,

61. REL to GWCL, Fort Hamilton, N.Y., December 18, 1845, photostat, LFP-WL. In another example Lee told his sons from Mexico that he hoped to "have the happiness of finding you much improved in all your studies on my return. . . . But oh, how much I will suffer on my return if the reverse has occurred!" REL to GWCL and WHFL, "Ship Massachusetts off Lobos," February 27, 1847, in Jones, *Life and Letters*, p. 40.

62. REL to ACL, February 25, 1853, LFP-VHS.

63. Clinton, *Plantation Mistress*, p. 134; Frank, *Life with Father*, p. 114–116; Griswold, *Fatherhood in America*, pp. 14–15. Note, for example, how similarly this letter from a North Carolina father reads: "I have so often (in conversation) recommended to you and my other children attention, industry and application to whatever you see hear & are about doing, that I do not mention them now as duties merely; but I point them out to you again and again, as conducive, nay as absolutely necessary to your pleasures, your happiness and your respectability." Griswold, *Fatherhood in America*, p. 18.

64. William L. Marshall to WHFL, Baltimore, April 14, 1853, William Henry Fitzhugh Lee Papers, VHS. This wonderful letter ends with the words: "Take care old fellow and keep those malignant influences of time down or you will spoil your fortune. There now I have tired you with a full sheet of nonsense."

65. REL to MFC, Baltimore, March 17, 1852, REL Letterbook #1, LFP-VHS.

66. REL to MFC, "On Board Ship Massachusetts off Lobos Isd.," February 22, 1847, DE-LC.

67. Among those who have made the connection between the lack of guidance Lee received from his father and his intense preoccupation with his own children are Connelly, *Marble Man*, pp. 177–80; Thomas, *Robert E. Lee*, pp. 37, 150; and Fellman, *Making of Robert E. Lee*, p. 8.

68. REL to MCL, Jefferson Barracks, Mo., August 20, 1855, Edmund Jennings Lee Papers, VHS.

69. REL to MFC, "On Board Ship Massachusetts off Lobos Isd.," February 22, 1847, DE-LC.

70. REL to WHFL, Arlington, January 1, 1859, in Jones, *Life and Letters*, pp. 95–96; and REL to "my precious life," Arlington, April 1, 1861, DE-LC.

71. ALJ, March 16 and March 27, 1856; and ACL to REL, Staunton, Va., May 21, 1856, both DE-LC; and ACL to Helen Bratt, Staunton, March 7, 1857, LFP-WL.

72. REL to "Precious Life" [MiCL], Indianola, Texas, March 22, [1857], DE-LC.

73. Coulling, *Lee Girls,* p. 169.

74. Lee Jr., *Recollections,* pp. 9–10; and Mildred Lee, "Recollections," July 20, 1890, in ALJ, DE-LC.

75. MCW Diary, December 31, 1854; Zimmer, ed., *Housekeeping Book,* p. 60.

76. The "tussle" quotation is in REL to Mrs. W. H. Stiles, Camp Cooper, Texas, August 14, 1856, Special Collections, UTA; also ACL to Helen Bratt, Arlington, May 3, 1855, and Staunton, Va., November [1856], in LFP-WL; MCL to Louisa Snowden, Lexington, Va., November 10, [c. 1868], BLA; Zimmer, ed., *Housekeeping Book,* pp. 50–51; and Coulling, *Lee Girls,* pp. 164–68. This issue will be discussed in more depth in chapter 12, "Black-Eyed Fancies."

77. MCL Diary, December 6, 1870.

78. REL to MCL, San Antonio, Texas, July 27, 1857, DE-LC.

CHAPTER SEVEN: **Pioneers**

1. REL to Jack Mackay, St. Louis, June 27, 1838, Gilder-Lehrman Collection, NYHS. The general mentioned by Lee was Charles Gratiot, the head of the Army Corps of Engineers. Horace Bliss, who came to work with Lee on the Mississippi, graduated from West Point in 1822. Cullum, *Biographical Register,* 1:279.

2. REL to Jack Mackay, St. Louis, October 22, 1837, typescript, Mackay-McQueen Papers, GHS.

3. REL to MCL, St. Louis, August 21, 1837, REL-UVa.

4. Eduard Zimmermann, "Travel Into Missouri in October 1838," *Missouri Historical Review* 9, no. 1 (October 1914): 33–34; Reginald Horsman, *Frontier Doctor: William Beaumont, America's First Great Medical Scientist* (Columbia: University of Missouri Press, 1996), pp. 213–14; Helen DaVault Williams, "Social Life in St. Louis from 1840 to 1860," *Missouri Historical Review* 31, no. 1 (October 1936): 10–11; Stella M. Drumm, "Robert E. Lee and the Improvement of the Mississippi River," *Missouri Historical Society Collections* 6, no. 2 (February 1929): 158; Elihu H. Shepard, *The Early History of St. Louis and Missouri* (St. Louis: Southwestern, 1870), p. 151; REL quoted in REL to John Lloyd, St. Louis, August 15, 1837, Lloyd Papers, LC; quotation REL to CCL, August 15, 1837, REL-UVa.

5. REL to CCL, St. Louis, August 15, 1837, REL-UVa. Lee's West Point acquaintance, Ethan Allen Hitchcock, who was also in town on army business, agreed with Lee's assessment of St. Louis, finding it a "forbidding place of shabby buildings, poorly kempt alleys and willful ignorance." Ethen Allen Hitchcock to "Miss Lynde," Saint Louis, May 24, 1839, EAH-LC.

6. James Neal Primm, *Lion of the Valley: St. Louis, Missouri* (Boulder, CO: Pruett Publishing Company, 1990), pp. 155–56; Drumm, "Lee and the Improvement of the Mississippi," pp. 159–61; John Fletcher Darby, *Personal Recollections* (repr., New York: Arno Press, 1975), pp. 220–21, 226–27. Some sources have stated that the initial appropriation was $15,000; in REL to Jack Mackay, St. Louis, October 22, 1837, typescript, Mackay-McQueen Papers, GHS, Lee states that $135,000 had been earmarked for the project; in Lee's June 27, 1838, letter to Jack Mackay he gives the figure as $50,000. What is known for certain is that none of the monies proved sufficient for the project.

7. John C. Calhoun's long tenure and enlightened leadership as secretary of war have been largely eclipsed by his reputation for states' rights oratory, but were instrumental in the early development of the U.S. Army. See "John C. Calhoun: The Expansible Army Plan," in Weigley, *Towards an American Army,* pp. 30–37; and Prucha, *Broadax and Bayonet,* pp. 194–97.

8. For the role of the army in western development, see Prucha, *Broadax and Bayonet;* Forest G. Hill, *Roads, Rails & Waterways: The Army Engineers and Early Transportation* (Norman: University of Oklahoma Press, 1957), pp. 35–36, 77; Coffman, *Old Army,* pp. 44, 56; quotation REL to Jack Mackay, St. Louis, August 8, 1838, typescript, Mackay-McQueen Papers, GHS. Lee again expressed wistfulness about the Topographical Corps in REL to Jack Mackay, Washington Engineers Office, July 23, 1840, typescript, Mackay-McQueen Papers, GHS. Nonetheless, the "Topogs" were considered less prestigious than the Engineer Corps. See Todd Shallat, *Structures in the Stream* (Austin: University of Texas Press, 1994), pp. 44–45.

9. Zachary Taylor quoted in Coffman, *Old Army,* p. 44; Russell F. Weigley, *History of the United States Army* (Bloomington: Indiana University Press, 1984), pp. 164–66.

10. New York's Rensselaer Polytechnic Institute granted its first engineering degrees in 1835, but this was based on a one-year course, far below the rigorous four-year program that had been developed at West Point. Pappas, *To the Point,* pp. 96–131 and 274–75; Skelton, *American Profession of Arms,* pp. 168–171; Hill, *Roads, Rails & Waterways,* pp. 205–14.

11. The *Oxford English Dictionary* gives the date 1615 for the first usage of the word *technology* in the sense of a treatise on an art, and 1859 for the first usage in England of its contemporary meaning—the study of the applied or useful arts. The word was evidently used in this latter fashion in America during lectures at Harvard in 1829 by Jacob Bigelow, later published as his *Elements of Technology.* Clark A. Elliott, *History of Science in the United States: A Chronology and Research Guide* (New York: Garland, 1996), p. 59.

12. "Letter from the Secretary of War: A Copy of the Survey and Report for the Improvement of the Hudson River," March 30, 1832, 22nd Cong., 2nd sess., House of Representatives doc. 189.

13. REL to Capt. A. Talcott, St. Louis, October 3, 1838, Talcott Papers, VHS.

14. "Report from the Secretary of War . . . in Relation to the Rock River and Des Moines Rapids of the Mississippi River," January 29, 1838, 25th Cong., 2nd sess., Senate doc. 139; and REL to Jack Mackay, St. Louis, June 27, 1838, Gilder-Lehrman Collection, NYHS.

15. REL to CCL, St. Louis, August 15, 1837, REL-UVa.

16. M. C. Meigs to Charles D. Meigs, St. Louis, August 5, 1837, MCM-LC; REL to MCL, Des Moin[e]s Rapids, September 10, 1837, DE-LC; Russell F. Weigley, *Quartermaster General of the Union Army: A Biography of M. C. Meigs* (New York: Columbia University Press, 1959), pp. 32–34; and David W. Miller, *Second Only to Grant* (Shippensburg, Pa.: White Mane, 2000), p. 13. For the devastating part Meigs played in the Lees' later life, see chapter 18, "Field of Honor."

17. REL to Henry Kayser, Arlington, February 1, 1838, quoted in "Letters of Robert E. Lee to Henry Kayser, 1838–1846," *Glimpses of the Past* (Missouri Historical Society) 3, no. 2 (1936): 6; Thomas, *Robert E. Lee,* pp. 91–92; "Report from the Secretary of War," January 29, 1838; and REL to Jack Mackay, St. Louis, June 27, 1838, Lee Papers, GHS. The maps drawn by Lee and Meigs are in RG77, NARA. For notes on Henry

Shreve and the originality of Lee's plan, see Fredrick J. Dobney, *River Engineers on the Middle Mississippi: A History of the St. Louis District U.S. Army Corps of Engineers* (Washington, D.C.: GPO, 1978). The textbook from which much of this was taken was Joseph Mathieu Sganzin's *Program d'un Course de Construction*, which contained a chapter on navigation that proposed the very options considered by Lee. Shallat, *Structures in the Stream*, pp. 93–95, 144–45.

18. REL to Jack Mackay, St. Louis, June 27, 1838, Gilder-Lehrman Collection, NYHS; Henry Kayser, Receipt for Property, St. Louis, October 8, 1839, in "Letters of Robert E. Lee to Henry Kayser," pp. 10–11; for Kayser's background, see pp. 1–2; the *Missouri Republican* quoted in Drumm, "Lee and the Improvement of the Mississippi," p. 162.

19. Darby, *Personal Recollections*, p. 228.

20. Ibid., p. 230; Primm, *Lion of the Valley*, p. 156; Lee, *General Lee*, pp. 28–29; *Glimpses of the Past*, p. 4; Freeman, *R. E. Lee*, 1:176; and REL to Jack Mackay, Washington, Engineer's Office, July 23, 1840, typescript, Mackay-McQueen Papers, GHS. The project was also controversial in St. Louis, where some citizens thought it should be paid for by local, not federal, funding. See "Internal Improvement," *Missouri Daily Argus*, August 2, 1839.

21. See for example REL to Henry Kayser, Des Moin[e]s Rapids, July 26, 1838; REL to Henry Kayser, Des Moin[e]s Rapids, August 4, 1839; and REL to Henry Kayser, St. Louis, April 3, 1839, all REL-MoHS.

22. REL to Henry Kayser, Arlington, February 1, 1838; March 9, 1838; and Baltimore, April 2, 1838, all in "Letters of Robert E. Lee to Henry Kayser," pp. 4–9.

23. "Report from the Secretary of War," January 29, 1838.

24. Charles F. O'Connell Jr., "The Corps of Engineers and the Rise of Modern Management, 1827–1856," in Merritt Roe Smith, ed., *Military Enterprise and Technological Change: Perspectives on the American Experience* (Cambridge, Mass.: MIT Press, 1985), pp. 90–103; and Peskin, *Winfield Scott*, pp. 66–68.

25. By 1866, 12.4 percent of those trained as army engineers had become corporate officials. O'Connell, "Corps of Engineers," pp. 103–14.

26. Darby, *Personal Recollections*, p. 228.

27. Freeman, *R. E. Lee*, 1:151; and Sanborn, *Portrait*, p. 119.

28. REL to Capt. A. Talcott, St. Louis, January 1, 1839, Talcott Papers, VHS.

29. Dobney, *River Engineers on the Middle Mississippi*, p. 26; and letters of REL to Chief Engineer Gratiot, REL Letterbook #1, LFP-VHS.

30. REL to Henry Kayser, St. Louis, April 3, 1839, MoHS.

31. REL to Mrs. A. Talcott, St. Louis, May 29, 1838, Talcott Papers, VHS.

32. Ruth Musser and John C. Krantz Jr., "The Friendship of General Robert E. Lee and Dr. Wm. Beaumont," *Bulletin of the Institute of the History of Medicine* 6, no. 5 (May 1938): 467–76; REL to Mrs. A. Talcott, St. Louis, May 29, 1838, Talcott Papers, VHS.

33. Hitchcock, *Fifty Years in Camp and Field*, p. 47; Sanborn, *Portrait*, p.125. For Lee's fine storytelling, see Hugh Mercer to "My dear wife," Savannah, March 20, 1849 Mercer Family Papers, GHS; and Lee Jr., *Recollections*, pp. 9–10; for Beaumont's personality, see REL to Mrs. A. Talcott, St. Louis, May 29, 1838, Talcott Papers, VHS; and Jesse S. Myer, *Life and Letters of Dr. William Beaumont* (St. Louis: C. V. Mosby, 1939), pp. 97, 239.

34. Hitchcock had an absorbing love of philosophy. He delighted in probing the meaning of life after death and the religious principles of Swedenborgianism. Dr. Beaumont and his wife also liked to discuss spiritual matters, in the tradition of the individualistic paths of Universalism and the Quaker faith. We do not know whether or not Lee participated in these debates; at this age he had not as yet embraced religiosity, and when he did it was of a doctrinaire nature, not given to spiritual questing. Musser and Krantz, "Friendship of Lee and Beaumont," pp. 467–476; Horsman, *Frontier Doctor,* pp. 228–29, 254–55; Herman Hattaway and Eric B. Fair, "Ethan Allen Hitchcock," in *ANB,* 10:867–68; quotation in REL to Mrs. A. Talcott, St. Louis, May 29, 1838, Talcott Papers, VHS.

35. REL to MCL, St. Louis, August 21, 1837, REL-UVa; REL to John Lloyd, St. Louis, March 22, 1839, Lloyd Papers, LC; Thomas Maitland Marshall, ed., "The Journal of Henry B. Miller," *Missouri Historical Society Collections* 6, no. 3 (1931): 224; Skelton, *American Profession of Arms,* p. 201; and "The Lewis and Clark Journey of Discovery," Jefferson National Expansion Memorial, National Park Service, at www.nps.gov/jeff/historyculture.

36. On the scientific method of the day, which eschewed theoretical or abstract work in favor of taxonomic fields, see George H. Daniels, *American Science in the Age of Jackson* (Tuscaloosa:University of Alabama Press, 1994), pp. 32–35, 65–66; and Nathan Reingold, "American Indifference to Basic Research: A Reappraisal," in George H. Daniels, ed., *Nineteenth Century American Science* (Evanston, Ill.: Northwestern University Press, 1972), pp 47–53; also Thomas, *Robert E. Lee,* p. 89.

37. REL to Jack Mackay, Des Moin[e]s Rapids, October 19, 1838, typescript, Mackay-McQueen Papers, GHS.

38. REL to Jack Mackay, St. Louis, October 22, 1837, typescript Mackay-McQueen Paper, GHS; and REL to CCL, October 8, 1837, REL-UVa.

39. Horsman, *Frontier Doctor,* pp. 1–3, 179–82; and Harvey E. Brown, comp., *The Medical Department of the United States Army from 1775–1873* (Washington, D.C.: Surgeon General's Office, 1873), pp. 161–62. Few questioned the ethics of performing experiments in a walking human laboratory. But perhaps Alexis St. Martin, who had suffered much pain and some embarrassment during the years of research, gave the ultimate opinion: he refused further experimentation after 1832, and when he died had heavy rocks placed on his coffin to prevent anyone from using his body for an autopsy. Ronald L. Numbers, "William Beaumont and the Ethics of Human Experimentation," *Journal of the History of Biology* 12, no. 1 (Spring 1979): 113–135; and "Life of Dr. William Beaumont" at www.james.com/beaumont/dr_lfe.htm.

40. Beaumont was less successful in his attempt to analyze the composition of the gastric juice; he knew it contained hydrochloric acid, but could break down the elements no further. He was not alone in his frustration. He sent a vial of St. Martin's gastric juice to the most famous biochemist of the day, Swedish scientist Dr. Jacob Berzelius, who also had to admit defeat, though Berzelius blamed it on the small size of the sample. See Mary Gillett, *The Army Medical Department, 1818–1865* (Washington, D.C.: Center of Military History of the United States Army, 1987), p. 25.

41. Over the years there has been a scholarly debate over the extent to which Beaumont's research was praised, some historians believing that European scientists recognized its importance, while it was generally ignored in the United States. Apparently there was appreciation on both sides of the Atlantic, but it differed in na-

ture. The Europeans lauded the scientific breakthroughs, and Americans generally recognized the benefits for nutrition and good health. Ronald L. Numbers and William J. Orr Jr., "William Beaumont's Reception at Home and Abroad," *Isis* 72, no. 264 (December 1981): 590–95.

42. Even this support was withdrawn soon after the 1839 appointment of a new surgeon general, Thomas Lawson, who dismissed Beaumont's work as an example of the excess privilege accorded some officers. Prucha, *Broadax and Bayonet,* pp. 196–97; and Gillett, *Army Medical Department,* pp. 32–34.

43. A few years after Beaumont's results were published, one journal lamented that "not one man" was continuing significant medical research; Richard Harrison Shryock, *Medicine and Society in America, 1660–1860* (Ithaca, N.Y.: Cornell University Press, 1972), p. 117; and Joseph F. Kett, *The Formation of the American Medical Profession* (New Haven, Conn.: Yale University Press, 1968) pp. vii–viii, 167; and Stowe, *Doctoring the South,* p. 8.

44. Myer, *Dr. William Beaumont,* p. 97

45. Horsman, *Frontier Doctor,* pp. 109–111; Charles E. Rosenberg, *The Care of Strangers: The Rise of America's Hospital System* (New York: Basic Books, 1987), pp. 71–93; and William G. Rothstein, *American Physicians in the Nineteenth Century: From Sects to Science* (Baltimore: Johns Hopkins University Press, 1972), pp. 43–52.

46. "Prescription for Yellow Fever," undated newspaper clipping [1855–61], REL Memorandum Book, DE-LC; and front page and overleaf to Shirley Plantation Book, 1828, SPP-RL.

47. REL to Mrs. H. Hackley, St. Louis, August 7, 1838, Talcott Papers, VHS; REL to Henry Kayser, Arlington, March 29, 1841, in "Letters of Robert E. Lee to Henry Kayser," p. 23; see also REL to MFC, St. Louis, March 26, 1839, to ACL, San Antonio, Texas, August 8, 1857, and to EAL, February 20, 1863, and April 11, 1863, all DE-LC; Hugh Mercer to "My dearest wife," Savannah, March 20, 1849, Mercer Family Papers, GHS; and REL to "My Beautiful Tasy," Fort Hamilton, N.Y., March 11, 1843, photostat, EA-LC.

48. See, among several examples, REL to MCL, Baltimore, July 12, 1837, photostat, AHA; and REL to Hill Carter, Arlington, January 25, 1840, SPP-RL.

49. MCL(d) to "Dear Mrs. Corbin," March 6, 1918, REL-GHS.

50. REL to Hill Carter, Arlington, January 25, 1840, SPP-RL.

51. REL to Henry Kayser, Washington, May 4, 1840, and Engrs. Dept., Washington, June 16, 1840, both in "Letters of Robert E. Lee to Henry Kayser," pp. 17–19.

52. Mark Twain, *Life on the Mississippi* (New York: Harper and Brothers, 1906), p. 221.

53. Dobney, *River Engineers,* p. 28; REL to Henry Kayser, Washington, January 15, 1844, in "Letters of Robert E. Lee to Henry Kayser," p. 32; and John O. Anfinson, *The River We Have Wrought: A History of the Upper Mississippi* (Minneapolis: University of Minnesota Press, 2003), p. 25.

54. Primm, *Lion of the Valley,* pp. 155–56.

55. REL to John G. Floyd, West Point, November 3 [?], 1853, Letterbook # 2, LFP-VHS. For a discussion of how all engineering builds on the success and failure of previous designs, see Henry Petroski, *To Engineer Is Human* (New York: St. Martin's Press, 1985).

56. The Mississippi boat race of 1870 was one of the most celebrated events of its time. Local papers called it "The Grandest Race on Record," and advised that the Iron Horse had better be "looking out for his laurels." The *Robert E. Lee* beat the

Natchez and *Princess* by more than an hour, and when the boat arrived at St. Louis, police could not restrain the crowds, which poured onto its deck "like a living torrent." Lee, then in the last months of his life, must have known about this race, but does not appear to have made any comment. Darby, *Personal Recollections,* p. 232; and "The Boat Race," *Missouri Daily Republican,* July 6, 1870.

CHAPTER EIGHT: **The Family Circle**

1. MCW Diary, February 27, 1854, and March 28, 1859, AHA.
2. REL to A. E. L. Keese, "Arlington, near Alex^a Va.," April 24, 1858, HL.
3. "Inventory of the Estate of G. W. P. Custis," January 1, 1858, Will Book No. 7, Alexandria County Records, Alexandria, Va.; Daniel W. Crofts, "Late Antebellum Virginia Reconsidered," *VMHB* 107, no. 3 (Summer 1999):261. In Alexandria County the number of slave owners was one of the smallest in the entire South, with slaves making up just 11 percent of the population and only one in seven Alexandria households holding a black servant. Kundahl, *Alexandria Goes to War,* p. 7.
4. Census records show that there were 58 slaves at Arlington in 1820; 57 in 1830; 52 in 1840; and 63 in 1850. In 1860 only 38 are listed as residing on the property—all able-bodied hands had been hired away to pay the estate's debts. Sixty-three slaves were attached to Arlington at Custis's death. See "Inventory of the Estate of G. W. P. Custis"; and Decennial Census of the United States, District of Columbia, 1820, 1830, and 1840, in Alexandria County, Virginia, 1850 and 1860, NARA.
5. Zimmer, ed., *Housekeeping Book,* p. 17. According to the Arlington stories, Mammy had great reverence for "Ole Mistis," as she called Martha Washington, but made little fuss over the Father of the Country, saying he "was only a man" and "she didn't suppose he was so much better than anyone else." See ALJ, "Sunday Morn. 23rd" [March 1856], DE-LC.
6. GWPC to T. S. Skinner, Arlington, March 23, 1827, HL.
7. Doug Pielmeier, "The Evolution of a Virginia Plantation," draft research report, 1996, p. 75, AHA.
8. GWPC to F. Nelson, January 17 and January 25, 1855, typescript, both AHA.
9. Over the years Custis devised several schemes that would accomplish the liberation of his slaves, including some plans for them to "buy" themselves through their labor, as well as the scheme he proposed to Lafayette. He never acted on any of them. Nelligan, "Old Arlington," p. 170.
10. GWPC to "Mr Bomley," Arlington House, May 25, 1824, LFP-WL.
11. Reports of the "cruel, inhuman and barbarous treatment of the slaves of Major George W. P. Custis, placed under [an overseer's] direction" circulated in 1824, just as earlier reports of "night balls" and "negroes out of control" had surfaced in 1804. Inattention to the management of the slaves continued through the years; in 1857 instances of unsupervised slaves becoming unruly were again recorded. Affidavit of Jonathan P. Walden, White House, n.d., Custis Papers, VHS; Lynch, *Custis Chronicles,* pp. 2:245–46; and MCL to REL, March 17, 1857, DE-LC.
12. For buying and selling slaves at Arlington, see Daybook of Charles Lee, account of George W. P. Custis, December 31, 1811, and December 31, 1812, and GWPC, note to Baldwin [?], n.d., in GWPC accounts, both CL-LC; also REL to A. S. White, Washington City, February 21, 1845, REL Letterbook #1, DE-LC. For giving slaves as presents, see GWPC to "My dear Children," Arlington House, August 14, 1838, CL-TPA.
13. Virginia law stipulated that freed slaves had to move out of the state, or be sup-

ported by their former master. For more on the consequences of this statute for slave owners, see chapter 16, "Theory Meets Reality." MCW Diary, "Tues. 15" [*sic* 16], 1853.

14. "Inventory of the Estate of G. W. P. Custis"; and Eugene D. Genovese, *Roll Jordan Roll: The World the Slaves Made* (New York: Pantheon 1974), pp 444–49.

15. Daybook of Charles Lee, account of George W. P. Custis, December 31, 1811, and December 31, 1812; and GWPC, note to Baldwin [?], n.d., in GWPC accounts, both CL-LC; quotation MCL to MFC, "Friday 12th" [1850], MCL-VHS.

16. MCL to MFC, Fort Hamilton, November 8, [1841–45?], SH. For slaves visiting their partners, see e.g. MCL to "Gen'l Sanford," May 30, 1861, in which she writes, "My gardener Ephraim also has a wife in Washington and is accustomed to go over every Saturday and return on Monday. My old cook also has a wife in the neighborhood." Typescript, AHA.

17. For an example of the slaves' despondency at the hiring away of their community members, see L. R. Nelson to MCL, White House, May 6, 1853, DE-LC. A longer discussion of this issue is in chapter 16, "Theory Meets Reality."

18. Early records for some of the Custis estates on the Pamunky River show that more than 90 percent of the slaves worked in the fields. See J. Anderson to GWPC, White House, March 10, 1806, MCL-VHS. For the role of work in a slave's life, see Ira Berlin and Philip D. Morgan, "Labor and the Shaping of Slave Life in the Americas," in Berlin and Morgan, eds., *Cultivation and Culture* (Charlottesville: University Press of Virginia, 1993), pp. 1–6; and Genovese, *Roll Jordan Roll,* pp. 313–21.

19. Zimmer, ed., *Housekeeping Book,* p. 7; and EAL to WHFL, Arlington, October 2, 1858, DE-LC.

20. Mary Custis Lee recorded the diversity of chores done by the slaves in an 1860 letter to Annie, who was then keeping house. She instructed her daughter to have the servants attend to the garden, clear out brush, water the flowers, wash and card a bag of wool, complete some knitting, haul manure for the strawberry bed, and pick and can tomatoes. MCL to ACL, Satturday [July 1860], LFP-VHS; also "Tour of Arlington with Mrs. Annie Baker and Mrs. Ada Thompson," n.d. [1920s], RG92, NARA, copy at AHA; and MCL to MFC, Fort Hamilton, October 27, 1844, DE-LC.

21. MCW Diary, June 3, 1856, and August 27, 1857, AHA.

22. MCL to MFC, Old Point, Friday [May 1833], REL-DU; and MCL and REL to "Mrs. Styles," Arlington, January 23, 1863, SH.

23. MCW Diary, October 31, 1853, AHA; and ACL to Helen Bratt, Staunton, Va., January 25 [1856], LFP-WL.

24. ACL to Helen Bratt, July 13, [1855], LFP-WL.

25. MCL to ACL, Satturday [July 1860], LFP-VHS; MCW Diary, June 3, 1856, AHA; MCL to MFC, Fort Hamilton, October 27, 1844, DE-LC; "Interview with James Parks," *Sunday Star,* November 4, 1928.

26. ACL to Helen Bratt, January 25 [1856], LFP-WL; and REL to MCL, San Antonio, Texas, March 3, 1860, DE-LC.

27. MFC to WHFL, March 15, 1853, William Henry Fitzhugh Lee Papers, VHS.

28. For more on slaves' resistance, see Berlin and Morgan, "Labor and the Shaping of Slave Life," pp. 2, 5–7; Genovese, *Roll Jordan Roll,* pp. 295–309; Thomas L. Webber, *Deep Like the Rivers: Education in the Slave Quarter Community, 1831–1865* (New York: W. W. Norton, 1978), pp. 94–99; Anne S. Frobel, *The Civil War Diary of Anne S. Frobel of Wilton Hill in Virginia,* eds. Mary H. Lancaster and Dallas M. Lancaster (Birmingham, Ala.: Birmingham Printing, 1986), p. 24.

29. MCW Diary, November 6, 1853, AHA.

30. REL to Captain A. Talcott, Washington, May 5, 1836, Talcott Papers, VHS; and Blanche Berard to mother, April 18, 1856, in Torrence, "Arlington and Mount Vernon, 1856," pp. 149, 162.

31. Blanche Berard quoted in Torrence, "Arlington and Mount Vernon, 1856," pp. 163–64.

32. WHFL to MCL, Cambridge, March 30, 1856, DE-LC; and MCL to ACL, Satturday [July 1860], LFP-VHS.

33. REL to "My dear Son," New Orleans, February 14, 1860, in Jones, *Life and Letters,* p. 109; and REL to MCL, Laredo, March 24, 1860, DE-LC.

34. MCW Diary, August 11, 1856, AHA.

35. ALJ, August 6, 1853, DE-LC; and ACL to Helen Bratt, Arlington, May 3, 1855, LFP-WL.

36. *The Slavery Code of the District of Columbia,* Section 53. The code can be found in its entirety at "American Memory," http:/hdl.loc.gov/loc.law/llsc002. Slave owners were fined for the first two offenses, but at the third the slaves were given their liberty.

37. MCL to "My dear child" [MiCL], [December] 5, [1860], and MCL to MFC, Fort Hamilton, "27th" [c. 1844], DE-LC; watercolor portrait of Lawrence Parks, AHA; "Account of the Estate of G. W. P. Custis," Will Book No. 7, Alexandria County Records, Alexandria, Va., pp. 488–90; and MCL to [Benson Lossing], July 20, 1859, WL. Former Arlington slave Jim Parks also remembers how the slaves "dressed up" in "Colored Servant of Adopted Son of George Washington," *Christian Science Monitor,* September 24, 1924.

38. GWPC to "Mr Bomley," Arlington House, May 25, 1824, LFP-WL.

39. Though G. W. P. Custis might extol the virtues of these "comfortable homes," there is evidence that by the 1850s they were in sad disrepair. Space was also at a premium. The Gray family, among the most privileged at Arlington, shared just one room, with eight children sleeping in a loft so cramped that they could not stand upright. The 1860 census lists five "slave houses" at Arlington for the thirty-seven black people who had not been hired away; when the estate's full contingent of sixty-three were all present, conditions must have been very difficult. "Tour of Arlington with Mrs. Annie Baker and Mrs. Ada Thompson," [ex-slaves], c. 1920, AHA; W. H. Peckham to "Dear Friend," October 10, 1861, quoted in Benjamin Franklin Cooling, *Symbol, Sword, and Shield* (Shippensburg, Pa.: White Mane, 1991), p. 88; for "comfortable homes," see MCW Diary, [November 2], 1853; and REL to GWCL, San Antonio, Texas, December 14, 1860, DU.

40. GWPC to Dr. J. Weems, MS Accounting Sheet, January 11–August 16, 1807, CL-LC; "Account of the Estate of G. W. P. Custis," Will Books Nos. 7 and 8, 1859, ACH; MCL to MFC, Fort Hamilton, June 13 [1846]; and REL Daybook, September 1–3, 1859, both DE-LC. Similar medical expenditures continued throughout the years, with nearly $400 spent for medical attention to the slaves in one sample year during Lee's executorship of the estate. Though this was well beyond the average for the time, it did not guarantee that the slaves enjoyed good health. The state of medical knowledge was primitive, and the treatments sometimes did more harm than good. Indeed, the slaves often preferred their own remedies. The high rate of sickness among the blacks may indicate another way the slaves got around unreasonable demands. See Robert William Fogel and Stanley L. Engerman, *Time on the Cross* (New York: W. W. Norton, 1989), pp. 120–21; and Todd Savett, *Medicine and Slavery* (Urbana: University of Illinois Press, 1978), pp. 149–84.

41. For an example of Lee's commiseration with ill servants, see REL to WHFL, San Antonio, Texas, September 7, 1860, DE-LC; and REL to CCL, CockSpur Island, January 4, 1831, REL-UVa, which confirms what had long been thought to be the legend of Lee's care of the servant Nat—in it Lee writes, "He is very weak and his cough is still bad, though I will not despair in the commencement of an experiment which I hope will prove successful." For long memories of this deed, see Sally Lee to MCL, Gordonsville, Va., November 10, [1870], DE-LC; and Emily V. Mason, *Popular Life of General Robert E. Lee* (Baltimore: John Murphy, 1897), p. 23.

42. REL to CCL, Engineer Department, Washington, D.C., May 2, 1836, REL-UVa.

43. "Account of the G. W. P. Custis Estate," Will Book No. 7, pp. 487, 489, ACH.

44. Ibid., 487; Nelligan, "Old Arlington," p. 62; and REL to MCL, San Antonio, Tex., June 3, 1860, DE-LC.

45. Nan Netherton et al., *Fairfax County, Virginia: A History* (Fairfax, Va.: Fairfax County Board of Supervisors, 1978), pp. 165–68; "Interview with James Parks"; and MCW Diary, November 2, 1853, AHA.

46. See "Interview with James Parks"; REL to A. E. L. Keese, Arlington near Alex[a], April 24, 1858, HL; MCL to "Gen'l Sanford," May 30, 1861, typescript, AHA.

47. Parks, in "Colored Servant."

48. Those studying runaways have found that they were rarely the most abused, indeed were often the most advantaged, either by education, because of the master's favor, or in material opportunities. A petition filed in neighboring Prince George County, Virginia, corroborates this, complaining that the ability of slaves to buy and sell products was a "great & most operative cause of the corrupting of habits & morals of slaves, & of infusing into their minds discontent & the spirit of insubordination & consequently of producing discomfort & unhappiness to themselves, & loss to their masters." Petition, Prince George County, Virginia, 1859, quoted in Loren Schweninger, "The Underside of Slavery: The Internal Economy, Self-Hire, and Quasi-Freedom in Virginia," *Slavery and Abolition* 12, no. 2 (September 1991): 8–9. For more on the relation of privilege and discontent, see Berlin and Morgan, "Labor and the Shaping of Slave Life," pp. 22–25, 40–41; and Gerald W. Mullin, *Flight and Rebellion* (New York: Oxford University Press, 1975), pp. 89–98.

49. Indenture between Mary Anna Randolph Custis and Anna Maria Fitzhugh, August 18, 1830, Deed Book, S#2, Alexandria County, District of Columbia, pp. 37f.

50. Former Arlington slave quoted in "To Arlington," *Harper's Weekly*, May 29, 1886. An undated letter from the farm manager states that "Mrs. Custis will be pleased to note that no children had been used as field hands." ? to GWPC, n.d., AHA.

51. Laura C. Holloway, *The Ladies of the White House*, 2 vols. (Philadelphia: Bradley, 1881), 2:58–60; and GWPC quoted in MCW Diary, November 2, 1853, AHA.

52. "To Arlington."

53. William Burke to REL, Baltimore, May 8, 1853, REL-DU.

54. "Old Nurse" quoted in MCW Diary, [November 3], 1853. For the servants' high regard for Mary Fitzhugh Custis, see also "Lilly" to "My Dear Mistress," n.d. [c. 1853], BLA.

55. Mrs. William Fitzhugh to Mrs. Abbey Nelson, April n.d. [1853], printed in "Funeral of Mrs. G. W. P. Custis and Death of General Lee," *VMHB* 35, no. 1 (January 1927): 22–23.

56. MCL to "dearest Mother," April 11, [1832]; ALJ, July 16, 1854 and May 13, 1855, all DE-LC; "Interview with Emma Syphax" and "Tour with Thompson and Baker,"

copies at AHA; MCW Diary, November 2, 1853, AHA; and Zimmer, ed., *Housekeeping Book,* pp. 19–20.

57. For Lee's skepticism about the learning ability of the slaves, see REL to WHFL, San Antonio, Texas, September 7, 1860, GBL-VHS; REL testimony to the Joint Committee on Reconstruction, *Report of the Joint Committee at the First Session,* 39th Cong., 1st sess. (Washington, D.C.: GPO, 1866). Examples of the slaves' ability to write are found in "Lilly" to "My Dear Mistress," n.d. [c. 1853], BLA; and William Burke to Rev. R. R. Gurley, Algashland, February 9, 1867; and Selina Gray to MCL, Arlington, Va., November 1872, both MCL-VHS.

58. ACL to Helen Bratt, West Point, November 7, [1854], LFP-WL.

59. ALJ, July 16, 1854, and MCL to "dearest Mother," April 11, [1832], both DE-LC.

60. MCW Diary, November 2, 1853, AHA.

61. MCW Diary, November 20, 1853, AHA.

62. MCW Diary, April 6, 1856, AHA. For more on attitudes toward slave instruction and the "alternative" education within the slave community, see Webber, *Deep Like the Rivers,* pp. 26–29, 246–49.

63. See Susan Maria Fickling, "Slave Conversion in South Carolina," *Bulletin of the University of South Carolina,* no. 146 (September 1, 1924): 12–13; Clinton, *Plantation Mistress,* pp. 161–62; and MCW Diary, October 30, 1853, AHA.

64. CCL, "My Boyhood" LoV; Fickling, "Slave Conversion," pp. 12–13; Webber, *Deep Like the Rivers,* pp. 44–56; sermon copied at end of MCW Diary. For Robert E. Lee's religious beliefs, see chapter 14, "Mutable Shield."

65. MCW Diary, November 6, 1853, March 28, 1857, and October 25, 1857, AHA.

66. MCW Diary, October 30, 1853, AHA; and Karen L. Byrne, "Our Little Sanctuary in the Woods: Spiritual Life at Arlington Chapel," *Arlington Historical Magazine* 12, no. 2 (October 2002): 41.

67. MCW Diary, November 20, 1853, AHA.

68. MCW Diary, June 29, 1853, AHA.

69. MCW Diary, March 12, 1854, AHA.

70. *District of Columbia Slavery Code,* Act 29th October 1836, sec. 18.

71. George M. Stroud, *Sketch of the Laws Relating to Slavery in the Several States of the United States of America* (repr., New York: Negro Universities Press, 1968), pp. 60–61, 66.

72. William Meade to MFC, April 9, 1823, and May 30, 1825, both Custis Family Papers, VHS; Lynch, *Custis Chronicles,* 2:246; Amos Beyan submits that Meade's motive was to secure the slave system in the United States, but his family letters, at least in the 1820s and '30s, do not bear this out. Amos Beyan, *American Colonization Society and the Creation of the Liberian State* (Lanham: Univeristy Press of America, 1991), p. 4.

73. MCL Diary, June 9, 1853.

74. Ibid.; Will of M. Lee, November 3, 1857, "Opened and Resealed after the War at Lexington," December 13, 1865, GBL-VHS; Calvert, "Childhood Days at Arlington," AHA; and REL to Rev. W. McLain, West Point, N.Y., February 8, 1855, Letterbook #1, LFP-VHS.

75. Pielmeier, "Evolution of a Virginia Plantation," p. 75, AHA; REL to Rev. R. R. Gurley, Arlington, December 24, 1835; REL to Rev. W. McLain, West Point, February 8, 1855; and W. McLain to REL, Washington City, October 18, 1853, all American Colonization Society Records, LC.

76. Among those who left Arlington for Africa were William Burke and his clan, all highly motivated individuals, who were educated and liberated by the Custis family, and, with shoemaking skills and a $100 gift from Mrs. Lee, landed in Liberia in the 1850s. Their brave letters attest to the difficulties of the artificially created colony, but show a willing spirit and stout heart. William C. Burke to "Dear Madam and Sir" [MCL and REL], n.d., quoted in John W. Blassingame, ed., *Slave Testimony: Two Centuries of Letters, Speeches, Interviews, and Autobiographies* (Baton Rouge: Louisiana State University Press, 1977), pp. 100–101; and William Burke to Rev. R. R. Gurley, Algashland, February 9, 1867, MCL-VHS.

77. Daniel Feller, *The Jacksonian Promise: America 1815–1840* (Baltimore: Johns Hopkins University Press, 1995), p. 61; Beyan, *The American Colonization Society,* pp. 2–3; Douglas R. Egerton, "'Its Origin Is Not a Little Curious': A New Look at the American Colonization Society," *Journal of the Early Republic* 5, no. 4 (Winter 1985): 479–80; Scott L. Malcomson, *One Drop of Blood* (New York: Farrar, Straus and Giroux, 2000), pp. 188–194; and REL to Rev. W. McLain, West Point, February 8, 1855, Letterbook #1, LFP-VHS. The objectives of the American Colonization Society, controversial in its own day, have remained an issue of debate among historians. For an excellent summary of who is on which side, see Beyan, *American Colonization Society,* p. xv (notes).

78. For examples of the difficulties with health, angry local populations, and adaptation, see R. R. Gurley to MFC, Baltimore, March 5, 1823; and R. R. Gurley to MFC, Office of the Col[onization] Society, Washington, D.C., June 23, 1831, both MCL-VHS.

79. MCL to MFC, "Friday 12th," [c. 1850], MCL-VHS; William Meade to MFC, May 30, 1825, and Ann Meade Page to MFC, n.d. [c. late 1820s], both Custis Family Papers, VHS.

80. MFC to MCL, Arlington, October 8, 1831, Custis Family Papers, VHS; and R. R. Gurley to MFC, Harford, November 9, 1842, MCL-VHS.

81. Eric Robert Papenfuse, *The Evils of Necessity: Robert Goodloe Harper and the Moral Dilemma of Slavery* (Philadelphia: American Philosophical Society, 1997), p. 63; *American Colonization Society Annual Report* 7 (1824): 7; Marie Tyler-McGraw, ed., "'The Prize I Mean Is the Prize of Liberty': A Loudoun County Family in Liberia," *VMHB* 97, no. 3 (July 1989): 356–57, 362; and Mary Frances Berry and John W. Blassingame, *Long Memory: The Black Experience in America* (New York: Oxford University Press, 1982), pp. 399–400. Mary Custis Lee was among those who witnessed a change in attitude away from colonization as a solution to slavery toward a northern commitment to abolition. See MCL to MFC, Fort Hamilton, N.Y., October 27, 1844, DE-LC.

82. Joel Williamson, *New People: Miscegenation and Mulattoes in the United States* (New York: Free Press, 1980), p. 56.

83. See James Hugo Johnston, *Race Relations in Virginia and Miscegenation in the South, 1776–1860* (Amherst: University of Massachusetts Press, 1970), pp. 192–94; Clinton, *Plantation Mistress,* pp. 87, 91, 202–4; James Hugo Johnston, *Miscegenation in the Ante-Bellum South* (Chicago: University of Chicago Press, 1939), pp. 6–8, 15; and Deborah Gray White, *Ar'n't I A Woman?* (New York: W. W. Norton, 1999), pp. 34, 43.

84. Marietta Minnigerode Andrews, *My Studio Window: Sketches of the Pageant of Washington Life* (New York: E. P. Dutton, 1928), pp. 68–69.

85. Reverend Ishrael Massie quoted in Charles L. Perdue Jr., Thomas E. Barden,

and Robert K. Phillips, eds., *Weevils in the Wheat: Interviews with Virginia Ex-Slaves* (Charlottesville: University Press of Virginia, 1976), p. 207.

86. George Calvert, first cousin of GWPC, had a liaison for many years with his slave Eleanor Beckett. Eventually he freed her and the children he sired, and made an effort to ensure their well-being. See Calvert, *Mistress of Riversdale*, pp. 379–81; quotation M[ary] Meade to MFC, Annfield, Monday 13th, [pre 1817], MCL-VHS.

87. In the District of Columbia the white partner was to be enslaved for seven years. *Slave Code of the District of Columbia*, vol. 2, sec. 59.

88. Williamson, *New People*, pp. 63–67.

89. John Custis quoted in Wiencek, *Imperfect God*, p. 74. The legal documents indicate that John Custis meant to favor Jack and to set him up independently. He stopped short, however, of acknowledging the relationship between them. According to the Custis family's version of the story, John Custis became fond of Jack because of his clownish ways, but wrote the will in irritation at his son Daniel, who hoped to marry someone not of his father's choosing. Neighboring planters created their own pressure by telling Custis that if he proceeded with the will "Among old friends & neighbors he should stand isolated & despised." Jack's early death put an end to the matter. Whichever version one accepts, the racial prejudices of the day are in high relief. Blanche Berard quoted in Torrence, "Arlington and Mount Vernon, 1856," pp. 159–60.

90. Wiencek, *Imperfect God*, pp. 84–85; Lynch, *Custis Chronicles*, 2:94–95; GWPC, Note to Bank to pay $10 to William Costin, April 5, 1836, TPA; and George Washington Williams, *History of the Negro Race in America, 1619–1880*, 2 vols. (New York: Arno Press, 1968), 2:192.

91. Lynch, *Custis Chronicles*, 2:4–5; GWPC Deed of Manumission, April 5, 1803, Liber E, 1803, and Deed of Manumission, May 14, 1818, Liber G, no. 2, 1818–1819, both ACH; E. Delorus Preston Jr., "William Syphax, a Pioneer in Negro Education in the District of Columbia," *Journal of Negro History* 20, no. 4 (October 1935): 450–51; and Dorothea E. Abbott, "The Land of Maria Syphax and the Abbey Mausoleum," *Arlington Historical Magazine*, October 1984, pp. 64–79, *Congressional Record* quoted p. 65. See also Evelyn Reid Syphax, "William Syphax, Community Leader," *Arlington Historical Magazine* 6, no. 1 (October 1977).

92. Powell, "Reminiscences of Our Childhood." "William Parke" likely refers to William Parks, listed on the inventory at Custis's death as being fifty-two years old.

93. Williamson, *New People*, p. 63; Fogel and Engerman, *Time on the Cross*, p. 132; Seventh and Eighth Decennial Censes of the United States, Alexandria County, Va., 1850 and 1860, NARA.

94. El Marquise de Monserrate to GWPC, Washington City, August 8, 1813, CL-TPA; MCW Diary, November 6, 1853, AHA.

95. The picture is in the collections at Arlington House, the Robert E. Lee Memorial, National Park Service.

96. Harriette C. Gillem Robinet, "Interview with Martha Gray Gillem," 1963, typescript, AHA.

97. REL to MCL, Camp near Parras, December 7, 1846, DE-LC.

98. For legal actions taken on behalf of the slaves see M. L. Custis to Philip R. Fendall, December 9, 1850, Fendall Papers, LC; for treats given to the servants see ALJ, February 23, 1853; and REL to "dearest Mother" (MFC), Baltimore, March 17, 1852, both DE-LC.

99. ALJ, December 31, 1854, DE-LC.

100. See MCL Diary, July 30, 1854; "Interview with Emma Syphax"; and MCW to MCL, Georgetown, D.C., July 25, 1862, DE-LC.

101. REL Jr. to MiCL, University of Virginia, January 5, 1862, DE-LC.

102. Vincent Syphax to Kendall Thompson, e-mail, August 30, 2002, copy at AHA.

103. "Interview with Emma Syphax."

104. See quotation in Webber, *Deep Like the Rivers*, p. ix; and Cooling, *Symbol*, p. 88.

105. Slave resistance at Arlington is discussed in chapter 16, "Theory Meets Reality."

CHAPTER NINE: Humanity and the Law

1. REL to MCL, Fort Hamilton, N.Y., April 18, 1841, REL-UVa. "Cuddies" were small ship cabins. "Hill" refers to Lee's cousin Hill Carter. "Boss Cropsy" probably refers to one of the landowning Cropsey family, who were prominent in Brooklyn. "Colross" was the home of Lee's brother Smith, whom he had nicknamed "Rose." Bernard Carter, his mother's brother, married Lee's sister Lucy Grymes Lee, making him both his uncle and brother-in-law.

2. The identity of the Lewis family is unclear here. This was a common local name—or it may have been the estate of Nelly Custis Lewis, though it is unusual that she would have been referred to as "Mrs. Lewis," rather than "Aunt Lewis." "Aunt Lewis" had been married to Lawrence Lewis, a harsh and trying man who sold his slaves South despite considerable popular pressure not to do so. It may have been on this estate that the problem occurred. Lynch, *Custis Chronicles*, 2:3, 212, 215; for the selling of the Lewis slaves to Louisiana see, for example, Lawrence Lewis to Major Edmund G. W. Butler, November 2, 1836 and January 18, 1837, typescripts, CL-LC. A discussion of the dichotomy between humanity and the law in slave/master relations is found in Phillip J. Schwarz, *Slave Laws in Virginia* (Athens: University of Georgia Press, 1996), pp. 5–7; J. Thomas Wren, "A 'Two-Fold Character': The Slave as Person and Property in Virginia Court Cases, 1800–1860," *Southern Studies* 24, no. 4 (Winter 1985): 417–431; and Stroud, *Sketch of the Laws*, pp. 12–13, 44. Philip Morgan has noted that there were two types of slaveholders: patriarchal masters who stressed order, authority, and duty and were quick to resort to violence when their authority was questioned, and paternalistic masters who expected gratitude, even love, from their slaves, and were keenly interested in their religious welfare. See Thomas D. Morris, *Southern Slavery and the Law, 1619–1860* (Chapel Hill:University of North Carolina Press, 1996), p. 263.

3. A number of contemporary historians have discussed Lee's racial attitudes. Michael Fellman (*Making of Robert E. Lee,* p. 54) says Lee had little to say about slaves, but goes on to cite excellent original research with many illuminating comments. Thomas Connelly describes the way Lee's myth-makers consciously erased anti-abolitionist statements from his writings in *Marble Man,* pp. 118–19; Alan T. Nolan has given us an excellent summary of those who simplified Lee's views, characterizing them as antislavery or relying only on the 1856 letter, in Alan T. Nolan, *Lee Considered* (Chapel Hill: University of North Carolina Press, 1991), pp. 9–10. Douglas Southall Freeman claimed that "nothing of any consequence" on slavery was said by Lee until the 1856 letter. See Freeman, *R. E. Lee,* 1:371.

4. Nolan, *Lee Considered,* pp. 9–10; Connelly, *Marble Man,* p. 118; Sanborn, *Portrait,* p. 283; and John Leyburn, "An Interview with General Robert E. Lee," *Century Magazine* 30, no. 1 (May 1885). One recent biographer even calls Lee an "emancipator," despite the fact that Lee did not free the slaves under his authority until a court

decreed that he must, as is discussed in chapter 16, "Theory Meets Reality." See Thomas, *Robert E. Lee,* p. 273.

5. For Richard Henry Lee's career, first as an antislavery orator, then as a slave trader, see Nagel, *Lees of Virginia,* pp. 81–84; Jefferson's discomfort with the issue is described in Schwarz, *Slave Laws in Virginia,* pp. 35–62.

6. REL to MCL, Fort Brown, Texas, December 27, 1856; and REL to MFC, St. Louis, March 20, 1839, both DE-LC. For a discussion of proslavery views, see Nolan, *Lee Considered,* pp. 13–19; Mark V. Tushnet, *The American Law of Slavery, 1810–1860* (Princeton: Princeton University Press, 1981), pp. 22–24; and Drew Gilpin Faust, ed., *The Ideology of Slavery* (Baton Rouge: Louisiana State University Press, 1981), pp. 6–12.

7. Examples of Lee's identification with the rights of the master and his disdain for the activities and goals of the abolitionists are found in REL to Captain A[ndrew] Talcott, Fort Monroe, June 6, 1834, REL-VHS; and REL to MFC, Fort Hamilton, N.Y., April 13 [1844], GBL-VHS. Lee gives a dispassionate account of Nat Turner's rebellion in a note to his mother-in-law, scribbled at the end of MCL to "My dearest Mother," Sunday, n.d. [1831], DE-LC; for his remarks on the Harper's Ferry incident, see REL to Henry Lee, Harper's Ferry, December 6, 1859, LFP-VHS; and REL to Captain George W. Cullum, Arlington, Washington City P.O., December 24, 1859, USMA; also REL-MCL, December 1, 1859, DE-LC.

8. For Lee's willingness to buy slaves, see REL to MCL, Fort Mason, March 28, 1856, DE-LC; and REL to WHFL, July 9, 1860, GBL-VHS. For defense of the methods of slave control, see REL to WHFL, Arlington, May 30, 1858, LFP-VHS; his unsympathetic treatment of slaves under his control at Arlington is dealt with in chapter 16, "Theory Meets Reality." See also remarks of Arlington slaves about Lee as "a harsh taskmaster" in Sneden Diary, September 12, 1862; and in Preston, *West Point and Lexington,* pp. 76–77. For postwar attitudes, see chapter 25, "Blurred Vision."

9. Leonidas Polk to Stephen Elliott, New Orleans, August 30, 1856, in Polk, *Leonidas Polk,* 1:239.

10. Boyd, *Light-horse Harry Lee,* pp. 207–9; CCL, "Recollections of Stratford," n.d., photostat, EA-LC; "Stratford Hall Slave Population, Preliminary Analysis," unpublished research report, n.d., SH; Deposition of Westmoreland Co. Sheriff Gerrard McKenny, April 28, 1807, *Lee vs. Rowand,* SC-H, 1822, Folder 2 of 7, Fredericksburg Circuit Court Records; Deposition of Randsdell Pierce, April 28, 1809, *Lee vs. Rowand,* photostat, SH; and Wiencek, *Imperfect God,* pp. 230, 278.

11. *Alexandria Gazette* quoted in Virginia Writers' Project, *The Negro in Virginia* (repr., New York: Arno Press, 1969), pp. 161–62. See Frederic Bancroft, *Slave Trading in the Old South* (repr., Columbia: University of South Carolina Press, 1996), pp. 45–49; and Donald M. Sweig, *Slavery in Fairfax County, Virginia, 1750–1860: A Research Report* (Fairfax, Va.: Office of Comprehensive Planning, 1983), pp. 62–69.

12. Mason's granddaughter, "Nannie," married Smith Lee. George Mason, "Extracts from Virginia Charters," in George Mason, *The Papers of George Mason,* ed. Robert A. Rutland, 3 vols. (Chapel Hill: University of North Carolina Press, 1970), 1:173.

13. REL to MCL, March 25, 1832, DE-LC; quotation REL to MCL, Old Point, April 17, 1831, in Cuthbert, "To Molly," p. 262.

14. MCL to MFC, March 19, 1833; and REL to MCL, Old Point, April 24, 1832, both DE-LC.

15. REL to MCL, Old Point, June 2, 1832, DE-LC.

16. REL to MCL, Old Point, April 24, 1832; and to MFC, St. Louis, March 20, 1839, both DE-LC; REL to GWCL, San Antonio, Texas, July 4, 1860, CL-LC; and REL to WHFL, Arlington, May 30, 1858, VHS.

17. REL to MCL, Camp Fred^g, December 7, 1862, DE-LC. This author has found only one instance in which Lee praised a slave. He called "Old Daniel," a servant on the White House plantation, "an excellent man." REL to WHFL, San Antonio, Texas, September 7, 1860, GBL-VHS.

18. REL Manuscript Will, August 1, 1846, photostat in CL-LC; Freeman, *R. E. Lee,* 1:371, n38; Joseph C. Robert, "Lee the Farmer," *Journal of Southern History* 3, no. 4 (November 1937): 429–30; and Robert E. Lee Jr. to Thomas Nelson Page quoted in William T. Rachel, "Some Letters of Thomas Nelson Page," *VMHB* 62, no. 2 (April 1953): 183–84.

19. See Elizabeth Brown Pryor, "Flexibility and Profit in the Slave Hiring System of Fairfax County, Virginia, 1830–1860," unpublished manuscript.

20. REL to "My dear Cousin Hill," Fort Hamilton, January 22, 1842, DE-LC; quotation REL to William O. Winston, Alexandria, July 8, 1858, William O. Winston Papers, VHS.

21. For the class structures of the time, see James Oakes, *The Ruling Race* (New York: W. W. Norton, 1998), pp. x, 210–18; also REL to MFC, St. Louis, November 7, 1839, DE-LC. Michael Fellman proposes that Lee was also anti-Semitic, citing a letter in which Lee criticizes a family staying near him at the White Sulphur Springs. The letter, however, does not mention the family's religion and carries a name—Hoffman—that was a common Dutch Christian name and, indeed, the surname of a family that married with one of Lee's favorite nieces. Professor Fellman could not cite other sources for this assumption when contacted. REL to MCL, White Sulphur Springs, W. Va., August 4, 1840, DE-LC; Fellman, *Making of Robert E. Lee,* pp. 55–57; and Michael Fellman, e-mail to author, April 16, 2004. For Lee's friendly comments toward the Hoffmans, see REL to "My Dear Mr. Bonaparte," September 19, 1850; and May 11, 1853, LFP-WL.

22. REL to John Mackay, National Palace, City of Mexico, October 2, 1847, USAMHI; and REL to MCL, Camp Cooper, Texas, July 28, 1856, DE-LC.

23. REL to Mrs. [Wm. Henry] Stiles, "Camp on the Clear Fork of the Brazos," Indian Territory, May 24, 1856, SH.

24. REL to Major Earl Van Dorn, San Antonio, Texas, July 3, 1860, CL-LC.

25. REL quoted in Fellman, *Making of Robert E. Lee,* p. 58; REL to Eliza Mackay Stiles, Arlington, January 23, 1836, SH; and to MCL, Camp Cooper, Texas, August 25, 1856, both DE-LC. For an in-depth analysis of the origins of class and racial prejudice in the early republic, see Winthrop Jordan, *White over Black* (Baltimore: Penguin, 1968), especially chapter 15.

26. Apparently even during the surrender at Appomattox Lee's racial expectations were evident. An eyewitness recorded that Lee's impassive face changed only once—when Colonel Ely S. Parker, chief of the Six Nations and an aide on Grant's staff, was introduced to him. "When he saw the swarthy features he looked at him with evident surprise, and his eyes rested on him for several seconds. What was passing his mind probably no one ever knew, but the natural surmise was that he at first mistook Parker for a negro, and was struck with astonishment to find that the commander of the Union armies had one of that race on his personal staff." According to one account Lee apologized to Parker for mistaking him for a black man, saying "I am glad

to see one real American here." The story is told by only one of those present and seems more of a slap at the Northerners than a recognition of native peoples. Horace Porter, "The Surrender at Appomattox Court House," in *B & L* 4:741; and Arthur C. Parker, *The Life of General Ely S. Parker* (repr. New York: AMS Press, 1985), p. 133.

27. See, for example, Hattaway and Fair, "Ethan Allen Hitchcock," in Garraty and Carnes, *ANB*, 10:868. Hitchcock, who served with Lee on the frontier, is quoted as saying, "I have been much with Indians and look upon them as part of the great human family, capable of being reasoned with and susceptible of passions and affections which, rightly touched, will secure moral results with almost mechanical certainty."

28. REL to W. H. Nettleton, Lexington, Va., May 21, 1866, REL Letterbook #3, DE-LC.

29. For Lee's thoughts on black inferiority, see Testimony of Robert E. Lee, *Report of the Joint Committee*; and Fellman, *Making of Robert E. Lee*, p. 58.

30. MCW Diary, November 7, 1853.

31. Mary Anna Randolph Custis to Mrs. Richard Lee, n.d. [prior to 1831], CL-LC; and MCW Diary, undated insert on slavery. Many historians have creatively discussed the way in which slaves either identified with their masters' views or repeated them when it was to their advantage. For an example, see Genovese, *Roll Jordan Roll*, pp. 113–115. For a further discussion of the difficult class distinctions among both whites and blacks in the antebellum South, see Elizabeth Brown Pryor, "An Anomalous Person: The Northern Tutor in Plantation Society, 1773–1860," *Journal of Southern History* 47, no. 3 (August 1981). There was also an understood pecking order among the slaves and hired servants. See Mrs. Roger A. Pryor, *Reminiscences of Peace and War* (New York: Macmillan, 1905), p.43; and Genovese, *Roll Jordan Roll*, pp. 337–39.

32. REL to Andrew Hunter, Head Quarters A.N.Va., January 11, 1865, SH. After the war, Lee continued to dislike aligning himself with African-Americans: "You will never prosper with the blacks, and it is abhorrent to a reflecting mind to be supporting and cherishing those who are plotting and working for your injury." REL quoted in Lee Jr., *Recollections*, p. 306.

33. For Lee's conformance to accepted thought, see chapter 11, "Crenellations." Bertram Wyatt-Brown quoted in Nolan, *Lee Considered*, p. 13; Jefferson quoted in Wiencek, *Imperfect God*, p. 5; James Henry Hammond, "Letter to an English Abolitionist," 1845, in Faust, *Ideology*, p. 202, also pp. 6–10; see also Thomas Roderick Dew, "Abolition of Negro Slavery," in Faust, *Ideology*, p. 55; and Eugene Genovese, *The World the Slaveholders Made* (New York: Vintage, 1971), particularly pt. 2, chap. 4.

34. For a longer discussion of Lincoln's views on race, see David Herbert Donald, *Lincoln* (New York: Simon & Schuster, 1995), pp. 633–34n; and William E. Gienapp, *Abraham Lincoln and Civil War America* (New York: Oxford University Press, 2002), p. 52, Lincoln quoted p. 65.

35. Thomas Dew, "Abolition of Negro Slavery," in Faust, *Ideology*, pp. 27, 52, 53; and Ira Berlin, *Slaves without Masters* (New York: Pantheon, 1974) pp. 182–88.

36. REL to MCL, Fort Brown, Texas, December 27, 1856, DE-LC; *Report of the Joint Committee*, p. 136; James Henry Hammond in Faust, ed., *Ideology*, pp. 202–203; quotation REL to MCL, Baltimore, July 8, 1849, LFP-VHS. Even Lincoln initially thought colonization of freed blacks was the only workable solution. He insulted a group of African-American leaders during his presidency by inviting them to the White House and declaring, "You and we are different races. It is better for us both, therefore, to be separated." He proposed a plan to send the freedmen to Panama and Haiti—a scheme that ended disastrously. See Donald, *Lincoln*, pp. 342–48, 367–68.

37. Alison Goodyear Freehling, *Drift toward Dissolution: The Virginia Slave Debate of 1831–1832* (Baton Rouge: Louisiana State University Press, 1982), pp. xii–xiii.

38. Patrick Henry quoted in Wiencek, *Imperfect God*, p. 5. Thomas Jefferson, George Washington, and Robert Lee's first cousin Hill Carter all agreed. REL to MCL, Fort Brown, Texas, December 27, 1856, DE-LC; Schwarz, *Slave Laws in Virginia*, p. 39; and Hill Carter, "On the Management of Negroes," *Farmer's Register* 1 (February 1834): 564–565.

39. Elijah Fletcher to father, New Glasgow, September 5, 1813, in *Letters of Elijah Fletcher*, pp. 77–78. Eugene Genovese notes, "There is no reason to believe that for every guilt-stricken, inwardly torn slaveholder there were not many who went about their business reasonably secure in the notion that they did not create the world, it existed as it existed, and that their moral worth depended on how well they discharged the duties and responsibilities defined by the world in which they, not someone else, lived." Genovese, *Slaveholders*, p. 147. Schwarz, *Slave Laws in Virginia*, pp. 36–39, also elaborates on this subject.

40. Washington's struggle with slavery in terms of eighteenth-century concepts of democracy is discussed at length in Wiencek, *Imperfect God*, quotation p. 272. Abraham Lincoln quoted in Albert E. Pillsbury, *Lincoln and Slavery* (New York: Houghton Mifflin, 1913), p. 33.

CHAPTER TEN: **Adrenaline**

1. REL to MCL, Hacienda [El Len]cero, April 18, 1847, REL-VHS.

2. For an excellent account of the cultural and social development of the time, see Robert W. Johannsen, *To the Halls of the Montezumas* (New York: Oxford University Press, 1985); also Frederick D. Schwarz, "The Time Machine: 1847," *American Heritage* 45, no. 5 (September 1997): 105–6; and Timothy Foote, "1846: The Way We Were—and the Way We Went," *Smithsonian* 27, no. 1 (April 1996): 38–50.

3. Peskin, *Winfield Scott*, pp. 133–34.

4. Foote, "1846," pp. 41–44; and David K. O'Rourke, "Our War with Mexico: Rereading Guadalupe Hidalgo," *Commonweal* 125, no. 5 (March 13, 1998): 8–9. Although Thoreau made much of spending time in jail as a protest, in fact his aunt paid the tax for him, and he was released after one day.

5. Anna Maria Fitzhugh to CCL, Alexandria, May 23, 1846, EA-LC.

6. REL to MCL, Fort Hamilton, N.Y., May 12, 1846, DE-LC.

7. REL to MCW, Governors Island, June 7, 1846, in Lee, *"To Markie,"* pp. 17–18.

8. Freeman, *R. E. Lee*, 1:202.

9. Lee had hoped to serve under General Zachary Taylor, who was brilliantly conducting the campaigns in northern Mexico, including the battle of Monterey. REL to CCL, Arlington, September 1, 1846, REL-UVa; also Major-General Zachary Taylor to Roger Jones, Adjutant-General of the Army, "Head-Quarters, Army of Occupation, Camp before Monterey," September 25, 1846, in Steven R. Butler, ed., *A Documentary History of the Mexican War* (Richardson, Tex.: Descendants of Mexican War Veterans, 1995), p. 96.

10. REL to MCL, "Camp near Alamos River," Mexico, October 19, 1846; and REL to MCL, San Antonio, Texas, September 25, 1846, both DE-LC.

11. REL to MCL, "Camp near Monclova, Reveille," November 20, 1846, DE-LC. Santa Anna quoted in REL to MCL, "Camp of Agua Nueva, 44 miles south of Monclova," November 26, 1846, DE-LC. Santa Anna signed his name "Santa Ana"; the En-

glish version, which Lee employed, has been used here. For more on Santa Anna's exploits, see Robert L. Scheina, *Santa Anna: A Curse upon Mexico* (Washington, D.C.: Brassey's, 2002); and Antonio Lopez de Santa Anna, *The Eagle: The Autobiography of Santa Anna*, ed. Ann Fears Crawford (Austin, Tex.: State House Press, 1988).

12. Richard Bruce Winders, *Mr. Polk's Army: The American Military Experience in the Mexican War* (College Station: Texas A & M University Press, 1997), pp. 52, 108, 140–44; *The Mexican War Diary of George B. McClellan*, ed. William Starr Myers (Princeton, N.J.: Princeton University Press, 1917) p. 19; and REL to MCL, "On board Steamboat from New Orleans to Savaca," August 13, 1846, DE-LC.

13. One historian has written that Lee was hardened to the realities of military life in the 1850s when he served with the cavalry in Texas, but it appears that the Mexican adventure was his baptism. See Carl Coke Rister, *Robert E. Lee in Texas* (Norman: University of Oklahoma Press, 2004); also REL to MCL, San Antonio de Bexos, September 21, 1846; "Camp of Agua Nueva, 44 miles south of Monclova," November 26, 1846; and "Camp near La Pastora," December 1, 1846, all DE-LC.

14. *Diary of George B. McClellan*, pp. 38–39. Grant liked the volunteers and refused to hear complaints against them. Ulysses S. Grant, *Personal Memoirs of U.S. Grant* (repr., New York: Da Capo Press, 1982), p. 84.

15. REL to MCL, Rio Grande, October 11, 1846, DE-LC; and Freeman, *R. E. Lee*, 1:208–09.

16. REL to MCL, "Camp near Monclova, Reveille," November 18 and November 20, 1846; and Sotillo, December 23, 1846, all DE-LC.

17. Lee apparently first told this story to Reverend J. William Jones after the Civil War; his version is found in Jones, *Personal Reminiscences*, pp. 288–90; also Freeman, *R. E. Lee*, 1:214–216.

18. Polk was a self-avowed one-term president, but his concern was that Taylor or Scott, both of whom were Whigs, would be able to garner enough support to defeat the Democratic Party in the 1848 election. This is, of course, exactly what happened, with Taylor the rather reluctant victor. The personal styles, strategies, and military views of Taylor and Scott could not have been more dissimilar, and the precipitous way that Scott had been placed over Taylor ensured that there would be little collegiality between them. Grant, who served under both during the Mexican War, would later diplomatically state that even with their contrasting characteristics, "both were great and successful soldiers." Peskin, *Winfield Scott*, pp. 141–42; and Grant, *Personal Memoirs*, pp. 56–57, 67.

19. For more on Scott, see Peskin, *Winfield Scott*, pp. 125–27; Thomas Fleming, "Birth of the American Way of War," *MHQ: The Quarterly Journal of Military History* 15, no. 2 (Winter 2003): 86–95; and Grant, *Personal Memoirs*, pp. 66–67.

20. Winfield Scott, *Memoirs of Lieut.-General Scott, Written by Himself*, 2 vols. (New York: Sheldon, 1864), 2:428.

21. Beauregard was among those who frequently ventured his opinion, on one occasion persuading the general to take a risky, but ultimately successful, approach at the battle of Chapultepec. P. G. T. Beauregard, *With Beauregard in Mexico: The Mexican War Reminiscences of P. G. T. Beauregard*, ed. T. Harry Williams (repr., Baton Rouge: Louisiana State University Press, 1956), pp. 68–72.

22. See Hitchcock's description of Scott, in Hitchcock, *Fifty Years in Camp and Field*, pp. 299–300.

23. REL to John Mackay, National Palace, City of Mexico, October 2, 1847, USAMHI.

24. Ethan Allen Hitchcock diary for August 19, 1847, in Hitchcock, *Fifty Years in Camp and Field*, p. 277.

25. Lt. Isaac Ingalls Stevens to "My Dearest Wife," August 22, 1847, in Grady McWhiney and Sue McWhiney, eds., *To Mexico with Taylor and Scott, 1845–1847* (Waltham, Mass.: Blaisdell, 1968), p. 196.

26. Keyes, *Fifty Years Observation*, p. 206 and Winfield Scott to J. B. Floyd, Headquarters of the Army, May 8, 1857 quoted in Jones, *Life and Letters*, pp. 127–28.

27. *Diary of George B. McClellan*, pp. 61–65; and REL to MCL, "Camp near Vera Cruz," GBL-VHS.

28. Jones, *Life and Letters*, pp. 46–47, quotation p. 46.

29. *Diary of George B. McClellan*, p. 67.

30. Ibid., pp. 66–67; and Raphael Semmes, *The Campaign of General Scott in the Valley of Mexico* (Cincinnati: Moore & Anderson, 1852), pp. 20–26; quotation p. 26.

31. *Diary of George B. McClellan*, pp. 66–70; quotation REL-MCL, Camp before Vera Cruz, March 27, 1847, both GBL-VHS.

32. K. Jack Bauer, "The Veracruz Expedition of 1847," *Military Affairs* 40 (Fall 1956): 162–169.

33. *Diary of George B. McClellan*, pp. 66–70.

34. Lee, *General Lee*, p. 33.

35. The Duke of Wellington quoted in Schwarz, "The Time Machine," p. 106.

36. Fleming, "Birth of the American Way of War," pp. 92–94; Freeman, *R. E. Lee*, 1:237–248; and Grant, *Personal Memoirs*, p. 63.

37. REL to MCL, Hacienda [El Len]cero, April 18, 1847, REL-VHS; *Diary of George B. McClellan*, p. 92n. Another source gives the losses as 30 officers and 387 men, with 64 killed. Fleming, "Birth of the American Way of War," p. 94.

38. Semmes, *Campaign of General Scott*, p. 267.

39. Lt. Isaac Ingalls Stevens to "My Dearest Wife," August 22, 1847, in McWhiney and McWhiney, eds., *To Mexico with Taylor and Scott*, p. 196.

40. Robert Anderson, *An Artillery Officer in the Mexican War* (1911; repr., Freeport, N.Y.: Books for Libraries Press, 1971), p. 191.

41. General David Twiggs and Bennett Riley quoted in Jones, *Life and Letters*, p. 49; General Winfield Scott quoted in Freeman, *R. E. Lee*, 1:247–48. Scott is also quoted in Jones, p. 47, but he omits the word *again*, which makes the commendation appear to be discussing Lee's work at Vera Cruz.

42. General Persifer Smith quoted in Long, *Memoirs*, p. 64.

43. Peskin, *Winfield Scott*, p. 180; Hitchcock, *Fifty Years in Camp and Field*, p. 277; and General Winfield Scott quoted in Long, *Memoirs*, p. 58.

44. Scheina, *Santa Anna*, p. 69.

45. Long, *Memoirs*, p. 66; REL to John Mackay, National Palace, City of Mexico, October 2, 1847, USAMHI; and Dowdey, *Lee*, pp. 93–94.

46. Freeman, *R. E. Lee*, 1:284; Duke of Wellington quoted in Schwarz, "Time Machine," p. 106.

47. For Lee's longing to hear from home and his dismay at not receiving any letters, see e.g. REL to MCL, "Camp near Monclova," November 14 and 20, 1846. Quotation REL to MCL, "Camp near Panas," December 7, 1846, all DE-LC.

48. For an example of Lee's rich descriptions of the Mexican landscape, see REL to GWPC, "Ship Massachusetts off Lobos," February 28, 1847, LFP-WL. Letters to his

children include REL to GWCL and WHFL, "Camp near Satillo," December 24, 1846, DE-LC; and REL to CCL, City of Mexico, February 13, 1848, REL-UVa.

49. REL to Smith Lee, March 27, 1847, in Lee, *General Lee,* p. 37; and REL to Smith Lee, City of Mexico, March 4, 1848, SH.

50. See REL to John Mackay, National Palace, City of Mexico, October 2, 1847, USAMHI; and REL to ?, Perote, April 25, 1847, quoted in Jones, *Life and Letters,* pp. 51–52. Lee anticipates Scott's movement across the interior in REL to MCL, "Camp near Monclova," November 18, 1846, DE-LC.

51. On his infatuation with Mexican chocolate, see REL to MFC, "On Board Ship Massachusetts Off Lobos Isd," February 22, 1847, DE-LC; the polished Mexican ankles are mentioned in REL to John Mackay, National Palace, City of Mexico, October 2, 1847, USAMHI.

52. REL to Mackay, October 2, 1847, USAMHI; similar comments in REL to Major D[elafield], "Ship Massachusetts, off Lobos," February 28, 1847, LFP-WL. For the common attitude of the army toward the Mexicans, see Winders, *Mr. Polk's Army,* pp. 167–85; and Johannsen, *To the Halls of the Montezumas,* pp. 164–70. E. Kirby Smith was among those who recorded attitudes similar to Lee's. He wrote to his wife in 1846 that Mexico "truly might be an earthly paradise were the inhabitants civilized. They, alas, are lost in the most groveling superstition and ignorance and are under a government that tramples them to dust." E. Kirby Smith, *To Mexico with Scott: Letters of Captain E. Kirby Smith to His Wife,* ed. Emma Jerome Blackwood (Cambridge: Harvard University Press, 1917), p. 69. George B. McClellan made similar comments; see *Diary of George B. McClellan,* pp. 11–12, 91.

53. REL to MCL, "Camp near Alamos river Mexico," October 19, 1846; and REL to MCL, Camp near Satillo, December 25, 1846, both DE-LC.

54. REL to GWCL and WHFL, Camp near Satillo, December 24, 1846, DE-LC.

55. MCL to Sarah Beaumont Irwin, Arlington, October 18, [1846], LFP-BLC.

56. MCL to Sarah Beaumont Irwin, Arlington, February 15, 1847; and January 1, 1848, both LFP-BLC; and MFC to "My dear Grandson," December 5, 1851, DE-LC.

57. REL to Mackay, October 2, 1847, USAMHI; also Skelton, *American Profession of Arms,* p. 194.

58. REL to GWPC, City of Mexico, April 8, 1848, DE-LC. It should be noted that by the time Lee was writing this letter, he was thoroughly disgusted with the treatment of the army after its victories in Mexico and in the midst of watching his esteemed General Scott be publicly humiliated.

59. CCL to "My dear Cousin Nat" [Nathanial Burwell], Richmond, February 1, 1848, LJF-WL.

60. Scott quoted in *Memoirs,* 2:500–501; and MCL to "My dear Caroline" [Peters], n.d. [c. late spring 1848], LJF-WL.

61. James May to REL, Theological Seminary of Virginia, April 22, 1861, SH.

62. REL to GWPC, City of Mexico, 8 April 1848, DE-LC; and REL to Smith Lee, City of Mexico, March 4, 1848, SH.

63. *Diary of George B. McClellan,* pp. 16–18; quotation p. 17.

64. REL to MCL, Camp near Satillo, December 25, 1846, DE-LC.

65. REL to MCL, City of Mexico, December 23, 1847, GBL-VHS.

66. REL to CCL, City of Mexico, February 13, 1848, REL-UVa.

67. REL to John Mackay, Fort Hamilton, N.Y., June 21, 1846, UTA.

68. Freeman, *R. E. Lee,* 1:288–89; Peskin, *Winfield Scott,* pp. 197–202.

69. REL to GWPC, City of Mexico, April 8, 1848, DE-LC.

70. Freeman, *R. E. Lee,* 1:290–91; and Keyes, *Fifty Years Observation,* p. 206. Scott may have been especially appreciative of Lee's fidelity, since some of the initial charges against him had been instituted by his former protégé, General Worth, which disgusted much of the officer corps. "His desertion of General Scott, his old friend and ally, his patron, the man who *made* him, but for whom he never would have been *known,* is the rankest ingratitude of which I have ever seen. . . ." See W. S. Henry to Ethan Allen Hitchcock, Onzara, Mexico, March 7, 1848, Hitchcock Papers, LC.

71. For Lee's prediction that the charges would be dropped, see REL to MCL, City of Mexico, March 24, 1848, DE-LC; quotation REL to CCL, City of Mexico, February 13, 1848, REL-UVa.

72. REL to CCL, City of Mexico, May 15, 1848, REL-UVa.

73. REL to MCL, City of Mexico, February 13, 1848, DE-LC.

74. REL to Col. Jos. G. Totten, City of Mexico, April 1, 1848; and to EAL, City of Mexico, February 12, 1848, DE-LC. For Lee's pride in the Spanish he had learned, see Judge D. Gardiner Tyler in Riley, ed., *General Lee after Appomattox,* p. 130.

75. REL to CCL, City of Mexico, February 13, 1848, REL-UVa.

76. *The Constitution of the Aztec Club to Which is Appended a List of the Members of the Club* (Mexico: Office of the *American Star,* 1848); and Richard Hoag Breithaupt Jr., *Aztec Club of 1847: Sesquicentennial History, 1847–1997* (Universal City, Calif.: Walika, 1998), pp. 5–8. The club charged $20 to join and $1 per month thereafter, and boasted a parlor, reading room, dining room, refreshment room, and card rooms. Lee's refusal to attend the dinner honoring him is in Freeman, *R. E. Lee,* 1:286.

77. REL to MCL, City of Mexico, March 24, 1848, DE-LC.

78. For examples of Lee's strategizing, see REL to MCL, "Camp near Monclova," November 11, 1846, DE-LC; and REL to MCL, November 20, 1846, LFP-VHS; also Lt. Isaac Ingalls Stevens to "My Dearest Wife," August 22, 1847, in McWhiney and McWhiney, eds., *To Mexico with Taylor and Scott,* p. 196.

79. For a lengthy description of the terrors of the Mexican War battlefields, see Winders, *Mr. Polk's Army,* pp. 162–63; quotations Lt. Isaac Ingalls Stevens to "My Dearest Wife," August 22, 1847, in McWhiney and McWhiney, *To Mexico with Taylor and Scott,* pp. 201–2; and Smith, *To Mexico with Scott,* p. 53.

80. Ethan Allen Hitchcock recorded Lee's brush with "friendly fire" in his diary on March 20, 1847: "Capt. R. E. Lee, one of the engineers, and an admirable officer, had a narrow escape with his life yesterday. Returning from a working party with Lieut. P.T. Beauregard, he turned a point in the path in the bushes, and suddenly came up on one of our soldiers who no doubt mistook him for a Mexican and the soldier challenged 'Who comes there?' 'Friend!' said Captain Lee. 'Officers,' said Beauregard at the same time, but the soldier, in trepidation and haste levelled a pistol at Lee and fired. The ball passed between his left arm and body,—the flame singing his coat, he was so near. The General was very angry, and would not listen to Lee's intercession in behalf of the man." Hitchcock, *Fifty Years in Camp and Field,* p. 243; and Long, *Memoirs,* p. 60.

81. Lee Jr., *Recollections,* p. 5; and REL to GWCL, Perote, April 25, 1847, DE-LC.

82. Quotation REL to "My dear Son" [GWCL], Vera Cruz, April 11, 1847, DE-LC. Apparently Lee burst into tears when he witnessed Johnston receiving the news of his nephew's death; see REL to MCL, Tacubya, Mexico, August 22, 1847, GBL-VHS; and Joe

Johnston quoted in Lee, "Character of General Lee," p. 384. For Lee's exaltation at large numbers killed, see REL to MCL, Hacienda [El Len]cero, April 18, 1847, REL-VHS.

83. For Scott's character, see Peskin, *Winfield Scott,* p. 164; Grant, *Personal Memoirs,* pp. 66–67; Semmes, *Campaign of General Scott,* pp. 168–70; and Lt. Isaac Ingalls Stevens to "My Dearest Wife," August 22, 1847, in McWhiney and McWhiney, *To Mexico with Taylor and Scott,* pp. 196–97. Quotation REL to John Mackay, October 2, 1847, USAMHI.

84. Scott, *Memoirs,* 2:454.

85. For more on Scott's remarkable military creativity, see Peskin, *Winfield Scott;* and Weigley, *History of the United States Army,* pp. 184–87.

86. Scott's occupation policy was laid out in General Orders 287, a prescient document. See Scott, *Memoirs,* 2:498–99; also Sanborn, *Portrait,* pp. 172–73; Weigley, *History of the United States Army,* pp. 188–89; and Peskin, *Winfield Scott,* pp. 159, 194, quotation p. 194.

87. In his memoirs Scott cited the War of 1812 and the Civil War as "just" wars, but pointedly omitted the Mexican War from this category. Scott, *Memoirs,* 1:53; Peskin, *Winfield Scott,* pp. 136–37; quotation in Semmes, *Campaign of General Scott,* p. 168.

88. Grant, *Personal Memoirs,* pp. 56–57; and Davis, *Jefferson Davis,* pp. 165–66. For Lee's view of Scott's political problems, see REL to GWPC, City of Mexico, April 8, 1848; and to "Mrs. A. M. Fitzhugh," City of Mexico, April 12, 1848, both DE-LC; and REL to CCL, City of Mexico, March 18, 1848, REL-UVa.

89. Weigley, *History of the United States Army,* pp. 186–95; and *Diary of George B. McClellan,* pp. 28n, 36–38. McClellan's mistrust of the volunteers and scorn for their lack of training may have influenced his obsession with army "readiness" during the early months of the Civil War.

90. Freeman, *R. E. Lee,* 1:295–300; Roland, *Reflections on Lee,* p. 14; quotation Grant, *Personal Memoirs,* p. 96.

91. The southern portions of present-day New Mexico and Arizona were sold to the United States in 1853 in what is known as the Gadsden Purchase.

92. REL to MCL, City of Mexico, February 8, 1848, DE-LC; and Foote, "1846," p. 43.

93. For Lee's anxiety to get home, see REL to MCW, City of Mexico, May 21, 1848, in Lee, "To Markie," p. 22; and REL to MCL, "Steamer Portland," June 14, 1848, LFP-VHS; quotation REL to Smith Lee, Arlington, June 30, 1848, in Lee Jr., *Recollections,* p. 4.

CHAPTER ELEVEN: Crenellations

1. REL to Jack Mackay, Old Point, November 3, 1831, typescript, Mackay-Stiles Family Papers, SHC-UNC. Hugh Mercer, also from Savannah, was one of Lee's special friends at West Point and graduated in the class of 1828, as did Robert Temple and "Dick T"—Richard Tilghman, who was a groomsman at Lee's wedding. Gustavus Brown was in Lee's class the following year, as, of course, were John Mackay and Joseph E. Johnston. "Bradford" was most likely James A. Bradford, a Kentuckian from the class of 1827. All of these men finished at the top of their classes, which was typical of those Lee chose as friends. Colonel Abram Eustis commanded the Artillery School at Fort Monroe, where Lee was assigned. Colonel William Jenkins Worth had been in charge of the cadets at West Point for the first three years Lee was there and at that time was the overall commandant of the Fort. Cullum, *Biographical Register,* vol. 1, pp. 389, 406–9, 425, 427–28, 432.

2. REL to Col. Joseph G. Totten, Fort Hamilton, N.Y., June 17, 1845, REL Letterbook #1, LFP-VHS.

3. REL to Gen. Joseph G. Totten, Fort Carroll, August 2, 1852, REL Letterbook #1, LFP-VHS.

4. Weigley, *Towards an American Army*, pp. 12–19; Prucha, *Broadax and Bayonet*, pp. 29–33; and Coffman, *Old Army*, p. 42.

5. "Internal Improvement," *Missouri Daily Argus*, August 2, 1839.

6. Peskin, *Winfield Scott*, p. 70.

7. [Davis], *Jefferson Davis: A Memoir*, 1:102; and Shallat, *Structures in the Stream*, p. 172.

8. Ibid.

9. Prucha, *Broadax and Bayonet*, pp. 31, 56; and Peskin, *Winfield Scott*, p. 10.

10. Quotation in Coffman, *Old Army*, p. 67.

11. [Davis], *Jefferson Davis: A Memoir*, 1:64–66; and Philip St. George Cooke, *Scenes and Adventures in the Army; or, Romance of Military Life* (repr., New York: Arno Press, 1973), p. 33.

12. Lee also described a situation in which he and Johnston had to help a fellow officer out of his clothing, only to find that in his inebriation the chap had appropriated the commanding colonel's clothes to sleep in. Another recollection of junior officers' quarters in 1856 described them as "drenched with whiskey from morning till night." Freeman, *R. E. Lee*, 1:114; Skelton, *American Profession of Arms*, p. 188. REL to Captain A[ndrew] Talcott, Fort Monroe, November 22, 1833, REL-VHS; and REL to "My Glorious Jack," Washington, February 18, 1835, excerpted in catalog of Robert Black, List Number 53, Pilgrim 4–6607, copy in Special Collections, USMA.

13. General O. O. Howard, "The Character and Campaigns of General Lee," in Brock, ed., *Gen. Robert Edward Lee*, p. 350.

14. For more on the subject of manliness in the Jacksonian era and the military reinforcement of it, see Donald J. Mrozek, "The Habit of Victory: The American Military and the Cult of Manliness," in Mangan and Walvin, *Manliness and Morality*; and Kimmel, *Manhood in America*.

15. See, for example, Jack Mackay to "Dear Mother," Pecolata, April 2, 1836, and Franklin, N.C., November 10, 1837, Mackay-Stiles Papers, SHC-UNC.

16. I have chosen to quote Fitzhugh Lee's transcription of this letter from *General Lee*, pp. 84–85, since the original (REL to MCL, [?] Bay, February 4, 1849, DE-LC) is badly damaged and partially unreadable. Fitzhugh Lee has changed some of the original spelling and punctuation.

17. Jefferson Davis called Lee "a general favorite" among the officers, Davis, "Robert E. Lee," p. 56; statement of Joseph E. Johnston, in Long, *Memoirs*, p. 71; also James May to REL, Theological Seminary of Va., April 22, 1861, SH; Erasmus Keyes quoted in Keyes, *Fifty Years Observation*, p. 189.

18. Lee, *General Lee*, p. 28.

19. REL to John Mackay, Fort Monroe, June 26, 1834, Gilder-Lehrman Collection, NYHS; and REL to Jack Mackay, Fort Monroe, February 27, 1834, typescript, AHA.

20. Keyes, *Fifty Years Observation*, pp. 188–89; and e.g., REL to Jack Mackay, Eng[r] Dept., Wash., March 18, 1845, Lee Papers, GHS; and REL to Genl. Jos. G. Totten, West Point, February 15, 1854, REL Letterbook #2, LFP-VHS.

21. Beaumont had built up a flourishing private practice in St. Louis, something tolerated under Surgeon General Joseph Lowell. Lowell's successor tried to curb this

as well as his independent research, and Beaumont began to play a game of chicken with the army. When the Medical Corps tried to assign him to Florida, he threatened resignation, which, to his shock, was accepted. Beaumont's biographer believes Lee tried to help him, but the chain of correspondence does not bear this out. See Myer, *Life and Letters,* pp. 251–258; REL to William Beaumont, Washington, D.C., May 19, 1840, quoted pp. 260–61; for Hitchcock's response, see p. 256; Horsman, *Frontier Doctor,* p. 241; and Ethan Allen Hitchcock to Dr. DeCamp, draft letter, August 1840, Hitchcock Papers, LC. On the back of the letter, where he marked his correspondence for filing, Hitchcock had written, "The Doctor was in trouble and I helped him."

22. REL to Col. R. S. Roberts, West Point, May 31, 1853; and to Chas. M. Perry, West Point, June 4, 1853, both REL Letterbook #2, LFP-VHS.

23. Diary of Eliza Johnston, March 31, [1856], in Charles P. Roland and Richard C. Robbins, eds., "The Diary of Eliza Johnston," *Southwestern Historical Quarterly* 60, no. 4 (April 1957): 494.

24. REL to MCL, West Point, August 31, 1849; and to Jefferson Davis, Baltimore, February 2, 1850, REL Letterbook #1, both LFP-VHS; REL to Mary B. Ball, Arlington, November 16, 1859, Ball Family Papers, DU; and REL to GWCL, February 15, 1858, in Jones, *Life and Letters,* p. 89. Lee also tried to place his younger cousins in engineering positions on the Orange and Alexandria Railroad. See REL to Dr. William Powell, Baltimore, May 22, 1850, to Henry Dangerfield, Sollers Point, May 28, 1850, and to Mrs. Eliza C. Turner, Baltimore, July 18, 1850, all REL Letterbook #1, LFP-VHS.

25. REL to CCL, Albany, May 29 and 31, 1835, both REL-UVa. Lee also declined to intervene for a young cousin in a matter of the heart, though from the apparent outcome, he may have been wise in this. REL to Z. Collins Lee, St. Louis, January 12, 1839, REL Letterbook #1, LFP-VHS.

26. Lee's excuse was that he might be posted away from Virginia; he also proposed that Uncle Bernard would actually want him to decline the service. That conjectural statement is hard to defend, since Bernard Carter had specifically wished Lee to serve as executor because of the contention among his children. REL to CCL, Arlington, January 30, 1840, REL-UVa; REL to Charles H. Carter, Arlington, March 7 and April [n.d.], 1842, to Bernard F. Carter, Fort Hamilton, N.Y., January 11, 1843, and to CCL, Arlington, February 14, 1843, all REL Letterbook #1, LFP-VHS.

27. REL to John Mackay, Fort Monroe, February 27, 1834, typescript, AHA.

28. REL to John Mackay, Arlington, February 6, 1843, Gilder-Lehrman Collection, NYHS.

29. There are many examples of Lee's interest in the politics that affected army matters. A sampling: REL to Capt A[ndrew] Talcott, Washington, November 25, 1835, and n.d. [February 1836], both Talcott Papers, VHS; REL to Jack Mackay, St. Louis, August 8, 1838, and Fort Hamilton, N.Y., June 21, 1846, both Mackay-McQueen Papers, GHS; REL to John Mackay, Arlington, March 18, 1841, and February 6, 1843, both Gilder-Lehrman Collection, NYHS.

30. Eliza A. Stiles to "My dearest Mother," Washington, April 3 and 14, 1844, Mackay-Stiles Family Papers, SHC-UNC.

31. REL to "My dear son" [GWCL], San Antonio, Tex., February 28, 1860, REL-DU.

32. For discouragement of officers' participation in politics, see Skelton, *American Profession of Arms,* pp. 283–90; and Shallat, *Structures in the Stream, pp.* 154–55. For assumptions about Lee's political leanings, see Fellman, *Making of Robert E. Lee,* pp. 78–81; and Thomas, *Robert E. Lee,* pp. 79–80. For Lee's dislike of partisan politics,

see REL to Henry Kayser, Fort Hamilton, N.Y., May 19, 1844, REL-MoHS; and REL to Jack Mackay, St. Louis, August 8, 1838, Mackay-McQueen Papers, GHS. Quotation REL to "Delectable Jack," Fort Monroe, June 26, 1834, Gilder-Lehrman Collection, NYHS.

33. REL to Captain A[ndrew] Talcott, Fort Monroe, July 2, 1834, photocopy, REL-VHS.

34. R. W. Johnson, *A Soldier's Reminiscences in Peace and War* (Philadelphia: J. B. Lippincott, 1886), p. 87; Skelton, *American Profession of Arms,* pp. 193–200; Prucha, *Broadax and Bayonet,* p. 54; and Coffman, *Old Army,* pp. 57–58.

35. REL to "My dear Jack," Washington, June 22, 1836, excerpted in catalog of Robert Black, List Number 53, Pilgrim 4–6607, copy in Special Collections, USMA. In November of the same year the promotions were finally approved, and both Lee and Johnston were moved up to first lieutenant. See Cullum, *Biographical Register,* 1:419–47.

36. Lee and Mackay were among those who accepted the seniority system, perhaps because it seems more equitable than one that could be easily misused by favoritism. See John Mackay to Mother, Milledgeville, Ga., November 6, 1836, CD-GHS; and REL to GWCL, Fort Brown, April 16, 1860, in Jones, *Life and Letters,* p. 114.

37. Roger Jones quoted in Prucha, *Broadax and Bayonet,* p. 54.

38. Peskin, *Winfield Scott,* pp. 9, 71, 76–77; and Skelton, *American Profession of Arms,* pp. 193–98.

39. Cullum, *Biographical Register,* 1:419–47; William Skelton has studied promotions in the classes of 1831–33 and found that it took twelve to thirteen years for most West Pointers to reach the level of captain, and that the average age to achieve major was fifty. Skelton, *American Profession of Arms,* pp. 197–98. Johnston's career, which had the greatest parallel to Lee's, is also difficult to compare, for he left the service for a period in 1837 to work as a civil engineer and then returned to the army. Like Lee, however, he had long periods of stagnation and then quick double promotions. Because of his leave he was not made captain until the outbreak of the Mexican War, but during that conflict he was given a full promotion to lieutenant colonel. He also claimed one of the four new positions created in 1855, holding the same position as Lee but with the 1st Cavalry. He, along with Lee, was one of four men considered for quartermaster general in 1860; he got the position, which brought with it the rank of brigadier general. Symonds, *Johnston,* pp. 34–35, 75, 88–94; and REL to GWCL, Fort Brown, Texas, April 16, 1860, in Jones, *Life and Letters,* p. 114.

40. Coffman, *Old Army,* p. 50. Quotations REL to CCL, Arlington, October 12, 1830, and Fort Monroe, December 6, 1833, both REL-UVa.

41. REL to CCL, Arlington, January 30, 1840, and February 14, 1843, both REL-UVa.

42. For the propensity of young officers to cultivate political sponsors, see Skelton, *American Profession of Arms,* p. 193. Characteristically generous, Lee wrote: "Joe Johnston is playing Adjt. Genl in Florida to his hearts content. His plan is good, he is working for promotion. I hope he may succeed." REL to Jack Mackay, Arlington, February 6, 1843, Gilder-Lehrman Collection, NYHS.

43. For Lee's colorful descriptions of Babcock, see REL to Mary Anna Randolph Custis, Cock-Spur Island, November 11, 1830, and January 10, 1831, both in deButts, "Yours Forever."

44. Quotation REL to CCL, St. Louis, December 24, 1838, REL-UVa; REL to Major R. Delafield, St. Louis, April 14, 1839, and to Mrs. Anne Gratiot, St. Louis, April 19, 1839, both REL Letterbook #1, LFP-VHS; Freeman, *R. E. Lee,* 1:289–292. For Winfield Scott's personality, see Peskin, *Winfield Scott,* pp. 70–78; also Thomas, "Young Man Lee."

45. REL to Joseph G. Totten, June 17, 1845, LFP-VHS; and REL to Capt. Fred Smith, Corps of Engineers, Baltimore, December 13, 1851, Benjamin Long Papers, LC.

46. REL to MCL, March 25, 1832, DE-LC; MCL to MFC, Fort Hamilton, October 26, 1842, MCL-VHS; REL to MCL, Camp Cooper, Texas, September 1, 1856, in Lee, *General Lee,* p. 61; quotation REL to MCL, Fort Brown, Texas, December 13, 1856, DE-LC.

47. Symonds, *Johnston,* pp. 88–92; REL to MCL, Fort Brown, Texas, December 13, 1856, DE-LC; Petition to the President, March 1856, DSF-LC; quotation REL to GWCL, Fort Brown, April 16, 1860, in Jones, *Life and Letters,* p. 114.

48. REL to MCL, San Antonio, Texas, July 27, 1857, DE-LC.

49. Symonds, *Johnston,* pp. 34–35; and Cullum, *Biographical Register,* 1:419–47.

50. REL to CCL, Fort Monroe, June 30, 1834, REL-UVa.

51. REL to Capt. A. Talcott, Washington, February 2, 1837, Talcott Papers, VHS.

52. William Brumley to GWPC, White House, June 4, 1833, MCL-VHS.

53. Eleanor Parke Custis Lewis to MFC, December 19, 1847, MCL-VHS, also see MFC to MCL, Arlington, October 8, 1831, Custis Family Papers, VHS; MCL and REL to MFC, n.d. [March 24, 1838?], DE-LC; MFC to "My dear Grandson" [GWCL], December 5, 1851, E. C. Turner to "My dearest Mary" [MCL], n.d. [1853], and MCL to REL, Arlington, May 22 [1857], all DE-LC.

54. S. S. Lee to "My dear Sister" [MCL], Navy Yard, Philadelphia, February 10, 1857, Fitzhugh Lee Papers, UVa.

55. REL to Capt. Ephraim Kirby Smithy, 1845, quoted in Coffman, *Old Army,* p. 62.

56. REL to CCL, City of Mexico, March 18, 1848, REL-UVa.

57. REL to Mrs. W. H. Stiles, Camp Cooper, Texas, August 14, 1856, UTA.

58. Quotation REL to CCL, City of Mexico, March 18, 1848, REL-UVa; also REL to MCL, San Antonio, Texas, August 12, 1857, DE-LC; and REL to Mrs. H. Hackley, St. Louis, August 7, 1838, Talcott Papers, VHS.

59. REL to Anna Maria Fitzhugh, San Antonio, Texas, June 6, 1860, Fitzhugh Lee Papers, UVa.

60. REL to Mary Anna Randolph Custis, CockSpur Island, December 1, 1830, in deButts, "Yours Forever." REL to E. A. Mackay, Cockspur, "Wednesday 13th" [1830?], CD-GHS; REL, Plan of Cockspur Island, 1830, RG 77, NARA; and Freeman, *R. E. Lee,* 1:96.

61. REL to Capt. A[ndrew] Talcott, Old Point, November 3, 1832, December 15, 1833, and April 7, 1834, all REL-VHS.

62. REL Letterbook #2, May–November 1842, LFP-VHS.

63. Many of Lee's engineering plans are in RG 77, NARA. REL to Gen. Joseph G. Totten, Baltimore, May 21, 1849; and Fort Carroll, August 21, 1852, both REL Letterbook #1, LFP-VHS. For the difficulties of nineteenth-century engineering, see David F. Noble, *America by Design: Science, Technology and the Rise of Corporate Capitalism* (New York: Alfred A. Knopf, 1977), p. 35; and Elting E. Morison, *From Know-How to Nowhere: The Development of American Technology* (New York: Basic Books, 1974), pp. 88–89. Among the equipment failures Lee endured was a piledriver that bounced off the wooden piles with such a force that it tore out the spikes binding

them together. For an example of Lee's continued frustration over lack of appropriations, see REL to Major John Saunders, Baltimore, April 13, 1852, USMA.

64. REL to "My dearest Son" [GWCL], Baltimore, May 4, 1851, in Jones, *Life and Letters*, p. 74.

65. REL to Henry Kayser, Arlington, February 1, 1838, in "Letters of Robert E. Lee to Henry Kayser," p. 6; REL to "Gentlemen," St. Louis, January 12, 1839, HL; and Zimmer, ed., *Housekeeping Book*, pp. 44–45.

66. REL to MCL, West Point, August 31, 1849, DE-LC.

67. For Lee's self-description as an "indifferent engineer," see Nagel, *Lees of Virginia*, p. 235; REL to Jack Mackay, Fort Monroe, February 27, 1834, typescript, AHA; REL to John Mackay, Eng. Dept, Washington, March 18, 1845, REL-GHS; and quotation REL to MCW, Baltimore, May 10, 1851, in Lee, *"To Markie,"* p. 26.

68. Shallat, *Structures in the Stream*, pp. 102–9; John G. Fredriksen, "Montgomery Cunningham Meigs," *ANB*, 15:256–57; and Miller, *Second Only to Grant*, pp. 18–54.

69. Morison, *From Know-How to Nowhere*, p. 91–93; and Noble, *America by Design*, p. 24–28, 33; see also Edwin T. Layton, "Science as a Form of Action: The Role of Engineering Science," *Technology and Culture* 29, no. 1 (January 1988):82–97.

70. In fact the class prior to Lee's had selected no one for the Engineer Corps, and a member of the Board of Visitors that year noted that a cadet who could immediately go into the corps "must be a man of superior talents." James W. Burbridge to W. G. Hawkins, West Point, March 18, 1828, typescript Sylvanus Thayer Papers, USMA.

71. The number of army engineers did not grow appreciably until the Civil War. After the passage of the new army bill in 1838, the figure rose to 43, and in 1860 there were 48. Skelton, *American Profession of Arms*, p. 222; Miller, *Second Only to Grant*, p. 12; Noble, *America by Design*, pp. 170–76. Virginia geologist William Barton Rogers was quoted as saying that life for scientists in his region was "as dull as a mill-pond in a deep hollow where no breeze can touch it." Ronald L. Numbers and Janet S. Numbers, "Science in the Old South: A Reappraisal," *Journal of Southern History* 48, no. 2 (May 1982), p. 176.

72. REL to Major R. Delafield, H. Brewerton, Captain Mansfield, Captain A. H. Bowman, Captain [George] Cullum, Captain William D. Frazer, and to Lt. M. C. Meigs, all Fort Hamilton, December 27, 1841, in REL Letterbook #1, LFP-VHS.

73. Robert Knox Sneden, who was part of the occupying force at Arlington in 1862, wrote on September 14 that he "spent most of the day in looking over the books in General Lee's Library. . . . Many valuable works on Military Engineering and Fortification were here, also which I eagerly studied for hours." Sneden Diary; also REL to Geo. W. S. Fly, Lexington, Va., November 23, 1866, UTA.

74. Davis, "Robert E. Lee," p. 56.

75. There has been an intense scholarly debate about what constituted a "middle class" in the early nineteenth century—if indeed one existed at all. This author found particularly helpful K. G. Davies, "The Mess of the Middle Class," *Past and Present*, no. 22 (July 1962): 77–83; and Stuart Blumin, "The Hypothesis of Middle-Class Formation in Nineteenth-Century America: A Critique and Some Proposals," *American Historical Review* 90, no. 2 (April 1985): 299–338. For those wanting to explore more of the give and take, see Burton J. Bledstein, *The Culture of Professionalism* (New York: W. W. Norton, 1976); Karen Halttunen, *Confidence Men and Painted Women: A*

Study of Middle Class Culture in America, 1830–1870 (New Haven, Conn.: Yale University Press, 1986); Edward Pessen, "The Egalitarian Myth and the American Social Reality: Wealth, Mobility and Equality in the 'Era of the Common Man,'" *American Historical Review* 76, no. 4 (October 1971): 989–1034; Edward Pessen, "Social Mobility in American History: Some Brief Reflections," *Journal of Southern History* 45, no. 2 (May 1979): 165–84; and John William Ward, "Jacksonian Democratic Thought: 'A Natural Charter of Privilege,'" in Stanley Coben and Lorman Ratner, eds., *The Development of an American Culture* (Englewood Cliffs, N.J.: Prentice-Hall, 1970).

76. J. B. Hood, *Advance and Retreat: Personal Experiences in the United States and Confederate States Armies* (repr., New York: Da Capo Press, 1993), p. 8.

77. REL to John Livingston, U.S. Military Academy, West Point, N.Y., October 20, 1854, in Major Charles R. Bowery Jr. and Major Brian D. Hankinson, eds., *The Daily Correspondence of Brevet Colonel Robert E. Lee, Superintendent, United States Military Academy, September 1, 1852 to March 24, 1855,* U.S. Military Academy Library Occasional Papers #5 (West Point, N.Y.: USMA Press, 2003), p. 231.

78. Lee, *General Lee,* p. 21.

79. Skelton, *American Profession of Arms,* pp. 190–92; also Edward Pessen, "The Egalitarian Myth," pp. 989–1034; Sean Wilentz, *Chants Democratic* (New York: Oxford University Press, 1984), pp. 14–16; Donald R. Adams Jr., "Wage Rates in the Early National Period: Philadelphia, 1785–1830," *Journal of Economic History* 28, no. 3 (September 1968): 404–26.

80. See REL to CCL, Fort Hamilton, N.Y., August 17, 1843, and July 13, 1846, both in REL-UVa; and REL to ?, August 22, 1860, in Jones, *Life and Letters,* p. 113.

81. For more on the pervasiveness of the new enterprising attitudes, particularly among the yeomen of the South, see Carl R. Osthaus, "The Work Ethic of the Plain Folk: Labor and Religion in the Old South," *Journal of Southern History* 70, no. 4 (November 2004): 745–83.

82. REL to MCL, December 5, 1856, DE-LC.

83. Katherine C. Grier, *Culture and Comfort: Parlor-Making and Middle Class Identity, 1850–1930* (Washington, D.C.: Smithsonian Institution Press, 1997); introduction and pp. 1–17; and Nelligan, "Old Arlington," pp. 379–81.

84. Halttunen, *Confidence Men and Painted Women,* contains an extensive discussion of deportment manuals and middle-class values of sincerity, politesse, and conformance.

85. Indentures of William and Beulah Craig and CCL and Bernard F. Carter, 1839 and 1840, CCL-LoV; and Robert E. Lee Will, 1846, copy in CL-LC.

CHAPTER TWELVE: **Black-Eyed Fancies**

1. Note at end of letter from REL to Eliza Mackay, Cockspur, [April] 13, 1831, typescript, Mackay-Stiles Papers, UNC. Eliza and Catherine were sisters of Lee's great West Point friend, Jack Mackay.

2. REL to Julia Gratiot, Fort Hamilton, N.Y., November 27, 1845, LFP-WL. Julia Ann Gratiot, whom Lee had known from girlhood, was the daughter of Chief Engineer Charles Gratiot. She married Charles Pierre Chouteau on November 7, 1845.

3. REL to Mrs. Julia G[ratiot] Chouteau, Lexington, Va., March 21, 1866, SH.

4. Emily Mason in Long, *Memoirs,* p. 30, Joseph E. Johnston quoted p. 71; Marietta Turner Powell to "My dear Nannie," Oakley, July 17, 1886, quoted in Andrews, *Scraps of Paper,* p. 203.

5. There are numerous copies of this portrait, but the beauty of the original is so great that it is worth a journey to see it in the museum at Washington and Lee University, in Lexington, Virginia. The exceptional quality of the picture was recognized at the time it was painted. "Your pictures, my dear Children are the principal ornaments of our parlour," G. W. P. Custis wrote in 1838. "Robert's is one of the best ever painted, of anyone. . . ." GWPC to "My Dearest Children," Arlington House, August 14, 1838, CL-TPA.

6. Howard, "Character and Campaigns of General Lee," p. 351.

7. Lt. Isaac Ingalls Stevens to "My Dearest Wife, August 22, 1847, in McWhiney and McWhiney, *To Mexico with Taylor and Scott*, p. 196.

8. Humphrey's Autobiography, Milton Wylie Humphreys Papers, UVa.

9. A northern newspaperman, describing Lee at Appomattox, wrote, "He is growing quite bald, and wears the side locks of his hair thrown across the upper portion of his forehead," and a southern neighbor called this description "entirely accurate." [Sallie A. Brock], *Richmond during the War: Four Years of Personal Observation by a Richmond Lady* (New York: G. W. Carleton, 1867), pp. 376–77. The side sweep and regressing forehead also show in pictures from the 1840s.

10. For Lee's interest in clothes, see REL to Saml Frost, Arlington, January 18, 1840, in REL Letterbook #1, LFP-VHS.

11. The picture can be seen in chapter 25, "Blurred Vision." From 1869 on Lee seems to have worn the four-in-hand tie, though it would not come into general fashion for several more years. See also pictures of him with General Joseph Johnston, and in a portrait by Frank Buchser in David J. Eicher, *Robert E. Lee: A Life Portrait* (Dallas, Tenn.: Taylor, 1997), p. 168.

12. John Mackay to "My dear Mother," October 4, 1830, typescript, Mackay-McQueen Papers, GHS.

13. CCL to Henry Lee IV, New York, April 19, 1831, CCL-UVa; and Ann H. Lee to Smith Lee, Georgetown, March 24, 1829 in Freeman, *R. E. Lee*, 1:90–91.

14. Chesnut, *Diary*, pp. 115–16, 226.

15. REL to MCL, Harper's Ferry, December 1, 1859, and to MCL, Richmond, May 16, 1861, both DE-LC. Mary Boykin Chesnut was among those who favored Smith, as she confided to her diary on more than one occasion. When she heard an officer telling Smith, "Don't be so conceited about your looks, Mrs. Chesnut thinks your brother Robert a handsomer man than you" she did not contradict him, but later wrote, "It was false. . . . I like Smith Lee better, and I like his looks too." Chesnut, *Diary*, pp. 115–16.

16. Long, *Memoirs*, p. 71; quotation "The Southern Confederacy," *London Times*, December 30, 1862.

17. Hugh Mercer to "My Dear Wife," Savannah, March 20, 1849, Mercer Family Papers, GHS.

18. Lomax, *Leaves from an Old Washington Diary*, p. 29.

19. REL to John Mackay, St. Louis, October 22, 1837, CD-GHS.

20. REL to John Mackay, Fort Monroe, November 8, 1833, typescript, CD-GHS.

21. For the speculation see Sanborn, *Portrait*, pp. 72–73; and Frank B. Screven, "The Letters of R. E. Lee to the Mackay Family of Savannah," unpublished typescript, 1952, at Armstrong State College Library, Savannah, Georgia; for lingering affection see REL to Mrs. [Eliza] Stiles, Camp on the Clear Fork of the Brazos Indian Territory, May 24, 1856, SH.

22. REL to Mary Anna Randolph Custis, Cockspur, April 20, 1831, in deButts, "Yours Forever."

23. REL to John Mackay, Fort Monroe, November 8, 1833, typescript, CD-GHS.

24. Ibid.; and REL to John Mackay, National Palace, City of Mexico, October 2, 1847, USAMHI.

25. REL to "My dear Mr. Caskie," Near Cartersville August 30, 1865, LFP-WL; and REL to Capt NG Evans, Fort Brown, December 15, 1856, REL-VHS.

26. REL to Mary Anna Randolph Custis, Cockspur, April 11, 1831, in deButts, "Yours Forever." See also REL to Mary Anna Randolph Custis, CockSpur Island, December 1, 1830, ibid.; and REL to Annie C. Lee, Savannah, March 1862, DE-LC. Robert E. L. deButts believes Lee's interest in plumpness had to do with a fear of illness and the association of slenderness with tuberculosis which had plagued his friends and family. Lee does not ever make this connection directly himself, however. The attraction might also stem from his mother, for her one remaining dress indicates a medium-sized build. Lee could also simply be expressing the prevalent Victorian fashion, which favored plump women. See Freeman, *R.E. Lee*, 1:91n.

27. REL to "My dear Mr. Caskie," Near Cartersville, August 30, 1865, LFP-WL.

28. REL to "My beautiful Tasy" [Sarah Beaumont], Fort Hamilton, N.Y., March 11, 1843, photostat in EA-LC.

29. REL to "My beautiful Talcott," February 21, 1833, quoted in Douglas [Southall] Freeman, "Lee and the Ladies," *Scribner's Magazine* 78, nos. 4 and 5 (October and November, 1925):345.

30. Eliza Mackay Stiles to "dear Kate," Baltimore, February 22, 1851, Mackay-Stiles Papers, SHC-UNC.

31. REL to A. Talcott, February 10, 1835, Talcott Papers, VHS.

32. MCL to Mrs. A. Talcott, St. Louis, January 1, 1839, Talcott Papers, VHS.

33. MCL to Sarah Beaumont, n.d. [c. 1840], BLC.

34. REL to Captain Andrew Talcott, Ravensworth, July 13, 1831, LFP-VHS.

35. Wyatt-Brown, *Southern Honor*, pp. 226–53, Steven M. Stowe, *Intimacy and Power in the Old South* (Baltimore: Johns Hopkins University Press, 1987), p. 50–65; Buza, "'Pledges of Our Love,'" pp. 9–10.

36. REL to "My beautiful Tasy" [Sarah Beaumont], Fort Hamilton, N.Y., March 11, 1843, photostat, EA-LC.

37. REL to Misses Mason, St. Louis, August 31, 1840, in REL Letterbook #1, LFP-VHS.

38. REL to Carrie Stuart, Camp Rapidan, November 21, 1863, quoted in Freeman, "Lee and the Ladies," p. 465.

39. REL to "My dear Miss Caroline," Philadelphia, November 20, 1851, LFP-WL.

40. REL to Eliza Mackay Stiles, Saturday night, [1831], typescript, McQueen-Mackay Papers, GHS.

41. REL to Eliza Mackay Stiles, Arlington, January 4, 1832, typescript in Mackay-McQueen Papers, GHS. Lee makes similar comments about being tempted to night-time sins in his correspondence with his fiancée Mary Anna Randolph Custis. See deButts, "Yours Forever."

42. REL to MCL, Old Point, April 24, 1832, DE-LC.

43. REL to MCL, Camp Cooper, Texas, May 25, 1857; and REL to MCL, Camp near Monclova, November 18 and November 20, 1846, all DE-LC.

44. REL to MCL, San Antonio, September 25, 1846, "Camp near Alamos river Mexico," October 19, 1846; quotations "Camp near Monclova, Mexico," November 4, 1846, and San Antonio, Texas, August 22, 1857, all DE-LC.

45. MCL to Caroline [Peters], n.d. [c. 1850–51], LFP-WL.

46. MCL to Mary Jones, n.d. [early November 1870], copy in MCW's hand, DE-LC.

47. Coffman, *Old Army,* pp. 105–110; Skelton, *American Profession of Arms,* pp. 188–190.

48. See for example, REL to Jack Mackay, Fort Monroe, May 3, 1833, ML; REL to Captain N. G. Evans, San Antonio, August 28, 1857, REL-VHS; and REL to CCL, January 4, 1831, CCL-UVa.

49. REL to Henry Kayser, Fort Hamilton, N.Y., June 16, 1845, in "Letters of Robert E. Lee to Henry Kayser," p. 38.

50. Peskin, *Winfield Scott,* p. 89.

51. See for example REL to WHFL, West Point, June 12, 1853, USMA; and REL to GWCL, January 12, 1852, copy in GWCL's hand, LFP-VHS.

52. See Bruce Haley, *The Healthy Body and Victorian Culture* (Cambridge, Mass.: Harvard University Press, 1978); Mangan and Walvin, eds., *Manliness and Morality,* pp. 38–40.

53. REL to MCL, St. Louis, August 5, 1837, to the Misses Mason, St. Louis, August 31, 1840, REL Letterbook #1; and to EAL, Near Fred[g], April 11, 1863, DE-LC.

54. REL to GWCL, January 12, 1852, copy in handwriting of GWCL, LFP-VHS.

55. REL to John Mackay, Fort Hamilton N.Y., January 30, 1846, Gilder-Lehrman Collection, NYHS.

56. REL to MCL, San Antonio, September 25, 1846, DE-LC.

57. REL to MCL, San Antonio, Texas, August 22, 1857, DE-LC.

58. REL to MCW, Fort Hamilton, N.Y., September 2, 1844, and September 17, 1845, both in Lee, "*To Markie,*" pp. 4, 13. For Markie's romantically sweet personality, see her diaries, 1844–58, AHA; and ACL to Helen Bratt, Arlington, May 3, 1855, LFP-WL.

59. REL to MCW, Baltimore, May 10, 1851; and REL to MCW, West Point, May 26, 1854, both in Lee, "*To Markie,*" pp. 26, 45–46; quotation REL to MCW, West Point February 28, 1854, SH.

60. MCW Diary, March 1, 4, 17, 1854, AHA.

61. MCW Diary, April 8, 1854, AHA.

62. MCW Diary, April 10, 1854, AHA.

63. Interview with Ada Thompson and Annie Baker, c. 1920, AHA.

64. See for example, REL to MCW, Fort Hamilton, N.Y., September 17, 1845; West Point, January 2, 1854; and Lexington, Va., April 14, 1868, all in Lee, "*To Markie,*" pp. 13–15, 38–39, and 80–81.

65. REL to MCW, Lexington, November 5, 1866, and February 5, 1869, ML.

66. REL to MCW, "Camp on Washington's Run," October 2, 1862, REL-VHS. Markie Williams did not marry until after Robert E. Lee's death.

67. Eliza A. Stiles to "My dearest Mother," Washington, April 3, 1844; and to "My dear Kate," Washington, February 25, [1845], both Mackay-Stiles Papers, SHC-UNC.

68. "Recollections of West Point in 1853, by an Officer's Wife," *Bulletin of the Association of Graduates of the United States Military Academy,* no. 3 (1903): 39.

69. MiCL, "Recollections," July 20, 1890 in ALJ, DE-LC.

70. Freeman, "Lee and the Ladies," p. 469; Charles DeKuy, "Captain Theophile

Marie D'Orenieulux," *Bulletin of the Association of Graduates of the United States Military Academy,* no. 3 (1903): 44; REL to MCW, Fort Hamilton, N.Y., December 14, 1844, and May 26, 1845, and Fort Mason, Texas, January 22, 1861, in Lee, *"To Markie,"* pp. 6–7, 10–11, and 59–60; and REL to MCL, Sollers Point, June 13, 1849, DE-LC. For interference in the affairs of others, see REL to W. H. Hoffman, July 3, 1852, DSF-LC; Elizabeth Blair Lee to Samuel Phillips Lee, Washington, January 16, 1865, in Elizabeth Blair Lee, *Wartime Washington: The Civil War Letters of Elizabeth Blair Lee,* ed. Virginia Jean Laas (Urbana: University of Illinois Press, 1991), pp. 463–64; and REL to MCL, Orange Co., April 21, 1864, DE-LC.

71. REL to Charlotte J. Wickham, San Antonio, Texas, October 10, 1857, REL Letterbook #1, LFP-VHS.

72. Lee, "Character of General Lee," p. 381.

73. Harrison, *Recollections Grave and Gay,* p. 127.

74. The phrase "Ithuriel spear" comes from Milton's *Paradise Lost,* in which the angel Ithruiel learns the truth of the devil's character by touching him with his spear. Christiana Bond, *Memories of General Robert E. Lee* (Baltimore: Norman, Remington, 1926), pp. 25–27, quotation p. 25. In typical postwar fashion Bond believed that Lee convened the group of young ladies out of kindness, to give them a good time. Though Lee's discouragement of potential suitors puts this in question, there is no reason the two motives could not have existed simultaneously.

75. EAL to Helen Bratt, n.d. [c. 1855]; and ACL to Helen Bratt, Staunton, Novem[ber 1857], typescript, both LFP-WL.

76. REL to "Sweet Meta & Carrie," Camp, September 11, 1863, quoted in Freeman, "Lee and the Ladies," p. 465.

77. REL to EAL, Lexington, Va., November 16, 1865; to MCL, Lexington, November 21, 1865; and to EAL, Lexington, Va., December 5, 1865, all DE-LC.

78. REL to WHFL, Lexington, Va., November 15, 1867, GBL-VHS. Other examples of overt matchmaking for his sons are in REL to Col. Chas S. Venable, Lexington, Va., March 8, 1866, Minor-Venable Papers, UVa; and REL to REL Jr., August 1867, quoted in Nagel, *Lees of Virginia,* p. 290.

79. Zimmer, ed., *Housekeeping Book,* p. 51; Mittie Williams quoted in George C. Rable, *Civil Wars: Women and the Crisis of Southern Nationalism* (Urbana: University of Illinois Press, 1989), p. 51; MCL to "My dear Letty," Warm Springs, July 19, 1868, CL-LC.

80. See Coulling, *Lee Girls,* pp. 164–67.

81. MCL quoted in ibid., p. 168.

82. MiCL to Lucy Bain, August 14, 1865, LFP-WL.

83. Blount, *Robert E. Lee,* pp. 172–74, 178; and Fellman, *Making of Robert E. Lee,* pp. 114–15.

84. Thomas, "Young Man Lee," p. 50.

85. Chesnut, *Diary,* p. 690.

86. Chesnut, *Diary,* February 16, 1864, p. 569; and Keyes, *Fifty Years Observation,* p. 205. For insecure male sexuality and aggression, verbal or otherwise, see Michael S. Kimmel, *The Gender of Desire: Essays on Male Sexuality* (Albany: State University of New York Press, 2005), pp. 39–40.

87. Jefferson Davis evidently had the same predilection for the company of children and women, and one of his biographers has surmised similar motives. Davis, *Davis: The Man and His Hour,* p. 219.

88. For more on the subject of masculinity in the nineteenth century, see Stowe,

Intimacy and Power in the Old South; Mangan and Walvin, eds., *Manliness and Morality;* and Lewis, *Pursuit of Happiness.*

89. Mary Custis deButts quoted in Zimmer, ed., *Housekeeping Book,* pp. 25–26.

90. Pryor, *Reminiscences of Peace and War,* p. 336.

CHAPTER THIRTEEN: **The Headache Bag**

1. REL to MFC, Baltimore, June 22, 1850, TPA. Robert Wood entered West Point with Custis Lee, but did not graduate. Jerome Bonaparte, the great-nephew of Emperor Napoleon, was a friend from Baltimore. He graduated eleventh in the class of 1852, later resigning to join the French army, fighting with distinction in the Crimean War. Laurence Williams, also in the class of 1852, was the brother of Markie Williams, and a cousin of Mary Custis Lee. John Shaff was a neighbor in Washington, D.C., who would graduate at the bottom of the class of 1851, as would Roger Jones, another Lee cousin. Cullum, *Biographical Register,* vol. 2. Mr. Lloyd is probably John Lloyd of Alexandria, Lee's cousin. "Mrs. B." is Mrs. Bonaparte, the mother of Jerome, and close friend of both the Lees and the Harrison family mentioned in the letter. "Sollers" refers to Soller's Point, where Lee was in charge of the construction of Fort Carroll. "The bath" was the Lees' first indoor bathroom—deliciously enjoyed by the whole family. "Cymblins," a variant of "cimlin" or "cymling," was the Virginia word for pattypan squash.

2. REL to Fred A. Smith, St. Louis, August 12, 1839, REL Letterbook #1, LFP-VHS.

3. REL to GWCL, Baltimore, April 13, 1851, DE-LC.

4. Report of the Board of Visitors to the U.S. Military Academy, West Point, June 1844, USMA; and Keyes, *Fifty Years Observation,* p. 188.

5. REL to Genl. Joseph G. Totten, Fort Carroll, May 28, 1852, and July 1, 1852, both REL Letterbook #2; and REL to Genl. Joseph G. Totten, Baltimore, July 25, 1852, Letterbook #1, all LFP-VHS.

6. REL to "My dearest Beaur^y," Baltimore, June 25, 1852, in "A Robert E. Lee Letter to P. G. T. Beauregard," *Maryland Historical Magazine* 51, no. 3 (September 1956): 249–51.

7. Ticknor, "West Point in 1826," p. 11.

8. Edward L. Hartz to father, Military Academy, West Point, N.Y., December 1, 1854, Hartz Papers, LC; Hunt, "West Point and Cadet Life," p. 197.

9. Strong, *Cadet Life,* pp. 302–3.

10. Pappas, *To the Point,* pp. 306–7; Freeman, *R. E. Lee,* 1:319–20; Ruben Ross Diary, September 1, 1852, USMA; and Edward L. Hartz to Father, Military Academy, West Point, November 18, 1852, Hartz Papers, LC.

11. Andrew Jackson quoted in Janowitz, *Professional Soldier,* p. 128; and Agnew, *Eggnog Riot,* p. 65.

12. The stable is pictured in Pappas, *To the Point,* centerpiece; for a list of architectural manuals borrowed by Lee from the West Point library in these years, see Freeman, *R. E. Lee,* 1:356–57; also Preston, *West Point and Lexington,* p. 40. REL to Genl. Joseph G. Totten, U.S. Military Academy, West Point, October 9, 1852, October 8, 1853, and October 7, 1854, all in Bowery and Hankinson, eds., *Daily Correspondence,* pp. 128–29, 225–26.

13. J. E. B. Stuart to Alexander Stuart Brown, West Point, March 27, 1854, J. E. B. Stuart Papers, VHS.

14. Preston, *West Point and Lexington,* p. 42; and Report of Board of Visitors, June 1853 and June 1854, USMA.

15. Quotation of the West Point surgeon in Preston, *West Point and Lexington,* p. 31; REL to Genl: Jos G. Totten, West Point, March 15, 1853, in Bowery and Hankinson, eds., *Daily Correspondence,* pp. 67–68.

16. "January Examinations," West Point, April 30, [c. 1853], copy in MCL(d) Scrapbook, LFP-VHS.

17. Preston, *West Point and Lexington,* pp. 43–46; Pappas, *To the Point,* pp. 307–8; and Report of Board of Visitors, June 1853 and June 1854, USMA.

18. Sylvanus Thayer to James Monroe, Military Academy, West Point, November 23, 1826, typescript, Thayer Papers, USMA.

19. General Joseph Wheeler quoted in Fleming, *Young Whistler,* p. 93.

20. Edward Hartz to father, Military Academy, West Point, N.Y., November 3, 1854, Hartz Papers, LC.

21. For parties at the Lee residence see ALJ, February 9, 1854, DE-LC; Howard, *Autobiography,* 1:54; and Edward L. Hartz to "Jenny," Military Academy, West Point, N.Y., March 25, 1853, Hartz Papers, LC.

22. REL to Genl Jos. G. Totten, West Point, January 29, 1853; and REL to Honble. H. B. Wright, U.S. Military Academy, West Point, January 11, 1855, both in Bowery and Hankinson, eds., *Daily Correspondence,* pp. 48, 264–65; and Preston, *West Point and Lexington,* pp. 22–29.

23. William Whitman Bailey, "General Robert E. Lee at West Point," n.d., USMA; "Recollections of West Point in 1853 by an Officer's Wife," *Bulletin of the Association of Graduates of the U.S. Military Academy,* 1903; Lomax, *Leaves from an Old Washington Diary,* p. 29; and quotation Hunt, "West Point and Cadet Life," p. 203.

24. REL to J. N. Bonaparte, West Point, November 4, 1854, photostat, LFP-WL; REL to Gen. J. G. Totten, U.S. Military Academy, December 19, 1853, and July 24, 1854, in Bowery and Hankinson, eds., *Daily Correspondence,* pp. 157, 216; Freeman, *R. E. Lee,* 1:324–25, 332–33; Ross Diary, June 7, 1850, USMA; Fitzhugh Lee to "My dear godmother" [Anna Maria Fitzhugh], West Point, April 1, 1855, Fitzhugh Lee Papers, UVa.

25. Ross Diary, August 21, 1852, USMA.

26. GW Cushing to father, West Point, December 29, 1854 and January 3, 1854 [*sic* 1855], both Cushing Files, USMA. The documentary record stands in contrast to the traditional belief that "discipline was at a high level during his superintendency." See, for example, Dowdey, *Lee,* p. 102.

27. Preston, *West Point and Lexington,* p. 32.

28. Ross Diary, September 3, 1852, USMA.

29. Pappas, *To the Point,* p. 297; and Edward L. Hartz to "Jenny," Military Academy, West Point, N.Y., February 17, 1853, Hartz Papers, LC.

30. Edward L. Hartz to Father, Military Academy, West Point, N.Y., November 18, 1852, Hartz Papers, LC.

31. Thomas, *Robert E. Lee,* p. 154.

32. REL to Genl Joseph G. Totten, April 7, 1854, in Bowery and Hankison, eds., *Daily Correspondence,* pp. 175–76.

33. Hunt, "West Point and Cadet Life," p. 196.

34. Edward L. Hartz to Father, Military Academy, West Point, N.Y., November 13, 1854, Hartz Papers, LC.

35. REL to Genl Joseph G. Totten, April 7, 1854, in Bowery and Hankinson, eds., *Daily Correspondence,* pp. 175–76; and REL to Genl J. G. Tottten, January 29, 1855, REL Letterbook #2, LFP-VHS. Douglas Southall Freeman, in a lecture about Lee and

leadership, quotes him as saying, "I have always regarded the cadets at West Point not as soldiers in the ranks but as individual gentlemen whose wishes and dislikes should be respected as far as is compatible with discipline," but gives no citation. If indeed Lee ever said this, it is a case similar to others in which his concrete actions were slightly at odds with his professed theories. *Douglas Southall Freeman on Leadership*, ed. Stuart W. Smith (Shippensburg, Pa.: White Mane, 1993), p. 114.

36. Edward L. Hartz to "Jenny," Military Academy, West Point, N.Y., February 17, 1853, Hartz Papers, LC.

37. Preston, *West Point and Lexington*, p. 29.

38. ACL to Helen Bratt, [West Point], February 22, 1855, LFP-WL.

39. Lomax, *Leaves from an Old Washington Diary*, p. 29.

40. Edward L. Hartz to "Jenny," Military Academy, West Point, N.Y., March 25, 1853, Hartz Papers, LC.

41. Wheeler Journal, June 1, 1854, John Hill Wheeler Papers, LC.

42. Edward L. Hartz to "Jenny," Military Academy, West Point, N.Y., February 17, 1853, Hartz Papers, LC; and G. M. Cushing to "My dear Folks," West Point, November 5, 1854, Cushing, Files, USMA.

43. G. W. Cushing to "dear Mother," W.P., July 16, 1854, Cushing, Files, USMA.

44. Lee allowed young Clay to resign rather than be dismissed for deficient conduct "in consideration of the name of his Gnd father. . . ." REL to Jos. G. Totten, U.S. Military Academy, West Point, January 20, 1853, in Bowery and Hankinson, eds., *Daily Correspondence*, p. 42.

45. Stanley Weintraub, *Whistler: A Biography* (New York: Weybright and Talley, 1974), p. 17–19.

46. Ibid., p. 22.

47. Fleming, *The Young Whistler*, pp. 95–97; and REL to Anna M. Whistler, U.S. Military Academy, West Point, N.Y., September 28, 1852, May 26, 1853, and August 31, 1853, all in Bowery and Hankinson, eds., *Daily Correspondence*, pp. 9, 92, and 117.

48. This is but a small part of Whistler's colorful demerit sheet; for additional deletions see Fleming, *Young Whistler*, pp. 84, 87.

49. Weintraub, *Whistler*, p. 19.

50. REL to Genl. J.G. Totten, U.S. Military Academy, West Point, July 18, 1854, in Bowery and Hankinson, eds., *Daily Correspondence*, pp. 203–4.

51. Whistler quoted in Weintraub, *Whistler*, p. 24; also Fleming, *Young Whistler*, pp. 103–5.

52. Whistler quoted in Weintraub, *Whistler*, pp. 23–24. Seeing a story about Whistler's successful exhibition in 1860, Lee wrote, in classic form, to his wife: "I also send you a newspaper slip which will give you some information of little Jimmy Whistler. I wish indeed he may succeed in his career. He certainly has talent, if he could acquire application." REL to MCL, San Antonio, Texas, July 15, 1860, DE-LC. Whistler evidently retained an affection for West Point's pomp and ceremony throughout his life and often spoke of it in affectionate terms. Twenty-five years after his dismissal, he sent a copy of a book of his illustrations to the academy library, inscribed, "From an old cadet whose pride it is to remember his West Point days." Fleming, *Young Whistler*, p. 108.

53. The textbooks developed by Mahan were very influential not only in military science, but in the development of engineering as a whole. Among the most notable in the prewar era were *Treatise on Field Fortifications* (1836); *Elementary Course of*

Civil Engineering (1837; rewritten in 1868); and *Elementary Treatise on Advanced Guard, Outposts, and Detachment Service of Troops* (1847; improved ed., 1862).

54. Twice Lee also borrowed a life of Benedict Arnold, who had committed treason by plotting to deliver the fort at West Point to the British. He also looked through material on other Revolutionary leaders, though there is no indication of a particular interest in Washington. Freeman, *R. E. Lee,* 1:355.

55. Pappas, *To the Point,* p. 301; Skelton, *American Profession of Arms,* p. 247; and "Dennis Hart Mahan: The Professionalism of West Point," in Weigley, *Towards an American Army,* pp. 38–53.

56. REL to "My dear Cousin Anna" [Anna Maria Fitzhugh], West Point, April 28, 1854, DE-LC; Freeman, *R. E. Lee,* 1:320, 358–59.

57. Howard, "Character and Campaigns of General Lee," 1:351.

58. Lomax, *Leaves from an Old Washington Diary,* p. 29.

59. Erasmus Keyes was one who wrote, "I will not deny that the presence of Lee, and the multiform graces that clustered around him, oftentimes oppressed me." Keyes, *Fifty Years Observation,* p. 205.

60. Howard, "Character and Campaigns of General Lee," p. 351. This account was written after the war, and Howard was no friend of Lee, but the material is balanced in its portrayal overall and tracks with other contemporary comments.

61. Preston, *West Point and Lexington,* pp. 29–35.

62. See Bowery and Hankinson, eds., *Daily Correspondence;* REL to MCL, "Clear Fork of the Brazos," Texas, April 19, 1856, DE-LC.

63. His "Iron Ram Rod" decision to deny cadet Wheeler leave, for example was overturned by Davis; Wheeler Journal, June 1, 1854, John Hill Wheeler Papers, LC; see also REL to J. G. Totten, West Point, February 1854, Lee Letterbook, #2, LFP-VHS; and Freeman, *R. E. Lee,* 1:326–27.

64. For the visit of Amelia Bloomer, see Edward Hartz to "Jenny," Military Academy, West Point, N.Y., September 15, 1852, Hartz Papers, LC; and REL to MCW, West Point, June 29, 1854, in Lee, *"To Markie,"* pp. 48–49; also REL to Mrs. A. M. Fitzhugh, West Point, April 28, 1854; and ALJ, November 8, 1853, both DE-LC.

65. REL to MCW, West Point, June 29, 1854, in Lee, *"To Markie,"* pp. 48–49.

66. Davis, "Robert E. Lee," p. 57.

67. ALJ, April 20, 1854, DE-LC; Lee Jr., *Recollections,* pp. 12–13; REL to WHFL, West Point, February 2, 1853, LFP-WL; and ACL to Helen Bratt, West Point, January 18, [1855], LFP-WL.

68. "MCG" [Mary Goldsborough] to MCL, Myrtle Inn, May 26, [1853], DE-LC; MCL quoted in Pappas, *To the Point,* pp. 291–92; and REL to Jerome Bonaparte, West Point, March 12 and May 11, 1853, photostats, LFP-WL.

69. REL to A. M. Fitzhugh, West Point, April 3, 1854, DE-LC.

70. REL quoted in Nagel, *Lees of Virginia,* p. 253; and REL to Jerome Bonaparte, West Point, March 12, 1853, and May 11, 1853, both photostats, LFP-WL.

71. ALJ, March 11, 1855, DE-LC.

72. General Joseph G. Totten to REL, Washington, March 21, 1855, typescript in USMA; and REL to MCW, March 14, 1855, in Lee, *"To Markie,"* pp. 52–53.

73. ALJ, April 17, 1855, DE-LC; and ACL to Helen Bratt, Arlington, May 3, 1855, LFP-WL.

CHAPTER FOURTEEN: **Mutable Shield**

1. Fragment of damaged letter, REL to MCL, Baltimore, 8 July 1849, LFP-VHS. The preacher was John Johns, later Episcopal bishop of Virginia, who would preside at Lee's confirmation in 1853.

2. REL to Rev. C. Walker, Richmond, May 2, 1861, DSF-LC.

3. Henry Lee to Henry Lee IV, Barbados, September 3, 1813, CCL-LoV; Henry Lee to Carter Lee quoted in Armes, *Stratford Hall*, p. 325; Letters of Elizabeth Randolph to Mary B. Carter, 1818–1820, in SPP-RL; Meade, *Old Churches*, 2:268–69.

4. John Ray, *The Wisdom of God Manifested in the Works of the Creation* (1691; repr., New York: Georg Olms Verlag, 1974). Lee evidently passed this volume along to his son Rooney, for it was listed in a bookseller's catalog as containing both the autograph of Henry Lee and the presentation line "To Wm. H. Fitzhugh Lee with much love your affectionate father RE Lee." Catalogue of the American Library Service, n.d., in DSF-LC.

5. See Jas G. Percival to Ethan Allen Hitchcock, Boston, June 28, 1825, Hitchcock Papers, LC.

6. CCL, "My Boyhood," CCL-LoV.

7. Henry Lee to Carter Lee quoted in Armes, *Stratford Hall*, p. 325.

8. REL to N[athaniel Burwell], Lexington, February 15, 1869, photostat, Burwell Papers, VHS.

9. See Robert Morell Schmitz, *Hugh Blair* (New York: King's Crown Press, 1948), Boswell quotation p. 1; and Hugh Blair, *Select Sermons* (Philadelphia: Robert Campbell, 1795), quotations pp. 11, 48, 144–50.

10. For background on the Second Great Awakening in Virginia, see Donald G. Mathews, *Religion in the Old South* (Chicago: University of Chicago Press, 1977); John Frank Waukechon, "The Forgotten Evangelicals: Virginia's Episcopalians, 1790–1876," Ph.D. diss., University of Texas at Austin, 2000; David L. Holmes, *A Brief History of the Episcopal Church* (Valley Forge, Pa.: Trinity Press International, 1993), pp. 50–59; William Wilson Manross, *A History of the American Episcopal Church* (New York: Morehouse-Gorham, 1950), pp. 215–46; Lewis, *Pursuit of Happiness*, pp. 65–68, 221–22; Gardiner H. Shattuck, *A Shield and a Hiding Place* (Macon, Ga.: Mercer University Press, 1987), pp. 2–11; Richard E. Beringer, Herman Hattaway, Archer Jones, and William N. Still Jr., *The Elements of Confederate Defeat* (Athens: University of Georgia Press, 1988), pp. 36–43; and Oates, *Ruling Race*, pp. 96–122.

11. Fox-Genovese, "Family and Female Identity," p. 28; Rosalie Stier Calvert to Isabelle van Havre, Riversdale, April 1, 1809, in Calvert, *Mistress of Riversdale*, p. 204; MCL to "My dear Mr. B," Lexington, December 11, 1870, REL-DU.

12. Henry Lee to Henry Lee IV, Barbados, September 3, 1813, CCL-LoV; Lee, *Revolutionary War Memoirs*, pp. 54–78; and CCL to Henry Lee, quoted in Sanborn, *Portrait*, p. 76.

13. Elizabeth Randolph to Ladonia Randolph and Mary B. Carter, Eastern View, April 25, [1818]. This and other letters expressing Elizabeth Carter Randolph's strong missionary bent at the time Robert Lee was being educated at Eastern View are in SPP-RL.

14. See D. H. Conrad to Philip Fendall, October 11, 1859, Fendall Papers, DU; R. R. Gurley to MFC, Arlington, September 20, 1825, MCL-VHS; and Meade, *Old Churches*, 2:269.

15. Meade went on to become bishop of Virginia and a major supporter of the

American Colonization Society. Waukechon, "Forgotten Evangelicals," p. 412–64. J. E. Booty, ed., "The Autobiography of William Meade," *Historical Magazine of the Protestant Episcopal Church* 31, no. 4 (December 1962): 379–94; Meade, *Old Churches*, 1:13–62; John Johns, *Address Delivered . . . on the Occasion of the Funeral of the Rigtt [sic] Rev William Meade, D.D., March 17th, 1862* (Richmond: MacFarlane & Fergusson, 1862); quotations William Meade to Mary Fitzhugh Custis, [Princeton, N.J.], August 9, [c. 1809], and Nassau Hall, "New Year's day," 1808, both MCL-VHS.

16. CCL, "My Boyhood" LoV; REL to MCL, Richmond, March 14, 1862, DE-LC; and REL to "Right Revd and dear Sir" [John Johns?], Lexington, Va., March 7, 1866, unfinished draft, REL-DU.

17. Elizabeth Carter Turner to MFC, Kinloch, May 26, 1833, GBL-VHS.

18. MFC to Mary Meade, Ravensworth, August 9, [c. 1839–45?], Jones Family Papers, VHS.

19. A. C. Robertson to MFC, Sudley, March 14, 1821, and n.d. [c. April 1821], MCL-VHS; Eleanor C. Stuart to MCL, Chantilly, June 7, [1853], DE-LC; and Lucy R. Mason to Mary B. Carter, October 22, 1822, SPP-RL. Also M. F. Powell to "My dear Nannie" [Lee], Oakley, July 18, 1886, quoted in Andrews, *Scraps of Paper*, p. 200; and "To Mrs Custis with a Moss Rose Bush," and M L Custis to CCL, Arlington, March 17, 1825, photostats, EA-LC.

20. Letter to the editor of the *National Intelligencer*, May 16, 1853.

21. Ibid., quotation Rosalie Stier Calvert to Isabelle van Havre, Riversdale, July 15, 1811, in Calvert, *Mistress of Riversdale*, p. 240.

22. See letters of Anna Maria Fitzhugh to Charles B. Dana, 1833–58, and many undated, in Charles B. Dana Papers, UT.

23. MARC to Hortensia Monroe, Arlington, October 14, 1830, AHA. Mary Custis Lee's lifelong commitment to religion infuses virtually every message she wrote. For some strong examples, see Mary Anna Randolph Custis Lee Diary, LFP-VHS; MCL to "My Dearest Mother," Sunday, n.d. [1831], DE-LC; MCL to MiCL, Arlington, "Friday 25th," [c.1860]; and MCL to "My dear Child" [MiCL], November 15, [1862], all DE-LC; MCL to "my dear Lettie," Lexington, November 15, 1870, SH.

24. For more on Southern women's role in evangelical religion, see "The Feminization of American Religion," in Welter, *Dimity Convictions*, pp. 86–101; Friedman, *Enclosed Garden*; Anne M. Boylan, "Evangelical Womanhood in the Nineteenth Century: The Role of Women in Sunday Schools," *Feminist Studies* 4, no. 3 (October 1978): 62–80; Colleen McDannell, *The Christian Home in Victorian America, 1840–1900* (Bloomington: Indiana University Press, 1986); and Barbara Welter, "The Cult of True Womanhood, 1820–1860," *American Quarterly* 18, no. 2, pt. 1 (Summer 1966): 151–74.

25. See Charles Pettit McIlvaine, "The Apostolical Commission: The Sermon at the Consecration of the Right Reverend Leonidas Polk, D.D.," 1838; and Church, *Personal Reminiscences*. For McIlvaine's style, which included using mercantile jargon of the time, see Charles Pettit McIlvaine, *Importance of Consideration*, No. 202 (Boston: American Tract Society, 1830), in which McIlvaine admonishes those who are "accustomed to compute the value of things. . . . Compute the *worth of your soul!* Calculate the price at which you can afford to sell it."

26. REL to Mary Anna Randolph Custis, CockSpur Island, February 14, 1831, in deButts, "Yours Forever."

27. See REL to Mary Anna Randolph Custis, CockSpur Island, November 19, 1830,

and postscript to REL to Mary Anna Randolph Custis, CockSpur Island, February 14, 1831, both ibid.

28. REL to MCL, Old Point, May 14, 1832, DE-LC.

29. See REL to CCL, Old Point, June 15, 1831, REL-UVa; REL to Jack Mackay, St. Louis, June 27, 1838, Gilder-Lehrman Collection, NYHS; and REL to Jack Mackay, National Palace, City of Mexico, October 2, 1847, USAMHI.

30. Lee Jr., *Recollections*, p. 12; MCL quoted in Nagel, *Lees of Virginia*, p. 237. These signs of religious ennui were not atypical of the time—evidently even devout men often found themselves uncomfortable in the church house and preferred to worship at home. See McDannell, *Christian Home*, pp. 77–79; and Rogin, *Fathers and Children*, p. 67.

31. REL to MCL, "Camp near Monclova, Mexico," November 4, 1846, DE-LC; and REL to MCW, Mexico City, October 28, 1847, REL-VHS.

32. Nagel, *Lees of Virginia*, p. 237.

33. Jack Mackay died on May 31, 1848. Cullum, *Biographical Register*, 1:425. For Lee's encounters with death and destruction in the Mexican War, see chapter 10, "Adrenaline."

34. See for example REL and MCL to GWCL, Baltimore, February 1, 1852; and REL to MFC, Baltimore, March 17, 1852, Letterbook #1, both LFP-VHS.

35. REL to MCL(d), West Point, April 25, 1853, MCL-VHS; and REL to WHFL, West Point, April 26, 1853, USMA.

36. REL to MCL, April 27, 1853, DE-LC.

37. MCW Diary, March 19, 1854, AHA.

38. REL to MCL(d), West Point, May 21, 1853, MCL-VHS; and REL to WHFL, West Point, April 26, 1853, USMA. Quotation REL to MCL, April 27, 1853, DE-LC.

39. REL to Edward Lee Childe, West Point, October 31, 1853, SH.

40. ALJ, July 20, 1853, DE-LC.

41. MCL Diary, July 7, 1853. Confirmation in middle life was not unusual during this era, especially among men. In the evangelical tradition it was a serious commitment, not an undertaking for children or for the halfhearted. Those studying religious conversion during this time have found indications that men were frequently persuaded into such choices and that spontaneous conversion was more common among women. Others thought that such gradual acquiescence to God's will was evidence of "unconscious" growth toward sanctification. Lee appears to have experienced some of both. For the trepidation with which confirmation was approached see letters to the rector of Christ Church, for example, Agnes Gray to Charles B. Dana, East Wood, December 23, 1839; and E. S. Hostin to Charles B. Dana, Alexandria, July 14, 1843, in Dana Papers, UT. The difference between male and female religious experiences is discussed in Susan Juster, "'In a Different Voice': Male and Female Narratives of Religious Conversion in Post Revolutionary America," *American Quarterly* 41, no. 1 (March 1989): 34–62; also Ann Douglas, *The Feminization of American Culture* (New York: Alfred A. Knopf, 1977), pp. 132–35.

42. REL to MCL, Jefferson Barracks, Mo., September 3, 1855, Fort Brown, Texas, January 9, 1857, and San Antonio, Texas, July 27, 1857, all DE-LC.

43. REL to MCL, Camp Cooper, September 1, 1856, DE-LC.

44. MCL to REL, March 17, 1857; and EAL to REL, Staunton, Thursday, April 9, 1857, both DE-LC. Intriguingly, Agnes felt she had been touched by God as she sat

reading *Evidences of Christianity,* by Charles McIlvaine, the very minister who had failed to sway her father at West Point. Coulling, *Lee Girls,* p. 63.

45. See Ethan Allen Hitchcock to Wm. G. Eliott, Jeff[erson] B[arrac]ks, September 15, 1840; and to Rev. Theodore Parker, Ship Massachusetts off Lobos, February 29, 1847, both EAH-LC; and Diary of Charles Mason, Sunday [December 30, 1855], Charles Mason Remey Papers, LC.

46. REL to WHFL, West Point, May 23, 1853, typescript, USMA.

47. For the appeal of rules and principles to evangelical men, see Juster, "'In a Different Voice,'" pp. 39–44; and Waukechon, "Forgotten Evangelicals."

48. Among those who have labeled Lee's devotion to duty "obsessive" are Fellman, *Making of Robert E. Lee,* p. 53; and Connelly, *Marble Man,* pp. 188–89.

49. REL to MCL, Camp Cooper, Texas, June 9, 1857, DE-LC.

50. See Charles A. Graves, *The Forged Letter of Robert E. Lee* (Richmond, Va.: Richmond Press, 1914). One of the most disturbing of the many anecdotes having to do with Lee's insistence on the primacy of duty was told by a mother who asked him to pronounce a blessing on her infant child. "Teach him he must deny himself," snapped Lee. Connelly, *Marble Man,* p. 189.

51. REL to MCL, Fort Brown, Texas, January 9, 1857, DE-LC.

52. For dislike of censure, see, for example, REL to MCL, St. Joseph's Bay, February 4, 1849, DE-LC; and Elizabeth Blair Lee to Phil[lips Lee], Silver Spring, July 30, 1863, in Lee, *Wartime Washington,* p. 293; for "breaking down a little," see REL to MCL, Richmond, July 12, 1861, in Lee Jr., *Recollections,* p. 36.

53. REL to ACL, San Antonio, Texas, August 24, 1860, DE-LC.

54. REL to MCL, Huntersville, August 4, 1861; and REL to MCL, Culpeper, June 9, 1863, both DE-LC.

55. REL to MCL, Savannah, February 8, 1862, DE-LC.

56. Meade quoted in Johns, *Address Delivered . . . on the Occasion of the Funeral;* and Rt. Revd. C. P. McIlvaine, *Christian Duty in Time of War* (Boston: American Tract Society, c. 1861). For the two men's friendship, see Waukechon, "Forgotten Evangelicals," p. 402.

57. REL to MCL, Camp Fred^g, May 31, 1863, DE-LC.

58. REL to MCL, Camp Fred^g, December 16, 1862, DE-LC.

59. Diary of Milton Wylie Humphreys, May 12–13, 1863, Humphreys Papers, UVa; and Drew Gilpin Faust, *The Creation of Confederate Nationalism: Ideology and Identity in the Civil War South* (Baton Rouge: Louisiana State University Press, 1988), pp. 23–30.

60. Humphreys Diary, May 12–13, 1863.

61. For an excellent overview of religious beliefs during the war see Shattuck, *Shield and a Hiding Place,* pp. 40, 96–106; also Bell Irvin Wiley, *The Life of Johnny Reb: The Common Soldier of the Confederacy* (Baton Rouge: Louisiana State University Press, 1978), pp. 181–82.

62. Jedediah Hotchkiss, a cartographer with the Army of Northern Virginia, noted numerous occasions when Lee attended church with chaplains or men; see for example notations for May 23 and 31, August 9 and 10, and December 10, 1863, in Jedediah Hotchkiss, *Make Me a Map of the Valley: The Civil War Journal of Stonewall Jackson's Topographer,* ed. Archie P. McDonald (Dallas: Southern Methodist University Press, 1973), pp. 145–46, 166, 168, 188. Lee's adjutant, Walter Herron Taylor, also

remarked on Lee's religious example; see Walter Taylor to [Bettie], Camp Orange County, March 25, 1864, in Taylor, *Lee's Adjutant*, p. 144.

63. For Lee's anti-Catholic bias, see REL to Jack Mackay, City of Mexico, October 2, 1847, USAMHI. REL to Mrs. Adele Fowler, U.S. Military Academy, West Point, N.Y., November 9, 1853, in Bowery and Hankinson, eds., *Daily Correspondence*, p. 141; and REL to Rabbi M. J. Michelbacher, "Hd Qtrs: Valley Mountain," August 29, 1861, "Headquarters Army of Northern Virginia," April 2, 1863, and September 20, 1864, in Herbert T. Ezekiel, *The History of the Jews of Richmond from 1769 to 1917* (Richmond: Herbert T. Ezekiel, 1917), pp. 161–63.

64. REL to MCL, Camp, July 10, 1864, DE-LC.

65. John B. Jones, *A Rebel War Clerk's Diary*, ed. Earl Schenck Miers (Baton Rouge: Louisiana State University Press, 1993), p. 289.

66. Josiah Gorgas, *The Civil War Diary of General Josiah Gorgas*, ed. Frank E. Vandiver (Tuscaloosa: University of Alabama Press, 1947), entry for July 17, 1863, pp. 50–51.

67. Samuel A. Burney to wife, in Samuel A. Burney, *A Southern Soldier's Letters Home: The Civil War Letters of Samuel A. Burney*, ed. Nat S.Turner III (Macon, Ga.: Mercer University Press, 2002), p. 107; Texan quoted in Faust, *Creation of Confederate Nationalism*, p. 23.

68. Thomas Claybrook Elder to wife, "Camp near Orange CH," August 21, 1863, in Thomas Claybrook Elder Papers, VHS (hereafter cited TCE-VHS).

69. Faust, *Creation of Confederate Nationalism*, p. 23–28; Jean V. Berlin, "Did Confederate Women Lose the War? Deprivation, Destruction and Despair on the Home Front," in Mark Grimsley and Brooks D. Simpson, eds., *The Collapse of the Confederacy* (Lincoln: University of Nebraska Press, 2001), pp. 170–82; Rable, *Civil Wars*, pp. 216–17.

70. REL notes on the back of letter to Mrs. W. C. Rives, n.d. [c. 1864], REL-DU. The quotations are from Psalms 16, 25, and 27.

71. REL to MCL, Gaines Mill, June 4, 1864, and Petersburg, February 21, 1865, both DE-LC.

72. REL to J. E. B. Stuart, "HdQrs, Fred^g," February 13, 1863, J. E. B. Stuart Papers, VHS.

73. REL to MCL, Camp Petersburg, August 28, 1864, DC-LC.

74. Faust, *Creation of Confederate Nationalism*, pp. 76–81.

75. Shattuck, *Shield and a Hiding Place*, pp. 41, 106–109; quotation Chesnut, *Diary*, p. 644.

76. See Beringer et al., *Elements of Confederate Defeat*, pp. 125–29.

77. Shattuck, *Shield and a Hiding Place*, pp. 112–114; quotation p. 113.

78. Ellen Renshaw House quote in Berlin, "Did Confederate Women Lose the War?" p. 182.

79. Shattuck, *Shield and a Hiding Place*, pp. 121–22.

CHAPTER FIFTEEN: Odyssey

1. REL to Albert M. Lea, San Antonio, Texas, March 1, 1860, Texas State Library. Lea was a close aide to Texas governor Sam Houston. Houston had demanded that something be done about Indian raids and cross-border incursions from Mexico, and President Buchanan had promised to protect the state. Lee, as acting head of the Department of Texas in 1860, was in a delicate position, for he knew well that he had been given inadequate resources to defend the area and satisfy Houston. Indeed, the

letter carries a handwritten annotation from Lea to Houston that reads in part: "This letter from Col. Lee arrived only last night. Although it is plain from his allusion to the 'Constitution and the Laws' that he wd not participate in any movement upon Mexico not expressly sanctioned by the Government, yet his expressions towards yourself are so justly complimentary that I tho[ugh]t you wd be glad to see them, coming as they do from a man of high intelligence and sincerity. You will be gratified to see also how anxious he expresses himself as to the repression of Indian depredations."

2. REL to ACL, San Antonio, Texas, February 22, 1860, DE-LC.

3. REL to Anna Maria Fitzhugh, San Antonio, Texas, June 6, 1860, Fitzhugh Lee Papers, UVa.

4. Scott, who was often at loggerheads with Davis, was among those who admired the high quality of the regiments' command. He told Kentucky senator William Preston "that the appointments were very good, but that the positions of Johnston and Lee should have been transposed." Scott later claimed that no one could have done better than Johnston, though he continued to favor Lee. See William Preston Johnston, *The Life of Gen. Albert Sidney Johnston* (repr., New York: Da Capo Press, 1997), pp. 184–85, Winfield Scott quoted pp. 185–86; James R. Arnold, *Jeff Davis's Own: Cavalry, Comanches and the Battle for the Texas Frontier* (New York: John Wiley, 2000), pp. 22–25; Rister, *Lee in Texas,* p. 14; and Lee, *General Lee,* pp. 54–55.

5. Hood, *Advance and Retreat,* p. 9.

6. Johnson, *Soldier's Reminiscences,* pp. 95–97; Arnold, *Jeff Davis's Own,* pp. 30–37.

7. The complexity of launching the regiment in an orderly manner was a challenge in itself for Lee. Those recruited for the rank and file were largely from disadvantaged elements of the society, and some were opportunists who simply wanted free passage to Texas. Lee confronted problems of sickness, clothing and provisions that did not arrive, and massive defections. In the month of July 1855, for example, there were thirteen deaths from cholera and ninety-two desertions. REL to CCL, Louisville, Ky., May 10, 1855, REL-UVa; REL to Lt. K. Garrod, Jefferson Barracks, Mo., August 1, 1855, REL Letterbook #2, LFP-VHS; Freeman, *R. E. Lee,* 1:361–63; Arnold, *Jeff Davis's Own,* pp. 28, 97–98, 102.

8. REL to CCL, Louisville, Ky., May 10, 1855, REL-UVa.

9. James R. Arnold gives a useful description of the Indian's predicament in the face of white encroachment in *Jeff Davis's Own,* pp. 54–67; also Charles Anderson, *Texas Before and on the Eve of the Rebellion* (Cincinnati: Peter G. Thompson, 1884), p. 4. For insights into Comanche culture, see Ernest Wallace and E. Adamson Hoebel, *The Comanches: Lords of the South Plains* (Norman: University of Oklahoma Press, 1986), pp. 39–45; for the fear of white settlers and demands that they be protected, see Dorman H. Winfrey, ed., *Texas Indian Papers, 1846–1859* (Austin: Texas State Library, 1960).

10. Frederick Law Olmsted, *Journey through Texas: or A Saddle Trip on the Southwestern Frontier* (1857; repr., Austin: University of Texas Press, 1978), pp. 298–99. A. S. Johnston quoted in Johnston, *Life of Albert Sidney Johnston,* p. 191.

11. Lee's disdainful description is in REL to MCL, Camp Cooper, April 12, 1856, LFP-VHS. See also Hattaway and Fair, "Ethan Allen Hitchcock," *ANB* 10: 868; and letters of John Mackay to Eliza Ann McQueen Mackay, 1836–38, in Mackay-Stiles Family Papers, UNC.

12. Robert Wooster, ed., *Recollections of Western Texas, Descriptive and Narrative . . .*

By Two of the U.S. Mounted Rifles (repr., Lubbock: Texas Tech University Press, 1995), p. 75.

13. "Report of R. S. Neighbors to H. R. Schoolcraft, The NA-Ü-NI, or Comanches of Texas; Their Trails and Beliefs, and the Divisions and Inter Tribal Relations," n.d. [c. 1859], in Winfrey, *Texas Indian Papers,* pp. 353–56; Skelton, *American Profession of Arms,* pp. 307–320; Thomas W. Kavanagh, *Comanche Political History: An Ethnographical Perspective* (Lincoln: University of Nebraska Press, 1996), pp. 354–55; Arnold, *Jeff Davis's Own,* pp. 58–61; and Hood, *Advance and Retreat,* pp. 12–13.

14. REL to MCL, Fort Brown, Texas, January 24, 1857, REL-DU.

15. For more on the contradictions inherent in attitudes toward the Indians, see Robert F. Berkhofer Jr., *The White Man's Indian: Images of the American Indian from Columbus to the Present* (New York: Alfred A. Knopf, 1978), especially pp. 150–60.

16. The spelling of Catumsah's name has also variously been interpreted as Katumsah, Ketumse, Ka tem a se, and Ka-tum-she. Kavanagh, *Comanche Political History,* pp. 352–56, 361; "Report of R. S. Neighbors to H. R. Schoolcraft," pp. 347–357; Rister, *Lee in Texas,* pp. 25–26; Olmsted, *Journey through Texas,* pp. 295–98; Francis Paul Prucha, *The Sword of the Republic* (London: Collier-MacMillan Ltd., 1969), pp. 193–99; and Arnold, *Jeff Davis's Own,* pp. 66–67, 136.

17. Lee, *General Lee,* pp. 72–73. Robert E. Lee's version of this story, which may have served as the basis for Fitzhugh Lee's recounting, is in REL to MCL, Camp Cooper on the Clear Fork of the Brazos, Texas, April 12, 1856, DE-LC; and "Report of R.S. Neighbors to H.R. Schoolcraft," in Winfrey, ed., *Texas Indian Papers.*

18. Freeman, *R. E. Lee,* 1:365–68; and Hood, *Advance and Retreat,* pp. 9–13.

19. A. S. Johnston quoted in Rister, *Lee in Texas,* p. 16.

20. Ibid., p. 52; REL to Major DC Buell, Camp Cooper, Texas, July 24, 1856, REL Letterbook #2, LFP-VHS; Arnold, *Jeff Davis's Own,* pp. 86–90, 98.

21. Olmsted, *Journey through Texas,* pp. 298–99.

22. REL to "My dear Son," [GWCL], Arlington, May 30, 1859 in Jones, *Life and Letters,* p. 99.

23. REL to Eliza Mackay Stiles, Camp Cooper, Texas, August 14, 1856, UTA; REL to EAL, Camp Cooper, August 4, 1856. LFP-VHS; and Rister, *Lee in Texas,* p. 66.

24. REL to MCL, San Antonio, Texas, March 17, 1856, DE-LC.

25. REL to "My dear little daughter" [MiCL], Camp, April 28, 1856, DE-LC.

26. REL to MCL, Camp Cooper, August 4, 1856, in Lee, *General Lee,* pp. 59–60.

27. REL to [MCL], Ringgold Barracks, Texas, October 3, 1856, in Jones, *Life and Letters,* p. 81.

28. REL to Captain N. G. Evans, Fort Brown, December 6, 1856, REL-VHS.

29. REL to John F. Lee, Fort Brown, Texas, December 11, 1856, DE-LC; REL Diary, February 18, 1857, LFP-VHS; and Freeman, *R. E. Lee,* 1:378. Quotation REL to J[erome] Bonaparte, West Point, February 28, 1855, photostat, LFP-WL.

30. REL to Captain N. G. Evans, Fort Brown, December 6, 1856, REL-VHS.

31. For examples of Lee's despondency, see REL to MCL, June 22, 1857; to ACL, San Antonio, Texas, August 8, 1857; and to MCL, San Antonio, Texas, August 12, 1857, all DE-LC; and REL to "My dear Cousin Anna," San Antonio, Texas, September 8, 1857, REL-DU. Quotation REL to MCL, Camp Cooper, Texas, June 9, 1857, DE-LC.

32. REL to MCL, San Antonio, Texas, August 12, 1857, REL to EAL, Camp Cooper,

Texas, August 4, 1856; and San Antonio, Texas, March 11, 1857, all REL-VHS; and Johnson, *Soldier's Reminiscences*, p. 105.

33. MCL to REL, September 2, 1856, DE-LC.

34. REL to MCL, Ringgold Barracks, Texas, October 3, 1856, in Jones, *Life and Letters*, p. 81; and REL to MCL, November 19, [1856], quoted in Rister, *Lee in Texas*, p. 71.

35. REL to ACL, San Antonio, Texas, Februay 22, 1860, DE-LC.

36. REL to MCL, San Antonio, Texas, August 12, 1857, LFP-VHS; REL to WHFL, quoted in Rister, *Lee in Texas*, p. 87; and REL to Capt. N. G. Evans, Fort Brown, December 15, 1856, REL-VHS.

37. REL to MCL(d), "On Rio Grande near Camp Cooper," Texas, n.d. [October 1857], fragment, MCL-VHS.

38. REL to MCL, Ringgold Barracks, October 24, 1856, DE-LC.

39. REL to Col. Albert S. Johnston, San Antonio, Texas, October 25, 1857, in Sibley, ed., "Lee to Albert Sidney Johnston," pp. 103–4.

40. REL to MCL, March 7, 1857, quoted in Coulling, *Lee Girls*, p. 62; and REL to WHFL, Ringgold Barracks, Texas, November 1, 1856, DE-LC.

41. REL to "My dear Cousin Anna," San Antonio, Texas, September 8, 1857, REL-DU.

42. For the death of his mother-in-law, see REL to MCW, June 23, 1853, in Lee, *"To Markie,"* p. 31; quotations REL to MCL, August 11, 1856, in Jones, *Life and Letters*, p. 80; and REL to Eliza Mackay Stiles, Camp Cooper, Texas, August 14, 1856, UTA.

43. Mildred was forty-six at her death, the cause of which appears to have been childbirth. REL to Edward Lee Childe, Ringgold Bks., Texas, November 1, 1856, SH.

44. REL to MCL, Camp Cooper, June 9 and June 22, 1857, DE-LC.

45. REL to MCW, West Point, January 2, 1854, in Lee, *"To Markie,"* pp. 38–39; and REL Diary, October 1, 1857, LFP-VHS.

46. REL to EAL, San Antonio, Texas, March 11, 1857; REL-VHS; REL to "Precious Life" [MiCL], Indianola, Texas, March 22, 1857; quotation REL to "My dear little daughter" [MiCL], Camp, April 22, 1856, both DE-LC.

47. REL to MCL, San Antonio, Texas, August 12, 1857, LFP-VHS; REL to MCL, Camp Cooper, June 22, 1857, DE-LC; REL to Eliza Mackay Stiles, Camp Cooper, Texas, August 14, 1856, UTA; quotation REL to WHFL, San Antonio, Texas, December 3, 1860, GBL-VHS.

48. Lee's experiences as executor of the Custis estate are found in chapter 16, "Theory Meets Reality."

49. REL to EAL, San Antonio, Texas, March 11, 1857, REL-VHS.

50. REL to GWCL, Baltimore, March 28, 1852, LFP-VHS.

51. REL to MCL, Fort Brown, Texas, December 20, 1856, REL-VHS.

52. For more on southern codes of honor that reflect many of Lee's values, particularly self-control, see Stowe, *Intimacy and Power in the Old South*. Charles Royster discusses the sublimation of disappointment by the pursuit of duty in relationship to Stonewall Jackson in *The Destructive War: William Tecumseh Sherman, Stonewall Jackson, and the Americans* (New York: Alfred A. Knopf, 1991), p. 71.

53. REL to MFC, Baltimore, March 17, 1852, DE-LC. For a discussion of Lee's moral pronouncements, see Fellman, *Making of Robert E. Lee*, pp. 34–53.

54. REL to Anna Maria Fitzhugh, San Antonio, June 6, 1860, Fitzhugh Lee Papers, UVa.

55. REL to "My dear Cousin Anna," San Antonio, Texas, September 8, 1857, REL-DU.

56. Torrence, "Arlington and Mount Vernon, 1856," p. 151. For other expressions of the general disarray at Arlington, see ACL to Helen Bratt, Arlington, July 13, [1856], and EAL to Helen Bratt, "Thurs. eve" [1855], both LFP-WL.

57. MCW Diary, October 11, 1856, AHA.

58. MiCL, "Recollections," July 20, 1890, in ALJ, DE-LC.

59. MCW Diary, May 2, 1857, AHA.

60. ALJ, October 13, 1857, DE-LC; Lomax, *Leaves from an Old Washington Diary*, p. 149; and Coulling, *Lee Girls*, p. 64.

61. Joseph Henry to GWPC, Washington, November 21, 1854, Rembrandt Peale to GWPC, Philadelphia, August 20, 1857, M. C. Meigs to GWPC, Washington Aqueduct Office, January 19, 1856, and Jared Sparks to GWPC, Cambridge, January 11, 1855, all CL-TPA; and MCW Diary, August 11, 1856, AHA.

62. MCW Diary, October 21, 1856, AHA.

63. REL to ACL, San Antonio, Texas, August 24, 1860, DE-LC. Lee made a similar self-pitying remark to his daughter Mary earlier that year: see REL to MCL(d), San Antonio, Texas, February 19, 1860, MCL-VHS.

64. REL to Mrs. Eliza Stiles, Camp in the Clear Fork of the Brazos, Indian Territory, May 24, 1856, SH.

65. REL to MCL, December 5, 1856, DE-LC.

66. REL to MCL, Fort Brown, Texas, December 20, 1856, DE-LC. Other moving letters written by Lee at Christmastime include REL to GWCL, Arlington, December 28, 1851, copy in hand of GWCL, LFP-VHS; REL to GWCL and WHFL, Camp near Satillo, December 14, 1846, DE-LC; and REL to MCL(d), Cossawhatchie, S.C., December 25, 1861, MCL-VHS.

67. Charles Marshall, *Lee's Aide-de-Camp*, ed., Frederick Maurice (Lincoln: University of Nebraska Press, 2000), p. 278.

68. Rister, *Lee in Texas*, pp. 137–42; and Fitzhugh Lee to "My dear Godmother" [Anna Maria Fitzhugh], Camp Radziminski, September 1, 1859, Fitzhugh Lee Papers, UVa.

69. REL to MCL, Fort Brown, Texas, May 2, 1860, DE-LC; Rister, *Lee in Texas*, pp. 113–14; and J. Frank Dobie quoted in Samuel P. Heintzelman, *Fifty Miles and a Fight: Major Samuel Peter Heintzelman's Journal of Texas and the Cortina War*, ed. Jerry Thompson (Austin: Texas State Historical Association, 1998), p. 17–19.

70. Juan Nepomuceno Cortinas, "To the Inhabitants of the State of Texas and Especially to Those of the City of Brownsville," quoted in U.S. Congress, "Difficulties on the Southwestern Frontier," 36th Cong., 1st sess., 1860, H. Exec. Doc. 52; Heintzelman, *Fifty Miles*, pp. 23–24.

71. REL to GWCL, San Antonio, Tx., March 9, 1860, CL-LC; quotation REL to GWCL, April 17, 1860, DU.

72. REL Diary, April 7, 1860, LFP-VHS; Col. M. L. Crimmins, "Colonel Robert E. Lee's Report on Indian Combat in Texas," *Southwestern Historical Quarterly* 39, no. 1 (July 1935): 21–33; and Rister, *Lee in Texas*, p. 128.

73. Ibid., p. 101; REL to GWCL, San Antonio, Texas, February 28, 1860; and "Statement of Equipment at Various Camps and Forts in Texas," 1860, both REL-DU.

74. The use of camels, as outlandish as it at first seems, was meant as a practical response to harsh desert conditions. The experiment was interrupted by the Civil War and ultimately abandoned when railroads began to be used for supply and transport. Apparently for years, however, the Native Americans reported seeing strange animal

apparitions in remote areas. Johnson, *Soldier's Reminiscences*, pp. 129–31; Davis, *Jefferson Davis*, pp. 233–34; REL to EAL, San Antonio, Texas, June 8, 1860, DE-LC.

75. Quotation by unidentified Texan in Rister, *Lee in Texas*, pp. 157–58.

76. Anderson, *Texas Before and on the Eve of the Rebellion*, p. 24.

77. Hood, *Advance and Retreat*, pp. 7–8.

78. Johnston, *Life of Albert Sidney Johnston*, pp. 150–51, 175, 185.

79. Freeman, *R. E. Lee*, 1:369; and REL to MCL, Fort Brown, December 27, 1856, DE-LC.

80. REL to Captain N. G. Evans, San Antonio, August 3 and August 28, 1857, both REL-VHS. Evans did not marry until 1860. See Herman Hattaway, "Nathan George Evans," *ANB*, 7:615.

81. Anderson, *Texas Before and on the Eve of the Rebellion*, pp. 24–32, quotation p. 32; Johnson, *Soldier's Reminiscences*, pp. 132–34; and REL to EAL, Fort Mason, Texas, January 29, 1861, DE-LC.

82. Johnson, *Soldier's Reminiscences*, pp. 132–33.

83. Arnold, *Jeff Davis's Own*, pp. 296–303; and Jeanne T. Heidler, "'Embarrassing Situation': David E. Twiggs and the Surrender of the United States Forces in Texas in 1861," in Ralph A. Wooster, ed., *Lonestar Blue and Gray* (Austin: Texas State Historical Association, 1995), pp. 28–44.

84. Lee quoted in Mrs. Caroline Baldwin Darrow, "Recollections of the Twiggs Surrender," in *B & L*, 1:36; Heintzelman, *Fifty Miles*, p. 36; Heintzelman Diary, March 25, 1861, Heintzelman Papers, LC; and Johnson, *Soldier's Reminiscences*, pp. 132–33.

CHAPTER SIXTEEN: **Theory Meets Reality**

1. Wesley Norris interview in "Robert E. Lee: His Brutality to His Slaves," *National Anti-Slavery Standard*, April 14, 1866. After being freed in 1863, Norris attached himself to the Union army and aided their efforts by offering information on local conditions and troop movements. U.S. War Department, *OR*, ser. 1, vol. 29, part 2 pp. 158–59.

2. Nelligan, "Old Arlington," pp. 407–13; Robert, "Lee the Farmer," pp. 424–26; Will of G.W.P. Custis, probated December 7, 1857, Records of Alexandria Co., Virginia; REL to GWCL, Arlington, July 2, 1859, quoted in Jones, *Life and Letters*, p. 102.

3. REL to "Cousin Anna," Arlington, November 22, 1857, REL-DU.

4. Nelligan, "Old Arlington," p. 408; MCL to "My dear Sir," Arlington, December 5, [1859], CL-LC; REL to GWCL, Arlington, February 15, 1858, REL-DU; and Schwarz, *Slave Laws in Virginia*, pp. 54–55. Freed slaves had been ordered out of the state of Virginia since 1782, and the law was reinforced in the new state constitution that was passed in 1851–52. See Stroud, *Sketch of the Laws*, pp. 98–99.

5. The best account of Lee's management of the Custis estates is in Nelligan, "Old Arlington," pp. 407–18; REL quoted p. 417; MCL to "Abby," Arlington, May 7, 1858, MOC; see also Roberts, "Lee the Farmer," pp. 438–39; and EAL to WHFL, "Arlington," October 2, 1858, DE-LC.

6. REL to Wm. O. Winston, Alexandria, July 8, 1858, Winston Papers, VHS.

7. Kenneth M. Stampp, "The Historian's Burden," in Harry P. Owens, *Perspectives and Irony in American Slavery* (Jackson: University Press of Mississippi, 1976), p. 162; and Fogel and Engerman, *Time on the Cross*, p. 73.

8. REL to GWCL, San Antonio, December 14, 1860, REL-DU; "Account of the Estate of G. W. P. Custis," Will Book No. 8, p. 93; REL to GWCL, January 1, 1863, quoted

in Sanborn, *Portrait*, p. 98; REL to GWCL, April 6, 1860, quoted in Robert, "Lee the Farmer," p. 432. In REL to Edward C. Turner, Arlington, February 13, 1858, REL-UVa, Lee reiterates a philosophy of relations between overseer and slaves that he had long held; see, for example, REL to Hill Carter, Arlington, January 25, 1840, photostat, EA-LC.

9. For a description of the slaves' anxiety at the death of a master, see Frederick Douglass, *Narrative of the Life of Frederick Douglass, An American Slave* (repr., New York: Penguin, 1982), p. 89–91; also John Hope Franklin, *Runaway Slaves: Rebels on the Plantation* (New York: Oxford University Press, 1999), pp. 18–19; AHA; Robert, "Lee the Farmer," p. 435, and MCL to ?, February 10, 1858, typescript, AHA.

10. Seventh and Eighth Decennial Census of the United States, Alexandria County, Va., 1850 and 1860, NARA; "Inventory of the Estate of G. W. P. Custis," January 1, 1858, Will Book No. 7; and "Account of the Estate of G. W. P. Custis," 1859, 1859, Alexandria Will Book No. 8.

11. REL to "My dear Son" [WHFL], San Antonio, August 20, 1860, GBL-VHS; slave interviewed in Preston, *West Point and Lexington*, p. 76; and Sneden Diary, September 12, 1862, VHS.

12. See Pryor, *Flexibility and Profit;* REL to GWCL, January 17, 1858, REL-DU; and REL to William O. Winston, July 3, 1859, Winston Papers, UVA. Among hired slaves, running away was a common problem, but it reached unusually high levels at Arlington. For example, Lee lists seven slaves missing in just one month, April 1858. REL to A. E. S. Keese, Arlington, near Alex[a], April 24, 1858, HL.

13. REL quoted in REL to Wm O. Winston, Alexandria, July 8, 1858, Winston Papers, VHS; and REL to GWCL, December 5, 1860, REL-DU.

14. MCL Diary, May 1, 1858.

15. REL to GWCL, Arlington, July 2, 1859, in Jones, *Life and Letters*, p. 102; and Robert, "Lee the Farmer," p. 435. For an in-depth study of Lee's use of slave hiring, see Pryor, "Flexibility and Profit."

16. See *Custis EXR vs Lee and Others*, "Note of Argument for Appellant," [1858], Supreme Court of Appeals of Virginia, in which Lee states that "it is with great difficulty that he can get some of them to discharge their duties, whilst others positively refuse to labor, saying that they had been advised that they were then free." Copy in VF Legal Papers, BLA.

17. CCL to Henry Lee, New York, December 1, 1830, CCL-LoV.

18. Custis quoted in Wiencek, *Imperfect God*, p. 358; Washington to Tobias Lear quoted p. 316.

19. One of the slave accounts, from the *Cincinnati Commercial*, which substantially agrees with Norris's story, is recounted in Preston, *West Point and Lexington*, pp. 76–77. This is a particularly interesting version because it indicates the way slave information traveled, and how it could be at once factual and distorted. The witness stated that she knew she had been freed but confuses the conditions with slaves on the Fitzhugh estate, who had also been promised freedom, and a start-up payment of $50 each. Custis had not provided for such a payment, but the story had gotten round that he had done so, adding to the disgruntlement. The witness in this case was one whose family had been broken up, and she does not distinguish between having her children "sold" South or hired out, another indication of the uncertainty hiring caused.

20. "The Slaves of Mr. Custis," *New York Times*, December 30, 1857; and "The Will of Mr. Custis," *New York Times*, January 8, 1858.

21. *Custis EXR vs Lee and Others,* "Note of Argument for Appellant," [1858], Supreme Court of Appeals of Virginia, copy in VF Legal Papers, BLA; and REL to WHFL, Arlington November 27, 1858, GBL-VHS.

22. MCL to W. G. Webster, February 17, 1858, typescript, AHA.

23. Ibid.; MCL to Mrs. William Henry Stiles, Arlington, February 9, 1861, SH; quotation REL to WHFL, Arlington, May 30, 1858, GBL-VHS.

24. MCL Diary, May 1 and May 11, August 8, and December 5, 1858.

25. MCW Diary, November 2, 1853.

26. MCL to [Benson Lossing], July 20, 1859, LFP-WL; and MCL Diary, May 1 and May 11 and August 8, 1858.

27. The slaves' "betrayal" of their masters is discussed in Leon F. Litwack, *Been in the Storm So Long* (New York: Vintage, 1980), especially pp. 152–54. Paul Laurence Dunbar quoted in John W. Blassingame, "Sambos and Rebels: The Character of the Southern Slave," lecture given at Howard University, May 4, 1972. Eugene Genovese also interprets the slaves' "put-ons" in *Roll Jordan Roll,* pp. 609–12.

28. For abolitionist activities around Washington, D.C., see Stanley Harrold, *Subversives: The Anti-Slavery Community in Washington, DC, 1828-1865* (Baton Rouge: Louisiana State University Press, 2003); REL to MCL, Baltimore, September 25, 1849, LFP-VHS.

29. Schwarz, *Slave Laws in Virginia,* p. 140; and MCL to W. G. Webster, February 17, 1858, photostat, AHA.

30. MCL to Mrs. William Henry Stiles, February 9, 1861, SH.

31. REL to MFC, Fort Hamilton, N.Y., April 13, [1844], GBL-VHS.

32. Feller, *Jacksonian Promise,* pp. 61–62; Franklin, *Runaway Slaves,* p. 251; Hill Carter, "On the Management of Negroes," p. 565; and REL to MCL, Fort Brown, Texas, December 27, 1856, DE-LC.

33. Franklin Pierce, "Fourth Annual Message, December 2, 1856," in James D. Richardson, ed., *A Compilation of the Messages and Papers of the Presidents* (Washington, D.C.: GPO, 1897), 2930–41; quotation, p. 2932; REL to MCL, Fort Brown, Texas, December 27, 1856, DE-LC.

34. For the role of abolitionists aiding runaways, see Larry Gara, *The Liberty Line: The Legend of the Underground Railway* (Lexington: University of Kentucky Press, 1961); and Harrold, *Subversives,* p. 73; REL to GWCL, Arlington, July 2, 1859, in Jones, *Life and Letters,* p. 102; and *Carroll County Democrat* (Westminster, Md.), June 2, 1859.

35. "Some Facts That Should Come to Light," *New York Tribune,* June 21, 1859; and "To the Editor of the N.Y. Tribune," *New York Tribune,* June 19, 1859; both printed in Freeman, *R. E. Lee,* 1:390–92.

36. Robert, "Lee the Farmer," p. 435.

37. See narrative from *Cincinnati Commercial,* recounted in Preston, *West Point and Lexington,* pp. 76–77.

38. Norris says there were "about 70" slaves at Arlington; probate and census records give the figures 63 and 67; the overseer's name is sometimes written "Quinn" but generally as "McQuinn." See, e.g., REL Daybook, August 12, 1859; MCL to MiCL, Arlington, January 17, 1861; and REL to MCL, Richmond, May 2, 1861; all DE-LC. *Carroll County Democrat* (Westminster, Md.), June 2, 1859, in Carroll County Historical Society establishes the facts and dates of the runaways' arrest; fees to slave catchers are in REL to A. E. S. Keese, Arlington, April 24, 1858, HL; for fees paid to Richard Williams, see "Inventory of the Estate of G. W. P. Custis," 1859, Will Book No.

7, pp. 488, 491. Witnesses describe a whipping post at Arlington, standing as a silent witness to the exercise of this punishment. Cooling, *Symbol,* p. 88.

39. *The National Anti-Slavery Standard* says Norris gave his statement to dispel the impression that Lee was a kind and humane slave owner. Historian Ervin L. Jordan Jr., who accepts Wesley Norris's story, adds that Norris "knew better: the proof was on his back." Ervin L. Jordan Jr., *Black Confederates and Afro-American Yankees in Civil War Virginia* (Charlottesville: University Press of Virginia, 1995), p. 162. This author has found no description of Norris carrying permanent scars. The value of slave narratives is discussed in Blassingame, ed., *Slave Testimony,* pp. xiii–xiv and xviii–lxv; Perdue et al., *Weevils in the Wheat,* pp. xi–xlv; and Stampp, "Historian's Burden," pp. 153–76. An example of a slave narrative that does not hold up under scrutiny is Rev. William Mack Lee, *History of the Life of Rev. Wm. Mack Lee,* 1918. Rev. Lee claimed that he was raised a slave at Arlington and served as cook to the general throughout the war. He is not listed on any inventory of Arlington slaves, however; places Lee (and himself) at battles such as First Manassas, and claims to have cooked for a group of southern officers "in de Wilderness" on July 3, 1863, that included Stonewall Jackson and George Pickett as well as Lee. On this date, Jackson was dead, and Lee and Pickett were fighting the last desperate throes of the battle at Gettysburg. Lee's letters make no mention of William Mack Lee. His personal servants and cook during the war were Perry and Lawrence Parks and Billy Taylor.

40. REL to GWCL, Arlington, July 2, 1859, in Jones, *Life and Letters,* p. 102.

41. REL to George K. Fox, April 13, 1866; and to E. S. Quirk, March 1, 1866, both quoted in Fellman, *Making of Robert E. Lee,* p. 67.

42. REL to MCL, April 18, 1841, REL-UVa; and REL to Genl. Jos. G. Totten, U.S. Military Academy, West Point, N.Y., December 9, 1852, and April 10, 1854, in Bowery and Hankinson, *Daily Correspondence,* pp. 27, 176.

43. Alan T. Nolan gives an account of this propensity in *Lee Considered,* pp. 53–54.

44. Douglass, *Narrative,* p. 113; Franklin, *Runaway Slaves,* p. 237; and interview with Frank Bell in Perdue et al., *Weevils in the Wheat,* p. 27.

45. See Robert B. Shaw, *A Legal History of Slavery* (New York: Northern Press, 1991), pp. 234–42; Tushnet, *American Law of Slavery,* pp. 12–13, 44; and Larry Gara, "The Fugitive Slave Law: A Double Paradox," *Civil War History* 10, no. 3 (September 1964): 235–36.

46. Tushnet, *American Law of Slavery,* pp. 68–72; Stroud, *Sketch of the Laws,* pp. 69–75; Schwarz, *Slave Laws in Virginia,* pp. 46–47, 60–61. For evidence that whipping was common practice in the neighborhood of Alexandria, see Elijah Fletcher to Jesse Fletcher, Alexandria, Va., August 29, 1810: "They whip them for every little offense most cruelly." Also Elijah Fletcher to father, Alexandria, Virginia, October 31, 1810, and Elijah Fletcher to "My best Friend and Father," Alexandria, January 11, 1811, all in *Letters of Elijah Fletcher,* pp. 14, 21, 25–26. Bertram Wyatt-Brown gives a factually incorrect account of the Norris incident in *Southern Honor,* pp. 371–72, but closes with a well-phrased description of the mindset that underlay such a situation: "It would not do for any slave to take flagrant advantage of a master's delicacy or conscience. To push too hard against the institution or against an owner's sense of self-esteem was to threaten the social order as it was then understood. Failure to react appropriately could be misinterpreted, not only by the compliant slaves but by the white community, too. . . . One simply could not be made to look inept, powerless, or squeamish."

47. REL to Major Irwin McDowell, "Arlington near Alex^a Va.," October 22, 1858, HL.

48. REL to MCL, Coosawhatchie, S.C., January 28, 1862, DE-LC; and REL to GWCL, Coosawhatchie, January 4, 1862, and January 19, 1862, both in Lee, *Wartime Papers*, pp. 99–101, 104–6.

49. REL to MCL, Camp Fred^g, January 8, 1863, DE-LC; REL to GWCL, Camp, January 11, 1863, in Jones, *Life and Letters*, pp. 285–86. Ervin Jordan believes that in freeing the Custis slaves, Lee "overcame his own private uneasiness" and bowed to his "strong sense of duty"; but the evidence indicates that Lee simply followed the orders of the court. Jordan also asserts that the slaves were put into "families" and given names at this time; however, Arlington records, including family correspondence and inventories made at the death of GWPC, show that the slaves had long been associated with family groups and were recognized by family surnames. See Jordan, *Black Confederates*, pp. 258–59; and "Inventory of the Estate of G. W. P. Custis," January 1, 1858, Will Book No. 7.

50. REL to MCL, Camp Fredericksburg, December 21, 1862, and January 8, 1863; Camp Rapidan, November 11, 1863; and Camp, January 24, 1864, all DE-LC.

51. See for example, the granting of 17½ acres of land along with the manumission of Custis slave Maria Syphax. Lynch, *Custis Chronicles*, 2:5. Technically, under Virginia law, Maria Syphax should have been sent out of the state. Virginia law would also have allowed Lee to petition to keep any freed blacks at Arlington had he emancipated them in 1857.

CHAPTER SEVENTEEN: **"Upon a Fearful Summons"**

1. REL to Lt. R. Jones, U.S. Army, Arlington, April 20, 1861, USMA. Jones was an 1851 West Point graduate who had served with Lee in Texas. He rose to major in the Union army and to brigadier general by the end of his career. Cullum, *Biographical Register*, 2:466–67. The title of the chapter is from William Shakespeare, *Hamlet*, act 1, scene 1. The play was one that Lee liked to quote; see, for example, REL to Jack Mackay, Fort Monroe, February 27, 1834, typescript, AHA.

2. William Orton Williams to General Winfield Scott, "Fort Columbia, Govrs Island, NY Harbor," May 14, 1861, typescript, AHA.

3. REL to Edward Vernon Childe, Fort Brown, Texas, January 9, 1857, SH.

4. Lee's transactions for the day are in Account of the Estate of G. W. P. Custis, Will Book No. 8, pp. 92–93; quotation from Parks in "Colored Servant."

5. REL pocket memorandum book, October 17, 1859, DE-LC; and J. E. B. Stuart to "My Dear Mama," Fort Riley, Kansas Territory, January 31, 1860, in Emory M. Thomas, ed., " 'The Greatest Service I Rendered the State': J. E. B. Stuart's Account of the Capture of John Brown," *VMHB* 94, no. 3 (July 1986): 345–57. Harper's Ferry changed hands many times during the Civil War. It became part of West Virginia when that state broke off from Virginia in 1861 and was made an independent state in 1863.

6. Like many other details of the event, the time of Lee's arrival varies with the person recording the episode. Stuart says they arrived about midnight, but does not say whether this was in Harper's Ferry or Sandy Hook; another eyewitness, Israel Green, says they met at 10 p.m. See J. E. B. Stuart to "My Dear Mama," January 31, 1860, in Thomas, ed., " 'The Greatest Service' "; Israel Green, "The Capture of John Brown," *North American Review* 141, no. 349 (December 1885): 564–70; National Park Service, *John Brown's Raid* (Washington, D.C.: GPO, 1973), pp. 36, 44; and Jordan, *Black Confederates*, pp. 1–2.

7. Alexander Boteler, the district's congressman, later wrote that when he called on Lee early that morning Lee knew Brown had identified himself during negotiations with the militia. Green also says that he knew the group's leader was Brown before he left Washington. These accounts are at odds with J. E. B. Stuart's assertion that he "proclaimed" the old man's true name to the world. It may be, however, that in order to keep his troops as cool as possible Lee did not admit who was in the engine house, and Stuart believed himself the first to recognize Brown. See Green, "The Capture of John Brown," p. 564; J. E. B. Stuart to "My Dear Mama," January 31, 1860, in Thomas, ed., "'The Greatest Service'"; and Alexander R. Boteler, "Recollections of the John Brown Raid," *Century Magazine* 26, no. 3 (July 1883): 408.

8. Oswald Garrison Villard, *John Brown: A Biography Fifty Years After* (repr., Gloucester, Mass.: Peter Smith, 1965), pp. 450-51.

9. "Colonel Lee's Report," in W. W. Scott, ed., "The John Brown Letters," *VMHB* 10, no. 1 (July 1902).

10. Freeman, *R. E. Lee*, 1:397–98.

11. J. E. B. Stuart to "My Dear Mama," January 31, 1860, in Thomas, ed., "'The Greatest Service.'" Some accounts have Lewis Washington shouting that the marines should "never mind us, fire" and Lee, a good distance away, remarking that "the old revolutionary blood does tell." None of the firsthand accounts mention this anecdote, however, and Lee, many yards away, seems unlikely to have recognized a voice in the din of the moment. However, Freeman includes the story based on a later, secondhand account. Freeman, *R. E. Lee*, 1:399.

12. One of the casualties of the first day was also a son of John Brown. Green, "The Capture of John Brown"; J. E. B. Stuart to "My Dear Mama," January 31, 1860, in Thomas, ed., "'The Greatest Service'"; and Boteler, "Recollections of the John Brown Raid"; quotation Green, "The Capture of John Brown."

13. Mary Glenn to Mrs. Andrew Low, n.d. [c. 1859–60], Mackay-Stiles Family Papers, UNC.

14. The author is indebted to Frank Cucurullo, a historian for the National Park Service, for pointing out the police tactics used by Lee at Harper's Ferry and for allowing me to use his notes from an excellent presentation given at Arlington House in October 2004. See also Green, "The Capture of John Brown"; J. E. B. Stuart to "My Dear Mama," January 31, 1860, in Thomas, "'The Greatest Service.'"

15. "Colonel Lee's Report," in Scott, ed., "John Brown Letters"; and REL to Col. S. Cooper, Arlington, December 24, 1859, in REL Letterbook #1, LFP-VHS.

16. REL to Mary B. Ball, Arlington, November 16, 1859, Ball Family Papers, DU.

17. J. E. B. Stuart to "My Dear Mama," January 31, 1860, in Thomas, ed., "'The Greatest Service'"; and Cucurullo notes. Stephen Vincent Benét was one of the first writers about Lee to catch his distaste for such work, in *John Brown's Body*, p. 34.

18. The congressional delegation consisted of Senator James M. Mason and Ohio congressman Clement L. Vallandigham, both strongly sympathetic to slavery. Mason later wrote an official report of the affair. Villard, *John Brown*, pp. 456–63; quotation p. 461; and REL pocket memorandum book, October 18, 1859, LFP-VHS.

19. "Colonel Lee's Report," in Scott, "John Brown Letters," p. 22.

20. MCL Diary, [December] 11, [1859]; and REL to George W. Cullum, Arlington, Washington City P.O., December 24, 1859, USMA.

21. REL to Henry Lee, Harper's Ferry, December 6, 1859, LFP-VHS. For other ex-

amples of Lee using dialect, see REL to "Precious Life" [MiCL], Indianola, Texas, March 22, 1857, DE-LC; REL to MCL; and Soller's Point, June 23, 1849, DE-LC.

22. "No part of my life has been more happily spent; then that I have spent here," Brown wrote from prison; "& I humbly trust that no part has been spent to better purpose." John Brown to Rev. Luther Humphrey, Charlestown, Jefferson Co., Va., November 19, 1859, facsimile in John Brown of Ossawattomie Papers, LC. For letters and diary entries of Emerson, Thoreau, and Bronson Alcott that discuss plans to rescue Brown and the advantages of his becoming a martyr, see F. B. Sanborn, *Recollections of Seventy Years*, 2 vols. (Boston: Richard G. Badger, 1909), 1:199–207.

23. Stephen B. Oates, *To Purge This Land with Blood: A Biography of John Brown* (New York: Harper Torch, 1970), pp. 318–19, 324–27, quotation, p. 327.

24. "Death Sentences of Jno Brown and Accomplices," n.d. [November 1859], John Brown of Ossawattomie Papers, LC.

25. A facsimile of Brown's note is in National Park Service, *John Brown's Raid*, p. 60.

26. Further accounts of Brown's execution can be found in C. B. Galbreath, "John Brown" and Murat Halstead, "The Execution of John Brown," *Ohio Archaeological and Historical Quarterly* 30, no. 3 (July 1921): 285, 290–99; William A. Link, *Roots of Secession: Slavery and Politics in Antebellum Virginia* (Chapel Hill: University of North Carolina Press, 2003), pp. 185–89; and Oates, *To Purge This Land with Blood*, pp. 348–52.

27. "Aunt Lizy" to John Brown, n.d. [November 1859], in Scott, "John Brown Letters," p. 163.

28. For Lee's involvement with Wise's plan to augment the militia, see REL to Col. T. J. August, Arlington, Washington City, D.C., December 20, 1859, REL Letterbook #1, LFP-VHS. Lee apparently initially tried to decline the honor, but ultimately did attend a session of the military committee of the Virginia General Assembly. See REL pocket memorandum book, January 13, 1860, DE-LC.

29. Another Lee cousin described the "terror" felt after the raid and the change it produced in the slaves: "we children were charged never to mention the fact before the negroes, but it was easy to see that from some source they knew something unusual was going on. . . ." "Reminiscences of Cazenove G. Lee," n.d. [post 1865], transcription at BLA. See also Jennie Chambers, "What a School-Girl Saw of John Brown's Raid," *Harpers Monthly Magazine* 104, no. 620 (January 1902): 318; and Link, *Roots of Secession*, pp. 184, 189–91.

30. C[onstance] C[ary] Harrison, "A Virginia Girl in the First Year of the War," *Century Magazine* 3, no. 4 (August 1885): 606–14, quotation p. 606.

31. Rister, *Lee in Texas*, pp. 156–62; Skelton, *American Profession of Arms*, pp. 348–58; Totten quoted in Coffman, *Old Army*, p. 46.

32. Coffman, *Old Army*, pp. 92–95.

33. REL to EAL, Fort Mason, Texas, January 29, 1861, DE-LC.

34. Scott quoted in Peskin, *Winfield Scott*, p. 233.

35. Hancock, *Reminiscences of Winfield Scott Hancock*, pp. 66–69; and Edmund M. Coffman, "The Army Officer and the Constitution," *Parameters* 17, no. 3 (September 1987): 2–12.

36. W. H. Cob, "Reminiscences of Washington in 1861," Simon Cameron Papers, LC.

37. Hancock, *Reminiscences of Winfield Scott Hancock*, p. 69. In all, 269 officers left the service to join the Confederacy between the election of 1860 and the following summer. Twenty-six more resigned, but declined to serve on either side. It consti-

tuted only about a quarter of the total strength of the corps, yet many think that it was the ability of this group that turned the Civil War into the costliest conflict in American history. Most of those who resigned were at the lower levels of the officer corps; higher-ranking officers who had more at stake were less likely to give up their commissions. The rank and file was also more reluctant to cut their institutional ties. See Skelton, *American Profession of Arms,* pp. 355–56; and Gerald A. Patterson, *Rebels from West Point* (Mechanicsville, Pa.: Stackpole, 1987), p. xiii.

38. REL to [GWCL], Fort Mason, Texas, January 23, 1861, in Jones, *Life and Letters,* pp. 120–21. The letter as reproduced by Jones is actually an amalgam of two letters, the above and one written by REL to MCL, on the same day. A transcript of the latter is in DSF-LC.

39. REL to "My dear Son" [GWCL], San Antonio, Texas, December 14, 1860, REL-DU; and REL to EAL, Fort Mason, Texas, January 29, 1861, DE-LC.

40. REL to Annette Carter, Fort Mason, San Antonio P.O., January 16, 1861, Lennig Collection II, WL.

41. Anderson, *Texas Before and on the Eve of the Rebellion,* p. 32; and Darrow, "Recollections of the Twiggs Surrender," p. 36. Yet another acquaintance wrote that when he spoke of secession, "he showed more emotion than is recorded of him when he had won or lost a great battle later on." George B. Cosby quoted in Col. M. L. Crimmins, "What General Robert E. Lee's Generals Thought of Him," *West Texas Historical Association Yearbook* 12 (July 1936): 99.

42. REL to MCW, January 22, 1861, in Lee, *"To Markie,"* p. 58.

43. Johnson, *Soldier's Reminiscences,* p. 133.

44. REL to "My dear Son," December 14, 1860, San Antonio, Texas, REL-DU.

45. Anderson, *Texas Before and on the Eve of the Rebellion,* pp. 30–33, quotation p. 31. For Lee's use of his father's model in determining his course, see Chesnut, *Diary,* p. 480; and REL to CCL, Lexington, March 14, 1867, MoC.

46. Lee, *General Lee,* p. 11; and Henry Lee quoted in Royster, *Light-Horse Harry Lee,* p. 99.

47. REL to [GWCL], Fort Mason, Texas, January 23, 1861, in Jones, *Life and Letters,* pp. 120–21; and REL to "My dear Son," December 14, 1860, San Antonio, Texas, REL-DU.

48. For Lee's racial views, see chapter 9, "Humanity and the Law"; quotation REL to EAL, Fort Mason, Texas, January 29, 1861, DE-LC.

49. REL to EAL, January 29, 1861, Fort Mason, Texas, DE-LC. Lee's affinity with secessionist principles is discussed at some length in Nolan, *Lee Considered,* pp. 46–49.

50. Lee speaks of this resentment in his letter to "My dear Son," December 14, 1860, San Antonio, Texas, REL-DU, but it was an old sore with him. See, for example, Lee's complaint that the "South has had to bear some hard kicks from all sides" on the issue of slavery, in REL to Capt. A. Talcott, Arlington, February 21, 1833, LFP-VHS.

51. One writer has gone so far as to say that Lee must have had a strong gift for self-delusion. Nolan, *Lee Considered,* pp. 50–52.

52. William Allan, "Memoranda of Conversations with General Robert E. Lee," in Gary W. Gallagher, ed., *Lee the Soldier* (Lincoln: University of Nebraska Press, 1996), pp. 9–10, and Keyes, *Fifty Years Observation,* pp. 205–6; REL to Reverdy Johnson, Lexington, Va., February 25, 1868, REL Letterbook #4, LFP-VHS; REL Telegram to Genl Philip St. George Cocke, April 23, 1861, in Executive Papers of Virginia, LoV; and Freeman, *R. E. Lee,* 1:476–77.

53. REL to EAL, Fort Mason, Texas, January 29, 1861, DE-LC.

54. Harrison, "Virginia Girl," p. 606; Elizabeth Blair Lee to Phillips Lee, Silver Spring, July 3, 1861, in Lee, *Wartime Washington*, pp. 55–56; quotation from Miss S. Lee, "War Time in Alexandria, Virginia" *South Atlantic Quarterly* 4, no. 3 (July 1905): 235.

55. Alexander Stephens quoted in William E. Brooks, *Lee of Virginia* (repr., Westport, Colo.: Greenwood Press, 1975), p. 99.

56. REL to MCL, Fort Mason, Texas, January 23, 1861, transcript, DSF-LC; and REL to MCW, January 22, 1861, in Lee, *"To Markie,"* pp. 58–59.

57. Cassius Lee to REL, Alex[a], April 23, 1861; James May to REL, Theological Seminary of Va, April 22, 1861; and REL to Cassius Lee, Richmond, April 25, 1861, all SH.

58. Daniel W. Crofts, "Late Antebellum Virginia Reconsidered," *VMHB* 107, no. 3 (Summer 1999): 253–286; Link, *Roots of Secession*, pp. 6–7; Henry T. Shanks, *The Secession Movement in Virginia, 1847–61* (repr., New York: AMS Press, 1971), pp. 116, 206.

59. Adams, *Education of Henry Adams*, p. 86.

60. Link, *Roots of Secession*, pp. 8, 138–40, 171.

61. MCL to "My Dear Helen," Arlington, February 1, 1861, LFP-VHS.

62. Gienapp, *Abraham Lincoln*, pp. 50–52; Heintzelman Diary, March 4 and March 5, 1861, Heintzelman Papers, LC.

63. Allan, "Memoranda of Conversations," p. 9.

64. Cob, "Reminiscences of Washington," Cameron Papers, LC.

65. "Reminiscences of John Caldwell Tidball," Washington, 1861. LC; Heintzelman Diary, March 13, 1861, Heintzelman Papers, LC.

66. The promotion was approved by Lincoln on March 20 and tendered to Lee on March 28, 1861. He accepted on March 30. Freeman, *R. E. Lee*, 1:433.

67. McPherson, *Battle Cry of Freedom*, pp. 272–75, quotation p. 274. Hunter is quoted in Pryor, *Reminiscences of Peace and War*, p. 124.

68. Shanks, *Secession Movement in Virginia*, p. 206.

69. Lomax, *Leaves from an Old Washington Diary*, p. 149.

70. "Reminiscences of Cazenove G. Lee," BLA.

71. MCL to [Benson Lossing], May 1, 1861, typescript, AHA; "Statement of Francis Blair," in James Ford Rhodes, *History of the United States from the Compromise of 1850 to the McKinley-Bryan Campaign of 1896*, 8 vols. (reprint; Port Washington: Kennikat Press, 1967), 3:252n. Elizabeth Blair Lee to Samuel Phillips Lee, May 18, 1862, in Lee, *Wartime Washington*, p. 148. Elizabeth Blair Lee was the daughter of Francis Blair and heard the story through him. This is the closest to a contemporary account that we have of the Blair–R. E. Lee meeting. Both Secretary Simon Cameron and Lee later wrote descriptions of the encounter, which substantially agree. See REL to Reverdy Johnson, Lexington, Va., February 25, 1868, REL Letterbook #4, LFP-VHS; Allan, "Memoranda of Conversations," pp. 9–10; and "Statement of Simon Cameron" in Jones, *Life and Letters*, p. 130.

72. Allan, "Memoranda of Conversations," p. 10; Keyes, *Fifty Years Observation*, pp. 205–6.

73. Keyes, *Fifty Years Observation*, pp. 205–6; A. M. L. Washington to Fannie W. Reading, Washington, May 13, 1861, AHA; Robert E. L. deButts Jr., ed., "Mary Custis Lee's 'Reminiscences of the War,' " *VMHB* 109, no. 2 (Spring 2001): 314; Mason, *Popular Life*, p. 73; Freeman, *R. E. Lee*, 1:437; "General Lee and General Scott," *National Republican*, July 12, 1861.

74. REL to Smith Lee, Arlington, Va., April 20, 1861, in Lee, *General Lee*, pp. 88–89; and "Reminiscences of Cazenove G. Lee," BLA.

75. Nelligan, "Old Arlington," p. 450; quotation in Lee, "War Time in Alexandria," p. 235–36.

76. EAL to MiCL, Arlington, April 19, 1861, DE-LC.

77. Though she would later be accused of having influenced her husband, not until Yankee troops threatened Arlington did Mary Lee become an unswervingly loyal Confederate. For accusations against Mary Lee, see "Remarks of Mrs. P. R. Alger, Annapolis, Md.," 1957, MCM-LC, LC; for the Lee daughters' remark that their mother was "such an awful Unionist," see ACL to EAL, White House, May 2, [1861], REL-DU; for MCL's Unionist statements, see MCL to "My dear Helen" [Peter], Arlington, February 1, 1861, LFP-WL; MCL to Mrs. William Henry Stiles, Arlington, February 9, 1861, SH; MCL to MiCL, Arlington, February 24, [1861]; and MCL to "my dear child" [MiCL], Arlington, [April] 19, [1861], both DE-LC; and MCL to [Benson Lossing], May 1, 1861, typescript, AHA.

78. Parks, "Colored Servant."

79. Upshur, As I Recall Them, pp. 16–17. Upshur was a cousin of the Lees. His book contains numerous errors, but his account of Lee pacing and praying corroborates other descriptions of the scene.

80. Agnes Lee quoted in Lee, "War Time in Alexandria," p. 235–36.

81. Allan, "Memoranda of Conversations," p. 10; Upshur, As I Recall Them, p. 17.

82. Freeman, R. E. Lee, 1:431; and Dowdey, Lee, p. 134. Even the most contemporary writers follow this theme. "Lee had no choice in the matter," writes Bertram Wyatt-Brown as recently as 2005. "Robert E. Lee and the Concept of Honor," in Peter Wallenstein and Bertram Wyatt-Brown, eds., Virginia's Civil War (Charlottesville: University Press of Virginia, 2005), p. 37.

83. DeButts, "Mary Custis Lee's 'Reminiscences,'" p. 314.

84. This version is from Lee's letter to his sister Ann(e) Marshall. REL to Anne Lee Marshall, Arlington, Virginia, April 20, 1861, in Lee Jr., Recollections, pp. 25–26.

85. Allan, "Memoranda of Conversations," p. 10.

86. Julia Tyler to mother, Sherwood Forest, Charles City Co., April 25, 1861, in Lyon G. Tyler, The Letters and Times of the Tylers, 2 vols. (repr., New York: Da Capo Press, 1970), 2:648.

87. John Robertson to Governor John Letcher, Richmond, April 23, 1861, Executive Papers of John Letcher, LoV; and Freeman Cleaves, Rock of Chickamauga: The Life of George H. Thomas (repr., Westport, Colo.: Greenwood Press, 1974), pp. 5, 67–69.

88. William Price Craighill to mother, West Point, August 20, 1861, USMA.

89. USMA Archives; Cullum, Biographical Register, vols. 1 and 2; and Skelton, American Profession of Arms, p. 358.

90. Peter L. Guth, "Dennis Hart Mahan," ANB, 14:338–39.

91. Skelton, American Profession of Arms, p. 355.

92. Elizabeth Blair Lee to Samuel Phillips Lee, Silver Spring, May 18, 1862, in Lee, Wartime Washington, p. 148; and Apolline Blair to Frances Preston Blair, Bethlehem, September 12, 1861, in Blair and Lee Family Papers, Special Collections, Princeton University.

93. Cullum, Biographical Register, 2:466–67. See letters of Elizabeth Blair Lee to Samuel Phillips Lee in Lee, Wartime Washington, pp. 15n, 302; Lee, Lee of Virginia, pp. 396–98; and Upshur, As I Recall Them, pp. 15–16.

94. Cullum, *Biographical Register,* 2:506; and George B. McClellan to MCW, May 24, 1862, copy in MCW's hand, Carter Papers, TPA.

95. Two of Fendall's sons also fought for the Union. Captain Philip R. Fendall served with the U.S. Marines, and Clarence Fendall, with the U.S. Coast Guard, developed maps for the U.S. Navy. A third son, Lt. James Fendall, was an officer in the CSA marines. Introduction to Fendall Papers, DU.

96. MCL to ACL, "H. Hill," August 20, 1862; and REL to MCL, Near Richmond, July 28, 1862, both DE-LC.

97. Chesnut, *Diary,* p. 480.

98. Elizabeth Blair Lee to Samuel Phillips Lee, Philadelphia, June 4, 1861, in Lee, *Wartime Washington,* p. 43; and Chesnut, *Diary,* p. 131.

99. MCL to "My dear Helen" [Peter], Arlington, February 1, 1861, LFP-WL; MCL to Mrs. William Henry Stiles, Arlington, February 9, 1861, SH; MCL to MiCL, Arlington, February 24, [1861]; and MCL to "my dear child" [MiCL], Arlington, [April] 19, [1861], both DE-LC.

100. Custis Lee was among those torn over the decision, reiterating his father's belief that "secession was nothing but revolution" and stating that if he had the power he would fortify Arlington Heights; he remained in the army more than a month after his father's resignation. For his and Rooney's dismay over Virginia's secession, see Lee, "War Time in Alexandria"; Bernice-Marie Yates, *The Perfect Gentleman: The Life and Letters of George Washington Custis Lee* (Longwood, Fla.: Xulon Press, 2003), 1:212–14, 223–26; and REL to MCL, May 13, 1861, in Lee, *General Lee,* p. 94. As he stated to Roger Jones and Orton Williams, Lee did not want to influence the decisions of others. "The present is a momentous question which every man must settle for himself and upon principle," he told his wife. Nonetheless, others did follow his lead. See Louise Humphrey Carter, "Reminiscences of War Days," Shirley, June 20, 1905, copy in DSF-LC; REL to "My Precious Life," Arlington, April 1, 1861, DE-LC; and Elizabeth Blair Lee to Samuel Phillips Lee, Silver Spring, July 3, 1861, in Lee, *Wartime Washington,* pp. 55–56.

101. REL to MCW, January 22, 1861, in Lee, *"To Markie,"* p. 58; and REL to Simon Cameron, Arlington, April 20, 1861, NARA.

102. REL to Smith Lee, Arlington, Virginia, April 20, 1860, in Lee, *General Lee,* pp. 88–89.

103. REL to Capt. A. Talcott, Arlington, February 21, 1833, LFP-VHS.

104. For more on the various notions of honor, and how they played into the debate on secession, see Bertram Wyatt-Brown, *Yankee Saints and Southern Sinners* (Baton Rouge: Louisiana State University Press, 1985).

105. Allan, "Memoranda of Conversations," pp. 8–10.

106. MCL to [Benson Lossing], May 1, 1861, typescript, AHA; John Robertson to Governor John Letcher, Richmond, April 23, 1861, Executive Papers of John Letcher, LoV.

107. John Robertson to Governor John Letcher, Richmond, April 23, 1861, Executive Papers of John Letcher, LoV; Lee, "War Time in Alexandria," p. 235; Harriotte Hopkins Lee Taliaferro, "Reminiscences of Robert E. Lee," typescript, BLA.

108. Alan Nolan has proposed that Lee's acceptance of a position in the Virginia forces could not have been made spontaneously in the thirty-six hours after he resigned from the U.S. Army, and has hypothesized that Lee had made prior contingency arrangements. Nolan, *Lee Considered,* pp. 44–50. However, Robertson's letter expresses great pride that no conflict of interest was in question; by the time Lee was

given an official offer, he had resigned voluntarily, and "he was wholly unapprised of the generous intentions of the Convention . . . until we met [on April 22]." John Robertson to Governor John Letcher, Richmond, April 23, 1861, Executive Papers of John Letcher, LoV.

109. On March 15 Confederate Secretary of War L. P. Walker offered Lee a post as brigadier general in the army being formed—the highest rank then available in the Confederate service. Fellow Virginian George Thomas also received queries from the prosecessionist forces in Virginia around this time, and Lee may have been contacted as well. Cleaves, *Rock of Chickamauga,* pp. 5, 64–66.

110. John Robertson to Governor John Letcher, Richmond, April 23, 1861, Executive Papers of John Letcher, LoV.

111. "Reminiscences of Cazenove G. Lee," BLA; and Allan, "Memoranda of Conversations," p. 10.

112. John Esten Cooke to J. E. B. Stuart, Richmond, April 4, 1861, J. E. B. Stuart Papers, VHS.

113. One account has Lee confiding to Cassius Lee after the meetings in the churchyard that he had been tapped to lead Virginia's forces. "Reminiscences of Cazenove G. Lee," BLA. Also W. W. Scott, "Some Reminiscences of Famous Men," *Southern Magazine* 4 (July 1894): 628; and Allan, "Memoranda of Conversations," pp. 10–11.

114. Untitled newspaper clipping, Richmond, Virginia, April 23, 1861, in REL Memorandum Book, DE-LC. For a discussion of the quick turnabout from northern to southern forces, see Nolan, *Lee Considered,* pp. 41–45.

115. Oaths quoted in *General Regulations,* p. 410; and Nolan, *Lee Considered,* p. 39.

116. Elizabeth Blair Lee to Samuel Phillips Lee, Silver Spring, July 3, 1861, in Lee, *Wartime Washington,* p. 148.

117. The louse drawing is found in "Portraits and Views of Men and Events Connected with the Civil War," Box I, #8, USMA; *New York Daily Tribune,* May 9, 1861; for Lincoln's assertion that Lee was among those who should have been arrested on suspicion see Abraham Lincoln to Erastus Corning and Others, Executive Mansion, Washington, June 12, 1863, in *Abraham Lincoln, Speeches and Writing, 1859–1865,* ed. Don E. Fehrenbacher (New York: Library of America, 1989), pp. 454–63.

118. Greene's words were "Arnold the traitor must fall!—Oh Lucifer! How great will be thy fall." Nannie Rodgers Macomb to Montgomery C. Meigs, n.d. [1861], MCM-LC; and Greene quoted in Johnson, *Nathanael Greene,* 2:40.

119. Henry Lee quoted in Royster, *Light-Horse Harry Lee,* p. 109.

120. Anna Maria Fitzhugh to CCL, November 12 [1830], Arlington, EA-LC.

121. Lee is reported as saying, "I cannot consult my own feelings in the matter." See *National Republican,* July 12, 1861.

122. This larger perspective was suggested to the author by David Halberstam's remarks in Thomas A. Bass, "The Spy Who Loved Us," *New Yorker* 81, no. 14 (May 23, 2005).

CHAPTER EIGHTEEN: **Field of Honor**

1. REL to MCL, Richmond, April 30, 1861, copy in MCL's hand, DE-LC. Mary Childe was the daughter of Lee's deceased sister, Mildred Lee Childe. "My poor Anne" refers to his sister, and perhaps to her receipt of his letter announcing his resignation. The reference to the Alexandria market probably refers to the hiring out of

the slaves, who were continuing to resist the family. "Helen" is probably Helen Peter, a cousin of Mrs. Lee. The phrase "bring peace to our distracted country" appears in a letter Lee received a few days before he wrote the April 30 letter to his wife and must have made an impression on him. James May to C. F. Lee, Theological Seminary of Va., April 22, 1861, enclosed in Cassius F. Lee to REL, Alexandria, April 23, 1861, both SH.

2. For Lee's comments on his new beard, see REL to MiCL, Charleston, November 15, 1861, DE-LC. The first known reference to "Robert E. Lee" is in a letter from Henry Lee, endorsing his brother's application to West Point. Henry Lee to ?, Fredericksburg, Va., March 6, 1824, in Freeman, *R. E. Lee*, 1:43. The U.S. Military Academy continued to occasionally refer to him in this way, but otherwise its usage was very rare until 1861. No papers in Lee's hand have been found that use this formulation. For Lee's claim of a passive role in being made commander of the Army of Northern Virginia, see REL to Reverdy Johnson, Lexington, Va., February 25, 1868, REL Letterbook #4, LFP-VHS.

3. Margaret Leech, *Reveille in Washington* (New York: Harper and Brothers, 1941), quotation Enoch Aquila Chase, "The Arlington Case," *Records of the Columbia Historical Society* 31–32 (1930): 175–76; and "Distances from Mansion House, Arlington," in Thomas Jefferson Cram, "Reminiscences," USMA.

4. Stories abound of the political divisions in the counties of northern Virginia. A majority of the voters had actually selected the Constitutional Unionists in the November 1860 election and moderate delegates to the secession convention held in the months thereafter. Others responded to Lincoln's call for troops by making Southern banners and uniforms, and joining the Mount Vernon Guard. Many in Alexandria stayed away from the polls rather than vote for secession, and two-thirds of those who did vote rejected ratification. Nonetheless, once the war began, Alexandria boys quickly joined the southern army. One Lee cousin, recounting the round of tattoos and flag-makings, reported: "No where was rebellion more rampant." Leech, *Reveille*, pp. 79–81; Noel G. Harrison, "Atop an Anvil: The Civilians' War in Fairfax and Alexandria Counties, April 1861–April 1862," *VMHB* 106, no. 2 (Spring 1998): 137–38; Charles O. Paullin, "Alexandria County in 1861," *Records of the Columbia Historical Society* 28 (1926): 109; Kundahl, *Alexandria Goes to War*, pp. 1–18; and Lee, "Wartime in Alexandria," pp. 234–48, quotation p. 234.

5. Charles Russell Lowell to mother, Washington, May 13, 1861 in Edward W. Emerson, *Life and Letters of Charles Russell Lowell* (Port Washington, N.Y.: Kennikat Press, 1971), p. 208. For a similar description of the contrast between early elation and war's reality, see Sam R. Watkins, *Company Aytch: Or, A Side Show of the Big Show* (New York: Plume, 1999), pp. 6–7.

6. MCL to [REL], May 12 [1861], DE-LC; Leech, *Reveille*, p. 80; and Benjamin Franklin Cooling and Walton H. Owen II, *Mr. Lincoln's Forts: A Guide to the Civil War Defenses of Washington* (Shippensburg, Pa.: White Mane, 1988).

7. It is unclear how consciously Lee considered the possibility that, should he accept command of Union forces, one of his first acts might be the seizure of his wife's property. Surely when he says he could not "make up my mind to raise my hand against my relatives, my children, my home" or that he wished to avoid "duty which I could not conscientiously perform," he must have thought of Arlington's strategic location. REL to Anne Marshall, Arlington, April 20, 1861, DE-LC; and REL to Smith Lee, Arlington, April 20, 1861, in Lee, *General Lee*, pp. 88–89.

8. Custis Lee quoted in Lee, "Wartime in Alexandria," p. 236.

9. REL to MCL, Richmond, July 12, 1861, DE-LC.

10. See REL to MCL, Richmond, April 30, May 2, 8, 11, and 16, 1861, all DE-LC.

11. MCL to [REL], May 12 [1861], DE-LC.

12. MCL to REL, May 9, 1861; EAL to ACL, May 6 [1861], and MCL to "My dear children," Arlington, May 11, [1861], all DE-LC.

13. MCL to "My dear little girl" [MiCL], Arlington, May 5 [1861], DE-LC.

14. DeButts, "Mary Custis Lee's 'Reminiscences,'" p. 315. Also MCL to REL, Arlington, May 9, 1861; quotation MCL to "My dear children," May 11, [1861], both DE-LC.

15. MCL to [REL], May 12, [1861], DE-LC; quotation in deButts, "Mary Custis Lee's 'Reminiscences,'" p. 315.

16. DeButts, "Mary Custis Lee's 'Reminiscences,'" p. 315.

17. Ibid., pp. 315–17; Nelligan, "Old Arlington," pp. 458–59; and MCL to MCW, May 26, 1862, CL-TPA. Though she would never again live at Arlington, Mary Custis Lee in fact visited it for a few minutes just before she died—a painful experience for her. See chapter 25, "Blurred Vision."

18. Cooling, *Symbol,* p. 33; Mary Custis Lee told the story of meeting a Union officer of long acquaintance in the streets of Washington and being told that he had "expected to see Jeff Davis with an army of at least 30 thousand men on the Arlington heights." DeButts, "Mary Custis Lee's 'Reminiscences,'" p. 314.

19. Cooling, *Symbol,* pp. 52–53, 59, 136; and MCL to [REL], May 12, [1861], DE-LC.

20. Among the most poignant documents remaining from this period is a telegram form written by Lee—apparently his first official order as commander of Virginia's troops—that tries to forestall Federal occupation of Arlington by convincing the Union that it had nothing to fear from his forces. The telegram reads: "It is not considered probable that the U.S. troops will occupy the Virg[a] shore opposite Washington unless they have reason to believe that preparations to attack Washington City are making. It is important that no such expectation should be raised, but that the troops in Alex[a] should be kept quiet & prepared & the movements in Washington be observed without attracting attention. The termini of the R. Roads in Alex[a] should be secured from attack. A portion of the troops at Harper's Ferry could be stationed at Gordonsville for service in Alex[a] if necessary. Ordnance &c will be forwarded as soon as practicable. Keep all movements secret if there is a likelihood of provisions being carried to Wash[a] from Alex[a]. Send them into the interior. It is important that conflict not be provoked before we are ready. R.E. Lee, Com in Chief." REL, telegram in hand to Genl Philip St. George Cocke, Executive Department, April 23, 1861, Executive Papers of Virginia, LoV. Also REL to Cassius F. Lee, Richmond, April 23, 1861, SH; and Cooling, *Symbol,* p. 35.

21. See MCL to REL, May 9, 1861, to "My dear children," Arlington, May 11, [1861]; quotation EAL to ACL, May 6, [1861], all DE-LC. Orton Williams was to pay for his continued interaction with the Lees. Soon after his early-morning appearance at Arlington he became suspect because of his proximity to both Scott and the Lees, and was, in Mrs. Lee's words, "branded as a traitor." When he tried to tender his resignation, he was refused a hearing and sentenced to confinement in the prison on Governor's Island, New York. Orton Williams to General Winfield Scott, May 14, 1861, TPA; and MCL to REL, May 9, 1861, DE-LC.

22. Nelligan, "Old Arlington," p. 463; General David Butterfield quoted in Paullin,

"Alexandria County in 1861," p. 113; Jim Parks quoted in "Interview with James Parks," *Sunday Star,* November 4, 1928.

23. Nelligan, "Old Arlington," p. 463.

24. Charles Russell Lowell to Mother, Washington, May 25, 1861, in Emerson, *Life and Letters/Lowell,* pp. 209–10; Cooling and Owen, *Mr. Lincoln's Forts,* p. 90; and Edward A. Pierson to "Dear Aunt," "Camp Essex, East Shore of Old Virginia & West End of Long Bridge," May 27, 1861, Edward A. Pierson Papers, NJHS.

25. Irwin McDowell to MCL, "Head Qu. Dept. N.E. Virginia, Arlington," May 30, 1861, typescript, AHA; and MCL to General Winfield Scott, May 5, 1861, in Lee, *General Lee,* pp. 93–94. Mary Custis Lee may have been right in her instinct to stay at Arlington. Those who remained with their houses, even when they were occupied by Federal troops, generally had a better chance of protecting them than those who left. Cousin Anna Maria Fitzhugh remained throughout the war at Ravensworth, despite Lee's intense anxiety. Britannia Peter also remained at Tudor Place, though it became a billet for Federal officers. Neither house was destroyed, and both families retained their property.

26. McDowell to MCL, May 30, 1861, typescript, AHA; [MCW] to "Dearest Cousin Mary" [MCL], Washington, D.C., July 13, 1861, DE-LC; and Nelligan, "Old Arlington," pp. 464–65.

27. Nelligan, "Old Arlington," p. 168.

28. Cooling and Owen, *Mr. Lincoln's Forts,* pp. 6, 90; and Nelligan, "Old Arlington," p. 473.

29. Edward Pierson to "Dear Aunt," May 27, 1861, Pierson Papers, NJHS.

30. Cooling, *Symbol,* p. 77; and William Howard Russell, *My Diary North and South* (Boston: T.O.H.P. Burnham, 1863), p. 396.

31. Cooling and Owen, *Mr. Lincoln's Forts,* pp. 90–91.

32. DeButts, "Mary Custis Lee's 'Reminiscences,'" p. 320. Mrs. Lee's description of the post-Manassas flight was scathing: "Northern Women had gone to that battle in open Barouches decked out like Jesebel to witness the slaughter & flight of the Rebels. They scarcely escaped to Washington with garments sufficient for decency. Men threw away in their panic, arms, & all that could impede their flight even their shoes upon which a bare-footed little Reb remarked 'Papa, I can always run much faster with my shoes off.'"

33. Cooling, *Symbol,* pp. 52–53.

34. Russell, *My Diary,* pp. 394–95; and Nelligan, "Old Arlington," p. 472–73.

35. U.S. Quartermaster Corps, *Arlington House and Its Associations* (Washington, D.C.: GPO, 1932); MCL to Fannie Nottingham, Lexington, Va., May 6, 1866, in "Letters from Old Trunks," *VMHB* 44, no. 4 (October 1936): 335–36; Virginia Clay-Clopton, *A Belle of the Fifties* (New York: Doubleday, Page, 1904), p. 227; Karen Byrne Kinzey, "Battling for Arlington House: To Lee or Not to Lee?" *Arlington Historical Magazine* 12, no. 3 (October 2003): 28; Mary A. R. Custis School notebook, 1823, with note on front page: "Taken from Arlington Garret during the war of rebellion by EMB," CL-LC; quotation REL to MCL, December 25, 1861, DE-LC.

36. Gienapp, *Abraham Lincoln,* p. 88; Paullin, "Alexandria in 1861," pp. 29–31; Harrison, "Atop an Anvil," pp. 139–40; and Mark Grimsley, *The Hard Hand of War: Union Military Policy toward Southern Civilians, 1861–1865* (Cambridge, England: Cambridge University Press, 1995), pp. 17, 21.

37. The term *rosewater policy* came from the *New York Times,* June 30, 1861, the ed-

itors of which were hankering for a fight. "By no government in the wide world other than this of ours is treason treated so kindly," they wrote, "or rebellion sprinkled with so much rosewater." Grimsley believes that the Federal position began as a policy of conciliation, but changed in the beginning of 1862 to a more "pragmatic" approach that embraced confiscation and emancipation of slaves as policies of war. Stephen Ash maintains that the early conservative policies were discarded in favor of radical, punitive actions in the second summer of the war, and that this position was designed to crumble the Confederacy. See Grimsley, *Hard Hand of War;* and Ash, *When the Yankees Came.*

38. Harrison, "Atop an Anvil," pp. 135, 143–45.

39. Frobel, *Diary of Anne S. Frobel,* pp. 8, 27; and Frobel quoted in Harrison, "Atop an Anvil," p. 155.

40. For officers' participation in pillaging, see Harrison, "Atop an Anvil," pp. 141–44, 159; and Francis Colburn Adams, *The Story of a Trooper* (New York: Dick & Fitzgerald, 1865), p. 200–201; Henry W. Halleck's *International Law; or, Rules Regulating the Intercourse of States in Peace and War* (New York: D. Van Nostrand, 1861) quoted in Grimsley, *Hard Hand of War,* p. 16.

41. Harrison, "Atop an Anvil," p. 142.

42. The story of Confederate looting of Southern citizens is one yet to be written. For the actions described here, see General Carl Van Dorn quoted ibid., p. 157; REL to General Milledge L. Bonham, Headquarters, Virginia Forces, Richmond, Va., May 22, 1861, and to General Joseph E. Johnston, Headquarters, Richmond, May 18, 1862, both in Lee, *Wartime Letters,* pp. 33, 176.

43. Harrison, "Atop an Anvil," p. 157.

44. Russell, *My Diary,* p. 398.

45. MCL to Mrs. [Wm. Henry] Stiles, White House, March 8, [1862], SH.

46. MCL to General Sanford, May 30, 1861, typescript, AHA.

47. Note from MCL quoted in Nelligan, "Old Arlington," p. 481. At first the Union officers responded to such messages, packing up the family's furniture and guarding the estate. Pressures of war—and enmity—grew over time, however, and the White House was burned as Federal troops retreated from the area in 1862. See "The Washington Relics," *National Republican,* January 28, 1862. The Washington memorabilia that was displayed in the Patent Office was largely saved.

48. REL to MCL, Coosawhatchie, S.C., December 25, 1861, DE-LC; and REL to MCL(d), December 25, 1861, MCL-VHS.

49. MCL to MiCL, [February] 19, [1861], LFP-VHS; and REL to MCL, May 25, 1861, DE-LC.

50. MCL to "My dear little girl" [MiCL], Arlington, May 5, [1861], DE-LC.

51. Ibid.; MCL to EAL, June 30, [1861], DE-LC; and deButts, "Mary Custis Lee's 'Reminiscences,'" pp. 317-318.

52. MCL to "My dear little girl" [MiCL], May 5, [1861], DE-LC.

53. William T. Sherman, *Memoirs, by Himself* (New York: Charles Webster, 1891), 1:219.

54. Ibid., 1:217–18.

55. Paullin, "Alexandria in 1861," pp. 126–27; and Julia Ward Howe, *Reminiscences, 1819–1899* (repr., New York: Negro Universities Press, 1969), pp. 273–75.

56. Nelligan, "Old Arlington," p. 469.

57. Sneden Diary, vol. 4, n.d. [c. November 20, 1862], Sneden Papers, VHS.

58. Ibid., pp. 487–88; *Harper's Weekly* 8 (May 7, 1864); Lt. Col. E. M. Greene to BG Montgomery C. Meigs, July 22, 1863, RG 92, NARA. In January 1862 it had been determined that the U.S. government should take on responsibility for the Arlington slaves, since the owners could not maintain them. Gen. L. Thomas to Col. J. P. Taylor, January 2, 1862, RG 92, NARA. Also Joseph P. Reidy, " 'Coming from the Shadow of the Past': The Transition from Slavery to Freedom at Freedman's Village, 1863–1900," *VMHB* 95, no. 4 (October 1987): 403–28. Although this article contains numerous factual errors, it offers an interesting perspective on some of the uncertainties faced by the inhabitants of Freedman's Village.

59. On Lee's early difficulties, see MCL to "My dear children," Arlington, May 11, [1861]; and REL to MCL, Richmond, June 24, 1861, both DE-LC; and REL to Henry Wise, Richmond, May 24, 1861, Eggleston Collection, HL. Lee's desire to be in the field and disappointment about Manassas are expressed in REL to MCL, July 27, 1861, in Lee Jr., *Recollections,* p. 37; for his "mortification" at Cheat Mountain, REL to MCL, Valley Mt., September 17, 1861; and REL to MCL, Camp on Sewell's Mountain, September 26, 1861, both DE-LC. Lee's early days organizing the Army of Virginia are described in Walter H. Taylor, *Four Years with General Lee,* James T. Robertson Jr., ed. (New York: Bonanza Books, 1962), pp. 11–19. Bishop Meade's remarks in W[illiam] Meade to John Stewart, Millwood, July 14, 1861, William Meade Papers, LC.

60. See MCL to [REL], May 12, [1861]; and MCL to ACL, September 21, [1861], both DE-LC. Dishonorable discharges were being given to those who resigned from the U.S. Army and joined the Confederacy. For one account of this, see Frobel, *Diary of Anne S. Frobel,* p. 2.

61. REL to MCL, Camp at Valley Mt., September 9, 1861, DE-LC.

62. MCL to "My dear little child," Richmond, "7th" (n.d.) [1861], DE-LC. Judith McGuire gives several descriptions of Mrs. Lee about this time in *Diary of a Southern Refugee during the War* (repr., New York: Arno Press, 1972), pp. 26, 65–66.

63. A copy of the seizure documents, dated July 20, 1863, is in BLA.

64. Whether the cousin did or did not make the payment also remains an open question. The Supreme Court decision that ultimately repaid the Lees for the property took as the chief argument for illegal seizure that Philip Fendall had attempted to pay the costs. But when he was informed of Arlington's confiscation in November 1863 by Cassius Lee, and requested to pay the taxes, pro-Union Fendall wrote that it would "not be convenient for me to advance the taxes." Whether he was persuaded finally, or they were never proffered, is unclear. C. F. Lee to Philip R. Fendall, with notation in Fendall's hand, November 27, 1863, Philip R. Fendall Papers, DU; and *U.S. vs. George Washington Custis Lee,* December 4, 1882, in *Supreme Court Reporter: Cases Argued and Determined in the U.S. Supreme Court, October Term 1882* (St. Paul: West Publishing, 1883), p. 247.

65. Ibid.; Chase, "Arlington Case"; "Sale of Confiscated Lands," *National Republican,* January 12, 1864.

66. In 1877 Custis Lee began a protracted legal battle to contest the tax procedure and reclaim the Arlington estate. After a difficult struggle, the Supreme Court ruled in favor of Lee, upholding the constitutional principle "nor shall private property be taken for public use, without just compensation." No longer habitable, Arlington was retained by the government, and Custis Lee was paid $150,000 for the estate. On April 24, 1883, he handed the "good title" to the then secretary of war—Robert Todd

Lincoln. See U.S. vs. GWCL, *Supreme Court Reporter*, 1882, p. 247; Chase, "Arlington Case," pp. 181–206; Miller, *Second Only to Grant*, pp. 258–61; statistics, Margaret E. Wagner, Gary W. Gallagher, and Paul Finkelman, eds., *The Library of Congress Civil War Desk Reference* (New York: Simon and Schuster, 2002), p. 304.

67. "Remarks by Mrs. P. R. Alger," Annapolis, Md., 1957, typescript, MCM-LC; Fredricksen, "Meigs," pp. 256–57; for the Lee-Meigs connection, see, e.g., REL to CCL, St. Louis, August 15, 1837, REL-UVa; REL to Saml Frost, Arlington, January 1840, REL Letterbook #1, LFP-VHS; and Journals of M. C. Meigs for March 17, 1856 and December 21, 1859, MCM-LC; for Meigs's critical contribution to the Union cause, see Hugh McCulloch, *Men and Measures of Half a Century* (repr., New York: Da Capo Press, 1970), pp. 269–74.

68. Journal of M. C. Meigs, May 23, 1861, MCM-LC.

69. M. C. Meigs to Charles D. Meigs, Washington, D.C., May 12 and June 1, 1864, and May 3, 1865, all MCM-LC.

70. Some people have surmised that Meigs took over the Lees' estate for a cemetery because of his anger at the death of his son. However, the decision to use Arlington for burials was made in June 1864, and Meigs's son was not killed until the following October. Others commented that he requisitioned Arlington because of a real or supposed slight at the hands of the Lee family. Charles D. Meigs to M. C. Meigs, Harris, May 29, 1864; M. C. Meigs to "My Dear General," Washington, D.C., August 22, 1865; Statement of M. C. Meigs, Washington, D.C., July 20, 1865; M. C. Meigs to Charles D. Meigs, Washington, D.C., August 26, 1865, and "Remarks of Mrs. P. R. Alger," all MCM-LC; and Fredricksen, "Montgomerency C. Meigs," p. 257.

71. Nelligan, "Old Arlington," pp. 489–90; for more on death and burial in the Civil War, see Drew Gilpin Faust, "'A Riddle of Death': Mortality and Meaning in the American Civil War," 34th Annual Robert Fortenbaugh Memorial Lecture, Gettysburg College, 1995.

72. The story is told that Meigs conceived the idea while riding to Arlington "late in the afternoon" of May 13, 1864, with President Lincoln. But Meigs's diary contains no such notation for either that day or those shortly before or after, and there is no record that Lincoln visited the Heights around this time. Karl Decker and Angus McSween, *Historic Arlington* (Washington, D.C.: Decker & McSween, 1892). This curious volume, which was written with the cooperation of cemetery officials and obviously with access to the Lee family, is the source of many assumptions-cum-legends about the establishment of the cemetery. It was published a few months after the death of Meigs, and there is no indication in the voluminous Meigs papers that he or his family was in contact with the authors. See also Journal of M. C. Meigs, May 10–14, 1864. Had Meigs gone to Arlington that day, it would have been uncharacteristic of him not to have noted the visit. See, for example, entry for June 7, 1864, and M. C. Meigs to Charles D. Meigs, Washington, D.C., May 3, 1865, both MCM-LC, for descriptions of his rides to Arlington.

73. "Remarks of Mrs. P. R. Alger," MCM-LC. For Lincoln's admiration of Meigs, see A. Lincoln to Lieutenant General Scott, Executive Mansion, June 5, 1861, typescript, MCM-LC. Lincoln wrote: "I have come to know [then] Colonel Meigs quite well for a short acquaintance, and so far as I am capable of judging, I do not know one who combines the qualities of masculine intellect, learning and experience of the right sort, and physical power of labor and endurance, so well as he."

74. Gen. M. C. Meigs to Edwin M. Stanton, and Stanton approval, June 15, 1864, both RG 92, NARA. Decker and McSween, *Historic Arlington,* p. 69; also William B. Skelton, "Edwin McMasters Stanton," *ANB,* 20:558–62. One persistent myth was that the first soldier interred at Arlington was a Confederate. QMG records, however, establish clearly that it was William Christman of the 67th Pennsylvania Regiment, who was interred on May 13. The first Confederate soldier, L. Reinhart of North Carolina, was buried a few days later. See Nelligan, "Old Arlington," pp. 491. Several hundred Confederate soldiers were buried at Arlington, originally interspersed among the Union dead. When the graves were re-marked in the decades following the war, those labeled "Rebel" were given the same marble stones as northern regiments, including names and military outfits, where possible. In 1901, after some persistent lobbying by southern leaders, the Confederate dead were removed to a special section of the cemetery. See Michelle A. Krowl, "'In the Spirit of Fraternity': The United States Government and the Burial of Confederate Dead at Arlington National Cemetery, 1864–1914," *VMHB* 111, no. 2 (Spring 2003): 159–64.

75. *National Republican* and *Washington D.C. Morning Chronicle,* both June 17, 1864; and deButts, "Mary Custis Lee's 'Reminiscences,'" p. 318.

76. M. C. Meigs to Sec. of War, August 5, 1871, and Memo of M. C. Meigs, April 12, 1873, both in RG 92, NARA; deButts, "Mary Custis Lee's 'Reminiscences,'" p. 318.

77. Decker and McSween, *Historic Arlington,* p. 66; and Miller, *Second Only to Grant,* p. 260. Among those still referring to the assertions of Decker and McSween is the official Arlington National Cemetery Web site at www.arlingtoncemetery.org.

78. David Hackett Fischer discusses what he terms "motivational fallacies" in *Historians' Fallacies* (New York: Harper and Row, 1970), pp. 214–15.

79. E.g., the *National Intelligencer* (June 18, 1864) wrote: "The people of the entire nation will one day, not very far distant, heartily thank the creators of this movement." For early difficulties see Captain Charles Moore to BG D. H. Rucker, Washington, D.C., November 11, 1864, RG 92, NARA. Evidently piles of bodies caused "unpleasant odors," and rumors circulated about undertakers who threw the corpses from the coffins and then stacked them up to use again, or discarded bodies on remote parts of the estate, causing "many stories."

80. Edward Dicey, *Six Months in the Federal States* (London: Macmillan, 1863), 1:95.

81. M. C. Meigs to Charles D. Meigs, Washington, D.C., May 23, 1865; and "Remarks of Mrs. P. R. Alger," both MCM-LC.

82. For the inspiring vista from the Capitol dome and natural beauty of the Arlington grounds, see *Washington D.C. Morning Chronicle,* June 17, 1864; and George Tuthill Borrett, *Letters from Canada and the United States* (London: J. E. Adlard, 1865), p. 220.

83. Will of Montgomery C. Meigs, July 8, 1885, MCM-LC.

84. Emerson, *Life and Letters/Lowell,* p. 210.

85. Benson J. Lossing to MCL, unsent draft, Poughkeepsie, N.Y., March 1866, Lossing Papers, HL.

86. Borrett, *Letters from . . . the United States,* pp. 235–36.

CHAPTER NINETEEN: "A *General* . . . Is a Rare Product"

1. REL to Jefferson Davis, H^dqrs: Near Richmond," June 5, 1862, USMA. The "experiment" witnessed by Davis was the battle of Seven Pines, at which General Joseph

Johnston was wounded. The brigadier general D. H. Hill complained of was Gabriel James Rains, who was censured during the Peninsula campaign for poor performance and did not hold further field command. The other brigadier mentioned was General Winfield Scott Featherston, whose brigade was made up of Mississippi regiments. The nature of Hill's complaint against him is not known. The title of the chapter comes from a letter of Jefferson Davis to his brother Joseph, May 7, 1863, quoted in William C. Davis, *The Cause Lost: Myths and Realities of the Confederacy* (Lawrence: University of Kansas Press, 1996), p. 48.

2. REL to General [Martin W.] Gary, Headqrs, September 20, 1864, MoC. Gary, a South Carolinian, was an officer in Hampton's Legion, a combined infantry and cavalry outfit that was known for the kind of "special force" operations Lee is requesting in this letter.

3. An informal sample of letters from the first six months of 1863 from Lee to his wife shows that he referred to Union forces as "the enemy" in virtually every letter, dozens in all, ranging from January 21, 1863, to July 12, 1863; all DE-LC.

4. The speech is reprinted in Freeman, *R. E. Lee*, 1:468.

5. Joseph Ellis discusses Washington's similarly self-effacing response upon his elevation to command, and his equally questionable qualifications, in *His Excellency*, pp. 70–71.

6. Lee's desire to be in the field, and disappointment about being absent at Manassas, are expressed in REL to MCL, July 27, 1861; for his "mortification" at Cheat Mountain, REL to MCL, Valley Mt., September 17, 1861; and REL to MCL, Camp on Sewell's Mountain, September 26, 1861, all DE-LC; also Hitchcock, *Fifty Years in Camp and Field*, p. 33.

7. A good overview of this period is in Thomas, *Robert E. Lee*, pp. 192–225.

8. Chesnut, *Diary*, pp. 54–55; quotation W. C. Rives to R. E. Lee, Castle Hill, Cobham P.O., April 28, 1861, REL-DU.

9. Thomas J. Jackson to wife, April 23, 1861, quoted in James I. Robertson, *Stonewall Jackson: The Man, the Soldier, the Legend* (New York: Macmillan, 1997), p. 218.

10. Diary of Edmund Ruffin, November 28, 1861, Edmund Ruffin Papers, LC.

11. Goree, *Longstreet's Aide*, p. 47; and John William Ford memoir from diary notes, LC.

12. Davis, *The Cause Lost*, p. 38; Chesnut, *Diary*, p. 70, quotation p. 230.

13. W. Randolph Smith to Mrs. James Bell, Camp Before Richmond, June 22, 1862, typescript, DSF-LC.

14. McPherson, *Battle Cry of Freedom*, pp. 462–64; J. F. C. Fuller, *Grant and Lee* (Bloomington: Indiana University Press), pp. 156–62; and Longstreet, *From Manassas to Appomattox*, p. 114.

15. Casualty figures are from McPherson, *Battle Cry of Freedom*, pp. 467, 471; also Daniel H. Hill, "McClellan's Change of Base and Malvern Hill," in *B & L* 2:383–95; quotation p. 394. For a discussion of Lee's intentions and our imperfect understanding of this battle, see William J. Miller, "'The Siege of Richmond Was Raised,'" in Peter S. Carmichael, ed., *Audacity Personified* (Baton Rouge: Louisiana State University Press, 2004), pp. 27–56.

16. Toombs quoted in Steven E. Woodworth, *Davis and Lee at War* (Lawrence: University Press of Kansas, 1995), p. 173; see also Hal Bridges, *Lee's Maverick General: Daniel Harvey Hill* (New York: McGraw Hill, 1961), pp. 149–50.

17. Lee was also disappointed that he failed to "destroy" the Union army; see McPherson, *Battle Cry of Freedom*, p. 471. For the pro-Lee stance, Jubal Early quoted

in Jones, *Personal Reminiscences,* p. 7; quotations F[rederick] Johnston to "dear Fan," June 29 and July 4, 1862, James Ambler Johnston Papers, VHS; and J. L. Johnston to Miss M. M. Green, Richmond, July 20, 1862, Mercer Johnston Papers, LC.

18. Edward Porter Alexander, *Fighting for the Confederacy,* ed. Gary W. Gallagher (Chapel Hill: University of North Carolina Press, 1989), p. 265.

19. John S. Mosby, "Personal Recollections of General Lee," *Munsey's Magazine* 45, no. 1 (April 1911): 67.

20. Goree, *Longstreet's Aide,* p. 123; quotation Taylor, *Four Years with General Lee,* p. 145.

21. REL to MCL, Camp Fred^g, December 16, 1862, DE-LC.

22. Connelly, *Marble Man,* pp. 206–8; Fellman, *Making of Robert E. Lee,* pp. 114–17.

23. Quotation CCL, "Lines Descriptive of the Fate of Gen Henry Lee," n.d., EA-LC. Perhaps one day we will know more of genetics, overweening hormones, and behavioral development, and how they operate to instill aggression. Peter Carmichael questions whether one could give a biological interpretation to aggression, but contemporary analysis indicates that it is indeed a physiological trait which highly colors perceptions and judgments in many situations. See Peter S. Carmichael, "Lee's Search for the Battle of Annihilation," in Carmichael, *Audacity Personified,* p. 4. On aggression, see Paul F. Brain and David Benton, *Multidisciplinary Approaches to Aggression Research* (New York: Elsevier/North-Holland Biomedical Press, 1981); and Neil R. Carlson, *Physiology of Behavior* (Boston: Allyn & Bacon, 1998).

24. Royster, *Light-Horse Harry Lee,* pp. 19–27. For a longer discussion of the influence of Light-Horse Harry on Robert E. Lee, see John Morgan Dederer, "The Origins of Robert E. Lee's Bold Generalship: A Reinterpretation," *Military Affairs* 49, no. 3 (July 1985): 117–23. Some of the comparisons are convincing, but Dederer probably draws too many conclusions. Henry Lee's small auxiliary command bore little resemblance to the overarching responsibilities faced by his son, and many assertions—such as the assumption that Robert "read and reread" his father's memoirs or that his mother portrayed Harry in an idealized light—are taken from Douglas Southall Freeman. Although Freeman states them as fact, he does so without citation, and there is no independent evidence that these assertions are true. Henry Lee's Commonplace Book and accompanying letter to Lee, n.d., is in LFP-WL.

25. McCaslin, *Lee in the Shadow of Washington,* discusses Lee's military relationship to Washington with more persuasiveness than his connection to Lee's personal life. Herman Melville, however, has the last word on this popular comparison.

> Who looks at Lee must think of Washington;
> In pain must think, and hide the thought,
> So deep with grievous meaning is it fraught.

Herman Melville, "Lee in the Capitol," in *The Battle-Pieces of Herman Melville,* ed. Hennig Cohen (New York: Thomas Yoseloff, 1963), p. 189.

26. REL to Smith Lee, City of Mexico, March 4, 1848, SH.

27. REL to John Mackay, National Palace, City of Mexico, October 2, 1847, USAMHI.

28. REL to MCL, Petersburg, March 28, 1865, LFP-VHS.

29. See chapter 10, "Adrenaline," for a further discussion of Mexican War influence.

30. Pope's orders allowed Federal troops to subsist on the population, who would

be repaid by voucher at the end of the war if they could prove their loyalty to the U.S.; called for the arrest of any male who would not take a loyalty oath; and provided that any persons found to be involved in guerilla activities, "either during the act or at any time afterward, shall be shot, without awaiting civil process." See General Orders No. 5, 7, and 11, 19, *OR,* ser. 1, vol. 12, pt. 2, pp. 50–52. The Confederate cabinet was outraged at what they considered barbaric behavior and retaliated by placing Union officers caught enforcing the policies under a code of "outlawry" rather than military law. According to Confederate secretary of the navy Stephen Mallory, who was present at the meeting, it was assumed that "the laws of the states will . . . hang all whites caught leading black troops. . . ." Diary of Stephen Mallory, August 1, [1862], typescript, LC.

31. REL to General Thomas J. Jackson, Headquarters, Army of Northern Virginia, July 27, 1862, in Lee, *Wartime Papers,* pp. 239–40; REL to MCL, Near Richmond, July 28, 1862, DE-LC.

32. Emory M. Thomas, *Bold Dragoon: The Life of J.E.B. Stuart* (New York: Harper & Row, 1986), pp. 143–48.

33. Milton Barrett to brother and sister, September 9, 1862, in J. Roderick Heller III and Carolynn Ayres Heller, eds., *The Confederacy Is On Her Way Up the Spout: Letters to South Carolina, 1861–64* (Athens: University of Georgia Press, 1992), pp. 74–75.

34. Hood, *Advance and Retreat,* p. 37.

35. The second battle of Manassas, or Bull Run, was fought August 28–30, 1862. The National Park Service battle description is at http://www.cr.nps.gov/hps/abpp/battles/va026.htm; McPherson, *Battle Cry of Freedom,* pp. 528–33. Fitzhugh Lee's assessment is in Lee, *General Lee,* p. 185–94; Fuller, who criticized Lee's strategy, doctors the statistics to make his point. Fuller, *Grant and Lee,* pp. 163–65; also Lee Jr., *Recollections,* pp. 76–77.

36. For Stonewall Jackson's early proposal to invade the North, see James A. Kegel, *North with Lee and Jackson* (Mechanicsville: Stackpole Books, 1996); Archer Jones, "Military Means, Political Ends, Strategy," in Gabor S. Boritt, ed., *Why the Confederacy Lost* (Oxford and New York: Oxford University Press, 1992); and Charles Royster, *The Destructive War.*

37. REL to General Gustavus W. Smith, Headquarters, Army of Northern Virginia, Camp near Fredericksburg, January 4, 1863, in Lee, *Wartime Papers,* pp. 383–84. Allan, "Memoranda of Conversations," p. 7; and REL to Jefferson Davis, Headquarters, Alexandria & Leesburg Road, Near Dranesville, September 3, 1862, in Lee, *Wartime Papers,* pp. 292–93. Years after the war General John Walker stated that Lee's goal was to reach Harrisburg and disrupt the rail systems. John G. Walker, "Jackson's Capture of Harper's Ferry," *B & L* 2:605.

38. Quoted in Roy Morris Jr. and Blaine Taylor, "Jefferson Davis May Have Approved of Robert E. Lee's Maryland Gamble—But Had Lee Shown Davis All the Cards?" *Military History* 15, no. 4 (October 1998): 72.

39. Jefferson Davis to Wiley P. Harris, Richmond, Va., December 3, 1861, in *The Papers of Jefferson Davis,* eds. Lynda Lassell Crist and Mary Seaton Dix (Baton Rouge: Louisiana State University Press, 1993), 7:433–34. Jefferson Davis to the Congress of the Confederate States, Richmond, February 1862; and Jefferson Davis to John Forsyth, Richmond, July 18, 1862, 8:100 and 293–94.

40. REL to Jefferson Davis, 13 Miles from Fredericktown, Maryland, September 6,

1862, in Lee, *Wartime Papers,* p. 296; see also Davis, *The Cause Lost,* p. 42. For the debate about a split between Lee and Davis, see Woodworth, *Davis and Lee at War;* Morris Jr. and Taylor, "Jefferson Davis May Have Approved of Lee's Maryland Gamble"; and James M. McPherson, "Was the Best Defense a Good Offense? Jefferson Davis and Confederate Strategies," in Gabor S. Boritt, ed., *Jefferson Davis's Generals* (New York: Oxford University Press, 1999), pp. 156–75. Michael Palmer also proposes that Lee purposefully obfuscated his plans; see *Lee Moves North: Robert E. Lee on the Offensive* (New York: John Wiley & Sons, 1998).

41. REL to Jefferson Davis, Headquarters, Alexandria & Leesburg Road, Near Dranesville, September 3, 1862, in Lee, *Wartime Papers,* pp. 293–95.

42. Elisabeth Lauterbach Laskin, "Good Old Rebels: Soldiering in the Army of Northern Virginia, 1862–1865," Ph.D. diss., Harvard University, 2003, pp. 261–73. For the enthusiasm of the soldiers for a northern invasion, see J. E. B. Stuart to Laura [Ratchliffe], March 17, 1862, James Ewell Brown Stuart Papers, LC; W. J. Pegram to Virginia Johnson [Pegram] McIntosh, Camp near Gordonsville, August 14, 1862, in James I. Robertson Jr., "'The Boy Artillerist': Letters of Colonel William Pegram, C.S.A.," *VMHB* 98, no. 2 (April 1990):226–29.

43. REL, General Order No. ?, HdQrs Army of Northern Virginia, Leesburg, Va, Sept 4, 1862, MoC; and James M. McPherson, *Crossroads of Freedom: Antietam* (New York: Oxford University Press, 2002), p. 100. Lee also complained of the straggling problem to Davis. Charles Marshall for REL to Jefferson Davis, Hd Qrs, Ten Miles from Frederickstown, September 7, 1862, REL-DU.

44. John Hampden Chamberlayne, *Ham Chamberlayne—Virginian,* edited by C. G. Chamberlayne (Richmond: Dietz Printing, 1932), p. 105.

45. Journal of John Dooley, September 14, 1862, GU. Thomas M. Garber to sister, September 17, 1862, quoted in Laskin, "Good Old Rebels," p. 270.

46. Dooley Journal, August–September 1862, GU. According to General John Walker, Lee gave this opinion of McClellan: "He is a very able general but a very cautious one. His enemies among his own people think him too much so. His army is in a very demoralized and chaotic condition, and will not be prepared for offensive operations—or he will not think it so—for three or four weeks. Before that time I hope to be on the Susquehanna." Walker, "Jackson's Capture of Harper's Ferry," *B & L,* 2:606.

47. Dooley Journal, September [17], 1862, GU; and J. G. Hooff to aunt, September 17, 1862, Ward Family Papers, LC.

48. Thomas Henry Carter to dear wife, Camp near Bunker Hill, October 4, 1862, Thomas Henry Carter Papers, VHS (hereafter cited THC-VHS); Osmund Latrobe Diary, September 17, 1862, VHS; and James Cooper Nisbet, *4 Years on the Firing Line,* ed. Bell Irvin Wiley (Jackson, Tenn.: McCowat-Mercer Press, 1963), pp. 107–8.

49. General Joseph Hooker, Commander, Corps I, Report on Battle of Antietam, Washington, D.C., November 8, 1862, *OR,* ser. 1, vol. 19, pt. 1, pp. 216–19; quotation p. 218. The casualty figure is from McPherson, *Crossroads of Freedom,* p. 3. The figures are imprecise, as always, but it is estimated that the Federals lost about 25 percent of their strength and the Confederates 31 percent. If the 12,000 Federal prisoners taken at Harper's Ferry are counted, the losses become proportional for the two sides.

50. A. Perrin to Governor Milledge Luke Bonham, Camp of McGowan's Brigade near Culpeper CH, Va., July 29, 1863, in Milledge Louis Bonham, "A Little More Light on Gettysburg," *Mississippi Valley Historical Review* 24, no. 4 (March 1938): 523–24.

51. Quotation J. L. Johnston to [Mary Green], Bivouac Martinsburg Va., September 22, [1862], Mercer Johnston Papers, LC. Statistic recorded in BG Cadmus M. Wilcox to "Dear John," September 26, 1862, Cadmus M. Wilcox Papers, LC. See also Thomas Henry Carter to dear wife, Camp near Bunker Hill, October 4, 1862, THC-VHS; and Walter Taylor to sister, near Martinsburg, Va., September 21, 1862, in Taylor, *Lee's Adjutant,* pp. 44–45.

52. Sidney J. Richardson and James Barrett Daniel quoted in Laskin, "Good Old Rebels," p. 270.

53. D. H. Hill to Rev. R. I. Dabney, July 19, 1864, quoted in Bridges, *Lee's Maverick General,* p. 128.

54. Quotations W. R. Smith to My Darling Wife, Richmond, September 24, 1862, Easby-Smith Papers, LC; and Walter Taylor to sister, Between Martinsburg and Winchester, September 28, 1862, in Taylor, *Lee's Adjutant,* p. 46. Also REL to The People of Maryland, Headquarters, Army of Northern Virginia, Near Fredericktown, September 8, 1862; REL to Jefferson Davis, Headquarters, Near Fredericktown, Maryland, September 8, 1862, both in Lee, *Wartime Dispatches,* pp. 299–301; and Richard E. Beringer, Herman Hattaway, Archer Jones, and William N. Still Jr., *Why the South Lost the Civil War* (Athens: University of Georgia Press, 1986), pp. 157–58.

55. Longstreet was affectionately called the "old war horse" well before Lee is said to have coined the title; see Edmund DeWitt Patterson, *Yankee Rebel,* ed. John G. Barrett (Chapel Hill: University of North Carolina Press, 1966), p. 46; Osmun Latrobe Diary, September 17, 1862, VHS; for Longstreet's valor ("a great soldier, a very determined and fearless fighter"), see Journal of Major Raphael Moses, n.d., typescript, DSF-LC; for soldiers' esteem ("When the men saw him coming, they mounted the breastworks and while he rode down the lines made . . . cheers for the 'old bull of the woods' as they love to designate him), see Goree, *Longstreet's Aide,* p. 137; and J[ohn] L Meem to Dear Ma, Camp Taylor, Orange CH, April 3, 1862, VHS. For Longstreet's attention to his men's comfort ("Longstreet always gets his corps into some comfortable quarters—while Jackson prefers the bleak outdoors"), see Thomas Henry Carter to wife, Camp near Middleton, November 18, 1862, THC-VHS.

56. R. Channing Price to mother, Head Qrs. Cavalry Division, October 15, 1862, and Journal of Raphael J. Moses, n.d., both DSF-LC; and REL description in George Taylor Lee, "Reminiscences of General Robert E. Lee, 1965–68," *South Atlantic Quarterly* 26, no. 3 (July 1927): 249–50.

57. Whether there was a rivalry between Lee and Jackson is a teasing question. Some have surmised that unspoken competition was the explanation for Jackson's lethargy during the Seven Days fight, and he later clearly resented it when Lee ignored his advice. Jackson commanded respect that equaled and sometimes surpassed Lee's, and his tactical talent was often thought to be superior. Davis, *The Cause Lost,* p. 170; for consultations, see Hotchkiss, *Make Me a Map,* pp. 87, 96–97; Nisbet, *4 Years on the Firing Line,* p. 88; and William B. Taliaferro statement in Mary Anna Jackson, *Memoirs of "Stonewall" Jackson* (repr., Dayton, Ohio: Morningside Bookshop, 1976), pp. 508–26.

58. Richard M. McMurry, *Two Great Rebel Armies* (Chapel Hill: University of North Carolina Press, 1989), p. 32; Hotchkiss, *Make Me a Map,* pp. 136, 149; and Bridges, *Lee's Maverick General,* p. 149.

59. REL to Genl Armistead L. Long, Lexington, Va., March 9, 1867, REL Letterbook

#4, LFP-VHS; REL to Jefferson Davis, Camp Fred^g, May 20, 1863, REL-DU; and Lee, "Reminiscences of General Robert E. Lee," pp. 249–50.

60. James Longstreet to Osman Latrobe, Gainesville, Ga., May 28, 1886, in Latrobe Diary, VHS; and E. Berkeley to Col [John S.] Mosby, Haymarket PO, March 20, [postwar], in DSF-LC.

61. S. R. Johnston to General L. McLaws, Jersey City, N.J., June 27, 1892, typescript, DSF-LC. E. Porter Alexander also experienced Lee's loose yet unbending instructions. See Alexander, *Fighting for the Confederacy,* p. 167. Another revealing description of Lee's discretionary orders stated, "I have frequently noticed . . . that Gen. Lee's instructions to his Corps Comrs are of a very comprehensive & general description & frequently admit of several interpretations—in fact will allow them to do almost anything, provided only it be a success. They caution them particularly against failure & very frequently wind up with the injunction to 'attack' whenever or where ever it can be done to advantage." Quoted in Carmichael, "Lee's Search for the Battle of Annihilation," pp. 15–16.

62. Bridges, *Lee's Maverick General,* pp. 85–86, 143; and Hotchkiss, *Make Me a Map,* p. 87.

63. [A. P.] Hill to J. E. B. Stuart, HdQrs. Opequon, November 14, [1862], J. E. B. Stuart Papers, VHS. For Lee's lecture to Early, see REL to Gen. Early, Hdqrs, April 27, 1864, MoC.

64. [A. P.] Hill to J. E. B. Stuart, HdQrs. Opequon, November 14, [1862], J. E. B. Stuart Papers, VHS.

65. James Longstreet to Genl J. E. Johnston, Camp near Winchester, October 5, 1862, facsimile in James M. Longstreet Papers, DU; Bridges, *Lee's Maverick General,* p. 92.

66. Bridges, *Lee's Maverick General,* pp. 148, 162–63.

67. Ibid., pp. 155–57. Hill might not be considered the most objective source—his quarrels with Lee's generalship being well known—but his reputation for irascibility was matched by one for courageous truth-telling. The assertion is also made by Jackson's earliest biographer, R. L. Dabney, in *Life and Campaigns of Lieut-Gen. Thomas J. Jackson* (New York: Blelock & Co., 1866), p. 549. Douglas Southall Freeman, who underplayed all disorders between Lee and his general staff, favored the reminiscences, twenty years after the fact, of John Walker, who claimed to be in Lee's tent when Jackson received his orders, and found him "in high spirits," but says nothing more. Walker "Jackson's Capture of Harper's Ferry," *B & L,* 2:606; and Douglas Southall Freeman, *Lee's Lieutenants,* 3 vols. (New York: Charles Scribner's Sons, 1942–44), 3:161.

68. Allan, "Memoranda of Conversations," pp. 11, 14; and Peter Carmichael, "Lee's Search for the Battle of Annihilation," p. 15.

69. Taylor, *Four Years with General Lee,* pp. 145–48. Douglas Southall Freeman's discussion of Lee's interaction with his top generals, which proposes Lee's passivity was due to diplomacy and courtesy, is in *R. E. Lee,* 3:218–39, and is a continuous theme in *Lee's Lieutenants.*

70. Thomas Henry Carter to wife, Camp near New Market, October 31, 1864, THC-VHS.

71. John Cheves Haskall Memoirs, DU.

72. REL to Genl S. Cooper, HdQrs, August 11, 1862; General Order No. ?, HdQrs Army of Northern Virginia, Leesburg, Va., September 4, 1862; Extract from General Order No. 17, HdQrs, No. Va. March 7, 1864; all MoC; REL to Maj. Genl R. S. Ewell,

Headqrs Richmond, Va., May 8, 1862; REL to HE Henry T. Clark, HdQrs, Richmond, May 18, 1862; LFP-WL; REL to HW William Smith, Hd Qr ANVa, September 24, 1864, Van Dyke-McBride Collection, LoV.

73. For more on the differences between military managers and heroic leaders, see Janowitz, *The Professional Soldier;* and Peskin, *Winfield Scott.*

74. Quotation in Gary W. Gallagher, *Lee and His Army in Confederate History* (Chapel Hill: University of North Carolina Press, 2001), p. 73.

75. Clara Barton quoted in Elizabeth Brown Pryor, *Clara Barton, Professional Angel* (Philadelphia: University of Pennsylvania Press, 1987), p. 107. A fuller description of the Battle of Fredericksburg is in McPherson, *Battle Cry of Freedom,* pp. 570–74.

76. John Esten Cooke, *A Life of Gen. Robert E. Lee* (New York: D. Appleton, 1871), p. 184.

77. Lincoln quoted in Gienapp, *Abraham Lincoln,* p. 121; Lee quoted in Gallagher, *Lee and His Army,* p. 70.

78. Bridges, *Lee's Maverick General,* pp. 143, 155–57. D. H. Hill's assertion of Jackson's disgruntlement was replayed in Dabney, *Life and Campaigns,* pp. 592, 595.

CHAPTER TWENTY: **Apogee / Perigee**

1. REL to CCL, Camp Fredericksburg, March 24, 1864, REL-UVa. "Fitz" refers to Fitzhugh Lee, Robert E. Lee's nephew and a brigadier general of cavalry. Lt. Colonel John Pelham was an Alabama artillerist who gained a great reputation for ardor and bravery. He was leading a unit of horse artillery when he was mortally wounded on March 17, 1863, at the battle of Kelly's Ford, described by Lee. "Mildred & them" refers to Carter's daughter and sons Henry and George, who is also later mentioned in the letter.

2. Notes passed between Generals James Longstreet and George Pickett, and Col. E. Porter Alexander, July 3, 1863, in Edward Porter Alexander Papers, LC.

3. Garnett, "General Robert E. Lee: The Battle of Fredericksburg and Chancellorsville," p. 247.

4. REL to MCL, Camp Fredᵍ, April 3 and April 19, 1863, both DE-LC; and Jones, *A Rebel War Clerk's Diary,* pp. 195–96.

5. Garnett, "The Battle of Fredericksburg and Chancellorsville," p. 247. Statistics vary wildly for this battle, and Lee was among those who doctored them to his advantage. Best estimates are that Lee had 61,000 men to Hooker's force of 133,000. Lee later said that the odds were 3 to 1.

6. A summary of the battle is in Peter J. Parish, *The American Civil War* (New York: Holmes and Meiker, 1975), pp. 275–79; a detailed account is in Robert K. Krick, "Lee at Chancellorsville," in Gallagher, ed., *Lee the Soldier,* pp. 257–80. An engaging memoir is contained in Alexander, *Fighting for the Confederacy,* pp. 194–218.

7. Thomas Claybrook Elder to wife, Camp near Fredericksburg, May 8, 1863, TCE-VHS.

8. W. S. Harrison Jr. to mother, Near Fred'burg, May 8, 1863, William Southall Harrison Papers, VHS.

9. For a discussion of the issue and relevant documents see Frederick Maurice's notes in Marshall, *Lee's Aide-de-Camp,* pp. 161–76; and T. M. R. Talcott, "General Lee's Strategy at the Battle of Chancellorsville," *Southern Historical Society Papers* 34 (1906). Both Maurice and Talcott conclude that Lee was the originator, though Hotchkiss's evidence stands in contrast. Jackson's first biographer, Rev. R. I. Dabney,

bowed to the assertion that Lee had been the one to formulate the plan—but Dabney had succumbed to pressure to uphold Lee on another occasion when the evidence was against it. (In a similar case, when Lee subtly assumed credit for Jackson's perspicacious actions at Boteler's Ford on the retreat from Maryland, Dabney wrote that though the final version giving Lee credit was at odds with other officers' recollections, "Gen. Lee himself required a modification. . . . You see in this case I was cornered; and could not avoid yielding to his account." Dabney quoted in Bridges, *Lee's Maverick General*, pp. 140–41.) See also Hotchkiss, *Make Me a Map*, pp. 117–18, 137; and Krick, "Lee at Chancellorsville," pp. 365–67.

10. REL to MCL, Camp, Fred^g, May 11, 1863, DE-LC.

11. Casualty figures, as always, vary; they can be found in McPherson, *Battle Cry of Freedom*, p. 645; http://www.cr.nps.gov/hps/abpp/battles/va032.htm; and http://en.wikipedia.org/wiki/Battle_of_Chancellorsville.

12. John Berryman Crawford, May 7, 1863, quoted in Laskin, "Good Old Rebels," p. 220.

13. Brigadier General James H. Lane quoted in Jackson, *Memoirs of "Stonewall,"* pp. 538–39.

14. Goree, *Longstreet's Aide*, p. 95.

15. Alexander, *Fighting for the Confederacy*, p. 92.

16. REL quoted in Carmichael, "Lee's Search for the Battle of Annihilation," p. 14.

17. Henry Calvin Connor quoted in Laskin, "Good Old Rebels," pp. 472–73.

18. Fuller, *Grant and Lee*, pp. 190–92; quotation Watkins, *Company Aytch*, p. 102.

19. For more on this idea of a decisive, all-determining battle, see Carmichael, "Lee's Search for the Battle of Annihilation," pp. 1–26.

20. REL to Jefferson Davis, Camp, Petersburg, July 6, 1864, in Lee, *Wartime Papers*, p. 816; and Dr. W. G. Howard, notes on conversaton with REL, c. 1870, George Gregg McIntosh Papers, VHS.

21. Parish, *The American Civil War*, p. 581.

22. Herman Hathaway and Archer Jones, *How the North Won: A Military History of the Civil War* (Chicago: University of Illinois Press, 1983), pp. 46–48; Gary W. Gallagher, "An Old Fashioned Soldier in a Modern War? Lee's Confederate Generalship," in *Lee and His Army in Confederate History* (Chapel Hill: University of North Carolina Press, 2001), pp. 151–90.

23. Carmichael, "Lee's Search for the Battle of Annihilation," p. 17.

24. Alexander, *Fighting for the Confederacy*, p. 222.

25. REL to James A. Seddon, Headquarters, Army of Northern Virginia, June 8, 1863; REL to Jefferson Davis, Headquarters, Army of Northern Virginia, June 10, 1863, and to James A. Seddon, Headquarters, Army of Northern Virginia, June 13, 1863; all Lee, *Wartime Papers*, pp. 504–5, 507–8, 513–14; quotation p. 505. For Seddon's disagreement and capitulation, see Gerard Francis John O'Brien, "James A. Seddon: Statesman of the Old South," Ph.D. diss., University of Maryland, 1963, pp. 368–79. For a suggestion that there was strong divergence between Davis and Lee over the advantage of moving north, and that Lee was duplicitous in his actions with Richmond, see Woodworth, *Davis and Lee at War*, pp. 237–45. Longstreet apparently joined Davis and Seddon in their opinion that the western front was now the priority, and even traveled to Richmond to advise them that a concentrated push in that region would secure the Mississippi and distract northern forces from Richmond. James Longstreet, "Lee in Pennsylvania," in Gallagher, *Lee the Soldier*, pp. 382–84. E. Porter Alexander, in retro-

spect, also believed this to be the right strategic decision. See *Fighting for the Confederacy*, pp. 219–20.

26. For the expectations brought about by Lee's entry into Pennsylvania, see McPherson, *Battle Cry of Freedom*, pp. 647–51.

27. Allan, "Memoranda of Conversations," pp. 13–14.

28. Hotchkiss, diary entry for June 26, 1863, in *Make Me a Map*, p. 155; and Lee quoted in Woodworth, *Davis and Lee at War*, p. 242. Lee's aides Charles Marshall and A. L. Long also believed that waging a battle was always part of the plan. Marshall, *Lee's Aide-de-Camp*, pp. 185–86; Long, *Memoirs*, p. 269.

29. Thomas Henry Carter to wife, Camp near Chambersburg, June 25, 1863, THC-VHS.

30. REL, General Orders No. 73, Headquarters, Army of Northern Virginia, Chambersburg, Pennsylvania, June 27, 1863, in *OR*, ser. 1, vol. 27, pt. 3, pp. 942–43; and Tally Simpson quoted in Palmer, *Lee Moves North*, p. 26.

31. Lafayette McLaws quoted in David G. Smith, "Race and Retaliation: The Capture of African-Americans during the Gettysburg Campaign," in Peter Wallenstein and Bertram Wyatt-Brown, eds., *Virginia's Civil War* (Charlottesville: University Press of Virginia, 2005), p. 141.

32. Chamberlayne, *Ham Chamberlayne*, pp. 191–92. Chamberlayne was intercepted by a group of Union cavalry after this episode and taken prisoner. He remained in northern prisons until March 1864.

33. Smith, "Race and Retaliation," quotation p. 143; and Peter C. Vermilyea, "The Effect of the Confederate Invasion of Pennsylvania on Gettysburg's African American Community," a well-documented article at www.gdg.org/Gettysburg%20Magazine/gburgafrican.html.

34. Lieutenant George Breck to the *Union and Advertiser*, In Camp near Guilford Station, Virginia, June 27, 1863, in Eric A. Campbell, ed., "Lee Is Playing a Bold and Desperate Game," *American History*, 2003 supp., p. 42.

35. For Meade's approach to the battle, see *OR*, ser. 1, vol. 27, pt. 3, pp. 460–62; and Steven E. Woodworth, *Beneath a Northern Sky: A Short History of the Gettysburg Campaign* (Wilmington, Del.: Scholarly Resources, 2003), pp. 47–69. Meade resisted any advance on Gettysburg, and even after the second day he called for falling back in a fighting withdrawal to Maryland rather than continue the battle. He eventually decided to wait and see what Lee would do, and by maintaining his advantageous defensive position, he was able to carry the field.

36. Lee's description of the reorganization is in REL to Jefferson Davis, Camp, Fredericksburg, May 20, 1863; also to J. E. B. Stuart, Headquarters, Army of Northern Virginia, June 23, 1863, both in Lee, *Wartime Papers*, pp. 487–89, 526–27; Longstreet, "Lee in Pennsylvania," p. 385.

37. Lieutenant George Breck to Alfred Reynolds, In the Field near Gettysburg, Pa., July 2, 1863, in Campbell, "Bold and Desperate Game," p. 43.

38. Garnett, "Gen. Robert E. Lee: The Great Confederate's Part in the Battle of Gettysburg," in Brock, *Gen. Robert Edward Lee*, p. 267.

39. Arthur J. L. Fremantle, *Three Months in the Southern States* (repr., Lincoln: University of Nebraska Press, 1991), p. 256; and Gary W. Gallagher, *Lee and His Generals in War and Memory* (Baton Rouge: Louisiana State University Press, 1998), pp. 65–66.

40. According to one witness, Lee waffled in his plans during the night, but finally returned to his original design. Gallagher, *Lee and His Generals*, pp. 67–70. With the

advantage of hindsight, Alexander thought Lee's argument about the inadvisability of remaining passively on the field, or the difficulties of withdrawal, was specious. Given their agile retreat after the devastating third day of battle, he wrote: "It does not seem improbable that we would have faced Meade safely on the 2nd at Gettysburg without assaulting him in his wonderfully strong position." Alexander, *Fighting for the Confederacy,* p. 233.

41. Longstreet, "Lee in Pennsylvania," pp. 388–89; and Fremantle, *Three Months in the Southern States,* p. 256.

42. Hotchkiss, diary entry for August 21, 1863, *Make Me a Map,* pp. 168–69. Charles Venable was another aide who remarked on Lee's tendency to overreach. See Charles S. Venable, "General Lee in the Wilderness Campaign," *B & L,* 4:242.

43. REL to MARC, June 3, 1821 [sic 1831], in deButts, "Yours Forever."

44. Quotation John Cheves Haskell Memoirs, DU; also Douglas Southall Freeman, "Why Was Gettysburg Lost?" in Gallagher, *Lee the Soldier,* pp. 457–58; and Allan, "Memoranda of Conversations," pp. 14–15.

45. Quotation in Garnett, "Battle of Gettysburg," p. 177. Napoleon would have agreed. "The loss of time is irreparable in war," he once stated. Quoted in Jay Luvaas, ed., "Napoleon on Generalship," *MHQ: The Quarterly Journal of Military History* 12, no. 3 (Spring 2000): 85.

46. Richard A. Sauers, *George Meade: Victor of Gettysburg* (Washington, D.C.: Brassey's, 2003).

47. Frank A. Haskell, "The Battle of Gettysburg," in *Two Views of Gettysburg,* ed. Richard Harwell (Chicago: R. R. Donnelley and Sons, 1964), p. 96.

48. Ibid., pp. 141–46; also McPherson, *Battle Cry of Freedom,* pp. 656–60.

49. Walter Taylor to sister, July 7, 1863, in Taylor, *Lee's Adjutant,* p. 59; and John Gibbon, "The Council of War on the Second Day," *B & L* 3:313–14.

50. Tom Carhart, *Lost Triumph: Lee's Real Plan at Gettysburg and Why It Failed* (New York: G. P. Putnam's, 2005), pp. 187–95.

51. Haskell, "The Battle of Gettysburg," p. 178. A Confederate soldier's equally evocative description is found in Dooley Journal, July 3, 1863, GU.

52. General Joseph Hayes quoted in James Edward Kelly, *Generals in Bronze,* ed. William B. Styple (Kearny, N.J.: Belle Grove, 2005), p. 135. The numbers are courtesy of Gettysburg National Battlefield Park. McPherson gives a larger estimate of those participating, stating that some 14,000 men were part of the charge. *Battle Cry of Freedom,* p. 662.

53. Susan Leigh Blackford, ed., *Letters from Lee's Army* (New York: A. S. Barnes, 1947), p. 188.

54. Dooley Journal, July 3, 1863, GU.

55. Quotation ibid.; Peter S. Carmichael, "Who's to Blame?" *Civil War Times Illustrated* 37, no. 4 (August 1998); and John Cheves Haskell Memoirs, DU.

56. McPherson, *Battle Cry of Freedom,* pp. 660–61.

57. Carhart, *Lost Triumph,* pp. 220–35.

58. REL to Jefferson Davis, Camp Culpeper, July 31, 1863, in Lee, *Wartime Papers,* p. 565; Carhart, *Lost Triumph*; and Palmer, *Lee Moves North,* pp. 52, 64, 131.

59. Haskell, "The Battle of Gettysburg," p. 145.

60. Statistics at http://en.wikipedia.org/wiki/Pickett's Charge. Overall casualties for the battle have been estimated at 23,000 for the Union and 28,000 for the Confederates. Margaret E. Wagner, et al., *Civil War Desktop Reference,* p. 282.

61. Fremantle, *Three Months in the Southern States*, pp. 267–68; Alexander, *Fighting for the Confederacy*, p. 266; and Lee quoted in Woodworth, *Beneath a Northern Sky*, p. 202.

62. REL to MCL, Camp near Hagarstown, July 12, 1863, DE-LC; A. Perrin to Governor Milledge Luke Bonham, Camp of McGowan's Brigade near Culpeper CH, Va., July 29, 1863, in "A Little More Light on Gettysburg," p. 525; Edward Porter Alexander, "Personal Recollections of the Knoxville Campaign," n.d., Alexander Papers, LC; J. D. Imboden, "Lee at Gettysburg," *Galaxy* 11, no. 4 (April 1871).

63. REL to MCL, Camp near Hagarstown, July 12, 1863; and Camp near Orange C House, August 23, 1863, both DE-LC; REL to Jefferson Davis, Camp near Culpeper, July 31, 1863; and Camp Orange, August 8, 1863, both Lee, *Wartime Letters*, pp. 564–565 and 589–90.

64. Jones, *Rebel War Clerk's Diary*, p. 269; REL to MCL, Camp Orange, CtH, September 4, 1863, DE-LC.

65. For an incisive discussion of this issue, see Thomas Goss, "Gettysburg's 'Decisive Battle,'" *Military Review* 88, no. 4 (July/August 2004): 11–16.

66. Robert Augustus Siles, July 29, 1863, quoted in Laskin, "Good Old Rebels," pp. 226–27. Laskin, who has conducted the most comprehensive research on the men of the ANVa, found that most men did see the battle as a defeat, but not the decisive one; p. 482n.

67. Montgomery C. Meigs to father, Washington, July 24, 1863, MCM-LC.

68. Henry Halleck to U. S. Grant, February 17, 1864, in Ulysses S. Grant, *The Papers of Ulysses S. Grant*, 13 vols., ed. John Y. Simon (Carbondale: Southern Illinois University Press, 1982), 10:110–11n.

69. Again, numbers are never fast, but estimates show Lee had about 75,000 troops to the Union's 83,000. Wagner et al., *Civil War Desktop Reference*, p. 282.

70. Ewell quoted in Donald C. Pfanz, "Richard Stoddert Ewell," *ANB* 7:641. Lee also reportedly criticized Ewell after the war: see Allan, "Memoranda of Conversations," pp. 11, 14–15, 18.

71. Allan, "Memoranda of Conversations," p. 18. Colonel John S. Mosby agreed that it was foolish to blame the loss on men who did not exist. "Possibly if Stonewall Jackson had been there the issue would have been different. Very probably, if Stuart could have been in front and rear of Hooker at the same time [at Chancellorsville] or if we had had two Stuarts the battle would have gone differently. . . . History deals with what was and is and is folly to discuss what might have been." John S. Mosby, "General Stuart at Gettysburg," [Philadelphia] *Weekly Times*, December 15, 1877.

72. Again, a Napoleonic maxim: "In war, men are nothing; one man is everything. The presence of the general is indispensable." Luvaas, "Napoleon on Generalship," p. 80.

73. A. Perrin to Governor Milledge Louis Bonham, Camp of McGowan's Brigade near Culpeper CH, Va., July 29, 1863, in Bonham, "A Little More Light on Gettysburg," p. 521.

74. John Sale, July 29, 1863, and Sidney J. Richardson, July 8, 1863, quoted in Laskin, "Good Old Rebels," p. 285.

75. Long, *Memoirs*, p. 269; and Allan, "Memoranda of Conversations," pp. 13–14.

76. Alexander, *Fighting for the Confederacy*, p. 415. Antoine-Henri Jomini, one of the interpreters of Napoleonic method, whose works Lee may have studied, thought the following conditions were needed to exist to sustain guerilla warfare: the war could be fought in the interior of the country; it was incapable of being decided by a

single stroke; the theater of operation was large; the country was rough and inaccessible; and the national character was suited to fighting this kind of war. Jomini's principles are paraphrased in Hattaway and Jones, *How the North Won,* pp. 21–23. Gary Gallagher disputes the plausibility of protracted partisan warfare, believing that the populace was not ready to fully embrace it. His findings are based on the Southern public's exultation in victory, which increased support for the war. However, as any evidence about the ability to endure under prolonged deprivation is nonexistent, it is impossible to state with certainty how a war of attrition would have been supported in the South. Gary W. Gallagher, *The Confederate War* (Cambridge, Mass.: Harvard University Press, 1997), pp. 115–53.

77. Among the works that have criticized Lee's grand strategy are Nolan, *Lee Considered;* Connelly, *The Marble Man;* and Fuller, *Grant and Lee.* More apologist assessments are found in Freeman, "Why Was Gettysburg Lost?" in Gallagher, ed., *Lee the Soldier,* pp. 447–73; and Gary W. Gallagher, "If the Enemy Is There We Must Attack Him," in *Lee and His Generals,* pp. 47–76.

78. REL to John Mackay, National Palace, City of Mexico, October 2, 1847, USAMHI.

79. Howard, "Notes on Conversation with REL in Baltimore," c. 1870, David Gregg McIntosh Papers, VHS. A War Department clerk concurred with this definition of leadership in referring to Lee after Gettysburg: "All generals are judged by the degree of success they achieve, for success alone is considered the proof of merit, and one disaster may obliterate the memory of a dozen victories." Jones, *Rebel War Clerk's Diary,* p. 248.

CHAPTER TWENTY-ONE: **Overwhelmed**

1. REL to MiCL, Richmond, November 3, 1862, DE-LC.

2. Anne Wickham to CCL, n.d. [c. July 1863], EA-LC. The Wickhams were cousins of the Lees through the Carter family. Rooney had married Charlotte Wickham in 1859. The General Corse mentioned was Montgomery D. Corse, a native of Alexandria and a brigadier in Longstreet's corps.

3. Lawrence W. Orton, aka Orton Williams, to "My dear Sister" [Markie Williams], Franklin, Tenn., June 8, 1863, copy in Markie Williams's hand, William Orton Williams Papers, TPA.

4. REL to MCL(d), n.d. [November 1862], quoted in Lee Jr., *Recollections,* p. 80.

5. Sneden Diary, September 11, 1862, Sneden Papers, VHS.

6. Ibid.; and WHFL to "My darling wife," Camp near Richmond, July 11, 1862, DE-LC.

7. On the same Federal retreat Shirley was plundered of its livestock, wagon wheels were cut through the spokes to render them useless, and wheat cradles destroyed so that the large ripening crop in the fields could not be harvested. Only the charity of the Carter women, who personally nursed wounded Yankees on their property, saved the exquisite house from the torch. See MCL to Mrs. W. H. Stiles, Richmond, July 6, 1862, Eliza Mackay Stiles Papers, GHS; and Louise Humphreys Carter Reminiscences, Shirley, June 20, 1905, typescript, DSF-LC.

8. For an example of comments on Annie's frailty—"she seems to be one of the doomed"—see [Anna Maria Fitzhugh] to Charles B. Dana, "Monday 22nd Aug" [1846], Dana Papers, UT; for Annie's spirited personality, see ACL to Helen Bratt, Staunton, Va., May 3, 1855; Arlington, November 28, 1856; and Staunton, Virginia, April 12, [1856–57], all LFP-WL; quotation ACL to EAL, White House, May 2, [1862],

REL-DU. In fact the Lee ladies were treated with great deference by the Union army during the early, courteous days of the war. Caught behind enemy lines, they were escorted to the Confederate forces. "They are well & will of course be kindly taken care of," General McClellan assured Markie Williams. George B. McClellan to MCW, May 24, 1862, copy in MCW's hand, Martha Williams Carter Papers, TPA.

9. ACL to MCL, [Jones], N.C., August 10 [1862], DE-LC.

10. The daily dose of blue mass pills contained more than 9,000 times the amount of mercury that is now considered safe. For more on blue mass, see http://sleep disorders.about.com/cs/insomnia/a/bluemass.htm.

11. Coulling, *Lee Girls*, p. 109.

12. MCL to "My dear child" [MiCL], Richmond, Saturday night, n.d. [October 1862], EAL to "Dear Sister" [MCL(d)], Petersburg, November 7, 1862; and MCL to MCL(d), October 18, [1862], all DE-LC. Modern assessments have suggested that in addition to pharmaceutical ignorance, Annie may have suffered from an unusually strong form of typhoid, which could lead to spinal meningitis or appendicitis. See Coulling, *Lee Girls*, p. 109.

13. MCL to MCL(d), Jones Springs, "Saturday Oct 18th" [1862]; and MCL to "My dear child" [MiCL], [October 1862], both DE-LC.

14. REL Jr., to MCL, "Camp four miles from Berriville Clark[e] Co Va," October 30, 1862, DE-LC.

15. Taylor, *Four Years with General Lee*, p. 76.

16. REL to MCL, Camp near Winchester, October 26, 1862, DE-LC.

17. [Anna Maria Fitzhugh] to EAL, n.d. [October 1862]; and EAL to "Dear Sister" [MCL(d)], Petersburg, November 7, 1862, both DE-LC.

18. REL to MCL, Camp near Winchester, October 26, 1862, DE-LC.

19. REL to "My dear Cousin Ellen," April 20, 1863, REL-MoHS.

20. REL to Mrs. WHFL, Camp, Fredericksburg, December 10, 1862, in Lee, *Lee of Virginia*, p. 442; and REL to MCL, Camp Fredg, December 16, 1862, DE-LC.

21. REL to MCL, Camp Fredg, March 9, 1863, DE-LC.

22. REL to MCL Camp Fredg, April 3, 1863, in Lee, *Wartime Papers*, p. 428; REL to EAL, Near Fredg, April 11, 1863, DE-LC.

23. Rooney had been doubly lucky, for it was thought he had been shot by a Spencer rifle. This new weapon used a bullet with a zinc cap, which became detached, lodging itself in the wound, where it invited infection. But the range had been so close that the bullet had flown clear through the thigh, giving him an excellent chance for recovery. REL to MCL, Culpeper, June 11, 1863, DE-LC; Coulling, *Lee Girls*, p. 126; for more on the battle of Brandy Station, see http://en.wikipedia.org/wiki/Battle_of_Brandy_Station.

24. McGuire, *Diary of a Southern Refugee*, p. 224.

25. Anne Wickham to CCL, n.d. [c. July 1863], typescript in EA-LC; and REL to Charlotte Wickham Lee, July 26, 1863, GBL-VHS.

26. See REL to MCL, Camp Orange Ct House, September 8 and September 10, 1863, both DE-LC.

27. Chesnut, *Diary*, p. 450; see also Rable, *Civil Wars*, pp. 65–66.

28. Rooney's captivity actually did provide leverage some months later when the Confederate government considered executing ninety Union soldiers in retaliation for a perceived plot to assassinate Jefferson Davis. Lee was asked his opinion of the proposed execution, but the consensus was that he would advise against it since his

"*son* is a captive in the hands of the enemy, designated for retaliation whenever we shall execute any of their prisoners in our hands." Jones, *Rebel War Clerk's Diary*, p. 346; and REL to MCL, October 28, 1863, DE-LC.

29. Chesnut, *Diary*, p. 450.

30. REL to MCL, Camp Rapp^k, October 28, 1863, DE-LC.

31. REL to MCL, December 27, 1863, in Lee Jr., *Recollections*, pp. 117–18.

32. Chesnut, *Diary*, p. 586; for more on widows and widowers, see Rable, *Civil Wars*, pp. 68–70; and Drew Gilpin Faust, *Mothers of Invention* (Chapel Hill: University of North Carolina Press, 1996), pp. 149–50.

33. REL to MCL, Camp, March 18, 1864, DE-LC. Mary Boykin Chesnut was another who recorded Lee's emotion at this time, noting that his eyes filled with tears whenever Rooney's ordeal was mentioned. Chesnut, *Diary*, p. 589.

34. For Lee's worry about the family, see for example REL to MCL, Camp near Winchester, Va., September 29, 1862; to MCL, Camp, April 23 and April 27, 1864; and to MCL, Gaines Mill, June 4, 1864, all DE-LC; for the precarious position of many women without their male "protectors," see Mary Elizabeth Massey, *Refugee Life in the Confederacy* (Baton Rouge: Louisiana State University Press, 2001), p. 75; Coulling, *Lee Girls*, p. 134; and Kundahl, *Alexandria Goes to War*, pp. 84–92.

35. MCL to Abbey L. Cook, n.d. [c. January 27, 1865], LJF-WL.

36. Chesnut, *Diary*, p. 138; and Taylor to [Bettie], Edge Hill, March 21, 1865, in Taylor, *Lee's Adjutant*, p. 236.

37. People fled for many reasons. Fear of the enemy was the most common, but others wanted to follow family members in the army, to remove themselves from potential battle sites, or to avoid the conscription laws. In a few cases, such as in post-siege Atlanta, inhabitants were ordered to evacuate. Harrison, *Recollections Grave and Gay*, p. 153; Brock, *Richmond during the War*, pp. 31, 320; and Massey, *Refugee Life in the Confederacy* pp. 5–7, 12–13.

38. Jones, *Rebel War Clerk's Diary*, pp. 174, 182; quotation p. 319.

39. Ibid., p. 357.

40. Some believed that even the "bread riot" of April 2, 1863 was trumped up, an excuse for looting. See Gorgas, *Civil War Diary*, pp. 28–29; Berlin, "Did Confederate Women Lose the War?" pp. 180–81; Charles W. Ramsdell, *Behind the Lines in the Southern Confederacy* (repr., New York: Greenwood Press, 1969), pp. 76–82.

41. Jones, *Rebel War Clerk's Diary*, p. 360; and Rable, *Civil Wars*, pp. 192–98.

42. Jones, *Rebel War Clerk's Diary*, p. 329.

43. Gorgas, *Civil War Diary*, p. 41.

44. See G. T. Beauregard to C. Cary, "H^dQuarters, 1st Corps, Army of the Potomac," August 28, 1861; and Fitz Lee to Constance Cary, "H^dQrs Lees Cav Brig," December 23, 1862, Burton Norwell Harrison Papers, LC; Chesnut, *Diary*, p. 475; also Constance Cary Harrison, "Richmond Scenes in '62," *B & L*, 2:439–48.

45. REL Jr. to MCL, Richmond, July 30, 1863, DE-LC.

46. J. E. B. Stuart to EAL, Camp Botele, September 11, 1863, DE-LC.

47. MCL to Abbey L. Cook, n.d. [c. January 27, 1865], LJF-WL.

48. K[itty] C. Stiles, to "my dear Aunt Eliza" [Mackay Stiles], n.d. [c. 1862–63], Mackay-Stiles Papers, SHC-UNC; also McGuire, *Diary of a Southern Refugee*, p. 66; Robbins, "Mrs. Lee during the War," pp. 330–34; and Harrison, *Recollections Grave and Gay*, p. 153.

49. Lee's remedy for the food shortages was to sacrifice Mildred's rambunctious

pet squirrel, named "Custis Morgan" after her brother and General John Hunt Morgan, who had heroically escaped from a Union prison. Like his namesake the creature would not stay in his cage, and Lee saw no peace for him but the stewpot: "squirrel soup thickened with peanuts," he recommended. "Custis Morgan in such an exit from the stage would cover himself with glory." MCL to Mrs. F. Dickens, n.d. [c. 1864], AHA; REL to MCL, Camp, March 24, 1864; REL to MCL, Camp Petersburg, July 10, 1864, both DE-LC; Coulling, *Lee Girls*, p. 138; for slave rations, see Leslie Howard Owens, *This Species of Property: Slave Life and Culture in the Old South* (New York: Oxford University Press, 1976), pp. 50–51.

50. Sarah Pryor quoted in Faust, *Mothers of Invention*, p. 23.

51. K[itty] C. Stiles, to "my dear Aunt Eliza" [Mackay Stiles], n.d., [c. 1862–63], Mackay-Stiles Papers, SHC-UNC; also [Brock], *Richmond during the War*, p. 151. Mildred Lee and her sister Mary had also treated wounded soldiers near the battlefield after First Manassas. See Coulling, *Lee Girls*, p. 91.

52. W. C. Corsan, *Two Months in the Confederate States*, edited by Benjamin Trask (Baton Rouge: Louisiana State University Press, 1996), p. 91.

53. For expectations of women during the war, see Rable, *Civil Wars*, pp. 55–56. Quotation in Robbins, "Mrs. Lee during the War," pp. 330, 334–35.

54. MCL to Mrs. F. Dickens, August 11, [c. 1863], AHA.

55. Robbins, "Mrs. Lee during the War," pp. 338–39.

56. MCL quoted in Coulling, *Lee Girls*, p. 147. The wonderful phrase "defiant dignity" is on page 146.

57. Faust, *Mothers of Invention*; Rable, *Civil Wars*; and Massey, *Refugee Life in the Confederacy*, all discuss in detail the reactions of women to war.

58. MCW to EAL, fragment, n.d. [post-1863], DE-LC.

59. REL to John B. Floyd, Arlington, February 1, 1860, REL Letterbook #1, LFP-VHS; and REL to MCL, Richmond, July 8, 1861, DE-LC.

60. The most complete accounts of Orton Williams's actions are William Gilmore Beymer, "Williams, CSA," *Harper's New Monthly Magazine* 119, no. 707 (September 1909): 498–510; Margaret Sanborn, "The Ordeal of Orton Williams, U.S.A., C.S.A.," *Assembly* 28, no. 4 (Winter 1970); and Kundahl, *Alexandria Goes to War*, pp. 167–79, quotation p. 179.

61. Britannia Peters Reminiscences, January 17, 1897, TPA; Coulling, *Lee Girls*, pp. 114–15, Harry Wickham quoted p. 115.

62. Kundahl, *Alexandria Goes to War*, pp. 172–73; Britannia Peters Reminiscences, January 17, 1897; and MCW to EAL, fragment, n.d. [post-1863], DE-LC.

63. *Richmond Examiner*, June 13, 1863; and REL to MCL, HdQrts, June 14, 1863, DE-LC.

64. Williams had been promoted to colonel of cavalry in the Army of the Tennessee under Major General Earl Van Dorn. Kundahl, *Alexandria Goes to War*, pp. 174–76. The official communications are in U.S. War Department, *OR*, ser. 1, vol. 23, pt. 2, pp. 397, 398, 425–27, 804; ser. 2, vol. 5, p. 763.

65. Col. Van Vleck quoted in Sanborn, "Ordeal of Orton Williams," p. 35.

66. Ibid.

67. Robert F. Saylor to MCW, Headquarters, July 7, 1863, TPA.

68. Ibid.; Beymer, "Williams, CSA"; and Kundahl, *Alexandria Goes to War*, p. 177.

69. *OR*, ser. 1, vol. 23, pt. 2, p. 398; Robert F. Saylor to MCW, Headquarters, July 7,

1863, TPA; and W. F. G. Shanks in *New York Herald,* quoted in Sanborn, "Ordeal of Orton Williams," p. 37.

70. For more on spies and spy systems during the war, see William Gilmore Beymer, *On Hazardous Service: Scouts and Spies of the Civil War* (New York: Harper Brothers, 1912); William A. Tidwell, *April '65: Confederate Covert Action in the American Civil War* (Kent, Ohio: Kent State University Press, 1995); Alan Axelrod, *The War between the Spies: A History of Espionage during the American Civil War* (New York: Atlantic Monthly Press, 1992); and Donald E. Markle, *Spies and Spymasters of the Civil War* (New York: Hippocrene, 2004). Lee was one who feared spies. He guarded against them by allowing no one into his camps without a personal pass from the president or secretary of war, and ordered that all of his dispatches be written in cypher. Jones, *Rebel War Clerk's Diary,* pp. 83, 163.

71. REL to MCL, Camp, Orange, August 17, 1863, DE-LC.

72. Beymer, *Scouts and Spies,* p. 161–63; Benjamin's letter in Beymer, "Williams, CSA"; and Jones, *Rebel War Clerk's Diary,* p. 262.

73. Tidwell, *April '65,* pp. 32–35.

74. See MCW Diary, 1862, and MCW to Benson Lossing, March 25, 1864, Williams MS, both TPA; and Cullum, *Biographical Register,* 2:506.

75. Harry Wickham quoted in Coulling, *Lee Girls,* p. 126.

76. REL to MCW, Lexington, Va., December 1, 1866, in Lee, *"To Markie,"* pp. 71–72.

77. REL to MCL, Richmond, March 14, 1862, DE-LC; also MCL to Mrs. W.H. Stiles, White House, March 8, 1862, SH. The quotation is a paraphrase from *Hamlet,* act 1, scene 2.

78. REL to MCL, Camp, April 23, 1864; and MCL to ACL, H. Hill, August 20, 1862, both DE-LC.

79. REL to Edward Lee Childe, Richmond, June 17, 1865, SH.

80. REL to EAL, Camp Fred^g, May 25, 1863; quotation REL to EAL, Petersburg, November 20, 1864, both DE-LC.

81. The largest collection of Lee's private wartime papers is at the Virginia Historical Society; many letters have been reprinted in *Wartime Papers of R. E. Lee,* or Jones, *Life and Letters of Gen. Robert E. Lee.* In nearly every instance the transcriptions are imperfect. Jones, for instance, omits the many amusing and touching references to Lee's deteriorating undergarments. For lowering expectations about receiving letters, see REL to MCL, Camp Fred^g, March 9 and March 19, 1863, both DE-LC.

82. REL to MCL, Camp Fred^g, March 21, 1863, DE-LC.

83. REL Jr., to MiCL, Camp near Hicksford, February 16, 1865, DE-LC.

84. REL Jr., to EAL, "Headquarters Lee's Brigade," November 17, 1863, DE-LC; and L. R. Garrison, "Administrative Problems of the Confederate Post Office Department," 2 parts, *Southwestern Historical Quarterly Online* 19, no. 2 (October 1915), and 19, no. 3 (January 1916).

85. Lee quoted in Garrison, "Administrative Problems," 1:12–13.

86. [MCW] to "Dearest Cousin Mary" [MCL], Washington, D.C., July 15, 1861; and MCL to "My dear child" [Mildred], Chantilly, June 19, 1861, both DE-LC.

87. REL to EAL, Camp Fred^g, December 26, 1862, DE-LC.

88. REL to Mrs. W. H. F. Lee, Culpeper, June 11, 1863, quoted in Lee, *Lee of Virginia,* p. 442.

89. REL to GWCL, Camp Orange, August 18, 1863, HL.

90. REL to MCL, Camp Fred^g, December 21, 1862, DE-LC.

91. REL to GWCL, Camp Orange, August 18, 1863, HL. According to a cousin, at Appomattox Lee told an old friend in the Union command that "he had not a dollar in the world—" Elizabeth Blair Lee to S. Phillips Lee, Washington, April 14, 1865, in Lee, *Wartime Washington*, p. 492.

92. REL to MCL, Camp, July 16, 1864, DE-LC.

CHAPTER TWENTY-TWO: The Political Animal

1. REL to Jefferson Davis, Head Quarters ANV^a, April 25, 1864, DU. "Mr. Newton" has not been identified but was probably a local citizen in the Northern Neck, a peninsula between the Potomac and Rappahannock Rivers.

2. Charles Marshall for REL to Richard S. Ewell, "H^d Q^{rs}, CS Armies," March 30, 1865, Richard S. Ewell Papers, LC. Lee may have dictated this letter to Marshall, as he often did; if not, it shows Marshall's close familiarity with his chief's style. Lee had had Ewell transferred to Richmond from his corps command after the battle of Spotsylvania, when he found Ewell trying to rally troops by beating their backs with his sword. For an account of this episode, see Paul D. Cardorph, *Confederate General R. S. Ewell: Robert E. Lee's Hesitant Commander* (Lexington: University Press of Kentucky, 2004), pp. 298–99, 308–9. Lt. Colonel Kirkwood Otey was colonel of the 11th Virginia Regiment. General Order No. 14, addressed to Jubal Early, was issued February 3, 1864. In it, Lee states how pleased he is with the large number of reenlistments among units of the Army of the Tennessee, and hopes it will be a model for other armies. The order is in U.S. War Department, *OR*, ser. 1, vol. 33, pp. 1114–15.

3. The Confederate States of America (CSA) was formed on February 8, 1861, by (in order of secession) South Carolina, Mississippi, Florida, Alabama, Georgia, Louisiana, and Texas; and joined by four more—Virginia, Arkansas, North Carolina and Tennessee—after Lincoln called up troops in April 1861. Kentucky, a border state, had two state governments during the war—one that backed the Union, and one that backed the South. Missouri also had a complicated secession history, and along with Kentucky sent representatives to the Confederate Congress. Both of those states are also often considered part of the CSA.

4. For a discussion of Confederate political culture, see George C. Rable, *The Confederate Republic: A Revolution against Politics* (Chapel Hill: University of North Carolina Press, 1994). Quotation W. R. Smith to "My Darling Wife," Richmond, February 8, 1863, Easby-Smith Family Papers, LC.

5. For a discussion of these issues, see Faust, *The Creation of Confederate Nationalism*; and Gary W. Gallagher, *The Confederate War* (Cambridge, Mass.: Harvard University Press, 1997). A copy of the Confederate constitution, marked to show the changes from the United States' version, is at http://www.civilwarhome.com/cscon stitution.htm. Quotation W. R. Smith to "My Darling Wife," Richmond, February 8, 1863, Easby-Smith Family Papers, LC.

6. Lee, *Wartime Washington*, p. 378n. See also Franklin, *Militant South*, pp. 21–25.

7. James A. Seddon quoted in O'Brien, "James A. Seddon," pp. 440–41. For an example of the tension between state and national interests, see Joseph E. Brown to Jefferson Davis, Canton, Ga., October 18, 1862, in *OR*, IV, pt. 2, pp. 128–31; and John D. Ashmore to Maj. C. D. Melton, Greenville, S.C., August 7, 1863, ibid., pp. 771–73; and Kean, *Inside the Confederate Government*, p. 55.

8. REL to MCL, Camp Fred⁸, December 25, 1862; and quotation REL to MCL, Richmond, July 27, 1861, both DE-LC.

9. REL to MCL, Camp, November 21, 1863, DE-LC.

10. REL to MCL, Richmond, April 30, 1861, copy in MCL's hand, DE-LC.

11. Davis, *Jefferson Davis*, p. 444; and Kean, *Inside the Confederate Government*, pp. 133–42.

12. Ibid., pp. 435–55; quotation p. 451.

13. Mallory Diary, August 11, [1861], Stephen R. Mallory Papers, LC; Taylor, *Four Years with General Lee*, pp. 11–12; quotation John Cheves Haskell Memoirs, 1860–65, Haskell Papers, DU.

14. REL to MCL, Richmond, March 14, 1862, DE-LC; quotation Stephen R. Mallory to Master S. R. Mallory, Fort Lafayette, September 27, 1865, Stephen Mallory Papers, LC.

15. Marshall, *Lee's Aide-de-Camp*, p. 7.

16. Chesnut, *Diary*, p. 100.

17. Jones, *Rebel War Clerk's Diary*, pp. 88, 103.

18. Ibid., p. 242; and O'Brien, "James A. Seddon," pp. 312–17.

19. Jones, *Rebel War Clerk's Diary*, pp. 471–72; WHFL to wife, Fredericksburg, February 27, 1862, DE-LC; quotation in Gallagher, *Confederate War*, p. 88.

20. Davis, *Jefferson Davis*, pp. 426–27.

21. Marshall, *Lee's Aide-de-Camp*, pp. 4–6; quotation in Kean, *Inside the Confederate Government*, p. 86.

22. Davis, *Cause Lost*, pp. 39–40; quotation in Nisbet, *4 Years on the Firing Line*, p. 236.

23. Davis, *Cause Lost*, pp. 14–34, quotation p. 45.

24. The story is told this way in Harrison, *Recollections Grave and Gay*, pp. 72–73. Other accounts have Lee asking Davis bluntly if he or the president were in charge on the field, or claim that Lee saved Davis's life by urging him away from the fire. Jones, *Rebel War Clerk's Diary*, pp. 86–87; and Ernest B. Furgurson, *Ashes of Glory: Richmond at War* (New York: Alfred A. Knopf, 1996), pp. 148–49.

25. Davis quoted in Woodworth, *Davis and Lee at War*, p. 180.

26. REL to Jefferson Davis, Headquarters, Army of Northern Virginia, Rapidan, December 7, 1863, in Lee, *Wartime Papers*, p. 642.

27. REL to Jefferson Davis, H⁴qrs, August 13, 1864, LFP-WL.

28. Examples of Lee's continual pleas for troops can be found in REL to Jefferson Davis, Headquarters, Army of Northern Virginia, May 11 and May 30, 1863; REL to Jefferson Davis, Headquarters, Army of Northern Virginia, March 25, 1864, all Lee, *Wartime Papers*, pp. 438–84, 495–96, and 682–84. His willful omission of important details was evident when he reported his movements into Maryland only after he had crossed the river, and during the 1863 Bristoe campaign, when he obscures the location of his army so that Seddon would not interfere with his developing plans. Quotations Lee, *Wartime Washington*, p. 293; and Kean, *Inside the Confederate Government*, p. 91. A firsthand account of the episode discussed is in A. Perrin to Gov. Milledge Luke Bonham, Camp of McGowan's Brigade, Near Culpepper CH, Va., July 29, 1863, Bonham, "A Little More Light on Gettysburg," p. 525. Lee's account is in *OR*, ser. 1, vol. 27, pt. 2, pp. 303–4, 310.

29. Jones, *Rebel War Clerk's Diary*, pp. 146–51.

30. Davis, *Cause Lost*, pp. 43–44; and O'Brien, "James A. Seddon," pp. 369–70.

31. Fuller, *Grant and Lee*, pp. 115, 124–25.

32. O'Brien, "James A. Seddon," pp. 457–61. Understatement and deference had long been part of Lee's style. See Bowery and Hankinson, eds., *Daily Correspondence*; also Max R. Williams, "The General and the Governor: Robert E. Lee and Zebulon B. Vance," in Carmichael, *Audacity Personified*, pp. 107–32; and REL to Henry Wise, letters of April–June 1862, Wise Family Papers, VHS.

33. Gallagher, *Confederate War*, p. 115–44.

34. See Janowitz, *Professional Soldier*, p. 322. Sun Tzu's philosophy had been translated into French in the late eighteenth century and was known in the West from that time.

35. See, for example, Frances Stebbins Ward to Jefferson Davis, July 27, 1863, in *Papers of Jefferson Davis*, 9:306.

36. These issues are discussed in James M. McPherson, "Failed Southern Strategies," *MHQ: The Quarterly Journal of Military History* 11, no. 4 (Summer 1999): 60–67; Thomas Lawrence Connelly and Archer Jones, *The Politics of Command* (Baton Rouge: Louisiana State University Press, 1973), pp. 31–48; Palmer, *Lee Moves North*; McMurry, *Two Great Rebel Armies*; Gallagher, "Home Front and Battlefield," pp. 135–68; Emory M. Thomas, "Ambivalent Visions of Victory: Davis, Lee and Confederate Grand Strategy," in Gabor S. Boritt, ed., *Jefferson Davis's Generals* (New York: Oxford University Press, 1999), pp. 27–45; and Roland, *Reflections on Lee*, pp. 45–98; and O'Brien, "James A. Seddon," pp. 314–17, 369–76. A diarist in Richmond who knew both Lee and Davis wrote after Appomattox that he doubted if Davis "will ever forgive Gen. Lee." Jones, *Rebel War Clerk's Diary*, p. 535.

37. Gallagher, *Confederate War*, pp. 72–79, quotation p. 91. Gallagher extends this argument to a larger conclusion: without the Army of Northern Virginia, there would have been no sustaining morale and therefore no nation; he contends that a guerilla war could not have been fought and won because the people's will would not have supported it. But one must ask: If there was no nation outside the army, what was the army fighting for, and why did it exist?

38. Sallie Minor to John Minor, May 15, 1864, quoted in Ash, *When the Yankees Came*, p. 75; see also Kean, *Inside the Confederate Government*, p. 215.

39. Taylor to "my dear Bettie," Camp at "Violet Bank," September 11, 1864, in Taylor, *Lee's Adjutant*, p. 191.

40. Lee's appointment is in General Orders No. 3 of the Adjutant General's Office, February 6, 1865 *OR*, ser. 1, vol. 46, pt. 2, p. 1205. Quotation *Richmond Times-Dispatch*, February 7, 1865.

41. REL to CCL, letter fragment, n.d. [c. 1862 or early 1863], CL-LC.

42. REL to MCL, Coosawhatchie, S.C., December 25, 1861, DE-LC.

43. REL to CCL, letter fragment, n.d. [c. 1862 or early 1863], CL-LC.

44. Mallory Diary, July 9, [1861], Stephen R. Mallory Papers, LC.

45. REL to GWCL, Savannah, February 23, 1862, photostat MoC. Another expression of frustration on the same subject is in REL to ACL, Savannah, March 2, 1862, DE-LC.

46. REL to MiCL, Camp Rapp[k], October 31, 1863; and REL to ACL and EAL, Washington's Run, September 30, 1862, both DE-LC.

47. S. S. Lee to CCL, Commandant's Office, Camp Bluff, March 28, 1863, Fitzhugh Lee Papers, UVa.

48. Quotation W. R. Smith to "My Darling Wife," Richmond, October 2, 1862, Easby-Smith Family Papers, LC; Beringer et al., *Why the South Lost*, pp. 64–81.

49. Jones, *Rebel War Clerk's Diary*, p. 174; quotation p. 259.

50. [Brock], *Richmond during the War*, p. 21.

51. Julia Tyler to mother, Richmond, June 16, 1861, in Tyler, ed., *Letters and Times,* 2:651.

52. For more on the rather bungled British debate on Confederate recognition, see Adams, *Education of Henry Adams,* pp. 100–42, 157–60; for civic discontent, see Gallagher, "Home Front and Battlefield," p. 155; and Rable, *Civil Wars,* pp. 74–81.

53. Jones, *Rebel War Clerk's Diary,* p. 338.

54. George T. Lee, "Reminiscences of General Robert E. Lee, 1865–68," typescript WL.

55. S[arah] J. Turner to MCL(d), Kinloch, January 17, [1865], MCL-VHS.

56. REL to Col. S[amuel] Bassett French, H^dQrs, August 8, 1862, LFP-WL.

57. Armistead L. Robinson, "In the Shadow of Old John Brown: Insurrection Anxiety and Confederate Mobilization, 1861–63," *Journal of Negro History,* 65, no. 4 (Autumn 1980).

58. Jordan, *Black Confederates,* p. 77.

59. For more on the problems caused by unsupervised plantations and the fear of black insurrection, see Armistead L. Robinson, "In the Shadow of Old John Brown: Insurrection Anxiety and Confederate Mobilization, 1861–63," *Journal of Negro History* 65, no. 4 (Autumn 1980).

60. Aaron Sheehan-Dean, "Justice Has Something to Do With It: Class Relations and the Confederate Army," *VMHB,* 113, no. 4 (Autumn 2005), pp. 357–60.

61. Jones, *Rebel War Clerk's Diary,* pp. 359, 440.

62. Goree, *Longstreet's Aide,* p. 137.

63. REL to Jefferson Davis, Headquarters, Army of Northern Virginia, January 19, 1864, in Lee, *Wartime Papers,* p. 655.

64. Marshall, *Lee's Aide-de-Camp,* pp. 32–33.

65. Deserters and draft dodgers were another running theme throughout Lee's correspondence with Richmond officials. See, for example, REL to Jefferson Davis, Headquarters, Army of Northern Virginia, January 13, 1864; and REL to General James L. Kemper, Headquarters, Army of Northern Virginia, January 29, 1864, both in Lee, *Wartime Papers,* pp. 650–51 and 663–64.

66. REL to Jefferson Davis, Headquarters, Petersburg, February 9, 1865; quotation REL to Jefferson Davis, Headquarters, Army of Northern Virginia, August 17, 1863, both in Lee, *Wartime Papers,* pp. 892–93, 591.

67. Another notorious case of Confederates slaughtering captured African-Americans was at Fort Pillow in 1864. Jordan, *Black Confederates,* pp. 62–64; Jay Winik, *April 1865: The Month That Saved America* (New York: Perennial, 2002), pp. 51–52; and McPherson, *Battle Cry of Freedom,* pp. 564, 634, 748n, 759–60.

68. W. J. Pegram to Virginia Johnson [Pegram] McIntosh, Petersburg, August 1, 1864, in Robertson, ed., "'The Boy Artillerist,'" pp. 243–44. A few of the Southerners admitted to being struck by the bravery of the African-American forces. "The story is the negroes fought better than their white Yankee brethren," one of Lee's soldiers told his wife. Thomas Claybrook Elder to wife, Camp near Petersburg, July 30, 1864, TCE-VHS.

69. Davis, *Jefferson Davis,* p. 541.

70. REL to Andrew Hunter, Headquarters, Army of Northern Virginia, January 11, 1865, SH.

71. Silas Chandler and Erastus Willis quoted in Laskin, "Good Old Rebels," pp. 86, 89.

72. Quotation in Rable, *Confederate Republic,* p. 290.

73. Daniel Cobb and Joseph Brown quoted in Beringer et al., *Why the South Lost,* pp. 386–87.

74. Berlin, "Did Confederate Women Lose the War?" pp. 172–73.
75. Thomas Henry Carter to wife, Fishersville, December 31, 1864, THC-VHS.
76. REL quoted in Long, *Memoirs*, p. 454.

CHAPTER TWENTY-THREE: Ragged Individualists

1. REL to Col. S[amuel] Bassett French, H^{d}Qrs, August 8, 1862, LFP-WL. As the letter implies, Samuel Bassett French (1820–1898), was an "extra" aide-de-camp to both Lee and Jackson. Bassett French later became known for his compilation of biographical materials on nearly 9,000 prominent Virginians, which he prepared for a volume to be titled *Annals of Prominent Virginians of the XIX Century*.

2. REL to William C. Rives, Camp Fred^g, May 21, 1863, Davis Collection, TU. Rives was a U.S. congressman and senator prior to the Civil War, and also served in the Confederate Congress.

3. Edward Richardson Crockett Diary, [May] "The 6th," [1864], UT. Crockett was 3rd sergeant in Company F, "The Mustang Grays" of the 4th Texas Infantry. He fought with distinction at Gettysburg, Chickamauga, the Wilderness, Spotsylvania, and Cold Harbor and surrendered with Lee at Appomattox. He was wounded slightly the day of this diary entry, and six other times, but never incapacitated. The 4th Texas Infantry, "The Hell Roaring 4th," was John Bell Hood's old regiment, famous for its valor, and frequently used by Lee as shock troops. Though the "Lee to the Rear" episode has been recounted in numerous memoirs, this is one of the few contemporary accounts. The regimental history is at www.texas-brigade.com.

4. Benét, *John Brown's Body*, p. 165.

5. Chesnut, *Diary*, p. 442.

6. References to the Army of Northern Virginia begin about February 1862. See A. L. Rives to J. E. Johnston, February 25, 1862, addressed to the "Commander, Army of Northern Virginia," *OR*, ser. 1., vol. 5, pp. 1081–82. Lee continued to hold his position with the ANVa after he was made general in chief of all Confederate forces in February, 1865. The order making Lee commander of the ANVa is in *OR*, ser. 1, vol. 9, pt. 3, p. 571.

7. Overall around 900,000 men fought for the Confederacy from 1861 to 1865. Statistical evidence is far from complete, but it appears about 38 percent of the ANVa came from Virginia itself, and two-thirds from the easternmost Confederate states. Unlike their northern foe, almost all were native-born, with fewer than 5 percent coming from outside the southern states. At the time of the Seven Days battles, soon after the creation of the Army of Northern Virginia, the ANVa contained 275 units, designated by state; 64 percent were from eastern states, 18.5 from western states, and 17.5 from the central states of the South. The figures changed as the composition of the forces changed over time. Robert Krick has calculated that 385 infantry, cavalry, and artillery units of battalion size or larger served with the ANVa, with similar distribution: 66.5 from the eastern states, 16.6 from the central states, and 16.9 from the western part of the Confederacy. Figures given in McMurry, *Two Great Rebel Armies*, pp. 88–89.

8. This data is based on statistics compiled by Elisabeth Lauterbach Laskin, based on a sample of 647 ANVa soldiers who wrote diaries or letters, and from regimental rolls and census data. She found that in her source sample 35 percent were farmers or planters; 38 percent professional men; skilled laborers and students each 8 percent. Biographical information was difficult to obtain, but of those possible to evaluate, the average age was 23.9 and the median 22. She found only 18 percent could be identified as slaveowners from their letters; but this figure jumped to 43 percent when

correlated with census data. The sample is biased toward the educated, who were more inclined to write letters. Laskin, "Good Old Rebels," pp. 4–5, 22–27, 117, 421–30; and Wiley, *Life of Johnny Reb*, pp. 322–25, 330–33. James M. McPherson and Bell Irvin Wiley also compiled figures for the Confederacy as a whole, based on letters and diaries. McPherson broke down his tables by officers and enlisted men, finding that 42 percent of the former were planters or farmers, compared with 79 percent of the latter. Wiley found an overall figure of 61.5 percent for the two. See table 3 in appendix of James M. McPherson, *For Cause and Comrades: Why Men Fought in the Civil War* (New York: Oxford University Press, 1997), p. 181.

9. Thomas Claybrook Elder to "my dear wife," Camp near Fredericksburg, December 21, 1862, TCE-VHS.

10. REL to GWCL, Camp, February 12, 1863, REL-DU.

11. Laskin, "Good Old Rebels," pp. 427–28; Philip Katcher, *The Army of Robert E. Lee* (London: Arms and Armour Press, 1994), pp. 91–98; quotation Fremantle, *Three Months in the Southern States*, p. 293.

12. Laskin, "Good Old Rebels," pp. 22–23. Laskin found few statistics available on the number of conscripts in the ANVa, but in one company that did keep records 44 of 138 men had been conscripted, or about 32 percent.

13. Laskin's study of the ANVa concludes that the men fought for preservation of rights; independence; avoidance of subjugation; the institution of slavery; and defense against northern aggression. They also responded to concepts of duty and to the honor their enlistment would bring, or conversely the shame of refusing to serve. These concepts changed as the war progressed; hardship at home, or flagging enthusiasm for the war effort, caused many communities to reverse their opinions of desertion or avoidance of army service. In her sample, preservation of rights was rarely mentioned, and fear of subjection increased as the war progressed. Bell Irvin Wiley and James M. McPherson have also found that a combination of idealistic, romantic, and pragmatic motives induced men to enlist both North and South. Laskin, "Good Old Rebels," pp. 34–55, 133–37; Wiley, *Life of Johnny Reb*, pp. 16–19; and Bell Irvin Wiley, *The Life of Billy Yank* (New York: Doubleday, 1952), pp. 37–44.

14. Quoted in McPherson, *For Cause and Comrades*, p. 109. McPherson believes Southern soldiers discussed the issue of slavery less frequently than their Northern counterparts because its existence was simply taken for granted; it was not debatable. Ibid., pp. 108–10.

15. Diary of Captain Robert Gaines Haile, June 12, 1862, typescript, DSF-LC. See also Richard Maury to "My dear Cousin," Fredericksburg, Va., November 4, 1862, Matthew Fontaine Maury Papers, LC; and Cadmus M. Wilcox to Sister Mary, Fredericksburg, Va., May 16, 1863, Wilcox Papers, LC. Charles Marshall, one of Lee's aides, was another who thought unequivocally that they were fighting the war over slavery. Marshall, *Lee's Aide-de-Camp*, p. 39.

16. Letterhead on James Keith to "My dear mother," October 2, [c. 1864], Keith Family Papers, VHS.

17. Joseph Valentine Smedley, "A Day at Genl Lee's Hdqrts," Richmond, June 9, 1864, Smedley Papers, DU.

18. For a longer discussion of the factors that brought unity to the ANVa, see Laskin, "Good Old Rebels," pp. 264–331, 424–79; McMurry, *Two Great Rebel Armies*, pp. 6, 25–27, 60; also Wiley, *Life of Johnny Reb*, pp. 308–14.

19. A description of Union army life, filled with lemons, brandy, shoes, and opera glasses, is in Goree, *Longstreet's Aide,* p. 87.

20. John Hampden Chamberlayne quoted in Laskin, "Good Old Rebels," p. 305.

21. Ibid., pp. 180–250 and McPherson, *Battle Cry of Freedom,* pp. 470–71.

22. Charles William McVicar quoted in Laskin, "Good Old Rebels," p. 236.

23. Viscount Wolseley, "A Month's Visit to the Confederate Head Quarters," *Blackwood's Edinburgh Magazine* 93, no. 567 (January 1863).

24. Micajah Woods quoted in Laskin, "Good Old Rebels," p. 481.

25. McMurry, *Two Great Rebel Armies,* pp. 92–104; Sherman quoted p. 99.

26. REL to MCL, Valley Mt., September 17, 1861, DE-LC. For a long discussion of this issue, see Marshall, *Lee's Aide-de-Camp,* pp. 33–39.

27. Sheehan-Dean, "Justice Has Something to Do with It," pp. 342–77; quotation Samuel B. Blymon to William Walter Christian, November 3, 1861, p. 346.

28. REL to James Lyons, Richmond, April 25, 1861, Brock Collection, HL.

29. See REL to MCL, Camp Orange, February 14, 1864, DE-LC.

30. A full list of Lee's staff members, written by Talcott, is in Stephen D. Lee to T. M. R. Talcott, Columbia, Miss., October 16, 1907, Talcott Family Papers, VHS. Lee's personal aides hailed from the Old Dominion, save Marshall, and he had been born and educated there.

31. E. Porter Alexander is among those who thought so. See *Fighting for the Confederacy,* pp. 236–37.

32. For the insiders' view of life on Lee's staff, see Taylor, *Lee's Adjutant;* Marshall, *Lee's Aide-de-Camp*; and Venable, "General Lee in the Wilderness Campaign," *B & L* 4:240–46. A discussion of Lee's staff arrangements is in Robert E. L. Krick, "'The Great Tycoon' Forges a Staff System," in Carmichael, *Audacity Personified.* Additional criticism of Lee's inadequate development and use of staff is found in Fuller, *Grant and Lee,* pp. 117–26.

33. A description of Lee's camp is in Venable, "General Lee in the Wilderness Campaign," p. 240; Wolseley, "Month's Visit," p. 20; and Walter Taylor to Bettie, October 25, 1863, in Taylor, *Lee's Adjutant,* p. 99, quotations Walter Taylor to sister, Camp near Orange, November 14, 1863, p. 83.

34. Taylor finally did get his much-sought recommendation for promotion to lieutenant colonel, and Lee wrote a tardy letter of appreciation after his chief of staff, R. H. Chilton, accepted a job in Richmond, but nurturing his personal staff could not be called his strong point. Walter Taylor to Bettie Saunders, Camp near Orange C. Ho., November 15, 1863, in Taylor, *Lee's Adjutant,* p. 89; REL to ?, Hd qrs, January 7, 1863, photocopy; and to R. H. Chilton, Camp, Orange Co., March 24, 1864, both MoC.

35. Venable, "General Lee in the Wilderness Campaign," p. 240.

36. Walter Taylor to Bettie [Saunders], Edge Hill, December 18, 1864, in Taylor, *Lee's Adjutant,* p. 212; and Krick, "'The Great Tycoon' Forges a Staff System," p. 93.

37. Venable, "General Lee in the Wilderness Campaign," p. 240; and A. R. H. Ranson, "General Lee As I Knew Him," *Harper's Monthly Magazine* 122, no. 729 (February, 1911): 328–32.

38. REL to MCL, Camp Rapidan, December 4, 1863; and REL to EAL, Camp Fred⁸, February 6, 1863, both DE-LC.

39. Venable, "General Lee in the Wilderness Campaign"; Ranson, "General Lee As I Knew Him," p. 332; Walter Taylor to Bet[tie], Camp at Violet Bank, August 15, 1864, in Taylor, *Lee's Adjutant,* p. 182.

40. Venable's remarks in Krick, "'The Great Tycoon' Forges a Staff System," p. 93; Taylor, *Lee's Adjutant,* p. 175, 182, quotation p. 134.

41. REL to John B. Floyd, Headquarters, Sewell Mt., October 15, 1861, HL.

42. REL to MCL, Rapp[k] River, October 19, 1863, DE-LC.

43. Marion Hill Fitzpatrick, *Letters to Amanda,* ed. Jeffrey C. Lowe and Sam Hodges (Macon, Ga.: Mercer University Press, 1998), p. 95.

44. Humphreys Diary, August 17–24, 1864, Humphreys Papers, UVa.

45. Thomas C. Brady to Jane A. Brady, Camp near Petersburg, Va., January 13, 1865, Brady Family Papers, UT.

46. REL Jr. to MiCL, "Camp near Hick's ford," February 16, 1865, DE-LC.

47. Taylor, *Lee's Adjutant,* pp. 73, 90, 143.

48. REL to MCL, Turnbell's, January 29, 1865; and REL to MCL, Camp, February 8, 1863, both DE-LC.

49. Jones, *Rebel War Clerk's Diary,* p. 307.

50. See Berlin, "Did Confederate Women Lose the War?"; Ramsdell, *Behind the Lines;* and Fuller, *Grant and Lee,* pp. 117–27.

51. E. P. Alexander to Lt. Col. Walter Taylor, April 24, 1864, with endorsements by J. Longstreet, April 25, 1864, and REL, April 26, 1864, LFP-WL.

52. Thomas Claybrook Elder to "My dear Wife," Camp near Rapidan Station, January 24, 1864, TCE-VHS.

53. REL to WHFL, n.d., [c. May 1863], GBL-VHS.

54. REL to MCL, Camp, January 24, 1864; and February 6, 1864, both DE-LC; Abram Hayne Young quoted in Laskin, "Good Old Rebels," p. 452.

55. Quoted in Laskin, "Good Old Rebels," p. 193.

56. Thomas Henry Carter to wife, Camp near New Market, October 26, 1864, THC-VHS.

57. McPherson, *For Cause and Comrades,* p. 50.

58. See Jones, *Rebel War Clerk's Diary,* pp. 100, 109; REL to Jefferson Davis, Headquarters, Army of Northern Virginia, August 17, 1863; and to James A. Seddon, Headquarters, Army of Northern Virginia, January 17, 1865, both in Lee, *Wartime Papers,* pp. 591, 886.

59. Thomas Henry Carter to "my dear wife," near Richmond, July 13, 1862, and Camp near Bunker Hill, October 18, 1862, both THC-VHS.

60. Genl B. T. Johnson to Maj Jno. W. Hensdale, "Hdqrts Port Salisb[y]," February 13, 1865, REL-DU. The authoritative source on Civil War desertion is Ella Lonn, *Desertion during the Civil War* (New York: Century, 1928). She estimated that a total of 103,000 soldiers deserted during the conflict. See also Marshall, *Lee's Aide-de-Camp,* p. 188.

61. Chesnut, *Diary,* p. 777.

62. Cadmus M. Wilcox to "Dear John," September 26, 1862, Wilcox Papers, LC; see also Wiley, *Life of Johnny Reb,* pp. 47–48.

63. S[arah] J. Turner to MCL(d), Kinloch, January 17 [1865], MCL-VHS.

64. Quoted in Wiley, *Life of Johnny Reb,* p. 47.

65. Jones, *Rebel War Clerk's Diary,* p. 319.

66. Hood, *Advance and Retreat,* p. 51; Taliaferro Simpson quoted in Laskin, "Good Old Rebels," p. 468. See also pp. 278–89, and Wiley, *Life of Johnny Reb,* pp. 47–48, for plunder during the Gettysburg campaign.

67. Mosby, "Personal Recollections of General Lee," p. 67. Mosby did not portray the remark as a joke.

68. For Lee's overoptimistic idea of controlling plunder, see REL to Gen. Joseph R. Anderson, Headquarters, Richmond, Va., April 29, 1862, photocopy, MoC.

69. Many heeded the admonition out of respect for Lee personally, but he established a military commission on the issue just to make sure. REL, General Order ?, Leesburg, Va., September 4, 1862, MoC; also REL to General Milledge L. Bonham, Headquarters, Virginia Forces, Richmond, Va., May 22, 1861; and to General Joseph E. Johnston, Headquarters, Richmond, May 18, 1862, both in Lee, *Wartime Letters*, pp. 33, 176; and *OR*, ser. 1, vol. 27, pt. 3, pp. 912–13, 942–43.

70. General Orders No. 116, "H'd-Quar's, Army Nor'n Va.," October 2, 1862, copy of original in MoC.

71. Dr. Harvey Black to wife, Orange CH, January 29, 1864, in Harvey Black, *The Civil War Letters of Dr. Harvey Black*, ed. Glenn L. McMullen. (Baltimore: Butternut and Blue, 1995), p. 83; also General Orders No. 7, Headquarters, Army of Northern Virginia, January 12, 1864 in Lee, *Wartime Papers*, p. 659.

72. The order allowing furloughs for two men per company is in General Orders No. 21, March 23, 1864, copy of printed order at MoC. REL to Jefferson Davis, Headquarters, Army of Northern Virginia, August 17, 1863; to James A. Seddon, Headquarters, Army of Northern Virginia, January 17, 1865; and to Jefferson Davis, Headquarters, Petersburg, February 9, 1865, all Lee, *Wartime Papers*, pp. 591, 886, 892. Also Thomas Claybrook Elder to "My dear wife," Camp near Orange CH, August 21, 1863, TCE-VHS; and Fitzpatrick, *To Amanda*, p. 114.

73. Douglas Southall Freeman believed that one of Lee's greatest challenges was to keep morale high in the face of lax discipline. See Freeman, *On Leadership*, pp. 62–82.

74. Fanny Roper Fendge, "Some Reminiscences of Gen. Lee," MS, n.d. [postwar], HL.

75. Quoted in Laskin, "Good Old Rebels," p. 467.

76. For an example of the inspiring tales told of visiting Lee's headquarters, see Freeman, *On Leadership*, p. 118.

77. James Dorman Davidson quoted in Sheehan-Dean, "Class Relations and the Confederate Army," p. 354.

78. Louis Leon and N. R. Fitzhugh quoted in Laskin, "Good Old Rebels," pp. 468, 471.

79. Hotchkiss, *Make Me a Map*, p. 136.

80. James Keith to "My dear mother," June 7, [1861], Keith Family Papers, VHS.

81. Diary of Lucy Rebecca Buck for July 22, 1863, in *Shadows on My Heart: The Civil War Diary of Lucy Rebecca Buck of Virginia*, ed. Elizabeth R. Baer (Athens: University of Georgia Press, 1997), pp. 236–37.

82. James Preston Chowder quoted in Laskin, "Good Old Rebels," p. 470.

83. For more on the nature and variety of leadership, see James MacGregor Burns's classic *Leadership* (New York: Harper & Row, 1978).

84. Thomas Henry Carter to wife, Camp near Melford Depot, March 19, 1863, THC-VHS; also "Journal of Raphael J. Moses," DSF-LC. Napoleon thought this one of the consummate skills of a great general: "The foremost quality of a commander is to keep a cool head, to receive accurate impressions of what is happening," he wrote, "and never fret or be amazed or intoxicated by good news or bad." Quoted in Luvaas, "Napoleon on Generalship," p. 82.

85. Few men had an opportunity to talk personally with the general—even a cousin who was a senior artillery officer wrote, "I never see him except on the battlefield." Thomas Henry Carter to wife, Camp near Morton's Ford, November 10, 1863,

THC-VHS. Only 16 percent of Laskin's sample ever even mentioned Lee in any of their writings. Laskin, "Good Old Rebels," p. 455.

86. Nisbet, *4 Years on the Firing Line*, p. 108.

87. Mosby, "Personal Recollections of General Lee," p. 66.

88. The conversation about wearing swords is in Horace Porter, "Surrender at Appomattox Court House," *B & L*, 4:742.

89. Marion Hill Fitzpatrick to Amanda, Near Orange Courthouse, Va., September 15, 1863 in Fitzpatrick, *Letters to Amanda*, p. 88.

90. For enthusiasm inspired by Jackson, see Thomas Claybrook Elder to wife, Camp near Dranesville, September 4, 1862, in TCE-VHS. Laskin discussed the reverence felt for Stonewall Jackson in "Good Old Rebels," pp. 455–66, quotation p. 458.

91. William Powell Hill to sister, Quarter Masters Office, Richmond, March 22, 1863, Hill Family Papers, VHS; and "Personal Recollections of the First Battle of Fredericksburg, Fought on December 13, 1862 as Seen from an Artillery Position on the Hill at Hamilton's Crossing," n.d. [from notes at the time], UT.

92. Edmund DeWitt Patterson, quoted in Laskin, "Good Old Rebels," pp. 475–76; also John Cheves Haskell Memoirs, DU.

93. Thomas Henry Carter to wife, Camp near Morton's Ford, November 10, 1863, and Camp near Summerville Ford, November 14, 1863, THC-VHS; and Harvey Black to wife, "Hospital, 2 Corps A.N.Va., Orange C.H.," November 9, 1863, in Black, *Civil War Letters*, pp. 67–68.

94. Walter H. Taylor to [Bettie], Camp near Orange, December 5, 1863, in Taylor, *Lee's Adjutant*, p. 94; and Venable, "General Lee in the Wilderness Campaign," p. 240. There is a long analysis of the fall 1864 campaigns, pointing up Lee's weakness on the offensive, in Palmer, *Lee Moves North*, pp. 89–120.

95. Jasper Gillespie quoted in Larkin, "Good Old Rebels," p. 452.

96. Walter H. Taylor to [Bettie], Camp Orange County, April 3, 1864, in Taylor, *Lee's Adjutant*, p. 148.

97. REL to Genl Braxton Bragg, Hdqrs, April 16, 1864, Eggleston Collection, HL.

98. Hotchkiss, *Make Me a Map*, pp. 198–99; and Goree, *Longstreet's Aide*, p. 123.

99. Walter H. Taylor to [Bettie], March 20, 1864, in Taylor, *Lee's Adjutant*, p. 139.

100. H. W. Halleck to U. S. Grant, February 17, 1864, in *The Papers of Ulysses S. Grant*, 10:110–12n.

101. The Overland Campaign lasted from May 5 to approximately June 24, 1864. The casualty figure is given in McPherson, *Battle Cry of Freedom*, p. 733, and covers the time of the greatest fighting, between the Wilderness and Cold Harbor. For a comparison of casualty estimates, see en.wikipedia.org/wiki/Overland_Campaign. For a discussion of the campaign, see McPherson, *Battle Cry of Freedom*, pp. 718–43; Walter H. Taylor to "my dear Bettie," Camp near Hanover Junction, May 23, 1864, in Taylor, *Lee's Adjutant*, pp. 162–63; and Robert McAllister to family, Battlefield near Spotsylvania Court House, Va., May 11, 1864, Robert McAllister, *The Civil War Letters of General Robert McAllister*, ed. James I. Robertson Jr. (New Brunswick, N.J.: Rutgers University Press, 1965), pp. 417–19; quotation p. 417.

102. U. S. Grant to H. W. Halleck, Spotsylvania Courthouse, May 11, 1864, *Papers of Ulysses S. Grant*, 10:422; and U. S. Grant to Julia Dent Grant, Cold Harbor, Va., June 6, 1864, ibid., 11:25.

103. Thomas Claybrook Elder to wife, Camp near Matawan, October 6, 1864, TCE-VHS.

104. Lee quoted in Carmichael, "Lee's Search for the Battle of Annihilation," p. 17.

105. U.S. Grant to Julia Dent Grant, Near Spotsylvania C.H. Va., May 13, 1864, and City Point, Va., October 28, 1864, *Papers of Ulysses S. Grant*, 10:443–44, and 12:362. For more on the conduct of the Overland campaign, see Gordon C. Rhea, "Lee, Grant, and 'Prescience' in the Overland Campaign," in Carmichael, *Audacity Personified*, pp. 57–81; Fuller, *Grant and Lee*, pp. 206–41; and Noah Andre Trudeau, "'A Mere Question of Time': Robert E. Lee from the Wilderness to Appomattox Court House," in Gallagher, ed., *Lee the Soldier*, pp. 523–58.

106. Marion Hill Fitzpatrick to Amanda, "In Line of battle near Spotsylvania C.H. Va," May 15, 1864, in Fitzpatrick, *Letters to Amanda*, pp. 143–44.

107. Crockett Diary, "The 3rd" [June 1864], UT.

108. Lee quoted in Jones, *Rebel War Clerk's Diary*, p. 370.

109. In absolute numbers, losses were greater for the North, giving the field the aspect of a Confederate victory, though proportionally the South suffered more. McPherson, *Battle Cry of Freedom*, p. 732.

110. U. S. Grant to Julia Dent Grant, Near Spotsylvania C.H., Va., May 13, 1864, in *Papers of Ulysses S. Grant*, 10:443–44; and Crockett Diary, "The 12th" [May 1864], UT.

111. In June 1864 REL described the conditions in Petersburg to his wife as "perfectly stifling & then the dust is so dense that the atmosphere is distressing." REL to MCL, Camp Petersburg, June 26, 1864, DE-LC; Marion Hill Fitzpatrick to Amanda, Near Petersburg, October 4, 1864, in Fitzpatrick, *Letters to Amanda*, p. 173. The quip about bacon is on p. 138.

112. Longstreet, *From Manassas to Appomattox*, p. 114; Thomas Henry Carter to wife, Camp near Bunker Hill, October 4, 1862, THC-VHS.

113. For more on the command situation during the Overland Campaign, see Gallagher, *Lee and His Generals*, pp. 75–98; Venable, "General Lee in the Wilderness Campaign," pp. 241–42; Trudeau, "'A Mere Question of Time,'" pp. 533, 537, 543–44. Chaplain William Jones claimed that at this time Lee told his subordinate generals they must give personal attention to the lines. Jones, *Personal Reminiscences*, pp. 148–50, 243–44.

114. Henry Robinson Berkeley, *Four Years in the Confederate Artillery: The Diary of Private Henry Robinson Berkeley*, ed. William H. Runge (Richmond: Virginia Historical Society, 1991), pp. 75–76.

115. For the officers' assessment of Lee's judgment, see, for example, Thomas Henry Carter to wife, Taylorsville, May 24, 1864, THC-VHS; and Walter H. Taylor to "dear Bettie," Edge Hill, February 20, 1865, in Taylor, *Lee's Adjutant*, p. 225.

116. Thomas Pollock Devereux quoted in Laskin, "Good Old Rebels," p. 470.

117. For demoralization, see Laskin, "Good Old Rebels," pp. 245–58; Thomas Claybrook Elder to wife, Camp near Spotsylvania CH, May 13, 1864, TCE-VHS; and Robert McAllister to "dear Ellen," Camp Tucker House, Va., March 22, 1865, in McAllister, *Civil War Letters*, p. 595. Quotation REL to James Longstreet, HdQrs, ANVa, March 21, 1865, typescript in Douglas Southall Freeman to Mrs. Henry Fairfax, February 3, 1937, in Fairfax Papers, VHS.

118. Henry Wise is quoted in John Sergeant Wise, *The End of An Era*, ed. Curtis Carroll Davis (repr., New York: Thomas Yoselof, 1965), p. 434.

119. Adj. Francis Boyle quoted in Laskin, "Good Old Rebels," p. 474; Humphreys Diary, [April] 11 [1865], Humphreys Papers, UVa.

120. Stephen R. Mallory, "Reminiscences," typescript, n.d., LC.

121. Diary of Margaret Junkin Preston, April 10, 1865, in Elizabeth Preston Allan, *The Life and Letters of Margaret Junkin Preston* (Boston: Houghton Mifflin, 1903), pp. 207–8.

122. Ibid.

123. Humphreys Diary, "Wednesday 12" [April 1865], Humphreys Papers, UVa.

124. Quoted in Philip R. Katcher, *The Army of Northern Virginia* (London: Reed International, 1975), p. 17.

125. Notes on conversation with REL, March 7, 1868, in Bean, "Memoranda of Conversations," p. 478.

126. The exchange between Lee and Grant is contained in Grant, *Memoirs*, pp. 550–54.

127. A description of the surrender, including the correspondence leading up to it, is in Grant, *Memoirs*, pp. 547–58; also Marshall, *Aide-de-Camp*, pp. 267–75; and Horace Porter, "Surrender at Appomattox Court House," pp. 729–46.

128. Marshall, *Aide-de-Camp*, p. 272.

129. George A. Forsyth, *Thrilling Days in Army Life* (repr., Lincoln: University of Nebraska Press, 1994), pp. 191–94. This account was written many years after the war, but its credibility is strengthened by the fact that Forsyth gave an identical description two decades earlier in an informal conversation with sculptor James Kelly—who scrupulously recorded it. See Kelly, *Generals in Bronze*, pp. 4–5.

130. Alexander, *Fighting for the Confederacy*, pp. 539–40.

131. Goree, *Longstreet's Aide*, pp. 166–67; also firsthand accounts, in J. Tracy Power, *Lee's Miserables* (Chapel Hill: University of North Carolina Press, 1998), pp. 282–84.

132. Goree, *Longstreet's Aide*, pp. 166–67.

133. "Narrative of the Appomattox Campaign," in McAllister, *Civil War Letters*, pp. 606–8, quotation p. 608; and Thomas Wilson to wife, n.d. [April 1865], LC.

134. Ranson, "General Lee As I Knew Him," p. 336.

135. Grant, *Memoirs*, pp. 555–56, and Thomas Wilson to wife, [April 1865], LC.

136. Chamberlain wrote the next day that his soldiers offered "the honors due to troops" with their weapons "at a shoulder & in silence." [Joshua] Lawrence Chamberlain to My dear Sae, Appomattox Court House, April 13, 1865, text in "Honor Answering Honor" (Brunswick, Maine: Bowdoin College, 1965); and J. L. Chamberlain, "The Last Salute of the Army of Northern Virginia," *SHSP* 32, suppl. (1904): 361–63. General John B. Gordon, who had the unenviable job of leading the Confederates in the surrender proceedings, confirmed Chamberlain's magnanimous move. John B. Gordon, *Reminiscences of the Civil War* (New York: Charles Scribner's Sons, 1904), pp. 443–45. A Virginian described the scene this way: "Had to march between two coluns of the enemy, one on each side. They did not look at us, did not look defiant, did not make disrespectful remarks. Our men marched up boldly and stacked arms and did not seem to mind any more than if they had been going on dress parade." Unnamed Virginian quoted in Power, *Lee's Miserables*, p. 284.

137. Many copies of this document were made as souvenirs, and a number bear Lee's signature. One of the most authentic, with original autograph, is at SH.

The text of General Orders No. 9 is as follows:

Hdqrs Army of No Va
10th April 1865

After four years of arduous service marked by unsurpassed courage and fortitude, the Army of Northern Virginia has been compelled to yield to overwhelming numbers and resources.

I need not tell the brave survivors of so many hard fought battles who have remained steadfast to the last that I have consented to this result from no distrust of them; but feeling that valour and devotion could accomplish nothing that would compensate for the loss that would have attended the continuance of the contest, I determined to avoid the useless sacrifice of those whose past services have endeared them to their Countrymen.

By terms of the Agreement officers and men can return to their homes and remain there until exchanged.

You will take with you the satisfaction that proceeds from the consciousness of duty faithfully performed, and I earnestly pray that a Merciful God will extend to you his blessing and protection.

With an unceasing admiration of your constancy and devotion to your country and a grateful remembrance of your kind and generous consideration for myself, I bid you all an affectionate farewell.

RE Lee

Genl

For a description of how this order was written by one of Lee's aides, see Marshall, *Lee's Aide-de-Camp*, pp. 278.

CHAPTER TWENTY-FOUR: A Leap in the Dark

1. MCL to "My dear Louisa," Richmond, April 16 [1865], BLA. Louisa Snowden was a distant cousin of Mary Custis Lee.

2. REL to J. A. Early, Lexington, Va., November 22, 1865, Davis Collection, TU.

3. "The End," *New York Herald*, April 10, 1865.

4. Quotation in Coulling, *Lee Girls*, p. 147.

5. M. F. Maury to Rev. F. W. Tremlett, City of Mexico, August 8, 1865, Mathew Fontaine Maury Papers, LC.

6. EAL to Sallie Goldsborough, Richmond, April 4, 1865, LFP-WL.

7. MCL to "My dear Louisa," Richmond, April 16 [1865], BLA; also McGuire, *Diary of a Southern Refuge*, pp. 356–57. Lee's arrival is more fully described in Flood, *Last Years*, pp. 36–40; Sanborn, *Complete Man*, pp. 242–43; and Freeman, *R. E. Lee*, 4:162–64.

8. Robbins, "Mrs. Lee during the War," pp. 340–42; Flood, *Last Years*, pp. 44–46; Sanborn, *Complete Man*, pp. 247–54.

9. Lee's parole is in RG 94, NARA. It can be seen online at arcweb.archives.gov.

10. Lee's statement on Lincoln's assassination is in Thomas M. Cook, "The Rebellion: Views of General Lee," *New York Herald*, April 29, 1865.

11. Ibid. Just how accurately Lee's views are expressed is not clear. Certainly there is nothing inconsistent with his other pronouncements at the time, but the reporter admitted that he took no notes, and the interview is written in narrative rather than question-and-answer format. Whether accurate or not, however, the remarks were assumed to reflect the views of the general, with the attendant stir.

12. Herman Melville, "The Martyr," in *Battle-Pieces*, p. 130.

13. See Dan T. Carter, *When the War Was Over: The Failure of Self Reconstruction in the South 1865–1867* (Baton Rouge: Louisiana State University Press, 1985).

14. "The Rebel General Lee's Opinions—The Old Virginia Fallacy of States' Rights," *New York Herald*, April 29, 1865.

15. Richard Maury to "My Dear Cousin," Richmond, Va., May 18, 1865, Mathew Fontaine Maury Papers, LC.

16. The quotation is from a friend of the Lees, Constance Cary Harrison, annotations on her diary written November 26, 1910, Burton Harrison Papers, LC.

17. Cook, "The Rebellion: Views of General Lee," *New York Herald*, April 29, 1865.

18. For Lee's continuing concern about Davis's condition, see REL to WHFL, Lexington, Va., March 30, 1868, GBL-VHS.

19. MCL to "My dear Lucy," April 26, [1865], EA-LC.

20. Flood, *Last Years*, p. 53. The convoluted history of the amnesty oaths, and the way they were used as a political pawn, are found in Richard Lowe, "Another Look at Reconstruction in Virginia," *Civil War History* 33, no. 1 (March 1986).

21. Flood, *Last Years*, p. 53.

22. REL to MCW, Richmond, June 20, 1865, in Lee, *"To Markie,"* pp. 62–63; also REL to WHFL, June 15, 1865, GBL-VHS.

23. Lee's letters to Grant and to Johnson are in Lee Jr., *Recollections*, pp. 164–65. Freeman believed that Lee intended from the first to hold himself up as an example to reconciliation, but Lee's actions do not support this until a few months later, when he became head of Washington College. Then he did take care to take the oath of allegiance, specifically as an example to the students and to avoid trouble for the college. For an argument that Lee deliberately omitted the oath from his original application to Johnson see Jonathan Truman Dorris, *Pardon and Amnesty under Lincoln and Johnson* (Chapel Hill: University of North Carolina Press, 1953), pp. 119–34. Quotation REL to REL Jr., Near Cartersville, July 10, 1865, DE-LC.

24. Channing M. Smith, "The Last Time I Saw General Lee," *Confederate Veteran* 35 (1927), p. 327.

25. GWCL note on REL to Andrew Johnson, Richmond, Va., June 13, 1865, copy in GCWL's hand, USAMHI.

26. REL to WHFL, Ringgold Barracks, Texas, November 1856, REL Letterbook #1, LFP-VHS.

27. REL to G. T. Beauregard, Lexington, Va., October 3, 1865, REL Letterbook #3, LFP-VHS; quotation REL to Fitzhugh Lee, Lexington, Va., August 5, 1869, Fitzhugh Lee Papers, UVa.

28. REL to Cap. Josiah Tatnall, Near Cartersville, Va., September 7, 1865, REL Letterbook #3, LFP-VHS. This letterbook carries a half dozen other letters on the same theme.

29. REL to A. M. Keiley, Near Cartersville, Va., September 4, 1865, REL Letterbook #3, LFP-VHS.

30. Colonel J. Stoddard Johnston, "Recollections of Robert E. Lee," *Louisville Courier-Journal*, June 3, 1900.

31. Quotation in Charles P. Roland, *Reflections on Lee*, p. 113.

32. I am grateful to Drew Faust and Martha E. Kinney's " 'If Vanquished, I Am Still Victorious': Religious and Cultural Symbolism in Virginia's Confederate Memorial Day Celebrations, 1866–1930," *VMHB* 106, no. 3 (Summer 1998), for suggesting many of these thoughts to me.

33. For more on Lee's influence in these crucial months, see Roland, *Reflections on Lee*, pp. 103–113; and Winik, *April 1865*. The latter book contains factual errors, but makes the point that Lee was instrumental in calming southern society during a critical moment.

34. Mildred Lee to Mary Cocke, n.d. [May 5, 1865], John Hartwell Cocke Papers, UVa.

35. REL to MCW, Lexington, November 5, 1866, ML.

36. Mildred Lee to Mary Cocke, n.d. [c. May 1865], Cocke Family Papers, UVa; and MiCL, "My Recollections of My Father's Death," August 21, 1888, LFP-VHS.

37. Edward Clifford Gordon, "Recollections of General Robert E. Lee's Administration as President of Washington College," in Franklin L. Riley, ed., *General Lee after Appomattox* (New York: Macmillan, 1922), pp. 75–76. For the assertion that Lee was inundated by offers of work "from every side," see, for example, Dr. Henry Louis Smith, "Tribute to General Lee as an Educator," ibid., p. 203; and Rev. Henry Field, "The Last Years of General Lee" in Lee, *Lee of Virginia*, p. 422, which claims that Emperor Maximilian offered to place Lee at the head of Mexico's army. Lee's correspondence, which was scrupulously responsive, gives no indication of offers until September 1865, and actually very few during the entire postwar period.

38. For Washington College's deliberations and their bold proposal to Lee, see Ollinger Crenshaw, *General Lee's College* (New York: Random House, 1969), pp. 146–48; and Flood, *Last Years*, p. 82.

39. *Richmond Whig* quoted in Crenshaw, *General Lee's College*, p. 148.

40. Jones, *Personal Reminiscences*, p. 146.

41. REL, "Report to the Board of Trustees of Washington College," June 20, 1867, Letterbook #4, LFP-VHS; Preston, *Lee: West Point and Lexington*, pp. 56–66; letters to students and parents are in REL Letterbooks #3 and #4, LFP-VHS; REL to Professor J. B. Minor, Lexington, Va., January 17, 1867, REL Letterbook #4, LFP-VHS; and Milton Wylie Humphreys, Autobiographical MS, Humphreys Papers, UVa.

42. Preston, *Lee: West Point and Lexington*, pp. 69–70; REL, "Report to the Board of Trustees of Washington College," June 20, 1867, and REL to Professor J. B. Minor, Lexington, Va., January 17, 1867, both REL Letterbook #4, LFP-VHS; REL to Cyrus McCormick, Lexington, Va., November 28, 1865, REL Letterbook #3, LFP-VHS.

43. REL to Professor J. B. Minor, January 17, 1867; and REL to Prof. L. Mankin, Lexington, Va., May 15, 1867, both REL Letterbook #4, LFP-VHS; quotation REL to Robert Beverley, Lexington, Va., July 6, 1868, photostat, LFP-WL.

44. Crenshaw, *General Lee's College* , pp. 166–68; Preston, *Lee: West Point and Lexington*, pp. 56–68, quotations pp. 62, 64.

45. Dr. Chalmers Deadrick quoted in Riley, ed., *General Lee after Appomattox*, p. 137.

46. Gordon, "Recollections of General Robert E. Lee's Administration," p. 84.

47. Samuel Hall Chester, *Memories of Four-Score Years* (Richmond: Presbyterian Committee of Publication, 1934), pp. 58–59.

48. Hugh Moran to Mrs. Nathan M. Moran, Washington College, Lexington, Va., April 6, 1867, Hugh Anderson Moran Papers, WL.

49. Hugh Moran to Nathan M. Moran, Lexington, Va., February 12, 1867, Moran Papers, WL.

50. The quotation is from Lee's administrative assistant who spent much of each day with him. Gordon, "Recollections of General Robert E. Lee's Administration," pp. 78–79; also Humphreys, Autobiographical ms., Humphreys Papers, UVa.

51. Humphreys, Autobiographical ms., Humphreys Papers, UVa; and recollections of John F. Ponder, in Riley, ed., *General Lee after Appomattox*, p. 127.

52. Recollections of W. H. Tayloe in Riley, *General Lee after Appomattox*, pp. 127–28.

53. Ibid., p. 126.

54. Chester, *Memories of Four-Score Years,* pp. 56–58; quotation Preston, *Lee: West Point and Lexington,* p. 89.

55. Ibid., p. 80; William Taylor Thom to "My Dear Father," April 28, 1866, William Taylor Thom Papers, WL; quotation Hugh Moran to Mrs. Nathan M. Moran, Lexington, Va., September 28, 1867, Moran Papers, WL.

56. Charles E. McCorkle Notebook, 1869–74, Charles E. McCorkle Papers, WL.

57. Preston, *Lee: West Point and Lexington,* p. 60. With the tuition fees he received, Lee was making double the salary he had received at West Point. Lee also told his brother of his comfortable financial situation, saying, "I am the recipient of rents instead of being in debt as I feared I was." REL to Smith Lee, Lexington, Va., February 20, 1869, Fitzhugh Lee Papers, UVa.

58. REL to Mrs. Wm H. Fitzhugh Lee, Lexington, Va., March 10, 1868, GBL-VHS; REL to Charlotte Haskell, White House, May 4, 1868, LFP-VHS; and Nagel, *Lees of Virginia,* pp. 290–91.

59. REL to Mrs. Wm H. Fitzhugh Lee, Lexington, Va., March 10, 1868, GBL-VHS; also MCL to [Nathanael Burwell], n.d. [post-1866], Burwell Papers, VHS.

60. MCL to "My dear Letty," Warm Springs, July 19, 1868, CL-LC; and Zimmer, ed., *Housekeeping Book,* p. 51.

61. MiCL, "Recollections, My Father's Death," Samuel H. Chester, "At College under General Lee," MS, WL; and Gordon, "Recollections of General Robert E. Lee's Administration," pp. 91–92.

62. MiCL to Lucia Blair, Lexington, February 7, 1866, LFP-WL.

63. See REL to GWCL, Ravensworth, Va., July 22, 1870, REL-DU; REL to MCL, Lexington, November 21, 1865; and to EAL, Lexington, Va., December 5, 1865, both DE-LC; and REL to Mrs. Wm H. Fitzhugh Lee, Lexington, Va., March 10, 1868, GBL-VHS.

64. Coulling, *Lee Girls,* p. 161.

65. T. S. Eliot, "Burnt Norton," from *Four Quartets* (New York: Harcourt Brace, 1971), p. 14.

CHAPTER TWENTY-FIVE: Blurred Vision

1. REL to "dear Sir," draft letter, Lexington, Va., July 9, 1866, REL-DU.

2. Mildred Lee was so described by Henry Adams in a letter of February 19, 1882. Marian Hooper Adams, *The Letters of Mrs. Henry Adams,* ed. Ward Thoron (Boston: Little, Brown, 1936), p. 349.

3. MCL to Florence Marshall, June 27, 1868, AHA.

4. MCL to Philip Fendall, n.d. [later marked September 1866], Fendall Papers, DU; and MCL to "My dear Ellen," Lexington, February 22, 1867, REL-MoHS.

5. MCL to Miss Betty Poulson, Derwent, September 21, 1865, MoC. The image of Arlington covered in a shroud is from Herman Melville's poem, "Lee in the Capitol," found in Melville, *Battle-Pieces,* pp. 188–93.

6. See REL to William H. Hope, Lexington, Va., April 5, 1866, in Jones, *Personal Reminiscences,* p. 246; REL to Francis S. Smith, Lexington, Va., April 5, 1866, SH; REL to Smith Lee, Lexington, Va., April 16, 1867, Fitzhugh Lee Papers, UVa; REL to Francis L. Smith, Lexington, Va., November 11 and November 14, 1867, quotation REL to Hon. J. L. Black, Lexington, Va., January 13, 1869, REL Letterbook #4, LFP-VHS.

7. REL to MCL, Lexington, Va., October 9, 1865, DE-LC; and to Ho. Geo. W. Jones, Lexington, Va., March 22, 1869, REL Letterbook #4, LFP-VHS.

8. MCL to Miss Emily Mason, Lexington, April 20, 1866, MoC.

9. MCL to Benson Lossing, Lexington, February 20, 1866, AHA; Benson J. Lossing to MCL, unsent draft letter, Poughkeepsie, N.Y., March 2, 1866, Lossing Papers, HL; and MCL to "My dear sir" [Benson Lossing], Lexington, April 4, 1867, CL-LC. Lossing may have misread Mary Lee's letter, for he interpreted the assertion in her characteristically untidy handwriting that the Washington letters had to be "buried to secure them from Hunter & his vandals" to read "*burned* [author's emphasis] to secure them." Either way the letters were destroyed, but to bury them with the hope of eventual recovery was certainly a far cry from willfully burning them.

10. Benson J. Lossing to Henry Wilson, "The Ridge," Dover, N.Y., July 19, 1870, Henry Wilson Papers, LC; and *Congressional Globe*, 40th Cong., 2nd sess., March 1, 1869.

11. MCL to Lucy Oliver Cocke, Hot Springs, June 20, 1873, Cocke Family Papers, UVa.

12. MCL to "Mrs Richardson," June 10, [1868], in Coulling, *Lee Girls*, p. 178; MiCL "Recollections of My Father's Death," August 21, 1888, VHS; and Mildred Lee, "Reminiscences of My Mother," Lexington, December 11, 1894, DE-LC.

13. This passage was suggested by Benét, *John Brown's Body*, p. 64.

14. See Faust, *Mothers of Invention*, pp. 238–50; and Berlin, "Did Confederate Women Lose the War?" pp. 169–73, 186–88, Sarah Morgan quotation pp. 186–87.

15. Claudine L. Ferrell, *Reconstruction* (Westport, Conn.: Greenwood Press, 2003), pp. 67–68; and James L. Roark, *Masters without Slaves* (New York: W. W. Norton, 1977), pp. 111–40.

16. As always, casualty figures cannot be known for certain, and this is a best approximation, taken from McPherson, *Battle Cry of Freedom*, p. 854.

17. For an overview of the reconstruction debates, see John Hope Franklin, *Reconstruction after the Civil War* (Chicago: University of Chicago Press, 1961); and Lowe, "Another Look at Reconstruction in Virginia," pp. 56–76.

18. MCL to "My dear Nat" [Nathanael Burwell], Lexington, "Easter Sunday," n.d., [c. 1868], LFP-WL.

19. MCL to ?, Lexington, typescript, December 1869, AHA.

20. MCL to "My dear sir," Lexington, June 12, 1867, LJF-WL. See also MCL to Mrs. R.E. Chilton, March 10, 1867, MoC; in which she refers to northern politicians as "scum" and rails against educating the freedmen.

21. Some confusion has existed about the return of Lee's "citizenship." Though his personal application had not been acted upon, it seems clear that Lee was included under Johnson's Christmas 1868 proclamation, which granted "universal amnesty and pardon" to "every person who directly or indirectly participated in the late insurrection or rebellion." Lee certainly believed so, and he began to travel and speak more actively at this time. However, archivists, searching for information about Lee during the centennial of the Civil War, came upon his application and concluded that he had never regained his civil rights. The discovery caused some latent fury, the *Richmond News Leader* proclaiming, for example, that "General Lee died a man without a country." Congress used the issue to make some stirring speeches about reunification, and on the eve of the bicentennial of the American Revolution passed a resolution granting Lee full citizenship. President Gerald Ford signed the unneccessary resolution on August 5, 1975. See Franklin, *Reconstruction after the Civil War*, p. 33; Elmer Oris Parker, "Why Was Lee Not Pardoned," *Prologue: The Journal of the National Archives* 2, no. 3 (Winter 1970): 181. For the views of the National Archives on the issue, see Delia M. Rios, "With Malice

toward None, with Amnesty for All: The Pardon of Robert E. Lee," in *We the People, Stories from the National Archives,* on the Web at www.newhousenews.com.

22. Michael Fellman, "Robert E. Lee: Postwar Southern Nationalist," *Civil War History* 46, no. 3 (September 2000): 193–94; and Crenshaw, *General Lee's College,* p. 154.

23. REL to Honorable Robert Ould, Lexington, Va., March 29, 1867, REL Letterbook #4, LFP-VHS.

24. General Neal Dow and the *Boston Evening Traveller* quoted in Crenshaw, *General Lee's College,* pp. 153–54.

25. Quotations REL to Genl J. Longstreet, Lexington, Va., October 29, 1867; and REL to Maj. A. I. Moses, Lexington, Va., April 3, 1867, both REL Letterbook #4, LFP-VHS; and Jones, *Personal Reminiscences,* p. 199.

26. See *Report of the Joint Committee on Reconstruction,* 39th Cong., 1st sess. (Washington, D.C.: GPO, 1966), pp. 129–36; Fellman believes the entire testimony was disingenuous, but given its early date (February 1866) and Lee's difficult political position at the time, it seems more that it was carefully understated. See Fellman, "Postwar Southern Nationalist." Quotation is from Melville, "Lee in the Capitol," in *Battle-Pieces,* p. 190.

27. See for example REL to A. M. Keiley, Near Cartersville, Va., September 4, 1865; and [P.] G. T. Beauregard, Lexington, Va., October 3, 1865, both REL Letterbook #3, LFP-VHS; and REL to John Letcher, Near Cartersville, August 28, 1865, in Lee Jr., *Recollections,* p. 163.

28. *Report of the Joint Committee,* p. 129; for awareness of press, see Allan, "Memoranda of Conversations," e.g., pp. 7, 15.

29. REL to Col. E. Fontaine, Lexington, Va., September 21, 1868; and to G. Taylor Webster, Lexington, Va., October 26, 1868, both REL Letterbook #4, LFP-VHS.

30. REL to Edward Lee Childe, Lexington, Va., January 5, 1867, and June 3, 1870, both SH.

31. Bond, *Memories of General Robert E. Lee,* p. 33.

32. "War," essay fragment in REL's hand, n.d. [c. 1868], MCL-VHS; additional unpublished political exhortations are found in "Govt" and "Men," essay fragments in REL's hand, n.d. [c. 1868], MCL-VHS; and REL to "My dear Sir," Lexington, Va, July 9, 1866, REL-DU.

33. For valuable discussions of the shift from moderation to more reactionary views in the South, see Carter, *When the War Was Over;* and Michael Perman, "Accepting Defeat: Historians and Reconstruction," *Reviews in American History* 14, no. 1 (March 1986): 83–90.

34. REL to Edward Lee Childe, Lexington, Va., January 22, 1867, SH.

35. REL to Annette Carter, Lexington, Va., March 28, 1868, LFP-WL. Annette Carter was both Lee's cousin and grandniece.

36. See REL to Genl. J. Longstreet, Lexington, Va., October 29, 1867, REL Letterbook #4, LFP-VHS; Bean, "Memoranda of Conversations," p. 479; and Fellman, "Postwar Southern Nationalist," pp. 198–99. For an overview of this attempt at a moderate coalition, see Lowe, "Another Look at Reconstruction in Virginia"; and Jack P. Maddex Jr., "Virginia: The Persistence of Centrist Hegemony," in Otto H. Olsen, ed., *Reconstruction and Redemption in the South* (Baton Rouge: Louisiana State University Press, 1980).

37. REL to Genl. J. Longstreet, Lexington, Va., October 29, 1867, REL Letterbook #4, LFP-VHS.

38. Bean, "Memoranda of Conversations," p. 479.

39. Lee et al. to William Rosecrans, White Sulphur Springs, W.Va., August 26, 1868, LFP-VHS. Many books, including Freeman, *R. E. Lee*, vol. 4, have selectively reproduced this letter. The original bears reading in full.

40. REL to George W. Jones, Lexington, Va., March 22, 1869, in REL Letterbook #4, LFP-VHS.

41. Bean, "Memoranda of Conversations," p. 483.

42. For examples of Lee's assertion that he was glad that slavery had been abolished, see *Report of the Joint Committee*, p. 136; Allan, "Memoranda of Conversations," e.g., p. 10.

43. For Lee's views see *Report of the Joint Committee on Reconstruction*. Many historians have written on this topic, among them Carter, *When the War Was Over*; Willie Lee Rose, "Masters without Slaves" in *Slavery and Freedom*, ed. William W. Freehling (New York: Oxford University Press); Roark, *Masters without Slaves*; and Litwack, *Been in the Storm So Long*, especially pp. 359–63.

44. Notes at back of REL Diary, n.d. [postwar], LFP-VHS.

45. See REL to MCL, Lexington, October 3 and 29, 1865, both DE-LC; and MCL to Florence Marshall, Lexington, January 30, 1867, AHA. MCL quoted in Zimmer, ed., *Housekeeping Book*, p. 47.

46. *Report of the Joint Committee*, p. 130.

47. Lee Jr., *Recollections*, p. 168.

48. REL to Col. Thos. H. Ellis, Lexington, Va., December 31, 1869, REL Letterbook #4, LFP-VHS. Lee also endorsed the idea of importing a European underclass in REL to Francis T. Anderson, Lexington Va., June 5, 1866; and REL to Hon Alex[a] Rives, Lexington, Va., June 21, 1866, both REL Letterbook #3, LFP-VHS.

49. For more on the European immigration movement, see Carter, *When the War Was Over*, pp. 170–75.

50. *Report of the Joint Committee*, p. 134.

51. REL to "Dear Sir," Lexington, December 18, 1868, in Jones, *Personal Reminiscences*, pp. 269–70.

52. Lee et al. to William Rosecrans, August 26, 1868, LFP-VHS.

53. REL to Amanda Parks, Lexington, Va., March 9, 1866, in Lee Jr., *Recollections*, pp. 222–23. In private the Lee family often ridiculed their former slaves, especially those who complained of mistreatment at Arlington. See, e.g., REL, Jr. to MCL, Headquarters near Culpeper City, Va., August 21, 1863, DE-LC.

54. Joseph Pierro, "Praying with Robert E. Lee," *Civil War Times*, February 2006, pp. 40–43. For separate places at the communion table, see Chesnut, *Diary*, p. 40: Philip Schwarz assesses the incident largely in terms of the invisibility of black people and the tensions inherent in the change from slavery to freedom. "General Lee and Visibility," a talk at Stratford Hall Plantation, August 4, 2000, at http://www.stratalum.org/leecommunion.htm.

55. John M. McClure, "The Freedmen's School in Lexington versus 'General Lee's Boys,'" in Wallenstein and Wyatt-Brown, *Virginia's Civil War*, p. 189.

56. *Lexington Gazette and General Advertiser*, January 15, 1868.

57. McClure, "Freedmen's School in Lexington," p. 191; and Flood, *The Last Years*, p. 98.

58. McClure, "Freedmen's School in Lexington," p. 195; and Crenshaw, *General Lee's College*, pp. 151–55.

59. McClure, "Freedmen's School in Lexington," pp. 195–96.

60. Hugh Moran to Mrs. Nathan M. Moran, Lexington, Va., March 29, 1868, Moran Papers, WL.

61. Preston, *Lee: West Point and Lexington*, pp. 80–87; and McClure, "Freedmen's School in Lexington," p. 194. For the students' dismissal, see "Washington College Faculty Minutes," February 17, 1868, WL.

62. Hugh Moran to N. M. Moran, Lexington, Va., May 10, 1868, Moran Papers, WL.

63. Hugh Moran to Mrs. Nathan M. Moran, Washington College, Lexington, Va., February 26, 1868, Moran Papers, WL; and Gordon, "Recollections of General Robert E. Lee's Administration," p. 84.

64. *Report of the Joint Committee*, p. 130; McClure, "The Freedmen's School in Lexington," p. 198.

65. *Montgomery Daily Advertiser* quoted in Faust, *Mothers of Invention* p. 4; also Roark, *Masters without Slaves*, p. 132.

66. REL to "My dear Sir," draft letter, Lexington, Va., July 9, 1866, REL-DU.

67. "War," essay fragment in REL's hand, n.d. [c. 1868], MCL-VHS.

68. REL to Cassius F. Lee, Lexington, Va., June 6, 1870, SH.

69. See [P.] G. T. Beauregard to REL, New Orleans, November 25, 1865, DE-LC; Marshall, *Lee's Aide-de-Camp*, p. 39; quotation William Burke to Rev. R. R. Gurly, Algashland, February 9, 1867, MCL-VHS. The letter was found among Lee's papers.

70. REL to George W. Jones, Lexington, March 22, 1869, REL Letterbook #4, LFP-VHS. More on the subject of postwar contrition, guilt, and evangelical thought is contained in Carter, *When the War Was Over*, pp. 88–92.

71. Mosby, "Personal Recollections of General Lee," p. 68; REL to Edward Childe, Lexington, Va., July 7, 1866 and July 10, 1868, both SH; and REL to W. W. Corcoran, Lexington, Va., August 23, 1870, at valley.vedh.edu/memory.

72. REL to Edward A. Pollard, Lexington, Va., January 24, 1867, REL Letterbook #4, LFP-VHS. Lee confided his thoughts about the war to several men, and in every case he was well aware of recent articles and reassessments on the war. See Allan, "Memoranda of Conversations"; Edward Clifford Gordon, "Memorandum of a Conversation with General R. E. Lee," in Gallagher, *Lee the Soldier*, e.g., pp. 25–27; and Bean, "Memoranda of Conversations."

73. REL to [P.] G. T. Beauregard, Lexington, Va., October 3, 1865, REL Letterbook #3, LFP-VHS; also REL to George W. Jones, Lexington, March 22, 1869, REL Letterbook #4, LFP-VHS.

74. For more on Light-Horse Harry Lee's nearly unequivocal pro-Unionist views, see Royster, *Light-Horse Harry Lee*, pp. 87–89, 94, 99–100, 109. His one hesitation came when he thought the states were being unfairly taxed; ibid., pp. 108–10.

75. REL to CCL, March 14, 1867, MoC; See REL to Mrs. T. J. Jackson, Lexington, Va., January 25, 1866, in REL Letterbook #3, LFP-VHS. He also revamped the story of Bolteler's Ford, an incident in the post-Antietam retreat, giving himself credit for ordering an ambush of Federal pursuers, though witnesses asserted it had been Jackson's decision and that Lee had been in a state of "indecision and embarrassment." See chapter 20, note 9, and Bridges, *Lee's Maverick General*, pp. 128–41.

76. REL to Genl Wade Hampton, Lexington, Va., October 30, 1866, REL-DU; and Bean, "Memoranda of Conversations," p. 483; quotation William Preston Johnston, "Memoranda of Conversations," in Gallagher, ed., *Lee, the Soldier*, p. 31.

77. See among many such letters REL to Col. Walter H. Taylor and REL to Genl. R.

H. Anderson, both Near Cartersville, July 31, 1865; and to Genl J. A. Early, Lexington, Va., March 15, 1866, all LFP-WL; and Allan, "Memoranda of Conversations," pp. 7–8. See also "Men," undated essay fragment, and undated battle notes in MCL-VHS.

78. Allan, "Memoranda of Conversations"; "Johnston Conversation," pp. 26–27; and Bean, "Memoranda of Conversations."

79. Nagel, *Lees of Virginia,* p 289; and MCL to CCL, Lexington, September 23, [1869], typescript, EA-LC.

80. For dislike of praise, see MCL to "My dear Mr. B," Lexington, December 11, 1870, REL-DU; REL to James M. Mason, Lexington, Va., March 3, 1870; quotation REL to MCL, Lexington, Va., October 9, 1865; and numerous letters of invitation, all Letterbook #4, LFP-VHS.

81. REL to MCL, Lexington, Va., October 19, 1865; and November 5, 1865; to EAL, Lexington, Va., December 5, 1865, and to MiCL, Lexington, October 29, 1865, all DE-LC.

82. George Taylor Lee, "Reminiscences of Robert E. Lee," pp. 236–51.

83. MiCL quoted in Nagel, *Lees of Virginia,* p. 299.

84. REL to MCL, Lexington, Va., October 9, 1865, DE-LC; and REL to John Stewart, Richmond, May 26, 1865, Bryan Family Papers, VHS.

85. Bean, "Memoranda of Conversations," pp. 481, 484; and Mosby, "Personal Recollections," p. 68.

86. MiCL "Recollections of My Father's Death," August 21, 1888, VHS.

87. For an example of his faltering hand, see REL to A. Minis, Lexington, Va., June 28, 1870, REL-GHS.

88. REL to WHFL, Lexington, Va., October 15, 1866, GBL-VHS.

CHAPTER TWENTY-SIX: **"If Vanquished, I Am Still Victorious"**

1. MCL to CCL, October 7, [1870], EA-LC. The title quotation is from "Address by General William Ruffin Cox, Army of Northern Virginia, Delivered before the Oakwood Memorial Association, Richmond, Virginia, May 10, 1911" (Richmond, 1911), p. 13, and was suggested to me by Kinney, " 'If Vanquished, I Am Still Victorious.' "

2. EAL to Lizzie Fuller, Lexington, December 27, 1870, LFP-WL.

3. REL quoted in Bond, *Memories of General Robert E. Lee,* p. 51.

4. Quotation REL to WHFL, Lexington, Va., September 28, 1868, REL Letterbook #4, LFP-VHS; and "Reminiscences of Cazenove G. Lee."

5. W. H. Tayloe and Judge D. Gardiner Tyler in Riley, *General Lee after Appomattox,* pp. 128, 131; also MCL to CCL, October 7, [1870], photostat, EA-LC.

6. REL to MCW, Lexington, Va., April 7, 1866; and January 1, 1868, both in Lee, *"To Markie,"* pp. 70, 78.

7. REL to MCL, Near Fredericksburg, April 5, 1863, DE-LC.

8. REL to MCW quoted c. 1869 in Upshur, *As I Recall Them,* p. 19; and REL to Edward Lee Childe and Marie Childe, March 8, 1870, SH.

9. Sanborn, *Complete Man,* pp. 358–59; REL to Edward Lee Childe, Lexington, Va., September 9, 1869, SH; and Lucia Yeaton Wagener to "My dear Mrs. Syres," Summerville, S.C., typescript, April 10, 1934, BLA.

10. Britannia Peters Reminiscences, March 13, 1897, TPA.

11. Lucia Yeaton Wagener to "My dear Mrs. Syres," April 10, 1934, BLA; WN Pendleton to Edmund Jennings Lee II, Lexington, Va., March 15, 1870, Edmund Jennings Lee II Papers, DU; and "Reminiscences of Cazenove G. Lee."

12. MiCL, "Recollections of My Father's Death," August 21, 1888, VHS; MCL to

Mary Meade, October 12, 1870, in "Funeral of Mrs. G. W. P. Custis," pp. 23–24; MCL to CCL, October 7 [1870], photostat, EA-LC; and William Preston Johnston, "Death and Funeral of General Lee," in Riley, *General Lee after Appomattox*, p. 208.

13. MCL to CCL, October 7, [1870], fragment, photostat, EA-LC; quotation MCL to "my dear Lettie," Lexington, November 15, 1870, SH.

14. MiCL, "Recollections of My Father's Death," August 21, 1888, VHS.

15. There has been a great deal of speculation over the years about Lee's last words. Mrs. Lee's statements to family friends "Mrs. Buiter" and Margaret Junkin Preston seem to be the best source, particularly as Preston, a serious author and poet, noted that she reconfirmed the statement with Mary Lee before writing a little poem about the nobility of moving on from earthly life. But modern historians have disputed this evidence, believing the words were contrived as "stage tricks, used to enhance drama" and concerned that they reminded one a little too much of Stonewall Jackson's final utterances. Some believe that given his condition, Lee would not have been able to say anything; however, both Mary Lee and Mildred recorded that he was able to speak a little. It is certainly clear that over the years the words were modified or embellished. If they were indeed manufactured, it was done almost immediately, both by Mary Lee and the doctors, who told a newspaper reporter just hours after Lee's death that he had "ordered his tent be struck, and at another time desired that 'Hill should be sent for,' " as well as corroborating Mrs. Lee's story of his battlefield dreams. See MCL to Mrs. Buiter, November 18, 1870, in "Extracts from Letters of Mary Custis Lee," in REL-DU; Diary of Margaret Junkin Preston, October 29, 1870, in Allan, *Margaret Junkin Preston*, p. 238; and Margaret Junkin Preston to Paul H. Hayne, Lexington, Va., November 2 and 17, 1870, Hayne Papers, DU; "General Lee: His Last Moments; The Feeling at Lexington, Special Telegram to the *Dispatch*," dateline Lexington, Va., October 13, 1870, SHC-UNC. Also Marvin P. Rozear et al., "R. E. Lee's Stroke," *VMHB* 98, no. 2 (April 1990): 291–308; the article errs in saying that William Preston Johnston was the only source of the deathbed quotes. For modification of the quotes, see e.g. statements of Reverend E. C. De La Moniere and Senator John W. Daniel in T. R. B. Wright, ed., *Westmoreland County, Virginia: A Short Chapter and Bright Day in Its History* (Richmond: Whittet & Shepperson, 1912), pp. 78, 83.

16. Richard D. Mainwaring and Harris D. Riley, "The Lexington Physicians of General Robert E. Lee," *Southern Medical Journal* 98, no. 8 (August 2005): 800–804; MCL to CCL, October 7, [1870], fragment, photostat, EA-LC; and MCL to "my dear Lettie," Lexington, November 15, 1870, SH.

17. The causes of Robert E. Lee's death have also been debated by scholars. At the time Lee's physicians attributed it to a "venous congestion of the brain, which, however, never proceeded as far as apoplexy or paralysis, but gradually caused cerebral exhaustion and death." However, they took pains to tell a newspaper reporter who interviewed them in the hours after Lee's death that they believed the true cause was "moral rather than physical," and gave ennobling speeches about the cares that had befallen Lee during the war and the "affliction" he felt at the condition of the South. Several modern doctors, examining the evidence, have suggested that Lee suffered a stroke, complicated by atherosclerosis, and that the paralysis suffered, though not completely impairing speech or movement, did sap his will. Such a condition could have hampered his ability to swallow and cough correctly, sending the lovingly administered food and medicine into his lungs, filling them with rotting matter, and ultimately killing him of pneumonia and toxins. Lest we should leave any dignity in-

tact, these physicians also maintain that Lee would not have gently closed his eyes, but that, given his malady, they would have popped wide open at death. Rozear et al., "R. E. Lee's Stroke," pp. 291–308. The quotation in the text is from MCL to Mary Meade, October 12, 1870, in "Funeral of Mrs. G. W. P. Custis," p. 25.

18. MCL to Mary Meade, October 12, 1870, in "Funeral of Mrs. G. W. P. Custis," p. 26.

19. *New York Tribune* quoted in Preston, *Lee: West Point and Lexington*, pp. 92–93; Richmond description in Sanborn, *Complete Man*, p. 381.

20. Preston, *Lee: West Point and Lexington*, p. 93; MCL to Mary Meade, October 12, 1870, in "Funeral of Mrs. G. W. P. Custis," p. 26; and William Nalle to Mrs. Thomas Botts Nalle, Virginia Military Institute, Lexington, October 16, 1870, Virginia Military Institute Archives.

21. Margaret Junkin Preston to Paul Hamilton Hayne, Lexington, Va., November 2, [1870], Hayne Papers, DU.

22. Mary Lee's wartime attitude was one example of this; another can be found in Mrs. William Fitzhugh to Mrs. Abbey Nelson, n.d. [1853], in which at the death of her beloved mother Mary Lee astonished her friends with her "calm and collected conduct." "Funeral of Mrs. G. W. P. Custis," pp. 22–23.

23. A cadet from the Virginia Military Institute who guarded Lee's casket and had seen him taking a stroll a few days before his seizure said that he never saw a greater change in a man: "he looked to be reduced to half his original size, and desperately thin." William Nalle to Mrs. Thomas Botts Nalle, October 16, 1870, Virginia Military Institute Archives; also Johnston, "Death and Funeral of General Lee," pp. 218–221; Chester, *Memories of Four Score Years*, pp. 63–64, 141. For Lee's dislike of pomp, see his comments on the funeral of George Peabody, in Sanborn, *Complete Man*, p. 384.

24. Johnston, "Death and Funeral of General Lee," pp. 220–22; quotations MiCL, "Recollections of My Father's Death," August 21, 1888, VHS.

25. Johnston, "Death and Funeral of General Lee," p. 217.

26. Wolseley, "Month's Visit," p. 12.

27. Alan Nolan culls a long list of fanciful stories about Lee from his various devotees, including, as he notes, some that are so improbable that if true they would cast doubt on Lee's own judgment. See Nolan, *Lee Considered*, pp. 171–72. REL quoted in Bond, *Memories of General Robert E. Lee*, pp. 47–48.

28. Chester, *Memories of Four-Score Years*, p. 56.

29. Newspaper article in MCL(d) Scrapbook, c. 1866, LFP-VHS.

30. MCL to "My dear Lettie," Lexington, November 15, 1870, SH.

31. See, for example, the efforts of the Comte de Paris to analyze Lee's Civil War role, which was promptly disavowed. Connelly, *Marble Man*, pp. 85–86; "The Military Career of Robert Edward Lee," n.d. [post-1870], copy in MCL(d)'s hand in MCL Scrapbook, LFP-VHS; quotation in John Hampden Chamberlayne, "Address on the Character of General R. E. Lee, January 19, 1876," *Southern Historical Society Papers* 3, no. 1 (January 1877), p. 35.

32. See Rev. Randolph H. McKim, "In Memoriam: Good Men a Nation's Strength. A Sermon Preached on the Occasion of the Death of Gen. Robert E. Lee in Christ Church, Alexandria, Virginia, October 16th, 1870" (Baltimore: John Murphy, 1870); and "Address of Rev. Randolph Harrison McKim," in Wright, ed., *Westmoreland County*, p. 33.

33. Charles Francis Adams Jr., was the great-great-grandson of John Adams, as well as a brigadier general in the Union army, president of the Union Pacific Rail-

road, and president of the American Historical Association. Riley, ed., *General Lee after Appomattox,* p. 224; quotation Charles Francis Adams in Wright, *Short Chapter,* pp. 76–77.

34. "The Military Career of Robert Edward Lee," copy in MCL(d)hand, LFP-VHS.

35. Senator John W. Daniel, at the unveiling of Edward Valentine's *Recumbent Figure of Lee,* Washington and Lee University, June 28, 1883, in Wright, *Short Chapter,* pp. 81–84; William. A. Anderson, "A Tribute to General Lee as a Man"; and Dr. Henry Louis Smith, "Tribute to General Lee as an Educator," both in Riley, ed., *General Lee After Appomattox,* pp. 199, 204–5.

36. Nolan, *Lee Considered,* pp. 172–73; and Gary W. Gallagher, "Shaping Public Memory of the Civil War: Robert E. Lee, Jubal A. Early and Douglas Southall Freeman," in Alice Fahs and Joan Waugh, eds., *The Memory of the Civil War in American Culture* (Chapel Hill: University of North Carolina Press, 2004), pp. 45–48. Gallagher contends that there were good grounds for Freeman and other apologists to venerate Lee, but Freeman's books are so full of conjectural error—all of it boosting Lee mythologies— and so devoid of criticism that their historical objectivity seems questionable.

37. CCL, "Autobiographical Sketch" and "My Boyhood"; Connelly, *Marble Man,* describes this period of Southern nostalgia at length, see especially pages 102–7; quotations in Bond, *Memories of Robert E. Lee,* pp. 11–13; also Pryor, *My Day,* pp. 10–12, 55.

38. See, for example, Michael A. Ross, "The Commemoration of Robert E. Lee's Death and the Obstruction of Reconstruction in New Orleans," *Civil War History,* vol. 51, no. 2 (June 2005), pp. 135–150.

39. Joan Waugh, "Ulysses S. Grant, Historian," in Fahs and Waugh, *Memory of the Civil War,* p. 20; Frederick Douglass quoted in Gallagher, "Shaping Public Memory," p. 57.

40. Gallagher, "Shaping Public Memory," pp. 42–45; and Connelly, *Marble Man,* pp. 72–78.

41. Connelly, *Marble Man,* pp. 41–42, 72–73, 82; Gallagher, "Shaping Public Memory," pp. 39–63; also Jones, *Personal Reminiscences;* and Jones, *Life and Letters.* Jones's books are an interesting blend of anecdote—much of which he legitimately heard from Lee—and conscious idolization. He was the first writer about Lee to see his great literary capability, and though he sometimes radically edited Lee's letters, he made them available to the public, and is still, remarkably, one of the most referenced sources on Lee's writings.

42. Charles Francis Adams Jr., "The Confederacy and the Transvaal: A People's Obligation to Robert E. Lee," address read before American Antiquarian Society, Worcester, Massachusetts, October 30, 1901 (Boston: Houghton, Mifflin, 1901); Woodrow Wilson, "Robert E. Lee: An Interpretation," in *Journal of Social Forces* 2, no. 3 (March 1924), quotation p. 1; the italics are the author's. Wilson originally published this commentary in 1909. Also Connelly, *Marble Man,* pp. 116–19.

43. Clipping from *London Standard,* n.d., in REL to Wade Hampton, Lexington, Va., October 30, 1866, REL-DU.

44. The figures are for total Union and Confederate casualties for Antietam and Gettysburg, given in McPherson, *Battle Cry of Freedom,* pp. 544, 664.

45. This imagery was first brilliantly devised by Joshua Chamberlain at a Fourth of July oration in 1884. See Harwell, ed., *Honor Answering Honor.*

46. See REL to MCL, Coosawhatchie, S.C., December 25, 1861, DE-LC.

Selected Bibliography

A Note on Sources
The research for this book was mainly based on the various collections of Lee family papers that exist in private and public holdings; however, to amplify those seminal sources I also consulted nearly 1,200 published works. I did the research entirely myself, and although it is doubtful that any person could rightfully claim to have seen all the published material relating to Robert E. Lee, the antebellum period, and the Civil War, I have tried to be as much of an omnivore as possible, especially in using firsthand accounts. All of these materials are not equal, of course, but all of them are informative on some level. For the chapters relating to the Civil War, where competing political agendas color so many accounts, I have relied as much as possible on the contemporary reactions recorded in diaries and letters, though secondary works and reminiscences also gave me many insights and alternative perspectives. The following list is complete for manuscript collections and selected thereafter for the works that most strongly influenced my thoughts. Exclusion from the list is by no means a comment on the quality of any given work.

Manuscripts
Arlington House, the Robert E. Lee Memorial, National Park Service
    Custis and Lee Family Papers
    Martha Custis Williams Diary
    Interviews with Arlington ex-slaves
    Eleanor Calvert, "Childhood Days at Arlington"
Alexandria, Virginia, Public Records
Alexandria, Virginia, Public Library, Special Collections, Kate Waller Barrett Branch
Duke University, Special Collections, Perkins Library
    Ball Family Papers
    Philip R. Fendall Papers
    John Cheves Haskell Papers
    Paul Hamilton Hayne Papers
    Edmund Jennings Lee II Papers
    Robert E. Lee Papers
    James Longstreet Papers
    Eliza Anna Mackay Papers
    Smedley Papers
Georgetown University, Special Collections

Causten Family Papers
John Dooley Diary
Georgia Historical Society
Colonial Dames Collection
Lee Papers
Mackay-McQueen Papers
Mercer Family Papers
Eliza Mackay Stiles Papers
Huntington Library
Brock Collection
Eggleston Collection
Nathanael Greene Papers
Benson J. Lossing Papers
Henry Lee Papers
Robert E. Lee Papers
Library of Congress Manuscript Division
Edward Porter Alexander Papers
American Colonization Society Records
Ethel Armes Papers
Clara Barton Papers
Blair and Lee Family Papers
John Brown of Ossawattomie Papers
Simon Cameron Papers
George Washington Campbell Papers
Custis and Lee Family Papers
DeButts-Ely Papers
Easby-Smith Family Papers
Richard Ewell Papers
Philip Fendall Papers
Douglas Southall Freeman Papers
Ulysses S. Grant Papers
Burton Norvell Harrison Papers
Edward L. Hartz Papers
John William Ford Hatton Papers
Samuel P. Heintzelman Papers
Patrick Henry Papers
William Heth Papers
Ethan Allen Hitchcock Papers
Thomas Jefferson Papers
John Lloyd Papers
Benjamin Long Papers
James Madison Papers
Matthew Fontaine Maury Papers
William Meade Papers
Montgomery C. Meigs Papers
Miscellaneous Manuscript Collection
Charles Mason Remey Papers
Edmund Ruffin Papers
James Ewell Brown Stuart Papers
John Caldwell Tidball Reminiscences
Ward Family Papers
John Hill Wheeler Papers
Cadmus M. Wilcox Papers

Henry Wilson Papers
WPA Manuscripts
Library of Virginia
Charles Carter Lee Papers
Executive Papers of John Letcher
Executive Papers of Virginia
Maryland Historical Society
Lafayette–Eliza Custis Law Papers
Missouri Historical Society
Robert E. Lee Papers
Morgan Library
Robert E. Lee Papers
Museum of the Confederacy, Eleanor S. Brockenbrough Library
Robert E. Lee Family Papers
National Archives and Records Service
Decennial Censes
Records of the Adjutant General (RG 94)
Records of the Quartermaster General (RG 92)
Records of the U.S. Corps of Engineers (RG 77)
New Jersey Historical Society
Edward A. Pierson Papers
New-York Historical Society
Gilder-Lehrman Collection
Princeton University, Goodyear Library, Special Collections
Blair and Lee Family Papers
Rockefeller Library, Colonial Williamsburg
Shirley Plantation Papers
Stratford Hall Plantation, Jessie Ball duPont Memorial Library
Edmund Jennings Lee Papers
Robert E. Lee Papers
Tudor Place House and Garden Archives
Britannia Peter Reminiscences
Custis and Lee Family Papers
Martha Custis Williams Carter Papers
William Orton Williams Papers
Tulane University, Manuscripts Department
George and Katherine Davis Collection
U.S. Military Academy
William Price Craighill Papers
Thomas Jefferson Cram Recollections
Robert E. Lee Files
Reports of the Board of Visitors
Ruben Ross Diary
Sylvanus Thayer Papers
"X" Files
U.S. Army Military History Institute
University of California, Berkeley, Bancroft Library
Lee Family Papers
University of North Carolina, Southern Historical Collection
Mackay Family Papers
Mackay-Stiles Family Papers
R. E. Lee Papers
University of Texas at Austin, Center for American History

Brady Family Papers
Edward Richardson Crockett Diary
Charles B. Dana Papers
"Personal Recollections of the First Battle of Fredericksburg"
University of Virginia, Albert and Shirley Small Special Collections Library
Cocke Family Papers
John Hartwell Cocke Papers
Milton Wylie Humphreys Papers
Charles Carter Lee Papers
Fitzhugh Lee Papers
Robert E. Lee Papers
Minor-Venable Papers
Stuart Family Papers
Talcott Family Papers
Virginia Historical Society
George William Bagby Papers
Bryan Family Papers
Nathaniel Burwell Papers
Thomas Henry Carter Papers
Cooke Family Papers
Custis Family Papers
Thomas Claybrook Elder Papers
John Walter Fairfax Papers
William Southall Harrison Letter
Hill Family Papers
James Ambler Johnston Papers
Jones Family Papers
Keith Family Papers
Osmun Latrobe Diary
Edmund Jennings Lee Papers
George Bolling Lee Papers
Lee Family Papers
Mary Custis Lee Papers
Richard Bland Lee Papers
Robert Edward Lee Papers
William Henry Fitzhugh Lee Papers
David Gregg McIntosh Papers
Robert Knox Sneden Papers
James Ewell Brown Stuart Papers
Talcott Family Papers
William O. Winston Papers
Virginia Military Institute, Manuscripts Division
Robert E. Lee Mexican War Map Collection
William Nalle Letter
Washington and Lee University, Leyburn Library, Special Collections
Driver Collection
Lee-Jackson Foundation Papers
Henry Lee Papers
Lee Family Papers
Lennig Collection
Hugh Anderson Moran Papers
Washington College Minutes of Board of Trustees
William Taylor Thom Papers

Newspapers
Alexandria Gazette
Boston Evening Traveller
Carroll County (Maryland) Democrat
Missouri Daily Argus
Missouri Daily Republican
National Intelligencer
National Republican
New York Daily Tribune
New York Herald
New York Times
Richmond News-Leader
San Francisco Post
The Spirit of Seventy-Six
Virginia Gazette and General Advertiser

Official Documents
Acts Passed at a General Assembly of the Commonwealth of Virginia. Richmond, Va.: Thomas Ritchie, 1831.
The Constitution of the Aztec Club to Which is Appended a List of the Members of the Club. Mexico: Office of the *American Star*, 1848.
Cullum, George W. *Biographical Register of the Officers and Graduates of the U.S. Military Academy at West Point, N. Y.* Boston: Houghton Mifflin, 1891.
District of Columbia. *The Slave Code of the District of Columbia.* Washington, D.C.: L. Towers, 1862.
Joint Committee on Reconstruction. *Report of the Joint Committee at the First Session,* 39th Cong., 1st sess. Washington, D.C.: GPO, 1866.
"Letter from the Secretary of War: A Copy of the Survey and Report for the Improvement of the Hudson River," March 30, 1832. 22nd Cong., 2nd sess. House of Representatives doc. 189.
"Memorial of the Inhabitants of the District of Columbia Praying for the Gradual Abolition of Slaves in the District of Columbia," 1828.
Potts-Fitzhugh House Historic Structures Report, September 1, 2000. Privately printed.
Richardson, James D., ed. *A Compilation of the Messages and Papers of the Presidents, 1789–1897.* Washington, D.C.: GPO, 1897.
"Report from the Secretary of War . . . in Relation to the Rock River and Des Moines Rapids of the Mississippi River." January 29, 1838, 25th Cong., 2nd sess. Senate doc. 139.
U.S. Congress, "Difficulties on the Southwestern Frontier," 36th Cong., 1st sess., 1860, H. Exec. Doc. 52.
United States vs. George Washington Custis Lee, December 4, 1882, in *Supreme Court Reporter: Cases Argued and Determined in the U.S. Supreme Court, October Term 1882.* St. Paul: West Publishing, 1883.
U.S. War Department. *The War of the Rebellion: A Compilation of the Official Records of the Union and Confederate Armies.* 69 vols. Washington, D.C.: GPO, 1880–1900.
Winfrey, Dorman H., ed., *Texas Indian Papers, 1846–1859.* Austin: Texas State Library, 1960.

Published Diaries, Letters, Manuscripts, and Memoirs
"A Robert E. Lee Letter to P. G. T. Beauregard." *Maryland Historical Magazine* 51, no. 3 (September 1956).
Adams, Charles Francis. *The Confederacy and the Transvaal: A People's Obligation to Robert E. Lee* [Address Read before American Antiquarian Society, Worcester, Massachusetts, October 30, 1901]. Boston: Houghton, Mifflin, 1901.
Adams, Francis Colburn. *The Story of a Trooper.* New York: Dick & Fitzgerald, 1865.

Adams, Henry. *The Education of Henry Adams.* Reprint, New York: Oxford University Press, 1999.

Alexander, Edward Porter. *Fighting for the Confederacy.* Edited by Gary W. Gallagher. Chapel Hill: University of North Carolina Press, 1989.

Anderson, Charles. *Texas Before and on the Eve of the Rebellion.* Cincinnati: Peter G. Thompson, 1884.

Anderson, Osborne P. *A Voice from Harper's Ferry.* Washington, D.C.: J. D. Enos, 1873.

Anderson, Robert. *An Artillery Officer in the Mexican War.* Reprint, Freeport, N.Y.: Books for Libraries Press, 1971.

Andrews, Marietta Minnigerode. *My Studio Window: Sketches of the Pageant of Washington Life.* New York: E. P. Dutton, 1928.

———. *Scraps of Paper.* New York: E. P. Dutton, 1929.

Battles and Leaders of the Civil War. 4 vols. New York: Century, 1887.

Bean, W. G. "Memoranda of Conversations between General Robert E. Lee and William Preston Johnston, May 7, 1868 and March 18, 1870." *Virginia Magazine of History and Biography* 73, no. 4 (October 1965).

Beauregard, P. G. T. *With Beauregard in Mexico: The Mexican War Reminiscences of P. G. T. Beauregard.* Edited by T. Harry Williams. Baton Rouge: Louisiana State University Press, 1956.

Benham, Mary Louisa Slacum. *Recollections of Old Alexandria and Other Memories.* Edited by Elizabeth Jane Stark. Starkville, Miss.: privately published, 1978.

Berkeley, Henry Robinson. *Four Years in the Confederate Artillery: The Diary of Private Henry Robinson Berkeley.* Edited by William H. Runge. Reprint, Richmond: Virginia Historical Society, 1991.

Black, Harvey. *The Civil War Letters of Dr. Harvey Black.* Edited by Glenn L. McMullen. Baltimore: Butternut and Blue, 1995.

Blackford, Susan Leigh, comp. *Letters from Lee's Army.* New York: A. S. Barnes, 1947.

Blair, Hugh. *Select Sermons.* Philadelphia: Robert Campbell, 1795.

Blassingame, John W., ed. *Slave Testimony: Two Centuries of Letters, Speeches, Interviews and Autobiographies.* Baton Rouge: Louisiana State University Press, 1977.

Bond, Christiana. *Memories of General Robert E. Lee.* Baltimore: Norman, Remington, 1926.

Bonham, Milledge Louis. "A Little More Light on Gettysburg." *Mississippi Historical Review* 24, no. 4 (March 1938).

Borrett, George Tuthill. *Letters from Canada and the United States.* 2 vols. London: J. E. Adlard, 1865.

Boteler, Alexander R. "Recollections of the John Brown Raid." *Century Magazine* 26 (July 1883).

Bowery, Charles R. Jr., and Brian D. Hankinson, eds. *The Daily Correspondence of Brevet Colonel Robert E. Lee, Superintendent, United States Military Academy, September 1, 1852 to March 24, 1855.* U.S. Military Academy Library Occasional Papers #5. West Point, N.Y.: USMA Press, 2003.

[Brock, Sallie A.] *Richmond during the War: Four Years of Personal Observation by a Richmond Lady.* New York: G. W. Carleton, 1867.

Buck, Lucy Rebecca. *Shadows on My Heart: The Civil War Diary of Lucy Rebecca Buck of Virginia.* Edited by Elizabeth R. Baer. Athens: University of Georgia Press, 1997.

Burney, Samuel A. *A Southern Soldier's Letters Home: The Civil War Letters of Samuel A. Burney.* Edited by Nat S. Turner III. Macon, Ga.: Mercer University Press, 2002.

Calvert, Rosalie Stier. *Mistress of Riversdale: The Plantation Letters of Rosalie Stier Calvert.* Edited by Margaret Law Callcott. Baltimore: Johns Hopkins University Press, 1991.

Campbell, Eric A., ed. "'Lee Is Playing a Bold and Desperate Game.'" *American History,* 2003 supplement.

Carter, Hill. "On the Management of Negroes." *Farmer's Register* 1 (February 1834): 564–65.

Chamberlayne, John Hampden. *Ham Chamberlayne—Virginian.* Edited by C. G. Chamberlayne. Richmond, Va.: Dietz, 1932.

Chesnut, Mary Boykin. *Mary Chesnut's Civil War.* Edited by C. Van Woodward. New Haven, Conn.: Yale University Press, 1981.

Chester, Samuel Hall. *Memories of Four-Score Years.* Richmond, Va.: Presbyterian Committee of Publication, 1934.

Church, Albert E. *Personal Reminiscences of the Military Academy from 1824 to 1831.* West Point, N.Y.: USMA Press, 1879.

Clay-Clopton, Virginia. *A Belle of the Fifties.* New York: Doubleday, Page, 1904.

Clemens, Samuel L. *Life on the Mississippi.* New York: Harper & Brothers, 1906.

Craik, James. "Boyhood Memories." Edited by Mary Craik Morris. *Virginia Magazine of History and Biography* 46, no. 2 (April 1938).

Crimmins, M. L., ed. "Colonel Robert E. Lee's Report on Indian Combats in Texas." *Southwestern Historical Quarterly* 39, no. 1 (July 1935).

Custis, George Washington Parke. *Recollections and Private Memoirs of Washington with a Memoir of the Author by His Daughter and Illustrative and Explanatory Notes by Benson Lossing.* New York: Derby and Jackson, 1860.

Cuthbert, Norma B., ed. "To Molly: Five Early Letters from Robert E. Lee to His Wife, 1832–1835." *Huntington Library Quarterly* 15, no. 3 (May 1952).

Darby, John Fletcher. *Personal Recollections.* Reprint, New York: Arno Press, 1975.

Davis, Jefferson. *The Papers of Jefferson Davis.* Vols. 7–9. Edited by Lynda Lasswell Crist, Mary Seaton Dix, and Kenneth H. Williams. Baton Rouge: Louisiana State University Press, 1993–95.

Davis, Jefferson. "Robert E. Lee." *North American Review* 150 (January 1890).

[Davis, Varina Howell]. *Jefferson Davis: A Memoir by His Wife.* 2 vols. New York: Belford, 1890.

deButts, Robert E. L., ed. "'Yours Forever, R. E. Lee': Engagement Letters to Mary Custis, 1830–31." *Virginia Magazine of History and Biography,* forthcoming.

Dicey, Edward. *Six Months in the Federal States.* 2 vols. London: Macmillan, 1863.

Douglass, Frederick. *Narrative of the Life of Frederick Douglass, an American Slave.* Reprint, New York: Penguin, 1982.

Fitzpatrick, Marion Hill. *Letters to Amanda.* Edited by Jeffrey C. Lowe and Sam Hodges. Macon, Ga.: Mercer University Press, 1998.

Fletcher, Elijah. *The Letters of Elijah Fletcher.* Edited by Martha von Brieson. Charlottesville: University Press of Virginia, 1965.

Foote, Henry S. *Casket of Reminiscences.* Reprint, New York: Negro Universities Press, 1968.

Forsyth, George A. *Thrilling Days in Army Life.* Reprint, Lincoln: University of Nebraska Press, 1994.

Fremantle, Arthur J. L. *Three Months in the Southern States.* Reprint, Lincoln: University of Nebraska Press, 1991.

Frobel, Anne S. *The Civil War Diary of Anne S. Frobel of Wilton Hall in Virginia.* Edited by Mary H. Lancaster and Dallas M. Lancaster. Birmingham, Ala.: Birmingham Printing, 1986.

"Funeral of Mrs. G. W. P. Custis and Death of General Lee." *Virginia Magazine of History and Biography* 35, no. 1 (January 1927).

Goree, Thomas. *Longstreet's Aide: The Civil War Letters of Major Thomas J. Goree.* Edited by Thomas W. Cutrer. Charlottesville: University Press of Virginia, 1995.

Gorgas, Josiah. *The Civil War Diary of General Josiah Gorgas.* Edited by Frank E. Vandiver. Tuscaloosa: University of Alabama Press, 1947.

Grant, Ulysses S. *The Papers of Ulysses S. Grant.* 28 vols. Edited by John Y. Simon. Carbondale: Southern Illinois University Press, 1982.

Grant, Ulysses S. *Personal Memoirs of U.S. Grant.* Reprint, New York: Da Capo Press, 1982.

Graydon, Alexander. *Memoirs of His Own Time with Reminiscences of the Men and Events of the Revolution.* Philadelphia: Lindsay & Blakiston, 1846.

Hallowell, Benjamin. *Autobiography*. Philadelphia: Friends' Book Association, 1883.

Hancock, Almira Russell. *Reminiscences of Winfield Scott Hancock*. New York: Charles L. Webster, 1887.

Harrison, C[onstance] C[ary]. "A Virginia Girl in the First Year of the War." *Century Magazine* 303, no. 4 (August 1885).

Harrison, Mrs. Burton [Constance Cary]. *Recollections Grave and Gay*. New York: Charles Scribner's Sons, 1912.

Harwell, Richard, ed. *Honor Answering Honor*. Brunswick, Maine: Bowdoin College, 1965.

Haskell, Frank A. "The Battle of Gettysburg." In *Two Views of Gettysburg*, edited by Richard Harwell. Chicago: R. R. Donnelley and Sons, 1964.

Heintzelman, Samuel Peter. *Fifty Miles and a Fight: Major Samuel Peter Heintzelman's Journal of Texas and the Cortina War*. Edited by Jerry Thompson. Austin: Texas State Historical Association, 1998.

Heller, J. Roderick III, and Carolynn Ayres Heller, eds. *The Confederacy Is on Her Way Up the Spout: Letters to South Carolina, 1861–1864*. Athens: University of Georgia Press, 1992.

Hitchcock, Ethan Allen. *Fifty Years in Camp and Field*. Edited by W. A. Croffut. New York: G. P. Putnam's Sons, 1909.

Hood, J. B. *Advance and Retreat: Personal Experiences in the United States and Confederate States Armies*. Reprint, New York: Da Capo Press, 1993.

Hotchkiss, Jedediah. *Make Me a Map of the Valley: The Civil War Journal of Stonewall Jackson's Topographer*. Edited by Archie P. McDonald. Dallas: Southern Methodist University Press, 1973.

Howard, O. O. *Autobiography of Oliver Otis Howard*. 2 vols. Reprint, Freeport, N.Y.: Books for Libraries Press, 1971.

Howe, Julia Ward. *Reminiscences, 1819–1899*. Reprint, New York: Negro Universities Press, 1969.

Hoyt, William D., Jr. "Some Personal Letters of Robert E. Lee, 1850–1858." *Journal of Southern History* 12, no. 4 (November 1946).

Hunt, E. M. "West Point and Cadet Life." *Putnam's Monthly Magazine* 4 (1854).

Jackson, Mary Anna. *Memoirs of "Stonewall" Jackson*. 1895; facsimile ed., Dayton, Ohio: Morningside Bookshop, 1976.

Johns, John. "Address Delivered . . . on the Occasion of the Funeral of the Rigtt [*sic*] Rev William Meade, D.D., March 17th, 1862." Richmond: MacFarlane & Fergusson, 1862.

Johnston, Eliza. "The Diary of Eliza Johnston." Edited by Charles P. Roland and Richard C. Robbins. *Southwestern Historical Quarterly* 60, no. 4 (April 1957).

Jones, Charles C. *Reminiscences of the Last Days, Death and Burial of General Henry Lee*. Albany, N.Y.: Joel Munsell, 1870.

Jones, John B. *A Rebel War Clerk's Diary*. Edited by Earl Schenck Miers. Reprint, Baton Rouge: Louisiana State University Press, 1993.

Jones, J. William. *Life and Letters of Robert Edward Lee, Soldier and Man*. Reprint, Harrisonville, Va.: Sprinkle, 1986.

———. *Personal Reminiscences of General Robert E. Lee*. Reprint, Baton Rouge: Louisiana State University Press, 1994.

Kean, Robert Garlick Hill. *Inside the Confederate Government*. Edited by Edward Younger. New York: Oxford University Press, 1957.

Kelly, James Edward. *Generals in Bronze*. Edited by William B. Styple. Kearny, N.J.: Belle Grove, 2005.

Keyes, Erasmus D. *Fifty Years Observation of Men and Events*. New York: Charles Scribner's Sons, 1889.

Lankford, Nelson D., ed. "The Diary of Thomas Conolly, M.P.: Virginia, March–April 1865," *Virginia Magazine of History and Biography* 95, no. 1 (January 1987).

Lee, Elizabeth Blair. *Wartime Washington: The Civil War Letters of Elizabeth Blair Lee*. Edited by Virginia Jeans Laas. Urbana: University of Illinois Press, 1991.

Lee, Fitzhugh. *General Lee*. New York: D. Appleton, 1898.

Lee, George Taylor. "Reminiscences of General Robert E. Lee, 1865–68," *South Atlantic Quarterly* 26, no. 3 (July 1927).

Lee, Henry. *The Revolutionary War Memoirs of General Henry Lee*. Edited by Robert E. Lee. Reprint, New York: Da Capo Press, 1998.

Lee, Mary Custis. "Mary Custis Lee's 'Reminiscences of the War.'" Edited by Robert E. L. deButts Jr. *Virginia Magazine of History and Biography* 109, no. 3 (Spring 2001).

Lee, Robert E. *Lee's Dispatches*. Edited by Douglas Southall Freeman and Grady McWhiney. New York: G. P. Putnam's Sons, 1957.

———. *The Wartime Papers of R. E. Lee*. Edited by Clifford Dowdey and Louis H. Manarin. New York: Bramhall House, 1961.

———. *"To Markie": The Letters of Robert E. Lee to Martha Custis Williams*. Edited by Avery O. Craven. Cambridge: Harvard University Press, 1933.

Lee, Robert E. Jr. *Recollections and Letters of General Robert E. Lee*. Garden City, N.Y.: Garden City Publishing, 1904.

Lee, Miss S[arah]. "War Time in Alexandria, Virginia," *South Atlantic Quarterly* 4, no. 3 (July 1905).

"Letters from Old Trunks." *Virginia Magazine of History and Biography* 44, no. 4 (October 1936).

Lewis, Nelly Custis. *George Washington's Beautiful Nelly: The Letters of Eleanor Parke Custis Lewis to Elizabeth Bordley Gibson, 1794–1851*. Edited by Patricia Brady. Columbia: University of South Carolina Press, 1991.

Leyburn, John. "An Interview with General Robert E. Lee." *Century Illustrated Monthly Magazine* 30, no. 1 (May 1885).

Lionberger, Isaac H., and Stella M. Drumm, eds. "Letters of Robert E. Lee to Henry Kayser, 1838–1846." *Glimpses of the Past* (Missouri Historical Society) 3, nos. 1–2 (1936).

Lomax, Elizabeth Lindsay. *Leaves from an Old Washington Diary*. Edited by Lindsay Lomax Wood. New York: E. P. Dutton, 1943.

Long, A. L. *Memoirs of Robert E. Lee*. Reprint, Secaucus, N.J.: Blue and Gray Press, 1983.

Longstreet, James. *From Manassas to Appomattox: Memoirs of the Civil War in America*. Reprint, New York: Da Capo Press, 1992.

Madison, Dolley. *The Selected Letters of Dolley Payne Madison*. Edited by David B. Mattern and Holly C. Shulman. Charlottesville: University of Virginia Press, 2003.

Marshall, Charles. *Lee's Aide-de-Camp*. Edited by Frederick Maurice. Reprint, Lincoln: University of Nebraska Press, 2000.

McAllister, Robert. *The Civil War Letters of General Robert McAllister*. Edited by James I. Robertson Jr. New Brunswick, N.J.: Rutgers University Press, 1965.

McClellan, George B. *The Mexican War Diary of George B. McClellan*. Edited by William Starr Myers. Princeton, N.J.: Princeton University Press, 1917.

McGuire, Judith W. *Diary of a Southern Refugee during the War*. Reprint, New York: Arno Press, 1972.

McIlvaine, Charles Pettit. *The Apostolic Commission: The Sermon at the Consecration of the Right Reverend Leonidas Polk, D.D.* Gambier, Ohio: G. W. Myers, 1838.

———. *Christian Duty in Time of War*. Boston: American Tract Society, 1861.

———. *Importance of Consideration*. Boston: American Tract Society, 1830.

McWhiney, Grady, and Sue McWhiney. *To Mexico with Taylor and Scott, 1845 to 1847*. Waltham, Mass.: Blaisdell, 1969.

Meade, William. "The Autobiography of William Meade." Edited by J. E. Booty. *Historical Magazine of the Protestant Episcopal Church* 31, no. 4 (December 1962).

Mosby, Colonel John S. "Personal Recollections of General Lee." *Munsey's Magazine* 45, no. 1 (April 1911).

Nisbet, James Cooper. *4 Years on the Firing Line*. Edited by Bell Irvin Wiley. Jackson, Tenn.: McCowat-Mercer Press, 1963.

Olmsted, Frederick Law. *A Journey in the Seaboard Slave States.* Reprint, New York: Negro Universities Press, 1968.

———. *A Journey through Texas: Or A Saddle Trip on the Southwestern Frontier.* Reprint, Austin: University of Texas Press, 1978.

Packard, Joseph. *Recollections of a Long Life.* Washington, D.C.: B. S. Adams, 1902.

Patterson, Edmund DeWitt. *Yankee Rebel.* Edited by John G. Barrett. Knoxville: University of Tennessee Press, 1966.

Perdue, Charles L. Jr., Thomas E. Barden, and Robert K. Phillips, eds. *Weevils in the Wheat: Interviews with Virginia Ex-Slaves.* Charlottesville: University Press of Virginia, 1976.

Pleasants, Lucy Lee, ed. *Old Virginia Days and Ways: Reminiscences of Mrs. Sally McCarty Pleasants.* Menasha, Wis.: George Banta, 1916.

Pryor, Mrs. Roger A. *Reminiscences of Peace and War.* New York: Macmillan, 1905.

Ranson, A. R. H. "General Lee As I Knew Him." *Harper's Monthly Magazine* 122, no. 729 (February 1911).

Ray, John. *The Wisdom of God Manifested in the Works of the Creation.* Reprint, New York: Georg Olms Verlag, 1974.

Robertson, James I. Jr., ed. "'The Boy Artillerist': Letters of Colonel William Pegram, C.S.A." *Virginia Magazine of History and Biography* 98, no. 2 (April 1990).

Russell, William Howard. *My Diary North and South.* Boston: T. O. H. P. Burnham, 1863.

Sanborn, F. B. *Recollections of Seventy Years.* 2 vols. Boston: Richard G. Badger, 1909.

Santa Anna, Antonio López de. *The Eagle: The Autobiography of Santa Anna.* Edited by Ann Fears Crawford. Austin, Tex.: State House Press, 1988.

Scott, W. W., ed. "The John Brown Letters." *Virginia Magazine of History and Biography* 9, no. 4 (April 1902); 10, nos. 1–4 (July–April 1902–3); and 11, no. 1 (1903–4).

Scott, Winfield. *Memoirs of Lieut.-General Scott, Written by Himself.* 2 vols. New York: Sheldon, 1864.

Screven, Frank B. "The Letters of R. E. Lee to the Mackay Family of Savannah." Typescript, 1952. Armstrong State College Library, Savannah, Ga.

Semmes, Raphael. *The Campaign of General Scott in the Valley of Mexico.* Cincinnati: Moore & Anderson, 1852.

Sherman, William T. *Memoirs of General William T. Sherman by Himself.* 2 vols. New York: Charles L. Webster, 1891.

Sherwood, M. E. W. "Washington before the War." *Lippincott's Monthly Magazine* 54, August 1894.

Sibley, Marilyn McAdams, ed. "Robert E. Lee to Albert Sidney Johnston, 1857." *Journal of Southern History* 29, no. 1 (February 1963).

Smith, E. Kirby. *To Mexico with Scott: Letters of Captain E. Kirby Smith to His Wife.* Edited by Emma Jerome Blackwood. Cambridge: Harvard University Press, 1917.

Southern Historical Society Papers. 38 vols. Richmond: Virginia Historical Society, 1876–1914.

Taylor, Walter H. *Four Years with General Lee.* Edited by James I. Robertson Jr. Reprint, Bloomington: University of Indiana Press, 1962.

———. *Lee's Adjutant: The Wartime Letters of Colonel Walter Herron Taylor, 1862–1865.* Edited by R. Lockwood Tower. Columbia: University of South Carolina Press, 1995.

Thomas, Emory, ed. "'The Greatest Service I Rendered the State': J. E. B. Stuart's Account of the Capture of John Brown." *Virginia Magazine of History and Biography* 94, no. 3 (July 1986).

Tickner, George. "West Point in 1826." *Annual Reunion of the Association of Graduates* [1886]. West Point: USMA Press, 1886.

Torrence, Clayton, ed. "Arlington and Mount Vernon, 1856, as Described in a Letter of Augusta Blanche Berard," *Virginia Magazine of History and Biography* 57, no. 2 (April 1949).

Tyler, Lyon G. *The Letters and Times of the Tylers.* 3 vols. Reprint, New York: Da Capo Press, 1970.

Upshur, George Lyttleton. *As I Recall Them: Memories of Crowded Years*. New York: Wilson-Erickson, 1936.

Valentine, Edward V. "Reminiscences of General Lee." *Outlook* 84, no. 17 (December 22, 1906).

Watkins, Sam. *Company "Aytch"; or, A Side Show of the Big Show*. Reprint, New York: Plume, 1999.

Wise, John Sergeant. *The End of an Era*. Edited by Curtis Carroll Davis. Reprint, New York: Thomas Yoselof, 1965.

Wolseley, Viscount. "A Month's Visit to the Confederate Head Quarters." *Blackwood's Magazine* 93, no. 567 (January 1863).

Wooster, Robert, ed. *Recollections of Western Texas, Descriptive and Narrative . . . By Two of the U.S. Mounted Rifles*. Lubbock: Texas Tech University Press, 1995.

Zimmer, Anne Carter, ed. *The Robert E. Lee Family Cooking and Housekeeping Book*. Chapel Hill: University of North Carolina Press, 1997.

Zuppan, Jo, ed. "Father to Son: Letters from John Custis IV to Daniel Parke Custis." *Virginia Magazine of History and Biography* 98, no. 1 (January 1990).

Secondary Sources

Allan, Elizabeth Preston. *The Life and Letters of Margaret Junkin Preston*. Boston: Houghton Mifflin, 1903.

Armes, Ethel. *Stratford Hall: The Great House of the Lees*. Richmond, Va.: Garrett and Massie, 1936.

Arnold, James R. *Jeff Davis's Own: Cavalry, Comanches, and the Battle for the Texas Frontier*. New York: John Wiley & Sons, 2000.

Ash, Stephen V. *When the Yankees Came: Conflict and Chaos in the Occupied South*. Chapel Hill: University of North Carolina Press, 1995.

Avey, Elijah. *The Capture and Execution of John Brown*. Reprint, Chicago: Afro-Am Press, 1969.

Axelrod, Alan. *The War between the Spies: A History of Espionage during the American Civil War*. New York: Atlantic Monthly Press, 1992.

Ayers, Edward L., and John C. Willis, eds. *The Edge of the South: Life in Nineteenth Century Virginia*. Charlottesville: University Press of Virginia, 1991.

Bancroft, Frederic. *Slave Trading in the Old South*. Reprint, Columbia, S.C.: University of South Carolina Press, 1996.

Bearss, Sara B. "The Farmer of Arlington." *Virginia Cavalcade* 38, no. 3 (Winter 1989).

Benét, Stephen Vincent. *John Brown's Body*. Reprint, New York: Rhinehart and Winston, 1967.

Beringer, Richard E., Herman Hattaway, Archer Jones, and William N. Still Jr. *The Elements of Confederate Defeat*. Athens: University of Georgia Press, 1988.

Berlin, Ira, and Philip D. Morgan. *Cultivation and Culture*. Charlottesville: University Press of Virginia, 1993.

Beyan, Amos J. *The American Colonization Society and the Creation of the Liberian State*. Lanham: University Press of America, 1991.

Beymer, William Gilmore. *Scouts and Spies of the Civil War*. Reprint, Lincoln: University of Nebraska Press, 2003.

———. "Williams, CSA." *Harper's New Monthly Magazine* 119, no. 712 (September 1909).

Blassingame, John W. "Sambos and Rebels: The Character of the Southern Slave." Lecture at Howard University, May 4, 1972.

Bledstein, Burton J. *The Culture of Professionalism*. New York: W. W. Norton, 1976.

Bleser, Carol, ed. *In Joy and in Sorrow: Women, Family and Marriage in the Victorian South*. New York: Oxford University Press, 1991.

Bloom-Feshbach, Jonathan, and Sally Bloom-Feshbach, eds. *The Psychology of Separation and Loss*. San Francisco: Jossey-Bass, 1987.

Blount, Roy. *Robert E. Lee*. New York: Viking, 2003.

Blumin, Stuart. "The Hypothesis of Middle-Class Formation in Nineteenth-Century America: A Critique and Some Proposals." *American Historical Review* 90, no. 2 (April 1985).

Boritt, Gabor S., ed. *Jefferson Davis's Generals*. New York: Oxford University Press, 1999.

———. *Why the Confederacy Lost*. New York: Oxford University Press, 1992.

Bowlby, John. *The Making & Breaking of Affectional Bonds*. London: Tavistock, 1979.

Boyd, Thomas. *Light-horse Harry Lee*. New York: Charles Scribner's Sons, 1931.

Boylan, Anne M. "Evangelical Womanhood in the Nineteenth Century: The Role of Women in Sunday Schools." *Feminist Studies* 4, no. 3 (October 1978).

Bradford, Gamaliel Jr. *Lee the American*. Boston: Houghton Mifflin, 1912.

Bridges, Hal. *Lee's Maverick General: Daniel Harvey Hill*. New York: McGraw Hill, 1961.

Brock, Robert Alonzo, ed. *Gen. Robert Edward Lee: Soldier, Citizen, and Christian Patriot*. Richmond: B. F. Johnson, 1897.

Brown, Richard B. *Knowledge Is Power: The Diffusion of Information in Early America, 1700–1865*. New York: Oxford University Press, 1989.

———. *Modernization: The Transformation of American Life, 1600–1865*. New York: Hill and Wang, 1976.

Burns, James MacGregor. *Leadership*. New York: Harper & Brothers, 1978.

Byrne, Karen L. "Our Little Sanctuary in the Wood: Spiritual Life at Arlington Chapel." *Arlington Historical Magazine* 12, no. 2 (October 2002).

Campbell, Edward D. C. Jr. "The Fabric of Command: R. E. Lee, Confederate Insignia, and the Perception of Rank." *Virginia Magazine of History and Biography* 98, no. 2 (April 1990).

Casdorph, Paul D. *Confederate General R. S. Ewell: Robert E. Lee's Hesitant Commander*. Lexington: University Press of Kentucky, 2004.

Carhart, Tom. *Lost Triumph: Lee's Real Plan at Gettysburg and Why It Failed*. New York: G. P. Putnam's Sons, 2005.

Carmichael, Peter S., ed. *Audacity Personified*. Baton Rouge: Louisiana State University Press, 2004.

———. "Who's to Blame?" *Civil War Times Illustrated* 37, no. 4 (August 1998).

Carnes, Mark C., and Clyde Griffen, eds. *Meanings for Manhood: Constructions of Masculinity in Victorian America*. Chicago: University of Chicago Press, 1990.

Carter, Dan T. *When the War Was Over: The Failure of Self-Reconstruction in the South, 1865–67*. Baton Rouge: Louisiana State University Press, 1985.

Cashin, Joan E. "The Structure of Antebellum Families: 'The Ties That Bound Us Was Strong.'" *Journal of Southern History* 56, no. 1 (February 1990).

Chambers, Thomas A. *Drinking the Waters*. Washington, D.C.: Smithsonian Institution Press, 2002.

Chase, Enoch Aquila. "The Arlington Case." *Records of the Columbia Historical Society* 31–32 (1930).

Cleaves, Freeman. *Rock of Chickamauga: The Life of George H. Thomas*. Reprint, Westport, Conn.: Greenwood Press, 1974.

Clinton, Catherine. *The Plantation Mistress*. New York: Pantheon, 1982.

Coffman, Edward M. "The Army Officer and the Constitution." *Parameters* 17, no. 3 (September 1987).

———. *The Old Army: A Portrait of the American Army in Peacetime, 1784–1898*. Oxford: Oxford University Press, 1986.

Collins, Bruce. *White Society in the Antebellum South*. London: Longman Group, 1985.

Connelly, Thomas L. *The Marble Man: Robert E. Lee and His Image in American Society*. Baton Rouge: Louisiana State University Press, 1977.

Connelly, Thomas Lawrence, and Archer Jones. *The Politics of Command: Factions and Ideas in Confederate Strategy*. Baton Rouge: Louisiana State University Press, 1973.

Cooling, Benjamin Franklin. *Symbol, Sword, and Shield*. Shippensburg, Pa.: White Mane, 1991.

Cooling, Benjamin Franklin, and Walton H. Owen II. *Mr. Lincoln's Forts: A Guide to the Civil War Defenses of Washington.* Shippensburg, Pa.: White Mane, 1988.

Coulling, Mary P. *The Lee Girls.* Winston-Salem, N.C.: John F. Blair, 1987.

Crenshaw, Ollinger. *General Lee's College.* New York: Random House, 1969.

Crofts, Daniel W. "Late Antebellum Virginia Reconsidered." *Virginia Magazine of History and Biography* 107, no. 3 (Summer 1999).

————. *Reluctant Confederates: Upper South Unionists in the Secession Crisis.* Chapel Hill: University of North Carolina Press, 1989.

Daniels, George H. *American Science in the Age of Jackson.* Tuscaloosa: University of Alabama Press, 1994.

————. *Science in American Society: A Social History.* New York: Alfred A. Knopf, 1971.

Davies, K. G. "The Mess of the Middle Class." *Past and Present,* no. 22 (July 1962).

Davis, William C. *The Cause Lost: Myths and Realities of the Confederacy.* Lawrence: University of Kansas Press, 1996.

————. *Jefferson Davis: The Man and His Hour.* New York: Harper Collins, 1991.

Decker, Karl, and Angus McSween. *Historic Arlington.* Washington, D.C.: Decker & McSween, 1892.

Dederer, John Morgan. "In Search of the Unknown Soldier: A Critique of 'The Mystery in the Coffin.'" *Virginia Magazine of History and Biography* 103, no. 1 (January 1995).

————. *Making Bricks without Straw: Nathanael Greene's Southern Campaign and Mao Tse-Tung's Mobile War.* Manhattan, Kans.: Sunflower University Press, 1983.

————. "The Origins of Robert E. Lee's Bold Generalship: A Reinterpretation." *Military Affairs* 49, no. 3 (July 1985).

————. "Robert E. Lee's First Visit to His Father's Grave: Re-evaluating Well-Known Historical Documents." *Virginia Magazine of History and Biography* 102, no. 1 (January 1994).

Demos, John. *Past, Present and Personal: The Family and the Life Course in American History.* New York: Oxford University Press, 1986.

Dobney, Fredrick J. *River Engineers on the Middle Mississippi: A History of the St. Louis District U.S. Army Corps of Engineers.* Washington, D.C.: GPO, 1978.

Donald, David Herbert. *Lincoln.* New York: Simon and Schuster, 1995.

Dorris, Jonathan Truman. *Pardon and Amnesty under Lincoln and Johnson.* Chapel Hill: University of North Carolina Press, 1953.

Douglas, Ann. *The Feminization of American Culture.* New York: Alfred A. Knopf, 1977.

Dowdey, Clifford. *Lee.* Boston: Little, Brown, 1965.

Drumm, Stella M. "Robert E. Lee and the Improvement of the Mississippi River," *Missouri Historical Society Collections* 6, no. 2 (1929).

Egerton, Douglas R. " 'Its Origin Is Not A Little Curious': A New Look at the American Colonization Society," *Journal of the Early Republic* 5, no. 4 (Winter 1985).

Eicher, David J. *Robert E. Lee: A Life Portrait.* Dallas: Taylor, 1997.

Ellis, Joseph J. *Founding Brothers.* New York: Alfred A. Knopf, 2000.

————. *His Excellency, George Washington.* New York: Vintage, 2004.

Emerson, Edward W. *Life and Letters of Charles Russell Lowell.* Reprint, Port Washington, N.Y.: Kennikat Press, 1971.

Fahs, Alice, and Joan Waugh, eds. *The Memory of the Civil War in American Culture.* Chapel Hill: University of North Carolina Press, 2004.

Faust, Drew Gilpin. *The Creation of Confederate Nationalism: Ideology and Identity in the Civil War South.* Baton Rouge: Louisiana State University Press, 1988.

————, ed. *The Ideology of Slavery: Proslavery Thought in the Antebellum South, 1830–1860.* Baton Rouge: Louisiana State University Press, 1981.

————. *Mothers of Invention.* Chapel Hill: University of North Carolina Press, 1996.

Fellman, Michael. *The Making of Robert E. Lee.* New York: Random House, 2000.

————. "Robert E. Lee: Postwar Southern Nationalist." *Civil War History* 46, no. 3 (September 2000).

Fickling, Susan Maria. "Slave Conversion in South Carolina." *Bulletin of the University of South Carolina*, no. 146 (September 1, 1924).

Finkelman, Paul, ed. *His Soul Goes Marching On*. Charlottesville: University Press of Virginia, 1995.

Fleming, Gordon. *The Young Whistler, 1834–66*. London: George Allen & Unwin, 1978.

Fleming, Thomas. "Birth of the American Way of War." *MHQ: The Quarterly Journal of Military History* 15, no. 2 (Winter 2003).

Flood, Charles Bracelen. *Lee: The Last Years*. Boston: Houghton Mifflin, 1998.

Fogel, Robert William, and Stanley L. Engerman. *Time on the Cross*. New York: W. W. Norton, 1989.

Foote, Timothy. "1846: The Way We Were—and the Way We Went," *Smithsonian* 27, no. 1 (April 1996).

Fox-Genovese, Elizabeth. *Within the Plantation Household: Black and White Women of the Old South*. Chapel Hill: University of North Carolina Press, 1988.

Frank, Stephen M. *Life with Father: Parenthood and Masculinity in the Nineteenth Century American North*. Baltimore: Johns Hopkins University Press, 1998.

Franklin, John Hope. *The Militant South American, 1800–1861*. Urbana: University of Illinois Press, 2002.

————. *Reconstruction after the Civil War*. Chicago: University of Chicago Press, 1961.

Franklin, John Hope, and Loren Schweniger. *Runaway Slaves: Rebels on the Plantation*. New York: Oxford University Press, 1999.

Fraser, Walter J., R. Frank Sanders Jr., and Jon L. Wakelyn, eds. *The Web of Southern Social Relations*. Athens: University of Georgia Press, 1985.

Freeman, Douglas Southall. *Douglas Southall Freeman on Leadership*. Edited by Stuart W. Smith. Shippensburg, Pa.: White Mane, 1993.

————. "Lee and the Ladies." *Scribner's Magazine* 78, nos. 4 (October 1925) and 5 (November 1925).

————. *Lee's Lieutenants*. 3 vols. New York: Charles Scribner's Sons, 1942–44.

————. *R. E. Lee*. 4 vols. New York: Charles Scribner's Sons, 1934–37.

Freehling, Alison Goodyear. *Drift toward Dissolution: The Virginia Slavery Debate of 1831–1832*. Baton Rouge: Louisiana State University Press, 1982.

Friedman, Jean E. *The Enclosed Garden: Women and Community in the Evangelical South, 1830-1900*. Chapel Hill: University of North Carolina Press, 1985.

Fuller, J. F. C. *Grant and Lee*. Reprint, Bloomington: Indiana University Press, 1982.

Fuller, Wayne E. *The American Mail: Enlarger of the Common Life*. Chicago: University of Chicago Press, 1972.

Furgurson, Ernest B. *Ashes of Glory: Richmond at War*. New York: Alfred A. Knopf, 1996.

Gallagher, Gary W. *The Confederate War*. Cambridge, Mass.: Harvard University Press, 1997.

————. "Home Front and Battlefield." *Virginia Magazine of History and Biography* 98, no. 2 (April 1990).

————. *Lee and His Army in Confederate History*. Chapel Hill: University of North Carolina Press, 2001.

————. *Lee and His Generals in War and Memory*. Baton Rouge: Louisiana State University Press, 1998.

————, ed. *Lee the Soldier*. Lincoln: University of Nebraska Press, 1996.

————. "Robert E. Lee at Cumberland Island and on the Analyst's Couch." *Virginia Magazine of History and Biography* 103, no. 1 (January 1995).

Gamble, Robert S. *Sully: The Biography of a House*. Chantilly, Va.: Sully Foundation, 1973.

Gara, Larry. "The Fugitive Slave Law: A Double Paradox." *Civil War History* 10, no. 3 (September 1964).

Garrison, L. R. "Administrative Problems of the Confederate Post Office Department." *Southwestern Historical Quarterly Online* 19, nos. 2 (October 1915) and 3 (January 1916).

Genovese, Eugene D. *Roll, Jordan, Roll: The World the Slaves Made.* New York: Pantheon, 1974.

———. *The World the Slaveholders Made.* New York: Vintage, 1971.

Gienapp, William E. *Abraham Lincoln and Civil War America.* New York: Oxford University Press, 2002.

Gillett, Mary C. *The Army Medical Department, 1818–1865.* Washington, D.C.: Center of Military History, U.S. Army, 1987.

Gordon, Michael, ed. *The American Family in Social-Historical Perspective.* New York: St. Martin's Press, 1978.

Goss, Thomas. "Gettysburg's 'Decisive Battle,'" *Military Review* 84, no. 4 (July/August 2004).

Greven, Philip J. *The Protestant Temperament: Patterns of Child-Rearing, Religious Experience and the Self in Early America.* New York: Alfred A. Knopf, 1977.

Grier, Katherine C. *Culture and Comfort: Parlor-Making and Middle Class Identity, 1850–1930.* Washington, D.C.: Smithsonian Institution Press, 1997.

Grimsley, Mark. *The Hard Hand of War: Union Military Policy toward Southern Civilians, 1861–1865.* Cambridge, England: Cambridge University Press, 1995.

Grimsley, Mark, and Brooks D. Simpson, eds. *The Collapse of the Confederacy.* Lincoln: University of Nebraska Press, 2001.

Griswold, Robert L. *Fatherhood in America: A History.* New York: Basic Books, 1993.

Haley, Bruce. *The Healthy Body and Victorian Culture.* Cambridge, Mass.: Harvard University Press, 1978.

Halttunen, Karen. *Confidence Men and Painted Women: A Study of Middle Class Culture in America, 1830–1870.* New Haven: Yale University Press, 1982.

Harrison, Noel G. " 'Atop an Anvil': The Civilian War in Fairfax and Alexandria Counties, April 1861–April 1862." *Virginia Magazine of History and Biography* 106, no. 2 (Spring 1998).

Harrold, Stanley. *The Abolitionists and the South.* Lexington: University Press of Kentucky, 1995.

———. *Subversives: The Anti-Slavery Community in Washington, D.C., 1828–1865.* Baton Rouge: Louisiana State University Press, 2003.

Harsh, Joseph L. *Confederate Tide Rising: Robert E. Lee and the Making of Southern Strategy, 1861–62.* Kent, Ohio: Kent State University Press, 1999.

Hattaway, Herman, and Archer Jones. *How the North Won: A Military History of the Civil War.* Chicago: University of Illinois Press, 1983.

Heidler, Jeanne T. " 'Embarrassing Situation': David E. Twiggs and the Surrender of the United States Forces in Texas in 1861." In *Lonestar Blue and Gray,* edited by Ralph A. Wooster. Austin: Texas State Historical Association, 1995.

Hill, Forest G. *Roads, Rails and Waterways: The Army Engineers and Early Transportation.* Norman: University of Oklahoma Press, 1957.

Holifield, E. Brooks. *The Gentlemen Theologians: American Theology in Southern Culture, 1795–1860.* Durham, N.C.: Duke University Press, 1978.

Holmes, David Lynn. *A Brief History of the Episcopal Church.* Valley Forge, Pa.: Trinity Press International, 1993.

Horsman, Reginald. *Frontier Doctor: William Beaumont, America's First Great Medical Scientist.* Columbia: University of Missouri Press, 1996.

Hunter, Dard. *Papermaking in Pioneer America.* Philadelphia: University of Pennsylvania Press, 1952.

Huntington, Samuel P. *The Soldier and the State.* Cambridge, Mass.: Belknap Press of Harvard University Press, 1957.

Jabour, Anya. "Albums of Affection: Female Friendship and Coming of Age in Antebellum Virginia." *Virginia Magazine of History and Biography* 107, no. 2 (Spring 1999).

Janowitz, Morris. *The Professional Soldier.* Glencoe, Ill.: Free Press of Glencoe, 1960.

Johannsen, Robert W. *To the Halls of the Montezumas*. New York: Oxford University Press, 1985.

Johnson, William. *Sketches of the Life and Correspondence of Nathanael Greene*. 2 vols. Reprint, New York: Da Capo Press, 1973.

Johnston, James Hugo. *Miscegenation in the Ante-Bellum South*. Chicago: University of Chicago Libraries Press, 1939.

————. *Race Relations in Virginia and Miscegenation in the South, 1776–1860*. Amherst: University of Massachusetts Press, 1970.

Johnston, William Preston. *The Life of Gen. Albert Sidney Johnston*. Reprint, New York: Da Capo Press, 1997.

Jordan, Ervin L. Jr. *Black Confederates and Afro-American Yankees in Civil War Virginia*. Charlottesville: University Press of Virginia, 1995.

Juster, Susan. "'In a Different Voice': Male and Female Narratives of Religious Conversion in Post Revolutionary America," *American Quarterly* 41, no. 1 (March 1989).

Katcher, Philip. *The Army of Robert E. Lee*. London: Arms and Armour Press, 1994.

Kavanagh, Thomas W. *Comanche Political History: An Ethnographical Perspective*. Lincoln: University of Nebraska Press, 1996.

Kegel, James A. *North with Lee and Jackson: The Lost Story of Gettysburg*. Mechanicsville, Pa.: Stackpole Books, 1996.

Kett, Joseph F. *The Formation of the American Medical Profession: The Role of Institutions*. New Haven, Conn.: Yale University Press, 1968.

Kimmel, Michael S. *The Gender of Desire: Essays on Male Sexuality*. Albany, N.Y.: State University of New York Press, 2005.

————. *Manhood in America*. New York: Free Press, 1996.

Kinney, Martha E. "'If Vanquished, I Am Still Victorious': Religious and Cultural Symbolism in Virginia's Confederate Memorial Day Celebrations, 1866–1930," *Virginia Magazine of History and Biography* 106, no. 3 (Summer 1998).

Klamkin, Marian. *The Return of Lafayette, 1824–1825*. New York: Charles Scribner's Sons, 1975.

Krowl, Michelle A. "'In the Spirit of Fraternity': The United States Government and the Burial of Confederate Dead at Arlington National Cemetery, 1864–1914." *Virginia Magazine of History and Biography* 111, no. 2 (Spring 2003).

Kundahl, George G. *Alexandria Goes to War: Beyond Robert E. Lee*. Knoxville: University of Tennessee Press, 2004.

Larkin, Jack. *The Reshaping of Everyday Life, 1790–1840*. New York: Harper and Row, 1988.

Laskin, Elisabeth Lauterbach. "Good Old Rebels: Soldiering in the Army of Northern Virginia, 1862–1865." Ph.D. diss., Harvard University, 2003.

Layton, Edwin T. "Science as a Form of Action: The Role of Engineering Sciences." *Technology and Culture* 29, no. 1 (January 1988).

Leavitt, Judith Walzer. *Brought to Bed: Childbearing in America, 1750–1950*. New York: Oxford University Press, 1986.

Lee, Cazenove Gardner Jr. *Lee Chronicle*. New York: New York University Press, 1957.

Lee, Edmund Jennings. *Lee of Virginia, 1642–1892*. Reprint, Baltimore: Genealogical Publishing, 1974.

Lee, H[enry] IV. *Observations on the Writings of Thomas Jefferson with Particular Reference to the Attack They Contain on the Memory of the Late Gen. Henry Lee*. Introduction and notes by Charles Carter Lee. Philadelphia: J. Dobson, 1839.

Leech, Margaret. *Reveille in Washington, 1860–1865*. New York: Harper and Brothers, 1941.

Lewis, Jan. *The Pursuit of Happiness: Family and Values in Jefferson's Virginia*. Cambridge, England: Cambridge University Press, 1983.

Lewis, Jan, and Kenneth A. Lockridge. "'Sally Has Been Sick': Pregnancy and Family Limitation among Virginia Gentry Women, 1780–1830," *Journal of Social History* 22, no. 1 (Fall 1988).

Link, William A. *Roots of Secession: Slavery and Politics in Antebellum Virginia.* Chapel Hill: University of North Carolina Press, 2003.

Litwack, Leon F. *Been in the Storm So Long.* New York: Vintage Books, 1979.

Lossing, Benson J. "Arlington House, the Seat of GWP Custis, Esq.," *Harper's New Monthly Magazine* 7, no. 40 (September 1853).

Lowe, Richard. "Another Look at Reconstruction in Virginia," *Civil War History* 22, no. 1 (January 1986).

———. *Republicans and Reconstruction in Virginia, 1856–1870.* Charlottesville: University Press of Virginia, 1991.

Luvaas, Jay, ed. "Napoleon on Generalship." *MHQ: The Quarterly Journal of Military History* 12, no. 3 (Spring 2000).

Lynch, James B. Jr. *The Custis Chronicles: The Virginia Generations.* Camden, Maine: Picton, 1997.

Lystra, Karen. *Searching the Heart: Women, Men and Romantic Love in Nineteenth Century America.* New York: Oxford University Press, 1989.

MacDonald, Rose Mortimer Ellzey. *Mrs. Robert E. Lee.* Boston: Ginn, 1939.

Maddex, Jack P. Jr. "Virginia: The Persistence of Centrist Hegemony." In *Reconstruction and Redemption in the South,* edited by Otto H. Olsen. Baton Rouge: Louisiana State University Press, 1980.

Malcomson, Scott L. *One Drop of Blood: The American Misadventures of Race.* New York: Farrar, Straus and Giroux, 2000.

Mangan, J. A., and James Walvin, eds. *Manliness and Morality: Middle-Class Masculinity in Britain and America, 1800–1940.* Manchester, England: Manchester University Press, 1987.

Manross, William Wilson. *A History of the American Episcopal Church.* New York: Morehouse-Gorham, 1950.

Mainwaring, Richard D., and Harris D. Riley. "The Lexington Physicians of General Robert E. Lee." *Southern Medical Journal* 98, no. 8 (August 2005).

Marcus, Alan I., and Howard P. Segal. *Technology in America.* Fort Worth, Tex.: Harcourt Brace College Publishers, 1999.

Markle, Donald E. *Spies and Spymasters of the Civil War.* New York: Hippocrene Books, 2004.

Mason, Emily V. *Popular Life of General Robert E. Lee.* Baltimore: John Murphy, 1872.

Massey, Mary Elizabeth. *Refugee Life in the Confederacy.* Baton Rouge: Louisiana State University Press, 2001.

Mathews, Donald G. *Religion in the Old South.* Chicago: University of Chicago Press, 1977.

McCaslin, Richard B. *Lee in the Shadow of Washington.* Baton Rouge: Louisiana State University Press, 2001.

McDannell, Colleen. *The Christian Home in Victorian America, 1840–1900.* Bloomington: Indiana University Press, 1986.

McDonald, Robert M. S., ed. *Thomas Jefferson's Military Academy: Founding West Point.* Charlottesville: University of Virginia Press, 2004.

McMillen, Sally G. *Motherhood in the Old South: Pregnancy, Childbirth, and Infant Rearing.* Baton Rouge: Louisiana State University Press, 1990.

McMurry, Richard M. *Two Great Rebel Armies.* Chapel Hill: University of North Carolina Press, 1989.

McPherson, James M. *Battle Cry of Freedom.* New York: Ballantine, 1988.

———. *Crossroads of Freedom: Antietam.* New York: Oxford University Press, 2002

———. "Failed Southern Strategies." *MHQ: The Quarterly Journal of Military History* 11, no. 4 (Summer 1999).

———. *For Cause and Comrades: Why Men Fought in the Civil War.* New York: Oxford University Press, 1997.

Martin, Samuel J. "Did 'Baldy' Ewell Lose Gettysburg?" *America's Civil War* 10, no. 3 (July 1997).

Meade, Bishop William. *Old Churches, Ministers and Families of Virginia.* 2 vols. Reprint, Baltimore: Genealogical Publishing, 1995.

Melville, Herman. *The Battle-Pieces of Herman Melville.* Edited by Hennig Cohen. New York: Thomas Yoseloff, 1963.

Miller, David W. *Second Only to Grant: Quartermaster General Montgomery C. Meigs.* Shippensburg, Pa.: White Mane, 2000.

Mitchel, F. A. *Ormsby MacKnight Mitchel: Astronomer and General.* Boston: Houghton Mifflin, 1887.

Morison, Elting E. *From Know-How to Nowhere: The Development of American Technology.* New York: Basic Books, 1974.

Morris, Thomas D. *Free Men All: The Personal Liberty Laws of the North, 1780–1861.* Union, N.J.: Lawbook Exchange, 2001.

———. *Southern Slavery and the Law, 1619–1860.* Chapel Hill: University of North Carolina Press, 1996

Musser, Ruth, and John C. Krantz Jr. "The Friendship of General Robert E. Lee and Dr. Wm. Beaumont." *Bulletin of the Institute of the History of Medicine* 6, no. 5 (May 1938).

Myer, Jesse S. *Life and Letters of Dr. William Beaumont.* St. Louis: C. V. Mosby, 1939.

Nagel, Paul C. *The Lees of Virginia: Seven Generations of an American Family.* New York: Oxford University Press, 1990.

Nelligan, Murray H. "Old Arlington." Ph.D. diss., Columbia University, 1954.

Noble, David F. *America by Design: Science, Technology, and the Rise of Corporate Capitalism.* New York: Alfred A. Knopf, 1977.

Nolan, Alan T. "Grave Thoughts." *Virginia Magazine of History and Biography* 103, no. 1 (January 1995).

———. *Lee Considered.* Chapel Hill: University of North Carolina Press, 1991.

Nolan, J. Bennett. *Lafayette in America Day by Day.* Baltimore: Johns Hopkins Press, 1934.

Numbers, Ronald L. "William Beaumont and the Ethics of Human Experimentation." *Journal of the History of Biology* 12, no. 1 (Spring 1979).

Numbers, Ronald, and Janet S. Numbers. "Science in the Old South: A Reappraisal." *Journal of Southern History* 48, no. 2 (May 1982).

Numbers, Ronald L., and William J. Orr Jr. "William Beaumont's Reception at Home and Abroad." *Isis* 72, no. 64 (December 1981).

Numbers, Ronald L., and Todd L. Savitt. *Science and Medicine in the Old South.* Baton Rouge: Louisiana State University Press, 1989.

O'Brien, Gerard F. J. "James A. Seddon: Statesman of the Old South." Ph.D. diss. University of Maryland, 1963.

O'Connell, Charles F. Jr. "The Corps of Engineers and the Rise of Modern Management, 1827–1856," in *Military Enterprise and Technological Change: Perspectives on the American Experience,* edited by Merritt Roe Smith. Cambridge, Mass.: MIT Press, 1985.

Oakes, James. *The Ruling Race: A History of American Slaveholders.* New York: W. W. Norton, 1998.

Oates, Stephen B. *To Purge This Land with Blood: A Biography of John Brown.* New York: Harper Torch, 1970.

Osthaus, Carl R. "The Work Ethic of the Plain Folk: Labor and Religion in the Old South." *Journal of Southern History* 70, no. 4 (November 2004).

Owens, Harry P., ed. *Perspectives and Irony in American Slavery.* Jackson: University Press of Mississippi, 1976.

Palmer, Michael A. *Lee Moves North: Robert E. Lee on the Offensive.* New York: John Wiley Sons, 1998.

Palumbo, Frank A. *George Henry Thomas, Major General USA: The Dependable General: Supreme in Tactics of Strategy and Command.* Dayton, Ohio: Morningside House, 1983.

Pappas, George S. *To the Point: The United States Military Academy, 1802–1902*. Westport, Conn.: Praeger, 1993.

Patterson, Gerard A. *Rebels from West Point*. Mechanicsburg, Penn.: Stackpole Books, 2002.

Perman, Michael. "Accepting Defeat: Historians and Reconstruction." *Reviews in American History* 14, no. 1 (March 1986).

Peskin, Allan. *Winfield Scott and the Profession of Arms*. Kent, Ohio: Kent State University Press, 2003.

Pessen, Edward. "The Egalitarian Myth and the American Social Reality: Wealth, Mobility, and Equality in the 'Era of the Common Man.'" *American Historical Review* 76, no. 4 (October 1971).

———. "How Different From Each Other Were the Antebellum North and South?" *American Historical Review* 85, no. 5 (December 1980).

Peterson, Merrill D. *John Brown: The Legend Revisited*. Charlottesville: University of Virginia Press, 2002.

Petroski, Henry. *Invention by Design*. Cambridge: Harvard University Press, 1996.

———. *To Engineer Is Human*. New York: St. Martin's Press, 1985.

Pielmeier, Doug. "The Evolution of a Virginia Plantation." Draft research report, 1996, Arlington House Archives.

Pierro, Joseph. "Praying with Robert E. Lee." *Civil War Times Illustrated* 45, no. 1 (February 2006).

Polk, William M. *Leonidas Polk: Bishop and General*. 2 vols. New York: Longmans, Green, 1915.

Pollock, George H. "Mourning and Adaptation." *International Journal of Psycho-Analysis* 42 (1961).

Powell, Mary G. *The History of Old Alexandria, Virginia, from July 13, 1749 to May 24, 1861*. Richmond, Va.: William Byrd Press, 1928.

Power, J. Tracy. *Lee's Miserables: Life in the Army of Northern Virginia from the Wilderness to Appomattox*. Chapel Hill: University of North Carolina Press, 1998.

Preston, Walter Creigh. *Lee: West Point and Lexington*. Yellow Springs, Ohio: Antioch Press, 1934.

Primm, James Neal. *Lion of the Valley: St. Louis, Missouri*. Boulder, Colo.: Pruett, 1990.

Prucha, Francis Paul. *Broadax and Bayonet: The Role of the United States Army in the Development of the Northwest, 1815–1860*. Reprint, Lincoln: University of Nebraska Press, 1953.

———. *The Sword of the Republic*. Bloomington: Indiana University Press, 1969.

Rable, George C. *Civil Wars: Women and the Crisis of Southern Nationalism*. Urbana: University of Illinois Press, 1989.

———. *The Confederate Republic: A Revolution against Politics*. Chapel Hill: University of North Carolina Press, 1994.

Ramsdell, Charles W. *Behind the Lines in the Southern Confederacy*. Reprint, New York: Greenwood Press, 1969.

Reed, James. *From Private Vice to Public Virtue: The Birth Control Movement and American Society since 1830*. New York: Basic Books, 1978.

Reynolds, Terry S., ed. *The Engineer in America*. Chicago: University of Chicago Press, 1991.

Riley, Franklin L., ed. *General Lee after Appomattox*. New York: Macmillan, 1922.

Rister, Carl Coke. *Robert E. Lee in Texas*. Reprint, Norman: University of Oklahoma Press, 2004.

Roark, James L. *Masters without Slaves: Southern Planters in the Civil War and Reconstruction*. New York: W. W. Norton, 1977.

Robert, Joseph C. "Lee the Farmer." *Journal of Southern History* 3, no. 4 (November 1937).

Robertson, James I. Jr. *Stonewall Jackson: The Man, the Soldier, the Legend*. New York: Macmillan, 1997.

Robinson, Armistead L. "In the Shadow of Old John Brown: Insurrection Anxiety and Confederate Mobilization, 1861–1863." *Journal of Negro History* 65, no. 4 (Autumn 1980).

Rogin, Michael Paul. *Fathers and Children: Andrew Jackson and the Subjugation of the American Indian*. New York: Alfred A. Knopf, 1975.

Roland, Charles P. *Reflections on Lee*. Mechanicsburg, Pa.: Stackpole Books, 1995.

Rosenberg, Charles E. *The Care of Strangers: The Rise of America's Hospital System*. New York: Basic Books, 1987.

———. *No Other Gods: On Science and American Social Thought*. Baltimore: Johns Hopkins University Press, 1976.

Ross, Michael A. "The Commemoration of Robert E. Lee's Death and the Obstruction of Reconstruction in New Orleans." *Civil War History* 51, no. 2 (June 2005).

Rothstein, William G. *American Physicians in the Nineteenth Century: From Sects to Science*. Baltimore: John Hopkins University Press, 1972.

Royster, Charles. "A Battle of Memoirs: Light-Horse Harry Lee and Thomas Jefferson," *Virginia Cavalcade* 31, no. 2 (Autumn 1981).

———. *The Destructive War: William Tecumseh Sherman, Stonewall Jackson, and the Americans*. New York: Alfred A. Knopf, 1991.

———. *Light-Horse Harry Lee and the Legacy of the American Revolution*. New York: Alfred A. Knopf, 1981.

Rozear, Marvin P., E. Wayne Massey, Jennifer Homer, Erin Foley, and Joseph C. Greenfield Jr. "R. E. Lee's Stroke." *Virginia Magazine of History and Biography* 98, no. 2 (April 1990).

Sanborn, Margaret. "The Ordeal of Orton Williams, U.S.A., C.S.A." *Assembly* 28, no. 4 (Winter 1970).

———. *Robert E. Lee: The Complete Man, 1861–1870*. Philadelphia: J. B. Lippincott, 1967.

———. *Robert E. Lee: A Portrait, 1807–1861*. Philadelphia: J. B. Lippincott, 1966.

Sauers, Richard A. *Meade: Victor of Gettysburg*. Washington, D.C.: Brassey's, 2003.

Scheina, Robert L. *Santa Anna: A Curse upon Mexico*. Washington, D.C.: Brassey's, 2002.

Schmitz, Robert Morell. *Hugh Blair*. New York: King's Crown Press, 1948.

Schwartz, Barry. *George Washington: The Making of an American Symbol*. New York: Free Press, 1987.

Schwarz, Frederic D. "The Time Machine." *American Heritage* 48, no. 5 (September 1997).

Schwarz, Philip J. *Slave Laws in Virginia*. Athens: University of Georgia Press, 1996.

Schweniger, Loren. "The Underside of Slavery: The Internal Economy, Self-Hire, and Quasi-Freedom in Virginia." *Slavery and Abolition* 12, no. 2 (September 1991).

Shallat, Todd. *Structures in the Stream*. Austin: University of Texas Press, 1994.

Shanks, Henry T. *The Secession Movement in Virginia, 1847–61*. Reprint, New York: AMS Press, 1971.

Shattuck, Gardiner H. *A Shield and a Hiding Place: The Religious Life of the Civil War Armies*. Macon, Ga.: Mercer University Press, 1987.

Shaw, Robert B. *A Legal History of Slavery in the United States*. New York: Northern Press, 1991.

Sheehan-Dean, Aaron. "Justice Has Something to Do with It: Class Relations and the Confederate Army." *Virginia Magazine of History and Biography* 113, no. 4 (Autumn 2005).

Shryock, Richard Harrison. *American Medical Research Past and Present*. New York: Arno Press, 1980.

———. *Medicine and Society in America, 1660–1860*. Ithaca, N.Y.: Cornell University Press, 1960.

Skelton, William B. *An American Profession of Arms: The Army Officer Corps, 1784–1861*. Lawrence: University Press of Kansas, 1992.

Smith, William Francis, and T. Michael Miller. *A Seaport Saga: Portrait of Old Alexandria, Virginia*. Norfolk: Donning, 1989.

Starling, Marion Wilson. *The Slave Narrative: Its Place in American History*. Boston: G. K. Hall, 1981.

Starr, Paul. *The Creation of the Media*. New York: Basic Books, 2004.

———. *The Social Transformation of American Medicine.* New York: Basic Books, 1982.

Stevenson, Brenda E. *Life in Black and White: Family and Community in the Slave South.* New York: Oxford University Press, 1996.

Stowe, Steven M. *Doctoring the South.* Chapel Hill: University of North Carolina Press, 2004.

———. *Intimacy and Power in the Old South.* Baltimore: Johns Hopkins University Press, 1987.

Stroud, George M. *A Sketch of the Laws Relating to Slavery in the Several States of the United States of America.* Reprint, New York: Negro Universities Press, 1968.

Symonds, Craig L. *Joseph E. Johnston: A Civil War Biography.* New York: W. W. Norton, 1992.

Sweig, Donald M. "Slavery in Fairfax County, Virginia, 1750–1860: A Research Report." Fairfax, Va.: Office of Comprehensive Planning, 1983.

Thomas, Emory M. "God and General Lee." *Anglican and Episcopal History* 60, no. 1 (March 1991).

———. "The Lee Marriage." In *Intimate Strategies of the Civil War,* edited by Carol K. Bleser and Lesley J. Gordon. New York: Oxford University Press, 2001.

———. *Robert E. Lee.* New York: W. W. Norton, 1995.

———. "Young Man Lee." In *Leadership During the Civil War,* edited by Roman G. Heleniak and Lawrence L. Hewitt. Shippensburg, Pa.: White Mane, 1992.

Thomson, J. Anderson Jr., and Carlos Michael Santos. "The Mystery in the Coffin: Another View of Lee's Visit to His Father's Grave," *Virginia Magazine of History and Biography* 103, no. 1 (January 1995).

Tillson, Albert H. Jr. "Friendship and Commerce: The Conflict and Coexistence of Values on Virginia's Northern Neck in the Revolutionary Era." *Virginia Magazine of History and Biography* 111, no. 3 (Summer 2003).

Torbert, Alice Coyle. *Eleanor Calvert and Her Circle.* New York: William-Frederick Press, 1950.

Tushnet, Mark V. *The American Law of Slavery, 1810–1860.* Princeton, N.J.: Princeton University Press, 1981.

Unger, Harlow Giles. *Lafayette.* Hoboken, N.J.: John Wiley Sons, 2002.

U.S. Quartermaster Corps. *Arlington House and Its Associations.* Washington, D.C.: GPO, 1932.

Van Doren Stern, Philip. *Robert E. Lee: The Man and the Soldier.* New York: Bonanza, 1963.

Villard, Oswald Garrison. *John Brown: A Biography Fifty Years After.* Reprint, Gloucester, Mass.: Peter Smith, 1965.

Wallace, Ernest, and E. Adamson Hoebel. *The Comanches: Lords of the South Plains.* Norman: University of Oklahoma Press, 1986.

Wallenstein, Peter, and Bertram Wyatt-Brown, eds. *Virginia's Civil War.* Charlottesville: University of Virginia Press, 2005.

Waukechon, John Frank. "The Forgotten Evangelicals: Virginia Episcopalians, 1790–1876." Ph.D. diss., University of Texas at Austin, 2000.

Webber, Thomas L. *Deep Like the Rivers: Education in the Slave Quarter Community, 1831–1865.* New York: W. W. Norton, 1978.

Weeks, Lyman Horace. *A History of Paper-Manufacturing in the United States, 1690–1916.* New York: Lockwood Trade Journal, 1916.

Weigley, Russell F. *History of the United States Army: Military Thought from Washington to Marshall.* Bloomington: Indiana University Press, 1984.

———. *Quartermaster General of the Union Army: A Biography of Montgomery C. Meigs.* New York: Columbia University Press, 1959.

———. *Towards an American Army: Military Thought from Washington to Marshall.* New York: Columbia University Press, 1962.

Weintraub, Stanley. *Whistler: A Biography.* New York: Weybright and Talley, 1974.

Welter, Barbara. "The Cult of True Womanhood, 1820–1860." *American Quarterly* 18, no. 2, pt. 1 (Summer 1966).

―――. *Dimity Convictions: The American Woman in the Nineteenth Century*. Athens: Ohio University Press, 1976.

Wiencek, Henry. *An Imperfect God: George Washington, His Slaves, and the Creation of America*. New York: Farrar, Straus and Giroux, 2003.

Wiley, Bell Irvin. *The Life of Billy Yank: The Common Soldier of the Union*. New York: Doubleday, 1952.

―――. *The Life of Johnny Reb: The Common Soldier of the Confederacy*. Baton Rouge: Louisiana State University Press, 1978.

Williamson, Joel. *New People: Miscegenation and Mulattoes in the United States*. New York: Free Press, 1980.

Winders, Richard Bruce. *Mr. Polk's Army: The American Military Experience in the Mexican War*. College Station: Texas A & M University Press, 1997.

Winik, Jay. *April 1865: The Month That Saved America*. New York: Perennial, 2002.

Winton, Harold R. "Toward an American Philosophy of Command." *Military Affairs: Journal of Military History* 64, no. 4 (October 2000).

Wishy, Bernard. *The Child and the Republic*. Philadelphia: University of Pennsylvania Press, 1968.

Wood, W. J. *Civil War Generalship: The Art of Command*. Westport, Conn.: Praeger, 1997.

Wren, J. Thomas. "A 'Two-Fold Character': The Slave as Person and Property in Virginia Court Cases, 1800–1860." *Southern Studies* 24, no. 4 (Winter 1985).

Woodworth, Steven E. *Beneath a Northern Sky: A Short History of the Gettysburg Campaign*. Wilmington, Del.: Scholarly Resources, 2003.

―――. *Davis and Lee at War*. Lawrence: University Press of Kansas, 1995.

Wright, Robert K. Jr. *The Continental Army*. Army Lineage Series. Washington, D.C.: Center of Military History, U.S. Army, 1983. Online at www.army.mil/cmh-pg/books/RevWar/SontArmy/CA-fm.htm.

Wyatt-Brown, Bertram. *Southern Honor*. New York: Oxford University Press, 1982.

―――. *Yankee Saints and Southern Sinners*. Baton Rouge: Louisiana State University Press, 1985.

Index

Notes: Page numbers in *italics* refer to illustrations. REL refers to Robert E. Lee.